"It is clear that *Shade of th...* ...to become
an American classic. . . . ...that it sees
nothing in idealism to ridicule; Larry Lockridge can make us feel it the way his
father did."　　—Richard Dyer, *The Boston Globe*

"A book whose stirring power and complexity would daunt any reviewer. . . .
If it were up to me, I'd give this book all the awards and literary rosettes that
Raintree County should have received . . . "
　　—Donald Newlove, *The Philadelphia Inquirer*

"A dramatic account of his father's life. . . . We get a large portrait of a sophisticated artist. . . . In the son's account the father's experience seems both har-
rowing and inevitable. . . . What impresses you is the sense of the reconciliation
the son conveys."　　—Christopher Lehmann-Haupt, *The New York Times*

"Larry Lockridge has written a moving account of his father's life."
　　—Lee Hamilton, Member of Congress

"In his breakdown and collapse Ross Lockridge, Jr. comes fully alive on the
page."　　—Scott Donaldson, *The Washington Post*

"A reading experience at once moving, candid, and hypnotic. *Shade of the
Raintree* is worthy of sharing the shelf with *Raintree County* . . . "
　　—Charles Lee, *WFLN*, Philadelphia

"Meticulously, unflinchingly, Larry Lockridge [has] created a biography that is
also a searching clinical study of depression; a remarkably objective essay in
literary criticism; an important contribution to rural American history; and
finally, a magnificent and compassionate act of forgiveness."
　　—Tim Page, *Newsday*

"In the annals of 20th-century American literature, there may be no act more
puzzling than [the suicide of Ross Lockridge, Jr.]. [*Shade of the Raintree* is] a
book that is, in its own way, as remarkable and compelling as *Raintree County*.
Larry Lockridge . . . has produced a wonderful hybrid: a solid, dispassionate
biography that is at the same time a tender and understanding homage."
　　—Roger Miller, *The Milwaukee Journal*

"[Larry Lockridge] is a lively, witty writer, who manages to find irreverent humor even in the aftermath of his father's suicide."
—John Blades, *Chicago Tribune*

"[Larry Lockridge] would not have wanted his father to have written a less ambitious book, nor to have given up the great egoism, which was also a great generosity, to have striven less high."
—Erika Duncan, *The New York Times*

"One senses that the novelist would be proud of his son: he has created a full portrait of life in the Midwest between the wars and of the collision of depression and the creative mind."
—*Publishers Weekly*

"[Ross Lockridge, Jr.] emerges as a brilliant and likable young man . . . "
—Olin Chism, *The Dallas Morning News*

"*Shade of the Raintree* is a riveting book, shattering and shot through with the powerful poignancy of a life undone. I have read my copy twice through already, and will turn to it again and again, as I read and reread *Raintree County* . . . "
—Robin Mather, *The Detroit News*

"Beyond any other standard, I tend to judge the quality of the biographies I read by the sense of loss I feel at the death of the subject. In this vein, I have seldom been moved more deeply than I was by *Shade of the Raintree* . . . "
—J. Kent Calder, *Traces* magazine

"Larry Lockridge has produced a major work on depression: a superb analytic description of clinical depression as it was understood vaguely in 1948 and more fully today. At the same time, he describes a great American tragedy. . . . An immensely moving book, deserving of the Pulitzer Prize . . . "
—*Kirkus Reviews*

"A touching, insightful and affectionate biography. It reveals much about his gifted father, his father's extraordinary family, and a vanished almost idyllic world—that of the Indiana heartland in the years between World War I and World War II. . . . This finely wrought, finely researched, moving and loving biography succeeds on all counts."
—Pauline Mayer, *The Cleveland Plain Dealer*

PENGUIN BOOKS

SHADE OF THE RAINTREE

Larry Lockridge, author and Guggenheim Fellow, teaches Romantic literature at New York University. He lives in Manhattan.

Shade
of the
Raintree

The Life and Death of Ross Lockridge, Jr.

Author of *Raintree County*

Larry Lockridge

PENGUIN BOOKS

to Marcia Scanlon

Frontispiece: Ross Lockridge, Jr. with his family in August of 1946, shortly after his prodigious novel, *Raintree County*, had been accepted for publication and eighteen months before his suicide. Courtesy of *Indiana Alumni Magazine*.

PENGUIN BOOKS
Published by the Penguin Group
Penguin Books USA Inc., 375 Hudson Street, New York, New York 10014, U.S.A.
Penguin Books Ltd, 27 Wrights Lane, London W8 5TZ, England
Penguin Books Australia Ltd, Ringwood, Victoria, Australia
Penguin Books Canada Ltd, 10 Alcorn Avenue, Toronto, Ontario, Canada M4V 3B2
Penguin Books (N.Z.) Ltd, 182–190 Wairau Road, Auckland 10, New Zealand

Penguin Books Ltd, Registered Offices: Harmondsworth, Middlesex, England

First published in the United States of America by Viking Penguin,
a division of Penguin Books USA Inc. 1994
Published in Penguin Books 1995

1 3 5 7 9 10 8 6 4 2

Grateful acknowledgment is made for permission to reprint excerpts from the following material: Houghton Mifflin Company correspondence, by permission of Houghton Mifflin Company; James Michener's letter to John Leggett, by permission of James Michener; Christopher Morley's correspondence, by permission of the Estate of Christopher Morley.

Photographs are from the author's collection, unless otherwise indicated.

Page 500 constitutes an extension of this copyright page.

THE LIBRARY OF CONGRESS HAS CATALOGUED THE HARDCOVER AS FOLLOWS:
Lockridge, Laurence S.,
Shade of the Raintree: the life and death of Ross Lockridge, Jr.,
author of *Raintree County* / Larry Lockridge.
p. cm.
ISBN 0-670-85440-9 (hc.)
ISBN 0 14 01.5871 5 (pbk.)
1. Lockridge, Ross, Jr. 1914–1948—Biography.   2. Novelists, American—
20th century—Biography.   I. Title.
PS3523.O246Z74   1994
813'.54—dc20
[B]   93–26712

Printed in the United States of America
Set in Postscript Perpetua
Designed by Ann Gold

Contents

Photograph sections follow pages 148 and 340
Genealogy   ix

PART ONE

I   Epilogue
Bloomington, Indiana, 1948–1993   3

II   "Avenue of Elms"
Fort Wayne Days, 1914–1924   41

III   "Legends in a Class-Day Album"
Early Bloomington Days, 1924–1933   68

IV   "A Richly Laden Festal Board"
France and Italy, 1933–1934   108

V   "Dream of the Flesh of Iron"
Bloomington, 1934–1940   142

PART TWO

VI   Starting Over
Cambridge, Bloomington, Boston, and Cape Ann, 1940–1943   193

vii

Contents

VII   Writing *Raintree County*
Boston, Cape Ann, and South Byfield,
Fall, 1943–Spring, 1946   235

VIII   Author in the Epic   271

IX   Snake Pit in Paradise
Manistee, Michigan, Summer, 1946–Fall, 1947   310

X   "Flu or Something"
Hollywood and Bloomington, Fall, Winter, 1947–1948   368

XI   "Hail and Farewell at the Crossing"
Bloomington, March 6, 1948–Spring, 1948   439

Notes and Acknowledgments   459

Index   487

Genealogy

(In the interests of brevity, names of many offspring, especially in the larger, older families, are omitted. Names of fictional counterparts in the novel *Raintree County* are given parenthetically in italic type.)

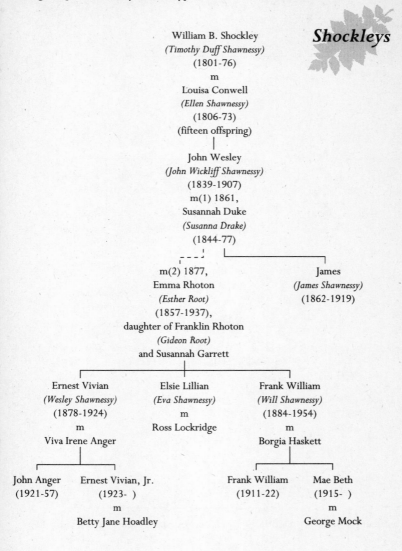

Shockleys

William B. Shockley
(Timothy Duff Shawnessy)
(1801-76)
m
Louisa Conwell
(Ellen Shawnessy)
(1806-73)
(fifteen offspring)

John Wesley
(John Wickliff Shawnessy)
(1839-1907)
m(1) 1861,
Susannah Duke
(Susanna Drake)
(1844-77)

m(2) 1877,
Emma Rhoton
(Esther Root)
(1857-1937),
daughter of Franklin Rhoton
(Gideon Root)
and Susannah Garrett

James
(James Shawnessy)
(1862-1919)

Ernest Vivian
(Wesley Shawnessy)
(1878-1924)
m
Viva Irene Anger

Elsie Lillian
(Eva Shawnessy)
m
Ross Lockridge

Frank William
(Will Shawnessy)
(1884-1954)
m
Borgia Haskett

John Anger
(1921-57)

Ernest Vivian, Jr.
(1923-)
m
Betty Jane Hoadley

Frank William
(1911-22)

Mae Beth
(1915-)
m
George Mock

Lockridges

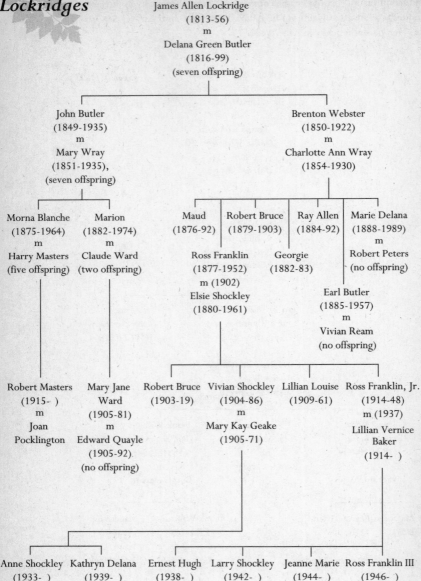

James Allen Lockridge
(1813-56)
m
Delana Green Butler
(1816-99)
(seven offspring)

John Butler
(1849-1935)
m
Mary Wray
(1851-1935),
(seven offspring)

Brenton Webster
(1850-1922)
m
Charlotte Ann Wray
(1854-1930)

Morna Blanche
(1875-1964)
m
Harry Masters
(five offspring)

Marion
(1882-1974)
m
Claude Ward
(two offspring)

Maud
(1876-92)

Robert Bruce
(1879-1903)

Ray Allen
(1884-92)

Marie Delana
(1888-1989)
m
Robert Peters
(no offspring)

Ross Franklin
(1877-1952)
m (1902)
Elsie Shockley
(1880-1961)

Georgie
(1882-83)

Earl Butler
(1885-1957)
m
Vivian Ream
(no offspring)

Robert Masters
(1915-)
m
Joan
Pocklington

Mary Jane
Ward
(1905-81)
m
Edward Quayle
(1905-92)
(no offspring)

Robert Bruce
(1903-19)

Vivian Shockley
(1904-86)
m
Mary Kay Geake
(1905-71)

Lillian Louise
(1909-61)

Ross Franklin, Jr.
(1914-48)
m (1937)
Lillian Vernice
Baker
(1914-)

Anne Shockley
(1933-)

Kathryn Delana
(1939-)

Ernest Hugh
(1938-)

Larry Shockley
(1942-)

Jeanne Marie
(1944-)

Ross Franklin III
(1946-)

x

Bakers

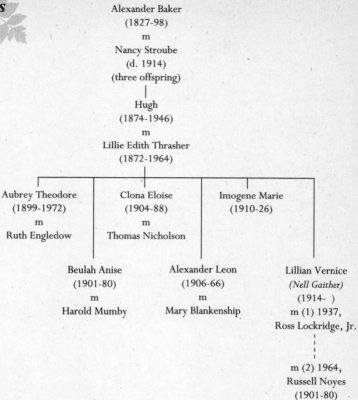

Alexander Baker
(1827-98)
m
Nancy Stroube
(d. 1914)
(three offspring)

Hugh
(1874-1946)
m
Lillie Edith Thrasher
(1872-1964)

Aubrey Theodore
(1899-1972)
m
Ruth Engledow

Clona Eloise
(1904-88)
m
Thomas Nicholson

Imogene Marie
(1910-26)

Beulah Anise
(1901-80)
m
Harold Mumby

Alexander Leon
(1906-66)
m
Mary Blankenship

Lillian Vernice
(Nell Gaither)
(1914-)
m (1) 1937,
Ross Lockridge, Jr.

m (2) 1964,
Russell Noyes
(1901-80)

Part One

I

Epilogue

Bloomington, Indiana, 1948–1993

My brother and I were horsing around on our twin beds, struggling over the small lead replica of the Empire State Building our father had brought back from the East. Ernest aimed it at me as if it were a gun—"Bang! Bang! Pow!"—and on my back I deflected the bullets, kicking up at him fearlessly. Our anarchy was the better for knowing we'd have to put on Sunday School penitentials before long. The door opened and in walked our mother and Grandma Lockridge, which stopped our play. They were sleepy-eyed. Ernest, aged nine, knew something was wrong. Our mother placed her hand gently on his shoulder and said, "Honey, your father is dead. He died last night."

Ernest screamed and fell sobbing on the floor and I, aged five, was puzzled and a little embarrassed, for Mom and Grandma didn't make it sound so bad. Our father had been tired, he needed a rest, he was now in a warm and sunny land, but no, he wouldn't be coming home soon.

I tried to see my father in a space above my own, walking care-free amid trees and flowers, and hoped he'd soon be rested up.

Later that morning Ernest still lay on the floor. He'd stopped crying but hoped his mother would come in and find him lying there—then she would know how much he had loved his father and how dead with grief he was. But she was busy with funeral preparations, and he was tired of lying on the cold floorboards and got up and dressed.

The death of fathers is a common theme, but the suicide on Saturday evening, March 6, 1948, of Ross Lockridge, Jr., author of the novel *Raintree County*, was improbable enough to be the subject of many editorials. At his death his novel was first on the New York *Herald Tribune*'s best-seller list, had won the enormous MGM Novel Award, had been excerpted in *Life,* and had recently been the Main Selection of Book-of-the-Month Club. He left a wife and four children.

"The death, apparently by suicide, of Ross Lockridge, Jr., author of *Raintree County*, has stirred a wave of shocked speculation among his countrymen," noted the Washington *Evening Star*. "What more, they wonder, could a man ask of life than had been granted this 33-year-old writer, whose first book, an unabashed attempt at the great American novel, brought him wealth and fame and recognition. . . . Curiously enough, one of the book's most notable aspects was its staunch repudiation, through its hero, of materialism, its repeated affirmation of faith in the American dream and the American destiny. How did the author lose the hope and optimism expressed by the hero who was presumably his spokesman? . . . We shall never know, since evidently the only testament he left is his questing, vital, sprawling book. He seems to have gained the whole world and then to have wondered what it profited a man. We can only pity the desolation and confusion of his going."

My book is a quest, four decades later, to overcome confusion and lay bare this desolate act—and, more so, the life and work that preceded it. Pablo Neruda wrote that, in death, Ross Lockridge had joined Melville, Whitman, Poe, Dreiser, and Wolfe as American writers who were like "fresh wounds of our own absence." They were all "bound to the depths" and "to the darkness," were "checked in their work by joy and by mourning"—and yet over them "the same dawn of the hemisphere burns." I'll tell the story of my father's life, from dawn to darkness, for the intensities of will and creative intellect we might find there. A full measure of them has not yet been taken. His was an American life of great aspiration, a life of prodigious labors ending in a sense of dead enormous failure even before the applause began. Few driven spirits give way to darkness so irrevocably, but I believe that in some ways Ross Lockridge's life is an allegory of the American writer.

~

I always took pride in the *The New York Times* giving him a front-page obit. The circumstances of the death were chronicled there. "Dr. Robert E. Lyons, Jr., Monroe County Coroner, who returned the suicide verdict, said he had not been able to determine a motive. Mr. Lockridge was found unconscious in his car in the gas-filled garage of the new home he built with part of a $150,000 movie studio award for the book. He wrote the novel in seven lean years of trying to break into the writing field. Dr. Lyons said that relatives told him Mr. Lockridge appeared to be in good spirits yesterday. . . . Mr. Lockridge left no letters or notes indicating he was despondent or ill. . . . Mrs. Lockridge became alarmed last night when her husband failed to return after a reasonable time from a trip to the post office. She went to the garage shortly before midnight to see if the car was back and found the doors locked and the garage lights on. The car was inside. She summoned neighbors, who smashed in the doors. They found the car's motor running and Mr. Lockridge sprawled in the driver's seat. The door was open and his legs were hanging over the running board. The garage was filled with carbon monoxide fumes."

This account permitted many of his friends to think it an accident. Maybe he was listening to the regional high school basketball tournament over the car radio and passed out, maybe he hit his head when exiting. Here was an exuberant writer known for thoroughness in all matters who hadn't left a note, who hadn't made out a will, who in a letter to his lawyer on the day he died alluded to future books. But our mother, years later, didn't encourage us to think it an accident. And I'd come to dislike the idea that it could have been. However bleak, suicide is a willed act invested with human meaning.

But if it was suicide, it seemed less premeditated than impulsive. Those legs exiting the Kaiser's front door even hinted at a last-minute change of mind. Somehow I wanted my father to have done what he fully intended to do.

Grandma Lockridge, a Christian Scientist with a master's in psychology, felt the four Lockridge children shouldn't attend the funeral, and our mother gave in on this, as she would later rue. But we were there for the wake. My younger sister, Jeanne, had, like the rest of us, been dispatched to relatives while funeral arrangements were being made. Aunt Lillian—an obese woman once photographed standing next to Revolutionary War cannons by my father, who wrote the caption "They shall not pass!"—was in charge of Jeanne. Barely four years old, she had little conception of what was happening.

She could see, arriving at our house, that the living room was full of flowers and she knew it had something to do with her daddy. "I want my daddy! I want my daddy!" she screamed as she fought to get free of Aunt Lillian. She ran to the coffin, was picked up by someone, and stared at the white skin, puzzled that her father was in a box and seemed to be sleeping. She satisfied herself that he was breathing. She and I then ran through the crowded living room, endangering floral displays with hide-and-seek around the coffin—she trying to wake him up—taking it all for a party until somebody subdued us. Jeanne would later be surprised that her breathing, sleeping father was simply *gone*.

Ernest returned from our uncle's home in Indianapolis. Furtively he reached into the coffin and touched his father, who felt like ice. On a piece of paper he wrote "Daddy I love you" and stuck it in the coffin. He could never again stand the smell of flowers, the taste of pineapple pie. Earlier, next to the typewriter in his father's bedroom, he had found a typed page entitled "Ultimate Philosophy" and scribbled guns all over it.

Not attending the funeral would have consequences for Ernest—it would complicate the work of mourning. Jeanne and I would gradually learn of death's finality. Terry Ross, two years old, would learn to mourn a father he could hardly remember. At the wake his mother held him above the coffin so he would see his father lying there. Later that day he saw his father's pajamas in the downstairs bedroom. "Daddy?" he asked.

Confident that we would learn in our own time and way what we needed to know, our mother set no agenda for discussing the dead father, but would narrate luminous moments of their life together. We children didn't much discuss him or ask many questions of our mother, though she answered what little we asked. Rather we began private dialogues with him that continued over the years. We had been thrown into a story so rich in vital promise that to allude to our father and his novel was to mourn a bright universe lost. We couldn't speak casually about this founding catastrophe.

The house at 817 South Stull Avenue, Bloomington, Indiana, contained a number of relics that prompted these dialogues. His dress shoes were in our mother's closet, his shaving mug and eye-wash cup in the bathroom medicine chest. We'd take our family picnics on his cream-and-crimson varsity blanket. On the walls there hung a drawing of the novel's hero, John Shawnessy, struggling to pull himself by a root out of the Great Swamp, a silkscreen of Senator Garwood B. Jones arriving at Waycross Station, and a painting of the book jacket after my father's design. Only when I reached puberty did I see that the green map of the county disclosed in its contours a woman's naked body.

I learned to play the piano with two pictures of him, one serious and one smiling, staring at me from atop the Acrosonic. And at the foot of the wooden staircase was a large publicity photograph—a handsome man seeming to smile with the self-assurance of a movie star, with FDR's posthumous *Nothing to Fear* cradled on his lap. When we went upstairs to our rooms for serious tasks or sleep, his eyes followed us as if in ghostly encouragement.

From time to time our mother would take us through the many photo albums of their marriage, including one of great poignancy he made shortly after his novel was accepted. The visionary landscape of Raintree County, sketched in pencil, merges with photographs of familiar Indiana pastoral scenes, and Ross and Vernice are smiling together in photos going back to their courtship days. " 'Tis summer and the days are long!" As my sister would write, his memory "has been carefully preserved for us by our mother and others, like a rare and beautiful life-form, long since extinct, preserved in translucent amber."

Once a year, on Memorial Day, we'd visit his grave at Rose Hill Cemetery in Bloomington, taking peonies, pulling weeds, and cleaning spider eggs out from his name on the simple granite marker.

We'd watch the parade and the DAR ladies reading poetry—"Ain't God good to Indiana? Ain't he, fellers, ain't he though?"—and adjourn to the radio broadcast of the Indy 500, which compounded our domestic tragedy with fresh deaths of its own.

Jeanne and I didn't find out our father was a suicide until she was ten, I eleven. A neighbor girl taunted her after school one day— "Your daddy killed himself! Your daddy killed himself!" My mother brought me into the room with Jeanne to say yes, the neighbor girl was right and it was time for us to know. He'd had a nervous breakdown and felt he would never be well again. Jeanne cried, but once again I silently wondered what this meant.

It still seems remarkable to me that there could have been so uniform a silence among Bloomington children and adults. I hadn't learned for six years what most townsfolk already knew and what Ernest knew instinctively from the beginning. We all know that silences are as compelling as words spoken—and suicide, insanity, sex, and unorthodoxy are matters that families and larger communities often decline to make more real through talk. I suppose the silence in Bloomington came out of cautious respect for family privacy. Amid genuine sympathies, people often presume that suicide survivors must feel some shame, and what good comes anyway from reminding others of their tragedies?

The most sacred relic around the house was the novel itself, which was anything but silent about sex and unorthodoxy. *Raintree County* had been prominently denounced as obscene and blasphemous, and to this day some Indiana folk think he "got what he deserved for writing that dirty book." A small portion of the original manuscript, which he wrapped up with a belt while burning the rest, was left untouched on top of Ernest's and my bookcase. The novel has gold antique lettering on a green cover, and a book jacket blurb that ends, "Through all vicissitudes of residence and travel, the Lockridges have considered Bloomington their home town." Shortly before he died he signed copies for each of us—with his signature only, no personal message.

Even so, the novel spoke to us like a testament from the grave and resuscitated its author in every reading. He left no instructions as to how we should carry on, and I recall my puzzlement as to how

I was to fill in this fatherless future. But he left a novel that some critics would read as the incarnation of an enormous vitality, with all sorts of implicit imperatives. Others would read it as an unusually gaseous suicide note.

Thus we grew up with a novel instead of a father—a novel attempting "no less than a complete embodiment of the American Myth," not just a chunk of it. So driven by the quest for ultimate meaning, so warmed by eroticism, so full of its own search for origins and fatherhood—ending with "a signature of father and preserver, of some young hero and endlessly courageous dreamer"—and so suffused with a sense of loss, Raintree County was to us a haunting. It was an extended letter left to us, with a hero who seemed like our father—exuberant, ambitious, maybe all too good—except that Shawnessy survives in the end.

In 1979 a critic said of Raintree County that it was "an ecological novel written before its time, and its time has finally come." He noted its impassioned evocation of this biological planet and its lament at industrial rape. In the Great Swamp, John Shawnessy sees the astonishing beauty of plants and insects as he searches for an Asian tree said to have been planted by Johnny Appleseed.

Though I never warmed to bugs, I felt a similar biological imperative and a sense of the land's pagan antiquity whenever the southern Indiana spring arrived. A few times as a young adolescent I set out on solitary journeys through river goo and poison ivy, reenacting the feverish pastoralism of the novel.

It is written like a decipherment, with parchment maps and an old county atlas and aboriginal swamp sounds that hint of generous meaning. These beckon its hero to return to origins in a landscape that wears a human face and has imprinted in the contours of its river his own initials. I suppose my adolescent reenactment was an attempt to find the signature of my father in the Indiana wilderness, and perhaps his blessing, but I knew at the time that this was too literal-minded a search for symbols.

I'd feel a rebuff whenever we drove through Henry County, Indiana—the prototype of the novel's county and ancestral home of my father's mother. Signs on the old National Road still inform confused drivers that they are entering "Raintree County." You will look

9

hard and wide for the Shawmucky River, Paradise Lake, and the Great Swamp, and they won't be there in this unarresting farmland some twenty-five miles east of Indianapolis.

You find human testimonials, though: "Raintree Auto Sales," "Raintree Bait and Tackle," "Raintree County Dairy," "Raintree Barber and Styling Shop," "Raintree Industries," and "Raintree Muffler Shop." My father enhanced Henry County with the Eel River, lifted from Miami County where his father had grown up, and with the raintree itself, lifted from the utopian community of New Harmony in the southwest corner of the state. But beyond this he transplanted the great Occidental myths and the great literary texts, from Homer, Virgil, and Shakespeare to Emerson, Hawthorne, Stowe, and Whitman—and the prophets Jesus and John Brown—into this improbable Hoosier landscape. To visit Henry County was to feel an uncanny nostalgia for a locale that never really existed.

Raintree County is not so much an idealization as a distillation of what Ross Lockridge thought worth acknowledging about Western culture—plus that Eastern tree. Yet the novel's principal character is an idealist, in both popular and philosophical senses. This compounded the temptation for us to idealize our dead father, from his personality to his novel to his final act. It's as if Ross Lockridge, Jr. stepped out of a script for the ideal hero, and from his brains to his morals to his good looks he seemed far beyond anything his homely kids could ever be. We took some kidding because both our parents were better looking than any of us.

Our father had excelled in most things—junior and senior class president in high school, state champ in shorthand and typing, member of Indiana University's championship cross-country team and holder of the highest grade point average ever recorded there, president of the Chess Club, winner of a Harvard fellowship, favorite teacher at Simmons College, author of one of the heaviest unsolicited manuscripts ever lugged into a publisher's office, winner of the biggest movie prize, et cetera. He had also been of exemplary character—even-tempered, witty, helpful, nonsmoking, faithful to his wife, hard-working, once described as "an unusually affable genius," who befriended the blind and in passing rescued at least three people, one drowning, one fainting, one marooned. Except for the small wrinkle of self-murder—to which one may add a writer's egomania—there was little to say against him.

And he *isn't* a candidate for the conventional moral demythologizing that underwrites modern biography. Our interest in him won't be found in revelations that he was a bad boy after all. His earlier biographer wrote that he had his sexual initiation at the age of twenty while in Paris. I was sorry to conclude that he probably came home a virgin!

It wasn't lost on us that our father had died at Christ's age and that his birthday, April 25, is one possible date for Shakespeare's. Had his death been a martyrdom—for art and for the philosophical and religious vision of his novel? Had he undergone a crucifixion in the press, denounced by the blind mouths of zealots and philistines? A literary New Testament is dangerous in more ways than the aesthetic—and though I've long since discarded the Christ and Shakespeare analogies, I haven't changed my mind that in a real sense he died for a book.

This book has hardly had the recognition of the King James Bible or, for that matter, of *The Naked and the Dead* and *Other Voices, Other Rooms*, both published in 1948. It stayed on the best-seller lists for a while and then slipped away by the end of the year. Howard Mumford Jones wrote that "the breath of life sweeps through its voluminous pages, and it may be that *Raintree County* marks at last the end of a long slump in American fiction." Charles Lee pronounced it "an achievement of art and purpose, a cosmically brooding book full of significance and beauty." Frank Brookhouser said it "is not merely the first big book of 1948; it is an event in American letters." William York Tindall observed that though it has the multileveled texture of *Ulysses*, it hasn't forsaken the common reader.

It also had plenty of detractors in 1948, including James Baldwin, who got his own career under way with a pan. "We might discover that affirmation consists of more than a handful of cheerful slogans. *Raintree County*, according to its author, cannot be found on any map: and it is always summer there. He might also have added that no one lives there anymore."

We kept the faith over the years and were disgruntled by a literary establishment that declined to canonize it, or maybe even read it, since isn't it a relief to hear that a 1,066-page book isn't worth the time? Couldn't these blockheads, whose profession I would join, see the Great American Novel staring them in the face? Ross Lockridge had written his life into this book, and for it to be neglected or out of print seemed a double death. He thought it a failure in the end, hearing only the pans, but we always hoped it would come to be firmly recognized as an American classic.

And I still do and can claim little objectivity in the matter.

Some critics back in '48 complained about the formal innovations—cinematic dissolves, temporal dislocations, and satiric juxtapositions of myth and journalism. Here I'm confident they were wrong, and it's unusual for a reader today to complain about its difficulty or formal intricacy. But some critics also complained about its lyricism, which they thought secondhand Thomas Wolfe. My father cried foul—it was Whitman he was invoking more than Wolfe, and there was more to his novel than lyricism. There were many other voices.

But rereading the novel after I had become a seasoned academic, I could see that my father might have carried still further his eleventh-hour blue-penciling. I toyed with doing it myself—a light "re-editing" to tighten things up a bit. Might he not have done this himself when he returned years later to the novel that launched a long career?

I decided not to. The novel wouldn't rise or fall because of stylistic unevenness, and besides, all great American novels have a little junk in them, so let it be. And who knows how a future age, if there continues to be a subclass of people reading long books, might receive its lyricism? Beyond this, the novel was what he left behind, and even a son's will-to-power over his father wouldn't sanction "refining" a personal testament. If there was greatness there, I reasoned, some strong critical voice would spread the word eventually.

We've continued to receive testimonials—from common readers more than from professors of literature—with language usually reserved for religious conversions. The novel remains a popular checkout at public libraries. And a few critics have challenged the canon—Joseph Blotner writing that "it may well be one of the five or six most important novels of this era," and Donald Greiner that it is "one of the ten best American novels published since World War II" and the one most neglected by the literary establishment. Another critic has called it, if not the Great American Novel, "indubitably the Great American *Studies* Novel," for what it tells us about American culture.

Greiner writes that "Lockridge's suicide was a stunning blow to American literature. . . . One can only read *Raintree County* and regret the loss of what his continued presence and writing might have offered to the spiritual life of the nation." And Darshan Maini, India's foremost critic of American literature, has recently called for a revival. The novel is "a fugitive American epic" that "has been *punished,* as it were, for its runaway, prodigal success on publication." He thinks it "a splendid example of language in visionary labor." Outside *Moby-Dick, Absalom, Absalom!,* and *Look Homeward, Angel,* there are "few other novels that set out to answer the assault of American reality through such an explosion of prose as does *Raintree County*," which he thinks "has assuredly a touch of greatness."

And on the occasion of the "centennial" of the novel's setting, July Fourth, 1892, Larry Swindell, a syndicated critic, wrote that "no myth is more imposing than the Great American Novel; but if it is truly unattainable, I believe that Ross Lockridge made closer approach than any other writer has, before or since."

On July Fourth, 1992, this "immortal novel," as Swindell called it, was out of print.

Like so many people who have lived in the aftermath of another's creative life, I've watched for signs of a revival. If James Baldwin was right and the novel *is* lamentably a celebration of America, why wasn't it dusted off for the Bicentennial? Since in 1948 it answered to a weary postwar America's need to reclaim a national vitality and sense of purpose, why wasn't it out there for our dispirited Vietnam homecoming? Or with its environmental, racial, feminist, and religious themes, why hasn't its continued bearing on our lives been proclaimed?

Sometimes I felt that Houghton Mifflin just wanted to forget about this curious item on its backlist, which has rarely been available in the author's hometown. But such whimpering about critical neglect or a publisher's marketing choices has expressed mostly a son's sad impatience that others should feel no special need to revive the book his father left behind or the life he took away.

~

Three episodes after 1948—involving journalism, Hollywood, and modern biography—helped keep author and title from oblivion.

In March of 1954 *Confidential* magazine featured an article, "The Sex Book Dr. Kinsey Didn't Sign!" This was the Golden Age of the scandal magazine, and *Confidential* was the most celebrated. "Don't look now, Dr. Kinsey, but we've got a secret that belongs to you. While you've been busy cataloguing our love lives, we've been doing a little research ourselves." During some months of 1948, the best-selling novel was *Raintree County* and the best-selling nonfiction title was *Sexual Behavior in the Human Male*. Improbably, Lockridge and Alfred Kinsey lived down the street one from the other in modest, proper, provincial Bloomington.

So Jay Williams uncovered the truth of the matter. "Until now, one of modern literature's best kept secrets was that Dr. Kinsey collaborated on another volume crammed with sex and titled *Raintree County*. In its way, it created an even bigger national rumpus. . . . Millions read the book when it burst on post-war America in 1948. It was so brutally frank about sex that thousands of readers wrapped their copies in plain brown paper. . . . It was banned in Boston and damned from church pulpits. Scores of southern editors ripped off enraged editorials recommending a bath of tar and feathers for its creator. . . . The book Lockridge created with Dr. Kinsey's help might have been more kindly received, if it hadn't advocated, at least indirectly, the marriage of blacks and whites."

Williams went on to reveal that Lockridge and Kinsey had been best friends, that the "two men got together on long hikes through the rolling hills of Indiana, over the dinner table and at late-night 'bull-sessions,' where they discussed their twin projects. Lockridge listened in youthful fascination as his guide and mentor unreeled for him a panorama of American sex life as it really is." And he modeled his cynical character "the Perfessor" after Kinsey. The Perfessor is "obviously a man who loves to jar people with a statement so frank it leaves jaws hanging: 'I wonder what the new America will be like when . . . the ladies have completely emancipated themselves and exchanged corsets for contraceptives. To the World of Tomorrow, a Feminist Fair / Where the liquor is Free and the Ladies are Bare!' " Kinsey was said to do his gardening in his undies, and Lockridge to have killed himself because of the public outcry over his dirty book.

The article renewed sales of the novel, if to people who must have been frustrated by the metaphysics. My mother was upset. Her husband and Kinsey had met just once, at a faculty musical tea. She asked our lawyer if the family should sue.

At a cocktail party many years later, I was introduced to Jay Williams, by chance as a son of the author of *Raintree County*, a connection I usually kept under wraps. I didn't recognize his name. Recognizing mine, he blanched and asked to be excused. He emerged from a back room half an hour later, still pale, to say that he admired *Raintree County* enormously and that in 1954 an article had appeared in *Confidential* with his by-line. In Europe at the time, he had called his agent to see if he should sue and was advised to let the matter drop.

I almost believed Williams, who had become a prolific novelist as well as theatre historian, art critic, and children's writer, and who died shortly after our meeting. Had he fessed up, I'd have been happy to forgive him, and even thank him for the surge in royalties.

Then there was the MGM movie that appeared in 1957 with the billing that here was an epic to outdo *Gone with the Wind*. The novel had won an enormous prize given by Loew's Incorporated in 1947 but was shelved in 1949. With the advent of TV and other problems, the company went into a disastrous slump in 1947–48. They were also having trouble coming up with a script, and the young author's suicide may have been a damper of sorts. In 1954 it was dusted off and the task of writing the script was given to Millard Kaufman, creator of the cartoon character Mr. Magoo.

In late August of 1956 my mother invited herself and the kids down to Danville, Kentucky, where an army of movie staffers was encamped for a summer of shooting. Indiana no longer looked enough like itself and to its dismay had been passed over in the location search. Montgomery Clift was still recovering from an automobile accident in May that interrupted shooting for six weeks. Leaving a party at Elizabeth Taylor's home in the Benedict Canyon hills, he had driven into a telephone pole, losing two front teeth, cutting a hole through his upper lip, and breaking his nose and jaw. He refused to drop out of the film, and, in constant pain, kept a gray satchel full of pills by his side. He stumbled through the rest of the film mostly in right profile; the left was lumpy and inert. In his off-camera life in recent weeks he had faked his own bloody death, run naked into the streets of Danville after a nightmare, broken a toe, and badly burned two fingers with a cigarette while out cold from an accidental overdose of sleeping pills.

Enter the Lockridge family hopeful of finding in Clift someone capable of playing John Shawnessy, who in many ways resembles his creator. I shook the hand of someone bent over, fidgety, gaunt, bloodshot, and much older than his thirty-five years. His efforts were heroic, but still the great actor mumbled, moved his wired jaw with difficulty, forgot his lines, and seemed by turns manic and drugged. The crew was shooting a scene that featured Shawnessy and Susanna Drake, the neurotic heroine played by Elizabeth Taylor. Both were lying drunk on the banks of the Shawmucky River following Shawnessy's great victory in the Raintree County footrace.

Taylor: "Let's go swimming." Clift: "In that thing? You'll sink." Taylor: "Then you can save me!" She grabs the oak leaf garland from his head and shrieks as Clift takes off in klutzy pursuit. Ten-year-old Terry Ross Lockridge, collecting tadpoles upstream, screams: "MOM, IS THAT ACTING?"

For the remainder of our stay we overheard staff muttering, "Mom, is that acting?" while director Edward Dmytryk called for take after take from his stuttering, shrieking leads. But in one scene of sentimental leave taking, Eva Marie Saint, playing the character Nell Gaither, wept excellently and later told my mother that her presence had helped. She knew that Nell was partly based on Vernice Lockridge.

A publicity campaign was supposed to include locally organized Raintree hunts and Raintree plantings, as well as nationally merchandised Raintree cufflinks, shoes, guns, luggage, good luck coins, hats, hairstyles, gloves, and petticoats. "THE GREAT AMERICAN NOVEL OF THE CIVIL WAR BECOMES THE MOST IMPORTANT SCREEN EVENT IN TWO DE-

CADES!" It was to be a movie of firsts: the most expensive ever filmed by MGM in the U.S.A., the first use of a 65 mm camera, the longest screenplay, the first movie to have an entire book about its making on sale simultaneously with its release, and the first Hollywood movie to be premiered in Louisville. Little mention was made of Ross Lockridge, Jr. in the vast promotional material, and certainly no mention of his suicide.

We waited in vain for invitations to the great premiere. Finally my mother once again invited us down herself—but no, she wasn't requesting five tickets, she wanted enough for all members of the collective family, which on her more prolific side included a miscellany of Bakers, Chitwoods, Mumbys, Nicholsons, and Kranstivers. MGM obliged.

Our hopes were raised by John Green's fine score, which arrived a week before the premiere. We hummed it as we drove down to Louisville in our secondhand oil-leaking Chevrolet. I was introduced to Van Johnson, imported as a friendly accessory star. "Gee, you look like me when I was a kid," he said. I almost asked him about the metal plate in his head. My mother was handsomely photographed with Eva Marie Saint. At the screening we sat behind Taylor and Mike Todd, who introduced himself as Mister Elizabeth Taylor. We breathed deeply as the overture began.

Critics agree that the movie we then watched is among the world's worst. "*Raintree County* begins in tedium and ends, 185 leaden minutes later, in apathy. Montgomery Clift, talking through his nose and expressing sensitivity of soul by seldom looking other cast members in the eye, jitters through the role of John Shawnessy," said the critic for *Time*. The film "is certainly not helped by a lot of symbolical gobbledegook about a tree called the raintree," said Hollis Alpert. "To say that it moves at a snail's pace is to insult the snail," said William Zinsser. "Millard Kaufman's screenplay is a formless amoeba of a thing, and therein lies the fatal weakness of this costly, ambitious film," said Bosley Crowther.

During the screening, one Hollywood interpolation caused my mother to lunge forward, her hands over her face, crying "Oh my God!," with Millard Kaufman sitting directly behind her. There was no applause in Louisville's Brown Theatre. Finding something positive to say, Todd whispered to Taylor, "It's your film, it's your film."

Her portrayal of a tormented southern belle would get her an Oscar nomination, for in this film she learned, as she said, "to climb up the walls and chew a lot of scenery." MGM studio head Dore Schary was canned shortly after the fiasco.

How had it happened? The director, Dmytryk, speaks of the novel as a "long, rambling, involved story of small-town life in Indiana." It was "assigned to a fine writer, Millard Kaufman, as a do-or-die project. He did pretty well, mostly by ignoring a good deal of the novel and striking off in new directions." Dmytryk would later tell a Canadian television producer that he himself never read the novel.

In newspaper interviews Mr. Magoo's creator said he thought *Raintree County* a magnificent novel but there were certain "confusions" in it. He outlined the novel on 1,791 separate pieces of notepaper, dropped the flashback structure, and focused on six years of the novel's fifty-three, the years 1859 through 1865 featuring the Susanna figure. As one critic would point out, the novel is constructed as if it were a film, but Kaufman wrote a film constructed as if it were a novel.

He confronted a novel in which the two principal heroines, as well as the hero's first son, die. With Hollywood at his back, he elected to preserve Nell's life and her virginity, which in the novel is lost to Shawnessy's rival. In the end Susanna conveniently drowns in swampmuck, the son is rescued, and Nell, a patient Griselda, is ready to forgive and forget.

Beyond such clarifications, the new direction in which Kaufman struck off was to supplant the novel's dialogue with his own. The moral of the piece is expressed this way by Kaufman's Shawnessy: "I've learned that to see the Raintree is not nearly as important as what you find looking for it, and I'm happy with what I've found—you."

Monty Clift agreed to do the film after three years of turning down better scripts. Elizabeth Taylor urged him to make the movie with her, and besides he was broke. He accepted only $250,000 of the offered $300,000 fee, though, asking that MGM make a better movie with the difference, because he felt the script read like "a soap opera with elephantiasis." Robert LaGuardia writes that Clift "sprawled the 1,066 page Ross Lockridge novel and two copies of Millard Kaufman's screenplay on his desk, and like a devoted Bob

Cratchit, with meticulous glare and tensely held pencil, he went from one to the other, taking dialogue from the book and enlarging or substituting for Kaufman's dialogue."

His efforts went unheeded. Though Clift is in virtually every scene, he doesn't speak a memorable or reflective line, leaving viewers to wonder why other characters think him some sort of literary world-beater.

Whatever the interventions of Hollywood, I still have to ask what there is about my father's novel that could yield such dubious spawn. That "gobbledegook" about the raintree, for instance. In the novel, the raintree is a symbol grounded in local legend and occasioned by the human need for myth-making, a symbol skeptically undercut by the "Perfessor." It is later authenticated in an indirect sort of way, rather like a Hawthorne story. In the movie it is improbably the skeptical Perfessor himself who introduces the raintree legend to the local aspiring bard, Shawnessy—who ought to have heard of it already—and sends him packing. For his troubles he would discover the secret of life and be proclaimed a hero. The distance between a compelling and a thick symbolism isn't very great. If it collapses, we gag.

Another problem of adaptation is that John Shawnessy of the novel sees lots of life but in a strictly dramatic sense doesn't do much of anything. He is merely a writer, which isn't fun to watch, and he doesn't manage even to *write*. Any adaptor would have a real challenge here.

The author feared what Hollywood would make of his novel. His cousin Mary Jane Ward, author of the 1946 novel *The Snake Pit*, would later say she became reconciled to his death only when she saw the movie—at least he had been spared this! Some friends in the film world tell me that I'm too hard on the movie, that some of the novel comes through, that Lee Marvin turned in his first superb character performance, that Taylor too comes of age here, that Green's score is one of the finest. The film has a cult following because of a ghoulish pleasure in spotting when Clift is pre-accident and when post. Patricia Bosworth thinks Clift's professional death occurred in his near-fatal accident, which lends the movie the dignity of a mausoleum. But I remember what my father brashly wrote to Louis B. Mayer in 1947: "I could sit down and write in one week-end the kind of corny scenario that *Raintree County* could be turned into."

In August of 1974 I found my father staring at me pleasantly from the front page of *The New York Times Book Review.* "Destroyed by Success," the caption read. Soon thereafter John Leggett appeared on the *Today* show talking about Ross Lockridge and Thomas Heggen, author of the novel *Mister Roberts,* whose death in 1949 was a probable suicide. Leggett's dual biography, *Ross and Tom,* was widely praised for its "marvellous feeling of reality" in narrating these "two American tragedies." Lockridge and Heggen, who never met, were said to have had parallel experiences. I had cooperated in the biography, but never guessed it would be so touted.

Time has worked its ironies. By the time I was ten, my father's death already felt like an anciently legislated event. And thirty-three years seemed a pretty fair allotment. As I've become older—older than he was at his death—he's become younger and his death has seemed increasingly premature. It has also come to seem closer in time as my sense of history has deepened. But even were I to outlive him threefold, he'll always seem older than I insofar as he remains my *father.*

So one jarring thing about this biography for *me* was that John Leggett called him "Ross" throughout and wrote of him as someone very young indeed. His early sense of kinship as an aspiring writer with Ross and Tom made it "remarkably easy for me to slip into their adolescent skins." He was now "an adult and a writer" looking back. How dare Leggett address my father as "Ross"! He had never even met him! As a son, I didn't like the tone of amiable paternalism with which Leggett ushers readers—all of whom are presumed wiser than the subjects of his biography—into a spectacle of adolescent self-destruction.

The portrait that emerges is fairly well summed up in the index, where the "character" of Ross is broken down into "ambition," "competitiveness of," "materialism," "self-confidence," "self-praise," and "single-mindedness." Having nothing else to go on, critics and readers tended to think the biography "deeply sympathetic and tactful," even "understated." Obviously Ross, a humorless figure, had brought it on himself and had become, as one reader put it, "a pain in the ass" by the time he did himself in. He and Heggen were "pictured as little boys in desperate pursuit of approval," wrote another, but at least Heggen had a sense of humor.

Epilogue

Leggett grants that "a *genuine* egoism is a writer's only defense against the enemies of indifference, disparagement, flattery, that are surely awaiting him. This was a discovery Ross had yet to make." Writers must ultimately write for themselves. Ross's egoism wasn't genuine because it was too bound up with his mother's will for him. It also coexisted with an extreme naïveté, even an inability to distinguish bourbon from sugar water. Leggett is an Easterner who draws on the Midwest Bumpkin paradigm.

Biographies, mine included, should not be written to reconfirm the idealizing of family members, who are rarely satisfied in any event. But idealizing in a moral sense wasn't the root of my problem with the biography. Rather, it was that Leggett's Ross comes off as such a lightweight!

Ross and Tom has two theses, one sociological and one psychological. The sociological has to do with what has been unhappily termed the "Bitch Goddess Success." Wishing to be first in everything, Ross pursued the commercial underside of the American Dream, writing a book to win the big prizes, dreaming of the pages of *Life,* rounding up "Houghton's startled flock and send[ing] it flying along the promotion trail." He couldn't live with what success brought.

The psychological thesis is Freudian. Encouraged by a strong mother to pursue a literary career, Ross wrote his novel as a "gift" for her in answer to Oedipal stirrings. It was an attempt to secure her love. His father, a local historian of mediocre intellect, had spent the better part of his career looking for work he could endure. He was a "dilettante" not respected by academic historians, despite his many books. His son thus suffered "patricidal guilt" for having demolished his father with something more glorious than *he* had ever achieved.

A similar reading of Tom Heggen's life prompted the novelist Wallace Stegner, Heggen's cousin, to reply that Heggen's "father never *exerted* any authority. He was the gentlest father I ever saw, and least likely to stir up filial revolt, and Tom's mother was not so ambitious and driving by half as the mother Mr. Leggett imagines. . . . I suspect that Mr. Leggett was imprisoned in a thesis, or a series of them, from the first, and resisted having his conclusions disturbed by awkward facts or by the quibbles of relatives."

We Lockridges kept silent about the biography, feeling that nobody would believe our quibbles either. And we hoped some of those who told us this wasn't quite the Ross Lockridge they remembered would make their views public. They didn't.

His father wasn't exactly a dilettante, as thousands of Hoosiers in the 1930s and '40s could have attested. Ross Senior went about his self-constructed career of populist historian with the passion of an evangelist. At the time widely known as "Mr. Indiana," he would be pleased that local history has now been admitted into academe, which concedes that history isn't necessarily something that happened in fourteenth-century France. Taking his measure with a conventional academic yardstick, Leggett didn't capture the extent to which Ross Senior was a *character* with a visionary agenda.

A son with ambitions of his own was bound to rebel against such a father. (He would also rebel against his mother.) But though *Raintree County* was admittedly better than *The Old Fauntleroy Home,* I find little evidence of patricidal guilt over it. This was a brave guess on Leggett's part, for the suicide begs for some bold interpretive act. But the evidence isn't there.

Before publishing any of his own novels, Leggett worked as an editor at Houghton Mifflin, and the central exhibit in this biography is Ross's correspondence with his publisher. It yields the portrait of a self-consumed, mean-spirited, and frenetic adolescent who thought his bravura piece greater than *The Republic* and *Ulysses*—and who had a temper tantrum over splitting the spoils with his publisher.

These letters are a sorry spectacle. Most writers have the good sense to camouflage their vanity somewhat. If there was ever any reminder that they had better betray it ephemerally over the phone, the embarrassments of *Ross and Tom* must be it. But written after initial drafting of the twenty-pound manuscript, the letters reveal an author on the brink of illness.

James Michener wrote to Leggett about this in 1974. "These are some of the damnedest letters I've ever read: they remind me of Marcel Proust and Theodore Dreiser launching and sustaining their pitiful campaigns for the Nobel Prize. A score of times in my reading I stopped to howl in disbelief. Another score of times I yelled to my wife in the other room, 'My God! Listen to this!' I simply cannot conceive of a grown man of 33, with the academic background that he had, behaving in such a jejune manner, and one that ultimately would have to be suicidal . . . My only question is whether he was not so sick, after his incredible self-persecution during the writing of his great book, that all of his acts from the date of finishing the manuscript must be judged as one grand, extended illness for which he was not responsible. I think so."

I believe that Michener's private surmise to Leggett concerning the onset of my father's illness, nowhere echoed in public critical discussion of *Ross and Tom,* was largely true. It was easy to read the biography instead as apt illustration of how pride goeth before a fall.

And pride for what? Just about the only evidence one finds in its pages that Ross had some talent is a couple of excerpts from letters written when he was nineteen and living in Paris.

My mother sent Leggett a few excerpts after he declined even to read the larger *family* correspondence from 1933 through 1947. (To be sure, he had his hands full in writing two biographies at the same time.) It is difficult to square these clever, spirited letters with the vain and benighted bumpkin who is said to have written them.

Some of our differences are a matter of perspective, and mine is necessarily that of a son. But I feel that Leggett's rendering of the life, work, and personality was limited by the modest number of family papers he thought relevant and the few people he interviewed. Despite the work he put into it—for which I am grateful—he wasn't enough of a sleuth. Instead of source materials beyond those letters to Houghton Mifflin, he preferred to rely on interviews and written recollections—and often on a novelist's hunches. Readers without intimate prior knowledge would never guess how much of this undocumented biography is "novelization." And it was governed early on by paradigms—the Midwesterner, the Innocent Abroad, the Bitch Goddess Success, and the Freudian Family Romance.

A strong implication throughout the biography is that Ross failed in art as in life. Leggett never suggests we should read or reread the novel, about which he says little. Upon reading it in 1948 he had asked himself, "Where did he get the brass and courage, to say nothing of the knowledge, for so heroic an undertaking?" But to acknowledge a gigantic ambition is hardly to concede talent or lasting achievement. Instead, this immense work collapses at last into the motive of its composition—it's a gift to his mother. And it's a period piece whose moment has come and gone. When asked on the *Today* show if either *Raintree County* or *Mister Roberts* is worth reading, he replied that it was a matter of taste.

This view may prevail. I won't be challenging it head-on—the value judgments of literary offspring are worthless. And I must allow the possibility that the novel's place on the edge of the canon is simply a measure of refined critical taste in the academy. But the life of Ross Lockridge, Jr. has implications well beyond the issue of his novel's stature. I'll narrate more intimately my father's life as an American *writer*. What was the vision? What sources from his own life did he tap? What was his writing like before he got to *Raintree County*? What decisions did he make as a writer driven to greatness? And what—be it greatness or rubbish—ended up on the pages of that novel?

Many of my father's friends objected to *Ross and Tom*. They said he'd been more likable than that, better than that, more sophisticated, with a greater sense of whimsy. Whether or not he was these things is of little critical interest. But I found it difficult to reconcile Leggett's reading of the life with my own reading of the work, published and unpublished, and with much of what I'd heard about my father over the years—which I thereafter had to hold under suspicion. I'd thought him, before his illness, a person of greater intellect—more impassioned, more reflective, more committed to a vision beyond personal ego, a better writer, and therefore more worth reading about.

Rehabilitation was thus a motive and a bias early on in my search, and I tried to be wary of it. Yet the evidence of a larger life, as narrated here, crowded in on me from the beginning.

Jay Williams, Millard Kaufman, and John Leggett were all initially taken with *Raintree County*. They were young men with large writing ambitions of their own when the novel appeared in 1948—and if there was envy, it was probably outweighed by admiration. Kaufman, who had already won two Academy Award nominations when given the screenplay assignment, said it was a "labor of love" on which he expended more of himself than on any previous task.

But in the popular media—journalism, film, commercial

publishing—we often pare down the objects even of our admiration. So the novel becomes an adjunct to the Kinsey Report, the movie a vehicle for Liz Taylor, and the author's life a cautionary tale about the perils of inflated success in America.

Today Ross Lockridge, Jr. is best known as a literary suicide and *Raintree County* as a late-evening soporific that Ted Turner uncorks every year on cable. Lockridge's survivors wish he were instead known as the author of a great novel found on every bookshelf, and we take heart that Penguin Books is publishing a new edition of the novel simultaneously with this biography.

Our wish has less to do with literary idolatry than with mourning—for to revive the novel would be to revive the dead author in his greatest hopes for himself. But mourning is a special kind of hunger—a hunger for something forever missing. And nothing could restore my father to his writing desk, sitting down to work again on the morning of March 7, 1948, as Ernest and I got ready for Sunday School, shaking his head at how close he had come to doing himself in the night before.

～

Ross Lockridge, Jr. killed himself in the bosom of his larger family—his parents, sister, brother, aunts, uncles, wife, children, and a large assortment of in-laws all living in or around Bloomington. His death has left a complex legacy felt in different ways by his survivors.

Shortly after his son's death, Ross Senior wrote a friend that, "resigned by faith" to his great loss, he was "more deeply devoted now than ever before to my work of Hoosier Historical promotion and shall give my remaining years to it with almost exclusive interest. This is what Ross Jr. wants and expects me to do. He made provision for it."

And out on the history stump he went eight days after the funeral, speaking in the summer and autumn of 1948 at dozens of historical sites—the battlegrounds of Mississinewa, and of Olde Towne on Eel River, the Constitution Elm at Corydon, Little Turtle's grave, Johnny Appleseed's grave, James Whitcomb Riley's house, the Angel Indian Mounds, and the Labyrinth at New Harmony. A student that autumn composed fifty-eight encomiastic couplets on the seasoned orator, who

> *Could quote each Indiana bard,*
> *And reel off speeches by the yard.*
> *We sat quite mute and held our breath*
> *At Patrick Henry's "give me death";*
> *Not just one line, nor even two—*
> *He said the bloomin' speech clear through!*
> *And 'fore we'd time to close the door*
> *He'd upped and said a dozen more;*
> *Amazed we sat and listened rapt*
> *As on the floor his specs he slapt!!*

Only weeks earlier Ross Senior had watched his dispirited son, shortly before his death, stumble through Patrick Henry's speech.

We children would visit the old Lockridge house on High Street, where at bedtime we could choose between Grandpa's old frontier stories or Grandma's Tommy and Zippy stories. Though I preferred the latter, I'd begun to feel sorry for my grandfather and gave him equal time. He slept alone in the tiny upstairs bedroom that had been his youngest son's. He had not been a dinner companion for the squeamish since he preferred fat to meat, and a lifetime of this vice was taking its toll on his heart. I'd sometimes go with him to the First Methodist Church. Breathing hard, he would take his medication halfway up the staircase. His Indian bearhugs were losing their crunch.

When he gave up directing the Hoosier Historical Institutes in 1950, some associates took pity and raised twenty-three dollars to replace the briefcase held together only by its straps—and though they got his initials wrong he was so moved at the surprise presentation that he was for once speechless. In retirement he taught recitation to my brother Ernest and cousin Kay and dictated to his daughter *The Story of Indiana,* his tenth published book, which remains the standard junior high history. Whatever its virtues, it occasioned a groan from my peers whenever the teacher told us to take it out. In the fiction section of his bibliography that includes titles by Dreiser, Booth Tarkington, Lew Wallace, and Marguerite Young, he didn't list *Raintree County.* Maybe he was still uneasy about those cuss words.

He died in 1952. The Hoosier Historical Institutes, his great legacy to the state, petered out a few years later under a new director.

Tommy and Zippy were two hand-sized elves who fell from the pocket of an extra-terrestrial giant onto the Indiana farm of Grandpa and Grandma. Elsie Lockridge made up dozens of episodes, often involving the abduction of these elves by local wildlife. Grandpa finally encircles their play area with an electric fence and binds the elves with a long rope. Fence and rope supplement the "Good Power" who protects Tommy and Zippy. In this fictional family all perils are overcome.

Could my grandmother look at her own family with this degree of cheer? Her eldest son didn't take rope to the river and drowned at sixteen, her youngest was a suicide at thirty-three, her only daughter was obese and celibate, and her second son had turned into a Republican.

After 1952 Elsie Lockridge lived with her daughter, kept up her Christian Science, read Thomas Mann, donated her husband's voluminous papers to the Indiana State Library, and gave her talk, "Henry County Real Life Background in *Raintree County*," at various clubs and historical societies. She too was never fully reconciled to the novel's indiscretions but was still proud that it was based on her father and that she was the prototype of the young girl Eva.

Elsie writes of her own girlhood: "She just did not like herself very well. She did not like her looks. She did not like her actions; many of the things that she did she knew were just plain horrid—*yet she did them.* . . . She wanted to be beautiful, gifted, and to have a winning personality—all for her beloved father's sake. *She wasn't any of these things.*"

Her son listened to such self-portraits and must have chuckled, she says, when he wrote of Eva that she "was a fat, bald, bugeyed thing that looked something like a toad in a dress." And he "must have been a discerning person to have seen possibilities in this dreadful child. That he did see them—or thought he saw them—is revealed by the infinite tenderness with which he depicts little Eva's questing—if tumultuous—nature, struggling to pull herself out of the Great Swamp—out of her stormy, unlovely childish self into—as he (the author) makes her—the beginning of a beautiful personality. For Eva of Raintree County will always remain at twelve years, just as the clock in the Court House Tower of the Raintree County Atlas is always fixed at nine o'clock. . . . I can almost believe I am little Eva at the year twelve, reading her father's poem, 'One Summer Morn' as told on page 757 of *Raintree County.* The author loved this poem. He used the last line of each verse, ' 'Tis summer and the days are long' again and again."

My father dedicated the novel to his mother, and on the printed map of his legendary county he shaped the contours of the Shawmucky River so that, in a mirror, the name "Elsie" may be seen. It joins the cursive initials, JWS, of his hero—her father. Late in life she said, "I loved my father—probably too much."

She spent her last months mute, paralyzed by a stroke. During her illness I played the piano for her, and to this day wish I'd played more Mozart and less Chopin. She died at the age of eighty-one. I challenged the Christian Science practitioner who told my Aunt Lillian that her grief was mere self-pity. She had spent most of her life with her mother, sharing the master bedroom, the nightlight always on. As if following a sad trite script to prove her grief was grief, Lillian died of a heart attack less than two months later.

For many years after the night of March 6, 1948, Vernice Lockridge thought she could smell the odor of car exhaust in the garage behind our house. The death instrument, a new Kaiser, had been hauled away by the police, never to be seen again. She would feel guilty about not sensing what was going to happen that night, about not having been more upbeat in her final conversation with her husband. And she'd wonder in deep pain if he might still be living had he married someone else. But she has never expressed any resentment at the desertion—he was convinced he would never get well and his death seemed to her a final act of love. He knew she'd understand. But if only he had held on till spring! she would say. His illness might have passed.

She was alienated for a time from Elsie Lockridge, who later in

1948 called in a medical doctor for Ross Senior, whereas she had, as a Christian Scientist, discouraged medical help for her own son.

And my mother alluded once many years later to a contract dispute my father had had with Houghton Mifflin that "broke him."

Guardian of the estate and the name, she maintained a dual existence as widow of the famed author and as hometown girl, who'd be rewarded for a trace of celebrity status by requests to serve as head of PTAs, women's clubs, and University organizations. And she was often asked to serve as secretary, on the assumption that her life with a writer had given her some credentials. My grandparents thought her not up to the task of raising all four kids, but she refused to farm any of us out and came to be known as a profile in courage, whatever the results of her parenting.

Her own girlhood was austere, and she had worked her way through college. She therefore ran a rather liberal household supported for many years by proceeds from the novel. Her children didn't have to take on summer jobs or submit to many constraints. Terry Ross kept a menagerie of wild and domestic birds, snakes, lizards, turtles, a skunk, and a caiman. Jeanne had a black lamb and maintained a rotbox for the roadside carrion she later pieced together into beautiful skeletons. (The Indiana University zoology department purchased them for ten dollars each.) Our sideyard became the neighborhood playground where we ran riot with nocturnal sessions of Kick the Can and Starlight Moonlight. I played the piano, Ernest the clarinet and sax, Terry Ross his cornet and guitar, while Jeanne had the voice in the family. We swam in the limestone quarries and went spelunking. My brothers and I peed in Kinsey's frog pond and shot up the woods with our .22s. Except for Jeanne, we could stay out all hours on dates.

We read whatever we liked, though little Jeanne was found out when she hid *God's Little Acre* under her bed. When a book report I did for Miss Gilstrap on *From Here to Eternity* came back with a C-plus and the reprimand that I shouldn't be reading portrayals of "commonplace, sordid human weaknesses," my mother objected to the censorship. Little occasion for parental revolt arose under our mother's gentle discipline.

She didn't go out on a date for sixteen years. The rather well-off widow received a few crackpot proposals in the mail. But she gave no encouragement to anyone—the memory of her husband stayed too fresh. The few pictures from her first year of widowhood show a wan young woman sitting on ragged grass, surrounded by small children. Instead of a new husband, her mother, Lillie Thrasher Baker, moved into the house, originally to help out with Jeanne's fifth birthday and then a family measles epidemic. She stayed until her death sixteen years later at ninety-two. Weighing less than ninety pounds and standing four feet ten, with deeply wrinkled cheeks and alert blue eyes, she was quick to smile, fun to tease, hard of hearing, and expert at navy beans and cornbread. "Land o' Goshen!" "Well forevermore!," she would say. She and her youngest daughter had not been particularly close but now they became so, at the quiet domestic center of a household overrun with kids and their friends.

As she did her household chores, our mother would sing unself-consciously in her high sweet soprano with slight vibrato—the same songs she sang with her husband when they did the dishes together, "Believe me if all these endearing young charms," "Beautiful dreamer, wake unto me," "Back home again in Indiana," and some French songs. Her intonation was always wistful, not bitter or impassioned. Singing "I dream of Jeanie with the light brown hair" to her daughter, she'd not go beyond the first stanza, since thereafter it becomes clear that Jeanie is dead. As the years have progressed she substitutes a whistle for forgotten phrases. These songs link her and us to earlier days in the spirit of elegiac acceptance.

About the time we kids were moving out of the house, I dropped a hint to a professor's secretary that my mother might be regarded as once again eligible. Russell Noyes had been my father's master's thesis director at Indiana University as well as my mother's own teacher. He was a widower with grown children of his own and at sixty-two was twelve years her senior. Within hours he telephoned, proposing a "social visit." She assumed it meant one of her children was in trouble at the University. At dinner Noyes passed inspection by the entire neighborhood, and he and Vernice Lockridge were married within the year. Noyes was given his charge—show our mother the world! The day before the wedding, she removed the conspicuous pictures of her first husband from the walls of the Stull Avenue house.

Though her children remain protective of her, she is made of sterner stuff than we. In her second widowhood she remains faithful to both husbands, dines with Bloomington friends going back to college and high school days—the old Lake Gang—and possesses the good humor and courage to confront the past with a precise memory that helps underwrite this biography.

In 1957 we five were invited to New Castle, Indiana, to see a new "Raintree Dining Room" with murals depicting episodes of the novel. The local newspaper sent a reporter. "When asked if any of the children would follow their father's writing career, young Ross upset his family grammatically by saying 'Ernest, tell about the two books you have wroten.' But Ernest [still a teenager] was reluctant to discuss anything he has written and so Ross again volunteered that 'he would some day write like his dad.'"

Had our father lived, we might not have pursued careers in literature and the arts. The force of his personality and achievement might have imposed too much, and there would have been no vacancy asking to be filled. One would have thought his fate cautionary, but the local assumption—and one we didn't really challenge—was that we would carry on the family trade. Except for Ross, who was dyslexic, we were fated for the IU English major. We didn't think of ourselves as crippled suicide survivors but as offspring of a great writer who died young. Staring at our father's hugely contradictory fate, we chose to read it as success, not failure, and hoped our careers would somehow take fire from his.

Ernest had wanted to write novels from a very early age but didn't admit it to himself for a time. "But when I was seventeen and had been writing all that time, I just said that's it. That's what I want to do." He took his doctorate at Yale and has wroten novels but not exactly "like his dad." They number more than one. And they begin and end with different assumptions. In its promo for one of them, Book-of-the-Month Club mentioned that Ernest was son of the author of *Raintree County*. Some readers took umbrage at his dark absurdist narrative, whose war of choice is not a distant civil war that feeds our national mythology, but Vietnam, and whose protagonist lives out a parodic nightmare of fame in an America where "endlessly courageous dreamers" are likely to go insane.

Extending another aspect of my father's career, I completed the

Harvard doctorate he abandoned in favor of novel-writing, and have wroten two books of philosophical criticism.

I labored on one of these for more years than he spent on his novel and produced a fat treatise on Romantic literature, with a manifesto for a new ethical criticism that I hoped would knock the socks off Derrida and Harold Bloom. When I approached my publisher's booth at the major professional convention, I found it wasn't being displayed—it was tucked into a side shelf. I weakly asked would they consider putting it on display? They agreed, but that afternoon it was again side-lined. A few months later the book seemed to have been peripheralized into nihility, so I wrote my editor, who replied, "Sales of the book have now reached 500 copies world wide, which is most encouraging . . ."

Forty-six of those *I* had purchased. Glumly I reflected that mine is the more common fate of authors, who may dream of my father's good fortune in prize-money, promotion, sales, reviews, and the movies—but who settle for getting into print. So what was *his* lament?

The modern talk of "belatedness" and an author's mortal struggle with literary predecessors has a curious twist here. Our father attempted a novel that would say it all. We genuinely hoped he had succeeded, but if he had, there would be nothing left for *us* to say.

If my younger siblings have diverged somewhat more, the father still has had great sway. With parents and older brothers holding literary degrees, Jeanne as an energetic teenager pursued an interest in biology, piecing together those skeletons and learning the body parts of paramecia, and I was cheered to think we had somebody doing something different. But female scientists weren't much encouraged in those days—a senior zoology professor to whom the family had lent money wouldn't even let her wash out his test tubes—and in an anguished moment she switched to English, loving books in any event. She went on to earn another Ph.D. from Harvard. Thereafter regarded as a faculty wife despite her literary roots, degree, and teaching experience, she took a more sensible degree and has had a career as an administrator in health care and higher education.

An artist and poet, Ross III reads his father's novel as environmental prophecy. He has worked to save the desert mountains of the Southwest where he lives. It was he who began the bibliographical work on his father's papers. Early on, his name was burdensome, if only because people didn't expect its bearer to be dyslexic. Grandmother Lockridge patiently tutored him in reading and spelling. His father had thrown all might and being into one overriding work, with consequences both wondrous and dire, so Ross has strategically divided his own ambitions between art and literature. For his published poems he uses a pseudonym.

Ross has no children, nor have I. Ernest's and Jeanne's offspring, now young adults, have only recently begun to express an interest in their grandfather's novel. When I began my research, only one of five had gotten around to reading it.

We all regretted not having this particular father about the house over the years. But we never morally *blamed* him for killing himself. We felt the motives and circumstances must have been compelling, even if we could never hope to dispel the dark sublimity that surrounded the night of March 6, 1948. We sensed it wasn't a petulant, small-minded, or selfish exit, and hoped he had silently said goodbye to us in his suffering. Oddly, the suicide seemed to teach us sympathy.

Suicide survivors often feel unexpressed resentment, rejection, and guilt, as well as grief. Therapists today look for such feelings, often obscured by denial. The therapeutic ideal is that suicide survivors should express all negative feelings openly within the family setting. Resentment toward the deserting family member is then less likely to turn inward. Many therapists believe the fact of a parent's suicide should no longer be withheld even from small children. Ideally, widows work through their grief within a year or so and become once again eligible, the pictures of the deceased and other relics tucked away. To the point of numbness in the popular media, we're all supposed to be "getting on with our lives." Families that do not talk it all out openly are declared more or less dysfunctional.

I quarrel with this thinking only insofar as it seems ideal in the extreme. How often can families talk everything out? And is it sometimes lost sight of that tragedies are tragic? In our protracted mourning, we didn't grow up with these enlightened interventions. We coped as best we knew how, within a broad range of survivors' responses. If we were dysfunctional, we somehow functioned. My siblings and I feel our mother did well by us.

And I enjoy the irony that had I resolved all the mourning and melancholy early on, this book would not exist. My father might have said something similar about his own book, because *Raintree County* is a meditation on time and loss in which protracted mourning has a creative as well as pathological dimension.

We grew up with an instinctive recognition of how the weight of tragedy disables easy moral censure. So none of us has thought it appropriate to speak of forgiveness. When he took his own life, he had to do it, and we didn't feel like crying, "Daddy, you bastard, you shouldn't have."

But he left us with a sense of blank desertion even so, and we improvised an image of him and his hopes for us. "I spent much of my idle time wandering the same country roads he had as a boy and young man," my sister writes. "As I walked the great rectangle of High Street, Moore's Pike, Sare Road, and Rogers Road, the same route he walked with his dog Skirtie, I often thought of him, wondering if he would have seen something of himself in me, if he would have liked me." With some anxious summoning, this father would appear as a benevolent and caring shade, who infused us with his own vitality from beyond the grave.

~

When I undertook this biography, I thought the first place to look was the FBI files. I'd get out of a lot of work describing the relationship of creativity and depression if the FBI was simply putting LSD in my father's milk. And he did fear at one point that something was wrong with his physical brain. Through the Freedom of Information Act, I obtained the forty-six-page file, which has to do exclusively with a letter postmarked May 1, 1948, Richmond, Indiana, addressed to the editor of *The Indianapolis News*.

"Sir: ROSS LOCKRIDGE did not die an accidental death. I killed him. The circumstances were these. He ruined my daughter. Superficially cultured, the swine had no more morals than a tom cat. He had a clandestine affair with my daughter. He thought it a joke—a broken heart and a bastard child were nothing to him. But he reckoned without me. He and all his male issue have to be killed. I have started the job. I shall complete it. I came upon him in his garage, intending at that time no more than to tell him that I was resolved on his death. But we had words as we sat in his car. I slapped him. He fainted. I saw my chance, turned on the motor, closed the door and came away. I think no one saw me. Now it is impossible for any to remember. It was the perfect murder. Yet his punishment was incomplete, for contrary to my plan his murder was not recognised as implacable justice. The killing of his sons cannot be carried out immediately without grave danger to me, and if in bringing him and his family to justice I am hanged by the law, justice will have miscarried. So I must wait till my killing can be completely anonymous. Then his sons will die, preferably one by one. Perhaps his too sudden execution—his very brief remorse—will be made up for by the expectation of retribution which his sons will suffer. The Bible says that we are to take an eye for an eye, but I am going to take three sons for a daughter. Did you know the circumstance, I am sure that you would agree with me that perhaps even less than justice is being done. Faithfully yours, WINSTON DONAHUE."

The FBI interviewed my grandparents and Aunt Lillian and were satisfied that the death could only have been suicide. They were unable to find any evidence of an affair with a young girl. Lillian told the FBI of her brother's devotion to his wife going back to schooldays. They didn't interview my mother—on advice of Lillian, who believed her sister-in-law too grief-stricken to handle yet more. She didn't learn of the threat to her male progeny until I sprang loose the file.

Whatever the circumstances of my father's death, the FBI still had reason enough to take the death threat against his sons seriously. The FBI office in Indianapolis failed for several months to inform the local Bloomington police, and was reprimanded by Washington in late August. "Winston Donahue" was never caught.

Meanwhile, as was common in small midwestern towns in those days, my brothers and I lived in a house often unlocked. Had Donahue prevailed, our sister would never have suffered the later humiliation of those mustaches we drew on her Elvis Presley posters.

I read this episode as symbolic of the absurd and dark aftermath of my father's buoyant endeavor to embody the American myth. And it crazily confirms the family mythology that there has been a curse on young males of the House of Lockridge. This was one of many revelations along a vast paper trail.

"The tragedy occurred more than three [now four] decades ago, but the suicide of Ross Lockridge, Jr. continues to echo through informed discussions of contemporary American fiction," writes Donald Greiner. The question of what Lockridge would have gone on to create "is forever moot, for Lockridge killed himself two months after publication of his masterpiece. Thus the question that subsumes all others about him is 'why?' "

With the recognition that the time was approaching when witnesses would no longer be available and when my father's letters would be casually discarded by his friends' offspring, I decided to confront this question, but only as one question among others.

In mid-adolescence my siblings and I had by turns gone through our father's filing cabinet and some drawers full of newspaper articles. These lent immediacy to both the prepublication triumphs and the desolations that followed. We felt the enormity of our mother's loss and our own. My biography has been a continuation of this search, expanded greatly beyond the filing cabinet and drawers. I opened a fortune cookie soon after I started—"The answer you seek is in an envelope"—and I've since then ransacked archives, closets, and attics.

Sartre portrayed the limits of biographical retrieval in his novel *Nausea*. The very bulk of old records, memoirs, and letters may reveal inconsistencies in the subject, as if the biographer is not always dealing with the same person. Biographers may simply be organizing such debris as an act of imagination, in a futile challenge to the pastness of the past, falsely living out their own lives in the lives of their subjects. It might be braver to acknowledge that those dead bones are truly dead. Narrative theorists today emphasize the fictive character of biography and, even more, autobiography.

To accept this skeptical view entirely would leave the biographer winded at the starting point. Why rummage through attics and archives if texts can embody only illusory traces, mere black marks on paper? And why tape all those interviews if one can record only revisionistic echoes? I sought to uncover the makings of a relatively seamless documented narration. I hoped the need for speculation, if not interpretation, could be minimized.

Epilogue

Sitting next to three large stuffed filing cabinets, plus some 230 hours of taped interviews with almost a hundred people who knew Ross Lockridge, and my correspondence with many others, I think I've partially succeeded. If I still don't ultimately know him—a tall order in any circumstance—I've become well-acquainted for the first time. Having been severed from him early on, I've continued the relationship by other means—in recovering his life from its traces and in writing this book.

People have asked me if I wasn't afraid of what I'd find—but all discoveries, however dark, have been exhilarating, confirming what the Greeks said about the pleasure that accompanies recognition. The torment has come with the occasional dead ends, loss of material, and the death of some people before I could talk to them. I've tracked Ross Lockridge, Jr., gathering his correspondence and other papers, visiting the old houses and apartments, driving coast-to-coast with a tape recorder, finding his last letter in the safe of our deceased family lawyer, and hearing from my mother what happened the night he died.

I've burned away some barriers. For instance, he entered Methodist Hospital in Indianapolis under an assumed name my mother couldn't recall, and the exact date of admission was lost. After months of futile correspondence with the hospital, I enlisted the retired chief of staff of another Indianapolis hospital—someone who had been a friend of my father. He, my mother, and I then went to Methodist Hospital and, after a full day of detective work, recovered the records.

My father had abandoned a 2,000-page manuscript in 1943, none of which I expected to recover. But a portion was found on the backside of the fragmentary *Raintree County* manuscript in the Lilly Library.

He was a state champ at Gregg shorthand, the obsolete 1929 version. His use of it became idiosyncratic over the years. I had to round up a world-class decoder to recover some dreams, notes, and marginalia.

Such episodes made me feel as if I were entering an inner sanctum that had always been just down the hall, but nobody had sought the key.

There have been some losses. My father maintained a literary correspondence during the last seven years of his life with someone my mother remembered only as "Don." In his half of the correspondence, Don never wrote his own surname on the envelopes. I finecombed the nearly illegible script of these many letters and finally came across his announcement of the birth of a son, Donald Edwin Blankertz, Jr. One hundred phone calls later, I traced Blankertz Senior to Phoenix, dialed the number, and asked tremulously about my father's letters. "Oh, Larry, your father wrote wonderful letters—they were *Joycean*—but when I moved out here in 1980 I threw them all away!"

He turned up ten a week later, and suggested I inspect a barn outside Philadelphia for others. Wading through gooseshit, a friend and I found an additional letter in a musty glass case. But up to fifty letters remain lost. With Blankertz and others, I confirmed what I had feared—that even those who admired him didn't place such a premium on his words.

Other losses. During the week before his death, he wrote a letter describing his state of mind to Aharon Arsenian, a friend now deceased. Arsenian and his wife Josephine were so alarmed that they were thinking of inviting my father East, whereupon the bad news arrived. The *Boston Post* subsequently found out about the letter and, according to his widow, offered Arsenian five thousand dollars. He replied, "I do not sell my friends." Two days of looking through this deceased man's property turned up original letters by Thomas Hardy, William Saroyan, and Reinhold Niebuhr, but I left with a deep sense of loss—probably the letter had been burned. I was in the dubious position of wishing Arsenian had been less scrupulous.

The letters my father wrote during the last two months of his life to the journalist Nanette Kutner were supposed to have been willed to a friend—as I discovered in the Surrogates Court of Manhattan. When I caught up with the beneficiary, she told me Kutner's extravagance had resulted in so many liens that all she got was a tattered cashmere sweater.

Many patterns will become evident in my story—including similar responses, across generations, to mourning, insanity, and sex. One pattern I've been much aware of is that just as Ross Lockridge searched through his grandfather's papers for the makings of a national myth, and just as the fictitious Shawnessy searches amid antiquities for aboriginal meaning, so I've searched for my father in faded envelopes, dusty manuscripts, and memories. Such searches must always fail if one has an absolutist's demand for the whole. We can search for lost fathers and mothers over hard roads and wide, and they won't be there. But I've found enough, for now.

What I've gathered are the many voices of an American archive—voices of my father and mother, their ancestors, their friends, neighbors, teachers, students, preachers, and doctors. I've sifted through farm journals, old newspapers, report cards, classroom notes, high school and college yearbooks, blue books, essays (historical, philosophical, literary, theological), epic poems, lyrical poems, short stories, plays, theses, rough drafts, family Bibles, marginalia, hospital records, city registers, county atlases, commonplace books, memory books, notebooks, diaries, memoirs, notes on reading, reviews, gossip columns, trash journalism, old photograph albums, checkbook stubs, autopsies, and obituaries.

But especially letters—personal letters, professional letters, love letters, and sympathy letters.

In exploring an American archive, I've had in mind the many voices of my father's novel, itself an American archive of love, tragedy, and visionary ambition. While writing one story, he was living another just as astonishing and even more resolute—for, unlike his fictional hero John Wickliff Shawnessy, he finished what he set out to do and gained a larger measure of recognition than he ever allotted his own hero.

Ross Lockridge's life isn't just a morality tale about the perils of success in America, from which those of us who don't try so hard may take some comfort. (I'm sure it contains this moral.) Nor is it an isolated pathology with little implication for those of us who have more successfully resolved our Oedipal conflicts or pre-Oedipal disorders—about which there's much to say. Nor merely a check list of everything that an aspiring writer should not do—though again it contains this. If there's a premise in this biography, it's that my father's experience differs only in degree from that of many dedicated writers—for whom writing is life-blood.

In its relentless course, his life realizes so many of a writer's aspirations and fates. It moves from the decision to *be* a writer, to an apprenticeship both repressive and enabling, to the sudden vision of a work that might answer to ambition. It continues through delays, false starts, and the resolve to abandon it all and start over. It entails the egoism that this work shall be great, yet the generosity of the work itself offered to a public. Then the perilous mediation of editors and publisher, the temptation to compromise and sell out, the dislocations of sudden fame, wealth, and critical recognition. And then also the disparagement and misreadings, the shame, guilt, and impoverishment of spirit, and the question that dogs the writer, "What next?"

Much of this is the experience of serious writers everywhere. But Ross Lockridge, Jr. is an *American* writer and his story has much of the American literary experience about it—the midwest writer who, through regional attachments, challenges the authority of the East Coast as well as Europe, the nervy ambition, hope, and a special kind of vital innocence, the wish to answer while young to a young country's need for a great literature of its own, the lure and curse of Hollywood, and a national press that shapes seasonal celebrities according to some very trite scripts. There is risk in all this, and John Updike remarks that there have been "very few American writers who haven't fallen apart from the age of about 35."

Not many writers decide on their careers at the age of seven, not many draft a 400-page epic poem in their early twenties or discard a 2,000-page novel a few years later. Not many attempt a novel as "a complete embodiment of the American Myth." Not many kill themselves at the height of their acclaim. But Ross Lockridge was as extreme as he was thorough. If thank god he doesn't typify the American writer's life, he may in some ways epitomize it.

The circuitous journey of leaving home, giving postwar America what he hoped was a visionary testament of beauty and meaning, and then returning home in a triumph turned nightmare lends his story an implacable tragic structure. But its daily texture is a blend of humor and spirited satire, affection, and a vitality that announces itself as clearly in Ross Lockridge's life as in his prose. If his experience is unusual in the degree of its aspirations and devastations, I think it speaks in kind to many of us—and it's a story that even those who never open the green and golden covers of *Raintree County* may find compelling.

II

"Avenue of Elms"

Fort Wayne Days, 1914–1924

Robert Bruce Lockridge, sturdy and fearless, took a swimming lesson from his friend John Crane, who told him to take a deep breath, lie face down, and learn that water keeps you afloat. But Bruce straightaway sank to the bottom, and after several dunkings Crane decided it must be the density of his body. He later received an exuberant letter from Bruce who told of having almost drowned in a gravel pit.

On Saturday, June 28, 1919, a few days after this close call, Bruce went to St. Joseph's River, Fort Wayne, for a boy scout overnight. He had just turned sixteen and graduated from high school, two years younger than most of his classmates. He wasn't yet a First Class Scout because he didn't have his swimming merit badge. His mother watched her son prepare to leave and *almost* said, "Well, Bruce, be sure to take the rope along." His younger brother Ross, aged five, followed him across the yard and watched him catch the streetcar at the corner of Creighton and South Wayne avenues. Laden with equipment, he was in his boy scout uniform.

The next morning Bruce and two friends left their campground for a swim in unsupervised waters. Bruce strode out first into the river well beyond his companions, probably to surprise them by swimming back. He straightaway went under, then surfaced screaming for help. But Ferdinand Vegler and Edward Hagadorn thought at first he was joking. He screamed again, "My God, help me!" and Vegler, who couldn't swim well either, dove in.

Bruce was taken out one hour and seven minutes later by drag hooks. The lungmotor revived Vegler, pulled much earlier, but not Lockridge. Hagadorn said Lockridge had surfaced twelve times before going under for good.

Late Sunday morning Rossie was reading the funnies with his older siblings Shockley and Lillian, his parents were washing dishes, when the telephone rang. He heard "scared, griefhoarse words," and his parents hurriedly left the house.

Rossie stayed next door during preparations for the funeral. The body was sent back from the mortician's for a service in the home. John Crane's brother George and a few friends stayed up all night with the body.

My father wrote of his five-year-old self: "On the day of the funeral, he was brought into the front room and approached the open casket and saw his older brother lying there very still in a boy scout uniform. The room was full of people. The black spider had sprung without warning, without reason. What had happened had happened. There were many tears, but there was no movement of the boy in the casket, and later when Rossie went with the family to Lindenwood Cemetery, as they did so often in after years, to see the grave, there was no stir nor sound nor token from the green earth or the mound or the stone that had on it the words Robert Bruce Lockridge and the Boy Scout Emblem."

He wasn't allowed in the living room for the funeral service proper. He sat at the top of the staircase and listened.

Several members of the community as well as Rossie noticed that the parents didn't seem to mourn. "Mother and Father never wept over this grave but were quiet and thoughtful. They believed that Bruce was going on in some purposeful afterlife simultaneous with their own, and this was also the belief of the little boy who accompanied them to the grave in beautiful Lindenwood Cemetery."

~

When his eldest son drowned, Ross Lockridge Senior at forty-two had not quite found the work that would absorb him the rest of his life. "A heavy, hearty, ruddy man," my father would write, "a man of velocity and purpose, a man of great laughters and strong words, this father was to the boy a creature of almost terrifying energy." Velocity and purpose had undergone several checks, but Ross Senior read his own life as always progressive.

"I was born [in 1877] and reared on a farm in Miami County, Indiana, on the banks of Eel River—the Kenapocomoco of the Miami Indians and home of Little Turtle, 'greatest Indian of all times.' I fished, swam, skated, trapped, and dreamed where Little Turtle fought so bravely and counselled so wisely."

His own father, Brenton Webster Lockridge, had been an indefatigable smallfry farmer, descended from Scotch-Irish immigrants who settled in Virginia, and had himself grown up on the Eel River farm at the tiny village of Paw Paw in a gaunt gray-board house. With some help from astrology he did everything that a farmer can do, raising horses, cows, poultry, pigs, corn, wheat, potatoes, and even fish, with road work on the side, and yet he was still forced to borrow money.

A one-year-old son, Georgie, died when Ross was five. His older sister Maud, who aspired to poetry and music, died of typhoid fever at sixteen. ("Oct 7 1893 by cash to Dr E. M. Bloomfield for one visett to council with Dr. Kidd when Maud was sick settled in full $12.00.") Two weeks later nine-year-old Ray died of diphtheria. Brenton Webster took out loans to pay for tombstones.

Besides the frequent entries for whiskey and tobacco—in violation of his Methodism—his farm ledgers contain only one extravagance: "February 21, 1885, by cash to Mr Johnson for making one paire of french high shoes for Mrs. C. A. Lockridge $3.25." His wife, Charlotte A. Wray, was from an industrious Virginia family undone by Yankee predators after the Civil War. There were suspiciously passionate denials from my Great-aunt Marie that Charlotte Wray's mother was part Cherokee, and from my Grandmother Lockridge that the Wrays had been slaveholders.

Charlotte Wray would get the larger share of credit from her son Ross, who dedicated his biography of Lincoln to her and never dedicated a book to his father. In a calamitous world she held the family together and encouraged her surviving children to leave the farm and get an education. This would be reparation for her own losses.

Strong-willed, optimistic, and quite a talker, she was the force behind the Lockridge family. Ross "was truly his mother's child," his
wife would write.

Diversions for the surviving Lockridges included the Bear Show
at the neighboring village of Roann, county fairs, "Demmocrat" ral-
lies, the Odd Fellows and Rebecca lodges, and trips to Kokomo and
Peru (pronounced PEE-roo). Ross attended a small red-brick country school whose ruins are now overgrown with trees and vines, and
he then gained a solid high school education at Roann under a poly-
math teacher, Noble Harter, who taught the country kids everything
from Caesar's *Commentaries* and Milton's *Paradise Lost* to music and
psychology. He began each day with readings in ethics.

Encouraged by Harter and his mother, Ross Lockridge, eldest
now of four surviving children, headed in 1895 for the State University at Bloomington, then a small southern Indiana town with dirt
streets and cobblestone-and-straw sidewalks. He could see ox teams
coming in on East Third Street. Majoring in history and political science, he compiled an academic record others in the family tree
would emulate, excelling in academics (Phi Beta Kappa), athletics
(catcher on the baseball team), and school organizations (Phi Gamma
Delta, class president, debating and oratory). He met Elsie Shockley
there, and they were married in 1902. After taking his degree, he
taught for five years at Peru High School, advancing to principal in
Cole Porter's hometown.

Meanwhile his younger brother, square-jawed muscular Robert
Bruce Lockridge (known in our family as the "first Bruce") was following in his footsteps at State University: class president, member
of Phi Gamma Delta, captain of the track team and the University's
best sprinter, left-end on the football and outfielder on the baseball
teams, president of the Athletic Association, president of the Independent Literary Society, et cetera.

In late March of 1903 Bruce went to Louisville for a short-term
high school coaching job, writing home concerning this legendary sin
city. "Mamma, you need not worry about me getting shot or going
to drinking. If a man wants to drink it can be done as easily in Indiana
as in Kentucky." When the streets of Louisville on Saturday night
proved too much "for a common ordinary clod hopper country Jake
like me," he retreated early to his room.

On March 28, Bruce was demonstrating the discus to a group of high school students, while several yards away the State University athletic director, James Horne, was demonstrating the twelve-pound hammer. On a triple turn the hammer left his hand early. Someone yelled "Look out!" Bruce turned, raised his head, and took the hammer in the middle of his forehead. Within minutes he died. Horne ran crazed around the practice grounds, darted through the gate with several in pursuit, and tried to brain himself on a fence.

When Elsie Lockridge gave birth a few weeks later, the infant was given the ill-fated name Robert Bruce.

Tragedy made my grandfather only more resolute. Back in Peru, he taught history and began a debating society at the high school that won all high school meets—one on "Whether the Tendency of Labor Organizations at the Present Time Is Dangerous to the Public," arguing the negative. His team then clobbered Indiana College on "Whether Educational Qualification Should Be Required of Foreign Immigrants," arguing the negative. He wanted out of high school teaching and got the position of law librarian at the State University. After taking a law degree, he moved his family in 1907 to Oklahoma, which was just on the verge of statehood and a land of opportunity for young lawyers.

The six years in Oklahoma challenged my grandfather's brand of idealism, which would always make him a popular commencement speaker. "Those who don't build castles of the brain will never build them in stone; and the riches of mind and heart are the most real and enduring. Who so rich, as he that has Aladdin's Lamp?" In Shawnee he won office as police judge, county judge, and public defender, running on the Democratic ticket.

Aladdin's Lamp had brought him from the buzzing cicadas, bean vines, and enchanted Native American artifacts of the Eel River to this desolate town, where real Native Americans lived in degradation. "It was my painful duty to incarcerate many a noble Redman, among them Jim Thorpe, America's greatest athlete. . . . The year after I fined him for drunkenness, he took most of the Olympic honors from the world's outstanding athletes in the Olympic Games at Stockholm, Sweden. I don't mean to suggest any causal connection between these two events, but . . ."

His speeches and writings during this period are sometimes puritanical. "In the lips of a child a cigarette is as a poisonous serpent in the very bosom of the home." "This matter of the conduct of pool halls is really a very important consideration from the standpoint of public welfare." He started a progressive juvenile court that sentenced delinquents to schoolwork, and his support of Prohibition was so absolute that he lost friends among his own party. A story was planted that he owed Pottawatomie County $3,462—he owed only $14.62—and he lost an election to a cabal of bootleggers, drunkards, crooks, Republicans, and Socialists who branded him "a radical and a fanatic." Concluding that the solitary reformer must be "devoted to martyrdom," he gave up running for office.

He was having more luck founding a club in Oklahoma for Hoosiers out of their element, and he now yearned for the banks of the Wabash. In several letters to the State University's President William Lowe Bryan and the board of trustees, he asked for some employment, preferably his own department and a full professorship!

He returned to Indiana in the fall of 1913 disillusioned with the legal and political life. He had decided to give up a career in law. But can an Indiana homecoming ever be a defeat? If ideals didn't catch on in Oklahoma, they could in Indiana. "I have visions of a great state, mighty in its civic spirit, united in all its vital parts and forces by the quick wires of public intelligence and civic virtue radiating from its beloved University." What he had always been passionate about anyway was "civic education," and he pursued this elsewhere than on the bench.

A full professorship he didn't get, but as head of Public Speaking he organized civic discussion groups throughout the state and then, for more pay, worked three years as executive secretary of the Citizen League of Indiana, which attempted to get a new state constitution that would, among other things, extend suffrage to women. The League gave up when the United States entered the Great War.

In Fort Wayne from 1917 to 1922, he earned a dreary living as employment manager and welfare director of Wayne Knitting Mills, where he established a program of industrial education for the eight hundred girls and boys, aged fourteen through eighteen, who worked there. Though he thought of himself as a progressive, he stayed with management during a failed strike of German knitters. It was his job, and anyway he thought they were asking for too much.

Elsie Lockridge kept her own more radical politics to herself for fear of ruining his career. (Where he was a democrat, she was a socialist who would vote for Norman Thomas.)

His fate was crying out for something beyond managing knitters. In 1922 he became a field representative for World Book Company. But for many years he tolerated this job only because he loved being on the road and could scout out historical sites along the way. He had adjudicated five hundred cases of vagrancy in Oklahoma but admitted to some envy—the vagrants "were dreamers, restless with wanderlust. In an earlier era, they might have been discoverers, pioneers. There is vagrancy in all of us: —an essential of our natures." This vagrant drove like a maniac.

Fort Wayne is the Indiana city richest in historical associations. It is the old Native American Kekionga at the glorious meeting of three rivers, where Mad Anthony Wayne established a stockade after defeating the Miami Confederacy, where Tecumseh, William Wells, and William Henry Harrison played their colorful roles in a drama of genocide, and where Johnny Appleseed and Little Turtle are buried. Aware of its history, the city had put on a pageant in 1916, the one-hundredth anniversary of statehood, with a cast of one thousand Fort Wayne citizens and fourteen thousand spectators.

Shortly after his arrival in Fort Wayne, Ross Lockridge was working historical speeches into his public speaking classes at the Extension Center, and began developing his own brand of "Historic Site Recital," combining public speaking, drama, and local history. He was a founder of the Fort Wayne Historical Society, and at one of its first meetings, in March, 1921, put on an historical revue, "Golden Era of Happy Kekionga and French Occupancy of the Site of Fort Wayne, 1614–1761," which began with the Spirit of History in the guise of Columbia and ended seventeen campy scenes later with the Passing of the Indians.

This was the beginning of his career as populist historian. He now looked to the past when there were giants in the earth. He tried to justify the idealizing—there was no necessary contradiction, he said, between an "objective" reading of history and an "heroic." "Why shouldn't the good, rather than the evil, that a man does live after him?" He would disinter the good buried with the bones of the dead by reciting the great words and deeds. These ritual exhumations were to be performed "on the spot," he always said, where history was made.

My grandfather didn't exactly whitewash history. He perceived tragic patterns and was adroit at verbal reenactment of massacres. But he certainly *edited* it. He attempted to bind people to their own local history through heroic narrative. Even as the word "religion" derives from the Latin *religare*—to bind or tie—his teaching was deeply religious. It meant reverence for the great people who had made the ground on which they strode enchanted. To feel a connection to your own soil, you must discover the local heroes who have left traces of themselves "on this spot" but who could fade away unnoticed if not called forth by the historian's deep-voiced utterance. His dramatic method shared something with Native American rituals of evoking the Great Spirit.

He would eventually take his act on the road, speaking at hundreds of sites throughout the state. He tried to sate his wanderlust with his historical pilgrimages—but he never aspired beyond Indiana.

He worked at preserving records and buildings, erecting monuments and roadside markers, and re-creating the great historical moments through pageantry. He didn't ask, What *good* is it for folks to know what happened on such and such a spot in Ouiatenon or Mississinewa or Terre Haute? He didn't have a refined philosophical brain. But his faith was in a collective awareness that preserves democratic vistas and purges the kind of meanness he'd witnessed in Oklahoma. Orating around giant bonfires, with audiences of up to two thousand for his "History on Wheels," he was both evangelical preacher and traveling salesman. His wife noted his "lack of self-consciousness." He had neither the perspectives of irony and satire nor their debilitations.

And he cast a spell with his story-telling and impersonation. I remember some of his performances—this resolute orator silhouetted against a bonfire, gesticulating grandly—and I've wondered what he'd think if he knew how hard it is for me to get up in front of a class.

Ross Lockridge Senior found his vocation and his voice, at last, shortly after the death in 1919 of his son Bruce, who shared many of his qualities of extroversion and hope. I think it was in part a consequence of that death. Preaching history as resurrection of the worthy dead was his idealistic, nonmetaphysical challenge to time and mortality, grounded in the tragedies of his own life and the pettiness of the contemporary scene. He didn't otherwise write or talk about Bruce.

~

Elsie Shockley Lockridge performed a piano duet with Bruce during a recital he gave the Thursday evening before he died. This was more in keeping with her own cultural values and hopes for her son than the boy scouts, her husband's idea. She would nurse some resentment that a scouting expedition had led to the tragedy. A few days earlier she and Bruce had a contest to see who could hold breath the longer, and she knew he must have held it stubbornly and in terror under water to the end.

Though Bruce was baptized at the Wayne Street Methodist Church the previous year, she gave him two months later a copy of Mary Baker Eddy's *Science and Health with Key to the Scriptures.* Where her husband taught the boy history, oratory, and debating, and had him learn typing and stenography—in good part to assist him in his own work—she tutored him with Montessori's methods.

Elsie Lockridge was known for her strange notions, yet she was civic-minded and a peacemaker. Within a year of arriving in Fort Wayne she became the first president of the Fort Wayne High School PTA, and subsequently president of a consortium of twenty-three Fort Wayne PTAs. Following her son's death—not giving way—she was also director of the League of Women Voters, legislative chairman of the YWCA, president of the Delphean Society, et cetera.

"She of the great thoughtful blue eyes, busy, purposeful, patient, great of soul"—her youngest son would say of her. But in her early years she had been, he knew, fretful, ambitious, jealous. And she was plagued by feeling unworthy of her father.

This father, John Wesley Shockley, was in many respects the antithesis of her father-in-law, Brenton Webster Lockridge. John Shockley had been a self-tutored small-town schoolmaster proficient in Greek, Latin, German, French, and Spanish, and knowledgeable of algebra, physics, botany, geology, zoology, music, medicine, philosophy, and the great literatures. Though nominally a Christian, he was allied to no particular sect and was known as a free-thinker. For a Hoosier hick, this was pretty advanced.

Above all he was a *poète manqué,* who composed a large portfolio of verse kept mostly to himself. He'd been divorced—Susannah Duke took their son James and moved to Mississippi. He then wooed Elsie's mother-to-be, Emma Rhoton, eighteen years his junior. In love letters smuggled in by friends, he turned on the poetry to unleash Emma from her father, who vehemently opposed the match, and from her dead mother, whose one dying wish had been that she never marry John Shockley.

"I wish you to consider *well* the sweet relation of two *Souls* whose path is one. . . . You are really a *Poet* I see. I don't like the word *Poetess.* You are *better* than a poet or a poet*ess, you are a poem.* . . . If we live right, if we seek only to help each other the days will roll on like the rich notes of a sacred song, and our lives will be sweetened by that pure love which we have already tasted. It is for us to live the life of heroes. . . . I have seen too many lives made desolate by obeying the dictates of parents." When Pa was looking the other way, they eloped.

John Shockley had a good deal of pride, but even so may never have guessed that Monty Clift would depict him on the silver screen as an unsung American Milton. Writing escapist poetry on the side, he settled into a humdrum school-teacherly life with Emma, a strict, reserved, and stubborn woman who bore him three children and didn't call him by his first name. He left the disciplining of the children to her.

Their daughter Elsie, born in Henry County in 1880, thought her father a minor deity. This high estimate may have compensated for her mother's early lack of warmth—and was implicated in her sorry opinion of herself.

As a girl she'd been in a surrey with her parents when her fierce dark grandfather, whom she'd never met, appeared in a buggy. "Emma, the old home's waitin' for you. Come on back." Her mother had replied, "Pa, I'll come back as soon as I can bring Mr. Shockley and the children," and Franklin Rhoton cracked his whip and rode off.

Elsie attended her father's school, where studying for one year with a lackluster teacher made her father seem all the more stellar. He made even geography come to life, emphasizing work with maps, and in second grade he had her recite one of his poems at the beginning of a Christmas program:

> *Now if you'll all be* young *again*
> *Just little lads and lasses*
> *And quite forget that you are men*
> *And women wearing glasses*
> *Remembering how* you *used to do*
> *Our faults you will not mention*
> *So here's a thousand thanks to you*
> *For your polite attention.*

Her idealization of her father didn't disguise the fact that early memories of him were invested with fear, guilt, and aggression. Coveting a doll given her younger brother, Frank, Elsie tricked him into baptizing it in a pond. The doll was ruined. She would remember this as her worst crime, but it was less haunting than a nightmare she had when about nine. She was returning from school and had just crossed the railroad tracks leaving Mooreland when she confronted a human head. Looking closer, she saw it was her father's, chewed by dogs and its mouth hanging open. Her father awakened her as she screamed. For weeks she felt guilty for having dreamt his death.

She *would* be worthy of him, so she practiced the piano six hours a day and put splints on her fingers when they were giving out. She even tried to prove herself a superior wrestler. She was the one of whom people said, "Well, I'll bet this one isn't sick much!" But when, with her father watching, she was thrown several times in quick succession by her older brother, Ernest, she wailed in shame and anguish.

She took her piano along to the State University in 1898, where she lived with Ernest and majored in English. She had written stories as a little girl and hoped that one day she might be a writer, finally proving herself worthy of her father's love. Soon she met Ross Lockridge. The romance was spoofed in the 1900 *Arbutus,* the college yearbook, as a meeting less of minds than of hicks. Her father approved the match—he thought Ross Lockridge's bright eyes betokened some intelligence—but he felt Lockridge wasn't a poet, wasn't deep.

Elsie returned to Henry County to teach in a country school prior to her marriage and didn't resume university studies for more than two decades. Instead she settled with Ross Lockridge in provincial Peru with not much more to do than bear children. The Peru High School yearbook, *The Narcissus,* of 1903—like many of this era full of satiric gossip—is our only direct evidence of how the marriage was faring. Assistant Principal Lockridge appears in caricature with spiked hair. "Here we have Rossie. Rossie was married last summer. He met Mrs. at I.U. We hear that he and Mr. Hall [the mathematics instructor] had quite a lively contest over her. . . . Some day Rossie is going to be a lawyer. He intends to make divorce cases a specialty. He is now studying the grounds for divorce. We would like to know why he doesn't ever bring Mrs. to class receptions."

Well, Elsie Lockridge, a nascent feminist, aspired to something higher than faculty wife. She was also pregnant that year. Giving birth to Bruce in the spring of 1903, she suffered a prolapsed uterus that would make child-bearing always difficult, reducing her to temporary invalidism. It was probably during her suffering after first childbirth that she turned to Christian Science.

Bruce started poorly—often sick and with barely enough flesh to cover his large bones. For the first year, sick Elsie carried sick Bruce around on a pillow. She bottle-fed her son with her own breast milk, enhanced by the beer some German friends convinced her to drink. Her husband must have given her short reprieve, because she was soon pregnant again and gave birth to Vivian Shockley—a name the kid didn't appreciate—in September of 1904.

The marriage was proving cooperative but not warm or physically demonstrative. Elsie's eyes were on an ideal world of literature, music, and intellect—sanctioned, she hoped, by her father. Ross's were on a more professionally determined sphere to which he brought his own visionary energies—sanctioned, he hoped, by his mother. Their eyes, cast outward, rarely met.

When the family returned to Bloomington in 1905 for Lockridge's stint in law school, Elsie kept a journal, "The sayings and doings of our two baby sons, Robert Bruce and Vivian Shockley." "Bruce at first wanted to hit Shockley on the head but he soon learned better. Bruce had a pencil one day and noticing Shockley's fair, bald pate he decided 'twas made to write on and tried it accordingly. Shockley howled & Bruce cried when he saw he had hurt Shockley. . . .

"On our trip from Straughn to Bloomington, Bruce was sitting with Ross when he suddenly arose and cooly knocked Ross' hat off. Ross scolded him pretty severely—(his hat was new). Soon Bruce came nudging up to his papa and in sweet little voice said 'Kiss papa smack.' He kissed Ross and quick as a wink he knocked off his papa's hat again. . . .

"Last Sun. eve I sang for Bruce a little song which I knew when a child—'The Little Babes in the Wood.' Bruce liked it, and I sang it several times and told him how the poor little babes were lost & couldn't find their papa & mama. Bruce became so sorry for the babes that he sobbed 'Oh, poor little babes—touldn't find papa & mama—o-o-oh poor little babes' and the tears stood in his eyes and his face fully told his sympathy with the babes. His papa later tried to put him to sleep but Bruce was so excited about the babes that he kept sobbing & talking of them & finally his papa bethought himself to change the story & he did so, telling Bruce the little babes finally found papa & mama. Bruce then was satisfied & went to sleep."

Throughout her journal Elsie takes pleasure in how her children gain power over environment and parents through language. Time and again Bruce gets the better of his father, once interrupting grace at dinner and, after a warm reprimand, coolly recommending, "Let's try it again." Bruce intercedes whenever she is about to punish Shockley, pleading that the punishment be lenient if at all. And he objects to her tactics, as when she declines to discuss a punishment: "Mama, you talk to me when I talk to you."

A more advanced pedagogue than her husband, Elsie respects these checks on her parenting, observing her children's experimentalism, their sympathies and aggressions, their word play and linguistic transfer of learning, and their literalist responses to storytelling—especially to stories of abandonment.

At the same time, there was something in her very habit of quiet observation that made her children feel as if they were loved mainly for their qualities and their deeds. We grandchildren remember how she would look closely at us, as if peering into our minds with a special psychometric lens, looking hopefully for signs of the family aptitude. As a little girl my sister sensed more inspection than warmth, and doesn't recall being held or touched by her grandmother, except for the occasional spit bath with linen handkerchief that her face endured. But we do remember the warm eloquence of her hands as she told us those stories.

I've found no record of how she took her father's death in 1907. She followed her husband to Oklahoma, where she gave birth to their third child, Lillian Louise, in 1909. They finally had a girl and decided against more children. Bruce and Shockley started in the public schools but Elsie withdrew them and vigorously tutored them herself, working them hard in the morning and letting them play in the afternoon. She gave positive reinforcement only and was never cross. When Montessori's method first reached the United States in 1912, she used it with her children and introduced it into a small kindergarten she had started, the only Montessori experiment at that time in Oklahoma. Decades later Shockley could still remember "matching the vari-colored skeins of silk and displaying spatial awareness by placing the round cutouts in the circular holes of a plaque."

With three children, a kindergarten, and various social commitments, she was wearing herself out in Shawnee, was frustrated at subsistence living in the squalid town and at the sacrifice of personal ideals for time-consuming housework. And despite all the hard work they were in debt.

She wrote about it in a short story of 1911. She portrays herself as a tired housewife in Oklahoma with three children—seven-year-old Brenton (Bruce), six-year-old Wesley (Shockley), and two-year-old Louise (Lillian)—and a husband who (wishful thinking) gets her father's name, John. Exhausted with housework, she feels guilty for not always having enough energy for her children. Their request for a bedtime story—to which they're addicted—is now frequently declined, and the kids retaliate: " 'I don't love mama. I never get tired,' said impetuous Wesley. 'If I ever have any little boys and girls, I'll not send them to bed without a story,' said philosophical Brenton." "She knew that both boys had longed for more expressed love than they had received." She vowed always to reciprocate love in little Lillian, but the "dear, plump body was a positive burden tonight."

This tired heroine comes across a magazine ad for a story contest with a $2,000 prize. She has always hoped to write, and her husband encourages her to enter. Were she to win, she would free up more time for her children, winning their confidence and encouraging in them "a love for the wholesome and beautiful." She begins to write her autobiography after the kids are tucked in. "She wrote better when alone. 'John, please, turn your back to me; you divert my thoughts.' And John, whose eyes and whole attention even then were riveted on his own work, considerately turned his back."

When first reading this story about the writing of a story, I awaited a bittersweet outcome, the dream punctured with a rejection slip and some lessons learned. But no! The mailman delivers the envelope, and her story, "For Things Worth While," has won first prize. Immediately she sends a telegram to her mother announcing the triumph. This heroine uses a nom de plume, "Lillian Western," just as Elsie's father had used "Will Western." Elsie's story ends with the prophecy of a brilliant career for her heroine. But there's no evidence that she herself, in the real world, submitted this story anywhere. I rather doubt it would have won a contest.

They left Oklahoma at last. Her child-bearing ordeal wasn't over. Accidentally pregnant, she gave birth at age thirty-four to Ross Franklin Lockridge, Jr. on April 25, 1914, in Bloomington Hospital. She would share a bedroom with her daughter, Lillian, for the rest of her life. It's unlikely her husband was ever invited back.

~

Ross Junior called the first few years of his life "The Unremembered!!"—the "mysterious period" that "supplies those vague images & recollections which recur to dreams & which unconsciously influence his responses to places & people & things all his life." He thought Keats was right to describe life as a "Vale of Soul-making," where human identity doesn't exist at birth but develops gradually as one buffets with circumstance.

The family lived briefly in a now-demolished house at 801 Atwater Street in Bloomington. Later in 1914 they moved to Indianapolis, site of Ross Junior's earliest memories. He would retain isolated images of playing on a high porch, probably their home at 3614 North Illinois Street, of being offered some pink and white candies, of some paper dolls, of a lost toy gun with a shiny black handle, of being with his mother—in his first recorded memory of her—next to a cluttered desk in an office building somewhere and looking out "the blackgrilled windows upon the streets of a city."

His conscious life "began in a street of majestic elms," the two-story brown-shingled house at 649 West Creighton Avenue, Fort Wayne. "The great elms flowered with black arms wide over the street where life had become a continuous stream flowing." The elms were protective and maternal—and he would always long for "the murmurous summery womb of the street" from which it seemed he had suddenly sprung into life.

He'd awaken in the night or early morning to the "sad iron wail" of the yellow streetcars that turned off Creighton Avenue, and he watched the "hollow jerky shapes of the cars go by, heard the clang of the footgong," and pondered the mysterious faces of people going off to work in factories.

It was wartime, 1917, and it seemed war had arisen with his life—"he did not know when there had not been a war." There was talk of his father going to war. "He cried at this thought of losing his father, for the war was something far-off and terrible." The war "reached in with inky fingers" of newsprint, lending something sinister even to the avenue of elms "in the valley of years."

Rossie played mostly by himself, often "a little wistfully and lonesomely," while his mother worked in her upstairs room. He would climb the box elder tree or sit beneath the bushes and watch the streetcars. Sometimes he'd wander off, fascinated by the fake antiquarian statuary and ironwork of the better houses with their remote and ghostly interiors. With his three older siblings he "was observer more than participant." He watched one day as Bruce with his pompadour haircut spent an afternoon taking a limb from the giant elm in the front yard. Rossie picked up the chips.

The surgery didn't work. I found this tree now reduced to a stump. And most of the large elms in the neighborhood have disappeared, though an enormous dead one still stands across the street.

His cousin Mary Jane Ward, nine years his senior, watched his father and older brothers as they "debated, teased each other, argued about American history and spelling. They quoted poetry (declaimed is the word) until some of the audience, like me, were ready to drop from exhausted admiration. They seemed never to run out of enthusiasm." Their idea of youthful war games was to act out the *Iliad* and the *Odyssey*. Elsie quietly observed her sons, while plain Lillian watched her handsome brothers from the sideline. Rossie watched too, but not in intimidation. When John and George Crane came over to play Crocinole with Bruce, he quietly watched to figure out the game.

John Crane, who went on to teach at Harvard and pursued an international career in journalism and diplomacy, says that he never again met anyone with so much "gusto for life" as Bruce. He came into a room "like a tornado," he *pounded* the typewriter, he always walked fast, his voice was "husky and rich." He *liked* everything.

And yet for all his fearless energy and friendliness, Bruce was socially naïve. Like Shockley and Lillian, he'd been kept out of public schools a good portion of his grade school years for his mother's tutoring. Upon entering the Fort Wayne school system, he was ahead of his class and skipped two grades, so his new classmates were two years older. He didn't go on bicycle hikes with the others, he had never dated. Despite his build he had never learned sports. He was, oddly, a stay-at-home extrovert.

In his senior year, he was making up for lost time. He joined the boy scouts, starred in local and regional debates as captain of the debating team, held office in the Mathematics Club, worked as a literary editor of the yearbook, joined the Platonian Literary Society, et cetera. He sang and yelled with friends on the train to a YMCA meeting in Chicago, where he joined in a three-hour pillow fight, and with George Crane he visited the dissecting room at a medical college. As he wrote in the 1919 Fort Wayne High School yearbook, *The Cauldron,* the "only thing that bothered us was the fact that they were all sliced up and moss was growing out of the eyes of one fellow."

Bruce saw nothing of himself in these corpses. Visionaries of denial that they were, his parents had not instilled in him an adequate sense of peril. He was immortal, omnipotent, someone who could swim even if he couldn't.

It was the family's expectation that Bruce was destined for a brilliant career, but despite his love of Webster's Dictionary it was probably not going to be literary. When he was three he was asked by a neighbor if he had prayed at Sunday School. No, he didn't pray. "Mrs. Castle—'Will you pray when you get big?' Bruce—'No, No, I'm going to be a lawyer!' "

Thirteen years later the class prophecy confirms the ambition. "Bruce Lockridge caused us the most trouble because he never came home. We ran upon him accidentally in Cleveland one day orating from a soap box. He and Eugene V. Debs were running an anti-everything law firm—Debs was still in jail." Elsie devoted enormous energies to her eldest son, but he was cut more in the mold of her husband than of her father.

Shockley, who also accelerated through the schools and would enter Indiana University at sixteen, thought about making a living. He worked hard at Wayne Knitting Mills, supplementing the family income, and found a negative example in his father, whose business sense was minimal. (Elsie would later take over the finances.) Growing up in the shadow of Bruce, he was quieter, less ostensibly happy, and less full of his parents' visionary optimism.

Lillian was out of the running—she was so shy that teachers at Miner School had to approach her desk to hear her recitations. In a spring pageant, she was given the part of Violet. I turned up a doctor's report of 1927 that alluded to tests revealing a thyroid problem. From adolescence on, Lillian was obese. But Elsie may also have overfed her daughter to compensate for doubts about the depth of her own love. Hoping to secure that love, Lillian was never able to separate from her mother. It is also doubtful that she felt secure in the love of her older brothers. Pretending to be Indians, they tied her to the stake one day and pondered setting it afire. Shockley would always feel guilty about it.

Lillian was born into a family unexceptional insofar as its sturdy, resolute women—from Charlotte Wray Lockridge to Emma Rhoton Shockley to Elsie herself—would find their own fulfillment mainly through child-bearing and the exploits of the menfolk.

Before the death of Bruce, Rossie wasn't given any special standing in the family. As Mary Jane Ward observed, the parents were used to having brilliant beautiful sons by the time he came along. But with Bruce's death, their larger hopes shifted to their youngest.

Shortly after his brother's drowning, Rossie was forced to ponder death again. One of his kindergarten friends died, and he was often asking his teacher about Dorwin. One day she saw Rossie on the swings, pumping with unusual vigor. He started going higher and higher, and higher and higher, and Ella Geake was alarmed and told him to swing a little lower. But he persisted, exclaiming, "If I swing high enough and reach the clouds, maybe I can see Dorwin!"

Bruce's death was the great wound in Shockley's life. He had elected not to go along on the overnight and felt guilty about it— might he not have saved him? He had often traipsed behind his exuberant oblivious brother who sometimes ignored him, but they were best friends even so. Shockley would rarely speak of Bruce, so the wound was inferred. He refused to see any movie that might involve drownings, for instance. His grades declined his senior year, but he managed to graduate an honor student at the age of fifteen and then spent a year working for a Fort Wayne newspaper. When he went off to Indiana University he flourished for a spell, writing papers for his upperclassmen in Phi Gamma Delta and making an impression in his English classes.

As a kid he had scribbled fairy tales and in 1921–22 he wrote a series of stories for Freshman Composition that he brought home. "Raucously through the vast meso-paleozoic mists, startling stray pterandons and ichthyornis, resounded the bellow of young perisso-dactyl condylarthra. . . . Briskly the amorous ungulate lingually sleeked his tawny whiskers and rasped his tusks on the gray face of the cliff."

Other stories were influenced by Poe and Maupassant, and included "How I Killed My Great Aunt," where the narrator enlists a dozen beggars to throw poisonous gas bombs at his great-aunt, the prima donna of the Paris Opera who has scorned him. He doesn't foresee that the bombs will also kill off the audience, including himself. Rossie loved especially the line, "Subtly amused, I floated away, emancipated from mundane bonds."

Another story he liked was "Them," a macabre paranoic dream-fantasy. Professor Douglas awarded everything an A, except the story "Why Not?," in which the dejected protagonist slips his red tie around the ceiling gas-jet and kicks away the chair. The prof gave this one an A-plus for style and a C-plus for plot.

It was upon reading these "haunting tone-poems" at the age of seven that Rossie decided once and for all to become a writer. We know for sure that he kept this decision from his parents.

He was returning from a birthday party down the street around this time when he found fire wagons surrounding his house. The attic and roof had burned away, and the firemen had removed charred and soaked family papers. He would remember spending "drunken days exhuming and reading old childhood manuscript of fairy tales written in unbelievable profusion by Shockley—and other charred books and relics of family life. Forbidden to read in bed, Rossie would hide the charred MS. under the sheets and read at night by flashlight."

The smell of wet charred paper stayed with him, flooding him with nostalgia. The fire left a scar "burned across his own life," for, unlike Bruce, he was learning something about mortality.

His cousin Robert Masters frequently played with him on weekends and they would exchange books. One year younger, Robert liked and admired his cousin, his role model. Together they discovered *The Count of Monte Cristo, Les Misérables,* and *Hiawatha.* Eight-year-old Rossie told Robert, but not his parents, that he was going to write an historical novel when he grew up. His personal hand-me-down library included *The White Indian Boy, Stories of American Life and Adventure, The Little Lame Prince, Tales of the Bark Lodges, Ned on the River, Poems of American Patriotism, Folk Stories and Fables,* a volume of *Pinocchio: A Tale of a Puppet,* inscribed by his Uncle Ernest, and many others. His mother gave him ten new words per week to use in conversation, an exercise he liked.

His father was tutoring him in recitation, of course, and Rossie wowed the PTA with "The Boy Stood on the Burning Deck." Father and son played a game, "The Rossiteers," based on a list they made of some 140 heroes from history and legend, grouped into Knights Errant, Sailors, Stalwarts, Scouts, Sharpshooters, and Messengers. As for Queens of Beauty, his mother and sister were listed above Helen of Troy, Lorna Doone, and Mary Pickford.

Ross Senior had his son play two parts in an historical pageant he directed, "The Peltiers," based on an old Fort Wayne family. For the first time, in May of 1922, Rossie saw his picture in the papers. And he and Robert would sometimes camp with Ross Senior at the old farm on Eel River, where they'd find arrowheads, shards, and tomahawks.

Robert felt his cousin an eager and very busy boy possessed of uncommon memory, who enjoyed this initiation into the heroic view of history. He wasn't a smartass, he was fun to be with. They never had a fight, they were never bored. Rossie was generally well behaved, having been physically punished only once by his mother, after he had climbed all over some visiting ladies, chewing at their dresses.

Throughout the Fort Wayne years Rossie went to the silent cinema, where he nearly lived the films he saw. Whenever he saw a violent film, he'd be too weak the next morning to get out of bed, and his mother would have to carry him downstairs. She began to regulate what he saw. The 1922 Paul Howell film *Borderland* haunted him years thereafter with images of a limbo where the heroine was doomed to roam "with other fleeting and lugubrious shades." She had left a preoccupied husband and her bothersome child for a lover, and the child had subsequently died in a fire. Rossie was haunted by images of separation and abandonment.

His love of music began with the piano and orchestral accompaniments in the Fort Wayne cinemas. One song that accompanied Sydney Franklin's 1922 film *Smilin' Through* became "invested with great sentimental meaning for me, such that whenever my mother played it, I would invariably go out and sit on the front steps where I became filled with the most extraordinary sentiments of destiny and other large notions, appalling to my childish imagination." His mother's playing evoked the "scenes of the old picture, the ghost of the dead sweetheart returning in her faded bridal gown to the garden where she was shot."

He would always prefer the dim, yellow appearance of the old movies to the "bright, photographic distinctness" of the new—"the image of a faded, dusty manuscript as compared with the morning paper." And he would come to believe that the power of art is "conditioned by *specific* childhood impressions. That is why we frequently feel a vague trouble when a certain piece of music is played. It is somehow reminiscent of some old scene of our childhood which is striving to win to consciousness but cannot quite succeed."

Frequently he visited his mother's old home in Straughn, where his parents had been married and where his Grandmother Emma Shockley had preserved her late husband's yellowing manuscripts, fading photographs, and a library filled with volumes antedating the Civil War. In the backyard was a sundial that read, GROW OLD WITH ME, THE BEST IS YET TO BE. I RECORD ONLY THE SUNSHINE. Time and again his mother and grandmother told him stories about this legendary grandfather John Wesley Shockley, who died seven years before he was born. He peered through the poems variously signed Seth Twigs, Will Western, John W. Shockley, and JWS.

Lillian Bradway Henley, oldest resident of Straughn, remembers the Lockridges' visits as occasions. All the kids in town would join in the play, except Lillian Lockridge, who kept to herself. To neighborhood kids Emma Shockley's house, with its exotic objects and large bookcases, seemed a palace, privy notwithstanding. Henley's own memory of John Wesley Shockley is less than flattering. He struck her as always "grouchy," and as a little girl she'd avoid the Shockley house if she knew the old grouch was there. The Shockleys were strict schoolteachers, especially Ernest, a dreaded substitute, but Lillian Bradway found Emma Shockley nice—so long as she wasn't teaching.

Rossie got less schooling from his mother than his older siblings had. She was happier with Fort Wayne's Miner School than she'd been with Shawnee's schools. And she recognized by then, as she would later confess to Shockley, that tutorials exclusively with Mom can limit a child's social development. Still she did set aside special time for Rossie after the death of Bruce.

He was permitted to skip only half a grade upon entering Miner primary school and would always be known for his affable, whimsical manner, smile, and dimples. He had a series of old-fashioned dedicated schoolmarms—Misses Vivian Withus, Katherine Dinklage, Alice Miller, Mary Shippen, Marie Bresnahan—who awarded him A's in most subjects, except for "conduct," where he often got the equivalent of B or C.

The school character was the principal of long standing, Celia Foley, a woman with unruly gray hair who would bring the student population to attention with a deafening clap and over on whom nobody ever put anything. With a passion for thrift, she was famous for coming unannounced into the classrooms, upending wastepaper baskets onto the teachers' desks, and rummaging through wastepaper to check that it was completely filled with writing, front and back. Teachers and students alike were in big trouble if six or seven lines were unused at the bottom of a page. Rossie picked up this thrift with paper.

Miner School was progressive enough to have its own school newspaper for a time. Looking through the few surviving copies at the local historical society, I came across "Our Flag." "George Washington wanted a flag to be made. He went to Betsy Ross to ask her to make one. He told her to have a blue field with thirteen stars in it, for the thirteen colonies. It had thirteen stripes. The stars were put in a circle. Ross Lockridge, 3A." Could I presume the wit and vision had been weeded out by the editorial staff?

The Miner Reporter has more searching columns. Mildred Crane of grade 7A was reporter for the school debate: "Resolved, That the Indian received worse treatment from the American people than the negro." The affirmative side won in the vote of the faculty judges, which decision produced so much applause that "with some difficulty Miss Foley regained silence among the happy children." Some on the losing side wept, however, and Mildred observed philosophically that we should not be "disheartened after having been defeated because we shall be defeated more or less in our life and we should be glad that the other side was happy."

First love hit Rossie hard in third grade. A new girl named Alicia Carpenter was introduced by the teacher, Miss Dinklage, to the solid old group of third-graders. Sitting next to Rossie, she promptly hid her face and cried. He was soon in love with her, following her home and rescuing this plump sweet-faced girl in his mind's eye "from a castle beset with ogres and circled with a hedge of thorns."

One day while carrying her books he confessed his love, but he never brought the matter up again. It was the "thornhedge of his own reluctance" that stopped him from crossing "the margin of his dreams," and he "confined the expression of his love to pathetic leaps and short wild sprints close to her play group in the schoolyard."

Near the end of the school term the class went to Forest Park for a picnic. Rossie had a painful sty in his eye and was unable to compete with a young pugilist, George Skeleton, who pushed Alicia in the swings. "Blonde hair flying, she rose and fell in vast pendulum

sweeps under the furious thinlipped assaults of Skelly the Strong."
Ross hid underneath a picnic table, while George and Alicia went off
hand in hand.

He had more luck in fiction. That year he wrote a quest romance, *The Demon with the Fiery Tongue.* Sir Mincer, nicknamed
Cherry, is one of four brother knights sent by the King to slay a demon who has been laying waste the countryside. He discovers the demon in a cave and "just as the demon opened his mouth to yawn
Cherry sprang up and cut his tongue off," whereupon it "cooled
down and disappeared." Going further down into the cave by various
iron-ringed holes and staircases, Cherry discovers the Princess
Eloise, whom the demon has abducted. The tongueless demon takes
a liking to his captor and somehow tips him off that his treacherous
brothers are plotting his death. Cherry cheerfully slays them.

Eloise is abducted again while Cherry is chasing after a stag with
golden horns. This time he must chop a giant's leg off to rescue her.
Back in the castle, he and Eloise surprise the King by jumping out of
a closet. His Majesty almost falls over, the demon is forgiven and becomes Cherry's servant, Cherry and Eloise have a three-month wedding ceremony, and soon produce a son, John.

"When John grew up he did greater deeds than his father ever
did before. John had a little son too and John's little son asked John
to tell him a story one night. John told him about the adventures of
Cherry and I was listening to the story too, or I would never have
written it down for you to read. End."

He requested a binding, probably to outdo his older brother, so
Elsie put scraps of upholstery leather around the twenty-five
handwritten pages of what her son would call the "first product of
my invention." He soon cut away enough leather to make a slingshot.

~

Through the mythic enlargements of early memory, Fort Wayne became for Ross Lockridge, Jr. the immemorial city, with its avenue of
elms in the valley of years. He would in memory return to it in his
final days. It was there that his mother and father, strong but dissimilar idealists, stirred in him the ambitions and ideals that in the beginning nourished his sense of power and identity. It was there that he

first experienced death and romantic love. Bruce's death and the loss
of Alicia fed an elegiac undercurrent not visible in his cheerful public
demeanor.

But the roots of his emotional life probably lay deeper in time
than these early recurrent memories, which may only have confirmed a preexistent sense of loss. They may have lain in the period
he called "The Unremembered!"—1914 through 1918, his first three
to four years, spent in Bloomington, then Indianapolis, and finally
Fort Wayne. Elsie probably didn't keep a journal on her youngest son
during this period when maternal influence is so crucial. But in his
twenties, thinking back on his earliest years, he would remember
that he was already "longing" for something with feelings of "tragic
love," with "a child's infallible sense of sadness." He couldn't say what
he was longing for.

It may have been for his mother's love, seemingly lost before it
was given. There's no evidence that Elsie did anything except care
for her four children during this period of time—as far as I know,
she wasn't much out of the house. There's also no evidence that she
didn't love them. But the story she had written in Oklahoma was in
effect a confession of her failure to be emotionally available—as well
as a resolve to improve on this.

She may have continued to fail on her own terms. Certainly the
last thing she wanted was another child. Ross Junior's birth capped
the physical estrangement of his parents. His presence confirmed that
she was stuck in motherhood, with no career of her own, married to
a sort of windbag. And to judge by the fates of her older children,
there was already something disconnected in her nurturing—Bruce's
dangerous sense of omnipotence, Shockley's deep reserve, and
Lillian's shyness and fear of separation. Elsie hoped her sons would
somehow fulfill the visionary promise of her father and have the brilliant career she never made good on. To this degree they were extensions of herself. (Neither she nor her husband had high hopes for
Lillian.)

I say this with sympathy for my grandmother—she worked hard
for her children, tried to instill in them her lofty conceptions of the
good and the beautiful, mesmerized them with her wonderful stories, and was surely entitled to lament her lack of a well-defined, independent career. Probably herself a victim of parental withholding,

she suffered from her own sense of failure, her unworthiness of her father's love.

As a Montessori pedagogue, liberal in principle, Elsie didn't insist that any of her children become one particular thing or another. She didn't program her youngest son to become a writer. She simply hoped that somehow he would be a great man.

He never said a word against her—he idealized her. But as with Elsie's idealization of her father, this may have compensated for something that seemed missing early on in the parent.

One tires of how often mothers take the rap for those first four years, while fathers as parental bench-warmers get exonerated. Ross Senior also tended to see his sons as extensions of himself and he too was a great idealist whose visions compensated for a tragic sense of loss, both personal and national. He hoped his sons would somehow continue his line of work. For them his energies were terrifying and coercive as well as infectious. But it was probably not until the death of Bruce that these qualities began to make themselves deeply felt in his youngest son, then already five.

My father was thrown into a family of considerably older, rather imposing males. He soon saw himself filling in for the dead brother, answering his parents' hopes for the eldest. He would feel some guilt, I think, in supplanting the dead sibling, having earlier been a rival for his busy parents' love and attention. Similarly, his career as a writer began in imitation and emulation of his other brother, Shockley. Unlike Cherry, he didn't slay these older brothers, yet one of them died and the other would step aside.

Both heroic fable and his position in the structure of this family cast him as heroic competitor, who would perform greater deeds than his father and brothers and who would, upon entering the House of Literature, cut off the tongues of competing writers—who remained nonetheless his close friends and benefactors. His competitiveness didn't show up as a loathsome personality trait—he was known as a likable kid and thereafter a "regular guy." Rather, it was a hunger of the soul to excel.

He came to have his father's great antiquarian lust. And he absorbed his mother's stories of his remarkable dead grandfather. In the midst of commonplace midwestern life, the parents conjured up ghostly idealizations that would inspire and torment their son from this time on.

Not until he was well into writing his novel did he tell his surprised parents how early he had committed himself to the writer's life. That this wasn't revisionary personal mythology is confirmed by Robert Masters, who heard him say it as a child. One year after his death, Elsie Lockridge remarked, "Most little boys pass through various stages in their choice of a life career. Little boys invariably want to be policemen, engineers, cowboys, something with a lot of action. We did not know until recent years how early Ross, Jr. had settled on his life work. He said that since he was between seven and eight years of age he had had one settled purpose in life. *He was going to write.* And he wanted to write a great, good book."

Why did he choose, at the improbable age of seven, to become a writer? In part it may have been to fulfill the special role he now had in the family, after the death of Bruce. In part it may have been an ego ideal that would compensate for some nameless maternal deficit. In part it may have been to emulate his father and older brother.

But I think it was principally grounded in a more positive inheritance from his parents. They were both wonderful story-tellers. They encouraged their son to read. Constitutionally he had a fierce sympathy with products of the imagination, whether stories, poems, plays, or movies. Aristotle long ago noted the intrinsic delight we take in imitation, and this child who loved stories wanted to make up stories of his own.

Keeping this commitment from his busy, ambitious parents was a strong child's instinctive claim to a sphere free for the imagination. It was his secret, kept in a self-defining resistance to the strong web of words and personality his parents spun around him. To tell them would have been to relinquish it—especially to his mother, who on a deep level may already have been identified with loss. The will to become a writer was the nucleus of his sense of identity, silently maintained throughout an apprenticeship where much of his writing would be for hire at the request of his father. The real book he had in mind to write would be the revelation of a fabulous secret.

III

"Legends in a Class-Day Album"

Early Bloomington Days, 1924–1933

Hoosier schoolmaster George W. Setser would pause in front of the Lockridge house on High Street to cut fresh switches on his way to Finley School. He arrived early to fire the coal furnace and ring the bell of the township school just southeast of Bloomington, where he taught grades four through eight in one of two classrooms. He spread the ashes to make separate paths to the girls' and boys' privies and served up cistern drinking water in a bucket equipped with a single tin cup. After hours he'd mop the floors.

Naomi Dalton—who would be my obstetrician—was upset to see new student Ross Lockridge stand unprotestingly in front of the class while Mr. Setser took a switch to his legs. Hardly an unruly kid, he had a nervous energy that could spill over in misdemeanors. Naomi's grandmother said he was "a caged lion" because he paced back and forth when he talked.

Mr. Setser's switches were mostly for show. He gave a lecture, "The Ideal Teacher," at a township school institute in early September of 1924, just as Ross Lockridge was entering his country school— and many of his students would so remember him. There was an advantage in strict single-room pedagogy: each grade went forward to the recitation bench at the front of the room for every subject taught, while the rest of the class had to sit still. Thus sixth-grader Ross Lockridge and others overheard the higher grades. Students who did all four grades in that classroom took in the same material four times, and would claim that even in college they were learning little that Mr. Setser had not already drilled into them. He taught the basics, plus heroic history, high moral values, and literary samplings. Sixty years later, one student would remember his enthusiasm for Whittier's *Snow-bound* and Gray's "Elegy."

Ross liked the school he would call his alma mater. Young Dorothy Smith, who visited one day from another school, watched the girls at lunchtime "trying to catch up with" this smiling new student who had prominent dimples, knew the answers, introduced the winter game Fox & Hounds, and told stories. Near the end of sixth grade, he tested out of seventh, but his parents refused to let him skip, and in the fall of 1925, he left Finley School, primed by Mr. Setser's catechism, and entered Bloomington High School, a large three-story red-brick building with a small replica of Winged Victory in the central staircase.

The Bloomington environment, more rural than urban, was making amends for his loss of that avenue of elms in Fort Wayne. The Lockridges' ample two-story frame house, built on a basement of huge unhewn limestone slabs, was graced with a barn, a fireplace encircled with rude stone benches in the south meadow, and a doghouse of mortared fieldstones large enough for several children. A local dog-and-pony circus had kept animals in the barn, and Ross could see the names Sparkle and Twinkle Toes on the stable doors. The surrounding acres had some virgin forest with a floor covered by mosses, may apples, jack-in-the-pulpits, wild strawberries, violets, poison ivy, and molehills. He played with Louise Moore, who lived on a nearby farm and had a Welsh pony named Girlie.

He soon had an animal of his own, an elderly black cow named June, purchased by his parents to encourage industry. A friend, Ben Siebenthal, was bemused by this singular boy with cow. His learned neighbor milked the barn's lone occupant twice a day for three years until she expired, and he sold surplus milk to neighbors. His mother kept after him in the matter of responsible milking. She would say, "Ross, June's out again!" whenever June jumped the fence, and he'd pull on boots and chase after his cow.

In the 1920s most of Bloomington, with a population of about thirteen thousand, was contained within a single square mile, beyond which were woods, pastures, and quarries where now there are malls and sprawl. The town was culturally more diverse and spunkier than Muncie, the dreary Indiana town documented in the mid-Twenties by the Lynds in their famous study, *Middletown*. The Twenties were the heyday of the local limestone industry west and south of town, where the hilly terrain was punctured by caves, sinkholes, and abandoned water-filled quarries—a karst terrain more picturesque than the flat Indiana to the north so many interstate drivers take to be the Hoosier landscape.

At 7 a.m., a thunderous blast from the work whistle of Showers Brothers, the nation's largest producer of bedroom furniture, woke up everybody in town who wasn't already reporting for work. The principal employer was Indiana University, which opened in 1825, only seven years after the town's founding. Subsequent historical and economic interweaving made for a greater-than-usual spirit of cooperation between town and gown. Still, much of Bloomington, with its practical-minded business and laboring classes, was worlds apart from academe.

There was also an eighty-acre shantytown called Pigeon Hill and a sin strip along the railroad tracks misnamed the Levee in riverless Bloomington. Pondering this ramshackle part of town, my father would later imagine "the dim gradual history of chicaneries, trades, puny hopes, insolvencies, sordid tragedies whereby this dead, gray, ugly assortment of malodorous and bug-ridden rooms had called its way into existence." But he also sensed its "excrementitious vitality." This vitality had waned by the time I was a kid, and the nearest whorehouse was rumored to be on Cherry Street in Terre Haute.

The country folk who came into Bloomington on Saturdays and helped bring the Levee to life were sometimes termed "aborigines" by the students, and the stonecutters were "stonies," but these folks "for their part were proud of the University, . . . a little city apart, of stone temples and Olympian figures," where many of them hoped to send their kids.

The Lockridges had come back for the University—Elsie, Shockley, and Lillian all working toward degrees and Ross Senior resuming an adjunct relationship with the University, whose history department would take a dim view of his populist brand of local narrative history. He was listed in the city directory as a "travelling salesman"—a field representative for the World Book Company.

In this busy household Ross Junior was often left to structure his own time. He would arrive home from school to find cookies his mother left him. With Ben Siebenthal he would hike down High Street to the old Covenanter graveyard and turn left down Moore's Pike to Jackson Creek for a shallow swim. At Louise Moore's farm on nearby Sare Road he collected crystalline rocks around a perpetual spring.

But he'd sometimes decline invitations to hike because he was deep into one of the many books that lined his small upstairs room—Kipling and Stevenson and other adventure tales—and Ben felt there was a disciplined reserve about this boy. He would read with his back against a comforting large maple so that nobody could creep up behind him when the reading got scary. But there were no maples in the moviehouse. When the heroine in *Phantom of the Opera* jerked away the mask from the hideous organist, he jumped headfirst onto the woman in the next row.

In the early part of his life my father emerged smiling from imaginary vistas of literature and film to lead a fluid social life in clubby Bloomington, and he was known for always *helping out*. It was only in his late twenties, when he closed the door to write, that he showed the world "a swiftly receding view of my derriere."

Not long after he turned twelve, he joined Troop One of the boy scouts, operating out of the Baptist Church. Having advanced from Tenderfoot to Second Class Scout he took a fourteen-mile hike to Ellettsville and back with a companion, and submitted a report for a hiking merit badge. "The road was covered with tar. Gilman [Morse] and I fell into singing the scout song Three Good Turns and tramped along to the time of it. . . . We reached a fork in the road and went straight on up a hill and turned north-northwest. As we hiked up the hill we noticed two stone quarries close together. Here we did our first good turn of the day. A lady and two girls were trying to get their Ford up a hill . . ."

The scout camp at Weimer Lake southwest of town was a popular site for regional camp jamborees. These provided occasion for out-of-town scouts to drop by Bloomington's main attraction, the cadaver room at IU's Owen Hall, where the female cadavers were sought out to supplement the scant material on sex in the scout handbook. Not always checking off good turns, Ross entered into the usual small-beer prankish conspiracies—hoisting the scoutmaster's undies on a flagpole, pulling the straw tick of a sleeping scout out to the public path so he'd wake up befuddled.

A higher art was story-telling. On an overnight, all scouts brought stuff for a hunter's stew—cabbage, canned beans, corn, cured ham. Ross had been reading *The City of the Sacred Well*, which describes Mayan sacrifice of brides to the Rain God. He pulled out a large carrot that had the configuration of a female—"Look, I have Claudie!" Malcolm Correll, Ed Fulwider, and many other scouts gathered around to watch as he set the scene for the sacrifice—inventing a dialogue of boy priest with Claudie the Carrot (instead of Ix-Lol-Nicte or Xkan-Xoc) before the sober witness of all and at last offering distraught Claudie to the stew.

The scouts often said "I dare you" to do this or that. One boy accepted the dare of wiping with poison ivy—and regretted it the next day. And one day Ross Lockridge was walking with a group of boy scouts past a large industrial chimney that the University was remodeling for its power plant. On a self-imposed dare, he announced he would climb it. To the surprise of all, he ran into the structure and started up the interior steel rungs. A few minutes later he emerged at the cornice, climbed out onto the platform, swaggered around it, smiling and waving to his frightened peers below, somewhat like Douglas Fairbanks Senior. He descended and bowed gallantly to their applause.

What he never told fellow scout Carl Martz and the others was that when he neared the top he panicked and felt he'd have to jump. The fear of death was intense enough to freeze him, and only through will and masquerade did he carry it off, forcing himself to climb to the top and descend despite the vertigo, squeezing the steel rungs for all his life. The derring-do was reminiscent of omnipotent Bruce leaping into the river, only to discover he couldn't swim. The terror of this moment on the chimney was swept into Ross's dreams.

It was in sharing a scout tent in late August of 1927 with Malcolm Correll that his longest close friendship began. Son of a local bookkeeper and housewife, Malcolm pursued interests less literary than scientific and mechanical. His father was a tinkerer, who cut out little horses and sleighs from cigar boxes to make a merry-go-round run by a sand wheel. Malcolm liked to see how things worked.

Their friendship was complementary from the beginning, each relishing the other for the dialogue—or simply banter. But Malcolm—intelligent, tall, broad-shouldered, with dramatic black eyebrows—was unduly modest about himself and thought his friend brilliant. Throughout their frequent bull sessions into the night, he never challenged the tacit superiority of his friend. They absorbed the culture of Bloomington together over the next several years—in scouts, sports, school, church-related events, and later the University.

I was surprised to learn that my father's illustrious high school career had its share of drubbings and second-place finishes. His freshman year he tried to make the wrestling team as a skinny kid contending at 108 pounds. "I was a very, very bad wrestler. It happened once that a series of mishaps befell the other contenders in my class. Shortly before a meet, two fell sick, another left town, and a fourth was ineligible. I was permitted to wrestle for Bloomington High School. For eight minutes I feebly fought off the assault of a short, blocky individual who persisted in hurling me to the mat and who would certainly have pinned my shoulders if I had had any." Malcolm cheered his glum friend after this defeat.

They both ran as freshmen for Prince of the all-school carnival—a fund-raising event in which the royalty were elected by local folk who put money behind a candidate's name. It was a lesson in power and privilege when the winning candidate was a "North Walnut Street" boy who beat out the field in the closing day. North Walnut and North College then boasted the peerage of Bloomington—the Showerses, the Hoadleys (in limestone), the Searses, deans of professional schools, various judges, and other top crust. Another losing candidate, for Princess, was a girl living in modest circumstances, Vernice Baker, whom Ross Lockridge had not yet met.

Malcolm and Ross made the best of that carnival as leads in a theatrical, "The Price of Love," in which Malcolm played Hector, the hero, and Ross in drag played Rosemarie. After much hamming and racing back and forth on stage, Hector rescued Rosemarie from the villain as the two exited on the same broomstick.

Their orchestral triumphs were only slightly more decorous. Malcolm and Ross both took up the violin and played in the high school and Methodist Church orchestras. Ross played second fiddle to his more accomplished friend. Their teacher and conductor was Fred Sharp, whom they called F#—an admirable eccentric with a slight one-sided grin reserved for those audible errors that didn't quite warrant bringing the performance to a halt.

On his way to a lesson Ross would pass the Violin Breaker-Inner, Sharp's invention whereby the frog of the bow was attached off-axis to a wheel belted to a motor. The moving bow rocked back and forth with the crank action playing *g-d-a-e-e-a-d-g-g-d-a-e* ad infinitum. Whenever Ross and Malcolm were ill-prepared for lessons, they'd ask F# about his capture by Mexican bandits or his efforts to demonstrate, by featureless old coins found near Jasper, that John Cabot had not only reached the North American coast but had penetrated to southern Indiana. Sharp's digressions would fill up most of the hour and they'd escape with the same assignment for next time.

One day Malcolm accidentally snapped Ross's bow in two against the music stand. Thereafter "to everyone's delight he would protect his instrument with his body whenever he had an audience and noticed that I was moving around." The BHS orchestra had some first- and second-place finishes in state competitions, but Malcolm and Ross had their own competition. They played a duet before a large audience in the high school gymnasium, a rendition of "Marche Militaire." "We had practiced and knew what we were doing," said Malcolm years later. "But somehow we got into a psychological state of competition. First one would think that he was dragging the time, so he would speed up; then the other would have the same reaction, and he would speed up. Faster and faster. When we had collapsed at the end Sharp declared the performance a photo-finish."

Contemplating a career in music, Malcolm spoke with F#— genuinely respected and a paternal presence. "During my conversation with Sharp, he opined that Ross was capable of doing anything he wanted to do. I wanted to be that kind of person and my envy of Ross was fed by Sharp's comment. I guess my inferences hurt a little bit."

When Ross first arrived at Bloomington High School, some teachers thought he was cheating because his recall on tests was so total. He didn't gloat or seem egotistical, so his classmates generally liked him despite his quiet bravura in the classroom. "I remember Ross in class because he had all the answers," said Georgia Adams. "I mean he had all the answers. The rest of us might just as well have stayed home. When he would get up to talk none of us knew what he was talking about because you needed the Webster's, and I'm not sure the teachers even knew what he was talking about." Some of the students wanted to kill him for this, "but you know he was a happy person. You very seldom saw him frowning. And he never seemed to get mad. We kidded him a lot. We really did kid him a lot about his wordsy talk."

Every six weeks the honor roll would be published in *The Optimist*, the school newspaper. Naomi Dalton's mother would say, "I see Ross beat you again," and Naomi would reply—overestimating the academic credentials—"Well, why not? He has two Ph.D.'s in the family."

He wasn't hounded for slippages or urged to excel by, as it were, a stage mom and a Little League dad. His parents' only recorded admonition was to tell him not to stay up so late reading. Rather, they exerted great influence by the sheer power of their disparate visionary energies, conjuring up heroic possibility in the stories they told. The parents didn't set his goals. They raised a son who would set them himself—large ones he liked quietly to fashion apart from them.

I find in this boy scout, church-goer, and eager student something other than happy sociability. He drove himself with the kind of egoism others would register as vitality of spirit. Without apology, he would acknowledge his own competitiveness, which he thought was part of what it meant to be American. He entered warmly into games and sports, and could usually be a good loser because these didn't much enter into his self-definition. It would be more threatening to come up short if the craft of writing were at stake.

Elsie did aspire to a Ph.D. but first she had to finish the A.B. begun in 1898, and decided on a psychology major. Her daughter, Lillian, academically three years behind her, decided on—psychology. Ross Junior buckled down to work for his high school diploma in this studious household. When he visited Malcolm, he'd organize the time between study and fun. Just for fun, he translated the entire *Aeneid*.

And under his father's tutelage, he started winning oratory contests. He visited Nancy Hanks Lincoln's grave in southern Indiana, where in a cold autumn rain his father asked him to recite the Gettysburg Address and other Lincoln excerpts. His father would drive him a hundred miles in any direction so that they "might discuss history and recite the living words of the past on the very soil where history was made."

At fifteen he began a working partnership with his father, who called him into his home office one day. "Scuffie, I understand that a couple of weeks ago you began taking a course in shorthand and typing." "Yes, sir." "Take a letter, Scuffie." Father handed son "a notebook and a pencil and began to dictate in his usual secretary-killing fashion." Ross Junior would eventually win state championships in both shorthand and typing.

Ross Senior dictated to various amanuenses a series of books for young adults—*George Rogers Clark: Pioneer Hero of the Old Northwest*, 1927 ("To my son, Ross Franklin Lockridge, Jr., whose boyish regard for genuine heroes of history has helped to inspire this book it is affectionately dedicated"); *A. Lincoln*, 1930 ("To my mother"); and *La Salle*, 1931 ("To the Lions Clubs of America"). For a wage Ross Junior typed the latter. All were published by World Book Company.

Shockley Lockridge joined the World Book Company also, having graduated as an English major in 1928 and marrying in 1929. He would stay with World Book the rest of his career. He'd begun drinking at the Phi Gam house during Prohibition and Hoagy Carmichael days—brew made in Pigeon Hill shanties or corn liquor distilled in Jasper County or Cokes spiked with alcohol from the medical school. Festive collegiate drinking turned compulsive on the road when he fell in with a crowd of well-oiled traveling salesmen. He'd wake up and be unable to account for whole days at a time. When he tried to pray for help, "I groped for speech like a drowning man."

Meanwhile, Ross didn't seem to resent working for his father. Fifty cents an hour was well above what his friends were getting as clerks or janitors about town. Sometimes he wished for yet more work. His friends felt he liked this character, his father, never expressing hostility despite the father's stubborn single-mindedness about his own work, his casting of son as adjunct, and his bossiness. The father-son relationship was more an unequal partnership expressed through a variety of projects than it was unadorned filial bonding.

In manner and person they were dissimilar. The father was a stocky unkempt man, his clothes wrinkled and baggy, not quite five foot seven, deep-voiced, with jowls and anarchic eyebrows. He was intensely physical in his manner—from his handshakes and hugs to his gestures and eating habits.

The son was leaner and, by the time he was sixteen, four inches taller. A quiet-spoken person, he had a voice more tenor than baritone. Elsie was always vigilant about diphthongs, so Easterners would notice only a slight Hoosier accent. With brown-black hair and pronounced eyebrows, blue-gray eyes, dimples, and perfect white skin and teeth, he was regarded by most as strikingly handsome, his features more refined than his father's. Some remarked on a likeness to Tyrone Power.

There was something of his physical person always in motion—whether hands, feet, or torso. He wasn't exactly jittery, just animated and expectant, with an animal energy that communicated well to others. His head pointed forward slightly, as if he were really going places. And he was peripatetic—I remember him pacing back and forth, by that time slightly stooped from years at the typewriter.

Though his warmer feeling was for the mother, there was little early evidence of withdrawal from the father. He genuinely *liked* history and memorials and cemeteries and speeches and camping. Still, he knew his father's work was different in kind from his own—and idiosyncratic. He was doing provisional work for hire. The father was slow to catch on.

~

BHS sophomore Vernice Baker had heard others speak of Ross Lockridge, one class ahead of her, and he was frequently mentioned in *The Optimist*. "ROSS LOCKRIDGE HEADS HONOR ROLL." "LOCKRIDGE ELECTED JUNIOR CLASS PRESIDENT." But it wasn't until Sunday evening, August 10, 1930, that they almost met. It was an Epworth League meeting in the basement of the First Methodist Church. He was there with Malcolm, who was president of this youth group and was to have a date later that evening with Becky Brown. Ross and Vernice were strongly aware of each other.

He'd seen her from a distance a few days earlier at the swimming pool, tanned from a recent stint at a YWCA camp. She was more often described as lovely than as beautiful. Delicate-boned, with brown-blond hair and a full figure, she had a musical soft voice and a grace of movement that owed something to her girlhood tree-climbing and dancing.

No one introduced them that evening, but Becky Brown was a mutual friend. She approached Vernice to see if she could join them after League. Vernice had already turned down Bud Miller for a date—having promised to join a bunch of girls at Martha Robinson's—so she had to say no.

That Thursday she was visiting an older brother when she got a call from Becky Brown renewing the offer. "And I said yes! So the four of us drove to Nashville and there was a drugstore right on the corner—the building is still there and looks very much the same—and we had a Coke. Well, it was fun because Malcolm and Ross were good cutups and they said a lot of funny things. We laughed a lot and had a good time. And drove back. And my mother was sitting on the front porch swing and I went up and I said, 'Mom, I have never had so much fun in my life!' That was my first date with Ross."

Ross and Malcolm would unload their F# stories, speak Pig Latin and Garfarble, sing scout and sailor songs, and make up words like "tooshomercartpeacerinksjinksrineofahorsepetedious." And on one subsequent ride through country roads, Ross recited Edgar Allan Poe's "The Raven" and all 625 lines of Coleridge's *The Rime of the Ancient Mariner*, memorized one rainy afternoon at Rivervale, the Methodist church camp. This might not have been to everybody's taste, but Vernice simply fell for him.

Like Ross, Vernice Baker was an accident, the youngest child of older parents. Their two families were a study in contrasts—the Lockridges visionary, ambitious, and wordsy, the Bakers practical, fatalistic, and quiet. Her father, Hugh Baker, was a gentle even-tempered man, never expressing anger, who loved his youngest daughter and gave her some needed advice in a world where there were few guarantees: "Always remember your good name and keep cheerful—the blues sap your energy and get no place."

In his early years he was variously a farmer, a quarry worker, a township school teacher and principal, a mail carrier, and a bookkeeper for a small loan company—frequently thwarted in his professional moves. When the Depression sent the loan company under, he was unemployed for a few years, while his older daughters, Beulah and Clona, worked in town, and he was lucky to supply the dinner table with an occasional bluegill.

He kept a diary over the years that narrates a life of dignity and hardship. His grandfather had "gained great fame as a local preacher in the Methodist Church, and a wild west farmer," while his father, who had hauled tobacco from Monroe County to Louisville in his early years, later became an itinerant preacher on horseback, journeying across the state and keeping a farm at the same time. Hugh was proud to be a third cousin of "*Sir Robert Fulton,* who invented the first Steam Boat in 1807 and floated it on the Hudson River from Albany to New York City." He attempted to leave the family farm near Smithville south of Bloomington, enrolling in Bloomington High School in 1890, but his father's death intervened. He resumed farmwork and pursued his education at the nearby normal school.

"In August of the same year 1891, after assisting with the harvest, I decided to try my hand at a Stone Quarry. Being of a timid disposition, I approached the place of business and stood awkwardly gawking around for a time. Finally mustering up all the courage possible I approached the overseer and said very inarticulately 'Have—you—got—any—thing—a—round—here—I—could—do?' 'I have some work to be done with a shovel and wheel-barrow. Do you think you are man enough for it?' "

His bride-to-be grew up in Smithville also. Lillie Thrasher was a tiny quiet person, eldest of five daughters whose mother died when Lillie was twelve, before some of the finer points of housekeeping were passed along, like cooking and sewing. The father, Theodore Thrasher, a stern patriarchal figure who was a station agent for the Monon Railroad, never remarried and let his daughters take over the domestic life. They all got along but Pa didn't permit a lively household. When she had a dancing party, he called out "Lillie!" from upstairs, and that put an end to that.

The five daughters did their own knitting but they took their stockings to an older person with the expertise to turn the heel. One day Lillie journeyed with a friend to Bloomington to pick out material for a dress, and she couldn't decide on what to buy. She had some teacher's training in Bloomington, but got cold feet when it came time to take the test.

Courtship in Smithville wasn't a bacchanal: a couple could walk up the railroad tracks a certain distance, and then there were basket dinners at church. Her marriage with Hugh Baker was harmonious and quiet.

Hugh liked best of all to teach, and had some success in country schools, but he wanted his kids to go to college and eventually took a mail carrier's job in Bloomington, where the family moved in 1905 and stayed, despite having fallen immediately into the hands of a real estate crook. It was a life of few rampant pleasures. Lillie served up cornbread and beans, cheese and tomato sandwiches, and sometimes swiss steak and butterscotch pie. Hugh records *not* being able to go to the 1904 World's Fair in Louisville and, in the single racy entry, writes: "I finished reading and burned *Sappho*, a novel. It gives vivid description of feminine debauchery in France. Not worth any body's while to read it. Retiring at 8:20 p.m."

He does take a trip out west and he does record seeing Halley's comet on a White River fishing trip. "Halley's comet was a grand sight to behold. As it appears so very seldom I will not be permitted to look upon it during my present incarnation, but I trust that it will be the good fortune of my progenity to read these pages and when they are permitted to behold the famous tailed star they may recall hereby the name of their far distant ancestor who had the same privilege while on the stage of action. To that end my name is here inscribed Hugh Baker 1874–1911 yet living."

And he inscribes the births of their six children, given exotic names to counterbalance the ordinariness of "Baker"—Aubrey Theodore, Beulah Anise, Clona Eloise, Alexander Leon, Imogene Marie, and Lillian Vernice. Nobody ever found out how he came up with "Clona."

Born March 19, 1914, in a small one-story house at 326 South

Fairview in Bloomington, a month before Ross Lockridge, Vernice Baker, like her husband-to-be, would find the backdrop of the Great War in her earliest memories. Her family assured her that her Uncle Henry was safe behind barbed wire in France, so she imagined him wrapped up in it. Life on Fairview Street was both ordinary and dramatic. There was the Bakers' first electricity—a bare lightbulb hanging from the ceiling. There was the great 1918 flu epidemic and Vernice felt grown-up while taking biscuits to her sick sister Imogene. When she stepped on a nail, her mother and a neighbor held her foot over hot wood ashes to kill the germs. Her father read the Katzenjammer Kids to her—there were few books in the house—and in later years whenever she sat down to read a book, her mother would say, "Don't you have anything to *do?*" She couldn't read without a vague sense of guilt.

At age four she watched her mother combing her hair in front of the glass cabinet the day they were moving to 534 South Lincoln Street. Though her mother would have liked to live on North College, this was a move to a better part of town—from west to east, literally to the other side of the tracks, thanks to Hugh Baker's industry. He whistled as he carried the mail, and was a good and honest man.

As a little girl, Vernice often got in the way of household tasks, once falling into a wash bucket. She got a spanking for that. The only other was for walking too far from home. One time her mother was talked into lying to the train conductor that Vernice was under six. She rode free back from Chicago feeling guilty all the way and sure she'd be told to get off. She learned to obey the rules.

Life on South Lincoln was challenging to a young girl's imagination. Not having store-bought props, Vernice and her friends climbed trees, traced animals in the clouds, made houses out of leaves and grass, pretended they were pursued by bears, played hopscotch, Touch the Icebox, and Statue, in which one kid would be whirled around by another and, upon landing, assume a stationary pose—"and you'd think you were very beautiful." They went barefoot in summer and, whatever the weather, took off their long underwear on the first of May.

Her friend Georgia Adams invited her to her father's farm near Smithville, where she slid down haystacks, scrambled up a maple tree to escape a billy goat, rode a Shetland pony bareback until raked off by a low limb, dressed a cat in baby clothes, drank coffee from a mustache cup, felt the chicken droppings between her toes, and in the outhouse found another use for a Sears Roebuck catalogue. Vernice thought the Adamses rich because they had a piano, and Georgia thought the Bakers rich because they had a Victrola.

And over the years they danced—the Powderpuff dance, the Rose dance, the Imp dance, the Doll dance, the Clown dance, the Old French Court dance, the Huntress dance, the Spanish dance, the Danish dance, at various picnics, convocations, 4-H club meetings, and theatres about town.

Paul Lentz, a fireman and neighbor, would watch her spirited comings and goings and say to his wife, "There goes my girl!"

One dance, the Boxing dance, she performed many times with her other close childhood friend, Nota Scholl. Nota's father worked as a laborer for Showers and they lived on the west side of the tracks. Nota was struck by how much Vernice's two oldest sisters, Clona and Beulah, adored her and yet how unspoiled she was—positive and uncomplaining, modest, nonjudgmental, with a catch in her voice that quickly turned to laughter. Nota was a comedienne when others wanted her to be, and she kept Vernice laughing. She was also philosophical and analytic, figuring people out.

One thing about the Baker household puzzled her, and Vernice didn't discuss it with her. Imogene, four years older than Vernice, was an odd person whose rough demeanor made her unlike the other Bakers.

Imogene had been a bright, pretty girl who read a lot and played with her younger sister, when at age ten she was diagnosed with encephalitis. She lay in a coma for some time and when she came out of it her personality and intellect had changed. If Vernice tried to play Parcheesi with her, Imogene would accuse her of cheating. They had to stop playing croquet because her tantrums could be dangerous. Georgia and Vernice would play up in the trees to hide from her. During some of these rages, Lillie Baker would have to hold Imogene down until she was quiet. Lillie was small, but as my mother would say, "You're given strength at certain times."

Vernice had to share a bed with Imogene in the room where the four girls slept. Her screaming could be heard outside the house, and the older siblings were sometimes ashamed to show their faces. At BHS an informal "I hate Imogene" club was started. The rest of the family, to prevent the rages, tiptoed around her.

Then one day when she was fourteen, Imogene chased Vernice with a butcher knife. Vernice proved the faster runner, and Imogene was sent to the mental hospital in Madison, Indiana. When the Bakers walked through the halls at Madison—known, of course, as a nuthouse—the mother placed hands over her youngest daughter's eyes. They once took Imogene to a nearby park, where Vernice tried gamely to teach her the Charleston. This small initiative failed and she worried what it would be like when Imogene came home.

When she did, Imogene was once again changed. Whatever they'd done, she was now devoid of personality. Unable to go to school, she'd sit on the porch and sing old hymns. A renowned doctor in Indianapolis was consulted, who decided something must be wrong with her bowels. He operated and she died three days later, November 11, 1926, at the age of sixteen. "A postmortem examination was performed which revealed the fact that sleeping sickness or Ensepholitus had again taken hold and had caused her death," wrote Hugh Baker in his diary.

At the wake in the Baker house, twelve-year-old Vernice sat on her brother Aubrey's lap and cried. She had learned caution and reserve during the six-year crisis. This aspect of her personality never undid the capacity to take pleasure in small things, or the laughter and the hope—but she would always have a sense of peril about what can befall innocent people.

Despite this family tragedy Vernice was very active in junior high and high school life, as well as church activities. In her high school years she was leader of the Canary Patrol in the girl scouts, president of the Junior Girl Reserves, head of Natural Dancing in the Girls' Athletic Association, Most Popular Girl of the Epworth League, president of Blue Triangle, and a member of Proscenium Players, National Thespians, the Girls' Council, the Patsies, the Spinsters, YPB, the Glee Club, National Honor Society, et cetera. As someone not admitted into the National Honor Society and never elected president of anything, I find this record daunting.

Way off in New York and Chicago, the Twenties may have been roaring, but the values and activities of BHS students suggest something closer to a chaste murmuring. The Girls' Council published a code dedicated to attaining "a higher, finer type of Christian womanhood." There was no strict line between school and church—Bloomington High School had several organizations whose religious orientation was unabashedly Christian. Religion *meant* Christianity. Beyond predictable high ideals there are several beatitudes encrusted with antique charm: "We believe that school shoes should be well fitting and with moderate heels," "We believe that performing one's toilet in public is ill-bred," "We approve of the policy of 'hands off' in friendship between boys and girls," "Gum chewing is in poor taste," "We believe in chaperones for all parties indoors and out," "WE BELIEVE THAT A WELL-BRED GIRL WILL DISCOURAGE SMOKING," "WE BELIEVE A GIRL WHO DOES NOT CONDUCT HERSELF IN A LADY-LIKE MANNER AT ALL TIMES REFLECTS ON HER HOME AND FAMILY" (emphasis theirs), "Knowing that a lady is recognized by a quiet inconspicuous manner, we shall try to conduct ourselves at school and on the street in such a manner as not to deserve criticism from others." And getting down to basics: "Avoid throwing anything on the grounds. Do not harm the shrubbery. Avoid excessive applause."

It goes without saying that most of the girls were virgins. Most of the boys too. Even in college one well-educated young woman still thought babies exited via the navel. The PTA conscientiously sent someone to explain sex to the girls. The explanation was metaphoric—the expert said sex was a matter of chemistry. So Alice Lloyd decided to take chemistry instead of physics. Word that a local girl had died after an abortion shocked classmates—this was a singularity that confirmed the perils of sex. The Spinsters were intent on getting married, but as an elite social club they regulated the social behavior of their members—anyone who stayed out too late with a boy could be suspended. The Patsies, the competing high school sorority, were more liberal—some members were seen smoking! And of course a girl who smoked was capable of anything.

But, as Byron would say, the "controlless core of human hearts" was alive in those days; it simply throbbed more discreetly. The BHS classes of 1931 and '32 would later say they were the Depression classes, yet "Were we depressed? Never!" They had a vitality as well as a relative innocence that justifies some nostalgia here. Ross and Malcolm joined forces with two other exceptional students—Donald

Binkley and Vincent Hippensteel—and christened themselves The Four Musketeers. At the sound of the opening bell, the four put arms around shoulders and strutted happily up the school steps—a gesture of schoolday eagerness that now seems prehistoric and forever lost.

I'm not very nostalgic for the BHS I was to encounter in the late 1950s. By then the boys were wearing black leather jackets instead of coat-and-tie, and rather than tease me for my sesquipedalians they chased me home with brass knuckles. Instead of that intellectual confraternity The Four Musketeers, we had The Black Aces—a gang of white punks with ducktails and switchblades who for me took any fun out of James Dean's rebellion.

Vernice Baker went out on dates with several boys before Ross Lockridge came along, and she liked many of them. But he wasn't to be confounded this time by anyone so formidable as his old Fort Wayne rival, Skelly the Strong. *Tuesday, January 14, 1930:* "Diary, I invited Fred to a party and *he can come!!* Oh! gee. I wished he liked me. It's Martha's surprise birthday party." *Wednesday, January 15, 1930:* "Dear Diary, I just came home from Martha's party. I had a pretty good time but I feel like I wouldn't want to have another date with Fred!!!"

Ross Lockridge dated a few other girls in high school. Only one—Peggy Bittner—seems to have made an impression. Peggy was a spirited intellectual, the daughter of a university administrator, who, like Ross, had a well-developed wordhoard. Between classes the two of them would sometimes compete before other amused students, each outdoing the other in a torrent of polysyllables. Ross Lockridge wrote that the junior class was "a microcephalic sodality of batrachian troglodytes" who "spue forth a cacoethes loquendi of echolalia"—and his banter with Peggy was of this ilk.

Vernice Baker, often on the honor roll but not at the top of the class, was present for some of these sessions and was anguished. Another girl with an interest in Ross Lockridge said the word "antidisestablishmentarianism" to someone in his vicinity, hoping he'd overhear her.

Looking back on his high school years he would speak cryptically of "a change in love." He may refer to having been drawn away from Peggy Bittner to Vernice Baker. The relationship otherwise covered

its teenaged tracks. Following graduation he and Peggy saw one another occasionally, but to judge by the single surviving letter—in
which he is apologizing for some unnamed offense—his courtship of
her was strained and oblique.

Following that initial date in August of 1930, Vernice and Ross
saw each other rather often, but their dates were tangential to other
functions, mostly Epworth League and YPB meetings. The former,
the Methodist youth group, was more social than devotional, and attracted non-Methodists looking for something upbeat on Sunday evenings. Following these meetings, Vernice would try to elude other
boys so that Ross could drive her home. Grimly programmed
courtship—where a solitary boy arranges early in the week to pick
up a girl on Friday or preferably Saturday under scrutiny of parents
and drives her to the movies or a ballgame, after which amorous
jousting begins under threat of curfew—was relatively uncommon.

Some representative dates: *Monday, September 29, 1930:* "Tonite I
went to Malcolm Correll's to help teach Ross Lockridge to dance—
then we went to YPB." *Sunday, January 4, 1930:* "After League Ross,
Malcolm, Doris Baxter, and I went to the show 'Reducing'—then
went over to Doris' home. Ross is the wittiest person I know." *Sunday, January 18, 1931:* "I took Ross to a pot luck supper that Georgia
gave at Grace's. It was so funny—every one brought *beans!*"

YPB was the Young People's Branch of the Women's Christian
Temperance Union. Temperance was notoriously widespread in this
subculture, enhancing the sense of occasion when people took their
first drinks. Ross Lockridge was secretary of YPB, which he called
the YP Beers. A member promised

> *not to buy, drink, sell or give*
> *Alcoholic liquors while I live.*
> *From all tobacco I'll abstain*
> *And never take God's name in vain.*

One of their missions was to stomp on any cigarette butt long
enough to tempt a child. The large, motherly adult leader, Mrs.
Barnard (known as Mrs. Barnyard), gave long-winded prayers during
which Ross, Vernice, Malcolm, Nota, Ruth Bradt, and others would
get tickled and pain their sides. These meetings threatened to be-

come saturnalias, because they'd begin with Ross's satiric minutes. Word of these minutes spread throughout Bloomington, and the ranks of YPB began to grow.

Some of these meetings were at the Lockridge house where Elsie Lockridge felt a strong attraction to this young girl, Vernice Baker. For her part, Vernice thought the Lockridge house a mansion and she was in awe of Ross Senior.

A good portion of the student body at BHS began monitoring the courtship. It became a community symbol—"we were all living in it ourselves," says Nota Scholl. A university psychologist, with Lord knows what agenda, visited the school and asked: "If you weren't yourself, who else in the school would you like to be?" The girls picked Vernice Baker, the boys Ross Lockridge. Vernice figured she was selected because she was going with Ross.

The Kunz family with twelve children moved in next to the Bakers on Lincoln Street, and Elloise Kunz talked with Vernice, who was often in the backyard "drying her feathers," as she put it. Vernice said she hoped to fill a backyard with children of her own. One day walking to school she laughed as she told Elloise about having dreamt she slept with Ross. Nota found out within minutes, and Vernice acted fast to restrain Elloise for fear it would get all over school.

Elloise's sister Majora felt the romance "had a fairy tale quality. Like a prince and princess, they seemed a couple chosen by Fate to enjoy all the best in life."

Friday, January 30, 1931: "Found out today that Ross and I have been chosen as leads in the Senior Review. Isn't that a coincidence?" Well, it wasn't a coincidence—rather, a fixup by Alice Thorne, theatrical coach.

The stars did have a long list of theatrical credits by this time. As a sophomore, Vernice Baker had leading roles in such productions as *Thanks Awfully*, *Hey Teacher*, *Gretna Green*, *On the Park Bench*, and by the end of her high school career she had appeared in at least twenty-five, often playing beside Catherine Feltus, who would have a brief career in films as Kay Craig.

Ross Lockridge's finest theatrical hour occurred the preceding month, when the lead of Katharine Kavanaugh's 1928 three-act farce *Who Wouldn't Be Crazy?* was taken ill and he was asked only two nights before the opening to learn the role. He memorized the many lines in a single afternoon and played Jack, alias "Speedy," very speedily in-deed, according to the rave notices in *The Optimist* and later *The Gothic*, BHS's yearbook. "Lockridge shines." The play was set in the courtyard of the Good Samaritan Sanitarium.

He and Malcolm, also in the cast, were chastened in this triumph by Edna Menger, Latin teacher, who asked them to reflect on the sensitivity of jokes at the expense of the mentally ill. They listened to her.

Collegiana, a three-act musical revue with a cast of one hundred and eighty-five, played to capacity audiences at the Harris Grand Theatre on February 26 and 27, 1931. Vernice always had stage fright and dreamt of not knowing her lines. Ross never confessed such fears to anybody, but I know he had them. He was George, "working his way through school," and she was Mary, "sweetest girl on the campus of Tate," and together they danced a minuet as book-ends and sang "There's something about an old-fashioned girl." Bud Miller sang "Tip-toe through the tulips," never to live it down, with dozens of campus nook girls, miniature golf girls, gypsies, and sailors striking up the chorus.

There were also sixteen Plantation Boys and sixteen Topsies in blackface. If any African-Americans attended those performances at the Harris Grand, they were required to sit in the rear balcony. In the photos of graduating seniors in the 1932 *Gothic*, the three black students—Francis Henson, Herbert Fearman, and Wade Chenault—are grouped together at the end. Black students in the first eight grades attended the black school, Banneker, until its closing in 1954. A KKK klavern had formed in Evansville in 1920, and by the middle of the decade the Klan was widespread in Indiana.

At BHS, attitudes toward race were more placidly embodied in organizational structures. The "Count On Me Reserves" was the black counterpart to the YWCA Girl Reserves, which included, in order of age, the Junior Girl Reserves, Silver Triangle, and Blue Tri-angle. When in 1931 Vernice Baker was president of Blue Triangle, the Count on Me Reserves were invited to the first joint meeting ever—a pre-Thanksgiving service. All agreed this was their best meeting, but thereafter the groups went their own way. Everyone understood that this was the way things eternally are.

When I grew up in Bloomington in the Fifties, my brothers and

I went to a black barbershop—the barbers were black and the customers were white. After hours, proprietor James Shawntee cut the hair of black people at his home. Had he permitted blacks to patronize his own shop, he'd have been run out of town.

Following *Collegiana*, Ross wasn't asking Vernice out very much. She was puzzled and thought maybe the theatrical had proved a downer. They did prepare food together for Epworth League one afternoon and he did accept her invitation to the Spinsters' Spring Dance for June. For her part, she applauded his performance in *Household Hints* and was enchanted when on April 16 he stepped forward at an orchestral convo and, spotlighted in a blue shirt, played Drdla's rapturous violin solo, "Souvenir." But something was wrong, and mutual friends began to talk and plot.

Study hall was taken very seriously in those days. The silence was so deep that when Vincent Hippensteel walked up the aisle one day in new shoes, everyone could hear the squeaks. But notes could be furtively passed back and forth. So in late April of 1931, sitting in study hall, Georgia Adams undertook on her own authority to find out from Malcolm Correll why Ross had seemed to fade away.

GEORGIA: Say, what is the matter with Vernice & Ross? I never do see them together any more. I asked Vernice yesterday what was the matter & she didn't say a thing so I thought maybe I had better shut up.

MALCOLM: He says they don't fit very well. He won't even date her. Don't spread it around though. I think he is a sap. Gosh! if I had a chance with any girl of such a standing—well I'd feel a lot different and be likewise. If he can get it he is having a date with her Thurs night for the Epworth League party. That is provided I can get one with Grace too. . . . He does like her. He just doesn't want to go steady with her. He still has dates with her; that is, until just recently. He has been too busy for them.

GEORGIA: . . . I sure think that Bake & Ross make a cute couple. Don't you? I've heard a lot of people say so. Alice Thorne sure thinks so.

MALCOLM: I'd give anything to get them to go together steady. I've never had as much fun on double dates as those I've had with them. . . .

GEORGIA: I asked Bake the other day if she *really* liked Ross & she said, "Oh, I don't know. I used to like him, but anymore I don't know." She said she never did see him when he was serious & that she would like him better if he were a little more serious—That's a laugh, isn't it?

MALCOLM: Well, for gosh sakes! That's almost exactly what he said about her.

That Thursday evening, April 30, Grace Rogers, Malcolm, Vernice, and Ross went roller-skating together. The problem in early spring of 1931 was simple enough. Still sixteen years old, Ross sensed what Vernice would later confess: despite the dignified reservations Georgia communicated to Malcolm, she had fallen for him beyond redemption. She was all too serious for this boy barely three years past puberty who had a writer's ambition that required some experience of the world. He hadn't yet told Vernice of this ambition—she had a vague idea he might become a lawyer and didn't really care what his professional goals were. Retaining portions of himself in bedrock privacy, he felt threatened by this early love and kept her and his own feelings at bay.

The fun he had with Vernice was ironically the problem. In some respects the "fit" was too good, as he would later explain it, and he backed away. He resisted the community script, the thornhedge of his reluctance now rooted in the fact that Vernice Baker was *not* an inaccessible Alicia Carpenter.

He would speak many years later of himself in the third person—"the love of another is fixed upon this boy, and this love follows him and adores him through these years. There is some slight passage [of time] between them." It would be four more years before he was fully committed. On page 118 of the 1931 *Gothic* appears a heart with photos of Ross and Vernice on the two crescents and a jagged line printed down the middle. "Busted Love" reads the caption. Some years thereafter Ross mended his copy with tape, writing in the margin, "Pulmonic valve O.K. Aortic valve O.K."

He kept a journal briefly in the spring of 1931 at the suggestion of his white-haired English teacher, Nellie Carrithers. There are no references to Vernice Baker. Though it's a fledgling writer's journal, full of comic Latinity, not a confessional log, it's revealing even so.

One finds the quiet verve his classmates saw, but also considerable frustration and performance anxiety that he kept hidden. His satiric invocation:

> *Imbue, celestial Muse, my feeble pen*
> *With thy supernal wisdom and inspire*
> *Such cadence as, withheld from humble men,*
> *Resounds so sweetly from thy deathless lyre.*

He ponders whether to call his journal "The Refuse Pit" or "Pen Drippings."

In this six-week period he appears in three theatricals, and where Vernice Baker in her diary is always the enthusiast for local productions ("Gee, it was swell"), he remarks, "I am only too conservative when I say it is idiotic. Fortunately the star of the *Gothic* does not rise or fall with the success of this production." Playing Prince Oesophagus opposite *Gothic* editor Peggy Bittner, "the cardboard crown collapsed during the second convocation and ended up by hanging around my neck like a halter. I spent the remainder of the day evading poorly-veiled insinuations as to my histrionic ability." Of *Collegiana*, "the dialogue is inane and spiritless" and he would like to escape from life's "unpleasant little burdens." He disposes "of many a haunting incubus among which may be numbered the eventful Senior Revue." During its production he "held scanty communion with Morpheus" and had to miss school.

Somewhat later "I gluttonized thirteen hours of sleep. Alexander the Great subsisted on a few minutes, Edison on three hours, Napoleon, on some like amount, and other geniuses commensurately. Draw your own conclusions. . . . Mother related at the evening supper table the case of a boy who had graduated from a university at the age of 15 with an I.Q. of 189, received his master's degree at the age of 16 and his Ph.D. at 19. Such a record, strangely enough, can serve either as a spur or an inhibition to scholastic advancement of less brilliant students."

Having taken her A.B. with High Distinction, Elsie was writing her master's thesis on intelligence testing. She read the journal, recognized the anxiety she had wrought, and scribbled in the margin, "But I wonder what we'll hear of him later?" To my knowledge, Ross never mentioned IQ again to anybody. I'm unsure whether she had him tested or merely tested him herself, but she would always claim he was off scale on the Binet test. Ross Lockridge had a fair estimate of his own intellect, yet was more uncertain than his mother that he was truly one of the elect.

The journal records an impatience with life's routines as he drags himself to Hi-Y banquets (he was president of the Southern Indiana Boys Conference, a consortium of YMCA Hi-Y's), crosses swords with his civics instructor, suffers a "pedal impairment" playing basketball, aggravated by his refusal to stop afterward, and endures a witless party. And at Epworth League, in charge of comestibles, "I tonsured potatoes, dimidiated apples, and delaminated celery."

Perhaps inhibited by a mother's eyes, he keeps affairs of the heart to himself and is left with little to write about. So he brings his journal to a close with a poem "which has been seeking egress for some time":

> *Pray come with me to a sylvan isle*
> *Bathed by Apollo's radiant smile*
> *Where numberless wavelets the hours beguile*
> *On the sands of a golden shore;*
> *And we shall reign in this wonderland,*
> *And fathom its secrecy hand in hand,*
> *Or unburden our souls on the aureate strand*
> *While the billows ceaselessly roar.*

I'm sure my father would kill me for quoting this. I do so for its stylized escapism and the clear imprint of his Grandfather Shockley's aureate verse. His grandmother Emma had shortly before given him a box containing the yellowed pages of his grandfather's effusions.

Except for brief forays to historical spots in adjacent states, he had escaped Indiana only once, in the summer of 1928, for a trip to Yellowstone with his parents, sister, and grandmother. He is photographed in his boy scout uniform holding a live prairie dog in the air by its paws. This trip gave him "the feeling of the spacious earth" and his own "awakening strength."

His subsequent high school writings, fictional and nonfictional, suggest an appetite for adventure that not even Bloomington answers fully to. He wrote with a sense of occasion. "To those resolute and sturdy spirits who braved the rigors of '49 to answer the magic call of adventure, [this essay on the Gold Rush] is respectfully dedicated." An essay on Melville has its appropriate dedication: "To the sea—vast, immeasurable—boundless setting for a mighty author's boundless conception." In *Moby-Dick*, the author "immolated himself with abstemious devotion on the altar of his immutable purpose."

Two lengthy high school stories tell of descents into vaults by a two-guys comedy team reminiscent of Ross–Malcolm, inspired partly by spelunking experiences. One of these, "The Mystery of the Many Skeletons," is faintly prophetic. Its narrator, Bob Drury, is trapped in his English family vault with a friend while searching for a treasure chest stashed away in Roundhead days. "Bacchus never forsakes his disciples," so they decide to get drunk. Drury delights in kicking at a family skeleton. Eventually they escape with the treasure through a false-bottomed coffin and end up back in the family library. Drury sees that a clever mechanism has been laid for an infinite number of Drury posterity in pursuit of treasure to end up trapped in the family vault. "The place would have been overflowing with skeletons, a reg'lar charnel house, no standing room, beastly overcrowded condition!"

He got published in *The Reflector*, the BHS literary magazine—tales of poetic justice. In "Extraction from 'Simian Memoirs,'" a boardinghouse hurdy-gurdy monkey named Cousin Jane is targeted by the obese Granadus McGeely with a ten-cent squirt gun filled with ammonia. The monkey outwits him by arranging for the ammonia to hit a pugilist, Bicep O'Dooley, who takes quick revenge.

In "The Iron Maiden," the tyrant Baron Grinmark is tricked into his own diabolic contraption by Lord Gaspard Kulben and Rocco the hunchback. "Suddenly, from the black tower above them, came a hideous noise—a raucous grating shriek—metal grinding against metal—such a noise as of rusty hinges slowly closing—closing—closing."

Students read their literary magazines in those days. It was somehow gratifying that sixty years later, many BHSers still recalled my father's first publications.

However one might psychologize these early efforts—womb-tomb fantasy, parental revolt, or familial entrapment—it's obvious Ross Lockridge didn't always think he had to write epics. He was in the story-telling tradition of his parents, but he had a satirical faculty they lacked.

For the next several years, his fondness for prose narrative would be preempted by the work he did for his father, by school essays, by playwriting, by versifying. It would be a journey through other literary genres before he returned to the narrative format that would find him an audience once again. Except that the narrator in prose would always be much alive in his letters.

On the evening of June 4, 1931, Vernice Baker and classmate Maxine Wesner—as honored juniors dressed in blue—led the commencement procession of the BHS Senior Class. Ross Lockridge, Jr., senior class president, rose to give the commencement oration, "The Tributaries." At that precise moment a Monon freight train rumbled by and a thunderstorm burst over the high school gymnasium. Vernice Baker watched his passionate gestures—sweeping now with the left hand, now with the right, now with both—but not a word was audible. His unheard metaphor for a high school career was "the course of a mighty river" to which many forces are "tributaries," including high school romance.

Vernice had been to two dances earlier that week with Bob Harrell but on June 6 she did have that Spinsters' Spring Dance to which she'd asked Ross months earlier. "Did I ever have fun. I never shall forget that 3rd dance!" she wrote in her diary.

During summers the most unbridled revels were to be found at Rivervale, the Methodist camp twenty-seven miles south of Bloomington. Though I was a militant teenaged atheist at the time, I went to Rivervale in the Fifties and remember little piety. Prayer circles gave me the chance to hold hands with girls, and on Sadie Hawkins Day I could hope to be caught by one. Vespers were secondary to amorous walks in the woods overlooking the White River and nocturnal visits to Inspiration Point. So it was in 1931. "Instead of a pious retreat for melancholy young spiritualists," my father called it "a jousting ground for youthful romancers." Throughout the week girls and boys looked forward to the Pajama Parade.

Ross and Malcolm spent a week together at Rivervale most summers, and Vernice was there at the same time in late July, 1931. At Ben Anna, the Bloomington cottage, the boys slept downstairs, the girls upstairs. There were the usual capers. Malcolm, Ross, and others snuck up the staircase to the girls' dormitory one evening and threw five pounds of beans in all directions. They could hear the tittering thereafter and beans dropping all over the floor. When Mrs. Miller, the chaperone, went up the same staircase to quiet them down, she was the mistaken target of an avalanche of retaliatory water.

But the Bloomington boys didn't date the Bloomington girls at Rivervale. The Bloomington girls, after all, could be found the year round. Instead, they dated the Bedford girls and the Bloomfield girls. And the Bloomington girls dated the Bedford boys and the Bloomfield boys. There was a heated exoticism about the new field, the license of summer romance that could lead to the holding of hands. Vernice Baker went along with the pattern—she skipped vespers for a date with Daniel of Bedford. Ross Lockridge dated Mary Black, a Methodist minister's blond daughter from Bedford, and more seriously a beautiful girl from Bloomfield, Mary Eloise Humphreys.

The daughter of a Dodge dealer, Mary Eloise was an intelligent girl with lovely long red hair—auburn, it was called—and winsome freckles and a flirtatious reserve Ross found arresting. Sometimes she'd let down her hair. They were seen walking hand in hand. One evening from a distance, Vernice saw Ross primping in advance of a date with either Mary Eloise or Mary Black, she wasn't sure which. Mary Eloise didn't yet know about Vernice.

Following Rivervale romances, the Bloomington boys would drive to Bedford or Bloomfield for occasional followup dates, and Bloomington girls would likewise receive Bedford or Bloomfield boys with cars. Ross began a correspondence with Mary Eloise, commenting on the "prosperous happy colony of chiggers" he was nourishing and rejecting her suggestion at their "tearful leave-taking" that she wouldn't be seeing him until next summer's Rivervale. But their relationship over the next four years would be mostly plans for getting together that didn't work out, with Ross writing of his disappointment in mock-heroics. He played the role of rejected suitor, writing that she had on one occasion given him "an expression such as the rock-bound fortresses of Pike's Peak must offer to hopeful westward adventurers."

For all the antics, Mary Eloise found him a serious young man who expressed pride in both parents when it was already becoming unfashionable to do so, and whose self-deprecation was meant to be seen through. He didn't tell her he intended to be a writer.

The literary spawn of the church camp that summer was a farce, "The Rivervale Robbery," produced August 4 at a "Rivervale Echo meeting." For once critical of Ross, Vernice wrote in her diary that it was "silly."

~

Entering Indiana University the fall of 1931, Ross Lockridge pledged the family fraternity, Phi Gamma Delta, and signed up for basic French, psychology, and English courses. His French instructor, Larry Wylie, five years his senior and a Phi Gam also, had just graduated from IU and was teaching his first course. It was the beginning of another lifelong friendship.

A Methodist preacher's kid, Wylie had grown up moving from one small Indiana town to another. The list of prohibitions in the Wylie household went beyond alcohol and tobacco to cards, dancing, and rolled stockings. His older brother, Jeff, disappointed parental expectations in not becoming a preacher. His junior year, Jeff worked his way to Europe on a cattleboat, sought out Parisian literary culture, and became a journalist and writer.

Larry Wylie assumed he ought to become a preacher, but something within him resisted. "And one night I was lying in bed, trying to sleep, and I couldn't stand it anymore. I got up and put some clothes on, went out and walked around the block saying 'God damn me, God damn me, God damn me' because I knew that if I were damned by God I could not be a preacher!"

His older sister, Katherine, had trouble with her mother for sitting in a car in daylight with a boy and for bobbing her hair. When she went to the University, she enrolled in French—already an affront. Episcopalians took French, a snob language, whereas Baptists and jocks studied Spanish, leaving upwardly mobile Methodists with Latin. Her American-born French teacher took ill in the middle of the year, and the University hired a young Frenchman as replacement. Her parents then forced her to drop the course because it would be immoral to study with a young Frenchman.

Thinking that French might somehow get him into the Foreign Service, Larry took up the language in his turn and spent a junior year abroad in France.

His low guilt threshold was one aspect of his personal charm. Nicknamed "Red" for the stigma of red hair, he was modest, affable, flirtatious, and informal. The informality and lack of pretension won the day for him in the classroom, which he approached the first day with the usual terror.

Sitting in class was Ross Lockridge, whom he'd describe decades later as the best student he ever had. They met outside class, often with a classmate, Edith Brown from Hobart, and became good friends.

Ross wrote Mary Eloise that he had met all his professors "on the field of combat" and that he was wearing that "coronet of nobility," the freshman beanie. Wylie would see Ross from time to time when visiting the fraternity, which Ross had pledged with Malcolm. From the west side of the tracks, Malcolm assumed he got in on his friend's coattails.

One professor Ross was jousting with was eighteenth-century scholar John Robert Moore, who had him in a writing course. "His first work was so absurdly polysyllabic that I sometimes read it aloud, for the other students to criticize by laughter—which Ross took good-naturedly, laughing with the others. He even began to admit that Swift's conception of style—'Proper words in the proper order'—was better than his own."

Chastening his style and his subject matter, Ross won a complete set of Robert Louis Stevenson, all too familiar to him, for the best freshman essay, "The Minor Characters of *Great Expectations*." At the end of the first term he had his characteristic grade card: 3 A's and

2 A-pluses. The ratio changed the second semester, with 2 A's and 3 A-pluses—and since grades had to be reported to the fraternity he became known about campus as "A-plus Lockridge."

One A per semester was for ROTC, a required course for freshman and sophomore men in this land-grant college. When I took ROTC at IU in the early Sixties, I registered a protest by aiming for the lowest passing grade. But whatever else he was, my father wasn't a reformer in the popular sense. He didn't protest ROTC. He was even admitted into Pershing Rifles, the elite drill squad.

And though he didn't like it or perpetuate it as an upperclassman, he didn't protest fraternity hazing. (I wasn't hazed but still depledged Phi Gamma Delta.) Not to be in a fraternity or sorority was widely regarded as being nothing at all—Bloomington had as yet little in the way of a supportive bohemian subculture—so he and Malcolm took the pledge proudly, polished the dance floor on Saturday morning, and endured the rituals, though both remained townies and lived at home.

Hell Week in the spring was only a thickening of the field of torture that extended throughout the year. It was easy to accumulate infractions that translated into paddlings, for instance failing to get cigarettes for an upperclassman with sufficient speed. When bending over, pledges *were* permitted to lift their testicles. In the Elephant Drill, they were stripped naked and ordered to follow one another around on all fours, goosing one another and then sucking fingers. They were blindfolded and made to eat peanut-covered bananas floating in johns, and were for routine defecation forced to sit on the john backward. They were confronted with live chickens, blindfolded, and ordered to open their mouths, into which stinky cheese was dropped. During Hell Week they were fed nothing but unseasoned beans three times a day and required to keep a Fart Chart on frequency and intensity of blasts. They were administered electric shocks on their buttocks.

And they were ordered to sit on the floor naked with their legs spread. An upperclassman read to them from *Nights in a Harem* while the other Phi Gams gathered around to monitor erections. Bets were placed and an incipient erection was cheered and hooted.

With his usual concentration, Ross Lockridge warded off any hint of arousal by silently reciting Tennyson.

The repressed homoerotic component of all this went unacknowledged. Any mention of homosexuality was pretty much outside the available discourse. An older man in religious and civic affairs had been too eager to pick Ross up after high school classes and usher him to the swimming pool, and his father put a stop to it. Homosexuality was known to exist but wasn't talked about.

Left behind at BHS for her senior year, Vernice Baker saw Ross Lockridge infrequently. Just before the term began, she had an eye-opening visit to Chicago with her cousin Sara Baker. She discovered that one wasn't necessarily slashed to death in Chinatown. The cast of *Green Pastures* was genuinely black. She danced with a date at the Aragon Ballroom, dined at the Palmer House, and toured Bug-House Square, where bohemians lived and someone was preaching rebellion from a soapbox. She discovered caviar, halibut, and finger bowls. "Gee I wish I could live like this all of the time. I suppose I wouldn't get so much 'kick' out of it if I were used to it as I do now, since I am a green little 'country-girl.' " And at a party all the girls smoked—"and they served beer too. I suppose that is nothing unusual and really not bad at all."

Back in Bloomington, Ross's Monday evening pledge meetings sadly preempted his and Malcolm's attendance at YPB. But she would bump into him here and there. One Friday in October she took Jimmy Coon to the YPB Banquet, and Ross was there acting as toastmaster. He had brought Louise Wylie (no relation to Larry Wylie), a BHS graduate who also had writing ambitions and was the great-granddaughter of IU's first president.

A few days later: "Gee I had a swell time tonight on the League Hayride. You see *Ross* was along and we roasted our wieners together and played games together and rode back." And the next week, she was with Bud Miller at a party when Ross showed up with yet another girl. "I feel so funny when Ross and I are together in the same crowd but with different dates—It doesn't seem right." By December 5, she asked Ross to a dance only after she'd been turned down by Jimmy Coon. Once again they had a grand time.

Determined not to be down about her ebullient but vanishing boyfriend, she threw herself into senior activities, playing leading roles in *Big Time*, *Not Quite Such a Goose*, *The Fool*, and *At the Stroke of Twelve*, going out with lots of boys, keeping up with her many clubs, making her grades, and seeing movies. "Nota and I felt wicked this afternoon so we broke the Sabbath Day going to a show—East of Borneo." One of her suitors struck out when his idea of a lively date was a visit with the Owen Hall cadavers.

In May she took Ross to a spring dance and "he wrote something in my memory book I wouldn't take a million for: 'Oh sweet are those hours of wonder and thrill / Whose memory never shall cease / Since first we travelled to old Nashville— / You and I—pretty Vernice!' "

And on Sunday, August 7, 1932, after another hiatus, they shared their first kiss.

Four days later Ross Junior joined his father's most ambitious historical tour ever, a caravan of older students in six touring cars and one truck that covered 2,400 miles in three weeks, gourmandizing sixty-five historical sites with as many Historic Site Recitals on fourteen different rivers, all for an enrollment fee of $8.30. Ross Senior was known behind his back as "The Big Chief," and he led the tribe to Chippewa-Nung, Black Hawk's Spring, Fort Crevecoeur, Lincoln's Tomb, New Harmony, Old Fort Harrod, and Pigeon Roost. Though there was some student participation, Mildred Neff recalls that The Big Chief played most of the parts himself—Tecumseh, Little Turtle, Mad Anthony Wayne, William Wells, Johnny Appleseed, Abraham Lincoln.

Elsie Lockridge went along as cook, and Lillian as malcontent. With lots on his mind, Ross Senior tended to be gruff, so Elsie ran interference as peacemaker. And Ross Junior with his mother's even disposition drove the truck, unloaded the luggage, pitched the tents, and set up the privy. This was a rather complex affair of wooden frames, stretched blankets, and church seat, about which he said, "I bet the cows have a hard time figuring that out." An older woman student wore the same dress every day, giving rise to speculation she was even sleeping in it. One day on the Ohio River in Kentucky, Ross saw the dress caught on a bush, thought she'd been abducted by a river beast, and ran to rescue her—"and there in sight of Louisville, Jeffersonville, and New Albany," he reported, "was Miss Hockersmith taking a bath."

Local people came to the campfire recitals—some two thousand at Clarksville and Harrodsburg. At night they sang songs—"Pretty little Indian Nap-a-nee / Won't you take a chance and marry me?"—and because Mildred Neff knew the words to "Silver Bells," Ross Junior gave her that nickname. (He himself accumulated many nicknames over the years—Rossie, Scuffie, Skunk, Claudie, Rip, Frank, A-plus, Punky—evidence of his social plasticity and a willingness to be domesticated by others.)

He got course credit through the Education School for his labors; his father gave him an A-plus. And he sent off postcards to Vernice, their first bit of correspondence: he was "just about fagged from driving a truck and throwing up tents. Were you ever sick enough to throw up a tent?"

Five days after his return, he played the part of Patrick Henry and his father played John Adams in a "Washington Recital" at the Indiana State Fair.

Still only small signs of filial displeasure in all of this. The son was not his father's puppet at such performances. He arranged for some speaking appearances of his own at Rotary Clubs throughout the state, hoping to pick up a few bucks. He'd practice on a stage in the barn—their "Bema," they called it—and Malcolm would watch his often satiric friend engage oratory as a serious art. But he never approached his father's ease of performance and lack of self-consciousness.

Not yielding to a sophomore slump, he threw himself once again into his studies. Upon entering the University, all freshmen took the American Council on Education Test that tried to measure intellectual aptitude in five categories—"completion," "artificial language," "analogies," "mathematics," and "opposites." Maurice Felger, lab instructor in chemistry during Ross's sophomore year, was impressed that this student had made a composite score of 100, which in Felger's eyes certified him a genius.

But he was not prepared for Ross's way of taking the first chemistry exam, where he wrote many more pages than requested. One question was "Give five uses of hydrogen." Years later Felger could still recall Ross's answer: "Hydrogen was discovered by Cavendish in

1766 and named by Lavoisier some years later. The name 'hydrogen' means 'water former,' from the Greek 'hydor' meaning water, and the suffix 'gen' meaning to make or do.' " Then Ross described how to *make* hydrogen and finally gave *ten* good uses for it. Felger told him he would henceforth read only two pages of exam, no matter how many Ross wrote. Once again chastened by an instructor, Ross complied. Despite hooking his Bunsen burner up by mistake to the water outlet one day, drenching classmates, he pulled off the usual grade.

Felger's admonition didn't transfer to a sophomore lit class with Dr. Carter, where he pumped out thirty-four typewritten pages on Chaucer and sixty-nine on Spenser. Concerning the late repentance for his sinful tales, he writes that Chaucer is "vexed by the glaring shades of an obscene Miller, a slanderous Reve, a voluptuous gap-toothed wife, a lecherous somnour, a licentious friar, and a score of lickerish, indecent clerks and loose, interesting wenches. These importunate spectres will not let him alone. He repents, and disowns them all! In the end, his deeply rooted morality and religious zeal ran him down and compelled him to renounce his best works."

Academics wasn't enough, so like many of his forebears he decided to go out for varsity track and cross-country, as did Malcolm. Ross tended to mingle the mental and the physical: in the summer of 1932, a bemused cousin watched him simultaneously read a book and mow the lawn. Unlike his Uncle Bruce, he wasn't a natural athlete, and he was up against many who were. Coaches E. C. Hayes and Sid Robinson turned out Olympic runners and NCAA champions. IU had won the Big Ten championship in cross-country for four consecutive seasons. Ross and Malcolm trained together, running out to the University reservoir and back, and both made the team.

Vernice began cutting out sports articles on Ross for her memory book. "Seven Indiana cross-country runners will make the trip Friday afternoon to Lafayette where the Hoosiers will bid for their twenty-second consecutive Big Ten victory Saturday morning against the long-winded Purdue harriers, Coach Sid Robinson announced last night. The harriers picked to go to the Boilermaker camp are Brocksmith, Watson, Neese, Hornbostel, Lockridge, Gettelfinger and Haymond."

"Lockridge, a Bloomington boy, finished in the first half of the Big Ten meet Saturday and is looking very promising. He came out for track just a year ago and has been under supervised training methods for just about ten months. Hornbostel, of course, will be a threat for first place honors in the meets of the 1933 season." "LOCKRIDGE WINS MAJOR LETTER IN CROSS-COUNTRY." Winning a varsity letter was a big deal then, and he wore the "I" sweater often for the rest of his life. Malcolm just missed winning a letter and took it like a philosopher.

On the road to track meets, Ross entertained the team with Burma Shave commercials, memorized and invented. Gettelfinger was impressed that he could get all the way to a meet and back without exhausting his repertoire. Specializing in the five-mile run, he wasn't upset at not being first in the pack—he plotted in detail with Robinson how to improve his personal best and was, as he said, "violently absorbed for a time." He never gave up. At the end of the 1932–33 season, the IU cross-country team once again won the Big Ten championship.

On the team was a runner superior to Lockridge—Charles Hornbostel. He was an Olympic finalist in the 880 in 1932 and set a world record in 1933, was on the USA National teams that set world records in the 4×800 and $4 \times$ mile relays, and was named the outstanding performer at the Millrose A. A. Track and Field Games in Madison Square Garden, having won the 1,000-yard invitational in 2:12.8 and anchoring the mile relay team with a winning final quarter of 49.2 seconds. Lockridge would write that he "won his varsity letter running behind (and rather far behind) such track immortals as Don Lash and Charles Hornbostel."

More to the point, Hornbostel met Vernice Baker when she was working at the IU bookstore in the spring of 1933, and they started to date.

Vernice had begun her freshman year at IU in 1932 working for 30 cents an hour at the bookstore to pay tuition, which was $37.50 for a full load. (Men were paid 35 cents.) She paid it off in five-dollar installments. Her family had persuaded her to enter the business school—Aubrey was in the termite business, Leon was an accountant, Clona was a teller, and Beulah a secretary. She got off to a bad start because bookstore employees had to miss the first two weeks of class, and Accounting proved a drag. But she loved the World Literature course for business majors, and would be a quiet rebel in the

Baker family in declaring an English major the following year. She pledged Pi Beta Phi, but as a townie who had to work all day, she didn't show up much and didn't feel at home. And since Ross Lockridge had once again faded away following that kiss in August, she began to feel her glory days were over.

Filling out a special order for Hornbostel at the bookstore in the spring of 1933, she was excited to meet the school's greatest athlete. A gentleman, Hornbostel didn't ask her out on the spot; he arranged a formal introduction through his fraternity. Ross was oblivious to this threat.

Larry Wylie had left to pursue his studies at Brown University and in early March, 1933, sent him a letter that had a profound impact. Wylie had been to a reunion of the Delaware Foreign Study Group with whom he had spent a year in Paris in 1929–30. "That year was crammed so completely full of things," he said, "that we talked all week-end sans relâche." Beyond great classes and great food, there were "trips to Corsica, the Midi and Algeria—warm sunshine, gorgeous views, fascinating natives and moeurs, only enough money to get from place to place and therefore a taste of true Bohemianism; back in Paris—shows, opera, concerts, cafés, the incomparable Parisian spring—walks in the parks and bois, along the quai and book-stalls, climbing to the top of the Eiffel tower and Notre Dame, dinner on a café terrace, and, of course, in love—but not enough to hurt. . . . Ross, try to place yourself there—and then let your mind wander."

Wylie had said enough. Ross was determined to go.

He applied to the International Institute of Education and won a scholarship. His father objected at first, mostly on financial grounds, but an additional amount was secured from his Uncle Earl—and of course there'd be one heck of a lot of historical sites for his son to reconnoitre. In his application he wrote that his "life has been somewhat cloistered. Travelling has been confined to short journeys in and about Indiana and one long trip to the West. . . . I have been active in the French Club of which I was recently elected president. . . . I have had the advantages of a rich library in the home, and have read extensively in the acknowledged classics of the world."

To stuff a bit more travel under his belt, he and Malcolm in mid-June set off for the Chicago Century of Progress World's Fair of

1933. Through Malcolm's father, they arranged for a ride on a flatbed chicken truck. Since there was no room in the cab, they were to be on top of seven layers of poultry crates full of chickens. They held onto ropes for dear life and endured the stench for ten sleepless hours overnight all the way to Chicago. The drivers took them in the early morning to a café across from the warehouse, where the waiter asked them if they wanted beer for breakfast.

Not wishing to be thought a country jake, Ross coolly said yes. The two were served, and ex-YPB Secretary Ross Lockridge swilled his down with nonchalance, while ex-YPB President Malcolm Correll found the going tough, almost gagging. From there they sacked out drunkenly for a few hours at the World Book Company headquarters, prearranged by Ross Senior.

At the fair their first stop was the Streets of Paris, advertised with a good deal of show-girl semi-nudity. They then went to Ripley's Believe It or Not, hardly in keeping with the "Century of Progress" motif, where they saw pygmies, giants, two-headed calves, a man who held up weights by slits in his nipples, and another who stuck hundreds of pins in his flesh. Malcolm fainted, and awoke to smelling salts administered by a nurse with whom Ross had already become very friendly. They then left the fair for the Rialto burlesque house, where they watched bare-breasted women on hollow pedestals singing Neapolitan love songs.

Four days later, having subsisted on cabbage and milk, "we rode home under a blistering sun on top the same accursed chicken truck, and fried like two herrings on a griddle." Deadpan, he told his parents, "We've seen some buildings that are higher than our barn." They had spent nine dollars each.

～

Vernice Baker was at a reunion for National Honor Society people when Catherine Feltus asked, "Oh did you see in the paper that Ross is going to the Sorbonne next year?" Her heart sank.

She was moping one evening soon thereafter when her friends Ruth Bradt and Elloise Kunz persuaded her to go to a rally down at the church. "And there was Ross!" Their relationship began again in earnest. In late July they were in Rivervale together, forsaking

Bloomfield girls and Bedford boys and wandering hand in hand by the White River. Conveniently, Mary Eloise wasn't there. Sitting together on a rock in the evening they listened through the woods to others singing hymns.

There followed an August of Indiana pleasures—tennis, swimming, swinging on the front porch, miniature golf, singing. They went to the circus and watched the sea lions, ate cotton candy, and bought a watermelon for the Baker family. Her Aunt Lizzie made a faux pas: "She invited us to California on our honeymoon. Ross didn't hear. I wonder how everything is going to turn out."

On August 29, her old friend Georgia Adams married Boyd Coppock. She wore Vernice's Blue Triangle ring for "something blue." *August 30, 1933:* "Mother reminded me that I am losing two of my best friends—Ross and Georgia—Georgia is going to Logansport and Ross is going to Paris. . . . Clona was awfully nice to us—she had a chicken dinner for us tonight. Ross is a big eater—he had chicken bones piled up all round his plate, bless his heart. We played noisy card games after that—Demon and Animal—Mrs. Eller's son had died and they brought him right next door. Ross said since there was somebody dead over there we had to have some life at Clona's. I hope the folks didn't mind. We went to Ross's for awhile and listened to his mother's club sing old songs around the campfire—it was beautiful—Ross was feeling mischievous tonight—We would just be sitting there and then before I would know it he would be curled up with his head on my lap. I don't know how I am going to stand it this winter."

August 31, 1933. With their friends Nota Scholl and Dan Sherwood she and Ross "played tennis from 9 to 12 this morning— Ross played six sets 3 hours without stopping—He is as good at tennis as anything else—I tell you Diary, I don't know what I am going to do—I'm lonesome."

Her relationship with Hornbostel had been put on hold during the summer. At an Alumni Hall dance in early September she and Ross ran into him, and Hornbostel exclaimed, "Oh, I didn't know you two knew each other!"

On parting, expressing a sense of peril himself, Ross gave her a leatherbound edition of Keats, inscribed with a Shakespearean sonnet of his own that ends with the couplet: "And though I move in death's pale equipage, / Think I am near to turn with you the page."

The final entry in Vernice Baker's diary: *September 12, 1933:* "We had our last date before he leaves, Diary—I wonder if it was the last we will ever have. Isn't that an awful thought? We visited all our trysting places (as we call them) for the last time—our two bridges on the campus—our dear old porch swing—east Third Street pike—you know when we had our first date we went to Nashville—we sang, too, Diary, we laughed, joked, sang—tried to get everything in in four hours. He left me at Clona's—He drove away slowly and we waved to each other and then he was *gone.* I'm afraid. He leaves for New York tomorrow and then for Paris Friday 15. His mother called me Wednesday and gave me his boat address. We are all going to write him tonight. S. S. Scythia, Cunard Line, Stateroom 109, Deck B, New York, New York."

IV

"A Richly Laden Festal Board"

France and Italy, 1933–1934

Elsie Lockridge wept privately with her son the morning of September 13, 1933, when he left for France, but she held in her tears at the train station, where she, Ross Senior, Larry Wylie, and a few others gathered for the send-off. Vernice Baker was not excused from her normal Wednesday hours at the IU bookstore. She heard the Monon pull into the station at 11:05, and accidentally shortchanged a customer one dollar at 11:15 when it pulled out. Lillian Lockridge was working normal hours in her new position as a parole officer for the Indiana Woman's Prison in Indianapolis—her own leap into the "tributaries" of life's purposeful great river—and would weep when, returning home on the weekend, she missed Ross's usual trail of hurriedly discarded clothes on the second floor.

"Woefully dejected" until he reached the transfer at Greencastle, her messy younger brother began to key himself for the great year abroad. On his own for the first time, he was eager to find in reality the culture and adventure he'd experienced through books and cinema.

A group of Dartmouth students was standing at the reception for the Delaware Foreign Study Group at the Hotel New Yorker when a smiling young man approached. "My name is Ross Lockridge and I'm from Indiana!" Curtis Lamorey, from small-town Barre, Vermont, liked him immediately—another lifelong friendship was under way—while some of the others were more cautious and wondered what, if anything, was behind the fresh and affable manner.

Ross was one of forty-two students—nine men and thirty-three women—mostly from prestigious Eastern schools. Only one other, Ruth Jackson of Winnetka, Illinois, a surgeon's daughter attending Wheaton College, was a Midwesterner. The idea of a "junior year abroad" was relatively new—this was the eleventh year of the program—and besides Delaware, only Smith College organized a year in France. It was newsworthy for a midwestern student from a state institution to be going. The University of Delaware itself was unrepresented.

Ross signed up for the lowest of the three rates and held one of five scholarships. He departed with $51 in his pocket and could expect an additional $110 spending money on deposit with the program to last the year. Much of this would go toward postage because he was encumbered with a correspondence list of forty-four addresses. One wonders how he could find time for adventures if so much time was spent writing them up. Vernice Baker headed the list of seven female friends, Malcolm Correll the list of nine male friends.

At orientation Miss Littlefield, Directrice, told them everything they shouldn't do in France, and the group assembled for a photograph—many of the women in fur and corsages and all of them except Amanda Macy of Mount Holyoke wearing stylish hats. Ross Lockridge stood in his best Sears Roebuck suit in the middle of the back row, flanked by Lamorey and Cloise Crane, a sophisticated Dartmouth student from Washington, D.C. In drizzling rain on September 15, the group embarked on Cunard Line's R.M.S. *Scythia* off the West 14th Street pier for what Ross Lockridge overadvertised to Larry Wylie shortly thereafter as "the strangest and most eventful ten days of my life."

The events included a storm at sea, nearly universal seasickness, and one elaborate seduction he and others monitored. Finding the "stiff aristocratic boobies" up in first class a bore, he often descended from his tourist-class cabin and joined the people in steerage. There he learned Irish songs and watched the spirited steerage class dance to a wheezy accordion. With Prohibition only recently repealed, the Delaware Group began to experiment with new drinks. Lamorey and he casually "drank a beverage called 'Tom Collins' which spread my toes apart."

Miss Littlefield enforced circulation of the men at the dining tables, so he quickly got familiar with the women. Practically everyone in the group drank and smoked except Ross, who drew the line at smoking. He wasn't regarded as an innocent by most, rather as eager, taking it all in as Larry Wylie had urged. Group members felt some moral admiration, if only because he took responsibility for Sydney Roseman, a blind student from the University of Pennsylvania, leading him around the steamer and conversing. Ross taught Charlotte Watkeys of the University of Rochester the "Indiana Hop," a polka mutation, which he performed whether the music was waltz, tango, or rumba.

Despite these social gestures, Amanda Macy, a more romantic spirit, judged him "deeply at home with the poets, the philosophers, the idealists." He complained to her that too many people aboard were reading *Lady Chatterley's Lover* and *Reader's Digest*.

After two days at sea the crew was complaining of the worst storm in twenty-five years. While others in the group were "casting their bread upon the waters," he found his own stomach the more demanding. A year of gusto in eating began.

Whatever the raw material, he converted it to epistolary narrative, with confidence his audience at home could sort out how much was fact, how much a concession to good story-telling. He asked Larry Wylie, "What usually happens, my friend, my old, sage, experienced, and canny friend—what usually happens when a number of boys and girls are thrown together in an impassible enclosure with nothing to do for ten days? Yes, that's what happened."

He was a "spectator" to a siege of Delaware Group women by Delaware Group men. But fate intervened, preserving maidenheads for a couple of days by seasickness, yet another day by the men's indecisiveness as to targets ("with nine boys and thirty-three girls, it was like trying to select a place for jumping into the ocean"), and yet a couple more days by female skittishness. Then the women recognized "they had perhaps consumed too much time parrying the initial thrusts of their companions," and "the situation became that of a party of besiegers who at last stood beneath the walls of a city which was dying to be sacked."

Well, only one seduction, mutual and Ivy League, was under way. His suitemate and a woman in the group were a case. The suitemate asked if Ross could find somewhere else to sleep, "so that our state-room might be converted into a pavilion of uninterrupted pleasure." With a mix of voyeuristic fascination and YPB conscience, Ross obliged, "and the old ocean murmured the tidings of good cheer, as the Scythia cut through the night to Liverpool."

Crossing by rail through England he felt that even the tree trunks were "green with age. When you are in England, you feel how young America is," he wrote Vernice, and in London he, Lamorey, and Edward Mitchell, another Dartmouth student, set out in search of beer and Westminster Abbey, "the greatest necropolis in the world." There the tombs made him feel "absolutely overwhelmed and stifled in fame and history . . . and who could care for else than to rest under that famous pile in the best company in the world?" He recited on the spot many passages of the mighty dead's own verse as he turned from monument to monument.

When he reached Paris he roomed within two hundred yards of France's own great necropolis, the Panthéon, at 19 rue Soufflot, in the fifth-story flat of Madame Pernot. She announced that he'd have to go by the name of Frank, because "a *rosse* is a poor, old, sick, mangy, broken-spirited horse, or by application, a worthless vagabond."

Looking from his balcony just before daybreak, he saw "a misty vapor like an old medieval robe [which] clings to the surface of the city, glowing here and there with rich spots of gold and hung with strange ornaments as where a tower or a palace breaks through. Le Panthéon stands not far away like a dour old guardian of the dead, a real personality, with grim jaws, a formless trunk, and long melancholy features. Only the faintest of murmurs animates the great corpse of the city, the long, low, rhythmic hum of millions of Frenchmen snoring in unison. . . . If you could look with my eyes now through the window, you would see it—a sad cemetery of old wars, old heroes, old hopes, and old sorrows, which quit their graves to mingle mournfully in the mist of the dying night."

He delighted in the antiquities of his own room. On the dusty nineteenth-century walls, in somber red wallpaper, hung two crossed sabres, one of them broken, and two oil portraits of Pernot ancestors in crude massive gilt frames. The one of Grandfather Pernot had taken a direct hit by an orange thrown by the previous American lodger. With an armoire capacious enough "for three or four French mistresses," a massive bed, and a broken antique clock on the fireplace mantel, he felt he would prosper, despite the fact that Cloise "Jack" Crane, to whom he took a dislike, was his co-lodger, in the adjoining room.

Madame Pernot was herself not prospering. Her husband, a career army officer, had died in the Great War sixteen years earlier. Thereafter, "Madame was left with two young ones, several beautiful military uniforms, a number of yellowing family portraits, a boxful of lustrous medals won at the cannon's mouth, several shelves of books treating of military science, two old sabres, and no money." Living on a small pension, she was forced to take in roomers and slept in the dining room after others were bedded down.

But there was an auspicious development. Her daughter, Jeanne, was engaged to an Italian marquis, Gennaro Dini, a rich dilettante who deposed the previous suitor, a German baron. "I hope to be able to announce some letters hence that the young lady has brought down something really remarkable, and that we dine Saturday nights with the King of England. . . . Although our charmer seems very much attached to the Marquis, I think if someone were to dangle a good, sleek, lively king before her eyes, we should soon have the best wine in the land on our table Saturday nights."

Dining with the French was a study in cultural contrasts. Elsie's cooking wasn't mouth-watering—utilitarian propriety was the norm at her table. Madame Pernot's table was different, as he wrote his parents. "I came to France with a long training in polite table manners, such as they are practiced in the refined circles of the Lockridge table; I came prepared to spend a year of small bites and slow movements. The first meal, I was nearly stabbed to death; the second, I was nearly choked; the third, I was hardly able to defend a place at the table to say nothing of eating. The French eat much; the French eat fast; the French eat skillfully. Madame's son, Felix, is large and hungry. Madame has long arms for a woman. The spinster sister-in-law of Madame is old and apparently feeble, but age has only quickened and subtilized the incredibly swift jab of her short, sure fork.

"Thrown into this family of vultures,—I, a tender, cloistered

Lockridge, soon discovered that I was going to have to change my style to keep from starving. Besides, my Lockridge honor burned indignantly along my veins. I could hear a thousand ancestral Lockridges, who had never failed their meat and potatoes, shouting for vengeance. . . .

"The evening meal usually goes along like this: The soup is in our bowls when we arrive. We toss this off with large spoons, exercizing care only when someone at the table has a new suit. The family then waits feverishly for the second course, moistening its eyebrows and humming nervously. Madame enters with the second course, a salad perhaps. A glitter of forks, a champing of teeth—and the salad is gone. We aren't even breathing hard as yet. Madame then enters with a dish of meat, swimming in a toothsome sauce. We murder the meat in remarkably short order. . . . Add to this that the French talk all the time they're eating, and you have some idea of our table."

He braced himself for the five-week preparatory session. One reason for a straight-A student not to go to France was the infamous French grading system, in which the top grade 20 is never given, 18 is reserved for the likes of Sartre, 16 is our A-plus, 15 our A, and a majority of French students have their self-doubts confirmed with 10s and 11s. Larry Wylie—eventually the C. Douglas Dillon Professor of the Civilization of France at Harvard—got B's and C's his year at the Sorbonne, killing his chances for Phi Beta Kappa. Ross Lockridge had had only two years of French, unlike most other Delaware students, who had also studied it in high school. So he geared up to outdistance the field with the same come-from-behind vigor he brought to his footrace with a streetcar down Boulevard St. Germain.

After two weeks of a cram course in French history, literature, and language, he placed tenth of forty-two in an examination, "first of the boys by a long margin, but there [are] 9 girls ahead of me whom it will be necessary to remove tout de suite." He began getting the highest grades in his *dissertations,* and during the final preliminary exam, "there quickly developed a very socialistic attitude. . . . The girl sitting beside me wrote right along with me, word for word, and line for line. When I stopped, she stopped. When I meditated, she chafed impatiently. To top this, she was smoking a malodorous Paris cigarette and held it so that the fumes entered copiously into my nostrils; I quickly developed a murderous stomach cramp. A long training in etiquette at last succumbed, and, forcing a weird smile, I said: 'I certainly have enjoyed smoking your cigarette.' . . . My paper went in as well thumbed as a stock-exchange sheet."

Scoring highest of the Delaware people, he made the Groupe Supérieur, but "I feel a little like D'Artagnan who began his career at Paris by having the stuffings beaten out of him with a club."

Two days later, on November 4, the Delaware Group entered *le Cours de civilisation française de la Sorbonne*. This was a high-powered curriculum for more than one thousand foreign students each year from some two dozen countries. Ross signed up for courses in French history, art history, contemporary literature, and modern drama, hoping that the worst was behind him and that he could put aside the books and see Paris.

One night he visited Les Halles, which he found "dark and deserted within, and emanating a peculiar odor formed of a thousand different essences of meats and vegetables, old and new. I had walked some time along the dark streets that separate the buildings, before I noticed a number of dim figures littered like dead men along the sidewalks, and against the walls of the building.

"I've never had such a stunning impression of wretched poverty. In the filth of the sidewalks, among the decomposing debris of the great market, breathing the impure odors of the district, these people lay in their filthy rags, covered with paper, sacks, straw, and even boards. There were hundreds, I noticed, as I threaded through the streets, and scarcely the slightest movement among them, so that they looked like so many corpses left unburied in the streets after a great plague. . . . I even saw one lying in a big box, half buried in the straw, so that only a hand and foot emerged.

"In one street, I ran into a fellow that hadn't yet retired for the night, but who was evidently arranging his quarters because he was carrying an armful of straw. As he approached me, I saw he was going to stop and say something to me, probably, as I thought, some beggarly plea or some vulgar sentiment. Instead he said something very pathetic and even lyrical. I don't know whether he took me for one of the fellowship in my old gray overcoat or not, but as he passed me, he said very distinctly in a deep, powerful voice, '*mon cher, c'est comme la mort à la tombée de la nuit,*' which translated literally means, 'My friend, it's like death at the fall of night.' "

In this letter to his parents he edited out the presence of his co-lodger, Jack Crane, who accompanied him on this nocturnal visit. Lamorey had noticed that his even-tempered friend became unusually blunt and argumentative with Crane on such pivotal issues as whether Racine is greater than Molière or whether good or evil predominates in the universe. Ross wrote home that his "roommate is the queerest and most insupportable bug I ever saw, and is acknowledged so by everyone in the group." The source of the tension was less intellectual than sexual. Crane was making advances—he would later allude to Ross Lockridge as "mon cher handsmacker." Not reciprocating, Ross kept this distraction to himself. He also edited out a trip with Lamorey to a bordello on rue Blondel, where they watched a floor-show that made Chicago burlesque look pretty anemic.

With Mitchell and Lamorey he visited Verdun over Armistice weekend and sent home a letter of several thousand words, omitting only his discovery of how French people on a bus handle the problem of urination. It's an epistolary Historic Site Recital narrating a pilgrimage "made every year by numbers of Frenchmen, for whom any ground is holy on which the Germans were defeated." He's most taken with the Tranchée des Baïonnettes, where several French soldiers were buried alive with only their bayonets protruding. Like his father who spent much of his life erecting them, he is fascinated by memorials and their eerie temporal play on presence and absence.

Back on the homefront his father was unhappy with what he took to be Scuffie's remissness in letter-writing. He'd hoped for at least two letters a week, but his son was inditing only one. This weekly letter was admittedly substantial, but "I thought possibly you could just sit down some midweek evening after a vivid experience in Paris and just dash off a single page in fifteen minutes recording that experience or episode and incidentally 'passing the time of day' so to speak, thus keeping us in more constant touch with you." Elsie had silently intercepted an earlier such request—there would be still others—penciling that one a week would suffice. Ross Junior quietly held his ground, and even let a week slip by occasionally.

His father liked the Verdun letter, yet thought his son needed more instruction. "I shall write you later concerning making record of your impressions on individual great sites." He was out on the history stump with a series of recitals he and family members referred to as "Herculean." Always enclosing a one dollar bill, he would write his son from downtown hotels all over the state as he plied his wares with a Willy Loman doggedness. With the blessing of Governor McNutt, he would try throughout the year to get the Ball Foundation to fund his Historic Site Recitals in some permanent way. The other continuing drama was the hoped-for state adoption of World Book Company mathematics textbooks. He assumed his son's close interest in these matters.

Truly missing Scuffie, he felt the stage in their barn was hallowed. "It is one of my best 'sites'—where I can stand on the 'spot' your feet have pressed. I wish I could wander with you on a day like this in Sunny France . . . to some of those world famed sites." He encouraged him to get away from his books and do the sites, preferably not with the eight men but with one or another of the thirty-three women. Though no communist, he was pleased that his son had briefly accompanied one. "I am FOR her. If her breath holds out, I should think she would make a fine walking (and talking) companion. However, I hope you won't make it necessary for the dames to do all the inviting."

Writing her own set of letters—dozens—Elsie Lockridge, who more than her husband had encouraged her son to take the year abroad, lavished maternal sympathy and accommodation, telling him that "Dad just doesn't stop to think of what you have on your hands to accomplish but he will always be Dad—he is just that way—so don't worry." She asked Malcolm to come over and mess up the house as a son-surrogate, and told her son that "maybe it isn't just the disorder I miss—it may have been the 'power' behind the disorder that leaves such an aching void at times." She was confident that he liked "clean, honest, straight-forward, beautiful and great things," was nobody's fool, and had "an excellent coat-of-armor to wear against those who would impose upon you." She told him not to worry about being first in everything.

What stories did *she* have to tell? Only that Lillian was making her way in the world and that one Hubert Akins seemed to be taking an interest in her beyond simple friendship. Lillian had lost at least twenty pounds and was down to 184. And Elsie continued her work as graduate instructor for Professor Yeager in the psychology department, where the emphasis was on stimulus-response studies and prosaic psychological measurement. And then she was monitoring the mental development of little Anne, Shockley's and Mary Kay's daughter, on whom she was beginning a psychological study. She wanted to measure how long it would take Anne to learn to grasp candy, then how long to stick it into her mouth.

So Elsie confronted the everyday paper-grading reality of her unfulfilled life, in contrast to her son's brilliant vistas. "I think you can't—I know you can't—have any conception of the pleasure your letters bring to me. In a life filled with many dreams, much inward rebellion against many circumstances in which I have been thrown—the usual general mixture of joys, sorrows, disappointments—the disappointments that come to one who has been reared in a highly idealistic home as a child—well into this life of vicissitudes that I have stumbled through—*you* have been a real comfort, a real pleasure and a genuine inspiration. Now that's saying a great deal—for I know but one or two other persons who have so functioned in my outwardly prosaic, yet inwardly dynamic career. You somehow seem *akin* to me—you answer some hopes, aspirations and dreams that I have not had the *ability* or *back*-bone (probably both) to develop into a reality. Your letters are just like you—full of life, fun, ambitious, yet withal so humanly considerate. You are a real satisfaction."

Even in this her warmest letter, Elsie speaks to her son, knowingly, as an extension of her own will. He can make real what she can only imagine. She conveys obligation as well as love.

Unlike her husband, who didn't mention the Baker girl in his letters, Elsie was a Vernice-loyalist, routinely sharing Ross's letters with her. (Knowing this, he satirized the Delaware Group women and somewhat underreported his social dealings.) Elsie thought Vernice "a dear girl, charming & with a marvelously fine spirit." She warned her son about women who didn't share his "ideals of desirable companionship."

And unlike Ross Senior, Vernice did have some reason to complain. After a letter from London in late September describing the trip over—it was addressed "Dearest" and was full of Irish, Scottish, and English love songs—she didn't receive another until mid-November. And this was only in response to a plaintive letter of her own, in which she hoped she was included in the "et cetera" tacked onto his formal salutation in a family letter. She gave him news about his niece Anne, the IU cross-country team, the thirteenth baby born to the neighboring Kunzes, but lamented that "all the things you do are so entirely different from anything I know or do that it doesn't seem real at all to me. I realize just how little and cramped my world is, making me have more desire than ever that maybe someday—but not on $35 a month." She offered to stop reading his letters home, but joked that doing so was the only way she had of checking up on him, just as she was sure his friends were informing on her.

Indeed Robert Masters, Ross's cousin whom she dated occasionally that fall, had dropped a hint about her doings. And Malcolm Correll about this time sent him the best wishes of the track team and added, "Charlie says, 'Tell Frenchie I'm taking his girl away from him.'" Not given to easy jealousy, Ross brushed this aside, but Vernice Baker was indeed seeing Hornbostel, and friends were gossiping about it and already taking sides. It was newsworthy to them that Vernice, so lacking in personal vanity, had her choice of the school's top athlete and the school's top scholar.

Ross assured her that her picture stood beneath a large candelabrum on his mantel. Several Delaware Group women were shown a snapshot of Vernice Baker, perhaps as a prophylactic against romantic entanglement abroad. He'd be dating even so—Ruth Jackson, Amanda Macy, Laura Thomas, Charlotte Watkeys, Huldah Smith, Marion Monico, and others. By late November such "rendezvous" had led "to the complete disembowelment of my purse."

The Delaware Group geared up for its biggest social event, the Thanksgiving dinner, a black-tie affair to be held at Le Plat d'Argent. Edward Mitchell wrote home to his mother: "We had a grand dinner, and this time it was American, turkey and all. However, we had two kinds of wine, and the waiters kept filling them up all the time. Well, the wine and the Pernod set lovely, and everybody was gay as the dickens. After dinner we sang songs. . . . Later Curt and Bill and I sang 'Les Gars de la Marine,' and received a nice round of applause. Just before we left, Ross Lockridge got up and gave a toast to Miss Littlefield, saying 'Come over and give me a kiss, Littley, old gal.' We had a good laugh out of that, and Ross wanted to know yesterday if he really had said that."

After dinner Ross, very tipsy, was escorting Charlotte Watkeys from the restaurant when he was accosted by Jack Parsons, a large-framed student with black hair and a fierce red beard from Rollins College who rarely said a word. Accounts of what happened next differ. From a small town himself, Parsons regarded Ross Lockridge not as a midwestern naïf but "rather as a wisecracking citified type. . . . I had one of the few fights of my life on Thanksgiving night 1933 when he started to *appropriate my girl*. I knocked him down and took her away with me—to the Hôtel des Deux Portes."

Charlotte Watkeys had a different reading. "Thanksgiving night Ross and I had a date to continue the evening after dinner with another couple. Walking down the street from the restaurant Mr. Parsons approached and made a grab for me. I resisted. Ross assisted. I explained. Mr. P., who had exceeded his champagne tolerance, may have struck out but I recall no blow landing. We left Mr. P. at the corner, hailed a cab and the four of us went to Montparnasse dancing and people watching. Ross joined in all phases and it was a gay time." Lamorey corroborates Watkeys's account.

Ross Lockridge's own was written up in a letter home, a *petite histoire* he entitled "The Battle of the Tux," which the family pronounced his most hilarious—but it was the one letter that got lost.

~

Armed with the Marquis's elegantly penned itineraries and a plebeian seventy dollars to last two weeks, and having "kicked" his co-lodger good-bye, Ross headed off for Rome with Curtis Lamorey over the Christmas break. Since he had spent only six or seven dollars out of pocket all the way from Bloomington to Paris, tipping porters with his "best smile," this sum seemed sufficient, but the earlier trip was mostly prepaid. Depression mentality and near poverty led him and Lamorey to decide in advance to tip charily if at all. They would try to sleep on trains to avoid hotel expenses and eat little.

The 40,000 words of his two Italian letters—enough for a novella, and not counting letters and postcards to twenty-two other parties—combine picaresque narrative and impassioned description, plus some dutiful site recitals. He shifts back and forth between satire and sublimity, as he confronts "a richly laden festal board" of European adventure. He also plays to the ethnic stereotypes he at this time shared in some degree with his audience. His Uncle Earl, whose hand-me-down beret he wore throughout the year, had been abroad for the Great War and, mustering his best wit, wrote his nephew, "All Frenchmen are Frogs to the Americans. Are you perfumed and powdered sufficiently to smell like a French yet? Have you learned to shrug your shoulders, look blank and act dumb?"

The Italians, whom Ross Lockridge preferred to the French, were less dumb than canny. For instance, an urchin sold them some bananas only to beg them back for resale. They complied but "in order that we not be forced to buy the same bananas over and over again until our money was exhausted, Lamorey and I, awed by this youngster's powers, hurried off the steps." Protecting their meager purse from native predators is one leitmotif of this comic narrative. Another is the ruins of time.

On the train to Rome they shared a compartment with Charlotte Watkeys and her parents. Mrs. Watkeys "reminded me of a boy in the University band who was extremely small but who blew a very loud trumpet," while Mr. Watkeys laughed gigantically at his own jokes. "Most people, who, like Watkeys, are continually emitting piteous, half-made-up cracks usually succeed at rare intervals in saying something droll. Watkeys never did." Worse, they flung their limbs around while sleeping, so Ross took refuge on the floor. To escape the Watkeyses he and Lamorey, stunned that sunny Italy was covered in snow, exited in the morning at Turin, where Ross got chilblained feet in a day of relentless sightseeing before boarding the night train to Rome.

Lamorey saw his friend's "eyes popping" at the Roman antiquities as they made their way around with a cheap American Express tour. It was as if all his training in Latin and history were a rehearsal for this confrontation and for the impassioned prose he loaded onto his parents. If he closed his eyes, "the ancient scene would raise in ghostly beauty her glittering forest of columns, her armies of colossal statues, her arches and ascending walls sweeping to southward as far as eye might reach, while down that marvellous vista with dull unceasing tramp, the stout legions of Caesar passed in grim triumph with golden chariots, bushels of precious plunder and beautiful captives, the whole long vision extending for miles so that the glittering spear-points twinkled even on the horizon."

If nothing else, this nineteen-year-old kid had facility. In the one hundred and eighty thousand words he wrote home to his parents

alone—for his own record as well as for communication—he didn't
blot a word or reformulate a single sentence.

In the Forum, he asked Lamorey to climb a podium and lie down
like the dead Caesar. He put his foot on Lamorey's shoulder and
within hearing of a group of tourists declaimed Antony's funeral oration, both of them sputtering with laughter. At the Protestant Cemetery, he approached the graves of Keats and Shelley with more
decorum, reciting "Ode to a Nightingale," "To a Skylark," and Shakespeare's "Full fathom five thy father lies."

Though raised a Protestant, Curt had Catholic grandparents and
wished to burn a candle to his grandmother. Ross thought this a species of voodoo. He couldn't reconcile the greatness of the cathedrals
and art with what he took to be the literalism of the sacraments.
"The morbidness of Christian worship extends to the point of butch-
ering, dissecting, transporting, and agonizing the remains of the mar-
tyrs to such an extent that the unfortunate saints are about as sadly
persecuted in death by those who love them as they were in life by
those who hated them."

He regarded nuns as no improvement over vestal virgins. As for
the skeletons in the Church of the Capuchins: "The poor devils are
clothed in the black hood of their order, girdled, and hung up in
their separate nooks to perpetuity—silent spectres of desiccated
flesh and pitted eyes, clutching in drawn and shrivelled hands each a
Christian crucifix. God defend me from a grave like that!"

To Lamorey, Ross quietly confided during this trip a secret he
had told virtually no one else. He wanted to write a great book.
Moby-Dick had just missed being the Great American Novel. Ross
thought maybe *he* could write it. He was going to try.

This seemed plausible enough to Lamorey, who didn't have much
interest in American literature in any event. He thought that Ross
could pull it off if anybody could. He had no idea how closely his
friend guarded this ambition.

His own was overseas business, for which he needed languages.
Like his Hoosier friend he had an independent streak and took his
own counsel, and he talked as fast as Ross wrote. Both of them
strong-willed and curious, neither imposed on the other. Ross liked
the element of dissimilarity in his friendships.

"Old phantom of faded grandeur, brooding on thy seven hills—

Farewell!" and they were off on a night train to Naples. They swilled Frascati, talked about their girlfriends, and emerged exhausted the next morning. For 60 lire each they hired an American Express guide to take them to Pompeii. The ruins would give rise to another epistolary effusion, with no mention of the delight they took in the lascivious frescoes.

It was time for dinner, included—supposedly with gratuity—in the tour price. Nobody else was in the restaurant. "A dozen plates of hor d'oeuvres were placed on the table. We ate them all. Waiters to left of us, waiters to right of us, waiters in front of us charged and retreated." Several other courses were set before them. The guide, sitting at another table, reassured them all was included, so they quickly cleaned off everything. "About this time, three musicians entered and began to play for us, while a honey-voiced tenor sang Sole Mio and other Italian melodies. We were afraid to look at him. We knew he would come around with a money plate later anyway. We crouched over the food without looking or talking. We were determined to give no tips."

When they didn't, the musicians punished them with deafening cacophony. Curt and Ross then devoured all the fruit, bread, and cheese set before them and prepared to decamp. The five waiters lined up hopefully. Ross and Curt feared that if they tipped one they'd have to tip all. Curt left first, followed by Ross, whereupon the waiters were "treated to the remarkably swift dissipation of my figure as I glimmered down the room and vanished through the door."

For the rest of the trip, physical and spiritual hungers made separate claims. The two Americans were living on bananas, chocolate, and an occasional plate of spaghetti. Above the Bay of Naples, they sought out the tomb of Virgil. "Through the ages he rests in the aged shaft of this gray cliff, from which his spirit may regard with immortal eye the sounding ocean, seeing there perhaps the spirit ships of Aeneas scudding before the wind or the flaming pyre of Dido."

On to other sublimities in Capri, Florence, Pisa. In Florence, starved, they splurged on two roast pullets, "well-salted, tawny, and exhaling warm odors," picked up two trenchers of bread, a bottle of wine and some bananas, and on the Ponte Vecchio devoured it all with such gusto they drew spectators. Then they starved their way to Genoa, where they again splurged on a feast, planning to pay for it by living the last two days of the trip on chocolate bars. That night, in a 16-lire hotel room, "we slept peacefully like wilted flowers, ignorant of the fact that on waking we were to face the toughest scrap of the whole voyage."

In the morning the proprietor handed Ross a bill for 29 lire, which would have left them with only seven lire and two sous for the balance of the trip. It wasn't merely a matter of survival, it was a *breach of contract*—and for the first recorded instance in his life Ross Lockridge got genuinely furious.

The fight was conducted in French. "He presented the bill. 'What's that?' said I. 'The bill, monsieur.' 'Well, the bill's only supposed to be 16 lire, everything included. It was arranged with your man last night.' 'No, monsieur, you can't possibly give a chamber for that. There's heating, bedding, service, and hotel tax to be considered. Look here—' and he started to show me what he had put the numbers down for. 'I'm not interested in that,' I said. 'We arranged for a room everything included for 16 lire and that's all we're going to pay!' 'No, monsieur!' 'Yes!'"

The fight augmented as the proprietor called in his reserves— gardener and elevator man—and Ross enlisted large Lamorey, who "removed his glasses and put them in his pocket, casting a calm eye on the elevator man and the gardener who accordingly shrivelled up to about half their original size. The proprietor started at me. I was twice as mad as he was. I was also twice as tall." The proprietor backed away and said he'd call the police, so Ross, calling his bluff, cried *"Bien! Dépêche-toi!"*—the familiar pronoun an insult in this context—knowing that the police were instructed to give tourists the break in such disputes. The proprietor capitulated.

On the train back to Paris, they performed a ceremony. "The five waiters of Pompeii, the handy-man at Florence, the bell-ringer at Pisa, and unsung others were crying for vengeance," and we readers cry with them! "Lamorey and I desired to prove that our spirits were as ample as our purses were lean. To this end, we had saved one sou apiece (five centimes, the smallest European coin) and, as we passed the Italian border, we sent these tokens of our bounty spinning out of the train—tipping all Italy at one time. . . . I don't suppose anyone ever went through Italy with a mouth more open and a purse more shut than—Your affectionate son, Ross Junior."

~

In a letter before the Italian trip, Ross had jokingly called Vernice "capricious," with the implication that he'd heard about her dates with Hornbostel. She retaliated by throwing, as she told him, "little wads of tin foil" at his portrait. He was addressing her as "Dearest," while she was reservedly coming back with "Dear," and where he smothered a postcard with more than five hundred "X" kisses, she responded with only twenty. Ross's letters had been few, however affectionate, and more poetical than intimate. She was receiving advice from her practical-minded older sisters Clona and Beulah to take the Hornbostel option seriously—and at this remove I find it hard to argue with the sisters.

Back in Paris he received somewhat reassuring word from Malcolm Correll, who gave a Phi Gam Christmas Formal guest ticket to his track teammate Hornbostel. "And whom should he bring to the dance but Vernice Baker. Alas, woe was me. I—a traitor to my best friend!" But Malcolm himself took Vernice to a dance later and, for four and one-half of their five hours together, she spoke of nothing except "her boy friend in France."

And she had spent New Year's Eve chastely, as lead in an allegory presented at the First Methodist Church. Mary Eloise Humphreys wrote Ross, "Vernice played beautifully the part of Christianity. She was dressed in pure white with an illuminated red cross on her breast." Malcolm played the part of Religion introducing his daughter Christianity to Fallen Man. Vernice felt somewhat hypocritical: on Christmas Day she'd broken the YPB pledge, first drinking some wine at a party and then confronting a gin rickey. "Being a curious person I took quite a large taste of that, too," she wrote Ross, trying to match his new worldliness.

Paris was in other ways a worldlier place than Bloomington. The Third Republic was imperiled by Fallen Man, and several governments were themselves falling—the Radical bourgeois government of Daladier in October of 1933, Sarraut in November, Chautemps in late January of 1934. Now Daladier as new premier was asked to form a cabinet. The Republican parliamentary system itself was under attack from the right, especially from L'Action Française, which Ross described as "a belligerent party" whose members "desire a king, something on the plan of the English monarchy, and advance descendants of the old royal family for election."

With his usual pedagogical thoroughness he explained the various political parties and the Stavisky affair to his parents. He saw the impending events as an orchestration of history in which disparate forces were imperfectly aware of the part they played. As yet rather apolitical, he didn't declare any sympathies of his own.

Early in January he and Felix Pernot attended a meeting of fifth arrondissement electors, where a fistfight broke out between a businessman and a communist, almost leading to a brawl—and Ross, who had begun regular boxing matches with a Finnish student, claimed he was eager to join in.

A *manifestation* against the Daladier ministry was called by the right wing for the evening of February 6 at Place de la Concorde, but other groups including communists were joining in—and so were the Delaware Group men, not for any political commitment but for the fun of it and in defiance of Mr. Brinton, Directeur, and Miss Littlefield.

Ross was the participant-observer, wondering if he was about to witness a new French Revolution. He and Lamorey took the Métro to Madeleine, "mounted the stairways, and dashed into the middle of a night dense with screaming citizens, soldiers, and policemen, running, fighting, and snarling at each other. Down the street just in front of us was a guard of mounted soldiers, the Garde Républicaine, breaking through the packed masses with difficulty and laying stoutly to right and left with their sabres, while the crowd drove sharp objects into the horses' sides or bowled the riders from the saddle with brickbats and bits of twisted iron. In the direction of the Seine, down the street, rue Royale, terrific outbursts of noise and occasional flashes of light exploded in the brisk air. The crowd was attempting to effect a crossing at the Pont de la Concorde, for just on the other side is the Chambre des Députés. We hurried down, came out into the Place de la Concorde and fell in with an immense movement of men and women of all ages singing the Marseillaise to make the heavens ring. Allons, enfants de la patrie!"

He saw that the little cops, not the big ones, were beating citizens over the head, and the smaller, weaker citizens at that.

They left the bridge and ran through the Tuileries, where they gained a view of the rue de Rivoli. "Women as well as men were running along this demolished area like a human cyclone. Arriving at the further end of the street, they launched a stinging, stunning cloud of stones and twisted bits of iron at the policemen, and repulsed them completely. However, when they had exhausted their ammunition and had nothing left but their hooting, the policemen recharged, and the citizenry took to its heels and went sweeping back down the street like jack-rabbits to renew their forces. This was repeated several times. Finally the crowds burst through a slender file of policemen, beating them back by sheer force of numbers, and, reaching the Ministry of the Marine, shattered the windows and threw flaming torches inside. Immediately a great triumphal cry went up.

"Just at this moment, a squad of horses came up, and rode ironshod into the middle of the crowd, which scattered on every side screaming with fear. Some of the horses were hamstrung by agile citizens, others were so infuriated by the stinging blows they received from everywhere that they got completely out of the riders' control and thundered up and down the street, bucking and kicking to the delight of the crowd. However, in the main, the horsemen triumphed, and quickly swept the crowd back along the street with the flat of their sabres. After they had passed, the street was completely empty except for one poor devil who had taken an open sabre blow on the head, and was running around in a circle clutching his hair and moaning.

"Just at this moment, Lamorey and I looked up and found ourselves standing in the middle of five grim looking policemen who had been patroling the garden. They had heavy, white batons. They had sneers on their faces. They were all little and dirty looking. We backed up against the wall, and the leader of the party advanced and started to prod me in the stomach with his baton, shouting at the same time—'Que faites-vous là?' I said 'Rien!,' backing away fast to keep his baton out of Madame Pernot's dinner. 'Nous sommes des étudiants américains.' We now continued to back away slowly together, assuring him in as bad accents as we could muster that we were just two harmless Americans who had come out to take the air. About this time, we saw another patrol coming down from the other direction. The chief of the squad that surrounded us made the mistake of

blinking. When he opened his eyes, we were gone. Ten French policemen were treated to the vanishing of four clean, American heels,
glimmering in the moonlight, down the garden and over the fence."

He and Lamorey looked for souvenirs, and Ross lugged a heavy
sign reading "Lavatory—W.C. Dans Le Jardin, En bas à Gauche" the
two miles back to rue Soufflot. Twenty demonstrators and one policeman were killed that night, and sixteen hundred people injured—
the greatest public violence in Paris since the 1871 suppression of the
Commune and a turning point in modern French history.

His father liked this letter.

Ross finished up the first term with the highest grades in the Delaware Group. Still he suffered his first and only B, in history—the
highest grade given by Professeur Guignebert, his "little goblin" of an
instructor. "Oh, well! let's be philosophical about it. After all it
doesn't make any difference to me if it doesn't to you." It didn't to
them, but I think it did to him. He had warned them that "it took
Caesar eight years to conquer La Gaule, and I surely can't be expected to do it in ten months." It was some consolation that Jack
Crane, destined to be a world-class linguist working for the OSS and
CIA, got three C's—and others in the Delaware Group, especially
the men, flunked many subjects.

In early March, Ross and Curt sang songs en route to Geneva,
rented skis, and took an autobus to the Jura. Ross's nose was freshly
broken from a recent boxing match with the Finnish student. He had
never skied before. "I got an extraordinary kaleidoscopic picture of
the Alps—sometimes, but very seldom, careening erect on my skis,
sometimes, and very often, humming comfortably on my posteriors,
sometimes on my stomach and face, sometimes on my back, whirling
always dizzily down the hillside with skis, tam, and batons lashing the
air. . . . All the veteran ski-runners declared they had never seen
such a diversity of positions, such an acrobacy of spills."

Back in Geneva, they decided to spend the night in the third-class
waiting room and see the city the next day, but they were evicted at
2 a.m. and ended up sleeping in two outdoor telephone booths in
freezing weather. Before the eviction, Ross wrote to Vernice. "The
French have an expression 'Loin des yeux, loin du coeur!' (Far from the

eyes, far from the heart.) The English say 'Absence makes the heart grow fonder.' The question is debatable, but I, who am of Celtic blood and temperament, hold that our English sentimentality has couched a truer phrase than the French skepticism. . . . You speak of my being closer far away from you. My male realism won't permit any such pretty spiritual conception." He writes some impetuosities about the New England courting custom of bundling and promises she'll have a "wild man" on her hands.

He left on another trip over spring break in late March and early April—a bicycle tour of the South of France, which Larry Wylie had visited. Lamorey preferred to go to Germany, where he was Heil Hitlered at every turn. In reply he'd mutter "To hell with Hitler." Nazi Germany was more hospitable to American tourists than was Republican France.

Ross's would be "a lone voyage, an unknown adventure." The larger Delaware Group was going to Italy. He toured Orange, Avignon, Nîmes, the Pont du Gard, Beaucaire, Tarascon, Marseilles, and Monte Carlo, writing up his adventures novelistically: "Chapitre II. Among the Roman Arenas and the Race with the Spectral Cyclist!!!!" "Chapitre III. On Assassin's Hill, or In the Vaults with Monte Cristo." "Chapitre IV: In the Game-Halls of Monte Carlo or Middle Ages for me!"

Five kilometers outside Arles, a cyclist "shot around me in the glimmering twilight like a ghost. . . . I hadn't been passed yet by a man on a bike, and, in spite of the fatigue I felt from the day's travelling, decided to call on my last resources for the honor of America and the Indiana Cross Country Team to see whether I could catch that scalawag on that bike. . . . I managed to nose about two feet to the front and was holding it very slightly when all of a sudden, a great many lights and a loud noise burst on my senses, and we swept together through a big medieval city gate into the town of Arles!"

That day alone he pedaled 116 kilometers, taking in four Provençal villages. Outside Marseilles he raced a cyclist who had been the 1926 champion of the Grand Tour de France, though twenty-eight kilometers later they gave up the race and had a beer.

In Monte Carlo he watched roulette but didn't gamble. Since this was April Fool's Day, he wrote his parents that he'd lost and then recovered two hundred dollars. When the wheel was spinning the last time he remorsefully "thought of old June, whose patient udder had borne my impudent assaults for three years."

From Monte Carlo he moved on to Carcassonne, Toulouse, Lourdes, Bordeaux, Angoulème, Poitiers, and the châteaux of the Loire, at one point going dutifully out of his way to see some boy Uncle Earl and his father were insisting on. Ross Lockridge, Jr. always discharged all debts. The connection proved amiable, and he spent some pleasant days with two French families. He typed up his account of the first half of this trip with the spectral cyclist's speed, dispatching some 18,000 words back to Bloomington, with generous effusions on antiquities and Provençal culture, the entire two-week trip having cost fifty-five dollars. His father was still suggesting some midweek letters would be appreciated.

A letter of April 3 from Malcolm arrived soon after his return to Paris. I regard this letter with holy dread since without it I might not be here to write this book. "Now, my friend, it becomes my most painful duty to tell you, as friend to friend, as crony to crony, as brother to brother, of your endangered interest." Hornbostel was now dating Vernice exclusively, was sending telegrams of his track victories to her, and had told Malcolm of his intention "to put his pin on her." "Just a few of those letters that only Lockridge can write and you'll be right back in there."

Ross wrote immediately. "Dear Vernice: Certain things recently called to my attention induce a somewhat different letter than you have been in the habit of receiving from me." He has heard about Hornbostel—not naming his informant—and fears his letters may have become embarrassments to her. "Although, if my memory trick me not, we used to dedicate the old porch-swing and sundry other dim-litten trysting places to certain sweet, breathless rites, we never made the age-old exchange of tokens and vows. I am now happy that I didn't because my belief that it wouldn't leave you any freedom— had you accepted it—has since been verified."

In deciding whether to accept Hornbostel's pin she should act as if he doesn't exist—he himself would not be able to offer a pin, tantamount to engagement, for quite some time—"considering my age, ambitions, etc." People with Hornbostel's qualities are hard to find,

129

whereas "of scamps like me there are many and many a one. The only thing that could induce some hesitation in your choice might be the fact of our pre-France relationship and our letter-writing—disposing you to a certain tenderness or mercy toward me." But he relieves her of all obligation toward him. "There! I did my dooty, and coldly cut my own throat. . . . Give my regards to your folks and all our friends. Push Hornbostel in a big lake for me, and tell him I hope he only loses *one* race this year. Affectionately, Ross."

Vernice saw the letter for what it was—a ploy. He had no intention of giving her up.

~

Shortly before his twentieth birthday, Ross Lockridge had to gather his belongings and move. Madame Pernot and her sister-in-law, La Reine or "The Old One," had accepted an invitation from the Marquis to move to the South of France, where he had purchased a villa near Cannes. Jack Crane moved in with Lamorey and another Dartmouth student across the street, while Ross elected to live without a roommate in the residence of Madame Vincent at 4 rue d'Ulm, no more than two minutes' walk. He wanted to be alone, though by this time an understanding had been achieved with Crane, and he wrote his folks that they were now "good friends." He lugged his stuff over on April 23 and spent the next two days helping Madame Pernot close up her home. She had become a second mother to him, and he had told her of his fears concerning Vernice.

Until now the Pernot household had been the butt of satire, especially the Marquis, whose egotism grated on Ross's egoism. When he wasn't boxing or racing streetcars, his aggressions were worked out in satire. "The marquis does now or has done everything, and always with genius. Is it a question of animals?—he has had lions in the house and likes these big fierce beasts because they challenge his mastery. Is it a question of drowning?—he saved three people once, flicking them out of the water before they had time to be scared. He paints, sculpts, and writes. He told us confidentially that in his youth he had a marvellous voice and could very possibly have been a Caruso."

But now Ross finds the Marquis's offer to his new mother-in-law a charitable act that could rescue her from a life he sees as pathetic and futile. He objects to Felix's treatment of his mother—he laughs at her idealism and gullibility. (Crane would recall her as "kind and sympathetic, our dreamer of Egyptian pyramids, Buffalo Bill, the Lost Atlantis.") Ross clearly feels *he* is the more understanding son.

I hear a new resonance in his letters as he begins to reach beyond both satire and stylized effusion to an authentic pathos. His language becomes less a performance and more an investment in its objects.

He was sorry to leave the Pernot household. "I actually felt as though I were in a family there, for [Madame Pernot] treated us as though we were her own children and insisted always that we consider her as our French mother. Her life is in the past.

"I visited them in the evening of the night before their departure. Madame was packing up the last things. The Old One was completely exhausted, but since there were no chairs to sit on, she was obliged to hold herself erect, and so went drooping about close to the walls and corners, like a resurrected ghost visiting the deserted abode of her childhood. They brewed me some tea and insisted on my staying with them awhile. Madame sat down on the floor in front of her trunk already bristling with odds and ends, and talking as she worked, showed me many old papers, books, and objects, recalling former grandeurs and long-forgotten happinesses. There were fine parchments attesting to the election of such and such a military ancestor to the Legion of Honor, signed by the Emperor Napoleon III; eagle feathers badly eaten by time which used to adorn Madame's more sumptuous headdresses in the blush of maidenhood or of young wifehood; several old books dating back to the time of Molière, Corneille, Racine—brilliant century of Louis XIV. Madame tenderly deposited packets of letters and postcards, ribboned and dusty, in the corners of the trunk, & showed me photographs of her husband, always the biggest and most handsome man in each photo, always wearing the most impressive mustache.

"Several family portraits, ignominiously rolled up in one, went in next, one or two half-destroyed albums, some children's garments, and at length her husband's military coat, with which I pleased Madame by showing that it was much too big for me. Many poignant memories were exhaled from the dust and clutter of the old trunk. She finally closed the lid on it, shutting many a sigh with its contents."

The emotion is anchored in his association of Madame Pernot's antiquarian debris with his own mother's and his grandmother Emma Shockley's. Confronted to an unusual degree throughout his early life with the paradoxes of time—the bewildering traces of the past in memorials, tombstones, old manuscripts, and memory itself that simultaneously promise and defeat acts of repossession—he saw in Madame Pernot's trunk of battered objects the potential "futility," as he put it, of human striving.

His mother's reading of her own life as disappointment was a parallel, with a husband not dead but absent. Her life too was in the past, as she looked to her dead father and sighed for her early ambitions. And his grandmother's box of old papers and photographs, now in his possession, was a coffin for his Grandfather Shockley's failed literary labors, alive only in the single witness of his own familial reading of them.

"I returned the next day [April 25] twice, once in the afternoon to take the last trunks to the station and help Madame secure her tickets, once in the evening to see them off finally. Along the boulevard that flanks the Seine, Madame made her last ride with a full heart and tearful eyes. I don't believe she's left Paris for 16 years. I finally got her through the station control with all her baggage, and hustled her and the Old One into an empty compartment of the train, where Madame nearly fainted away every time the train whistle blew. I felt pretty sad when I said good-bye to them. Madame said 'Embrassez-moi, Frank,' so I kissed her à la française. The Old One got up for hers. The train started off, so I skipped out and stood on the platform waving until they had gone. Then I returned to my new apartment. I was twenty years old that day, and it seemed to me that in many ways I was just as big a baby as I had been twenty years ago."

Aware of his own rite of passage through time, of human departures, and—with Vernice still very much on his mind—of the loss of potential futures, he was put into a sad perplexity that brought on sudden vision. Madame Pernot was not, after all, a tragic figure—she was to be whisked off to the South of France to live in style with a marquis. And his mother, in the midst of her lament, had written of feeling "*akin* to" her son, in whose brilliant career she might have a vicarious fulfillment.

In 1947, at the request of the publicity people at Houghton

Mifflin, my father immodestly described in third person the vision that fell upon him at this time. "One day in the spring of 1934, in a small bedroom-and-study of a third floor apartment on the Rue d'Ulm in Paris, a nineteen-year-old American boy sprang suddenly from his typewriter and began to pace excitedly back and forth. This was the idea-genesis of *Raintree County*. . . . It was on that day that Ross Lockridge, Jr. awakened to the fact that certain Nineteenth Century backgrounds in the life of his own family could be transmuted into the content of a novel, which, if it fully realized the possibilities of its content, might really merit the title of 'The Great American Novel.' "

If we accept "nineteen-year-old" as accurate, the only date for this event would be April 24, probably in the evening after he watched Madame Pernot pack her trunk.

To write the novel is a way of transmuting and reanimating those nineteenth-century parchments and objects, of removing them from the trunk of memory, of investing them with vitality and significance. It's a way of supplementing some fragmented and disappointed lives—those of his mother, his grandmother Emma Shockley, and his grandfather John Wesley Shockley. At fifty-four, his mother had become dowdy and looked older than her years. Her son was deeply aware of her mortality.

His novel was thus conceived in a struggle with time. For our life to be only in the past is strictly pathetic, but the past has uses beyond sentimental antiquarianism. He would convert it into the perpetuity of a strong fiction, his grandfather restored and his mother a girl forever.

This vision he kept to himself. I find only one allusion to it in his surviving French notebooks. Amid other literary projects he should "certainly begin laying bases for *Gr. Sh*," which I think refers to its working title, *Grandfather Shockley*.

~

In the spring he was frequently at Shakespeare & Company bookshop, where he presumably met its owner Sylvia Beach, whose name appears in one of his notebooks. He started reading *Ulysses*, jotting down words that interested him. "Meatfaced" he found occasion to deploy in a letter home. Beach may have been as close as he got to the Parisian emigré literati of the 1930s. But he was already deciding that modernism was wanting and a "new voice" was needed in "this age of desolation."

In training, he'd been sweating out his own verse in a notebook he called "Follies of France." These short lyrics, mostly sonnets, were composed against the clock in keeping with the Longinian idea that poetry originates in inspiration, a *furor raptus*. "Composed in 15 minutes, morning, Dec. 15, 1933." "Composed with furious passion 15 or 20 minutes, Monday, January 15, around 4:30 to 5:00 p.m." "Composed in 3 minutes at desperate speed, the afternoon of the 31 of May, 1934."

None of these efforts is "Ode to a Nightingale" and he tried to be his own hanging judge. With any composition, "convince yourself by a pitiless criticism that it is essentially poor in comparison with what you might have done and shall subsequently do." With this maxim in hand he slaughtered his own verse, writing in the margins: "conventional," "old stuff," "neither anything detailed nor anything large and synthetic," "muddy, ragged, abortive," "nothing new musically, nothing flavored with personality," "rotten," "horrid," "a very crude morbidity," "a discouraging puerility." He set Shakespeare's "When in disgrace with fortune and men's eyes" next to Lockridge's "Oh, for a truce to over-cruel disdainings" and pronounced the former "good" and the latter "awful."

Finding a new voice was no easy matter, and he saw that what felt like a torrent of fevered originality soon congealed on the page as a pastiche derived from Shakespeare, Hugo, Browning, and especially Keats. Like Keats he hoped to apprentice himself into the company of great writers and earn a noble fame, and he looked nervously for signs of his own genius, in "Follies of France" finding none. He started to revise the poems but felt that adding "superficial correctness to a thing so constitutionally feeble" was like "putting rouge on a dead man." He vowed to confront mediocrity, the "father of oblivion," head-on.

All the love poems are to Vernice Baker except "To a Dark Sweetheart," who turns out to be not somebody from Vassar but Death personified. Love and death are the two principal themes, fitting in a youthful poet. In "Ballad of the Grave-diggers," the speaker confronts the corpse of his own mother.

More impressive were the *dissertations* he was turning out for his coursework at the Sorbonne, which he'd finish and dash over at the last minute, racing traffic. One of his instructors was giving him by turns "extravagant compliments" and "terrible lacings." In one, "she told me my style had nothing of the offensive American odor about it, that I had the ability to concentrate my thoughts in few words, in striking formulas, and that in short my style reminded her a lot of Paul Valéry." But for the next, "Mademoiselle was unable to choose any French author, even among the most inferior, to whom I might be compared."

He shared a tutorial with another Delaware student, Walter Pruden, whose papers would be returned with many marginal corrections. "With this horrible marmelade of blunders and red-marks in his hand, the impassive Pruden will stoutly argue with Mademoiselle about its merits—much like a murderer standing over his victim with bloody knife in hand and professing entire innocence of the crime."

Most of his critical work in literature was on assigned topics asking *les étudiants* to discuss French authors in terms of period characterizations: classicism, romanticism, realism. Ross Lockridge obliged in finding much that was classical about Corneille, much that was romantic about Hugo, much realistic about Flaubert. But in increasingly periodic prose and essays twice the required length, he spoke his mind on his reading, enormous during the year.

He admired the vast, imperfect canvas of the Romantics and (in French) wrote: "Let us consider, for example, *Les Misérables*, which contains almost all of Hugo's qualities—the best and the worst—this immense work, full of interminable descriptions, digressions, superfluous episodes, offering us realism, romanticism, sentimentality, artificiality, lyricism, satire—in short, everything—manages even because of this amplitude to give a sensation of epic nobility and diverse genius. . . . The more a genius aspires to the sublime, the more he risks falling heavily into the ridiculous." The Romantics had *"une imagination audacieuse"* he found enviable. (He scored 16/20 for this 12-page effort.)

As maker of audacious lists, he pondered a number of intermediary literary projects, from a "great comprehensive epic poem of the Middle Ages to equal the *Iliad* and the *Odyssey*," a "Tragedy of Pompeii," "a poem on Virgil and the tomb overlooking the Med.," "a great poem dedicated to Vernice & love undying," and a play depicting the struggle between a dreamer and a censor, to—time permitting—a "Poetisation of the History of the World."

But meanwhile *la vie quotidienne* must be dealt with. As the second term wore on, other members of the Delaware Group watched the lean 130-pound runner add twenty pounds. They saw him always wearing his striped scarf and his beret, which had become quite dirty and given his hair a permanent crease. Lamorey and he would often eat fresh raw garlic chased with red wine before running off to lecture. Huldah Smith noted that he became "not particularly neat in dress, loping around Paris with his tie loose, his coat flapping open, and a generally slap-happy informality." Her *propriétaire,* somewhat discommoded by the informality, admired his mastery of the language. By spring, he was sometimes taken for a native Swiss speaker of French.

He drank and talked with Delaware men at Demory's, a brasserie on rue Broca near the Delaware headquarters, where the beer cost only 75 centimes. He and Lamorey often discussed politics and women, spread their schoolwork out on the large tables, and actually tipped 25 centimes per beer. He spoke with no apology of his great competitive spirit, and following one of their sessions, on three or four beers he raced Lamorey's bus the mile to the Latin Quarter, never giving up though he lost by some thirty seconds and was admonished by a gendarme as he wheezed on the curb.

Lamorey was struck by how much Ross seemed to love his family. He had a complete picture gallery of Lockridges plus Vernice on display in his flat. When Lamorey brought over the son of his *propriétaire,* he asked about these family pictures. Lamorey told the boy, as Ross wrote his folks, that these pictures were "my wife and child, that I had married some years ago, and had come to France leaving a wife and three kiddies to guard the fireside. The urchin went home and told his parents who know me quite well, seeing me frequently with Lamorey. They questioned Lamorey about it, and he continued to uphold the story, even to increasing the number of the children from three to four. Madame, remarking about my youth, said—'Il va vite,' meaning, 'He's working fast.' I told Lamorey I thought this was carrying things a bit far. I began to feel like a parent. But you'd be surprised at the hushed awe with which my youthful person is now perceived in the Baudry family." He called himself "The Fictitious Father."

Discussions with Crane at Demory's were often literary and philosophical. Crane described Ross as life's "bubbling young optimist" while he was "the stern and dramatic young pessimist." He'd remember Ross's arguing that it's "not sensible to be pessimistic, because we're licked before we start!" Crane argued a dour fatalism.

Ross did understand the threat of that view. He read *Jude the Obscure* in early March and, as his initial entry in a notebook, mentioned the doomed hero's return to Alfredston: "Old milepost, nearly obliterated by moss—visionary longing of his childhood—on that gray day refound in silence, misery, and dead enormous failure."

As the term wore on into early May, Ross was increasingly concerned about Vernice. It took easily a month to get a reply in the mails. There's only one entry in his notebooks to suggest any concurrent Parisian involvement, with an unnamed woman he owed eight francs. "Take it easy. Don't offer to kiss her. Talk with her. Get her to talk—Talk! Talk! Talk! Learn to analyse the female character." Malcolm received a letter, now lost, in which Ross described a feverish moment in the back row of a Parisian cinema. He was wary of erotic entanglement, and the women of the Delaware Group registered this. One of them thought him "of a warm intelligence, alert and involved. Still, he always seemed somewhat detached in the manner of one who is gently laughing. He never paired off with one girl for long." He handed Amanda Macy a volume of *Sonnets from the Portuguese* with some lines suggestively underlined, but didn't follow up.

Finally, on May 16, the letter from Vernice arrived, a dignified letter with some contrition and some challenge. "Dear Ross." She hadn't felt like dating others when he left in the fall, but with no vows having been made there was little reason not to. Charlie had emerged as the most plausible of the men she began seeing. Far from concealing her prior relationship, she even mentioned receiving letters from Paris, and Hornbostel had gamely read the letter sent to the Lockridge family about French table manners.

"You say you are glad we never exchanged the age-old tokens and vows because it would have deprived me of my freedom——I believe that you are absolutely sincere——for I felt, too, that there was a strong possibility that you would change your mind. I have flattered myself sometimes by thinking that maybe you have used this policy in our relationship as long as we have known each other. I could never understand why you would go with me for awhile and seem to like me perfectly well and then suddenly, without apparent reason, drop me completely. I believe that perhaps you did this in order to preserve our pleasant relationship. . . . But freedom was absolutely the last thing that I wanted this fall."

She'd have preferred to receive his fraternity pin, and remembers how her heart sank one evening when she thought it might be forthcoming, only to have him decide to drop off his pin-bearing vest at home. She doesn't offer to stop seeing Hornbostel. "Sincerely, Vernice."

Within two hours Ross wrote a reply, with no talk of sentimental trysts and only a little poetry—indeed some pretty straight talk. "Dearest Vernice, . . . Two days ago a letter from Mother indicated that you had expressed joy at the receipt of my last letter, which confirmed my worst suspicions." But "it seems that you are not really so taken up by Charley as he merits and as I had begun to suppose." He hadn't meant to reproach her, only to free up her decision about accepting a pin, and he assumes she'll continue dating Hornbostel.

"Now all we have to do is await my return to see how things will go. Above all, we must remember that we're young & that life is long and that there's no use denying oneself the privilege of perfect freedom at our age." Marriage is something he can't contemplate now— maybe at age twenty-four or twenty-five—and the conventions of pin-giving he regards as absurd.

"The difficulty that exists over here and everywhere is the absolute lack of finer and freer perception in such matters as love and sexual relationships. Don't you see how little, how sordid, how silly, pitiful, and brutalizing most university as well as high school 'loves' are, with arguments & constant interchange of pins?" Such people hang around together "until they've either stultified each other by too long familiarity and broken up—as usually happens—or gotten married off to each other like two truck horses. There's nothing audacious, free, sublime in that. Better for two people to meet, to yield because they desire—without heeding the pointing finger of convention and the regular wrestling bouts of jealousy & explanation." She shouldn't expect an offer of a pin upon his return, but their relationship has already affirmed its integrity and promise.

He finally explains his disappearances—they were brought about when he sensed their relationship "had ceased to be quite as free." Confessing that he isn't "entirely a liberated soul," doing many things he'd prefer not to and "chafing under forced labor," he has acted on his own will in matters of the heart, and when he periodically returned to her it was because "I couldn't help it. I wanted to—that's all." Many of those who are most constant have married only because "they got the habit." As for sex in Paris, "I could never bring myself to it, for the mere physical ecstasy of it. It would be a duty, a crying, cramping, unlovely task."

His own ideal of a relationship "is a kind of loving *friendship*," whether it assumes sexual form or not. If it does, it is "the perfect communion of two unquestioning virginal minds who in that way feel a kind of ultimate intercourse with each other." After all, "friends seldom break up but lovers frequently. Do people exchange vows and demand explanations in friendship? No! . . . Now I am dying to come back. I cannot conceal it—dying to come back to you, my own dear friend and more than friend."

~

Back home things were not faring very well. Elsie feared that Hubert Akins and Lillian didn't have "a very hot case" and Lillian had started gaining back the weight. For several months Ross Senior had been writing to his son of the two pending matters of great import for the family: the Ball Foundation support of his Recitals and the state textbook adoption. Foundation support "will not only bring safety (and luxury) to the family and immortality (modestly) to me but will help also to give you a *place in the sun*—offering a great stage for all your present preparation."

No clearer statement exists that the father hoped the son would carry on his own career of historical evangelicalism. Elsie may not have made the prospect of homecoming the more alluring when she wrote, "Dad is planning to have you occupy the platform in the barn & deliver an inspiring speech."

But, alas, both great hopes failed: the Ball Foundation decided somebody else should pay for those Recitals, and as for the state adoption of World Book mathematics texts, "Some of the other companies bid prohibitive prices in a throat-cutting price-cutting war that made our books impossible." Elsie felt that her husband should stop his Historic Site Recitals and try harder to convince World Book Company that he was truly interested in their less glamorous work.

Ross Junior had greatly hoped to stay over an extra month after the term ended—and Ross Senior had thought his son should stay at least for Bastille Day—but now a family powwow was convened. Since the family would be in financial straits, he should save the hundred dollars he had tucked away for the extra month and return with the rest of the group on June 30. Next year he'd greatly need that hundred dollars, which was mostly some extra money his parents had sent during the year. Elsie intimated it could still be his choice. He agreed to return, having an additional motive in any event.

He dug in to finish the term. Where some students were working hard to stitch together convincing plagiarisms, he said he was taking the easier route of writing his own, and had devised an original topic for his Groupe Supérieur term thesis: a comparison of the French Théâtre Libre and the English Court Theatre. He read minimally sixty-four plays to which he added those he'd been seeing in Paris throughout the year, getting unlimited English texts at Shakespeare & Company for a twelve-francs-per-month rental. He galloped over his seventy-nine pages in first draft three or four minutes late on June 8. Professeur Gaiffe gave it a "19." The play he was most taken by was *Riders to the Sea*. The copy he read was quite possibly the same that Joyce himself had borrowed from Shakespeare & Company on July 12, 1920, the day after his first meeting Sylvia Beach. In this play the mother confronts the drowned body of her youngest son, and Ross comments: *"La mère, qui avait considéré cette mort comme inévitable, se plie, sans trop pleurer, à la fatalité"* (The mother, who had considered this death inevitable, yields to the fatality without much weeping).

He still had the habit, developed in high school, of lamenting his poor performances on exams only to be told thereafter that he'd scored highest after all. This honked off some Delaware men. He met all his professors on the battlefield of written and oral examinations, and this time scored six A's for the term. On June 29, hundreds of students in *le Cours de civilisation française* convened in an amphitheatre. When the highest honors among the participating nations were awarded, an English woman and Ross Lockridge, Jr. were asked to step forward. They were given a standing ovation.

He wrote his parents that the year had been of "incalculable value." He himself couldn't know the extent of it. Culture, language, and adventure apart, he'd begun to discover a writer's voice in those letters home, written less for his parents than for authorial self-discovery. Getting out of Indiana had prompted a verbal explosion. He had had the vision, anchored in human pathos and his sense of time, that would come to fruition thirteen years later in his novel. And he had had a love affair—an epistolary one. He would always hope to return to France, the "second country of my soul."

In the days before boarding the *Mauretania,* he visited Versailles with some Delaware people and took another bicycle trip, into the north of France, to see Chantilly, Senlis, Beauvais, Rouen, and other places. From Cannes, Madame Pernot wrote to express relief that Frank was *"tranquille maintenant"* about his girlfriend back in the States.

And on June 28, he bade farewell to Lamorey, who along with only a small number of people was staying a few weeks longer in Europe. "I feel awfully low just now—having run around Paris a good part of the afternoon to return this evening and say goodby to Lamorey, who is leaving on a little trip from which he won't return until I shall have left. I just left him, feeling utterly miserable to say goodby to such a good friend with whom I have spent such memorable hours. I suppose I shall never know those vagabond travelling days again—never with Curtis, who is the best travelling companion in the world. Saying goodby to a friend here is like saying goodby to Paris, for the city is dear to us by the associations we have made and the memories we have made with other people. Fortunately, I am going home,—to a place where my associations, friendships, and memories are even more numerous, and my sadness is of course only momentary—to be uplifted when the last sight of France's olden coast dims on my eyes and the year will have ended. Well, it's always harder to leave people than it is places."

In a notebook he recorded that he wept uncontrollably after this leavetaking.

"War, War, War is brewing in Europe from all indications. I may be getting out just in time to miss the German invasion. Love to all, Ross."

V

"Dream of the Flesh of Iron"

Bloomington, 1934–1940

Returning to the United States aboard the R. M. S. *Maure-tania* in early July, 1934, Ross Lockridge, Jr. took notebook in hand and set about revising his persona. He figured that after a year abroad he should "give the impression of having reached maturity." "Talk less. Smile seldom. Revise laugh." In the company of males, he'd henceforth "talk in a deep, quiet way and make no efforts toward studied brilliance," while with females he'd attempt to be manly and "insist on entire equality," not bending so much to their will. *"No more swearing."* "Keep hair neat, shoes shined. SMILE LITTLE."

Still clutching a nominal liberty in affairs of the heart, he hoped to make headway with various Indiana women—"Edith with the golden hair, Vernice, the womanly one, Peggy, the fascinating." And he'd "try to conquer the irritating outward manifestation of my competitive spirit."

The Conquerer of Gaul also vowed to master the English language and renovate English expression. "Let energy, force, and incantation be the ends of my style." Though he'd be thinking always of his novel based on his Grandfather Shockley's life, he projected also a series of sonnets, plays, innovative essays, and by all means an epic poem. This proved to be not idle jotting.

He again took responsibility for blind student Sydney Roseman, but found a serious distraction on board in Marion Monico, a sophisticated Italian-American woman from what became Douglass College

142

of Rutgers University. She had a classic Roman profile and long dark hair in a braided coronet. On the night of July 4, they danced together up in first class and felt quite a rush. Disembarking, they decided to write but seemed to agree the relationship would not go beyond the epistolary friendship they kept up for the next several years.

From his summer job at a seaside New Jersey resort, Larry Wylie came to New York to meet Ross and the two spent a day traipsing about town. Though only a brief tour, its images would be drawn on heavily in his work. To save money, he boarded a bus instead of a train for his homecoming.

On Sunday, July 8, having just been to church, Vernice Baker was at the northeast corner of Fourth and Washington with her friends Nota Scholl and Wilma Jean Schmaltz, getting ready to cross the street, when Ross Lockridge and his parents saw her and stopped their car. Just back, he asked if he could see her that evening. Weak in the knees, she had to be helped across the street by her friends.

That evening she was less struck by any new maturity than by the twenty-pound weight gain. Though plump, he looked good to her. It was the same effervescent, smiling Ross with whom she strolled the campus in a happy reunion. He gave her a bottle of perfume, "Dans la Nuit."

One habit he hadn't vowed to break was Rivervale, so later in July the traveler over ancient parapets was once again at the local Methodist church camp. He and Malcolm walked southeast from the dormitory to a steep root-laddered path down to the White River's sandy beach, where they swam naked. Lying on the sand they watched the opposite shore for hippopotami and talked about sex. Both were still wondering what it would feel like.

Ross wrote Vernice midweek. Their happiness depended on when her boss, Mr. Biddle, would let her off bookstore duty— normally she had to work through Saturday morning. Mr. Biddle relented. The friend who drove her that Friday turned off the engine at the top of hills to save gasoline, and spent so much time restarting it in every valley that Vernice feared she'd never get to the camp.

Even with her there, Rivervale had lost some of its charm for Ross, just as he himself had lost his "boyish timidities." He had outgrown it. More severe chastenings would follow.

In August, he spent a week visiting his grandmother Emma Shockley at her home in Straughn, where his cousin Mae Beth Shockley, one year his junior, was also visiting. They enjoyed the pictures of Great Masters that Emma had plastered over the interior of her privy. This was the grandmother who would haul her dictionary all the way to Pittsburgh when visiting her son Frank, a university administrator. She'd bushwhack the family with it at the dinner table, pouncing on betrayals of pronunciation or usage whenever they auditioned their English.

A nonlinguistic lapse occurred right under her nose: in the coal cellar, Mae Beth and Ross finished off the grape juice, which, unbeknownst to teetotaling Emma, had fermented.

The August heat and fermentation fueled a pivotal letter to Vernice. The house at Straughn seemed haunted by his passionate ancestry, and he thinks it triggered the dream he relates. He and Vernice float through a limbo of time and space only to find themselves in the feather bed at Straughn, trying to restrain their laughter so as not to alert the bodily Dream Censor, Grandmother Shockley.

Worried that she might find them out, they begin "to embrace as though we never should see each other again. Then I began to lose you, and I was so full of sorrow, my heart felt all hollow." Ross awakens bereft, and "went searching about the bed. No—alas—I was awake & you were gone and I lay long awake and so melancholy." He wishes the impetuosity of dreams could overcome the conventions and ennui of the waking state. A new student of Freud, he knows the argument for dreams as wish-fulfillments. And yet this dream in its vanishing has only reminded him of yearning and loss.

Uncanny odors of love and death penetrate the quaint gingerbread house in Straughn, acting as catalysts to his will. He feels that only in the last couple of years has he been truly capable of falling in love, and even then "convention, ennui, misunderstanding" have blocked him. In this letter, for the first time, he tells Vernice that he "might as well sign Yours in love. Ross."

Ruminating on Freud, he will speak of the problem of "mother fixation" in "object choice," and early on has instinctively guarded against it. He went to the Old World only to find his hunger for this Indiana woman deepening. The dream of the feather bed has placed Vernice within his family structure, in a subversive sort of way. Now, within the symbolic enclosure of this ancestral house that will feed his art—and often freer in his writing than in his speech—he has declared himself for Vernice. Perhaps he finds in her someone whose nonjudgmental empathy is qualitatively unlike what he had sensed early on in his mother.

His "quixotic grandfather" lived a life of erotic promise and literary castles in air, and yet the aged widow Emma and yellowed manuscripts are testimony to time's check on dreams. Ross seeks a life larger and more durable than his grandfather's yearnings and scribblings, and a relationship warmer and more passionate than his parents'. Couldn't he enlarge those dreams and redress those disappointments—in a continuance of desire across generations, but one that finds a larger life?

In early fall of 1934, he accompanied his parents to another ancestral house—on the other side, so to speak, of the family tree. His grandfather Brenton Webster Lockridge had died in 1922, shortly after selling his farm and moving to Peru, Indiana. His grandmother Charlotte Wray Lockridge died in 1930. The family hadn't yet broken up the house in Peru. Ross Senior's two younger siblings, Marie Peters and Earl Lockridge, were to join the Bloomingtonians in dividing up the furniture and personal effects.

Aunt Marie had married a doctor, and was famed for her great square jaw, boisterous opinionated talk, and being always astonished by something. Born on Christmas Day, she loved to lavish gifts picked up at bargain sales. Her collection of old Christmas wrappings, boxes, and other debris would eventually smother the upper rooms of her elegant Indianapolis home. (She lived to a hundred, a sort of shopping bag lady *manquée*.) For one Christmas, Ross Junior received from this Dickensian aunt "one good shirt and three shapeless chestbags to make up for it; a scarf that must have come from a boy scout rummage sale; a picture of George Washington striving to hold a pair of false teeth in his mouth; a sweater that was only slightly scorched by the flames and discolored by the chemicals; a pair of pajamas from which the price tag had been wisely removed; and two books that were won in a raffle." Uncle Earl was an engineer and surveyor.

The two-story house at 315 East Main Street was musty and

coated with cobwebs. Dried flowers left over from the funeral were in a basket in the upstairs bedroom. Ross Senior hoped to get some books, family photographs, and especially the old cherry dresser. He used to practice speaking before its mirror. Elsie thought they could use some of the other furniture too, since the siblings were better off and without children. They braced for the arrival of Marie and Earl, and in a short play written a few days later Ross Junior recreated what happened, deleting himself from the cast of characters. He said *The Inheritors* was a "bit of realism" with "very little embroidery of imagination or rhetoric."

EARL: Hello, Elsie. Glad to see you, Rossie. Say Rossie, I thought you'd traded that old car in, till I saw it out there. Well, it still holds together in places, doesn't it, Rossie? Haw, Haw, Haw!

MARIE: Stop it now, Earl! You're always teasing Rossie about the car. (She looks around her.)

EARL: (looking around him) Gad, isn't it awful the way the old house has run down. I guess we should have got around to this sooner. (He glances at Marie.)

MARIE: It always just seemed to me like a kind of favor to dear Mamma to leave it the way it was when she lived here. Dear Mamma has been dead four years now. (She sniffs a little.) We haven't none of us been back since the funeral, I guess.

ROSS: This is my first time. But I thought maybe you folks had. There seemed to be a few things gone—the big chiffonier that stood in the front room upstairs. I thought maybe you'd taken it for better keeping. That is—I thought— (He hesitates, looking from one to the other.)

MARIE: (looking uneasily at Earl) Oh yes! Well, to tell the truth, Doctor and I did stop a time or two. I wanted to see the old place. We did take some little things I thought the rest of you wouldn't have any use for. (Earl starts to speak, but she goes on in a louder voice.) I SUPPOSED YOU HAD STOPPED TOO, EARL. I NOTICED THE VICTROLA AND TRIMMINGS ON THE MANTEL WERE GONE! (Earl subsides.)

[They have also taken the silverware but assure Ross and Elsie that the division of property is a matter of no import.]

ROSS: Here are the old photographs. There are some mighty funny ones too, aren't there, Elsie?

ELSIE: There are quite a few of the children. I guess you don't mind if I keep the ones of my children, of course, do you?

EARL: Of course not. Take what you want to. Of course, I reckon everyone will take any pictures of hisself. Haw, Haw, Haw! As for the old family pictures—well, I hate to see them divided. (Ross is looking uneasily back and forth from Elsie to Earl.) Well, Rossie, I see you want them pretty bad. Shall we let Rossie have the old pictures, Marie?

MARIE: (graciously) Sure. Take them all, Rossie. Take what you want; it makes no difference to me—although I should rather like to have the antiques.

ROSS: (very much pleased at the generosity of his brother and sister) Thanks! Thanks a lot for the pictures. I like very much these old photographs. (He puts them down and dabbles in them.)

ELSIE: I wonder if Ross and I could have some of this other furniture.

ROSS: Oh, say, Marie, do you want that old dresser that was in my room? You know, the old cherry dresser. I used to keep my—

MARIE: OH, ROSSIE, YOU DON'T WANT THAT OLD THING! THAT'S ONE OF THE OLDEST PIECES! I'M SURE DEAR MAMMA . . . WOULD WANT ME TO HAVE THAT! I DON'T CARE ABOUT THE REALLY VALUABLE THINGS, BUT DEAR MAMMA . . . WOULD LET ME HAVE THAT. SHE KNEW HOW MUCH I ADORE ANTIQUES!

[Ross sadly relinquishes his old dresser and all the other antiques to Marie.]

EARL: That's it. Let's don't argue. Mamma's last words were something about not squabbling over anything after she was gone. God knows we did enough of it while she was living. HAW, HAW, HAW! (Changing suddenly) Say, Rossie, how about those books?

[Earl doesn't read many books but for that very reason would like to start a fashionable little library. This time Ross prevails and gets the books, but to Elsie's dismay Earl takes the bookcases. After the siblings have left, Ross and Elsie have only the books and some photographs.]

ROSS: It was nice of old Earl to let me have the books without any argument.

[He looks forward to rereading *Two Years Before the Mast* and *She*. Upon parting he notices a wall photograph of his mother and hesitates to take it.]

ROSS: I imagine they both wanted it. I like this picture very much. They must have overlooked it.

ELSIE: Oh, go ahead, Ross. They took some things without telling you.

ROSS: (slow and a little sheepishly) Well, they told me to take the pictures. It's a wonderful picture of Mamma. I'll just take it, and we won't say anything about it. . . . She always thought I had great promise because of my university record. (He laughs at the contemplation of his own accomplishments.) But I guess I wasn't much of a satisfaction to Mamma.

Ross Junior has recreated this episode in sympathy and exasperation. He knows his father will always feel himself a disappointment to his own mother, despite his many books and children. The reversals the Wray family suffered at the hands of Yankee predators after the Civil War led Charlotte Wray Lockridge to insist on a different script for her children. Her eldest son ended up in the most impractical of professions—vagabond pedagogy—but in his own mind could any achievement really have answered?

Similarly, Ross Junior knows that Elsie is someone who will always feel herself a disappointment to her father, John Wesley Shockley. And no matter how long her husband's *Who's Who in America* column grows, he can never surpass her father, who rated only passing mention in *Henry County, Indiana: Past and Present*.

Ross Junior finds himself in a family where parental expectation, real or imagined, powers a relentless motive-spring. His father fashions an eccentric visionary career not sanctioned by his mother and for that reason feels all the more judged by her ghost. The self-possession he displays within the magic circle of his dramatic recitals doesn't carry over to the larger arena of life's exigencies, where he is a pushover—impractical and unable to perform his mother's implicit bidding. His son sees that he is naïve about the predatory nature of others. For all his energies, his kind of idealism makes him vulnerable, and in this implicitly judgmental family context he goes downright limp.

My father's fastidiousness about contracts and his thrift find their origins in the contrary precedent of his own heedless, trusting father. Far from naïve, he is wary of being taken or exploited. But I think

John Wesley Shockley, summer of 1893, aged fifty-four. The maternal grandfather of Ross Lockridge, Jr., he was the Hoosier schoolmaster and poet who inspired the portrait of John Wickliff Shawnessy, hero of *Raintree County*.

John Shockley with a copy of *The Indianapolis News* in his yard at Straughn, Indiana, renamed Waycross as the setting of the Day sections of *Raintree County*.

LEFT: Emma Rhoton Shockley, John Shockley's second wife, aged fifty, photographed in 1907, the year her husband died.
RIGHT: Charlotte Wray Lockridge urged her children to go to the state university. Her son Ross gave her all the credit for his own career.

Elsie Shockley in a college portrait, 1899. She aspired to a life of intellectual and spiritual ideals. For her day she was a feminist, but her progress toward a college degree would soon be interrupted by marriage to Ross Lockridge and childbearing.

LEFT: Ross Lockridge, Sr. in a college portrait of 1899. He compiled an academic record that would set the standard for the family.
RIGHT: Ernest Vivian Shockley, uncle of Ross Lockridge, Jr.

LEFT: Robert Bruce Lockridge in football garb. Younger brother of Ross Senior, Bruce was killed in 1903 at a track meet.
RIGHT: The younger Robert Bruce Lockridge, in a photograph taken June 19, 1919, one day after his high school commencement. Ten days later, Bruce drowned in St. Joseph's River, Fort Wayne.

LEFT: Ross Lockridge, Jr. in his first known photo, aged one.
RIGHT: Lillian Lockridge suffered from obesity, never married, and slept in the same room with her mother, Elsie, until late in life.

The Peltier Historical Pageant of May 1922 featured Ross Lockridge, Jr.

The two Rosses worked as an unequal partnership, with son from an early age assisting father in his populist history projects. Eventually Ross Junior made it known he could no longer go about his father's business.

LEFT: The Thrasher sisters lost their mother early in life and banded together to run the household as best they could. *Back row at right:* Lillie, mother of Vernice Baker.
RIGHT: Vernice Baker in 1928, aged fourteen. In *Raintree County* she would inspire the portrait of Nell Gaither.

LEFT: Breaking of camp at Clarksville on the Historic Site Recital tour of 1932. Ross Junior won high marks for always helping out.
RIGHT: At Rivervale Methodist Church Camp, summer of 1933, Vernice Baker and Ross Junior renewed their relationship.

Le Jardin du Luxembourg is the setting for this April 1934 photograph of Ross Lockridge, Madame Pernot's older sister ("the Old One"), Madame Pernot, and Cloise Crane.

In Campo Santo, Genoa, winter of 1934. My father's inscription on the back of this photograph draws attention to the "suddenly resurrected corpse who has just burst from his tomb with hideous aspect." He loved cemeteries and recited Gray's "Elegy" on this spot.

Ross Lockridge, Jr. with his mother outside the Indiana University wellhouse, spring of 1935. Known as "A-plus Lockridge," he graduated with the highest grade-point average ever accumulated at the University.

he also senses a deep unstated identification with his father in this play. He himself has felt, since his earliest years, the gaze of maternal judgment.

~

Charles Hornbostel had graduated in the spring of 1934, but was briefly back in town near the end of the summer, having asked Vernice not to accept a pin from Ross until he had a chance to see her again. Now Vernice explained her feelings about Ross and sadly walked with Hornbostel to the Monon station to say good-bye. She had been uncomfortable rather than buoyed up with her embarrassment of riches—star athlete and star scholar. But she warmly liked and admired Hornbostel and was sad to relinquish him.

After work one evening in the fall, she was driven by Clona and her husband, Thomas Nicholson, to the old Smith farm, where an Epworth League hayride would be concluding. Deprived by work of the hayride, she was to have a compensatory date with Ross afterward. Upon arriving she found him having somewhat too merry a time with Mary Eloise Humphreys—who didn't know of Ross's upcoming date—and Vernice departed much vexed. Embarrassed, Ross was now persuaded of the need for some clarifications of his own. His intermittent romance with Mary Eloise and all others soon came to an end.

During the 1934 fall semester, he resumed a busy university life, academic and social. He kept up with most of his old friends. But one member of the old Four Musketeers had faded. Vincent Hippensteel was a talented malcontent who signed Ross's 1931 high school yearbook with a large script that commenced with a flourish in the upper left-hand corner and plummeted to a fizzle in the lower right. He delayed his own high school graduation to edit the 1932 *Gothic* and lost touch with his old classmates. His father had died when he was two, and an older brother died of Bright's disease. Vincent lived with his mother and was working hard as a journalism student. On October 25, Vernice ran into him near the bookstore and noticed nothing wrong.

Later that afternoon, while climbing a fence northeast of the city, he shot himself through the heart with the .22-caliber rifle his father had left him. The coroner declared it an accident. Ross thought it more likely a suicide staged as an accident—to spare in some measure his mother's feelings. Hippensteel had a depressive tendency, after all, and he had ample intelligence to figure out how to fool a coroner. Very upset, Ross and Vernice offered condolences to Mrs. Hippensteel, now totally alone.

Throughout the year Ross Junior was in demand as a speaker. Greater Bloomington wished to hear about Europe. "Lockridge said he had participated in many riots while studying in Paris," reported the *Indiana Daily Student*. His set piece was the *manifestations* of February. The French had a passion for politics that far exceeded the Americans', he said, proving the point by keeping his own talks politically neutral.

In other collegiate pursuits his industry continued in kind: he took minor roles in *The Merchant of Venice* and *Ladies of the Jury,* was reelected president of Le Cercle Français, had a brilliant second-place finish at a major cross-country meet "under the inspiration of my girl's presence in the stands," and became a member of Blue Key, Skull & Crescent, and the Board of Aeons, whatever these are.

But the big event along these lines was to become Indiana University's contender for a Rhodes scholarship. He was one of two winners in the state competition and, with some local hoopla, went to Chicago as one of twelve finalists in the Great Lakes group of states. In early January, 1935, shortly before the final interviews, he wrote to Lamorey reminiscing about Europe, detailing his courtship of Vernice, and anticipating defeat in the Rhodes. He'd hope to win if only to join Lamorey in Europe the following year, but "I'm genuinely afraid that I haven't much chance for aforesaid honor. I haven't any particular pull, and, then, aside from my intellectual handicaps, I guess I'm a little too immature to receive the scholarship. . . . I'm afraid just one of us will be sailing for Europe next summer."

Well, for once he was right to lament his inadequacies—he lost. Louise Wylie, a friend from high school days, found Vernice Baker weeping in a college restroom—weeping, she thought, because Vernice couldn't understand how anybody could fail to appreciate Ross. She was actually weeping from relief, because Rhodes scholars are not permitted to marry and she had feared the two-year absence would be final.

Ross expressed disappointment to Vernice but didn't dwell on it and turned his energies elsewhere. There was a psychic momentum that would normally carry him through setbacks. It was grounded in his self-elected career of writer, still seeking material evidence of itself. He could confront a typewriter elsewhere than at Oxford. And it would take more than loss of a Rhodes competition to bring on debilitating self-doubt. What doubt he had only made him work the harder. If his was a strategy for protecting the ego, it worked for the time being. He would be in jeopardy only if it became clear to him that he was *no writer*.

His letter to Lamorey had been concerned more with love than academe. He was so much in love that people were feeling sorry for him. He had to write to somebody about it to avoid going mad. "As for my case with Vernice—the only English word adequately expressing it is—POW!!!"

The rest of this letter describing his courtship has been scissored away, probably by a prudent member of the Lamorey household sometime in the intervening years. In Lamorey's memory of it, Ross was hardly analytic. He would later say he'd found in Vernice someone who embodied the carnal and the spiritual equally, someone expressive of the Indiana landscape he loved, and—beyond mere symbols—someone who had loved him faithfully through his own waverings and betrayals.

He and Malcolm double-dated, and Malcolm's new girlfriend, Ruth Armstrong of Popcorn, Indiana, listened to Ross and Vernice singing in the front seat while they were parked: "When I grow too old to dream, I'll have you to remember." The two of them never seemed happier. Throughout the spring semester he tutored her in European history. "He just knew all that stuff, he just knew it!" Vernice was making up for loss of the Rhodes. On March 10, 1935, he offered his fraternity pin and they were engaged.

The concerns of his emotional life spilled over into his intellectual. His academic and creative work over the next five years would find him attempting to affirm a set of values contrary to modernist culture. It would also show how very conscious he was of his own personal and creative vulnerability as "dreamer" and "idealist." He learned that bright vision had to be wrested out of negation.

Throughout his senior year he was reading in modern philosophy and began to fashion a severe critique of twentieth-century culture in the light of what he regarded as the ideal human capability. He was attracted to the aesthetic idealism of Benedetto Croce, the intuitive vitalism of Henri Bergson, the voluntaristic idealism of Josiah Royce. Isn't Mind a force more powerful than the world of unapprehended physical objects? But he was also a critical student of idealism and didn't find anyone holding the key to it all.

Royce's Infinite Knower, for instance, he found a dead-beat egoist. This so-called Knower knows that we humans know very little, knows that seeming evils like earthquakes and plagues are part of a larger design, and knows that It will go on knowing when we mortals are gone.

Ross has some objections that are typical of his philosophical reasoning once he gets into gear. "I fail to see how good becomes triumphant over evil by the simple fact that it exists forever in suspension with evil in the mind of an Infinite Knower who, by Royce's own admission, creates neither the good nor the evil and who does nothing to realize the triumph of the one over the other except insofar as both are eternally present to the Infinite Consciousness. If it be argued, as Royce would appear to argue, that the good being always present is always triumphant, so also the evil, always present, is also always triumphant. We have simply a description of the world as we know it. . . . For ourselves, our whole religious enjoyment [according to Royce] must be in the knowledge that in God all our problems are solved. They are solved not for us, but for *Him!* . . . Royce's religious precepts seem pitifully inadequate to maintain the triumph of good in a world where the worst evils are not those that we overcome within ourselves but those that destroy, enslave, murder, and ravage human beings without their consent."

Ross sought a religious philosophy warmer and less notional, with its optimism grounded more firmly in human will and full acknowledgment of the evil that engulfs the planet.

He distrusted the way idealism makes a Taj Mahal out of the solitary ego, collapsing into solipsism. He found Poe's couplet a night-marish possibility: "Is all that we see and seem / But a dream within a dream?" The idealists don't sufficiently bother themselves with the fact that there are other minds in the world.

Whatever its inadequacies, he also saw idealism as the most eligible metaphysical tool for undercutting the spirit of the age, which he blandly termed "materialistic." As someone who delighted in flesh and the natural world, he wasn't hostile to matter, nor was he targeting Marxism or atomism. He meant consumerism, unenlightened capitalism, and industrial blight.

Such weighty issues should be reflected in art, he thought, and he was beginning to feel that modernist culture—art, music, and literature—is symptomatic of what ails us where it should be offering a therapy. It retreats from the public into the solitary ego and a world of private symbols. Contrary to intent, it fails to communicate our collective myths and history. Modernist culture is out of touch with the planet.

Under Stith Thompson, the great folklorist uncomfortably lodged for the time being in the English department, he studied twentieth-century poetry, and when he wrote a term essay in the fall of 1934 he selected not Eliot, Pound, or Yeats, but Stephen Vincent Benét. *John Brown's Body* points the way to a modern American epic not yet written, he thinks. Benét's effort is "a magnificent failure"—magnificent in its telling of the Civil War, the energy and flexibility of its verse, its mélange of "lyric, ballad, elegy, and even prose," and "an awareness of vast issues." But it's a failure in its prolixity, lack of progressive unity, and inability to leave anything out.

If *John Brown's Body* is merely experimental, a "more classic talent" might revitalize the epic. The Civil War remains the most likely subject for a truly great American epic, and "the huge energies of our modern industrial America" could also serve. To talk this way is, in his mind, to be less the cultural reactionary than the prophet. He didn't confess to Thompson that he had in mind to draft this epic himself.

Well, can we know for sure that blind Homer was older than twenty? He did tell Professor Stephenson in Advanced Composition that he'd like to write an epic poem, or possibly a play or two. The professor said he didn't care for poetry and to write plays instead. So

Ross Lockridge obliged and spent a good part of his senior year writing plays and scenarios.

Most of these, in variations on the theme of abandonment, portray Ross-figures whose Vernice-figures are endangered by Hornbostel-figures. In a three-act farce entitled *Metchnikoff,* the hero spouts a liberal free-love philosophy based on a theory of sex and the unconscious—a theory severely tested when he hears a false report that his loving, patient wife has taken a lover. He resolves on suicide through lethal injection of diphtheria germs, and goes through the motions only to learn that his lab assistant has substituted a placebo. "I insist on dying! I insist I am full of deadly germs! Can't a man kill himself without some booby coming along and spoiling the scheme?" "But you have all the glory of the gesture," replies the assistant, "without the necessity of dying!"

Except for the Susanna character in his novel, this absurd play is Ross's only explicit handling of suicide.

A more sober effort is *Wanderfell: A Tragedy in Four Acts.* Thought by others a brilliant clairvoyant poet, Wanderfell "tends to play feverishly and strangely over the objects of experience." Impoverished in Greenwich Village, he's writing a series of poems, *The Illuminations,* that purports to look deeply into the diseased unconscious. He comes to the attention of a literary mogul who invites him to move into his townhouse. It's a House of Modernism. There he meets the lovely Estella, the generous Vernice-like daughter of the mogul. He prefers her over Marcia, an exotic intellectual who may take some shadings from Marion Monico. He falls in love when Estella is about to abscond with suave Clappington, the Hornbostelesque figure.

Estella is the only one in the house capable of love, and she also has a better instinct about literature than these modernists. She doesn't like *The Illuminations*—a cranky obscure pessimistic work (with a title preempted by Rimbaud)—and encourages Wanderfell to write something that would communicate more wholesomely with the human race. He burns *The Illuminations* but in the sorry imbroglio that follows, Estella's father mistakes her in the dark for the faithless Marcia and shoots her. The good lose out in this perverted modernist culture.

Ross wrote a detailed scenario for this tragedy but finished only the first act because it was sounding too much like *The Importance of*

Being Earnest. He did write a fragment to be used in Act Three that adds a dimension here. Wanderfell tells Raggleton, his Correllian sidekick, that he has looked into the mirror and seen an "imposter."

"All those little dreams, those fantastic visions, those illuminations—they vanish—they are nothing. They were reared by conceit to seem a massive edifice, they took color from the brush of imagination, they became stupendous things." But he sees them now as "the hobgoblins of a sick imagination. The great thing, Raggleton, is to live in other people, in all people. The man who digs down into himself shuts the door of his mind, pulls down the blinds of his conceit, and turns off the light of reason, is in a prison—nay, more—a madhouse."

Like many driven spirits, Ross Lockridge wondered from time to time whether he too was an imposter. He knew enough to supplement any presumed talent with hard work and strategy. And he confronted the threat of isolation and egoism early on—writers can perish in their pride. The assumption of privileged vision—of idealism—risks its own pathology.

In Benét he found a precursor whose influence would only dwindle as the century wore on. He would soon find a greater one in Whitman, who was, however, no story-teller.

His alma mater didn't judge him an imposter. On June 8, 1935, with 25.5 credit hours of A-plus making up for that B at the Sorbonne, Ross Lockridge graduated with the highest undergraduate grade average ever recorded at Indiana University, a 4.04. In today's climate I fear that such a student would be recommended for psychological counseling.

~

In late spring of 1935, he enrolled in summer graduate courses and took a job as secretary in the English department during a period when Agnes Elpers, legendary secretary, was away. Thanks to his father he possessed uncommon secretarial skills. He had a toothache and sore throat but didn't let that stop him from carrying filing cabinets up and down the staircase in the old chemistry building where the English department was forced to hole up.

He tried to run off the sore throat at the track field, but it worsened and he was confined to bed. A local doctor suspected something contagious, so when Vernice visited she spoke to him through the screen of a first-floor window where he was lying. It had a hole so they could touch fingers. Declaring himself recovered within a couple of weeks, he was carrying a new gramophone into the house one afternoon when he collapsed.

His uncle, Dr. Robert Peters, was called down from Indianapolis, saw that Ross's hands were peeling, and diagnosed scarlatina, a mild form of scarlet fever. He discovered significant heart damage. A terrified Vernice was told the valves were "sloshing around." For the next three months he was flat on his back. A cardiologist has rediagnosed it for me and believes it was minimally scarlet fever, not scarlatina, and possibly rheumatic fever.

This was a new kind of challenge. Malcolm found his friend not depressed but bloody impatient to get moving again. But there were times early on, as he briefly records in a notebook, when he thought he was going to die—as did his doctors in the early stages.

This was somewhat more literal an imitation of his beloved Keats than he had bargained for. Holding as best he could to his sense of identity and purpose, he gave way in faint script to feelings not expressed to Vernice, Elsie, or Malcolm. "There's a dead man in the house. Who? I am he. Illusion was my life. The illusion gone I am no better than dead——." But he counters: "Cheer yourself, old man. Buckle your belt about you and start again." Perhaps he can still find "the courage to sustain the magnificent dream."

The dreams were more likely to be nightmares, of which he recorded one. "The singular dream of the colossal stone figures standing out of the water of the underground stream as I in the boat swept swiftly by them & finally went into the air at an incredible speed to find myself against a huge female figure leaning down, built out of some unfathomable upper vault of air. Feeling that I must be dead at last."

He kept the agony to himself. Vernice, Elsie, and others found him cheerful and uncomplaining. Vernice took the school year off, visiting daily after her hours at the bookstore, and Elsie stopped her own career in its tracks, giving up teaching and doctoral work to nurse her son back to health.

His illness would become the central metaphor of the epic poem he'd begin in 1938. But he didn't fully describe the interior experience of it, my mother says, until he wrote *Raintree County,* where the hero lies close to death of an infection in a Washington, D.C. military hospital. John Shawnessy was variously diagnosed but "knew that something more profound and terrible had happened to him. His fever fevered everything he saw. . . . His morale seemed good. He complained little, made no undue demands on the help, seemed to be a rather sweet-tempered, soft-spoken person."

But "from his own point of view, Johnny went down into hell and stayed there for weeks. No one knew it, because he never told anyone, but there were whole days when it seemed to him that he was dying. Death was approaching all the time, touching with a gradual hand all around him. . . . Whether he died now or not, he knew what death was, and he knew that he could never wholly escape it. Death was an impersonal thing that happened to a person who was alone . . . He knew also the awakenings at night, when he was covered with cold sweat and his heart beat hard and swift, as if to run its course and expire in a rush of failing palpitations. At such times, he wanted to talk with someone or have someone rise up and say, 'Johnny, you're all right. It's probably just the air in here. I feel it too.' He wanted people to lie to him about his condition, as if words were facts. . . . He came to love the beautiful, holy sound of the word 'normal' . . . And so the days went by, and Corporal Johnny Shawnessy lingered on while that impersonal thing, his body, tried to make up its mind whether to live or die. As for himself, he had never had a more terrible passion to live, to stand up, to walk, to move about in sunlight, to touch human hands, to laugh, to smoke a cigar, to mosey downtown. It seemed absurd that the affair was going to be decided for him by a hundred some-odd pounds of sweating clay. . . .

"Some of [his] dreams had a frustrate sweetness as when it seemed to him that he was back in the old Academy Building and he saw the cool, pale form of Nell Gaither standing in the ivied yard and looking at him from eyes alive with love and tenderness. Sometimes too he dreamed that he lay sick in his bed at home. He hoped that now he would be really healed, that she who had given life to him once could give it again. The irregular, vivid face of his mother Ellen Shawnessy bent over him in his dream, a lock of loose hair hung from under her cap, her eyes were full of belief in his recovery. He felt that here was a great strength from which he could draw inexhaustibly."

Other dreams were nightmares as he fought reptiles while sinking down into a swamp.

"As Corporal Johnny Shawnessy lay there chattering, sore, weak, soaked in a cold sweat, there came to him with more than usual vividness the memory of the younger Johnny of before the War, the boy who had believed that he would one day be a greater poet than Shakespeare, a faster runner than Flash Perkins, a lover for whom waited the most passionate of women, a hero for whom the Republic reserved her wildest applause. He remembered this Johnny—his strong young arms and legs, his inexhaustible vitality, his happy smile, his strong competitive heart; and then he thought of the miserable shrunken creature who lay in a makeshift building a thousand miles from home, perhaps dying."

During his convalescence Ross listened to music, read, wrote dark lyric poems and, with his mother, Burma Shave commercials, none of which ever won a contest. He asked his friend Ted Grisell, Rivervale chum, to bring over some books on chess, which he took up in a serious way, playing Grisell and Professor Robert Moore, faculty sponsor of the IU chess team. Moore wrote that Lockridge "didn't know the pieces or the moves or the rules at the beginning of October; next April he was nearly the best player in the state."

Elsie was ever optimistic and nurturing. Ross was listening to an exciting basketball game one day when Vernice became alarmed at his rapid heartbeat—but Elsie, never skittery, calmed both of them down. "Now everything is going to be just fine."

He had visitors, including the paternal Professor Carter and the forgiving Mary Eloise Humphreys. Later in his convalescence Elsie paid seven dollars for a puppy, which Ross named Skirtie for the white fur on her haunches. Teaching her tricks, he felt through her a vicarious vitality and came to love the dog.

As he began to improve, he could make his way up and down the stairs with Vernice, sitting down and taking them slowly one at a time, catching his breath. The nursing of mother and fiancée helped bring him around. To Vernice he wrote a simple quatrain:

"Dream of the Flesh of Iron"

I lay in fever and sore distress;
You came in dreams and soothed away the pain.
Calm in the presence of your loveliness,
I was ennobled and took heart again.

During the year of illness and convalescence he read a dictionary from start to finish, making a list of words he might use. His favorite was "callipygian." He kept a list of books read—a miscellany of seventy-six titles including *Anthony Adverse, Archy and Mehitabel, Gone with the Wind, Main Street, The Titan, The New Harmony Movement, Point Counter Point, The Last Puritan, The Physiology of Mind,* some histories of philosophy, some books on chess, and some French titles. By his standards this was reading to kill time. But he read an obscure 1931 French novel, Serge Simon Held's *La Mort du fer*—"The Death of Iron"—that would bear strange fruit a few years later.

He also planned a novel that would, at least in part, answer to the vision he had in Paris. It was "conceived when I believed that I had not long to live and scarcely enough time even to write it." He would foist his own life onto the person of an uncle he had as a child seen on occasion in Straughn but never really known, Elsie's older brother, Ernest Vivian Shockley. After a distinguished career at IU, where he proved that the Shockley side of the family could excel in both academics and sports, this uncle served in Italy with the YMCA near the end of the Great War. Thereafter as the YMCA regional director in Rome he ran a big operation with eight chauffeurs, tried to make himself unpopular with the Pope, and wrote warm letters home to his mother, Emma Shockley, signed "With all my best love, Your dearest first born boy Ernest." He spoke fluent Italian, French, German, and even Latin, and played the piano, mandolin, violin, and guitar. Returning to the United States in 1921, he became a history and economics professor at Grove City College in Pennsylvania, where he worked himself to death by 1924 at the age of 45.

A few days before he died—technically, of pneumonia—Dr. Ernest Shockley wrote his mother in Straughn: "I seem to [be] busy every minute of the day & too many of the night. I have 304 enrollments in my 5 classes, with 156 in U.S. history alone." He had collaborated on that three-volume classic, *Courts and Lawyers of Indiana,* but otherwise left little to suggest a great literary career.

Since Ross had no intimate connection with his dead uncle, he could shape him to his own will—so he made numerous notes for a novel with a most unpromising working title, *Ernest.*

It was to be a tragedy taking its cue from *David Copperfield,* a novel of development; Browning's *Childe Roland to the Dark Tower Came,* a nightmarish quest romance; and Wagner's *Tristan und Isolde,* especially the great agonized prelude. He would seek additional inspiration in his brother's stories, his own letters from Paris, and his Grandfather Shockley's poems. The chapter titles conformed to Ross's own life to that point: "The Unremembered," "The Street of Elms," "Borderland," "State University," "The Old World, Paris!!," "Pastoral Interlude," "Fever!!," and the chapter he had not yet lived, "Being Who?"

The "great flaw" in Ernest's character is his "inordinate competitive spirit," which will drive him to his death. He pursues the heroine Estella, but is everywhere dogged by "his immortal enemy—Parsons"! (Jack Parsons might have hesitated to engage the Battle of the Tux in Paris had he known he'd be thus mythologized.) Thinking of Vernice, Ross will portray "the sweetheart friend—the one he abandoned, betrayed, yet always came back to—& with what a sigh of shuddering relief the last time." His novel will be an "exposition of the great mystery of sex," played out in the pastoral Indiana landscape, especially Rivervale.

But "the great emotions, passions, etc which [Ernest] felt & hoped to translate in language—killed him at last. This is the great tragedy of the book . . . from love to love, from despair to despair to the inevitable gaping grave." He imagines the protagonist playing a game of chess with Death. And yet Ernest "dies with an absolute conviction of immortality—a conviction based upon the impossibility of conceiving himself as reduced to nothing."

He wrote to his old Paris roommate Jack Crane while convalescing. He was now inclined to see some truth in Crane's dark argument. Crane replied, "Your illness and unhappiness—I don't exaggerate, surely!—dropped you smack into things that had best be learned gradually. But of this much I am sure: that from all that you have gone through will come much good, and that with your sensibility and your poetry you will come to something very worth having."

For his part, Crane had decided the best ethical view is tactically to assume we have some power over our own lives, because the very belief shapes a world in which we can better live, whereas "the static and amoral pliability inherent in pessimism" leaves us impotent. This supportive talk from his one-time philosophic rival was appreciated.

His suffering changed him. Certainly his track days were over, and he would never fully regain his physical strength. To many he seemed quieter and more reflective. He had now internalized the reality of death as a personal matter, quite beyond the aesthetics of cemeteries or something that can happen to somebody else, even a brother.

In May of 1936, he was well enough to get back to work for his father, who was gathering materials for a book on New Harmony, the nineteenth-century Indiana utopia.

Doing his father's business was perilous in more ways than one. He wrote Vernice about the new speed record his father set for the Bloomington to Indianapolis course. "As soon as he hit the city limits, Dad began to punish the accelerator . . . He gestured vaguely with either right or left hand, delivering no doubt a commencement address to some unseen audience," a lifelong habit at the wheel. When they barely missed two cars while passing a truck, he protested and his father replied: " 'Do you think I haven't been driving for years? I see those cars.' . . . My pulses went gallop, gallop, gallop, gallop, but Dad just went right on with the commencement address, unperturbed. . . . On the straightaways Dad got that poor old Plymouth to run over 80 miles per hour. . . . After about forty minutes of this kind of thing there was a big jolt, a lot of noise, a vision of some street car conductors with white faces putting on the brakes, then a big jerk, and there we were sitting in front of the State House, while Dad composedly got out of the car and said, 'Well, Scuffie, we'll have to get down to business now.' "

Scuffie worked that week on twenty-six packets of old manuscripts dealing with the twenty-six original members of the Minerva Society, the women's salon in New Harmony. His task was to "brush the mould off" and write in effect an obituary of each. So far he had "embalmed 13 of them."

His way of silently challenging his father's authority was the satiric voice, which originated, I think, in filial dynamics.

No longer simply his father's amanuensis but his ghost writer, Ross adopted his father's voice and prose style, with only the suggestion of a more elegant syntax or more critical sensibility. Of the nine chapters that eventually made up *The Old Fauntleroy Home*, Ross Junior drafted chapters three through eight plus a hundred-line "Salutation" in blank verse, for two hundred dollars, to be saved up for his forthcoming marriage. He was acknowledged in the preface. His father went over the draft and, wherever his son had written of "the communistic experiment in New Harmony," substituted "the community experiment in New Harmony."

Rarely, a hint of subversive satire does emerge, as when Ross Junior writes that the poets of the Minerva Society "indited lace-like images of pastoral love and fastidious word-traceries in nocturnal church-yards."

The metaphor of this volume is to look at New Harmony's history from the perspective of the Old Fauntleroy Home, across whose porch an indefatigable parade of local characters had marched. The occupant at the time, seventy-eight-year-old Miss Mary Emily Fauntleroy, wanted some people not mentioned "in my book." "Their residence in New Harmony brought to it no credit, their removal no loss. . . . *Nothing more need be said of them*." And furthermore, "it is audacious in Louise [a local resident] to *inject herself* and her childish schoolgirl compositions in my book." Ross Senior was also reprimanded for sending the manuscript to a local authority for a reading. "For the manuscript of my book of my home to be sent to some one to criticize with out my *knowledge* or *consent* or *presence*. Mr Lockridge I feel you were thoughtless and feel you made a grave error."

He replied that she should understand it was *his* book, written for the New Harmony Memorial Commission, and that she shouldn't take him for her amanuensis. "I cannot conceive of myself as an amanuensis. I have had an excellent amanuensis in the person of my son, Ross Jr., but I am sure I would make a funny-looking amanuensis for anybody." She returned his letter with indignant scribbles all over the margins.

The book's dedication to Miss Fauntleroy, together with a campy photograph of her sitting at Jane Dale Owen Fauntleroy's harp in Minerva parlor, made amends. But paying off the censor didn't mean the book would be a bold examination of the New Harmony experiment. Ross Senior had his own internal censor. Certainly no mention is made of the legendary rumor that Father George Rapp, original founder of Harmonie on the banks of the Wabash, had taken a knife and castrated to death his own son John for breaking the chastity vow.

It was "the melancholy duty of the historian to record" that Robert Owen's experiment in communal living, following the departure of George Rapp, had flopped. But Ross Senior still wished to speak of an "afterglow," as the Owens and Fauntleroys and other remarkable characters kept this eccentric community going to the present day. Elsie and Ross Senior regarded the Minerva Society as a landmark in the history of feminism.

The Old Fauntleroy Home—its outer cover beautifully embossed with a golden raintree and historic maps of the town inside—didn't prove a landmark book. When I visited the home in 1987, the curator regretted never having seen a copy.

~

Vernice Baker would never forget how in late summer of 1936 her fiancé ran down the bank on the north side of the chemistry building toward the waiting car, exclaiming to her and his mother that he'd been given a teaching job in the English department. The five hundred dollars he'd be making that year, along with a green light from his uncle, the family physician, meant they could go ahead with marriage plans.

He quickly became known as an enthusiastic teacher, often seen walking about campus in a hurry, breezing into the classroom at the last minute, color uncoordinated—yet relaxed in his presentation, sometimes looking out the window, his feet on the desk while he talked. He was also very demanding, had a passion for literate punctuation, drew heavily on his historical erudition, and didn't win his popularity through his grading. A representative slice of final grades: C+ F B- B C+ B C+ D D F.

During the next three years he'd teach as many as four classes a semester in composition and literature for $125 per course, each class averaging over thirty students and meeting three times a week with weekly papers. Always rigorous in time management, he did his grading efficiently and never complained to Vernice, even when stuck with remedying the English of a score of subliterate men housed on Henderson Street. Such forbearance wasn't passed along to his progeny.

With Malcolm now at the University of Chicago, Ross reconstituted The Four Musketeers with a new membership—graduate students Henry Remak, Leo Dowling, and Dan Sherwood—and directed a series of skits at Le Cercle Français, where he played the fencing master in *Le Bourgeois Gentilhomme,* leaping about the stage and thrusting his foil to warm applause. He and Mademoiselle Billant, faculty sponsor, carried on intimate discussions in French that many others could only watch in exasperated envy.

He was also president of the Chess Club. Robert Sturgeon, a younger student on the team, was struck at his powers of concentration—"it was absolute, deep! When he played chess, as with other things, there was nothing else going on in his mind but *that!*" He won every competitive match for the IU team over the next few years, except one. An opponent from Indianapolis had developed a strategy he called "The Indiana Haymaker," whereby he sacrificed half his pieces only to produce a checkmate out of nowhere. Forewarned, Ross sat down confidently, decided on a fancy maneuver of his own, and was drubbed in a flash. Professor Moore, who was furious whenever his own son lost at chess, remembered that Ross "made a half-hearted apology, but he continued to show how he would have won by his own subtle method."

The IU English department emphasized old-style literary history and was hostile to the formalist analysis of Yale and Chicago. In his graduate work Ross pretty much tailored his work to expectation, though he turned out more of it than other students.

Like all English departments, Indiana's had its share of eccentrics. The popular bald Southerner Will Taliaferro Hale told his students they were not permitted to indulge in anything smacking of "interpretation" or "literary criticism." Ross obliged with an essay on interpolated chapters in *Pickwick Papers* and received a grade of

96999324925. Edwina Patton obliged with one on clothing in *Vanity Fair* and received an 835026481672. Professor Hale's code was itself resistant to interpretation; no student ever cracked it.

Ross did some more personal work, writing a series of essays for Professor Carter in the spring of 1937 that expressed his emerging view of literature and language. One of these, "Lockridge's Leaden Treasury," is cast as a parody of Aristotle's *Poetics*. He proposes to "treat of bad modern poetry, its nature and its kinds; and the manner of its avoidance. . . . We, who perfectly recognize the defects in the poetry of one hundred years ago, are too often hoodwinked by a legion of literary fakirs in our own time."

Arguing that badness is not only privation but a positive force in its own right, he divides bad poets into several groups—the Pretty Poetic Spirits, the Fiery Declaimers, the Garrulous Word-Weavers, the Clever Journalists, the Humble Vernacularists, the Mawkish Sentimentalists, the Morning Paper Moralizers, and the Hocus Pocus Mystifiers. Illustrations are drawn from Edwin Parker, James Randall, Kipling, Swinburne, Barton Rees Pogue, Eugene Field, Edgar Guest, and e. e. cummings. He reserves his keenest satire for the Mystifiers. The "true poet is never deliberately obscure."

In another essay for Carter, he's become more critical than he was in Paris of the Romantics. He now dislikes Victor Hugo's "tendency to reduce all things to symbol." The Battle of Waterloo in *Les Misérables* is "a glorious adventure, a romantic fiction—but it is scarcely a real battle in which men are horribly mangled by cannon and rifle shot, in mud and water." If we are to write in symbols, we must get something into them besides nobility.

He's drawn to the idea that art has "renewed its strength at that inexhaustible source of pure energy that Tolstoy loves—the earth and its simplest forms of life. . . . While we scoff at the practical applications of Tolstoy's theory, it is yet an undeniable fact that men do, like the giant Antaeus, take renewed energy from a return to the earth."

He prefaces this with the admission that his own experience with nature, as family gardener, has been a struggle with weeds and rodents. Neighbors have confirmed this: moles always ravaged the Lockridge yard, and driven to desperate measures, Ross was sometimes seen hooking a vacuum cleaner hose to the car's exhaust pipe and ruefully asphyxiating the poor creatures in their holes.

His literary judgments come from silent comparisons of previous writers with the writer he hopes to become. He sees himself as growing beyond Romanticism and yet out of step with Modernism, seeking a more elemental and direct literary form.

His most engaging short piece, written on his twenty-third birthday, is "Rhapsody in Words," a comic dream allegory based on *The Divine Comedy* that gives his search a linguistic grounding. It resonates with the later quest of John Shawnessy. Gazing on his dictionary one evening, the narrator becomes morose thinking of how words are nothing but "an arbitrary convention and, in themselves, utterly devoid of meaning. They are a gibbering noise, a ludicrous cluck made by clicking the tongue, the teeth, and the palate adroitly together," or they are "ink-monsters," mere black marks on paper.

Dozing off, he finds himself before a yawning portal where a quaint old man in a faded black suit, but somehow authoritative, introduces himself as the narrator's old Dictionary. Like Emma Shockley at the dinner table, he pounces on the narrator's use of pleonastic expressions, "rooted to the spot" and "natural talent," and other blunders, and inducts him into Wordland.

"As I gazed into this pit, I saw fantastic forms that were also sounds, so strangely does the primeval air of dream—a region of vast emotions and archaic wishes—blend the different worlds of sense and thought. It did not at that moment seem strange to me that a word could go about clothed in shape, strangely human, or that the mere sound of vocables and consonants hissing together should be accompanied by a sensuous content or image of the word." He encounters several word families—onomatopoeic, musical, cacophonous, Latinate, grotesque, degenerate, erotic, misused.

The Dictionary informs him that words, though they may have the appearance of mere conventions, "are only valuable as keys to some magical region that is not far from the heart of reality." Behind a colossal closed door "is the answer that all the poets have sought and all the literary critics. There may be found the secret of the very source of words and symbols and conventions in the heart of reality itself."

The old man is only the custodian of this door and cannot open it. But the narrator is seized with a hunger to enter, and smites it resoundingly—only to awaken to the sound of his alarm clock, still staring at the old tattered dictionary.

This allegory has roots in medieval theology and Romantic poetics. Instead of an arbitrary sign, a word is potentially the incarnation of thought, and capable of taking us to the interior of its represented world. The word is a *living thing*. This is a poet's faith and it was Ross Lockridge's—in the face, he knew, of theoretical objections from most modern linguists.

He was completing something else on his twenty-third birthday, which Vernice wouldn't hear about until she read of it in the newspaper. His secrecy here was fraught with implication. During the evenings of a single week in April, 1937, he tossed off *A Pageant of New Harmony* in seventeen scenes of blank verse, some thirteen hundred lines. Following the synopsis of his father, who engineered this job through the New Harmony Memorial Commission, he casually orchestrated a cast of 250, portraying the story of New Harmony from Tecumseh's stand—

> *The Great Spirit gave this island not to one tribe*
> *But to all tribes to roam whither they willed.*
> *He placed the white men on the other side*
> *Of the Big Water. They were not content*
> *To keep their own. One day they came across*
> *The dancing waves in great white-winged canoes,*
> *Stepped on our shores and settled in our land.*
> *Since then the white men, greedy and depraved,*
> *Have driven us little by little back.*
> *We left the seashore, and we left the hills*
> *Behind the shore, and now at length are come*
> *To the Great Lakes.* We can retreat no more—

to the building of the Labyrinth—

> *With mystic vision, Father Rapp*
> *Designed a labyrinth, a wondrous coil*
> *Of winding paths enclosed in shrubbery.*
> *Whoever entered there might wander long*

With endless divagation round and round
As though by fairy wand bewitched, until
By happy chance, reaching the inmost round,
He found a temple, rude with shaggy bark—

to the coming of the Owenites and the Boatload of Knowledge—

Through trackless forests where the catamounts
Still screamed by night, into a country where
But few could read or write, they made their way—

to the founding of New Harmony institutions and the rapid decline
of the community in the absence of Robert Owen—

Rascals and thieves
Lived on the labor of the virtuous.
Even the honest and industrious
Were loath to work where others were at ease.
Pigs ran in the street, and discord was
The leading pastime in New Harmony—

But then the "Afterglow," with founding of the Workingmen's Institute, the Minerva Society—and let's not forget the Murphy
Endowment!—and then the zoologist Thomas Say's planting of the
raintrees—

And there
The first gate-trees grown in America
Took root and sprang aloft. And now, behold!
The trees of Golden Rain, as they were called
In far-off China, blossom everywhere.
Each year, when summer with her dulcet airs
Brings on the sylvan pageantries of June,
We hold this festival. It ushers in
The Season of the Rain of Gold.

His father interpolated some lines on Miss Fauntleroy that show he
didn't know blank verse requires ten syllables.

Ross Junior also wrote a seventy-one-page adaptation "for Purposes of COLOR FILMING," because the New Harmony folk had arranged for one Captain Hubbard of Muncie, Indiana—said to be an accomplished cinematographer—to make a silent film version. And for those not partial to blank verse, he wrote a prose narration to be read at screenings. His "Foreword in Explanation to Directors of Film" would have been suitably penned to D. W. Griffith and Cecil B. DeMille. For his threefold effort, Ross agreed to be paid fifty dollars, another welcomed increment to his marriage fund.

Rehearsals began as soon as the script arrived in New Harmony, and pageant fever was in the air. The local newspaper reported proudly that someone from California had booked a room in the hotel, enclosing a five-dollar bill. On June 20, three thousand spectators made a pilgrimage to New Harmony for the great Pageant. When they asked where in town it was to be held, they were surprised to hear "in the cemetery."

The 250 actors were all in place at the old Rappite Cemetery, where 230 people are buried without markers. In the audience were Elsie, Lillian, and Ross Senior, along with Vernice Baker and her parents, for the earnest choreography over the graves, the singing and declamation, and the planting of the raintree. The local paper thereafter raved and said the Pageant was destined to become New Harmony's Oberammergau. "Ross Lockridge, Jr. gave to the world a masterpiece of historic composition."

Ross Lockridge, Jr. had preferred not to come. Just as he hadn't mentioned he was writing it, he didn't say much to Vernice about why he preferred not to see it, except that he wasn't feeling very well. Vernice knew that her fiancé kept many things to himself. He was a private person.

I suspect he acted from dread of a large-scale fiasco, made to his father's order, to which he had lent his own name. He was ashamed of it. And as a no-show he also tacitly signaled his father that this was not his own work. He dissociated his own career as writer from his father's as impresario. He would never see his pageant, produced many times over the years. He had dealt with failure directly in his illness, in his unfinished play *Wanderfell*, in the account of his father breaking up Charlotte Wray Lockridge's house. Now, in the first real exposure of his work before a public, he distanced himself from potential failure in the most literal way—he wouldn't be around for it.

~

On July 11, 1937, Ross Lockridge and Vernice Baker walked together down the aisle of the First Christian Church. (In May they had sadly watched the First Methodist Church burn.) They exchanged vows in a simple Depression-days ceremony. Ross had saved up six hundred dollars, while Vernice had saved fifty cents, had purchased a new coat, and had already visited the dentist. She wore a white organdy dress made by her sister Clona, and Ross wore a dapper white suit.

At the reception they visited the bedside of Emma Shockley, now living in the High Street house. She said she hoped they'd be as happy as she and Mr. Shockley had been.

Off they went in the better family car, sabotaged with the customary legends in white paint. Ross had taken a cottage called "Who's Next?" on Lake Manitou in northern Indiana for a week. On the way they tried to remove the paint with gasoline, and were relieved the next morning to find it had washed off in a rainstorm. They began a pleasurable eight-week honeymoon that was Ross's only respite of any duration for the remainder of his life. They went fishing and boating, Vernice tried out some cooking, and Ross practiced being lazy for a change. After the week on Lake Manitou, they spent time with relatives in other waterfront cabins and did some more fishing. One night Ross awakened from a nightmare screaming, "Watch out for the hook!"

Then they drove to Straughn for a rent-free week in the old Shockley house. They had it to themselves, in an improvement on Ross's dream of August, 1934. He had another week with his Grandfather Shockley's faded antiquities, which languished about in contrast to the rituals of honeymooning. The apple tree in the backyard furnished applesauce, they ate an awful lot of pork chops, and sang songs at dinner.

At the end of the week, Frank Shockley and Elsie Lockridge arrived to break up the house. Ross went through the Shockley library and selected books to remain in the family. He was especially pleased to have *An Illustrated Historical Atlas of Henry County, Indiana*, published in 1875.

Later that summer he and Vernice visited the famed cinematographer Captain Hubbard of Muncie and were treated to the film version of his pageant, the production values of which would make any other home movie look like Bertolucci. They did their best to be polite when some dour Rappites ran in circles double-time grinding grain. Once outside they gave way to laughter. Ross was learning that the production end of things can't be left to the producers.

The "Lake Gang"—a group of friends who often spent vacations together in northern Indiana—then asked Ross and Vernice to join them at Lake Webster. The women wanted some time alone before the men arrived, so Vernice reluctantly left Ross for a few days. He took the opportunity to visit Malcolm in Lowell, Michigan. The future physicist, now engaged to Ruth Armstrong, was working for a company that made photoelectric sorters for peanuts and coffee beans. Malcolm was pleased to hear how happy Ross was in his marriage, yet the two felt nostalgic for their old bull sessions and knew those days were pretty much over.

In early September, 1937, Vernice and Ross moved into an authentic log cabin at 612c Park Avenue in Bloomington which rented for twenty-five dollars a month. The landlord had moved it in from the country and spruced it up for the newlyweds with a thick coat of red creosote on the interior walls and floor. The place stank and there were no screens to keep out flies and the stove didn't work right and there was an icebox instead of a refrigerator and there was no heat in the morning and no hot water in the kitchen sink—and they loved it.

In the morning Ross would stick a finger from out the blankets and estimate the temperature within a degree or two, and then the two leapt out with hopes of starting a fire in the woodstove. The stench permeated everything and they called themselves "The Creosote Kids." Some mornings, faithful Skirtie walked the mile into town from the old Lockridge house to bark them out of bed.

With the money he'd saved, Ross was able to liberate Vernice from the bookstore so she could devote more time to finishing her degree. He diligently tutored her in English literature. Swamped with academic work, life became less social for both of them and Ross's writing was on temporary hold. He kept up a correspondence with Malcolm, as well as with Curt Lamorey and Marion Monico, asking them for news of the Delaware Group. He was wistful for Europe. Writing from Paris, Marion envied him his marriage and romantic log cabin, while he envied her her "academic idylls overseas" and proximity to *le Boule Mich, les pâtisseries, le Luxembourg.*

These things seemed to be moving farther and farther away from him in his new domesticity. Old friends and family members signed their guestbook over the next few months, and they gave a chili party for the Lake Gang. (The midwest convention in Depression days was either a chili or a waffle party.)

Shortly before Christmas in 1937, Emma Shockley died of a stroke. Vernice wept, but Elsie didn't, saying that weeping made it harder for departed souls to make an adjustment to the afterlife. She expected to see her mother again and said she couldn't bear life if such losses were permanent. "I have always seen all those I love *living on,*" she would write. She was a woman of powerful feelings, but from her early years these feelings—of love, sex, grief, jealousy, ambition—were identified with deep pain, and she had learned to control them.

Ross penned a eulogy, quoting from Emma's letters and her husband's poems, which he read without tears at the church in Straughn. During the thirty years of her widowhood she'd led a productive life, he said, becoming more liberal-minded and pursuing studies in art, science, literature, religion, and astronomy, even attending Oberammergau in 1930. She showed how a widow could work through grief to a full happiness. John Wesley Shockley, poet of eternal summer, awaited her, as he had written during their courtship: "Our dust must mingle together, and our souls march hand in hand forever more."

In late February, 1938, Vernice became pregnant and the two were delighted. Despite the Depression, they never considered postponing children. His early recognition of personal mortality may have contributed something. But he was also someone who needed and valued the structures of domestic life.

In the spring Vernice confronted the infamous undergraduate comps. With the excited dread of an expectant father and loving husband, Ross kept asking secretary Agnes Elpers whether the senior faculty had returned the results. Though Vernice lacked confidence about her scholarship, she passed all sections with honors. At graduation in June, Ross put on his white suit again, proudly adjusted Vernice's mortar board, and staged some pictures.

His closer friends were all out of town during these years, and Ross made a new friend in Donald Blankertz, a young instructor in the business school whose first love was poetry. He invited Ross to an all-male dinner party of spirited cynics in various disciplines. They had degrees from Harvard, Yale, and the University of Michigan, and felt somewhat déclassé in this cultural backwater. Ross seemed one Hoosier who didn't fit the mold.

Blankertz's "first reaction was that Percy Bysshe Shelley had come to dinner. I was at quick amaze at this young, handsome fellow. He was a remarkable conversationalist—far, far better than I could ever hope to be. He was never obtrusive, but when encouraged flowed as a freshet with English as it was meant to be spoken and so seldom is. His laugh had bells in it." Ross saw this group of intellectuals off and on, and arranged for Blankertz's cosmopolitan poetry to be published in *Folio*, the IU literary magazine he helped edit but did not himself contribute to.

For all Ross's exuberant talk when encouraged, Blankertz found the young instructor somewhat shy, humble about his accomplishments to date, and very secretive about his literary ambitions.

In the summer of 1938, after a trip to Kentucky with Vernice, Elsie, and Lillian, Ross drafted some preliminary chapters of the novel that would merge his own life with his Uncle Ernest's and feature his mother prominently in the cast of characters. He also started work with Professor Russell Noyes on his master's thesis, *Byron and Napoleon*.

A great enthusiast for the Romantic poets, Noyes was at thirty-seven a tall, handsome, confident New Englander—Greater Boston's first Eagle Scout—with a degree from the University of Massachusetts at Amherst in landscape architecture and a Harvard doctorate in English. He surmised that Ross could write and organize on his own, and turned him loose on the topic Ross thought up. Vernice had taken a course with Noyes, her favorite professor, getting a respectable B.

Since she would be entering the final stages of pregnancy, they moved out of the chilly log cabin in September, and, for economy's sake, moved back to the Lockridge house.

Vernice wept when they left the cabin. This had been their first home, and it was filled with good memories. The marriage was loving and playful, without quarreling or jealousy. It wasn't a marriage that seemed to require negotiations or analysis.

Ross stopped work on the preliminary draft of his novel—I think it was difficult for him to write about his mother when she was in the next room—and began work on another item he'd listed on his voyage home from France, an epic poem.

Vernice's periods of gestation would always parallel Ross's, and on November 28, 1938, she gave birth to Ernest Hugh Lockridge. Like most Ernests, my brother wouldn't appreciate the name, but my father was tone-deaf to any humor in it. This was homage to his dead uncle, as "Hugh" was to Vernice's beloved father.

Throughout this period of routine daily life, academic and domestic—in which time and movement seemed to slow—Ross Lockridge kept his ambition alive, but he didn't discuss it with anybody, including his wife. To talk about it would be to spend it fruitlessly. He read for what he could learn from other writers, not letting himself become anybody's acolyte. He would, Blankertz said, "keep things close to the vest so that Stephen Crane's seven mad gods that rule the sea would not rule his work."

Working on Byron and Napoleon was a fruitful compromise of the writer's vision and academic tasks, because here were two figures who bestrode the world like colossi, whose ambitions were played out relentlessly on the world stage, whose lives "belong to an epic poetry of human achievement." But his is a critical study, and, to the extent Ross may have identified with Byron, it is self-critical.

His politics, quiescent up to this time, had been inherited from his parents. In 1936, he had struck a deal with Vernice, who came from a family of Republicans. He was willing to vote for the local Republican dogcatcher if she would vote for Roosevelt. And he had written sardonic lyrics on the ironies of war:

> *René Adolphe Edouard Cali,*
> *Do you remember gay Paree?*
> *You, who were stuck with a bayonet*
> *And duly lamented in the gazette?*
> *Do you remember the midinette*
> *With the passionate eyes, petite Jeannette?*
> *René Adolphe Edouard Cali,*
> *Do you remember gay Paree?*

But with the rise of Hitler and the tragedy of the Spanish Civil War, which showed that good doesn't always prevail, he was becoming more politically inquisitive. He begins his master's thesis with a lengthy comparison of Hitler and Napoleon.

He then sets himself the task of explaining how Byron, with his revolutionary sympathies, can admire Napoleon—who has seemingly so much in common with Hitler. It's because Napoleon is still the heir to the French Revolution, still the thorn in the side of kings, still the hero of the oppressed, and Byron is pained at seeing him toppled. Napoleon *does* much of what Byron—who always claimed he'd rather be a man of action than a scribbler—can only write about.

Ross in turn admires Byron the liberal who speaks in favor of Catholic Emancipation, and Byron the revolutionist who joins the Carbonari in Italy and the Greeks in Missolonghi. His earlier hero, Keats, was too insulated from his age, he thinks.

Politics aside, Byron and Napoleon have much in common—even down to the same initials (i.e., *N*oel *B*yron)—and in describing how so, my father anatomizes the Romantic personality, which is, to a degree, his own. Both titans are driven by an egoism grounded in a "childlike" assumption of special destiny. Byron's heroes, from Childe Harold to Lara to Cain to Don Juan, are projections of various aspects of his psyche, and Napoleon himself becomes one of these. Withdrawing from his comrades to seek out cemeteries, Byron gives us "perhaps the most complete negation of the social ideal in English literature." Fatalism ironically encourages a kind of recklessness, a "careless speed"—seen in Byron's poetic composition itself, the gushing of lava that prevents an earthquake, some of it terrible verse.

Framed by a fatal destiny, these "imprudent dreamers" see themselves as handsome figures at the center of a vast stage. Napoleon's warfare is theatrical, his oratory spell-binding, and Byron has an antique Greek helmet fashioned for his voyage to Greece. Fame goes to their heads and they then discover the reverse side of it: "one moment in obscurity and the next, the thunderers of the scene, wearing the imperial velvet as if born to it. But such men create around them terrible hostilities." Ultimately they bring grief to all they touch, blighting everything in their path. They then expiate their satanic notoriety in homecomings of death.

Byron and Napoleon are testimony, though, to the public's need for the signature of creative personality. "How much of glamour would the Italian victories of Napoleon have lost had they been won by a pot-bellied, ridiculous old gentleman like the exiled Louis XVIII! How much of fascination would have gone out of *Childe Harold's Pilgrimage* if the public had discovered that its author was the withered Samuel Rogers!"

I'm a Byron scholar myself but admit to avoiding my father's 242-page screed until I set about writing this chapter. It's pretty good, I think, and should have been published at the time, and would still add something to Byron studies. But he got a rebuke from his committee, on which sat John Robert Moore, his old teacher and chess partner. Moore spent most of his life trying to prove that certain anonymous political pamphlets were written by Defoe. (Scholars now are trying to prove they weren't.) He thought there was too much interpretation in the thesis, too much talk of analogies between the two titans, and he hated the "naked grandeur," as Ross put it, of the title, *Byron and Napoleon*.

Rarely expressing anger, Ross wrote to Noyes that Moore's comments "are for the most part simply irrelevant or incorrect. I believe Dr. Moore has recently read Scott's *Life of Napoleon*, an acknowledged tissue of inaccuracies and biased interpretations."

But he himself didn't think his thesis very good, and because it would be better to have 150 than 275 pages of bad prose, he was willing to cut the first five of ten chapters, call it *The Influence of Napoleon on Lord Byron's Writings and Political Convictions*, and inter it "in the mausoleum of dead dissertations where it belongs." Noyes intervened, and Vernice retyped the longer version.

He acknowledged only two people in the preface, Russell Noyes and Vernice Baker Lockridge. I suppose it never occurred to him that these two would later marry.

Besides his own work, he had still more work coming from his father, with monetary offers he couldn't refuse. Ross Senior had in no way let up. He compiled a seven-volume local history of the entire state of Indiana, county by county, to assist in setting up roadside historical sites, for which he wrote dozens of markers. In 1939, he became director of the New Harmony Commission—agreeing to accept half-salary—and undertook to preserve the old buildings and get Hoosier folk keyed up about this historic site. He was a controversial figure down there. Miss Fauntleroy described him as a "visionary" who was good at spending other people's money, with an eye for pretty ladies.

The writer Marguerite Young was in New Harmony during summers and often went with him down to the Wabash, where they watched the sandpipers. They visited the nearby Indian mounds amid "the flowering trees, the chokecherries, the moss-covered logs, the golden atmosphere, the beautiful river." He would kick the ground and turn up arrowheads. To her, he was oracular, possessed by the spirit of place, worshipful of his youngest son, emotionally distanced from his wife, with "an eye for the exotic and romantic side of life to which he never fully yielded! He opened up New Harmony to me in a fabulous way. Nothing is so appealing as lost utopias. People cry when they go there."

He managed to get a replica built of the Rappite Labyrinth, publishing a history of labyrinths from Cretan to Hoosier for the occasion. He whipped books up more than he wrote them, and writing was always for him a pale substitute for speaking. He put enormous energies into New Harmony but had to settle for a fraction. How could they not preserve the old Rappite Tavern! He should have been listened to.

One somewhat more visionary project was to rebuild the historic Boatload of Knowledge. At a commission meeting attended by the lieutenant-governor, he brought along a boat-builder from New Albany and described with the intoxicated vision of a Noah how the keelboat could be reconstructed and the arrival of this celebrated company of Owenites reenacted. Whereupon Governor Schricker exclaimed, "Now, Ross, we're not going to do that. Why, it's the craziest thing I ever heard of!"

In the basement of the High Street house and down in the south field near the bonfire site, Ross Junior was amassing page upon page of his epic poem. His parents had no idea what he was writing—Vernice at least knew it was a long poem—and his father didn't hesitate to enlist him in two more projects. He had long nourished the idea of writing an historical novel, and had thumped one out, *Black Snake and White Rose*, a romantic tale of Miami Native Americans and white empire builders set near his childhood home on the Eel River. He portrays Native Americans in stylized terms as Rousseau's children of nature, noble but doomed by the Juggernaut of Civilization—their plight tragic but ultimately necessary. Would Scuffie write another verse prologue?

Scuffie wrote a poem about the Eel River, a river he loved. "Kenapocomoco" extends to fifty-one stanzas, and he added quatrains for each of the twenty-six chapters, and an epilogue. The river runs through cornfields,

> And as it goes it gathers up the rains
> And light brown leaves in silting multitude,
> Green river, serpent of the valley plains,
> River of snake-fish excellent for food!

Ross Senior sent the manuscript to New York houses and wasn't any more successful getting his novel published than he was in getting the state legislature to restore original Native American names to all Indiana rivers. "We feel that perhaps you have made a mistake in selecting the novel as your vehicle." Like his son, he brushed off setbacks and turned his energies elsewhere.

The other project came with a promise of two hundred dollars, with which Ross Junior would be able to finish paying off his Uncle Earl's high-interest loan for his trip abroad. As a member of the Benjamin Harrison Memorial Commission, his father arranged for him to write a family history of four Harrisons as part of the commission's official report to the United States Congress. He wrote it in five weeks the summer of 1940, basing it mostly on his father's research, and collected the money, but not without paying a price.

The ground rule coming from the commission was that nothing ill could be said about any of these Harrisons—and since Benjamin the Signer and William Henry Harrison helped suppress Native Americans, while John Scott Harrison was rather conciliatory toward slaveowners, and Benjamin Harrison was the most boring President ever elected, this assignment wasn't easy. But write it he did, deploying his father's prose style. Published under his own name as *The Harrisons*, Exhibit 2 of the Report, its 191 pages might be considered his first printed book. It was a severe compromising of his reading of history and a prostitution. He never complained to anybody, but clearly it was time to stop working for this character, his father.

That same summer he wrote in response to certain major public policy issues, such as a school board decision to terminate wrestling at Bloomington High School. His lengthy letter of protest was published in installments in two Bloomington newspapers. (His in-law Harold Mumby was wrestling coach.) The second no less pressing issue was whether the United States should get into the war, and he wrote a letter to the editor opposing isolationism.

The war was very much on his mind. He drafted a satire, "To Adolf Hitler, by An American Admirer, The First of Some Modest Proposals for Strengthening his Great Totalitarian War Machine." Concerning America's evident distaste for Hitler, "Is it not indeed a strange morality that libels as a brute the liberator of millions of Danes, Norwegians, Belgians, and Dutch from British aggression? No one but an American would mouth such an absurdity. If, with any shadow of reason, you, mein Führer, can be called a brute, then I will take my oath on it, Mussolini *is* a coward."

He wrote to the *Saturday Evening Post* about his willingness to write a series of satires around this conceit, with such installments as "A contrivance whereby the Führer can obtain the English and French navies" and "A method whereby the Führer can fertilize his fields for better crop production." Perhaps the *Post* feared its readership might not catch the irony.

That he could write this satire in the same breath and backyard as he wrote *The Harrisons* shows how fractured his writing career was becoming.

There were other disgruntlements. The dressing-down given his master's thesis was compounded by the department's awarding a position, earlier promised him, to a couple of Ph.D.'s imported from eastern schools. He'd pretty much exhausted the resources of the English department anyway and had been branching out, taking more philosophy and language courses. Beyond Latin and French, he'd learned Greek, Italian, German, and Old English. With ten hours of A-plus in Greek, and no B's this time, his grade point average for his graduate years had improved somewhat over his undergraduate—a 4.07.

Don Smalley, a Harvard doctoral candidate from northern Indiana, spoke to him about Harvard, as did Russell Noyes. And Larry Wylie was teaching at Simmons College in Boston. So Ross applied to Harvard and Yale, received fellowship offers from both on the same day, and picked Harvard.

On September 16, 1940, Lillie and Hugh Baker, Clona Nicholson, Lillian Lockridge, Elsie and Ross Senior—all very long-faced—accompanied the young family to the train station. Ross Junior wore his three-piece suit and Phi Beta Kappa key, and Vernice wore a stylish hat and flowers on her blouse. Ross would be strategically escaping his father, losing his mother, sister, and Skirtie, and perhaps finding in the East the vantage point from which to finish his poem and resume his novel. This would be Vernice's first extended period away from home.

Wife and child notwithstanding, my father later alluded to these years of his sickness and graduate work as "lost years." It seems more apt to say they were years of challenge: he'd encountered the kind of resistance out of which a writer might be made. On the *Mauretania* he vowed, half in jest, to smile little and give evidence of a new maturity upon arrival. He found out through a more severe discipline that, to be sure, the world didn't always give much to smile about. And in the sylvan south yard on High Street, this cheerful young man had been writing a book of nightmares.

~

He had begun recording his and Vernice's dreams in shorthand shortly after their return to the High Street house in the fall of 1938. Immersed in Freud, especially *The Interpretation of Dreams*, he was apparently less interested in self-analysis than in raw material for a dream epic. Only a few recorded dreams survive, all from the summer of 1939, narrated without commentary. To my father, such dreams were symbolic self-revelations. I think they at least announce his preoccupations at this time, and I apologize to his spirit for this supreme invasion of privacy.

So preoccupied with dreams themselves, he is aware of himself *as* dreamer in them. "I was trying to analyze the dream as I went along and I think also trying to wake myself up." Confronting a yellow flower left for him on his office desk, "I thought it was a phallic symbol in my dream and probably a homosexual invitation." Leaving, he encounters a group of men—the Don Blankertz confraternity—but Vernice intervenes, "and put arms around my neck." Subsequently he sees an old school acquaintance named Julie and wishes to dance with her, "also being afraid Vernice would find out about it." This low guilt threshold deprives him of Julie and he finds himself walking about campus instead, composing a poem in free verse, as if sublimating. He is self-consciously the dreamer-*poet*.

Following the departure from the Park Avenue cabin and return to his parents' house, with the birth of Ernest, there was a brief hiatus in my parents' physical relationship. Some of his dreams find his eye wandering—and Vernice herself is momentarily in the clutches of a ringmaster enclosed in a large top—but even in this dream world, as recorded in dim shorthand, he doesn't break his marital vows.

His sense of potency is instead grounded in writing. In one dream a Bloomingtonian reduced to lawnwork "would perhaps ask me to help him, or get him a job. That I would have authority after I was famous to go in anywhere and pull strings for people and get them jobs. I thought somewhere along in here . . . how famous my poem would make me." But most of these dreams find him powerless: "Tried to speak but my voice was no good—just a squeak, at which [Dr. Hale] laughed—like a little boy's."

It is often a sinister dream world threatening to the dreamer in its violence and polymorphous sexuality. Sometimes he is the potential aggressor, as when he carries a revolver into a sordid shooting parlor full of women and men with their guns removed. "When I first went in—my gun was showing & I was rather proud of it—thinking how fast I could draw, etc." This scene yields to Creighton

Avenue back in Fort Wayne—a city with a large German population—where he and his mother encounter Hitler's limousine. A bodyguard who at first appears to be a young man transposes into Hitler's wife, a "well-formed woman" on skates. "A little boy, also on skates, cuts loose & comes toward us in the street & I think he will be in the movies"—an uncanny self-projection.

In another he is in a large gymnasium, which is somehow also a theatre, where the principal actor walks around naked except for a shirt, his hairy buttocks showing, and a woman more agreeably transposes into "strawberries in a glass." He "walked through the door, knowing it to be a dream. . . . Behind me, along the floor came a little red thing, just like the head of a tumescent penis, with a little red string behind it. It was as though the penis were entering a body— . . . It came in behind me along the floor & passed me." He tries to wake himself up.

The vulnerability of women is as much dramatized as his own. That summer he and Vernice had visited Indianapolis to purchase her a new bathing suit. After some near-misses they found one and happily exited to the street at Monument Circle. Vernice wasn't used to the one-way traffic around the circle and, with her husband blocking vision to her right, stepped off the curb at North Meridian directly into the path of a speeding taxicab. Ross yanked her out of the way as the driver screeched to a halt, looking back at the terrified couple. Ross reflected on how the casual comedy can so quickly turn to death.

Thus, in one dream, "I heard an auto crash & a skidding sound. I up and ran as fast as I could in that direction. . . . I found that the girl had been picked up badly damaged . . . It appeared she was all cut up." He talks his way into the building where she is being worked over. It turns out she has only a slightly injured nose. His own relationship to her is variously father, brother, and lover. In another dream, a girl jumps off Bloomington High School with a parachute intending to land on the hedge but screams as she is carried beyond, with the dreamer looking helplessly on.

And he dreams the death of his father. "Dad died—we got word that during the night he was dead & had been treated in all the necessary undertaking manner. . . . Then this was disputed by the fact that he was walking right along with us." Rather than an elegy he composes a rhymed pastoral quatrain and is promptly attacked by a large dog. "I hit it once on the nose. Then I swung myself along a great distance—grabbed beech-tree limbs & threw the dog off." One might read this encounter with dog as a self-inflicted punishment for having wished the death of his father—or perhaps it was symbolic of his father himself, who kept *dogging* him.

These recorded dreams and probably hundreds of others that didn't survive were only one tributary to the large poem he projected. Most twenty-four-year-old poets in the history of letters are still sweating out lyrics and pastorals, not yet stepping up to epic. Keats is an exception who proves the rule—he despaired of finishing his *Hyperion.* And epic writers themselves are often modest enough not to cross national boundaries.

But Ross Lockridge conceived *The Dream of the Flesh of Iron* not as an American poem but as a vast international epic—a spiritual history of twentieth-century American and European consciousness from 1914 to the present, from the First to the beginnings of the Second World War, with a prophecy of apocalyptic destruction.

This prophecy may have been a lucky guess. Rather than epic of an era, his poem is better understood as a *psychomachia,* the history of his own internal struggle with a dark muse.

Whatever the literary merit of this unreadable 400-page poem, it's a phenomenon. He gave it a simple plot with only three principal characters, but the episodes number a hundred thirty-four, and each character has a floating identity with multiple costume changes. In yet another variation on the Ross–Vernice–Hornbostel/Parsons triangle, we now meet the Dreamer, whom the author calls Freud's "Beloved Ego."

He pursues the Beautiful One, who is the object of the Dreamer's will-to-value in a convulsive world. She has something in common with what Freud calls the "ego ideal"—an image of perfection and aspiration that begins to form in early childhood in compensation for frustration and maternal withholding. She is also an exalted Eros. The Dreamer hopes for a love that can spill beyond ego, but the Beautiful One always eludes him. First she appears as a little girl in a park, much like Alicia Carpenter of Fort Wayne days; then vari-

ously as an actress in a high school theatrical, a factory worker, a dan-
seuse, a midinette saying good-bye to her departing soldier, a Salva-
tion Army Lassie, and—always in danger of taint—a burlesque en-
tertainer, a vamp, and so on.

Wherever the Dreamer chases after her, he encounters the Rival,
a Thanatos figure threatening Eros. (I'm sure Charlie Hornbostel and
Jack Parsons would say their classmate is stretching things a bit.) As
a paranoic fantasy, the Rival is variously the rival suitor, the factory
boss, the army officer, the rapist, the diplomat, the capitalist, and the
face of Hitler that becomes nightmarishly larger and larger. He is aggression, ambition, violent sexuality, and death-wish.

The Rival as well as the Beautiful One is a component of the
Dreamer's own mind: "Nazi Germany is after all the monstrous image of something the individual human soul is capable of." The
Dreamer is himself a killer, and his other roles include a submarine
officer, a soldier in the trenches, a cabby in a besieged city, a gambler
at the roulette table, a spy, a pilot, a prisoner in a concentration
camp, a falsely accused traitor. It's a violent poem, with nightmarish
renderings of both great wars, and it is the author's tacit acknowledgment of his own aggressions.

Ross's illness of 1935–36 is behind the poem's bizarre symbolic
action. All the world's machines have become ill, their iron surfaces
encrusted like diseased flesh and their cores rotting. The Beautiful
One asks,

> *Have you not seen*
> *The sickness of the iron,*
> *The strange disease that eats the flesh of it?*
> *I saw the blue steel split*
> *And burn like rotten wood*
> *And they are afraid,*
> *The fat bosses and the capitalists.*

Dreamer and Beautiful One are both infected, and heroic pursuit is
the search for a cure, always calamitous. If they are in a dirigible, it
ruptures; if in a submarine, it implodes; if on a ship, it sinks; if on
a train, it derails. As in the dreams Ross recorded, his hero, though
of great aspirations, is often helpless and passive.

Freud and feverish imagination apart, where did all this come from? He's influenced by quest literature—*The Faerie Queene*, *Alastor*, *Childe Harold's Pilgrimage*—and by Keats's letter on Soul-making and Hugo's and Rimbaud's phantasmagoria. Fairy tales too; his poem isn't that far removed from his own juvenile *Demon with the Fiery Tongue*, where Cherry the Dreamer rescues Eloise the Beautiful One from the Demon as Rival.

And in drafts he alludes to *Frankenstein* as a touchstone. *The Dream of the Flesh of Iron* exploits the Gothic sensibility we've seen in his writings going back to high school days. It's a portfolio of Gothic conventions: womb-tomb fantasies, a chaste woman pursued by a man of satanic sexuality, the decay of social structures made literal in the crumbling of buildings, the protest of lovers against institutional tyranny, the rise of corpses from graves, the descent into the crypt of the unconscious.

But I discovered the main narrative source to be the futuristic novel by Serge Simon Held, *La Mort du fer*, read when he was ill back in 1936, of which only a few copies exist in the United States. He initially thought of writing a poem as "a series of fragments" based on this novel, in which French industry is mysteriously debilitated by a phosphorescent rot in all its iron and steel, leading to apocalyptic social dislocation and collapse. He later took this metaphor—a weird equivalent of the fallen sensibility he terms "materialistic"—and built his own plot around it.

I think this obscure novel made such an impact because he happened to be ill when he read it, and it somehow projected his own debilitation onto the modern world. He would always think of materialism thereafter as a "disease." Though someone who liked cars and gadgets, he came to see the growth of industry as spiritual illness and literal blight. The fiery iron mills were like diseased hearts and the contagion spread deep into the ground and into people's skin and bones. The antidote to all this was a renewed spiritual link to the body and the natural world. He had emerged from his sickbed a worshipper of nature.

Not wishing his poem to be too "literary," he also drew on cultural history, the history of warfare, journalism, and science. His ambition was encyclopedic. Vernice photographed him in the basement writing the poem with copies of *Life* on the cardboard table. To enhance descriptions of women walking down a city street, he culled hundreds of words from the fashion pages of *The Indianapolis Star*. To give an insider's view of the City, he researched the engineering history of New York City. He was always working things up, filling pages with what he called "raw material."

In the opening episode, "Emergence," he puts to use a geology course he took in 1935, extending his childhood interest in rocks. He narrates the allegorical passage of the human ego through the stages of embryonic development, paralleling it with the evolution of species in various geological eras. Not having taken college biology, he makes copious notes on *The Science of Life* and botanical textbooks. We watch the human ego emerging from a prenatal lake of amniotic fluid, a "warm hydrosphere," traveling down the birth canal river and gasping for air, surrounded by ferns, cycads, great golden spore-cones, giant dragonflies, fish, reptiles, birds.

Thinking this much of a muchness and worried that his poem might read like a biology textbook, Ross consigned dozens of stanzas to the cutting room floor.

My metaphor is apt: the principal nonliterary source besides Freud is cinema, especially the film he thought the greatest ever made, D. W. Griffith's *Intolerance*. He and Vernice joined the Campus Cinema Club in 1936, when he first saw this silent masterpiece of 1916. He observed that "several interwoven stories move slowly together, then increase in speed and interest, grow shorter and faster in pace, and at last approach a stupendous climax as history itself seems to pour like an irresistible torrent across the screen." Following Griffith, he mixes scenes in ironic juxtaposition, as when he narrates a strike of left-wing workers along with the collapse of the giant chandelier at the opera house, an image borrowed from another silent film, *Phantom of the Opera*.

In a draft of the episode "Borderland," he writes that "our consciousness is like a screen on which our own lives and their events and those of others—the world objective and subjective—are seen to flow and fade like the phantoms of the screen—and yet all retained in the imperishable celluloid of memory, the undying pictures." The poem has much the feel of a silent melodrama in which the hectic phantoms of the screen pour out their uncanny screams and unheard lamentations.

As for sources in the life of Ross Lockridge besides his illness and rudimentary romantic triangles, many are obvious and show he's drawing on whatever exotica he's experienced—I'm sure partly to take his mind off the fact that he's once again sitting in his parents' backyard. He would always find in the magic circle of writing a retreat from the domesticity he otherwise relied on, where he could give free expression to powerful, anarchic feeling.

At first the City is Fort Wayne, with its avenue of frame houses and elms, but it blends improbably with the Manhattan he did with Larry Wylie—ghettoes and skyscrapers and townhouses. A burlesque theatre is rather like the one he visited in Chicago; a café near the theatre of war smacks of Demory's in Paris; rioting workers are modeled on the right-wing Paris manifestations of 1934, except that the politics of the rioters have shifted to the radical left. The many episodes of warfare owe much to his trip with Lamorey to Verdun; a roulette episode comes from his lone visit to Monte Carlo; the "Ship of the Night" episode from his voyage home with Marion Monico aboard the *Mauretania*. A spy episode takes place in a room strikingly similar to his room at 19 rue Soufflot. The New Harmony Labyrinth, though merely Hoosier, is exotic enough to gain admission, transformed into the Iron Labyrinth of the Nazis' war and propaganda machine.

But the autobiographical dimension of *The Dream of the Flesh of Iron* is more compelling in what the author has omitted. Ross Lockridge conjures up his childhood scenes in Fort Wayne, but his Dreamer has no mother, no father, and no siblings! Tellingly, the house on Creighton Avenue is bereft of any familiar domestic face. I think the poem magnifies Ross's early sense of not quite connecting with his own family, not finding his place there.

In another sense, though, the mother is everywhere. She is the maternal lake of the opening poem, "Emergence," from which the Dreamer is born and to which he returns at the poem's end. Implicitly she is the prototype of the Beautiful One. Ross was seeking in this poem to break the memory barrier, to peer back into the period he called "The Unremembered." As he knew, Freud discusses intra-uterine dreams and links the sense of déjà vu to the genitals of the mother, "the home of our nostalgia."

The poem is thus more pre-Oedipal than Oedipal. The Dreamer

ultimately seeks to regain a total symbiosis with a maternal power, before any father intervened. The maternal aspect of the Beautiful One isn't balanced by any paternalism in the Rival.

For my father the torments of family romance were secondary— Ross Senior, during the Oedipal years, wasn't a full rival. He always slept alone and Elsie, after the death of Bruce, lavished attention on her youngest son. The awe Ross Junior felt at his father's energies in those early years, and the fun of historical vagabondage, had slowly been yielding to unspoken resentment at having to wield his pen for the greater glory of this midwest Thucydides. And with self-defining scrutiny, he hoped not to become the same well-intentioned push-over. He would always insist on the "Junior" in his name, which was otherwise not his own.

The Boss at the Mill offers the closest parallel to Ross Senior, since he was personnel manager at Wayne Knitting Mills during a strike. But I don't hear much of our Indiana orator in this speech:

> —Listen, you little bitch, I guess you know
> That I own half this mill and pay your wage.
> If there's one goddamned thing that I can't stand,
> It's to see little workin' sluts like you
> Playin' the priss. Oh, Hell, I guess you want
> To have me make the offer plain and fair.
> Well, here it is, by God. I don't mince words.
> There's somethin' about that pretty puss of yours
> That makes me want you bad.

In effect Ross Junior tries to write his father out of this poem.

The Dream of the Flesh of Iron is structured as a homecoming, but ironically to a home without domestic associations. After free-falling through two world wars and the cultural life sandwiched between, the Dreamer returns to the City to find it, like most of the planet, in ruins. Eventually he carries the lifeless body of the Beautiful One back to the primordial maternal lake. She revives, and as the Dreamer sinks into the warm waters, embraced by a white radiance, her "great eyes are shining with love and hope."

He doesn't exactly drown. "The Dreamer rises into some more august day, with the knowledge that the Quest for the Beautiful One never ends and that the Dream can never be ended in the heroic fight which the Soul carries against its antagonists."

But before coming to these straits, the Dreamer has had a confrontation less programmatic, where I believe we find Ross Lockridge, Jr. breaking through the persona of this universal Dreamer, grasping for a personal identity, and seeking deep in his memory for the early attachments that elude him. Near the end, the Dreamer confronts the Rival, who has abducted the Beautiful One to the top of a crumbling skyscraper. "For a moment the Dreamer feels a temptation to surrender the dream entirely rather than feel the agony and the fear." But he gathers strength from sight of her and flings the Rival off the roof. He must then confront the elevator shaft.

The moment in Ross's midteens when he panicked near the top of the industrial chimney at the Indiana University power plant had turned up in his dreams. He wrote up one as a "symbolic prose poem" that he then recast in Spenserian stanzas for the climactic skyscraper episode. He was in the top story of the Woolworth Building in downtown Manhattan, looking into a profound shaft where ladders were dangling. "I had been deceived in the ladders, and instead descended by a chain of old miscellaneous abandoned articles which clung flimsily to each other by their own projections."

He falls but catches himself "on a trunk whose contents spilled crazily into the void. Books, papers, marbles, clocks, vases, pictures, pencils, and typewriters—and all unbelievably old and decomposed—were loosed in my descent . . . I reflected that I had seen all of these objects many years before, but thought them erased from memory . . . I could see the floor now far below me, and in my frantic desire to reach it loosed a veritable rain of articles. These fled through the air turning and jostling one another and—wonder of wonders—struck the floor without noise, bounding again and again into the air. I turned my mind to salvaging some of these treasures, which, in the remarkable mutations of time, had found their way into this unremembered nerve of the building.

"And it was as though I lived my childhood all over again. At length I found myself on the floor clutching in my arms a load of old letters, shining marbles, books, locks of hair, and tarnished gold coins which with an unutterable hunger of regret I knew I could never bear away with me."

Triggered by sudden fear of death, this is a hunger for a personal past forever lost except in the "celluloid of memory, the undying pictures." This is Ross Lockridge, Jr., not a universal Dreamer, looking once again at his old marbles and books and the miscellanea of the Creighton Avenue house and in sorrow recognizing limits to repossession. He returns in time to recover sources of old memories that have all along, without his knowing it, informed the structures of his emotional life. Sadly, they have the appearance of debris.

They are probably tokens of a still deeper nostalgia that doesn't reveal its object—the mother, absent from the cast of characters and transmuted into the maternal lake. She is buried, I think, in what Ross calls an "antique preexistence"—those early years when children most require the presence of their mothers and when he may somehow have missed his own.

This poem was not the format in which such recognitions could be pursued. Estella had bluntly told Wanderfell she didn't like *The Illuminations*—that pretentious descent into the diseased unconscious—and he burned it. Vernice never advised Ross in this way—she always had total faith in his powers—and he cheerfully went ahead with his book of nightmares, onto which he tacked a positive if macabre ending. His poem risked the dangers Wanderfell described when he repudiated his earlier work as a "massive edifice" of sick dreams. "The great thing, Raggleton, is to live in other people, in all people."

In seeking a universal Dreamer, Ross Lockridge explored the dangerous idealism he had himself warned against a few years earlier. When all human selves are absorbed into the single self, that self is ironically diminished. He had written a long work unlike anything in the canon and had purged himself of it. *The Dream of the Flesh of Iron* is a cautionary tale he writes to himself. It is a nightmare of grandiose self-projection and emotional isolation—and the kind of poem he shouldn't write again, just as the illness it narrates is not to be endured again. He would soon turn to creating another cast of characters, which would reflect a greater range of his sympathies.

Part Two

VI

Starting Over

Cambridge, Bloomington, Boston, and Cape Ann, 1940–1943

Vernice Lockridge had never seen the sea, so Revere Beach was the first excursion after the young family was settled into 18D Shaler Lane, Cambridge. She and Ernest watched Ross in his three-piece suit skip stones on the water. From South Ferry in Boston Harbor they saw the old wharves and skyline. Cambridge, with its elegant gabled houses, its labyrinth of streets and mix of populations, made Vernice feel as if she were now living in a foreign country. And it was exciting to be alone with Ross and Ernest, after the two-year spell of domestic life with parents.

If their new environment seemed exotic to her, its revelations weren't exactly proof of how an advanced eastern culture brings wide-eyed Midwesterners up short. At a party for Shaler Lane residents—married Harvard graduate students and younger married faculty—she and Ross found themselves the only Roosevelt supporters in the room. All others were voting for IU graduate Wendell Willkie (B.A. '13, LL.B. '16) in the upcoming election. When his good-humored arguments on behalf of the welfare state dumbfounded his peers, Ross decided he and Vernice had better sit on their politics if they were going to make friends.

He was delighted when early in the term they were walking by the Charles River and he saw someone whose politics he admired. "Take a good look at that man," he said to Vernice, pointing to a white-haired gentleman. "That's Bertrand Russell."

Harvard had in residence some giants of art and intellect, but my father, like many graduate students, found it a large and disparate community without an intellectual center. The 1940 bulletin for the Department of English listed on its faculty the likes of Robert Frost, Wallace Stegner, Delmore Schwartz, and John Berryman, but where *were* they? There's no evidence he became acquainted with these luminaries, present and future.

The great philologist George Lyman Kittredge, recently retired, walked with fine hauteur across Harvard Square waving his cane at traffic. "Hey, Santa Claus!" yelled a truckdriver, "where the hell yah think you're goin'? Yah wanna get killed?" Kittredge was much alive in the curriculum, still heavily philological. A fellowship student with many languages, Ross Lockridge, Jr. was permitted to design an interdepartmental course of study. He signed on to one course in Plato, where he could use his Greek, and another in the philosophy of religion. As if to punish these forays outside the department, he was "dragooned" into the infamous year-long English 186, Bibliography, under Mister Jackson, as well as a course in Elizabethan poetry under philologist Mister Rollins. (Professors were called Mister, while untenured tutors were called merely Doctor.)

As one of relatively few graduate students already married and a parent, he was on the periphery of the graduate community. Fellow student Jack Bate recognized his name at the annual cocktail party given by Mister Rollins. He too was from Indiana and had heard Ross Senior during a high school assembly speak on Lewis and Clark and early Indiana settlements. Jerry Buckley, a Canadian student, found Ross gentle and poised in a way he associated with southern manners, yet he was outgoing, intense, and somehow charismatic. Dick Scowcroft shared some classes with him. As a family man, Ross Lockridge didn't "socialize in the lousy cheap restaurants where we all ate. He was genial, liked by teachers, seemed far better adjusted to the dreary life of graduate school than the rest of us drones." Though liked well enough by other students, the gentleman from Indiana kept some distance from the Harvard community.

It was self-imposed discipline. During the first semester he and Vernice were preparing *The Dream of the Flesh of Iron* for submission to a publisher, and he was giving much more time to this epic poem than to coursework. He had been dutiful secretary in his father's workshop for many years; he now created his own in the Shaler Lane apartment. A typical afternoon would find him typing in the living room, Vernice retyping in the kitchen, and two-year-old Ernest, a fledgling copy boy, running back and forth singing "Nobody knows the trouble I've seen."

Vernice loved this work. During the crisis in their relationship when Ross was in Paris, she had written of how a life without him would probably consign her to a secretaryship at the Showers factory. She now felt she was making a contribution to humanity. She was typing the work of someone she loved, someone she thought had genius. She wanted to do it.

It felt like a partnership, although Ross was dominant. She felt privileged to be his first reader and she helped create his sense of audience. Sometimes he asked her to read and summarize books for him. He'd later say that she provided "an atmosphere of faith." This was hardly a relationship that would rank high in the annals of feminism, but Vernice never felt exploited.

A soft-spoken taskmaster, he expressed no impatience at her moderate typing speed, slowed further by the three carbons that compounded any error. Instead he *dreamt* a reprimand, as he recorded in shorthand: "V. was copying from [a textbook] or resuming it & called me in to see if she had done enough. I told her that she wasn't going fast enough——."

Frugality was a tyranny they cheerfully accepted. With only the five-hundred-dollar fellowship from Harvard and a matured insurance policy of a thousand dollars, they could afford no luxuries, including baby-sitters. When they arrived they found a telephone in place. They had it removed—with social consequences—and wouldn't pay for a private telephone until early 1948. The ghost of Brenton Webster Lockridge smiled when a nickel given an Italian hurdy-gurdy went into their account book.

His letters home were no longer the bravura pieces of his year abroad. They were matter-of-fact and utilitarian, turning his parents into truck horses by frequent requests that books and furniture be shipped East. His linguistic energies were being directed elsewhere, there was less he was willing to tell his parents, and he no longer felt the need of epistolary self-display. It was witness to a disparity of feeling that most of these letters were addressed to his mother alone. Ross Senior was often tucked into "et al."

Early on he asked for his bicycle. The local grocer charged too much, so he put a large basket on the bicycle and routinely pedaled to the other side of town. Vernice cooked simple fare and the two sang harmony as they did the dishes. Their routine amusement in Cambridge was to knock off work Sunday evenings and listen to Walter Winchell, Jack Benny, Edgar Bergen and Charlie McCarthy, and *Inner Sanctum,* with tea and crackers.

And they sometimes saw friends, most of them with Indiana connections. There was a young departmental tutor, Gordon Ray, whose family was in the Bloomington limestone business. He arranged to get them a spare typewriter and a radio. Charlotte Martin—a good friend of Vernice who'd worked at the bookstore and was now at Radcliffe—had greeted them the night of their arrival in Cambridge, giving them blankets, and feeding them a late supper of chipped beef and potatoes.

And Louise Wylie of Bloomington was now working in the college department of Houghton Mifflin. She visited the Lockridges in November and wrote home to her mother about it at that time. "When I arrived at Shaler Lane—Incubator Alley they call it— . . . I found only Vernice as Ross and the baby were out for a walk. Vernice looked as sweet as ever. Their apartment was large, a tremendous living room with a bookcase made of an orange crate painted by Vernice into a most attractive thing, tables both unfinished and finished by her. We talked for a bit and then pretty soon she opened the door and there stood Ernest Hugh; he is so tiny and so sweet and so good and so bright. The first thing Vernice said to Ross was 'Honey, you let him fall.' Ross was very sheepish and said 'Yes, and it was a bad one, because he cried.' On the baby's forehead was an awful big blue place. He dashes forward so fast and hates to be held by the hand. . . . Ross kept saying 'Poor little thing' because he did look peaked from his bump. He is very blonde and pale.

"As for Ross and Vernice, I found Ross much more gentlemanly than I had remembered him; up he'd pop when Vernice entered or left the room to get us tea and cookies and he gave her the best chair. They seem very devoted to each other although Ross said he would like to go to Europe and be a war correspondent but he couldn't because of Vernice and the baby. This he said nicely, but it seemed as if the old gay cocky Ross was completely gone. He was quite modest about his work; admitted that at Bloomington he didn't have to work hard to get by, but that here he did in order to make a good record. They have only enough money for the one year. He says nothing could drag him back to Indiana to teach."

She later offered to baby-sit so they could join Larry Wylie and his wife at the symphony. Louise was planning a literary career of her own, so the next morning after breakfast, Ross showed her some of his poem-in-progress. "Vernice said he could compose poetry as fast as he could type and I think much of the poem sounds like that," Louise wrote her mother. "He certainly works hard and has in his head a tremendous store of accurate information. Vernice adores him and types for him; his mother thinks he is brilliance personified, so he has lots of encouragement."

Ross and Vernice did the touristy things only when they had out-of-town visitors—with Lillian it was Historic Boston and with Curtis Lamorey the waterfront. Ross was greatly pleased to see Curt after six years and the two talked Vernice's head off about the Delaware Group. Vernice was often quiet around Ross's friends, yet Curt found them a happy couple—they "got along like a house on fire."

Shortly thereafter, their circle of friends was diminished. On her way back to Indiana over the holidays, Charlotte Martin—whom they referred to as their "good angel"—came down with "brain fever" and died. Ross wrote home that she had been "in good—though not suspiciously good—spirits" when she fell "into the strange exhilaration and incoherence that characterized the rapid course of her illness." He and Vernice were the first people in the Cambridge community notified by the Martin family, and in shock they trudged through beautiful new snow to her Brattle Street dormitory to inform her friends and the University.

Larry Wylie had married and was now living in Boston. Ten years Larry's junior, Anne Stiles was a vivacious Simmons student from a well-off Michigan family. She liked both Ross and Vernice but was more critical than Louise and Curt of their domestic setup. Wishing to maintain a sense of independence in her own marriage, she couldn't believe that any woman could, without resentment, be so wholly devoted to her husband as Vernice seemed to be. She sensed that, wrapped up in his own projects, Ross was asking too much of his wife and must be neglecting his son. They exchanged a few dinner parties, and she found Vernice's cooking plain in the extreme—based as it was on Ross's frugal shopping. Poverty was no excuse for those beans and frankfurters.

But they shared a memorable evening that season. "The Majestic Chandelier" section of *The Dream of the Flesh of Iron* required a ballet scene, so Ross had set to work, checking out twelve library books on ballet and working up a scenario. The Beautiful One, "clad in the traditional tarlatan skirt, but more graceful, pure and classic in her pas," dances from out "the vague boskage that walls in the garden lawns," pursued by the Dreamer, who "braids his feet back and forth in entrechats. The crowd applauds his unbelievable jetés. He makes tours en l'air, three at a time . . . They dance a pas de deux," and the Dreamer watches as the Beautiful One "spins on down the garden and around the statue in vertiginous pirouettes and fouettés."

He had just drafted this when Vernice heard over the radio that the Ballet Russe de Monte Carlo was in town that weekend. They asked the Wylies to pick up tickets. Ross told them beforehand that he'd never seen any ballet.

At intermission, cutting up for the bemused Wylies, he rendered a seasoned estimate of the corps de ballet, the line of each of the principals, the degree of finesse with which they had executed their adagios, allegros, cabrioles, entrechats. He remarked on their excellent *ballon,* the unmistakable influence of Nijinski as *danseur d'élévation,* the englamoured plastic movements of this classic Mediterranean troupe.

He didn't let on why he happened to know so much about ballet. Neither he nor Vernice mentioned to the Wylies or the folks back home that they were compressing 2,500 pages of rough draft into a presentable 400-page epic. Throughout January of 1941 they undertook the *"big drive"* to get a submission ready—not the finished poem but a version to suggest the larger work he had in mind, with many episodes sketched in prose. In a 19-page "Apéritif," he discussed his poem, noting that there were four levels of interest and meaning— narrative, psychological, historical, and philosophical.

Attempting to preempt criticism, he said he was aware of the many imperfections. Some of the verse is "pretty, precious, formal, stilted, or glutted with romantic adjectives. Some of the episodes as planned and a few as written should perhaps be omitted." He has been more concerned with structure than with details.

After a month of punishing both typewriters, they had the manuscript ready to go, and it was simply a matter of finding a suitable publisher. Ross made a long list of New York houses. But of course there was that respected house just across the Charles—Houghton Mifflin—and their friend Louise Wylie worked there. Why not send it to Houghton Mifflin? So on February 20, 1941, Louise delivered the manuscript by hand to Two Park Street, and Ross and Vernice began their wait.

By February 22, he was having real doubts about his poem and set about formulating what was wrong with it and how it might be more radically revised. "Probably almost all of the formal verse in the present draft should be jettisoned. The story's the thing." All those Spenserians should go and be replaced by total "metrical fluidity." The "long, powerful, Whitmanesque" line should fuel the crescendo near the end, as the Dreamer finds his way "back to the dawn in which the poem was born, from regularity to the great free stream of the rhythmical universe." He'll junk the "sickness of iron" motif. His poem "is a view of life. It does not need that sensational amazing element."

And maybe the characters should have proper names after all. Certainly he should do more by way of getting readers into it, as if to say: "This is the way I dreamed it, but in a way it is your dream too." Readers should be like brothers and sisters who have been through all this too, the shared nightmare of the twentieth century. "The language—every kind of language—not just book language—not just Joycean word-carpentry." It should have more conversation and especially "more wit all the way through—there isn't a particle of wit. The Dream ought to be full of wit, like life."

And most telling: "Take a few clear artistic themes and hammer away at them—this will give unity. You can't do everything."

This was both shrewd self-criticism and a preemptive strike. Now that his poem was being exposed to others, he could see where it was vulnerable, and by extension where *he* was. He would safely distance himself from it and be his own hanging judge.

For reasons of its own, Houghton Mifflin was following suit. The in-house reader's memorandum of March 7 in its entirety read: "An immensely long narrative poem, divided into short lyrics, interspersed with frequent prose passages of exposition. This is all about War and the Machine, human depravity and human aspiration, pretty well tangled up together and expressed through symbols that aren't very fresh. To decline. R[uth]. P. H[arnden]."

On March 11, Louise Wylie returned the manuscript to Ross, without the reader's report, which he never saw. It was unclear to him if the poem had even been read. Louise explained that in any event Houghton Mifflin wasn't publishing epic poetry.

Ross registered no visible disappointment at all to either Louise or Vernice, herself surprised and disappointed—she figured it was Houghton Mifflin's loss. Ross didn't permit himself to mourn a work he had already decided wasn't any good, despite the two-and-one-half years of labor. He would start over. "Okay, well if they don't want poetry, I'll write something they *will* want." He laid the poem aside and never picked it up again.

~

Ross wrote Blankertz that "most of my artistic output recently has been expended on shaping new profanities to characterize the kind of graduate work I've been obliged to do this year." For instance, Hyder Rollins was doing a variorum edition of Shakespeare's sonnets and asked Ross to research their vogue in Italy. He put his Italian to work and cranked out an exhaustive 70-page treatise, which Rollins later summarized in his edition. It must have felt like working for his father all over again. What he got out of this exercise was the opportunity to memorize the sonnets. "Most *graduate* English is a waste of time," he wrote his mother.

It was time to return to his original ambition—to be a novelist. At Indiana and now at Harvard his literary studies had been the canonical dose of "Eng Lit." His reading of American literature had been wide over the years but haphazard. Now he'd had about enough of Eng Lit, so over the next two years he self-administered an ambitious course of reading in American literature. If he was to enter the lists with major American writers, he had better check out the competition. He started with two he admired enormously, Hemingway and Saroyan, typing up critical notes and plot summaries as he went, and moved on to Willa Cather, John Dos Passos, Frank Norris, Upton Sinclair, Theodore Dreiser, Gertrude Stein, Sinclair Lewis, F. Scott Fitzgerald, Marjorie Rawlings, Sherwood Anderson, Ambrose Bierce, Thomas Wolfe, William Faulkner, Stephen Crane, and many on the fringe of the canon.

In none of these was he finding the equal of Tolstoy, Joyce, and Mann—or for that matter Hawthorne, Melville, and Mark Twain. Wasn't America still awaiting a modern novelist of their stature?

When Larry Wylie told him of a possible teaching position at Simmons College beginning in fall of 1941, he leapt. For one thing, he'd be getting more than twice the top thousand-dollar fellowship Harvard offered him for the following year. Simmons offered him $2,000, and unlike his father he requested still more—$2,400. They settled for $2,200. "I hate that brute Hitler," he wrote his mother, "but he has taught me the advisability of asking for what you want. What a great feeling it will be next year to be *rich!*" Another plus was that he had sold himself as an Americanist.

He met many of the faculty, some from prestigious universities including Harvard, and thought the associations there "would be of the most pleasant sort imaginable." Vernice wrote Lillian, "Of course it *is* a girls' school. I tease him and threaten to buy him a wedding ring." But Ross was able to invite even Marion Monico to dinner at Shaler Lane, when she was in town for a conference, without triggering jealousy in Vernice. He just seemed in every way devoted.

Spring of 1941 was a period of crisscrossing ambitions not fully sorted out. He resolved to return to writing a novel based loosely on the life of his dead uncle Ernest Vivian Shockley. The expansive, bland working title would now be *American Lives*. But there remained the nuisance of a doctoral dissertation. Mister Rollins thought he had the makings of a first-rate philologist. But he disappointed this mentor and decided to write on Whitman, perhaps "The Brood of Whitman: The Great Betrayal," on how the great Whitman legacy had been exhausted in the decadent American poets who followed him.

But must he write the thesis? When Byron's publisher advised him to switch to some work nobler than the scurrilous *Don Juan,*

Byron replied, "I hate tasks!" Writing the master's thesis had been a task. Did he have to do that all over again? Hemingway never got a doctorate, he told Vernice.

He was also looking beyond the academy to the sinister progress of the war in Europe and was keeping up on his Italian, German, French, and Spanish in the event of foreign service somewhere. He toyed with the idea of spending part of the summer in Mexico to improve his Spanish. Maybe he could knock off a quick dissertation there by writing up the influence of Whitman on Spanish literature.

His Harvard philosophy courses were providing a better format for thoughts that matter. In one essay, a study of the Greek concept of *techne*—art or craft—he satirized the Department of English. Devoid of any "aesthetic sense," the folks at Warren House talk about Shakespeare "in the manner of someone dissecting a mummy. . . . They are very deep in philology—which is often but a way of designating a man who has surrendered himself to a complete nominalism, a slavery to the word as a word only, little regardful of the realities that are shadowed forth in words." The doctoral dissertation is "a hideous and dismal monument erected to the god of a false techne." The philologists "are worse than an ignoramus who has acquired no knowledge at all, for they have devoted great energy to the acquisition of something not really knowledge. . . . And indeed I find that I must make a reappraisal of my own position in regard to this techne, for I have myself at times been a follower of the false gods."

So much for Rollins and his kindly paternal gestures.

He continued his critique of modern times in a series of essays and Socratic dialogues written for Mister Wild in the Department of Philosophy. In one of these, "A Platonic Masque," he recasts Plato's critique of the state in *The Republic* and laments that American democracy has in the 1920s and '30s been threatened by oligarchy. The real rulers are the Fords and Rockefellers, who in their money-lust become paradigms for us all. "The crash of 1929 is only the chariot of the soul coming to earth. . . . The drone-like desire for mere consumption wars with the narrow, competitive, avaricious spirit, and we are alternately dynamos of misdirected energy and ragbags of acquiescence." As we have drifted into war, we see that this Platonic masque of the soul "is in reality a tragedy."

Brought up in the principles of Jeffersonian democracy and progressivism alike, my father read America as an experiment that was betraying its early promise.

He finished up the term, suffering a humiliating B-plus in his bibliography course. When his parents wired some money in payment for Vernice's having typed one of Ross Senior's new books, the family was down to four cents. Mexico would have to wait. Besides, they were homesick. They headed back to Bloomington on July 4, 1941, stopping in Manhattan to visit Curt Lamorey, recently married. They had a great time riding the double-decker bus and visiting the Cloisters. This was the last time Curt would ever see Ross Lockridge.

He planned to work on his novel. More than a habitat, Indiana was now a literary backdrop. They arranged a swap with Don and Ruth Smalley, who needed to be in Cambridge for the summer. The Smalleys' house, at 1919 Maxwell Lane, was just around the corner from the Lockridge house on High Street. And just a few doors away a new house was being constructed by Russell Noyes.

The Smalleys had shortly before taken in an untamed orange cat who chased dogs. When the Lockridges arrived, they discovered an invasion of sandfleas, who "had multiplied far beyond their ability to get sustenance, and somewhat like Hitler's legions before Munich were hungry for lebensraum." Ross consulted with Jim Pennington, gas station owner and famous Bloomington raconteur, who sent him "to a certain Clyde Reem." With Reem he "set some jars of sulphuric acid in the basement, poured cyanide balls in, and skedaddled after closing up the house hermetically. *Resultat:* next morning, I went over and swept up some hundreds of very dead and pitiful little brown carcasses and one exceptionally dead cricket."

It was a sociable summer, with reunions of the Lake Gang, now expanded with marriages, and the Bakers. Ross continued his methodical reading of American literature and did some editing but no writing for his father.

He also told his mother for the first time that he had in mind to write a novel based on her side of the family. Elsie was greatly pleased. A pedagogue who had long known the value of visuals, she suggested they make a tour of old family sites up in Henry County.

She herself had not visited many of them since she was a young girl. Apart from the initial vision he'd had on rue d'Ulm, my father would consider this visit the launching of his novel.

They took the Pontiac and drove up the old National Road—now Highway 40—to Lewisville, where they visited the graves of John Wesley Shockley, Emma Shockley, and their son Ernest Vivian, and then took narrow country roads to the old Harvey graveyard. Emma's father, Franklin Rhoton, a "stiff cocoon of seventy years of passionate begetting and goddamning," was buried there. They pressed through poison ivy and myrtle to the fenced-in lot only to confirm that no stone had ever been erected to the tyrant. A ground-hog hole funneled into the grave and Ross imagined that animal and corpse cohabited. As they left, the groundhog emerged and perched on his hind end, watching them.

The next day they visited the old conservatory house at Bluntsville where Elsie had lived two years as a girl, and then went to Mooreland, where she had dreamt of her father's severed head being chewed by a dog, and "on down the narrow dirt road and across the R. R. tracks again to a jog where Pedee College, at Dan Webster, Indiana, was, . . . passing the so-called old Messick place where Grandfather Shockley was born, and then to the Old Home Place where W. B. Shockley lived and had his office and where Mother and Uncle Ernest were born and, I think, Uncle Frank, which they left when Mother was about six. Then away from there to Messick not far down the road where the old Messick Graveyard is."

It was at the Messick graveyard that Ross was stricken with something like death nausea. "I like to mess around in old graveyards about as much as anything I know," he told his mother, and joked about wishing he'd brought along a spade. He thought of his mother as a little girl riding around this countryside in late August with her older brother, Ernest. Then he thought of the graveyard, now lost, where his great-grandfather W. B. Shockley had spent the Great War and all the intervening days—"all that time was as nothing to the perpetuity of his sleep."

They asked some locals how to find the graveyard. "Yeh, awhile back, Rabb was talkin' about plowin' the place under. I reckon he will too sometime, if he ain't already." They ended up in a cowfield. "Is that a bull?" asked Elsie. "Yes," replied Ross. They weren't dressed for cowfields—Elsie in a trim black dress and silk stockings and elaborate hat, he in his better pants. She tucked her large red pocketbook on the far side, away from the bull. "Here he comes!" cried Ross, who liked to kid his mother, a real sucker at times. She jumped a fence and endured her son's laughter while the bull calmly cropped grass in his corner.

They made their way through thistles, ironweed, horseweed, and marsh grass to the railroad embankment, crossed several fences and finally saw "out of the tangled ground the tips and corners of a few gray stones, fallen." "This is old W. B.'s grave alright," said Ross, and he thought, "Out of your mother's girlhood you have torn this fragment and got it back. . . . You had no more profound sentiment of the past and the buried days when you stood before the crumbling, moss-covered tomb of Virgil high on a cliff over-looking the Bay of Naples."

They stood the stone upright and cleared out the pillbugs. "You get close to a life at the grave where it ended," he reflected, looking at the matted wild growth of dewberries and ground roses interlaced with myrtle and bluegrass. They looked in vain for the stone of Susannah Duke, John Shockley's mysterious first wife. And then he returned to the grave of his great-grandfather W. B. Shockley in the southeast corner and imagined "wisps of the burial clothing perhaps still adhering for flesh to his limbs. You stand amid these shards, butts, tips, lettered fragments, gray scobs, flinders, slabs, and chips of stone, with the hungry tide of the earth coming up over them . . . with its green foam and spray-fingers of ivy and grass."

And then he looked at his mother and saw that she was tired and that only her "blue wide fearless eyes" were still young. He was seized by the sense of her mortality. He wondered if the "green-wave surge of the grass and the ineluctable bulge and tidal swell of the land wash out all recollection after all, after all, if we wait long enough!"

Suddenly the alien burst of the train, only yards away, magnified his dark astonishment. It wasn't that he'd confronted some new truth about death, but he'd never registered its granite finality quite so intimately, and he left the graveyard feeling all the more "how necessary it is," amid the implacable movement of time and earth, "that something be and endure."

~

Opposite 46 Mountfort Street in Boston's Back Bay was a row of three-story tenements and behind it the railroad tracks. An alleyway funneled some of the blast across the street to the Lockridges' apartment. During the war years heavy munitions were moved at night, and it sometimes felt like life in a train station. Ross and Vernice, with Ernest excitedly sitting in the front seat of the moving van, moved there in mid-September, 1941, to be within walking distance of Simmons College. They took a three-room apartment (number 19, now 4A) at $40 a month on the top floor of this utilitarian brick four-story walk-up.

Ross wrote his mother that it might have been a fashionable lodging place in the 1880s and wasn't "a bad old trap now." The high-ceilinged apartment with rooms of respectable size, hallway, and tiny kitchen seemed immense to Ernest. It was soon filled with wicker furniture from the old Shockley house in Straughn and other items the folks back home obligingly crated up and shipped. After the genteel ivied row of Shaler Lane, this was a dingy urban environment with dirty alleys and tough kids. Ernest grew up hating the neighborhood, but it was the beginning of a period of great vitality for Ross and Vernice, the happiest years of their life together.

When I revisited the apartment in 1989, the Boston University student occupants had heard that "a man wrote the longest American novel here." They didn't know author or title.

Ernest was getting on to three and my parents decided it was time to have another child before the age gap became a problem. Vernice became pregnant around the first of October. With any luck, they'd get a girl this time.

At $183.33 per month, my father was feeling expansive and wealthy, capable of feeding an additional mouth. There was also a large providential supplement. Fifty-six-year-old Dr. Thaddeus Hoyt Ames had studied with Jung in Zurich, Freud and Rank in Vienna, and Adler in New York, had published articles on hysteria, war shock, and childhood mental disorders, and had recently given up his Park Avenue office in New York to write a book. This was proving no easy matter, so from a list of candidates Ames selected Ross

Lockridge to give him a hand. My father was stunned to be offered five dollars an hour to chat as an "idea-man" with this amiable rich psychiatrist, who rented enormous office space in Boston.

"There Dr. Ames has assembled a number of tables and shelves where he has carefully filed his material," Ross wrote his mother. "He uses immense cardboards expressly designed for his purpose. Each cardboard is devoted to a subdivision of his subject. The cardboards carry little packets of manuscript, each packet carefully labelled at the top so that its subject-matter can be read at a glance. Thus, at any time, the ingenious Dr. Ames can take one sheaf of papers from one cardboard and place it on another where for the moment it seems more properly to belong. Or he can take one entire cardboard and carry it over to another table placing it on top of other cardboards with which it, as a larger division of the work, more aptly belongs. It is a regular assembly line."

Ross would go to Dr. Ames's office at 2 p.m. on Thursdays and chat learnedly about psychiatry while being served tea by one of Dr. Ames's many secretaries, switching to cocktails come evening, then he'd be taken out to wine and dine lavishly, all at five dollars per hour. Ames looked and talked "like a very genial and refined Protestant clergyman" through all of this, and the relationship continued over many months, with Ross taking guilty delight in the huge sum he received for being treated to dinner. He was feeling so rich he casually dispatched $150 to help pay off his parents' mortgage. And on the cheap he purchased 20,000 pages of typing paper.

The only wrinkle was that whenever he hinted that now might be the time to begin actually writing the book, the kindly psychiatrist evinced hostile symptoms.

This association prompted Ross's reflection that no great literary work ever came out of a collaboration. "Creative work on the highest level has to come from a single source, don't you think?" he asked Blankertz. Wordsworth "wisely withdrew" from work on *The Ancient Mariner*. In the few instances of successful collaboration, he thinks each writer must have taken responsibility for discrete parts. Writers need "searching criticism" from friends, they don't need collaborators.

He found a new friend in Warren ("Steve") Tryon, an assistant professor of history at Simmons thirteen years his senior. From Connecticut, with schooling at Dartmouth and Harvard, Tryon was a friend of Larry Wylie. Like Blankertz, Crane, and Lamorey, he had a cynical streak within a larger gusto and was a popular professor at Simmons, admired for wit and irreverence. Ross and he quickly hit it off, Ross enjoying repartee with this learned cynic, and Tryon enjoying what he felt was the creative vitality of the younger man.

Steve thought Ross found in him someone closer to a bona fide historian than his own father was. Ross now sometimes spoke of his father patronizingly as somebody to get off his back. In a school that emphasized professional skills, they sensed their kinship as guardians of the humanities. Though Ross continued to drink beer with Larry Wylie at nearby pubs after teaching, he and Steve began to pair off, and Larry Wylie was a little pained to see less of these two friends he had brought together.

Part of the problem was that Steve and Larry differed, to the degree of straining their friendship, on what individuals should do about the war in Europe. Ross had less trouble with Larry's pacifism—this was his friend's decision—but he and Steve were closer on the key issue of the day. He described his feelings about his own possible role in the war in letters to Blankertz and to Malcolm Correll, another pacifist.

After the attack on Pearl Harbor, he wrote Blankertz, "The truth is I would like to get into it in some active way, though I have no desire (nor any aptitude) for bouncing around in a tank turret. I know that I shall be ashamed to say, however, fifty years from now that I spent these epochal years tickling the risibilities of adolescent girls in a skirt-school in Boston. . . . I really would like to set my teeth in something that might by a series of rebounds and indirections cause a little discomfiture to the Axis cause."

He recalled what Hemingway had said of Thomas Wolfe, that what he "needed was to have someone shoot him in the ass or spend a year in the Siberian salt mines. Might make a writer out of him, Ernest said. . . . I envy the writers who have been at war—and survived. It gives you a certain authority to speak."

He was reading *War and Peace* in February of 1942 and for a couple of months conducted an epistolary debate with Blankertz on the nature of heroism. He was puzzled that a generation of young men brought up on the values of the Lost Generation could face fire in the foxholes of Bataan. It wasn't abstract, it was one real war multiplied by the number of individuals fighting it. As a soldier sights down the "brainless barrel of a Garand," he sees real enemies coming after him. "He really *sees* them, and it is no dream. And he has to make up his mind whether in the sum of things he is under any obligation to hold his ground . . . after all, it's his life. Well, I try to project myself into that frame of mind so that I will have some humility as I go about performing the diurnal asininities."

Blankertz replied that heroism has nothing about it that differs in kind from human behavior in everyday contexts. "Men dig a trench under fire with the same casualness and curses as they dig ditches anywhere . . . What makes a hero . . . is, I believe, not a state of mind, not any conceivable philosophy, and is not to be predicted. It is largely accident, a mood, a combination of circumstances, and anything but a decision or a conscious state of mind."

Citing *The Red Badge of Courage*, Ross replied that Blankertz leaves fear out of his analysis. Fear of death is hardly a daily nuisance. To be sure, fear arises among soldiers partly in response to "a social law whose infraction seems more formidable to [them] than death itself. Besides, deserters are killed." But he thinks there is "so much more than this obedience to compulsion . . . There often develops among the troops that competition in valor . . . which in the language of citation 'goes beyond the requirements of duty.' "

My father worried that he might not stand the test as well as all those soldiers who had never read Crane, Tolstoy, Dos Passos, Hemingway, and Sassoon. "I keep wondering, is it for Americans like me the boys are dying on Luzon." He had an example of soldierly dedication in his own family: his cousin John Shockley, a dyslexic who had a terrible time learning to spell, was calmly mastering the art of dropping depth charges on German subs.

Back in 1939, he had had a dream, recorded in shorthand, of being a French soldier who cuddled a pretty little baby girl in a domestic setting. "There was some question how I could spend all my time at this house, away from my regiment."

Since his wife was now pregnant, he decided for the time being not to volunteer but to wait for the draft, and not escape active duty by applying for a government desk job. If he were going to be in the war, he'd prefer to wear a uniform. Now a physicist at the University of Chicago, Malcolm advised him that he could surely make a bigger contribution to humanity in the field of literature than on the battlefield. Meanwhile, my father was actually on alert, in the event of enemy attack, "to defend one half of the fourth-floor library from incendiary bombs!"

His novel was piling up. After the IU teaching ordeal, his load at Simmons seemed light. He had to teach only four days a week, and he was once again in a writing mode. Most of his comments to Blankertz—the only person to whom he ever spoke in substance about *American Lives*—were disparaging. "On the creative front I have been making steady progress with the novel. It will never come to anything, but if success in these matters were measured by productivity, I would be right on top of the game. I have about 500 pages of sinisterly bad prose, typewritten, to show for a few months of work. If both the toilet paper and the dollar bills give out, I'll have a last recourse. . . . It is acquiring a sort of glacier-like mass and it moves about that quickly."

He was supposed to be writing his thesis. During the fall semester, he'd taken a reading course in Whitman with Perry Miller and had selected as his thesis topic "Whitman and the Idea of Democracy in American Literature." He had no intention of writing the thing and never wrote a page. His surviving copy of *Leaves of Grass*, purchased in December, 1941, is richly annotated with "N," his code for the novel-in-progress. He was reading Whitman to infuse his novel with this great predecessor.

His Widener Library call slips during this period include many titles on Whitman, and a larger number on agrarian and midwest culture and literature by Hamlin Garland, Frank Norris, and James Whitcomb Riley. Also a slew of titles like *The Country Cousin*, *R.F.D.*, *Flight from the City*, *Fifty Million Strong: Our Rural Reserve*, *The Country Boy*, *Farm Festivals*, *The Country Dance Book*, *Photography and the American Scene*, *American Architecture*, *Railroad Transportation*, *A Country Doctor*, *The Country Town*, and, because Widener is well-stocked, *History of Henry County, Indiana*.

He also read his mother's favorite sentimental girlhood novel, Edward Payson Roe's *Barriers Burned Away*, published in 1872. Whenever she and her brother Ernest visited their Aunt Frankie in their youth, they'd race from the fringed surrey to see who'd get hold of

the book first. Aunt Frankie had only two others, the Bible and an almanac. Elsie and Ernest would each read the novel during every
visit, never registering who wrote it. Ross Lockridge admired the
green and golden cover and wrote his mother, "What a book!"

He had a theory of what was lacking in modern American
literature—what he was revving up to supply. Right or wrong, it was
his way of clearing ground. Blankertz had begun reading modern
French literature, thought offhand it was feeble stuff, and asked his
friend for guidance. My father replied in part, "On the side of fiction, you don't do justice to some of the figures you name and leave
out others. After all Balzac, Flaubert, De Maupassant, Zola, the Fils
Goncourt, etc. are the predecessors and founders of our modern
school of naturalism or advanced realism or whatever you want to
call it. You compare Hemingway and Zola to the latter's disadvan-
tage, but remember there wouldn't have been Hemingways without
Zola. . . . Confining myself to the moderns, I should observe that all
or practically all of the classifiable contemporary trends in poetry, as
in art, take their rise in nineteenth century French. . . . If it were
not for Rimbaud, Baudelaire, Verlaine, Mallarmé, etc. there would
have been no MacLeish, Jeffers, Hart Crane, etc. . . . Anyway, don't
underestimate the poor Frogs."

But at the same time he thought the influence of French literature on American was much of the problem. Poe had exerted great
influence on these nineteenth-century French writers, especially
Baudelaire, and ironically these writers were in turn linking modern
American writers to this weaker, less "American," more pathological
figure in their own heritage.

Rather than to Poe and his French successors, American writers
should look back to the greatest American poet, Walt Whitman, and
to the great Emersonian tradition out of which he sprang. The
Franco-American tradition was ideologically bankrupt and decadent.
Pound, Eliot, and Dreiser were among the greatest offenders. He
told the Simmons Cercle Français, "The American writers have
learned maturity and subtlety from the French, but they must seek
an expression that will rescue them from the pessimistic determin-
ism of Zola and the artistic cul de sac of decadent poetry."

In Eliot, for example, one sees that the "modern ersatz for pro-
fundity is unintelligibility. Any one can thus win an easy victory over

his reader, who feels baffled as though confronted with a superior intellect, deep in lore, deep in mysteries and insights which he—the reader—does not possess." The failure of *Sweeney Agonistes* shows that "Let a man go long enough, let him imagine himself idolized, invulnerable, and he will finally reveal himself in his true colors."

What takes away his entitlement is that "the life-stream is exceedingly feeble in T. S. Eliot."

Lockridge did find Whitmanian vigor here and there—in Robinson Jeffers, Stephen Vincent Benét, Vachel Lindsay, Carl Sandburg, John Dos Passos, and Thomas Wolfe—but these were not in his opinion truly major writers.

All his reading in regional and agrarian literature made him long for Indiana. "I will be glad to shake the dust of this degenerate Athens off my feet and get back to the lush pastures of the Middle West," even to the point of working on a farm and pitching hay, sucking up "inspiration Antean-like from the soil of my birth," he told Blankertz. Also, "I want to be around when one of my means of immortality passes beneath the arch we all have passed. It is somehow wonderful to me how life goes on blindly creating itself in the midst of convulsions—serene, inscrutable, seeking far destinies."

Vernice returned with Ernest, accompanied by Lillian, to Bloomington in mid-May, 1942, to stay with her parents during the latter stages of her pregnancy while Ross stayed on in Boston to finish up the term at Simmons.

His favorite associate left town also. Dr. Ames was flabbergasted when boy scout Ross Lockridge showed up free of charge to help him move. "Nobody but someone from the Middle West or far West would do such a thing!" he wrote thereafter. "In the last thirty-three years I have lived in the East nobody before has ever come in spontaneously as you did simply to 'help out.' "

He was alone for the first time since the rue d'Ulm in Paris in spring, 1934. "I must confess that although at heart a family man I rather looked forward to the prospect of being on my own for a while in a big City," he wrote Blankertz. "Well, I have been that way two weeks, and it has practically wrecked me. My ego, for some reason or other, has shrunk like a prick in a cold shower; I have been melancholy (unusual for me), pessimistic, defeated." He had walked down Commonwealth Avenue one dreary night. "It seemed to me

212

somehow a symbol of our time to see the rain coming down steadily in the night on the deserted parking lots, empty buildings, abandoned filling stations, etc. A world drained of its blood—the corpse of the 1930s in the rain."

He wrote several plaintive letters to Vernice and Ernest, describing his predicament. "Just fixing a breakfast of bacon and eggs has me rushing wildly around like a man caught in a revolving door." He showed up for a Midwestern Rally at the Hotel Vendome only to be told there was no such event. He got the laundry all screwed up.

Ernest received several stories of neighborhood people and creatures who missed him. "I have a story for you. When I woke up this morning in our apartment on Mountfort Street, I thought, 'Well, I must go in and get Ernest up.' But when I got into Ernest's room, there was no one there. The little bed in the corner was empty. There was no little blond boy named Ernest in the bed or anywhere else in the apartment. Then I remembered that Ernest had gone off with his Mamma and Aunt Kiki to Pittsburgh and Bloomington. I felt very sad when I found no little Ernest and I had my breakfast all alone. While I was having breakfast, I heard something go 'Whurr, whurr-r-r-r,' in a very low musical way. 'Oh, I know what that is!' I said. I went to the window, and sure enough, there was—guess who! Yes, it was old Pidgy Pidgykins. He strutted back and forth on the ledge, and cocked his head, and peered through the glass. He was looking for someone. I brought some bread crumbs to him and said, 'Pidgy, guess what. Ernest is gone.' Pidgy looked very forlorn and lonely, just like Daddy. He pecked on the window with his beak, and said 'Whur-r-r-r,' which was his way of saying that he hoped Ernest would come back again and that he Pidgy would miss Ernest very much."

Ernest asked his mother to read these letters again and again. He would say, "Poor Daddy!"

Ross finished the term and managed to pull out of his slump to write 125 pages of the novel in five days before leaving in mid-June, 1942. Vernice had felt it the longest month since he'd been in Paris. He set up his card table in the south yard at the Lockridges' and wrote, breaking most days to walk his three- or five-mile circuit with dog Skirtie.

During one ramble on the outskirts of Bloomington, he encountered an old farmer who was ruefully looking at college litter: "beer cans, chewing gum and cigarette wrappers, and on a bush, hung by someone with a touch of the dramatic, two long, dangling, lewd-looking rubbers, looking like some kind of vulgar fruit," he wrote Steve Tryon. "I said, 'Hello,' and he said, 'It's a gol-derned shame, ain't it?' I said, 'Yes. It's terrible, isn't it?' He said, 'They come out here every night and hang these things on the weeds. Why, I've found as many as three or four in one spot.' 'It's a dirty shame,' I said. He said, 'They ought to have a place for them to do it, instead of them coming out here and wallowing around in my fields.' 'There sure ought to be a place for it,' I said. He said, 'One of these nights I'm goin' to come out here with my shotgun and I'm a-goin' to blow someone's ass right up a tree!' "

Other summer pleasures included visits with friends, many pregnant. Naomi Dalton, Vernice's obstetrician, told her to expect the child around June 25. Ross insisted the child would arrive on July 1, and challenged the professional opinion all over town. Wise-cracking husbands asked him to feel the stomachs of their pregnant wives to predict when their babies would be born—and incidentally sex and hair color. The 25th passed, and Vernice thought she was going into labor the next day. "Impossible," Ross said. "The baby won't be born until July 1st." The 27th, 28th, 29th passed, on the 30th Vernice went into labor, and I was born 12:46 a.m., July 1.

"Dear Steve: Your morose prediction came true; we have another boy, whom we have named Larry Shockley Lockridge, thereby concocting undoubtedly the most cacophonous name that ever a person of poetic sensibilities achieved. Larry—in spite of the fact that it alliterates with Lockridge; Shockley—after my mother's maiden name and my brother's Christian name, in spite of the fact that it contains a sound like that in Lockridge. The whole name sounds like a trunk falling downstairs. But we don't care. We think it's cute, and after we thought of the name Larry, nothing else would satisfy us. So Larry it is—not Lawrence, just Larry."

My father was being diplomatic. I was named after Larry Wylie. The Wylies had lost a baby a few months earlier. And Larry Wylie from Indiana was the long-standing friend who had made a real difference, encouraging him to go to Paris. Stephen or Malcolm or Curtis Lockridge would have been a more dignified name, but I've always been proud to be named after Larry Wylie.

Except that his name is really Laurence.

~

In late August, 1942, Ross revisited the old Lockridge farm on the Eel River—Kenopocomoco. With his father and Ernest, he camped for three days. Ross Senior told Ernest stories of Old Black Wolf, Old Dobbin, Kablu, Chingachgook, and Little Uncas. Little Chief Mosquito Bite, now three and a half, took a picture of the two Big Knives standing in front of the tent. Ross Junior looks relaxed, affectionate, in his element. The picture contrasts with one taken a month earlier of Ross Senior and Elsie on their fortieth wedding anniversary—Elsie folds her hands protectively in front, and her husband stands beside her, not touching, as if to say, "Did we really marry once upon a time?"

The campers visited the old homestead, now boarded up, and Paw Paw Church and cemetery, where Ross Senior was photographed next to his parents' and brother Bruce's graves, then to his old alma mater—the little red-brick structure known as the Lockridge School, beginning to be overtaken by vegetation—then to the house in Peru where Charlotte Wray Lockridge had died, and finally to the great covered bridge at Roann, which my father's cousin Mary Jane Ward, now a novelist, had visited many times as a girl. Ross Senior was also photographed next to a Miami County farmer. My father added the caption, "Two Old Deadbeats Compare the Ravages of the Years."

He wasn't directly writing about this side of his family, and didn't have the same sentiment about it. The mortality of that deadbeat, his father, didn't haunt him. But the landscape did, and the Eel River, its banks rife with vegetation and buzzing insects, was becoming for him a sacred emblem of fecund life. As he would write in *Raintree County*, "Flowing from distant to distant summer, the river was a place of archaic lifeforms and primitive sounds . . . the oldest pathway of the County, a place of frogs, fish, waterbirds, turtles, muskrats, coons, wildcats, groundhogs. The life within and upon its banks had not changed for centuries. And the river's name was the oldest name in Raintree County . . . a vagrant Indian word, a name never spelled but only spoken, a relic of pure language, the utterance of a vanished people."

That August, my father and Ernest visited his alma mater, Finley School, and with the Baker side of the family they walked through the streets of Smithville, where Lillie and Hugh Baker had grown up and courted. With the closing of its Monon station, Smithville was now pretty much a deserted village. The feel of small-town desolation stayed with my father. "Here lies the memory of a little town, of golden and agrarian days and sainted elders on the porches in the evening talking of the Union."

When we packed up for the summer and headed to the train station, no one guessed it would be another four years before we were back home again in Indiana.

Before the fall term began my father visited Steve Tryon in Rockport out on Cape Ann, northeast of Boston, to work out a course they were giving jointly that semester—American Issues, or as they termed it, "Whiskey Sour 10." It would be a colloquium in American history and literature mostly of the nineteenth century, centered around such topics as "The Frontier," "Industrialism-Capitalism," "The Rural Laborer," "Children and Education," "War and Literature." President Bancroft Beatley was cheered by this interdepartmental initiative and put coffee and cookies at their disposal. *Simmons News* would give it good press: "How would you like to join a class which is really different? Come down to the lunch room, help push the tables together, draw out a cigarette, and feast on coffee and cookies—while listening to an inspiring discussion! . . . With two instructors things are really lively, and arguments are long and intense."

His lament to Blankertz notwithstanding, my father was really enjoying Simmons College and was proud enough of the connection to begin signing his books "Ross F. Lockridge, Jr., Simmons College." He wrote a piece for the Simmons review *Fenways* contrasting Simmons favorably with IU, Harvard, and the Sorbonne. He wrote the college's promotional material on what Simmons graduates from various fields could do out there in the professional world. Though he was maintaining library privileges at Widener and was still thought to be writing his dissertation, only one book signed "Ross Lockridge, Jr., Harvard University" has turned up.

Simmons students would hear from him early in the term that he was from Indiana. Sometimes when they arrived he'd be reading his hometown newspaper, which Vernice's sister Clona was mailing East. "Don't laugh!" he said. And he told a couple of students he liked the idea of someday stepping out from a Pullman car in Bloomington wearing a white suit. Few Simmons students ever heard of his Harvard connection.

In the late 1960s, though a student protester committed to egalitarian ideals, I was sickeningly proud to be at Harvard. My father's lack of elitist feeling in this matter I'd tack onto the column of his virtues.

He was comfortable and informal with students, meeting them in his small basement cubicle, but maintaining a certain reserve. By all evidence he maintained his professionalism. One Simmons graduate said, "It was a shame that someone who looked a little like Tyrone Power was so goddamned uxorious."

Early into the fall term, there was a family tragedy back in Bloomington. My father recorded it in one of our picture albums. "Last Picture of LITTLE SKIRT LOCKRIDGE going down the long long road TAIL UP! On October 12, 1942, Skirtie Lockridge, 'Old Sweet Skirtie,' a born lady, was killed by the postman's car." And also on that page, "Skirt's master and trainer on the road he and Skirtie walked a hundred times together."

Back in 1941, he had advised his father that the vanity biography of Theodore Thieme, his former employer at Wayne Knitting Mills, might not leave a favorable impression of the old coot. "It would appear that Mr. Thieme had more affection for [his] dogs than for any human beings mentioned in the book. More attention is devoted to the passing of these dogs than to Thieme's marriage to Mrs. Thieme." But now Ross himself mourned a toy shepherd.

Even Elsie Lockridge permitted herself to mourn. A month after the accident, she wrote, "We still grieve over Skirtie." In detail she described the "sad services" she conducted and the weeping neighborhood girls who paid respects. No such document exists for any of her other losses.

Skirtie could be freely mourned because Skirtie was *gone,* unlike her son Bruce or mother or father. When losses were as great as these, she was compelled to deny the fact of loss—they were all still *"living on"*—and Denial found a handmaiden in Christian Science. My parents denied loss to the extent of deciding not to tell Ernest about Skirtie until they returned to Bloomington, but "it is quite pathetic for us to hear him still talking about 'Skirtie girlie' as though she were alive."

In a few other respects it was proving a calamitous fall and winter. Writing his novel and doing three new course preparations plus freshman composition, my father contended also with one of his frequent bouts of "flu," as he always called it. I was off my feed and Ernest had colds. The Coconut Grove fire in late November, which killed 492 Bostonians, left him "quaking." Living close to the mortuary, he and Vernice watched truckloads of caskets go by. "Somehow, today, more than ever before, I am feeling the insecurity of human life. My God, what a great lottery it is!" he wrote Blankertz.

This friend had himself been undergoing major surgery on his posterior. Ross extended sympathy for his "gluteal crucifixion" and praised him for the "note of comedy with which you tempered the indignity of it all." To the extent one can objectify the experience of "pain and anticipated death—there is good hope, isn't there, against the swallowing depression you felt along with it. . . . Why don't you read a little Whitman," he suggested. "That marvellous old windbag always does me a lot of good in dark moments." And he quoted his favorite lines:

O despairer, here is my neck,
By God, you shall not go down! hang your whole weight upon me.
I dilate you with tremendous breath, I buoy you up . . .

"The old bastard does too. They can still have Keats, for all of me. Give me old Walt—and American to the core."

Beyond these local calamities, America was not in a swallowing depression and seemed ironically buoyed up by the war. "Most of us live an accelerated life during wartime, and so far as I can tell most Americans are happier. For the first time in years, perhaps in a lifetime for some, they identify themselves with great objectives," he

218

wrote Blankertz. Back in Bloomington, Elsie was in charge of point rationing for Monroe County and would be keeping a Victory garden. Except that she was president of the local chapter of the American Association of University Women, her professional career had ended. The illnesses first of her son, then of her mother, weakened her resolve to continue teaching and finish the degree. But the war mobilized her, as her husband wrote: "Mother is doing *Herculean* war work all over *the home front.* Just now, she is ramrodding Point Rationing for Monroe County—*and is she ramrodding it!*"

· Ross Senior's New Harmony Commission was shelved for the duration of the war, but he was trying to get the house assembly behind a statewide patriotic "rabble-rousing program." He was pleased that his son wished to get into the war and recommended Intelligence somewhere on the French front.

By some reckonings, though, the *only* durable success story in the larger family was now in the making. Replying to an AA ad his wife, Mary Kay, had saved and taking his last drink on November 30, 1941, Shockley Lockridge remained on the wagon, had had a second daughter, Kay, was leading World Book Company in sales, and was well on his way to becoming a wealthy vice-president.

My father felt some shame in being one of the few young men on the street out of uniform. His cousin John Shockley coolly survived the sinking of his destroyer, the U. S. S. *Walke,* and told him, in so many words, to leave the fighting to those who know how. His cousin Bob Masters, now a major in the Air Force, visited in February of 1943. My father got a kick out of watching privates, lieutenants, and captains saluting Bob as they walked the streets of Boston. He encouraged his students at Simmons, many with boyfriends and fiancés abroad, to write about the war and reflect on what is noble and mean in American culture.

And he got into trouble over it. When he assigned Dos Passos's *U.S.A.* to his freshmen, some students and parents objected and the matter went to the dean. "Apparently few of us had ever read anything stronger than *Little Women*," wrote one undergraduate. He defended his selection in a lengthy letter, as usual covering all bases. "It is true that the Victorian Age would have rejected this book, but this age has rejected the Victorian Age. . . . A book may contain examples of immorality without being itself immoral. *U.S.A.* could not possibly debauch anyone. . . . A world that within the space of a quarter-century has been convulsed by the two most devastating wars in the history of mankind is a world in which imperfection perhaps outweighs perfection. . . . I point out the manner in which the book reproduces in a way impossible for the historian and sociologist the living, plastic stream of life in the American past."

The dean didn't wholly buy this, so a compromise was struck. As one student wrote shortly after my father's death, "My freshman year in English under Mr. Lockridge's instruction was one of the most delightful courses I had ever imagined. He tried to give us a broader outlook on life. . . . When instructions came from 'higher up' that John Dos Passos' *U.S.A.* was not suitable for young ladies, he told us, with a twinkle in his eyes, '*not* to read between page so-and-so to page so-and-so, but to read the following pages . . .' Of course, as he had anticipated, we ran to our rooms to read the forbidden pages." (They were surely disappointed.)

He spent some time just reading aloud from great works, and his rendition of Molly Bloom's soliloquy was a hit. One student said she "went after Joyce like a dog after that." Quite unlike his father's histrionics, his style was received by Simmons students as "companionable," "informal," "funny," "quietly dramatic." He perched on his elevated desk or sometimes teetered back and forth, heel to toe, on the edge of his platform. "Don't worry. I did this all last year and haven't fallen yet." They liked his "loping, kicky walk," battered old-fashioned briefcase, hair always falling over his forehead, and even his Phi Beta Kappa key, which they took to be tacit encouragement.

They didn't think him naïve. Rather, countering the sophistication was a quality many called "boyish"—it had to do with the playful informality, ebullience, and that damned dimpled smile he'd vowed to mothball while on the *Mauretania* in 1934.

In his American literature courses he emphasized Emerson, Whitman, Hawthorne (beginning with "The Great Stone Face"), Mark Twain, Hemingway, and many women writers—Wharton, Stein, Millay—often commenting on the extent to which such writers were truly American or derivative of foreign models. Thomas Wolfe, an American writer if there ever was one, was perhaps supplanting Dreiser and Hemingway in degree of influence on younger writers.

And *Hiawatha*, he said, only reminded one that America still awaited its great epic.

~

To the disappointment of their parents, Ross and Vernice decided to spend the summer of 1943 in the East. My father gave as an excuse "transportation difficulties and the general insecurity of our affairs," but in reality he wished now to keep his distance, especially from his father's projects, and finish the novel.

Through Steve Tryon they rented a remodeled barn at 8 Pasture Road in Pigeon Cove, the eastern end of Cape Ann. One hundred and fifty dollars for the summer, "Cleaves Barn" had four large rustic rooms and a big country kitchen, divided by varnished matchboard walls and with a Franklin stove in the common room. In the front room upstairs, my father set up a plain kitchen table and could look out through large Palladian windows to the sea, where the rock formation known as the Dry Salvages could be seen.

It was a wonderful place for a writer, especially one like my father, who wasn't bothered that nearby Rockport was a dry town. Surrounded by dramatic granite formations and old quarries, Pigeon Cove was fragrant with lilacs, pines, and cool sea breezes. Around the Cleaves Barn were pear and apple trees and blueberries, and a path leading off to the swimming holes. Not far away, the Tryons lived at the rocky beach with enormous granite blocks extending out into the water. My parents walked down at night and watched the full moon make a path in the water. My mother would have preferred to live there year round.

The war encroached even here. From time to time we would hear depth charges off the coast, and just out of earshot was a tool factory making munitions around the clock. Coast Guard sentries and navy blimps went up and down the coast. My parents were instructed to shut the blinds in the evening so house lights could not be seen from the sea. And there was virtually no meat in the grocery stores.

During the day my father would write while my mother tended the kids and did the housework. She had not been asked to retype a single page of the huge novel-in-progress. In the late afternoon he would take a break and walk with Steve Tryon to a large remote quarry where the water was clear and warm, surrounded by a granite amphitheatre topped with pines. Here they'd swim naked. Ross liked to swim across the entire pit, perhaps to prove to himself that he had recovered from his illness of 1935–36. Steve was more cautious.

Afterward they usually played chess, and of the hundreds of matches, this summer and the next, Tryon won only one—which single defeat put my father much out of humor with himself for several hours. He didn't talk much about his work at this time or show Tryon any of his novel.

Through Tryon, my parents became acquainted with Aharon and Josephine Arsenian, cultivated Armenian refugees who gathered around them a circle of artists and singers. Josephine had been educated in Constantinople and greatly enjoyed talking to Ross in French about Paris and Russian novelists, especially Turgenev. He told her how much he hoped to return to Europe and was quite the courtier with this handsome romantic woman some fifteen years his senior, to whom he paid extravagant compliments. She thought the Lockridges dreadfully poor, so she and her husband brought some beer up to the barn one day as a treat.

A communist sympathizer, Aharon Arsenian was a philosophical man of a certain gravity, very well read, with whom Ross discussed weighty issues, political and philosophical. With a magnificent voice he had hoped for a singing career but ran the valet service in a Boston hotel. Their son John and his American wife, Jean, were also in residence. John met Ross the first time when Ross was "busy picking apples and acting so *cheerful* about it. He summoned me to share them and we had a jolly time."

Less enthusiastic about Ross Lockridge was Rachel Tryon, who thought him insufficiently grateful to her husband for arranging the summer rental and to her for some hand-me-downs, thought he faked his professorial poverty, thought him egotistical, unfair to his wife, and uncaring of his son, whom she judged disturbed. Indeed, Ernest had dunked Mrs. Cleaves's cat in a bucket of red paint. She was upset when the two couples were leaving a theatre in Gloucester

and five Simmons women recognized Instructor Lockridge. Encircled by these admirers, he kept the three of them waiting for several
minutes.

Uncaring of his son? Anne Wylie thought this also. What kind of
father was Ross Lockridge proving to be? I'm not sure what it implies that an author, wrapped up in the great work, would take time
out to help with the baby books, or even beget babies in the first
place. They get in the way, after all, especially if authors live in confined spaces and have no funds for nannies. Blankertz was bemused
by my father's "philoprogenitiveness" and Malcolm Correll was delighted to receive baroque instructions on changing diapers—albeit
the final laconic advice was to call for help "and Ruth comes and puts
on the diaper."

He was probably projecting an honesty about himself, though,
when he wrote of the hero of *Raintree County*, "At first Johnny didn't
love his son. He had a strong feeling of pity and a sense of
responsibility—but no love."

Like his own mother, my father was concerned with child development, wondering what manner of spawn the genetic gamble had
given him, and he monitored Ernest and me pretty closely in our in-
fancies. He filled out the "Aptitudes" section of Ernest's baby book.
"Ernest showed early on a marked verbal facility. He memorized
easily whole books of rimes before or shortly after the age of two.
Now (at the age of three yrs, 10 mos), he rimes and composes little extempore chants fitting words to a preordained rhythm. His
sentences have for long been very pure, precise, and periodic. An
example of the last, recently noted: 'Mamma, when you get through
with your work, out of my tinker toys will you build me a wind-
mill?' " On Pigeon Cove Ernest pleased his parents by announcing
one morning that "it didn't take long for the sun to drink up the
darkness."

I, on the other hand, proved a sorry disappointment after the
Simmons News prematurely announced I had the makings of a whiz
kid. At the age of ten months I hadn't begun to speak, was still sucking my thumb, and slept through the night. He feared he had a dull
normal on his hands. Ernest, after all, had been able to distinguish
between the pictures of Beatrice Cenci and Pauline Bonaparte at that

age. Elsie broke the news to him that he himself hadn't begun to speak at ten months and still sucked *his* thumb.

I soon got out of my rut. My first word was "Da Da" and my first combination of words was "Daddy's book."

His letters home from the fall of 1940 on are full of stories about Ernest, with whom he spent a lot of time explaining how words are formed, telling him stories, teaching him to read and write by age four, and reading him Saroyan's *The Human Comedy*, which little Ernest professed to like.

He was a less patient instructor with his son than with his students. "He brought a blackboard home from Simmons, which he set up in the living room. He had a pointer. He had chalk and he started to try to teach me the alphabet. After about two minutes when I didn't get something, he exploded. He couldn't understand how I could be so stupid! I blacked out everything that followed, except that I could then read. He taught me to read." Elsie advised him, "Don't push the little fellow."

He found Ernest's response to poetry remarkable. He started the child out on James Whitcomb Riley. "One of the poems I read to him was a little elegy, 'The Little Red Ribbon, the Ring and the Rose.' I read it to him just before he went to bed and sometime after the lights were out in his room, we heard him sobbing and went in to discover that he was all heartbroken about the little girl whose death was commemorated in the poem. 'I'm a little bit sad,' Ernest said."

He memorized a good portion of Vachel Lindsay's "The Congo" when he was four and went down the street "leaving a wake of wide-eyed citizens" as he recited "Then I got religion, then I had a vision, / I could not turn from their revels in derision. / THEN I SAW THE CONGO CREEPING THROUGH THE BLACK / CUTTING THROUGH THE JUNGLE WITH A GOLDEN TRACK!"

Like his parents, Ernest was growing up amid reports of a war and they noted how it infiltrated his imagination. "We try to keep the war out of his thoughts," but "he has merged his two imaginary worlds of Japs and fairies into the most fearful tangle imaginable. Japs are attacking fairies, and fairies are defeating Japs, so that his psychic world is a frightful mixture of irreconcilable elements— Japs, Nazis, fairies, elves, Fascists, all whirling around together."

It hadn't taken long for a sense of responsibility and pity and a clinician's interest in child development to merge with love. He was frequently seen carrying Ernest around on his shoulders, even in museums and galleries. His dealings with his children may have seemed cold to some because he didn't use baby talk.

He wrote of his transformation of feeling in *Raintree County*, in which the character Little Jim is an unholy alliance of Ernest and me. By the time Jim was one year old, "Johnny was very proud of his son. He spent hours with him, talking with him, teaching him the names of things, carrying him around the town on his shoulders. . . . He lost all personal vanity in this son. . . . [L]ong after the physical fact of parenthood, he became a father by touching the form of a little boy, by dressing him, holding him, carrying him, watching him run, telling him stories. . . . No caution was too great, no tenderness too deep, no loyalty too lasting, no patience too enduring, for the saving and education of this little being." That bit about "patience" was revisionistic, but Ernest would mostly remember him this way. "He was a good father, a good father."

It would be my signal contribution to add—the following summer—the insight that "Johnny didn't suspect the depth of his love for Little Jim until a series of happenings seemed to imperil the child's safety."

My mother is still dismayed at the impression left in *Ross and Tom* that her husband didn't fully love their children, that he was "indifferent" to them. She simply doesn't believe it: of course he did, but how do you prove love? Leggett's biography apart, the burden of proof tends to be placed on self-murderers to show, as it were, that they actually loved those left behind. But surely this doesn't take into account what it's like to perceive the world through suicidal depression. My mother thinks that when her husband was writing *Raintree County*, he was compelled, like any responsible writer providing for his family, to close the door as best he could. There was less time for his children. He was otherwise always in our midst. She believes that neither time management nor suicide implied lack of love—and the tragedy was the greater for it.

Rachel Tryon and Anne Wylie were registering something real, though. For a writer as committed to his vision and craft as my father, the book's the thing. He wanted it, he wanted it. It was his life. He had sufficient wealth of personality, expressed both through the book and beyond it, for us to feel the affection and concern, especially Ernest. And some of us got *into* the book. But the great flow of personal feeling was directed through that typewriter. The growing circle of family he was gathering about him would have to remain, in some degree, peripheral.

~

Through the summer of 1943, Vernice was again pregnant. Beyond this form of productive life she was doing some canning in the late summer and watching her two sons play in the brilliant sunshine, and still not doing any typing for her husband. He was relieved that I was showing some motor skills beyond thumbsucking. And I reiterated the word "light," he said, "with many shades of meaning." He told his mother that I could have won the Rockport baby contest. Tanned, healthy, and unusually cheerful, Ernest helped out with the harvest of radishes, lettuce, and tomatoes.

All was well with the family but not with the book. My father had gone to Pigeon Cove hoping to revise and finish it. This would put him in the clear for military service, once the new baby arrived. To heck with the Ph.D. that his father was urging he finish. He'd begun the revision back in November of 1942, when he wrote his mother at length, requesting "authentic details" concerning her father that would "illustrate his character." He was content to let the character of her dead brother Ernest remain largely a product of imagination, but the character of her father he wished to anchor in historical sources.

He wanted also the kind of detail that would flesh out the "decor" of the novel. "Of course, it isn't my purpose just to write a 'period piece'; far from it." But he needed "little things like the kind of books people were reading, the kind of subjects they were talking about, the kind of clothes they were wearing," especially in the 1890s. Elsie replied that she'd send him all this as it occurred to her.

So now the novel had accreted to some two thousand pages. Nobody, including Vernice, had read a page of it. Behind a writer's secrecy, in addition to other motives, is a certain fear—that *this might not be any good.*

Don Blankertz and his wife, Eloise, visited for a couple of days in early August. The two couples didn't hit it off—Blankertz, a rather choleric person, had expected Vernice to be more literary. At his friend's insistence, Ross handed over a chunk of the manuscript. He was making few claims for it and was downright diffident. Blankertz told him the novel seemed "well-launched."

I'm sure my father sensed the praise was qualified. Forty-six years later, all Blankertz could remember about the novel was the character Ernest as a boy sitting on a fence engaged in a kind of interior monologue. It seemed an autobiographical sequence—Ross's life and concerns projected onto the character Ernest—influenced by both Wolfe and Joyce, and playing fast and loose with time. It didn't seem to be coming together as a novel yet, a judgment Blankertz tried to keep to himself.

Until my brother Ross noted it in the surviving *Raintree County* manuscript in 1984 and I reassembled some 210 pages in 1989, nobody besides Blankertz ever read a paragraph of *American Lives*. He was right: among the dozens of other novelists Ross Lockridge was reading in the early 1940s, Wolfe and Joyce were the two with whom he was locking horns. The likes of Hemingway, Saroyan, and Mann he simply admired. Joyce was by far the greater writer, he thought, but Joyce and Wolfe had equal and opposite defects.

Wolfe's were egoism and formlessness. This "strange, pathological subjectivism and egotism" is "not to be objected to in itself, but for what it does to the author's artistry and his feeling for existence." Incapable of love and obsessed "with himself and the charmed circle of his experience and acquaintanceship," Wolfe is unable to write convincingly of love relationships or even to create character. His characters "are all drawn in fits and starts of rhetoric and contradiction." "It is the *moral* world that does not really exist for T.W." Evidence of this is his almost complete lack of humor, which Wolfe imagines he has in great supply. His constructions do not go beyond the randomness of mere autobiographical reminiscence. The "dreary richness of the style" and its lack of diversity show an artistry swallowed up in egoism.

So if he's no good on character or plot, why was my father in '42 and '43 reading all those Wolfe novels? The southern writer expressed one thing very well that resonated deeply with his own sensibility—a tragic sense of time.

But even this was limited: it is "not so much a sense of time in all its mysteriousness, future, present, and eternity—but rather time that is gone—the ghost residence of the dead events." By means of this single intuition, Wolfe creates "the anchorless soul, wandering, grieved and adrift . . . He returns with real poetic feeling and passion and metaphysical intuition to this theme again and again," and it compensates for the "terrible crippled artistry."

When in *The Web and the Rock* Wolfe describes George Webber's childhood home on Locust Street, which seemed "fixed for him into the substance of immemorial antiquity," Lockridge thinks of his own Creighton Avenue in Fort Wayne and makes the marginal shorthand note, "Strange how Wolfe anticipates me in many things."

My father did not know, when he encased *You Can't Go Home Again* in disparaging marginalia, that Wolfe's embittered novel would in some measure prove prophetic for him, not just retrospective for Wolfe. Reading his copy, I find the dramatic irony painful.

If Wolfe had too little form and artistry, Joyce had too much. His defects are outlined in two fragments where my father is most intense in grappling with a predecessor, and most willfully clearing ground for his own novel. The first, written in September, 1942, is entitled "From the Point of View of the Aspiring Writer—The Virtues and the Faults of *Ulysses*." He thought better and struck "The Virtues and."

"One does not get creation in its highest forms in Joyce. It is a case of the mind analytical, the mind catalogical, the mind enumerative, the mind curiously weaving and unweaving of word webbing. But forms and wholes are not created. Characters are broken down and presented in bits and fragments and buttends and tips rather than as a series of impressions or in the shining wholes of action, motion, accomplishment." He has given us a work of "exhaustiveness" and "patience," but at a great sacrifice.

With the mind analytical in control, Joyce fails in communication. "The emotions are there, but not for the reader, who is too busy deciphering." The "objective details of Stephen's thought or Bloom's" do not result in a "forceful and pathetic equivalent" in the mind of the reader, who lacks the "subtle interconnections" that lend them significance for the characters. Expression is "both expanded and contracted" in Joyce, who "teaches freedom in the inner transformations of the word, but in the larger applications of language . . . it seems to me that he fails." Instead, we get life "staled with wordpiss." For all his Shakespearean comprehensiveness, he doesn't communicate "a sense of humanity." "It is good that Joyce did the job so completely. It need not to be done over. But what a goldmine for afterfollowers."

I recall the fatigue of some painter friends after they had braved the Picasso and the Matisse exhibitions that spread through the entire Museum of Modern Art in New York. What was there left to paint? My father was contending in his own way with the achievement of Joyce.

The other commentary on Joyce followed his systematic reading of *Finnegans Wake* in the spring of 1943 as he was getting into gear to revise *American Lives*. It's his single most revealing critical pronouncement, written like the earlier one for himself alone and first uncovered by my brother Ross. In part he elaborates his mixed review of *Ulysses*: critics "get a vicarious pleasure of creativity by repeating in reverse the intellectual processes by which Joyce created *Ulysses*. Of course, this is a cul-de-sac in itself. The intellect alone never created a great work of art, and without the obvious humanity and emotional and religious renunciations of *Ulysses*, it would not be great. As it is, it has a maimed and terrible greatness about it."

Joyce remains "a slave to his mentors, Vico, Aristotle, Aquinas. Having rejected the Jesuitical discipline, he really remains a slave to it." The book is too damned *"literary."* And in *Finnegans Wake* Joyce is too much like Jesus in assuming his disciples and publicity staff will mop up after his "enormous intellectual arrogance."

Still, my father would not have either of these novels different. "It simply *is* now, immutably like all other existential facts."

So why was he reading Joyce? Well, beneath the obscurities of that Irish philologist's novels are some simple yet powerful myths. He's learned from Joyce "the secret to the greatest writing. It is to pervade all scenes and characters with mythos—with a sense of the symbolical character of human life, with the feeling of reiterated and perpetual mystery that informs all acts of human life. . . . The thing to do is to discover the mythical character inherent in any given age or nation or people, for myth is domesticated in each country. So far, I think, America has not evolved very clearly her own mythos."

229

Then he gets more personal. How uncover the mythic character of his own experience that he will write of in his own fiction? He thinks himself essentially religious, more so than Joyce, "a vague, undefined religion, I fear, based on a sort of blind optimism, the inheritance of my blood and my surroundings, but nevertheless loving and so adoring the miracle of humanity and of being." His God, though, is not the transcendent God of the Old Testament but the divine potential in each human being. His novel-in-progress—a tragedy which has at its core a ritual slaying of the father—implies a repudiation of Old Testament values.

But he already looks beyond this novel to the next one, where he plans to exploit through indirection the mythic values of the New Testament. These values he thinks are immanent, human-centered, and "self-realizing." Myths are more than "primitive fragments" left over from earlier cultures. The "source of myths" is always with us, we create them anew in "the still continuous world of the human emotion with its ancient fixations."

Creative genius is simply the ability to bring to the surface and express the mythic structures that lurk in all human beings. The New Testament expresses one set of mythic values that are partly transcultural and are felt in moments of intense psychic awareness.

How recover and create anew for fiction those values in the ordinariness of his own midwestern life?

His answer startled me. It would be a novel based on his mother's response to the death of her son Bruce.

Just as one sees in Mary mother of Jesus and her circle "the terrible anguish of the women and the refusal to acknowledge the death," so he sees in his mother, Elsie, the "resurrection symbolized in [her] intense faith and conviction." It is a conviction that fastens to the mythic divinity she sees in her own dead father, who isn't really dead for her and whose perpetuity extends to her drowned son.

Beginning with this framing circumstance in his own life, he plans to explore in a new fiction the mythic character of American society, its wars, industry ("The Wayne Knitting Mills"), art, motion pictures, its insights and illusions. The novel-in-progress uses mythic parallels such as the Garden of Eden rather bluntly—the "symbolism here less disguised than it will be in the later book, involving Ft. Wayne and the drowning of my brother Bruce."

So Bruce was lurking enormously in his consciousness all along. I hadn't expected to find so direct a confirmation of what I had been wishfully projecting onto my father. Like me, he was five years old at the time of a catastrophic death in the family and, like me, he had tucked it away, in a child's hiding place of memory, only to have its significance grow. Now he conceived an entire book on this early death, an American New Testament, beyond the Old Testament aspirations of the work-in-progress. He would see in his mother's anguish and refusal to acknowledge the death of her son not pathology, as Freud would say, but creative mourning. Its roots were deep in American culture, which had, he felt, domesticated the Christian myth on many levels.

An artist of prophetic memory, my father hoped to redeem that early death through literary apotheosis and, like his mother, not let that boy die. In bearing witness to the fragility yet tenacity of dear human life, the drowned brother Bruce would be cast as a sacrificial figure, reviving in his homey way the myth of Jesus.

What about the novel at hand? Wolfe and Joyce reinforced my father's passionate evocation of the past and his mythic rendering of everyday life. But their faults, as he read them, were also evident in his own novel, *American Lives*. Instead of a single unified work, it seemed to him more like a "series of novels" in its two thousand pages. Had he solved the Wolfean problem of form, or was this not a heap of words without radiant focus or center, an inert "glacial mass"? And was there not a pretentious Joycean complexity about it that would make it fail to communicate? And there were other problems.

Set mostly in the 1890s but extending well back into the nineteenth century and as far forward as summer, 1941, the novel was plotted around a series of days, apparently July first through fourth, 1891. The principal character was based on his uncle Ernest Vivian Shockley, as he had planned while he was sick back in '35 and '36. But there were several other characters—his mother, Elsie; his grandmother Emma Shockley; his grandfather John Wesley Shockley; and purely fictitious characters like the Reverend Hezekiah Grubb, a murderous pharisee, and Mrs. Desmore Brown, a hot-to-trot widow. Each of these characters assumed, by turns, the novel's center of consciousness—each had dreams and interior monologues, each was involved in a string of episodes.

A miscellany of such episodes has survived—competitive boy-hood sports, a Decoration Day parade, a piano recital, some family funerals, an arrival at the State University, Bloomington on Saturday night. And a miscellany of dreams and daydreams, from sexual initiations, to the search for ancestral origins, to homecomings. In one, Ernest Shockley returned to walk naked down the streets of Straughn, the "naked, shivering, unhoused ego" most vulnerable on its own turf. Many episodes depicted Elsie's youth. And the author himself was in it—not just his personality projected into his Uncle Ernest but the literal Ross Lockridge, Jr. driving his mother through her childhood scenes in Henry County in late summer, 1941.

The complexity of this was compounded by the main structural metaphor, the palimpsest. As he wrote Blankertz, he was working with "conversations that have beneath them some older conversation of years ago, faintly present like the all-but-obliterated words of a palimpsest." The narrative was conducted by means of layering—thus while Ross drove Elsie to the grave of Franklin Rhoton in the summer of 1941 and confronted a groundhog hole in lieu of a tombstone, there were periodic cinematic dissolves to the funeral of Rhoton many years earlier, seen within the consciousness of the dead Uncle Ernest, who ruminated on still earlier events.

For someone who wished to communicate directly with that humanity he told himself he loved so much, my father was putting together a forbidding many-layered concoction difficult either to prepare or to consume.

There were problems that went beyond form, that went to the heart of his relationship to his material. The main character, Ernest, would die young and thus the novel was structurally a tragedy. As in the Wolfe novels, time was being portrayed mostly as time past, the "ghost residence of the dead events." The past makes its claims on us: "the dead hands are on those lives," he wrote of Franklin Rhoton. But he resisted writing a tragedy. There was too much Wolfe and not enough Whitman in the novel, and too much Gothic melodrama, which he'd already gone through in *The Dream of the Flesh of Iron*.

The countervailing force to time past was sex and the fecundity of land and swamp. He thought of new titles for the novel, including a corny one more suited for simple agrarian fiction, *On the Breast of the Land*.

The real-life Ernest was proving an awkward vehicle for all this—a learned and impassioned man but also a doctrinaire Christian, an administrator and co-author of a book about lawyers, and someone willing to work himself to death grading papers. His legacy included a dyslexic son now bombing German subs. The war in which he had participated behind the lines—the Great War—was the unredeemable nightmare my father had already exploited in his epic poem.

Surviving fragments of the novel suggest that he was having trouble in the collision of that personality with his own. The fictional character Ernest wasn't coming clear and, in his failed life and early demise, wasn't a spur to inspired composition. Ernest, like his mother Emma, "never got angry, just shut up like a clam, and refused to discuss the matter any further." It was proving more difficult than my father had imagined to wrest meaning from this premature death.

One evening, late in the summer of 1943 at Pigeon Cove, he looked at the manuscript and thought it over. There was one character in the novel with whom he felt a greater kinship in every way, someone directly filial, not merely avuncular—his grandfather John Wesley Shockley. Because of his audacious teaching of pagan myth in the schools, his early marriage and subsequent divorce, his free-thinking, his poetry, his participation in the Civil War—a war already entered into the mythic consciousness of the American people—John Shockley was energizing this desultory novel whenever he made an appearance. But his voice, in the end, was to be a ghastly emanation from his own grave, in the climactic dream where he blesses his son, the doomed character Ernest, and wishes him well.

My father recalled the vision he had on rue d'Ulm in the spring of 1934. He had supposed the novel-in-progress answered to it—he was writing about his mother's family, and John Shockley was a prominent character. But he suddenly recognized that the original vision was still "slumbering," and had done so for almost a decade. He had not been writing that visionary novel. These two thousand pages had been another stage in his apprenticeship all along, masquerading as the real thing. This wasn't the novel he felt destined to write. Some saving instinct had led him to swerve from the main task until he'd be ready for it.

In a matter of minutes the entire scope and structure of a new novel was laid bare to him—a novel in which he'd try to express the American myth, building on the Garden of Eden and the Fall of Man, and merging this with an American myth, the Great Stone Face. The hero would be John Wesley Shockley, the century the nineteenth, when there was still great promise and when humanity had not yet come into the desolation of reality. It would be a novel that, through the same "great restorative" power of art he felt in Tolstoy and Whitman, would remind a people of that original promise, stunted but alive.

My mother was working in the kitchen that night canning fruit, and Ernest and I were asleep. She hadn't heard any typing and figured her husband must be contending with one of his "bottlenecks." She heard him come down the stairs. Very excited and happy, he appeared at the kitchen door. He announced that he'd made a breakthrough. His strongest character was his grandfather John Shockley and his most vivid material the wealth of stories about him. He was going to move the novel back in time, away from the twentieth century altogether. He was going to abandon the novel he'd been writing and start over.

The next morning he did. Celia Foley, principal of Miner School, had inveighed against wasting paper. Rather than throw his defunct 2,000-page novel away, he turned it over, and started a new novel on the other side.

VII

Writing *Raintree County*

Boston, Cape Ann, and South Byfield,
Fall, 1943–Spring, 1946

Dual gestations were once again under way, new novel and new baby. My mother was expecting the third week of February, 1944. My father wrote home in October, 1943, to say that "Uncle Sam and the stork will arrive in a dead heat"—he'd be obliged to report for a preinduction physical that same week, with induction in March. "I would really like to get into the fuss before it's over." This gave him just a few months to get a good portion of the novel drafted before *he* was, and he geared up for it with an energy unlike any he'd felt since Paris days.

Simmons College wasn't about to stand aside for Pegasus. My father was saddled with four different course preparations each semester and was further handicapped by his elevation the previous year to head of freshman English. The next few months would surely prove the axiom that, whatever the circumstances, writers *write*.

The renewed vision he had in Pigeon Cove had quickly translated into a new structure for the novel. Taking a cue from the Greek dramatists and Joyce, he would now center the action around a single day, July Fourth, 1892, during which there would be cinematic dissolves to episodes in the life of the fifty-three-year-old protagonist John Wickliff Shawnessy. Quite unlike *Ulysses,* these "flashbacks" would be totally narrated episodes, arranged mostly in chronological sequence. During the morning, the dissolves would be to episodes in the early life of the hero, during the afternoon to episodes of his young manhood, and so forth. He was simplifying the design.

This easy chronology would give way, though, to a psychological and symbolic crescendo—he planned to postpone a few episodes to the end. These would be glorious or tragic events that the hero conjures up only in revelatory moments later in the "synoptic day" but that have silently exerted their explanatory force all along.

He didn't wish the novel to have a single perspective, so some episodes would be seen through the eyes of other characters, especially those based on his mother and grandmother. His Uncle Ernest, who had starred in the earlier novel, was to make only a cameo appearance or two.

Beyond the fireworks display at the end of the day, he planned a Dream Section that would owe less to Joyce, he said, than to Freud. He'd attempt to usher the reader to "the wellsprings of human personality" in a panoramic and symbolic reprocessing of the day's events.

As with *The Dream of the Flesh of Iron,* the structure was inspired by cinema. Griffith's *Intolerance* would be the model for temporal juxtapositions and the torrent of events that pours over the pages near the end.

He and Vernice had also seen *Citizen Kane,* which he went back to see a second time, writing up a lengthy analysis. He loved the "segment method of reviewing a life. A flash here, a flash there, with something establishing continuity. Overlapping of scenes. Clapping of hands in one scene for a banquet becomes applause of a crowd for a political speaker in the next. . . . The guardian of the boy wishes him a Merry Xmas at the end of one scene and completes the phrase 'And a Happy New Year' in the beginning of the next scene without any time lapse in the running of the film, but the man's face has aged twenty years and he is dictating a letter now to the boy, grown up."

He resolved to tie Day passages and flashbacks together by such verbal segues, highlighting the ironies of time and memory.

He wrote a synopsis of all episodes and set about writing the flashbacks first, researching the historical matrix for each. The Boston Public Library became the scene of these labors. It had a first-rate collection of nineteenth-century newspapers from all over the

country, including many from Indiana—if not from Henry County—
and he started reading his eyes out in the dim light. Over the next
several months he took thousands of pages of shorthand notes, supplementing dozens of synoptic histories with this more immediate
and local kind of historical record. He'd say that without shorthand
the novel would have taken years more to write.

In one sense he was the diligent student working up a series of
assignments for Independent Study. But his conception and practice
of the act of composition itself remained bardic and inspirational. Beginning with a brief synopsis of each episode, he "set all preoccupations of research and pedantry aside," and sat at the typewriter. He
kept in mind Matthew Arnold's saying about Homer that true epic
should be "noble, simple, swift." Those typing skills, like the shorthand, were now harnessed to the full.

In the initial composition of the larger number of episodes of
Raintree County, my father would try not to rise from the typewriter
while he lived through some day or period in John Shawnessy's life.
He composed at up to one hundred words per minute and thought
the novel's narrative momentum owed much to this volcanic purging
of imagination onto page. Among my earliest memories is the ceaseless drone of the typewriter coming from the small bedroom where
my father tried to hole up. He'd pencil a quick revision of each episode, noting weaknesses to tend to later, and would stash it away for
the time being.

The manuscript started to stack up here and there around the
bedroom-study with a messiness quite unlike the orderly filing system of Dr. Thaddeus Hoyt Ames. This, however, was a book getting
written.

He said I made a contribution of my own early on. I may have
been the one who ripped off a page of the first flashback and tossed
it in the wastepaper basket, its exact language forever a "lost chord."
But he'd say also that while still one year old I "toddled into the
work-room during Daddy's absence," climbed aboard a stack of
manuscript, "and completely drenched his father's handiwork," ex-
hibiting thereby "the only advanced critical faculty in the family."

When in 1989 I was working on the fragment of *Raintree County*
manuscript in the Lilly Library, the staff admonished me for manhan-

dling the pages, as I held them up to the light, felt their texture, and sniffed. It was too unseemly, in the elegant hushed reading room, to explain that I was seeking traces of my own antique urine.

I reported disappointing results to my mother, who gently informed me that the story was my father's embellishment—the promotion people at Houghton Mifflin wanted good copy. I always treasured stories of any impact I had made on my father. So there went a supportive stone from the edifice of my personal mythology!

During this period my father maintained his correspondence with friends—most of which would be forever lost—and was a busy affable presence at Simmons, where he still saw much of Steve Tryon and made a number of new acquaintances. But with Larry and Anne Wylie now at Haverford and with no private telephone, my parents' social life was minimal. The book was the thing.

Death in Venice prompted a rumination on the paradox of the private and social in the life of the artist. My father thought that "the impulse to save and justify the creative 'I' " in its isolation is "a social impulse." The creative ego is justified whenever it reaches toward "a feeling of human brotherhood." "This feeling is at the core of the creative process. One loves the human creature because he has a hard time, and because one is human oneself." Out of a sustaining egoism the artist creates something of beauty in an act of sympathy for the human race in its suffering.

My father was of course struggling to justify his own egoism. This is no easy paradox to sustain—he thought it had to remain a "problem." Egoism puts artists in moral jeopardy. They also become vulnerable to the contingent world in their visionary labor. "The menace of beauty remains for the artist. From some ambush a fatal arrow can fly."

Like many writers and athletes, Ross Lockridge had quasi-sexual superstitions. He believed that "in the process of talking about the book he would burn up some of the creative energy, all of which he needed for the great design." He had to be parsimonious with this energy—how could he guess his own allotment? Not many of his friends—not even Larry Wylie—knew about the book. Blankertz objected to the retentiveness, urging him to send portions and assuring him that he could be trusted with his friend's writings. He hadn't even heard of the demise of *American Lives*.

My father made an exception for his writing students at Simmons. He told many of them he was writing a novel—to convey, they thought, that they were all in this together as fledgling members of the family of writers. He imparted to them "an air of conspiratorial joy."

To one student, Naomi Scott, with whom he sometimes strolled and chatted after class, he imparted something else about himself. She too had lost an older sibling and sensed that this created an affinity between her and her instructor. He spoke of his brother Bruce and how he felt a strange kind of duty toward his parents to fill in for the dead sibling.

Dozens of established members of the family of writers, from Homer and Moses to Harriet Beecher Stowe and Whitman, crisscross the pages of *Raintree County,* but he felt especially buoyed by those obscure writers within his own family tree. The Shockley family archive was there at hand in Boston, a treasure that gave him a sense of fellowship and potency. He had the Henry County *Atlas* with its fine lithographs showing the old courthouse with the hands of its clock forever fixed at nine. He had tintypes of the Shockleys standing at the Old Home Place and of a reclining John Wesley Shockley musing on life and holding a copy of *The Indianapolis News.* He had the family's Civil War letters, the love letters of John Wesley Shockley and Emma Rhoton, and specimens of handwriting with sentimental posies exchanged at Henry County's vanished Pedee College. He had the old ledger of his great-grandfather William B. Shockley—doctor, preacher, farmer—with its botanical recipes and testimonials.

It was this Shockley who began the family tradition of versifying, and my father treasured the parchments of his two lengthy "pomes" on tobacco, which begin:

> *A weed among the plants we find*
> *That hurts the body and the mind,*
> *Yet in the way of self-abuse,*
> *We see it constantly in use.*
> *Unpleasant to the smell and taste,*
> *Yet men for it their money waste;*
> *The reason why I scarce can tell*
> *For none at first do like it well.*

Some do it chew and some it smoke
Whilst others in their nose it poke.

And he had more than a hundred poems in elegant calligraphy by his grandfather John Wesley Shockley, who aspired to a more genteel and visionary utterance than his own father's but never thought of sending these effusions beyond the local newspapers. My father would gain a wider audience for him.

Not vanquishing his literal predecessors, he would create within the covers of his book a family reunion, where the vagaries of John Wesley Shockley are converted, by means of an American mythology, into something rich and strange. Ross Lockridge Senior, not invited into the cast of characters, would undergo a sea change of his own and be everywhere apparent.

He asked his mother for the family's old ten-volume pictorial history of the Civil War that he'd grown up with—"I need them for some research I am making." She, Lillian, and the pictorial history took the train East for the new arrival. On the 16th of February, 1944, they were on a stopover at Frank Shockley's in Pittsburgh when they received a telegram from Ross requesting immediate "reinforcements"—the baby had arrived. When they entered the Mountfort Street apartment, I was "walking back and forth over the living room with a peculiar limp like old Dobbin," as my grandmother wrote. "Well, it turned out that he wasn't permanently crippled, just so excited he had to do something."

"The new baby girl is to be called Jeanne Marie," my father wrote his brother Shockley and Mary Kay. "She weighs 7 lbs 3 oz and is expected to be pushing Betty Grable any time out of the top spot as Army Pin-Up Girl. Vernice feels fine and went through very nicely. . . . My preinduction physical is next Tuesday, Feb. 22, the Army having decided to use its secret weapon at last."

He was feeling so upbeat about joining the Army that he talked Steve Tryon, less the patriot, into taking the preinduction physical with him. "I said, 'Ross, they'll never take us. You've got three kids and I've got two kids. They're not going to take us.' " They didn't. They asked forty-three-year-old Tryon, "Why do you want to enlist?" He replied, "Well, I don't particularly want to," and that ended that.

Ross emerged very glum. The doctor had first uncovered his pre–Pearl Harbor perforated eardrums. Then the doctor listened to his heart. He called in a colleague, who listened also. They declared him 4-F.

My mother was greatly relieved and my father humiliated. And as someone gearing up to write the Civil War portion of a novel, he felt deprived. The next day he brought his wife and infant girl home from the New England Hospital for Women and Children. Giving birth was still regarded as a species of invalidism. The hospital doctors he listened to, the Army doctors he ignored: he carried first the baby girl and then his wife up the staircase to the fourth floor.

Over the next few months my father, like Stephen Crane, fought the war from his writing desk. Not being literally in it, he lifted his imagination in a frenzy of composition, as Allied forces prepared for D-Day and he took his hero John Shawnessy on Sherman's March to the Sea.

Lillian left soon after Jeanne was born, while Elsie stayed for six weeks to help out with domestic chores. She too wasn't invited to read a page of this new novel. Her son took four days off to show her Historic Boston. With Lewis Mumford he thought Christian Science was the nineteenth century's theological equivalent of ether. But he respected his mother's religious convictions enough to make their first stop a visit to the grave of Mary Baker Eddy in Mount Auburn Cemetery.

Back in Pigeon Cove for the summer of 1944, I logged my first memory, an act of primal disobedience. Sally Fitz was a half-year older and, tiring of our sandpile, suggested we take a stroll to the sea. No problem, let's go. My mother was at her chores in the kitchen, checking every few minutes. She saw we'd disappeared. Panic-stricken, she and my father started running up and down paths, alerting neighbors, who joined in. An hour or so later, Sally's mother found us by ourselves a half-mile away at a solitary beach, sitting fully clothed in the water and playing with pebbles. I remember being warmly received by my parents and wondering what the fuss was about. I wasn't punished.

My father didn't rescue me but did rescue a drowning boy floating face down in the water that summer—an episode played up in the local paper though, modest hero, he didn't leave his name.

Later a hurricane passed through Pigeon Cove. Perhaps thinking of Odysseus, he braved the gale outdoors amid crashing tree limbs. After the storm, the doors were sticking, and Ernest failed to close one completely. My last excursion had been a lark, so I again strutted out barefoot and took a path to a fork. By now I was "a young, obstreperous bullcalf."

I could either turn right and head for a deep swimming quarry, or go straight into a field beyond which was a fifty-foot precipice into a dry quarry. My desperate mother, alone at the time, followed my tiny footprints to the fork, running up one path and then the other. As my father wrote, I was "standing in philosophical meditation on the brink of a quarry, where Vernice finally saw his little golden head shining in the sun. Larry obviously believes in living dangerously." I was playing with flowers.

These episodes got into the book. As a little boy, Johnny Shawnessy walks south away from his farm "hoping to see a Negro." He runs instead into little blond Nell Gaither, who invites him down to the Shawmucky River, where they play a long time "building little mud and stick huts. . . . When he started down the road that evening, he ran into a lot of people, and they all rushed at him and grabbed him and took him home. . . . 'Poor Ellen!' people said, 'Johnny, you pretty near killed your poor mother.' "

Years later, it is Shawnessy who is panic-stricken. His wife Susanna Drake, near mental collapse, absconds with Little Jim, and he begins a long and futile search. She too was like a child, and "two helpless children, entrusted to his care, had been lost. As in the old poem, they had wandered away on a bright summer's day. Bitterly, he reproached himself." My father improved on his raw material: this son would soon die in a fire.

And still later, remarried and father now to Eva (Elsie Shockley) and Wesley (Ernest Shockley), John Shawnessy is once again in search of lost children. On a camping trip with their parents, the two children get up early and steal away for a botanical excursion. Eva gets separated and lost for the better part of the day, passing once near a flowering tree and gathering up some yellow blossoms. This time John Shawnessy finds his child: "I've found her! I've got her!" "Her mother took the little dirty dress off and bathed her. Papa picked up the dress and shook it and the little yellow flowers fell out of the pockets. . . . He stood with a strange look on his face sifting the tiny flowers from one hand to the other." Eva had somewhere stumbled onto the mythical raintree her father had sought so many years and would never knowingly find.

It was a quality of my father's emotional life, as of John Shawnessy's, that his love for persons and things became fully apparent to him in their vanishings.

This motif of the raintree, and the name Raintree County, hadn't occurred to him until midsummer. Well into the composition he was still using Henry County place names. But one day he was sitting at his worktable in Cleaves Barn, "juggling words and trying out proper names by a process of sound-resemblance and free association." Saying the word "Henry" again and again, he stumbled onto "raintree" by the slight phonetic resemblance.

Eureka! The word touched off "a whole chain of slumbering associations." He thought of New Harmony and that damned Pageant. He took some pride that "the State of Indiana was the first in the Nation where these oriental trees were seeded and grown." Since he'd been working with the Edenic myth, "the motif of the Raintree instantly fused with the already existing pattern of the book. Almost as if by magic the whole landscape of Raintree County . . . sprang into being." It felt to him less a creation than a discovery. He seized a pencil and in a few minutes sketched the first map of Raintree County.

~

By late summer, 1944, he finished drafting the flashbacks. In the eleven months since he'd started the new novel—twenty-nine years old and turning thirty—he had written two-thirds of what would eventually be published as *Raintree County*. He wondered if he'd set some new records, "though such was far from his intention," he insisted. In the tradition of his parents, it had been daily story-telling.

Right away he started in on the Day passages, all set on July Fourth, 1892. Though already sketched out, shorter, and telling one continuous story of their own, these would be more resistant: they entailed many passages of philosophical dialogue, of remembering and yearning, of silent lyricism in the mind of small-town school-teacher John Shawnessy. Nevertheless, by October, 1944, he had drafted almost half of the Day passages and started to burn the candle at both ends, revising the flashbacks and handing them over to his wife for retyping while he continued with the Day passages.

Vernice hadn't done this kind of work since early 1941 and was happy to resume. After the kids were tucked in and the two had done their singing-dishwashing routine, she would type in the living room, about ten pages an evening. Ernest soon perceived that his mother was a better writer than his poor father. His pages were full of pencil smudges, arrows, and crumples; hers were beautifully printed and made tidier piles.

Mostly she could make her way through the labyrinth. From time to time she'd call in—"Honey, what comes after 'The muscles of his cocked arms'?" and he'd call back "bulged circularly," proud of his verbal recall. He asked her to read passages to him, especially the lyrical ones. But he called it "fanatical self-control" that he didn't dis-cuss the book with her or let on where the plot strands were going.

He also asked her not to read ahead. If he heard her typewriter stop for a suspicious interval, he'd call in, " 'No fair. Stop reading the manuscript, honey.' . . . In this way, she lived the book as she copied it, and next to the author himself, knows the story of *Raintree County* as no one else ever will." He explained that consciousness of any nor-mal reading audience at the time, even his wife, would throw him off his creative stride. This rule had the effect of making my mother type the faster to discover the sequel.

It was also grounded, I think, in a writer's fearful retentiveness and a desire to dictate the way in which he'd be read, beginning with his own household. Those words were *himself* on the page.

Early in her labors my mother objected that the character Nell Gaither bore a physical resemblance to Mary Eloise Humphreys, with her long red hair and a tiny, sexy gold filling. She was jealous. My father explained that all his characters had some composite fea-tures and he asserted the rights of authorship. Of course if she pre-ferred not to type the book, he could always ask some woman from Simmons College to take over. She raised no more objections. But her husband silently changed the color of Nell's hair to blond, and in lieu of the gold filling—symbolizing the mortality of beauty—he gave his callipygian heroine a penny-sized mole on her hinder. (My mother says this was a fiction.) The generation of adolescents who read *Raintree County* in the late 1940s and early ' 50s had a low arousal threshold and—I've been told—stirred to that penny-sized mole.

The Simmons College *Fenways* did a feature article that fall on Vernice Lockridge, "Meet the Missus." She "looks hardly older than a Simmons freshman," but has long since finished her college career and has three kids. Ambitious Ernest shoots the reporter with his tommy gun and expresses a desire to be a policeman. "Quite the opposite of his brother," Larry expresses no desire at all. And Jeanne smiles constantly, resembling "one of Raphael's cherubs." Vernice Lockridge prefers life in Pigeon Cove to Boston, considers Simmons "the most pleasant place in which Mr. Lockridge has taught so far," and confesses, "I hate to write. We'll leave that to my husband."

I am struck dumb by the fact that during this period of most intense work on his novel, my father didn't let up on his teaching. One of his four courses in the fall of 1944 was "Imaginative Writing," and some of his students have given me their stories and poems with his detailed commentary. It hints at some of his own concerns at the time.

A sampling: "This is emotionally and psychologically very convincing. One has the feeling, however, that it is a *literary* reinterpretation of childhood instead of the actual experience. You have a tendency toward stiffness and 'over-writing.' " "Effective, but your style is still too lush. It spoils the effects otherwise possible in describing a fascinating character like this." "This sentence got away from you. Break it up here or here or somewhere." "Simplicity and a more direct approach would be more effective." "It lacks something that I find hard to define. I think it is unity of impact. . . . We do not care much about Ruth's problem, because *she* does not seem to care much." "This is probably a very accurate study of social mores among the contemporary college fauna; it has some gaiety and go to it. But the blind-date story with the usual accessories is not a very challenging theme any longer and it doesn't seem to me you do anything very new with it." "So far, you have everything necessary except a story." "Your story seems not inconclusive, as life often is, but simply *unfinished*." "Both poems have a great many truly poetic qualities—

245

sensuousness of language, occasional sharpness and freshness of imagery, an ability to see the world slightly 'off-center' for a renewed vision of people and things. Probably both poems would be improved by sharpening and shortening, without losing the deeper intuitions."

Three years later he would be coming in for some of the same commentary—overwriting, discursiveness, literariness, diffuse plotting, sentences that get away, use of stock situations and characters, and a novel unfinished since we don't find out what happened to John Shawnessy—and it even lacks a period at the end. He would reply that he knew what he was doing, that it was all part of the design.

Family distractions continued from all sides. Elsie Lockridge was becoming more and more grandmotherly and domestic, sending large parcels all the time, including a large Christmas package of nuts-and-bolts, navy-building toys, bathrobes, sandpen outfits, spool-dolls, and the usual socks and shirts for her son and clothes for Vernice. "Such a hammering, pounding, riding, throwing, and thundering as we have had in this apartment for the last two days," he wrote her, "hasn't been heard outside of a professional rodeo." But he was to his novel as he had been to the chessboard: his concentration was absolute.

He would protest that he wasn't John Shawnessy, but admitted to having put himself in the novel. He was E. R. Ross, the photographer from Freehaven, who was taking pictures throughout the fabulous Fourth of July. "The Photographer was a pleasant young man with unusual blue eyes, shiny darkbrown hair, and dimples, who did not seem at all disturbed by the confusion in which he worked. People kept coming up and asking him questions about his apparatus, and every now and then, while he was under the hood correcting the focus, a small boy would come up and peer into the lens. Unperturbed, the Photographer waved him away and went on with his work, walking swiftly back and forth from his covered cart to his camera, carrying plates, making adjustments, bobbing in and out of the hood. In this scene, he alone was the artist-contriver as he prepared to trace with a radiant pencil a legend of light and shadow, some faces on the great Road of the Republic."

Another distraction came from his father, who was beginning a new campaign to enlist his son in various projects. He sent him a friend's enormous unpublished epic history of George Rogers Clark cast in eighteenth-century heroic couplets, asking if he'd supply a testimonial. My father declined. "I'm not at all sure that you would be doing the author a service if you made him think he was a world beater."

Gramps then asked him if he'd write another poem about an Indiana river to embellish his new book. "Dear Dad. Thanks for your letter. I am involved in a good deal of creative work just now that I am trying to push toward a culmination of some kind before long, and I'm afraid I wouldn't be able to do the Wabash thing justice."

His father upped the ante. He had good news. The New Harmony Commission was back in business and asked him to write six more books, beyond the three already completed, for the handsome sum of five thousand dollars for the lot. He could have up to three years to complete them. Naturally "I will be on my own expense for stenography, paper, etc.—also travel." Could he count on Scuffie to be back in Indiana for a "literary summer" with good pay? Elsie wrote independently to say, "If you do turn Dad down don't feel too badly about it. In any case he'll have to reduce at least the heavy lecturing." Shockley wrote to encourage him to accept his father's offer. This was a major domestic confrontation.

My father replied that he'd be staying East. "It would be very congenial work, I know, and the offer is generous. But I have some work of my own to finish up, and this is the time for it."

This was a deep blow to Ross Senior.

Another was the death of Roosevelt. Elsie forbade her visiting granddaughters Anne and Kay to play out in her yard during the period of mourning. Their father, Shockley Lockridge, had become a Republican and said "Damn Roosevelt!" upon bumping into a table. During the 1944 election there had been a fracas on High Street. When Shockley's wife, Mary Kay, and Dr. Robert Peters said the Democrats were running a dying man for President just to stay in office, Ross Senior—backed up by Lillian—called them Nazi traitors and ordered them out of the house. Elsie soothed tempers and arranged a truce.

My father wrote home eulogistically on April 26 that "even those who disliked [Roosevelt] felt as though they had lost something important, because hate is a way of life, as well as love. After the first few days, I felt a strange feeling of exultation. I managed to consign the man to History, where of course the verdict of his greatness is assured. How fortunate we were that the Republic was able to find and fashion such an instrument during twelve years of need. . . . The moral force will continue, more or less undiminished, for the man will go on as myth about as forcefully as if he were present in person."

That evening he and Steve Tryon were feted at the senior faculty supper as Simmons College's two "Favorite Professors." He finished up the school year with a flourish. On May 8, V-E day, the "Variety Show Melodrama Has 'Em Rolling in the Aisle. Pay-the-mortgage or I-have-you-where-I-want-you, Rudolph Rassendale Lockridge pursued his elusive handle-bar mustache and beauteous Murgatroyd Hendrickson, as Pa 'See' Palmer stood helplessly by."

Thereafter an anonymous student sent him a tongue-in-cheek note signed Miss Marion Haste, requesting an assignation. He placed a reply in the student mailbox under "H," telling her how his quarters at the Spink-Rialto might be reached via several intermediaries: e.g., "shortly thereafter, an organ grinder, pudgy and plain but with unusual blue eyes, will go by, playing A Toccata of Galuppi's. Follow him. . . ."

Simmons College obituaries appearing in 1948 would best remember him as "Slip-and-slide Lockridge," who played second base in the faculty-student baseball games, and was photographed once with his shirttails out because he had ripped his pants stealing base.

～

In early July, 1945, at an intersection on Highway One, my family and I gathered up bags and typewriters, climbed off the bus, and walked half a mile to an eighteenth-century country house rented for the summer. The Cleaves Barn was no longer available but South Byfield, Massachusetts, four miles from the sea, was an ideal writer's sanctuary. Situated close to the Governor Dummer Academy for Boys, the two-story New England house had a fireplace in every room, beamed ceilings, wide plank floors, and shutters. My mother felt for the first time that she'd like to have a house of her own. There were enough rooms for my father to take cover from hubbub.

A pasture next door featured a woebegone, cross-eyed cow, and there were blueberry patches, some black snakes, and an invasion of elm tree beetles to rival the sandfleas at the Smalleys' back in 1941. But the dignified landlady, Mrs. Helen Noyes, said, "The elm tree beetle, of which we seem to have a few this year, is not a *dirty* bug, if you know what I mean, Mr. Lockridge. After all, he eats elm trees."

"My secret conviction," thought my father, "is that the little bastard feeds exclusively on dung and corpses."

My mother was once again pregnant, expecting in February, and this time the race was to finish the novel before the arrival of the stork. Knowing virtually nobody in the neighborhood and as usual having no telephone, they found it a good quiet place for work. "Everything out here is so goddamn peaceful and wholesome that I'm going nuts," he wrote Steve Tryon. Once a week Mrs. Noyes drove him or my mother into nearby Newburyport for groceries.

During the war only the locals were normally favored with meat. Then one day out of the blue my mother's brother Leon and his young son David dropped in. My mother wept. She hadn't recognized till then how much she'd missed her family the past three years. Her husband, deciding the occasion called for steak, talked the Newburyport butcher into relinquishing the only meat we had that summer—a piece so tough we might as well have been eating that ancient cross-eyed cow.

The Lockridges on High Street were similarly bereft of family. Elsie wrote Vernice that "we all want to see the children & you and Ross so much. One Sunday morn Dad came out into the kitchen where Lillian & I were working & asked to see Jeanne Marie's picture. I couldn't leave my work then so Lillian said she would get it. I told her where it was on my desk. For some reason she failed to find it & Dad apparently had to see it instanter. So I went to my desk & soon located it. Dad looked at all three, wished he could see, *actually* see, Larry so he could see what he looked like & how he acts, said he would love to tell Ernest his history stories. Then he again went into raptures about Jeanne Marie."

Often thereafter my grandfather suffered these "severe wishing spells," asking that pictures be immediately found and that his wife tell him stories about their distant grandchildren. She was running out of material.

Of course, in his mind's eye Ross Junior hadn't really left Indiana and was writing about it every day. Steve Tryon would be passing through the Hoosier State that summer and got some advice from his friend. "For Christ's sake, do not mention to anyone that you know Ross Lockridge." He'd be besieged by hearty back-slapping Hoosiers who would yell, "Put her there, son! How in the Hell is Ross?" He might even be asked to speak at a local Rotary Club and be batted back and forth "like a bewildered tennisball" between the DAR, the Drop and Pearl Club, and Ladies Aid.

Hearing that Tryon might leave Simmons College, he composed an impromptu sonnet for a bronze plaque, beginning:

> Lo! where is Stephen, whose elusive sprite
> Did once flit blithely in these cloistered halls?
> Behold, this clay-pent faun has taken flight,
> With clouds of glory clinging to his balls.

He added a note that stands in contrast to what he had written Blankertz concerning the "glacier-like mass" of his previous novel. "Here in South Bugfield, life goes on at a terrific pace—and so does the Great Work. 1200 copied pages of incandescent prose, at this reading."

The summer passed fruitfully and happily in this "rural Shangri-La." I was protective of my sister, opening doors for her and guarding her if I heard a distant automobile. "Jeanne is entirely unspoiled, at least for the moment. She likes Larry very much and her demonstrations of affection are very violent."

Then in early August the bombs were dropped on Hiroshima and Nagasaki. My parents felt that a demo model might first have been shown the Japanese. But the war in the Pacific was over, they hugged, and Ernest carried a cowbell to the top of the big hill behind the house and rang it. There had been strict gas rationing and no joy rides. Now Mrs. Noyes drove with my mother into Newburyport with no purpose loftier than to celebrate with an ice cream cone.

Back in Boston and reflecting on the fact that the war had come and gone and he'd done nothing but scribble, my father wrote Tryon. "I feel very unheroic these days. The streets are stiff with heroes, bristling with campaign bars. I feel restless as all hell. Don't be surprised if I rush off overseas to bandage the wounds of Polish children."

A child in his own family was suffering some wounds. When Ernest entered the second grade at William McKinley School in the fall of 1945, the terrorism in neighborhood and school increased. Ernest had always been high strung and subject at times to tantrums. The contrast with my own exquisite placidity was dramatic from the beginning. "Larry is a very gentle and obedient little creature, being in this respect the complete antithesis of Ernest."

The war deeply infiltrated Ernest's consciousness, and next to vacuum cleaners he was most fascinated by guns. His grandmother received from him the following one-sentence letter: "Dear Grandma, I want the real rifle to be sent over to Boston. Signed Ernest." His father wrote independently to warn of this "pathetic little scrawl" and suggest she think of some pedagogically correct way of declining. He asked his parents to send something for Ernest's birthday "that doesn't involve killing other children with guns, the main preoccupation with small fry along our street."

Ernest was tyrannized by his classmate Lee Oliver, whose father had been killed by the Germans and whose mother worked as a waitress in the corner coffee shop on Mountfort Street. He was class bully, often accompanied by three or four henchmen. Many days going to and from school, Ernest would encounter Oliver and Company lying in wait to beat him up. His friend Henry Miller was too much a wimp to help out, and Ernest had imbibed enough of his grandpa's frontier lore to know he should stand his ground. One day, during one of these maulings, his father appeared and yanked the bullies off his son, holding Lee Oliver by the collar in righteous fury, chewing him out. Oliver cringed and whined and begged for mercy.

Ernest then made a big mistake: he took pity on his enemy and asked his father to let poor Lee Oliver go. "And Dad was just furious at me, just furious. You're not supposed to feel that way about people who are beating you up!"

William McKinley School was worse than Lee Oliver. The female principal routinely hit him and other delinquent students on the head. One cold drizzling day in late fall our obviously pregnant mother tried to pick Ernest up at the school, a task usually performed by our father. Not recognizing her, the principal ordered her back out in the rain.

My father wrote home to say that Ernest had become "quite a personality problem, and we sometimes wish we had an expert like Grandma Lockridge to turn loose on him." Diagnosing it as sibling rivalry, my grandmother replied that Ernest "shouldn't be permitted to be disobedient," and that when "boys change from model little boys to 'real boys' as they grow older—they have more plans & ideas of their own, more initiative, are less amenable to *gentle* control." It was sometimes necessary to spank, and she had spanked her son Ross that time in Fort Wayne when he chewed at some ladies' dresses.

His father would pick up Ernest from McKinley School and often speak with his teacher, who probably exaggerated Ernest's indiscretions in keeping with the school's pandemic sadism. He would calmly spank his son back home as a matter of principle. Ernest was unclear about the principle and sensed injustice. His father may have decided Grandma Lockridge was wrong for once—it was proving a failed experiment in child-rearing. Late in the school year he stopped it.

Ernest had some difficulty, though, reconciling this stern father with the gentle one who encouraged his fantasy with Pete and Repeat, the adventurous cut-out puppets who came to life every night while he was sleeping.

His handling of Ernest's problems shows both the high regard he gave his mother's opinions, and his steadfast devotion to principle as he saw it—to the extent of losing his flexibility. Several months later, both of these would get *him* into greater trouble than they ever got Ernest.

This regard for his mother's powers was tellingly reconfirmed in the fall of 1945. Elsie wrote him about a young family friend, Billie Rice, who had been institutionalized for depression following the amputation of a leg and, home now, still couldn't stand to be with people. He visited the Lockridges, though, and with her characteristic optimism, Elsie wrote thereafter, "Good old Bill! He'll come out OK." My father replied, "If a stay with you doesn't bring him around,

I can't imagine what would. Like the sunshine and the spring, you have a general revivifying effect on human nature."

But Billie Rice shortly after this visit had a relapse and was once again back in the sanitarium. Elsie worried she might have upset his "precarious balance" in some way. His son reassured her, "You gave him three days of happiness and a hope of ultimate recovery."

To my parents, Boston was less than sunny, springlike, and revivifying. We did have some friendly neighbors in the building on Mountfort Street—Kingdon Grant, for instance, a philosophical spirit whom my father now and then dropped in on for a chat and the only resident from that era still living there in 1989. He continued his colloquies with nearby Aharon Arsenian, and my parents enjoyed the Arsenians' New Year's Eve parties. But Ernest's experience in the school and neighborhood was confirming their feeling that big East Coast cities were not for them. The novel-in-progress owed much to the pastoral tradition—and pastorals from Theocritus's *Idylls* on have been written by city dwellers yearning for the countryside.

In December, 1945, Ross Lockridge started the Dream Section, the finale to his novel, which had grown now to 1,650 retyped pages. The stork was going to win the race, but given his exuberant compositional energies as he went down the stretch, it would be close. He was barely slowed by a case of pneumonia over the holidays. I fell asleep to the drone of typewriters and figured this is what parents must always do at night. Ernest asked his mother if he'd have to write a book when he grew up.

On January 20, 1946, Hugh Baker wrote his daughter a letter. "I lost 3 days work in December 17th, 18th, & 19th. I worked all the time since then up to Tuesday evening. I have been off & at home since that time. I have had a relapse or something which has wound me down. A numbness in my left arm developed & then pains extending through the chest to the shoulder blade. I, fearing that my heart has *gone bluey,* called the Dr. He examined me & said there was not much wrong with me & to go to work if I felt like it."

After his difficult period of unemployment during the Depression, Hugh Baker had made a real comeback. For the past several years he'd been bookkeeper at the respected Seward Foundry and a Master at the Masonic Lodge. He had missed Vernice greatly in recent years, but all his other children had stayed in the Bloomington area. His letter was a gentle warning to this beloved daughter, who immediately sent him recent pictures of us kids playing in the snow.

Elsie Lockridge arrived once again for the delivery. Then on February 14, word came through the building superintendent—who had a telephone—that Hugh Baker had died suddenly that morning. His last words were "It's snowing." He hadn't trusted the doctors and had picked out a black suit and scripture for his funeral.

My mother was grief-stricken. It was all the worse because she hadn't seen him in so long and he'd never know the outcome of her pregnancy. And it was too close to term for her to go home for the funeral. "Ross consoled me. We went for a walk, and he tried to paint the good part—that Dad had had a happy life in the main and that he didn't have to linger and suffer. He was very consoling to me."

A few days later she went into labor and on February 21 gave birth to a boy, named the next day. My father sent telegrams. "ROSS FRANKLIN LOCKRIDGE TERTIUS DIMPLED DARKHAIRED BOY BORN YESTERDAY RESEMBLES DADDY AND GRANDDADDY OTHERWISE PERFECT VERNICE FINE." Ross Senior, pleased and flattered, quoted an old English epitaph: "Here lies James Mather who had a son greater than his fayther and eke a grandson greater than ayther."

I don't believe the naming was egoism. It was in part a compensatory gesture to his father for bowing out of those history projects. And to pass along a name is also a symbolic act of family consolidation. My father was nothing if not a family man. My mother worried that they might have made a mistake.

They had now exactly duplicated his own sibling structure in sex, sequence, and number: Bruce was to Ernest as Shockley was to me as Lillian was to Jeanne as Ross Junior was to Ross Tertius. As if to defy genealogical imperatives, though, Ernest didn't drown young, I am no Republican, Jeanne hasn't gotten fat, and Ross will never kill himself.

Elsie stayed another four weeks, taking us kids for walks along the Charles River, holding tight to the reins she fastened to our backs. She left just before a siege of chicken pox. Neither sickness, death, birth, visitors, teaching, nor even paper-grading was going to slow my father in his labors, as he pushed forward the Dream Section that would be the culmination of that sudden vision he had had in Paris in the spring of 1934.

Though writing phantasmagoria at the time, he recalled that he hadn't yet investigated the phase of the moon for the night of July 4, 1892. Widener Library had an almanac for that year and he was greatly pleased to discover the moon had set at 12:39, just after he had planned to have John Shawnessy bid farewell to his old friend Jerusalem Webster Stiles at the train station.

As Vernice Lockridge steadily typed, she felt she was living through all John Shawnessy's years. When she remembered his childhood experiences, it was as if they had happened several years ago in her own life. On she typed, cheating only a bit on the ground rule of not reading ahead, and gradually catching up with her husband in the Dream Section.

In late April, she typed this passage: "He would be that dreamer, and he would have perhaps again his ancient and eternal dream. . . . Of a quest for the sacred Tree of Life. Of a happy valley and a face of stone—and of the coming of a hero. Of mounds beside the river. Of threaded bones of lovers in the earth. Of shards of battles long ago. Of names upon the land, the fragments of forgotten language. Of beauty risen from the river and seen through rushes at the river's edge. Of the people from whom the hero sprang, the eternal, innocent children of mankind. Of their towns and cities and the weaving millions. Of the earth on which they lived—its blue horizons east and west, exultant springs, soft autumns, brilliant winters. And of all its summers when the days were long. So dreaming, he held the golden bough still in his hand. So dreaming, he neared the shrine where the tree was and the stones and the letters upon them. And the branch quivered alive in his hands, unrolled its bark, became a map covered with lines and letters, a poem of mute but lovely meanings, a page torn from the first book printed by man, the legend of a life upon the earth and of a river running through the land, a signature of father and preserver, of some young hero and endlessly courageous dreamer "

My father heard the typewriter stop for a suspicious period and was about to call out, "No fair, honey. Stop reading that manuscript."

Instead he went into the next room. His wife was in tears, having typed the last page. Her weeping seemed to sanctify that page and he vowed never to change a word of it.

On April 24, the day before his thirty-second birthday, he put the twenty-pound 2,000-page manuscript, divided up among five large punchhole binders, into a suitcase and headed for Houghton Mifflin. For once, he took a cab.

~

It was not supposed to be a cold submission. Steve Tryon was writing a publishing history of Ticknor & Fields, the parent company of Houghton Mifflin, and contacted an editor about his friend's novel-in-progress. This editor, Edward Hodnett, had encouraged my father in early April to drop off the manuscript, but within days he left the company. Another editor, Dorothy Hillyer, also heard of it from Tryon and called my father at Simmons College about a possible submission. But he didn't call ahead to them in late April to say, yes, he was bringing it in.

On April 24, Betty Underwood, a junior editor, was told by her secretary that "there's a guy out there with a *big* manuscript." Several years later she would write of the encounter to her son. "A handsome man—late twenties, early thirties—got up. Even after all these years I remember how remarkable looking he was. He had an absolutely fresh face with the look of a scholastic Billy Budd. Fine blue eyes, dark hair and, as I remember, good color and skin. . . . That first instant I reacted to him the way I always did afterwards—he radiated some special quality of goodness, integrity. I hoped the world wouldn't hurt someone who looked and seemed like that. He was straight-forward, not shy really, but self-effacing. At his feet was a battered suitcase. He had, he said, brought something we 'might have a little interest in looking at.' We chatted a minute longer, then he left. I remember carrying the suitcase up to the little balcony where our Irish clerk (10 years at $22 a week) worked like a navvy 'entering manuscripts' . . . When I left the suitcase behind I figured it would take somebody only a half hour to assess it but I remember I kind of remarked to myself it was unusual he hadn't accompanied it with the standard kook spiel that it wouldn't be possible for the world to manage another day without that particular piece of writing!"

Figuring he had done all that was required of him, my father went home and began the vigil.

The manuscript was first unloaded onto Austin Olney, a new young employee, who was asked by emeritus editor-in-chief Ferris Greenslet to report on the novel. Olney thought the novel obscure in its symbolism and Proustian. "I am sure this would never sell enough to make it a practical venture, but on a chance that it might draw a small but passionate following, I think someone else should look at it." Hearing this on May 3, Greenslet was inclined simply to reject the manuscript.

But the logistical chore of mailing back a stuffed battered suitcase may have weighed in its favor, for it was still asquat the premises of Two Park Street when there were two timely interventions. My father's old Harvard acquaintance Dick Scowcroft, who had published a novel in 1945 with Houghton Mifflin, ran into him, asked about his novel, and was dismayed to learn he'd simply dropped it off cold. Scowcroft told him to write to Dorothy Hillyer, using his name, and let her know the novel was somewhere in the house. Scowcroft then called her, and upon hearing that it had had a discouraging reading, told her to have a look herself.

And Steve Tryon, often at Houghton Mifflin doing research for his publishing history, dropped by the office of Dorothy Hillyer to ask how his friend's novel was faring. She said not very well and gave him the impression it was already rejected.

Tryon went to bat. He had hastily read through only the first of the five volumes and the novel wasn't to his taste—it was too symbolic. But he informed her that it was "either one of the great books of our time or a pile of nonsense." It was therefore in Houghton Mifflin's interest to give it a serious reading. He added that Dick Scowcroft had told Lockridge that Houghton Mifflin had underpublicized his own first novel and that a New York house would be a better place for it. She listened and decided to channel the novel for more readings and read it herself.

Not one to mince words in any direction, Tryon reported all this back to my father, who was as upset with Tryon as he was with Houghton Mifflin, fearing the manuscript had been more endangered than rescued by that talk of "a pile of nonsense." On May 10, 1946, he wrote a momentous letter to Dorothy Hillyer.

His charming friend Tryon seems to have been "a self-appointed ambassador" who "has a way of overplaying his hand." His estimate of the book presented "rather somber alternatives. The book may or may not be one of the great books of our time—it certainly isn't a pile of nonsense." It needed some "cutting, sharpening, rearranging" and some of the "corn taken out of it," but it was hardly "a huge chaos crying for the knife. It's as solid as a rock. . . . I can hardly keep from assaulting it now with the black pencil. *Bref,* what I want is a chance to liberate the classic that is in it." Contrary to the young first reader, the book is written for a large audience and "will be talked about, written about, and read, read, read!"

Moreover, the common impression is that Houghton Mifflin "is timid and conservative about taking and pushing a work that doesn't conform to some easily recognizable and saleable genre." He has a connection in his cousin Mary Jane Ward, author of the current best-seller *The Snake Pit,* to New York houses with more "dash and dare." "The MS has been nearly three weeks at Houghton Mifflin and can stay as long again. But after that, if you're not taking fire from it, I'll want it, as school will be out on the Fenway, and I shall be off on my adventures, after five years of sackcloth and ashes." Since the novel wasn't knocking them dead at Houghton Mifflin, he silently sent a carbon to Prentice-Hall.

How reconcile this letter—and many of those that follow—with the self-effacing young man standing a few days earlier in front of a battered suitcase? Some of it was the medium of communication. In person and over the telephone he continued to be reasonable, soft-spoken, witty, willing to make compromises—and usually, not always, easy to deal with. But behind the writing desk he was once again that epic poet who had aspired unremittingly to enshrine a vision in a book and who wanted it out there in the world being read, the sooner the better. This same visionary ambition now funneled into the epistolary format, with ultimately disastrous results. I've even wondered if he'd be alive still if he'd had a telephone during the next several months, with no qualms about long-distance calls. It was a false economy, whatever a writer's need for insulation.

Blankertz thought the completion and acceptance of the novel was Ross Lockridge's ego getting at last out of its cage. The metaphor is apt up to a point. But I'll go this far in extenuation of my father: I think it unlikely for a thirty-two-year-old author to have just completed this particular manuscript and, be it greatness or nonsense, *not* think it a masterwork. The same ambition that produced the novel—which I think had roots in a will-to-create deeper than personal ego—sustained him for a time thereafter and sought confirmation of itself.

It seems to me that most editors today would already have told him to take his manuscript and shove it. But with that three-week ultimatum, Houghton Mifflin's readers now began to confirm his own hopeful estimate. His letter was so audacious it worked. Editor Dale Warren gave the novel its first enthusiastic reading—"Anyone here who has ever read a manuscript should take a crack at this"—and thereafter Ferris Greenslet, Dorothy Hillyer, and others chimed in as the manuscript made the rounds.

One wrote, "Having finished Volume I, I want to write down quickly that this is the most exciting manuscript I have read since I have been here. It is a work of genius." Upon completing it this reader added, "I am even more impressed . . . The book is 'overwritten,' but this is no more a criticism than to say that the Mississippi is swollen with spring floods."

Another wrote that the novel "does not strike me at first glance as a work of unmistakable genius. At the end of Volume II, I am still holding my judgment in abeyance, though I have pretty well made up my mind that Lockridge is the man from Mars." Upon completing it, this reader added that "my respect for the intentions of the writer began to go up sharply. . . . Whether *Raintree County* is a great American novel or not is beside the point; we need more of this kind of courageous stab at it."

Another wrote, "This is a very difficult book to criticize. There is the spirit of Whitman—full of a melancholy wonder at the young, virile, and immense character of our country; there is a Stephen Benét 'sweep of American history'; there is the satirical and debunking strain of a Sinclair Lewis; there is a W. H. Hudson school of nature; there is the symbolism of James and Hawthorne carried almost to its logical conclusion; there are Grant Wood pictures of the Middle West; there are de Maupassant passages which are brutally earthy. Some will find the satire harsh; the nature writing too lush; the symbolism overpowering. But when all of this is said, there remains a work whose boldness takes your breath and through whose great length your interest is held fast."

Dorothy Hillyer thanked Dick Scowcroft and told him "it smells of money." He would be sent $250 by the company for his intervention.

Having dispatched his own novel, my father found time to read his cousin's. Mary Jane Ward's *The Snake Pit,* a largely autobiographical novel based on her nine-month stay as a mental patient at New York's Rockland State Hospital in 1941, was on its way to No. 2 on the nation's best-seller lists. He liked it and wrote home that "apparently Mary Jane lost an awfully long week-end. It really is a frightfully competent little book, given the object." It is "considerably more than a mere clinical record. The realization of character and the emotional atmosphere of the mentally 'sick' is the work of an artist rather than the mere psychological reporter. I think we may be justly proud of our cousin's book—if not of the experience that made it possible."

Responding to yet another request from his father, he said he once again couldn't help out this summer—he'd be "pressing some matters of my own."

Waiting to hear from Houghton Mifflin, he was so anxious he sought out a masseur, an unprecedented indulgence. He had to cancel a couple of classes. It wasn't only whether the outcome would be positive or negative. Having so much of himself being read and judged for the first time felt rather like being walked on. He thought of writing Mary Jane to see if she had some ideas about other publishers. Hating the idea of being thought a "poor relation," he refrained.

Edith Helman, a professor of Spanish and member of the "Rockport Group," was sitting in her office on Monday, May 27, 1946, when her friend Ross Lockridge walked by to make a call at the pay telephone near the main entrance of Simmons College. He was well known for not having a home telephone and being unreachable. She was among the few to whom he'd spoken, with great hopes, of his novel-in-progress. He finished his call, loped into her office, and in great elation exclaimed, "Edith, they're taking it! They say it's terrific and I know it *is!*"

~

Dorothy Hillyer told him how enthusiastic the editorial response was, though there was some question about the fifth volume, the Dream Section, that would have to be discussed. Despite the slow start and my father's sense it was taking forever, editor-in-chief Paul Brooks gave this twenty-pound heap an imprimatur only one month and a few days after its submission.

In his report to the executive committee, he noted that the novel had had seven in-house readings, including his own. "In contrast to the thinness and narcissism of a great deal of recent fiction by young writers, this is refreshingly rich, exuberant, alive and surprisingly objective. I believe that it can be built into big sales and that the author will go on to write smaller and better books. Recommendation: To publish."

Assistant Professor Ross Lockridge was too excited to hold class and ran home to tell an elated Vernice. He even bought a bottle of champagne.

Jean and John Arsenian were walking by the Mountfort Street building and decided to drop in unannounced. "And there was Ross in a state of glee, euphoria. He didn't immediately say what it was about but it emerged that on that day his novel had been accepted and they were about to toast the event." Jean and John, both Harvard Ph.D.'s in psychology, had known he was writing a novel but assumed it was a potboiler to feed his family. John himself was thinking of writing a detective novel, and Jean had been encouraging him to read one first. Ross described his novel to the Arsenians, who were surprised to hear it was a real assault on Mount Parnassus.

As he talked on, he spoke of how much work he had yet to do, and Vernice saw he was already getting anxious about it, the euphoria of the day fading a little. That night he sent a telegram to his folks. Now they would have proof that he could write, he told his wife.

Two days later, he packed Vernice and the kids off to Bloomington as planned, tipping the porter of our Pullman compartment as his mother had advised. On the train I kept saying, "I'm very sorry Daddy isn't coming with us." Jeanne, Ernest, and I lay on the lower berth and peered out the window, staying awake as long as we could. We sensed that life was accelerating toward some unknown adventure.

The telegram had miscarried, so my mother broke the good news to the Lockridge family upon arrival. She was saddened to return to the little house on Lincoln Street for the first time in four years and see her mother now living there alone.

My father was lonely surveying the family debris: "torn magazines, bits of crayons, small cast-off garments, holes in the wall that go through almost to the sunlight, Ernest's Picasso-like drawings. . . . I don't know how many times since I came home I've heard children's voices in the street and have involuntarily gone to the window to see if Ernest is alright. It seems quite implausible that little Larry and Jeanne aren't sitting there in the adjoining room pulling beds to pieces and yelling Clementine at the top of their lungs."

He promptly got letters of congratulation from his parents and Lillian. Elsie Lockridge wrote, "The emotional reaction I have been experiencing is complex. I have known of your work on The Book. The years, the hours, the difficulty of doing such type of work surrounded by little banditti—but also the inspiration such a family and Vernice are to you. Many times I have wondered how you could create with such a multitude of responsibilities which had to be met—and which you did meet. Well, I have hoped and had faith. Then I know how happy you are now—how a future has opened up to you which will continue to give you work you love."

Her own career had been largely folded into her husband's by now. She was helping him on a series of historical articles for the New Harmony newspaper. She continued to be active in the Conversation Club, wrote a history of Women's Clubs in Indiana, worked to integrate Finley School, and still composed an annual Spring Poem, with mixed results:

> Each spring, I've written verse on verse!
> And tho I sweat, & toil, & curse,
> Each spring they've gotten worse and worse!
> My husband read my latest verse.

His answer was extremely terse.
"Elsie, this stuff is getting worse."

Ross Senior congratulated his son but cautioned against great expectations for the novel. "What you have already accomplished is enough for a beginning." And Lillian asked him to send along *The Snake Pit* so she could read it in time for Mary Jane's autograph when she visited Bloomington that summer.

He was to prepare for meetings with Houghton Mifflin's top brass a few weeks later on July 1 and 2 to discuss revisions, promotion, and contract. He'd been offered an advance of $3,500 and with this enormous monetary reserve was confident about his next move.

As he wrote Larry Wylie, "I finally did my long postponed but all the sweeter act of kissing the unsightly pile of Simmons College farewell. It was a wonderful place to have been, and my whole attitude toward it is sweetly elegiac. Mr. Beatley graciously granted me a leave of absence, which we both knew was just an academic gesture. I verbally applied the toe of my shoe to the seat of [Chairman] Wylie Sypher's pants, and showed the whole world of teaching a swiftly receding view of my derrière."

Tryon thought he should keep his toe in teaching just in case, and Larry Wylie felt some pain at the satiric put-down of the school where he'd helped engineer a job for his friend. But my father felt his career was now *writer,* and having accepted patiently the sacrifice of countless hours in paper-grading and lecturing, he was now "free as the wind—and almost Gone With It." I suppose billions of people teaching in literature departments fantasize such a moment.

This was, he told Wylie, the payoff of a ten-year gamble, "as I've had a masterwork on the boards ever since college days. I don't know what the world will make of it, but at any rate, I tried. My whole strength was thrown into it without stint." He told Wylie the book owed much to him, France having given him cosmopolitanism and Simmons the sinecure necessary to keep his family afloat while he was writing.

To Malcolm Correll, now collecting cosmic rays in Colorado, he wrote that his publishers had told him "they never had a novel like it, it's the book America has been waiting for, etc., etc. Since I'm only an amateur in these matters, I suppose I will just have to sit modestly back and accept their judgment. . . . They are going to try to make a best-seller out of the book, although I didn't fabricate a single line with that in mind. . . . Now that I've finished the darned novel, think I'll conduct a research to see if I can find out what's causing all these children. Yours, Claudie."

Remarkably, he told everybody he expected to revise the entire novel that summer so the book could be out for the 1946 Christmas trade.

Houghton Mifflin was giving him highest praise to his face, and entrusting their doubts to internal memos. Dale Warren had him to his apartment June 4 and told him more of Houghton Mifflin's enthusiasm. As Ross wrote Vernice, "They are absolutely gaga about it. He commented on passage after passage—for example the famous bullpasture scene, which he thinks is one of the most wonderful things in all literature, etc., etc. Johnny Shawnessy's homecoming from the war, he said, had strangely reminded him after many years of a fantasy he used to have when he was a soldier in World War I—that he would come back and everyone would think that he was dead, etc. He said that all soldiers have fancies of that kind, even when they aren't in serious combat, and he considered the war scenes inimitable. Apparently, darling, you and I have built a book that America needs and of which we may be immensely proud."

But one week earlier, in an internal memo, Warren had expressed grave doubts about the Dream Section—he thought it imitative of Joyce's Walpurgisnacht and likely to sink the novel as popular fiction.

Dorothy Hillyer initially told Ross of reservations about this part, so during the first week of June he sat down and wrote two lengthy documents. In one he told them what revisions he was prepared to make. He'd decided the title of the novel should be simply *Raintree County;* he had submitted it with a misleading one, *The Riddle of Raintree County.* There were other sensible revisions but he didn't wish to cut for the sake of cutting. And first and foremost he didn't wish to drop the Dream Section, giving an exhaustive defense of it.

The second document was—from an editor's point of view— even more fatiguing, a single-spaced 32-page "skeletal outline" of the entire novel. These two texts, he proposed, could be the basis of the editorial meetings in July. Writing them exhausted him. Upon receipt, Dorothy Hillyer wrote Paul Brooks, "I am quite dubious as to whether we can persuade Lockridge to omit his fifth volume."

It's clear he was beginning an orchestration of the publisher's handling of his novel, and also a profusion of words *about* his novel, as if he were continuing to write it by other means, and as if he could shape readers' perceptions by what he said about it. He wrote Hillyer on June 9 that his "attitude toward the book is a little that of a crusader. It is a book that Americans need to read. It will do them good—goddam them—." It was a moral fiction with its own work to perform in the world, a book he thought an America in decline needed as soon as possible.

Prentice-Hall had asked him to let them know if negotiations with Houghton Mifflin broke off. He now told Hillyer, "You took the book right out from under Prentice-Hall . . . I much prefer Houghton Mifflin to any other publisher"—as if he had vast experience.

Some of this was blarney he'd learned from his crusading Rotarian father. But he meant it, as is clear in letters to Vernice—he quickly came to *love* Houghton Mifflin and thought he'd been granted license to say and divulge anything to them. Family man that he was, he'd begun to think of this publishing house as a family—one in which he was extremely well regarded. By June 9 he was already calling Dorothy Hillyer his "fairy god-mother."

He was something more and other than the youngest, most promising son; he felt early on that he'd been granted unusual authority. After all, Dorothy Hillyer told him "that I have succeeded in doing what Thomas Wolfe wanted to do but could never pull off" and that *Raintree County* was "the novel Walt Whitman might have written." As my mother would say years later, "He had thought they liked him there."

Thus, in giving great encouragement and well-intentioned praise, and in politely not challenging Ross Lockridge's self-estimate (authors will be authors), the company at the beginning unwittingly fanned an Olympian flame that could quickly gutter.

That month my father sought out Dick Scowcroft to talk shop. Scowcroft had thought Ross Lockridge "the most normal person in Harvard" when he'd known him as a graduate student—he "dazzled his teachers, wasn't bothered by the routine, and was a guy in total control." At Scowcroft's apartment on Garfield Street in Cambridge, they talked for five hours, drinking bourbon, before going out for a sandwich.

Scowcroft was struck that Lockridge "talked about the book almost as if *he* hadn't written it." He talked about the preparation, the reading of great world writers, and yet the attempt to uncover quintessential *American* themes by means of his own family scribblers and history. He said "nothing grandiose about himself, but simply talked excitedly about how a writer writes a book. He wasn't manic, but eager, capable. We shared excitement about the novel."

They talked a little about Europe and then, as they got deeper into the bottle of bourbon, a little about sex. Ross spoke of his total fidelity and "how marvelous his wife was, how their sex life had improved over the years." He claimed—a stretcher, I've suggested—that he'd lost his virginity in Paris to a girl from an Eastern school, but "he had married a wonderful girl who became more wonderful with the years."

He disagreed with a mutual acquaintance that all friendship has a necessary component of homosexuality. Despite Freud's talk of friendship as aim-inhibited eros, he didn't feel it in his own warm friendships. "He wasn't bothered by poverty, growing family, small-time job. Personal problems—or complications—seemed not to exist. He was still the good-looking, bright, genial, totally well-adjusted young man I had thought him years before." Scowcroft walked my father to the subway after this exhilarating evening. He was one of many who would see a change in him a few months later.

Lockridge looked out on Mountfort Street at the "poor little deadbeats playing up and down it" and decided he could never bring the family back. He wrote his wife to begin looking around Bloomington for a place to live. With his career opening up, he'd be well situated in Indiana for travel both east and west, and the family would be well taken care of in his absences. As always he arranged to sublet the Mountfort Street apartment and was pleased to have the young couple move in with him right away on June 8.

From Bloomington, Ernest wrote his friend Henry Miller a one-sentence letter: "Dear Henry, I have two bunnies, a turtle, and the mumps. Signed Ernest." Even with mumps Bloomington was an improvement over Mountfort Street, with Grandma telling Tommy and

Zippy stories and Grandpa Old Northwest frontier stories, grue-
some in the extreme.

Vernice wrote that Bloomington's *World-Telephone* had wind of
the novel and was asking them about it—could he prepare a statement? He sat down and wrote "*Raintree County*: a Critical Estimate,"
a lengthy document in which he said the novel, appearing "at the out-
set of the Atomic Age . . . is a nostalgic farewell to the America in
which so much began that is sublime and tragic in the democratic tradition." It is "one of the longest novels ever published," "aspires to be
the greatest of the sentimental novels," and treats "erotic love" with
a "candor perhaps unequalled by any other American book."

Vernice cautioned him on the self-praise, saying that maybe that
sort of thing should come directly from the publisher, and even Ross
Senior agreed. My father replied that he was mostly parroting what
his publishers were telling him, but then addressed a couple of letters
to Houghton Mifflin on the question. It was agreed the publisher
should handle all such requests.

There were some uprisings as spring turned to summer, all with
Indiana connections. He learned that his "god-awful pageant" had
been given again in New Harmony to an audience of four thousand.
He was learning the old Horatian truth that a word once sent forth
can never be recalled. "I wonder if I can buy it back from them for
the $50.00 they paid me."

Ross Senior received a letter from Mary Jane Ward, offering to
write a blurb on her cousin's novel and telling him she'd be in
Bloomington in July to give a workshop at the annual writers' conference. Ross Senior replied, "I understand he will bring the book
manuscript with him and then I hope we can get a peep at it. I have
never seen any of it or talked with him about it. All I know is the little that I have been able to 'corkscrew' from Vernice. He will no
doubt attend the Writers Conference. I think he ought to enroll in
your workshop and probably one or two others—but, who am I to
tell him anything. These 'big hit' authors in the family have me buffa-
loed. . . . In fact, I feel considerably 'shaded' by these new
Lockridge literary lights."

Hearing of this, my father immediately wrote Mary Jane and a
busy new correspondence began. He confessed having traded shame-
lessly on her name during the dark moments of waiting to hear from

Houghton Mifflin. Her offer to write a blurb was innocent in the extreme, he said, since the novel would be the longest ever published in one piece in America. "You see, I was a cross-country runner in college." He told of the novel's acceptance, adding that "from what people have told me since, I had fabulous nerve for an unknown first novelist."

And he reviewed the history of their own relationship—indeed he hadn't seen her since he was about sixteen, when she and her mother were in Bloomington, she wearing big shell-rimmed glasses and naughtily smoking cigarettes with her mother. "And my mother actually tried smoking a cigarette too—a legendary occurrence. . . . I think it was many years later that your first book appeared—*The Tree Has Roots*. Like your recent and very famous book, it was completely genuine and natural—and, as I remember it, tinged with wisdom and sadness—qualities not characteristically Lockridge, if you know what I mean. As for your last novel, it filled me with admiration—and envy." He looked forward to seeing her at the writers' conference.

And then a still bigger uprising. My father had loyal friends. From Haverford, Larry Wylie spoke to his older brother Jeff, who was now New England bureau chief for Time-Life. Jeff had already had an indirect influence on my father, setting off a train of events by his own enthusiasm for Paris, which encouraged his brother to go, which . . . He had known Shockley Lockridge at the Phi Gam fraternity, had briefly dated Vernice's older sister, Beulah, and had taken a psychology course in which Elsie Lockridge was a fellow student. (Earlier, at Bloomington High School, he took Physical Geography and sat at the same table with an older student named Carmichael. One day the teacher asked, "Hoagy, what are the isotherms?" Hoagy improvised an answer in syncopated rhythm: "There's ice in the isotherms / And it's cold up north!")

After serving as president of Epworth League and deciding not to be a minister, Jeff tried his hand at disillusioned poetry, was an art critic for the Louisville *Courier Journal,* and Kentucky correspondent for Time-Life before coming to Boston.

Hearing of Ross Lockridge's novel, he tried to call him, discovered he had no telephone, and on June 28 sent a telegram from his office. "JUST HEARD ABOUT THE BOOK FROM LARRY AND HAVE TALKED TO

HOUGHTON MIFFLIN ABOUT MY DOING A POSSIBLE ARTICLE ON YOU FOR LIFE I'LL BE IN BLOOMINGTON THROUGH MOST OF JULY AND UNDERSTAND YOU WILL BE THERE TOO HOPE WE CAN DISCUSS IT FURTHER. JEFF WYLIE, 1318 STATLER BLDG." Within three hours Ross Lockridge appeared at his office.

Jeff didn't know this particular Lockridge but liked him immediately, and they set to "like a couple of kids talking about building a tree house." It was a case of mutual aid—Hoosier helping Hoosier—because Jeff, relatively new at his position, hoped to find good stories. They were quickly on the same beam, wisecracking their way through the possibilities.

Younger generations may not know of the immense influence of *Life* in those vintage years. Twenty-six million people read it or looked at the pictures every week. Turning America into a global village in its own way, it made people aware of how remarkable their own backyard barbecues were, their own high school dances. It gave the signal for new fads. It had come of age covering the Second World War, influencing my father's discarded epic poem. For any publicist to get a story placed there was a triumph, and Jeff Wylie was besieged with story ideas—including one from a foot fetish artist hoping to have his images of shoes and toes spread throughout America. But the story on Ross Lockridge originated within Jeff's own circle and he undertook it warmly.

The next day my father sent off an epic epistle to Jeff to be used as ammunition with the central office in New York, summarizing the story possibilities they'd discussed and rhapsodizing on *Life* as cultural history. The article could appear in a July Fourth issue with pictures dramatizing great institutions such as the old G.A.R. parades. Or the real-life background in Henry County could be featured, and "perhaps some quaint old family photographs might be exhumed to advantage here." Or, with the influence of *Intolerance* and *Citizen Kane* in mind, the "motion-picture possibilities of my book might be foreseen . . . but there I go—already halfway to Hollywood!" Or there could be a story on how he wrote the novel, "with pictures illustrating a fairly elaborate text. It's just possible that the author of the book would be available for this feat."

The air was promise-crammed. Vernice wrote that "we are all eager to see again the Hero of Raintree County" on July Fourth, by chance the legendary day of his novel. His conferences on July 1 and 2 seemed to go well. He was sticking to his guns on the Dream Section but would try to pare it down. They hoped he would drop it altogether. Paul Brooks called it "a very pleasant and fruitful get-together."

My father wrote his wife that she outclassed Lana Turner, whom he'd recently seen in a movie. "Decidedly, I'll have to write the screen version of my own book. Even pearls poured into the Hollywood hopper can come out corn." He hurriedly packed trunks with the Shockley family archive and his manuscript.

He'd been away from Indiana for four years and in that time had fashioned a visionary narrative he hoped embodied both the spirit of his home state and the spirit of America. He was now launched as a writer and prepared for a great homecoming. It would be a relief to get out of the overheated city apartment and return "to the cool breezes of Indiana. And to the arms of my darling sweet wife. Love, Love, Love, Love, Love, Love, Love! Ross."

VIII

Author in the Epic

Departures and homecomings give rise to the pathos of *Raintree County.* Reported dead, John Shawnessy returns from the Civil War to confront two new tombstones in Danwebster graveyard, his sweetheart Nell's and his own. Years later he returns from New York City upon news his mother is dying. His friend the Perfessor surmises that all myths of homecoming are really myths of death. Shawnessy never enjoys a triumphant homecoming and spends most of his life anyway in the county of his origin.

But the larger novel narrates triumphant homecomings of several of his friends, back in Raintree County for the 1892 Fourth of July celebration in Waycross (i.e., Straughn), Indiana—a politician, a financier, and an army general. They've all made it out there in the world and can now enjoy an afternoon of hometown applause. Also stepping off the train that day, to no applause, is the infidel Perfessor, chased out of the county many years earlier.

Ross Lockridge takes his plot from a short story, "The Great Stone Face," which turns on an obvious irony. Nathaniel Hawthorne's stay-at-home, idealistic, lowly Ernest is seen by local people in the end to have a nobler profile than four returning hometown heroes, yellow-faced and weather-beaten. He himself thus fulfills the local prophecy that a great and noble personage would someday appear whose face resembles a face shaped by nature in the side of a mountain.

Throughout the Fourth of July, in a series of flashbacks, fifty-three-year-old Shawnessy reviews his life, which began in great expectations but has seemingly come to little beyond a wife, three kids, and a small house in a hick town. Despite this, amid fireworks and exclamations of children at the end of the day, the Perfessor hoarsely declares, "Behold! John Wickliff Shawnessy is himself the Hero of Raintree County!"

On his own triumphant Fourth of July homecoming to Bloomington, Lockridge played ironic counterpoint to his fictional hero, a would-be poet who never finishes his great work. Was Lockridge outstripping the sad wisdom of his own novel? Perhaps an American epic could be written after all. And perhaps this homecoming signaled a new life—recognition, a career free of paper-grading, the liberation of his wife from the typewriter and of his children from Mountfort Street, and no more sackcloth and ashes.

As if to confirm that his euphoria must have been anchored in sand, I'll have to assume here that my own reader has never read *Raintree County* and, if lucky, has never seen the MGM "film."

In my academic writing I've been urging, to an audience of tens, a renewed ethical criticism, pretty much swept under by reigning critical agendas. One of my plainer assumptions is that a literary work provides writers with an arena of moral experimentation, where they can ask of themselves "What if?" and "What then?"—concocting premises of character and situation and seeing what follows.

Formalist critics in the Forties and Fifties warned us against literary biographers, who have nothing to tell us about literature in itself. Who cares why Shakespeare willed his second-best bed to his wife or whether he had anything in common with Hamlet or what he intended in *Troilus and Cressida?* What matters is what ended up in the plays. Now the formalists are themselves in disgrace, sent packing by historicists, deconstructionists, and neo-Freudians.

With due respect to two maligned parties, I think a critic can still combine the formalist's delight in fictional structures with the literary biographer's passion for authorial self-revelation. Writers invite this critical flexibility because they often test dynamics of their own personalities, finding their material very close to home, altering it in various ways, and in effect asking "What if?" and "What then?"

My metaphor for authorial composition is less the familiar one of "playing" than of "testing."

Lockridge insisted he makes only a cameo appearance in his own novel—on page 555 as the Raintree County photographer, E. R. Ross—but the novel is in part a continuous testing of aspects of his own personality, parceled out to various characters in situations of opportunity and crisis. This is only one dimension of *Raintree County*—the one of interest to us here—because, as Paul Brooks said, it is also "refreshingly objective" in contrast to all the "narcissistic" fiction that was deluging the American public.

A private person, Lockridge wrote a novel in no way private, where he opened up to public view all he most valued, all he most feared. The novel takes us on a journey into an interior only hinted at in his earlier writings and correspondence.

We can make our way there first through contrasts between Lockridge himself and a few characters both historical and fictional—contrasts that lie embedded in the novel's origin and structure.

When his mother called his deceased grandfather John Wesley Shockley a great man, Lockridge didn't challenge the estimate. His grandfather's learning *was* uncommon for someone with almost no formal training beyond primary school.

Certainly he spelled better than his brothers. During the Civil War his brother Elisha wrote another brother, Franklin: "Since I rote to you we hav had A picknic here A man by the name of Mikel Cornelle was shote fore shootin at A corprele it look hard fore A man to follow his coffin around and to stand by the side of his coffin and twelv men shoot at him but we must obey orders. . . . you want me to write to you whither I wold let Henry go an live with you I will tell you whot I think About that. . . . I hav no objetion to him living with you fore I know that you will take care of him right I want him rais right It wod greav me to here him sware an talk as other boys do I want him and sis sent to school and not be rais in ignorunce fore if you was here and see the negros you wold say giv me education."

John Shockley cultivated a different discourse:

Shade of the Raintree

My muse and I, one summer morn,
Built, dreaming we were cunning fays,
A castle on a cloud-isle borne
Adrift on blue, ethereal bays.
Our blessed isle was far away
From earth. It swam down eastern skies,
Whereon in bright pavilions lay
Glad choristers with joyous eyes,
And from their sweet throats woke the song—
'Tis summer, and the days are long.

Far east o'er pure empyreal seas,
Our happy souls that morning sailed,
Light-seated on our isle at ease,
Unheeding earth from whence we hailed.
Forgotten was all touch of care.
An age was lived in one sweet dream
As in our castle built in air
We swam the blue celestial stream
Safe into daybreak with the song—
'Tis summer, and the days are long.

While acknowledging its quaint Tennysonian echoes, Lockridge loved this poem, especially the last three lines.

I'd call it a species of Hoosier Orientalism. John Shockley's poems are escapist, many of them dream visions. They often find him choosing among an embarrassment of riches. When twelve beautiful maidens descend in a basket, our poet swiftly marries the youngest and best-looking. In "The Two Girls" the poet spies on Katie and Mat swimming in the nude, prefers Katie, and marries her. He tries his hand at the short story: After cheating death in a Nashville hospital, Alfred Kline becomes a New York bohemian poet, woos Jennie on Lake Tahoe over the objections of her parents, who would rather she perish at the hands of Indians, rescues her from an inundated tree, whereupon they drift out into the Pacific Ocean and live happily ever after. There are some folksy coups de plume with more local color, but John Shockley often deploys his imagination to get the hell out of Indiana and away from his sober wife Emma.

I find no unfinished epic in his surviving works to suggest a larger literary ambition. The closest is "An Indian Idyll," which exists in three unfinished drafts and concerns an ancient temple of twelve large slabs, on which an epic legend has been etched in an Indian language now lost. Another lengthy narrative poem, "A Summer Dream," mingles Spenser, Coleridge, and Keats, as my brother Ernest notes, in an Edenic quest romance full of birthing monstrosities.

Adapting his grandfather to the role of leading character, Lockridge asks, in effect, what if we give him true epic ambition and what if we bolster somewhat his literary pedigree? John Shockley was born on April 29, so he nudges the gestation back a few days and gets his hero, John Shawnessy, born on Shakespeare's official birthday, April 23, improving on his own near miss of April 25. (We know for sure only that Shakespeare was baptized on April 26.)

He also slips in an old family legend that his great-grandfather William B. Shockley was a bastard son of Thomas Carlyle. His fictional counterpart, T. D. Shawnessy, strongly hints this in confessing his bastardy to his son. (There are only two problems with this legend. One is the common opinion that Carlyle died a virgin. The other is that Carlyle was born in 1795 and W. B. Shockley in 1801, so even if the Victorian Sage was unacknowledged stud to all the lasses of Ecclefechan, it seems unlikely he got started by the age of six.)

Other tailorings of his grandfather show that Lockridge was in effect asking, What if I make Shawnessy more like me? Where John Shockley had been born eighth in a family of fifteen children, Lockridge makes John Shawnessy the youngest in a somewhat smaller family and, like himself, an accident. Shawnessy like Lockridge decides on a career of writer at the age of seven.

More telling are the many personality parallels. Both Lockridge and Shawnessy are fascinated by words and totally absorbed as readers, are students of classical literature and myth, and ponder time, antiquities, and old photographs. Both entertain a sense of special destiny as writers, in a clash of native humility with egoism. Their keen interest in sex chafes against an inner check. They have a capacity for friendship, male and female, yet give the impression of holding something in reserve. They are fast runners and competitive in a self-punishing way. They are smiling, handsome, rather soft-spoken and shy, heterosexual, attractive to women, and possessed of a vitality and optimism sometimes seen by others as naive. They are idealist in philosophy, nonliteral in religion, liberal socialist in politics, and are always trying to do the right thing. Except on occasion, neither smokes or drinks or swears. Neither tells his parents off.

Beneath this formidable miscellany is a trait Lockridge lays out schematically early in his novel. His hero is "plural"—on the one hand he is Mr. Shawnessy, "a dutiful citizen of the Republic calling for his mail," and on the other he is mr. shawnessy, "a faunlike hero poised on the verge of festive adventures." Mr. Shawnessy is the public family man bounded by custom who lingers on thresholds without crossing and acts as "a large comfortable mask" for his twin.

"mr. shawnessy," in turn, runs into naked women on stone slabs in post offices, crosses all boundaries of time and space in an "eternal vagabondage," and feels his mythic participation in the history of the human race from Genesis to Revelation. "His face peered furtively from a frieze of the Parthenon, passed in mob scenes in the reign of Justinian, crossed with crowds on Brooklyn Ferry ever so many centuries hence. . . . Mr. Shawnessy had made the turn north onto the County Road. But the insouciant twin had kept the westward bias."

They are of course one person, the narrator concedes, but it is largely mr. shawnessy who hopes to write the great epic of his people.

When *Raintree County* appeared, some of Ross Lockridge's friends and acquaintances were surprised by the novel's depth of feeling. They had known him as someone with "a delightful sense of whimsy and of relaxed fun," who "carried a truly impressive fund of erudition as naturally as breathing," as Don Smalley would write his wife, Ruth. "In contrast and in conflict there lived the other Ross who felt driven to greatness, a Ross carefully hidden from friends and colleagues, I would judge, certainly from me"—and this Ross, Smalley thinks, must have been punishing to the other. I agree.

Lockridge attempted half-seriously to revise his persona when returning from Europe in 1934, to make the smiling young man more consistent with the serious consciousness within, if only to impress the girls. He was annoyed by his affable public self, satirizing it as Mr. Shawnessy, and yielding his pen to the lyrical, memory-haunted self within. Only in his novel was this self permitted to speak.

Given these resemblances in personality between author and main character, Lockridge transforms the circumstances and happenings of his own life, as if to put himself by proxy through a more severe testing.

What if, for example, he had like Bruce confronted death by drowning? Johnny Shawnessy at seventeen tries to follow the Shawmucky River down to Paradise Lake and gets lost in the Great Swamp, where he drops neck-deep into ooze, at the last moment grabbing an exposed willow root. "He clung to the willow, gasping with a fear he hadn't felt during the struggle. Around him, impassive, secret, beautiful, the Great Swamp shimmered and stank. With a brutal indifference, his own earth had nearly killed him."

For a youth who has been reading Shakespeare on the banks of his beloved river and dreaming of noble fame, the experience is chastening. Nature, which had worn a nurturing human face, must now be engaged without sentimentality.

And what if Lockridge had lost Vernice Baker to a rival? Shawnessy watches as Nell Gaither makes out with Garwood Jones backstage at a performance of his own temperance play. In a privileged life, this would be a momentary discomfort overcome by love and perseverance. But though Johnny and Nell do love one another, he is at first hemmed in by the thornhedge of his reluctance and then dogged by a series of mishaps—including the bad luck that her aunt is still up when they try to sneak into Nell's bedroom. Nell eventually marries Garwood, with disastrous consequences for her and Johnny.

And what if Lockridge had not been declared 4-F for the draft and had got into the fuss, confronting real enemy in combat? John Shockley's own military service was as an assistant surgeon in the 134th Regiment of Indiana Volunteers. He didn't enlist until late spring of 1864 and may have seen no action. Once again Lockridge enhances the raw materials. Shawnessy fights all the way from Chickamauga to Missionary Ridge to Atlanta to the Sea. He discovers that half of courage is fear, that battles can be lost and depend largely on chance, that heroic ideals disappear on the battlefield, where men shyly hold their own guts in their hands, and that even he, Shawnessy, can simplify his concepts and learn to hate.

In his single most telling pronouncement to his publisher, Lockridge made clear the autobiographical thrust of his novel and laid the grounds for the reading I offer here. "For my part," he told them, "while the Republic was bleeding, I hid behind a thousand skirts and let J.W.S. bleed for me all over the thousands of MS. pages of *Raintree County.*"

And what if Lockridge hadn't recovered from scarlet fever in 1935? What would have happened to the world in the aftermath of this terrible loss? Falsely reported dead, John Shawnessy has a rare opportunity to gauge public reaction. The man who discovers him still alive is disappointed because he'd been named trustee of an educational fund in his name. Nell Gaither recovered enough from the bad news to marry his rival, Garwood Jones, almost in time to make use of the funeral baked meats. Garwood's terrible poetic tribute ("Lo, where is Seth, that erst did fill these glades / With laughter and rejoicing blithe and brave?") appeared with typos on the back page of the *Clarion.* And his mother has stopped wearing black. Life goes on in Raintree County. "After all, what did the dead expect? Did the dead have any rights?"

Such chastenings, contrasted with the better luck of the author, could be extended: Shawnessy never recovers *his* lost son, *he* doesn't win any elections. And though he does win the great Fourth of July footrace in 1859—while Lockridge was always eating dust—he pays for his victory tragically.

Most important, *he* never finishes the great work. In his youth Shawnessy writes a conventional temperance play and some derivative sentimental verse. While living in New York City he attempts a play, *Sphinx Recumbent,* but is unable to finish the fifth act. And now the great epic of America languishes. Politely assuming lack of genius isn't the problem, the Perfessor speaks like a modern-day historicist: "All so-called great men are the result of human collaboration before, during, and after the fact. With a little cooperation from Fate, you might have been America's Shakespeare, John, but you lacked the human context. A whole age worked to create the Plays, which are not unwisely attributed to a dozen other men besides the man who penned them." As we have moved from the Age of Lincoln to the Age of Senator Garwood B. Jones, the epic potential has withered.

The Perfessor's judgments, always incisive, are never sufficient. Exactly why Shawnessy can't otherwise get on with his epic isn't made explicit. In a passage Lockridge deleted, perhaps for being too explicit, Shawnessy reflects that Shakespeare didn't himself suffer the fates of Hamlet, Othello, Macbeth, Lear, or Cleopatra, and enjoyed an enabling aesthetic distance. Whereas, "I lived perhaps too deeply to give back what I have lived."

This is the rub. Shawnessy is too haunted by his own tragic past to make the conversion from life to art, to be the artist-contriver who, with radiant pencil, converts memory into "a legend of light and shadow, some faces on the great Road of the Republic." Although another kind of creative power will be ascribed to him, he is too steeped in his own unfinished life to see it whole and write his way out of it. Instead of the artist he is "the rememberer."

Lockridge is an innocent compared with his proxy Shawnessy, who suffers many irreparable losses—his sweetheart Nell Gaither, his first wife, Susanna, and their son, James, his parents, and his army buddy Flash Perkins, "the most affirmative being Johnny Shawnessy had ever seen."

Because his suffering is more through imaginative identification than literal mishap, Lockridge can write, in a trial of his projected selves, the life that Shawnessy only dreams of writing. *Raintree County*, as some critics have pointed out, becomes that paradoxical creation an epic about the impossibility of writing an epic. It's the novel that stands in for the epic poem its own hero would have written, had he been able.

In the novel, Lockridge thus undercuts his own sense of entitlement and special destiny. Shawnessy is repeatedly chastened—by nature and circumstance, and by the fact that there are other people in the world. Yet Lockridge's own lucky exemption from literal tragedy is enabling for the artist in him—he must "lift the soul," in Coleridge's phrase, to create through empathy what he has not shared.

The novel's most vivid character is not Shawnessy but Professor Jerusalem Webster Stiles. He was initially the spawn of Shawnessy himself. He made his first appearance, same name and same costume, in
one of Shawnessy's dreams in the abandoned novel, *American Lives*. He
and Shawnessy share the initials J.W.S. Lockridge asks in effect,
What if, in addition to the plurality of his inner selves, I create for
Shawnessy an alter ego who challenges him every inch of the way?

As elsewhere, there's no single real-life counterpart to the
Perfessor. Lockridge had many cynic-skeptics among his friends:
scientist Malcolm Correll takes a dim view of religious and metaphysical moonshine, sophisticated Cloise Crane argues a dark deter-
minism, international businessman and adventurer Curtis Lamorey
accepts no wooden nickels, Quaker pacifist Larry Wylie is skeptical
of religious dogma and militaristic flag-waving, economist and poet
Donald Blankertz has a world-weary suspicion of claims to heroic
motivation, and historian Steve Tryon finds much about American
history that gives us little reason to cheer. Correll told me that in
quirky mannerism and physical bearing—a "huge vivid insect," tall,
thin, angular, black-haired, with a Malacca cane substituted for a
baton—the Perfessor owes much to BHS orchestral conductor Fred
Sharp. Some other pedagogues may add a trait or two. Lockridge
told his wife that the Perfessor, like other characters, was a composite.

I think, though, that the Perfessor is deep-seated in Lockridge's
own personality. The satiric voice developed from high school days
on. In degree of virtuosity it was dominant. With something like the
division of labor one finds in Byron—between the heroic quester
Childe Harold and the satiric narrator of *Don Juan*—Shawnessy and
Stiles conduct a dialogue throughout the novel and test contrarieties
in the author who created them both.

Similarly, the dialogue of Castorp and Settembrini in *The Magic
Mountain* impressed Lockridge greatly. "It's like a symphony," he said
to his wife after reading Mann's novel in 1943. Despite its "time-
tranced existence" and portrait of European life in decay, it doesn't
fall into negation. "Living is dying, and smells like it too," Lockridge
noted, paraphrasing Hans Castorp, "but life keeps the form through
change of substance. . . . Life, its tremendous hovering instability,
and yet an inner principle always controlling and generating form. A

pullulation, something called flesh and becoming form, beauty, a lofty image, and yet all the time the essence of sensuality and desire." In the dialogue of *Raintree County*, Lockridge tries to give Shawnessy the upper hand over the Perfessor. His hero argues the continuance of life amid instability and negation.

In unpublished notes growing out of his earlier novel, Lockridge speaks of the Perfessor as a philologist, a pagan Easterner who transplants Classicism to the Midwest in a quaintly "Latinized America." He's a latter-day Hermes, messenger of the gods to Pedee Academy, Raintree County. The Perfessor speaks "the word Latin, sonorous, reverberant, the word capable of becoming a thing in itself, the word containing a kind of purple, stiff vitality, the word a tool of inhibition and reflection." The spirited classicism of *Raintree County* is Americanized, for though the novel invokes all the great epics from Homer to Joyce, Lockridge is attempting an *American* epic. In this largely Christian culture, classical myth and literature have an anachronistic gentility. But they have bearing on us still and the Perfessor is their messenger.

In the flexible mythic overlay of the novel, he takes on more sinister roles as well. He is the Grand Inquisitor, the Mysterious Stranger, Mephistopheles. When he departs on the night train, "the glare from the furnace showed a long, thin body in a soiled white suit, a face old and cunning, black eyes shining through pince-nez glasses."

A master of outrageous utterance, the Perfessor satirizes what Raintree County holds dear and does so with such gusto that he thrives on the targeted fatuities. He has neither a reformer's hope nor the animus of a severe moralist. Some of his pronouncements— for instance, that "Religion's a vast ritual of remorse for the unhappy discovery of pain and death"—flummoxed the American clergy in 1948.

In religion he's an agnostic, in politics a Marxist, in natural history a Darwinian, in psychology a Hobbesian and pre-Freudian, in personal morals a sexual opportunist (who, however, rarely gets any), in metaphysics a determinist, in history a debunker—and, for all this, a loyal friend to Shawnessy, his best student, whom he enormously likes.

Theirs is a relationship of mutual need. When the Perfessor is about to be lynched for having absconded with a juiceless preacher's succulent young wife, Shawnessy outruns the mob to tip him off. And when Shawnessy is himself about to be tarred, feathered, and falsely accused of adultery with a local Waycross feminist, the Perfessor confronts the mob led by a preacher. After helping unmask the Rev. Lloyd G. Jarvey, who has indulged in some adultery of his own that day, he "rapped the Preacher sharply on the head with his cane or jabbed him in the seat of the trousers. So doing, he had appeared to ship the whole struggling mass through the gates, which he promptly slammed to."

Farce has its allegorical meaning in *Raintree County*. The Perfessor, with his enlightened skepticism, routs the myopic preacher, whose name echoes Lord God Jehovah. The novel challenges Old Testament authoritarianism, as well as New Testament literalism. As Lockridge writes of Henry Adams, the Perfessor has the "tenacity of genius." Yet like Adams's his vision is inadequate.

The Perfessor's limitation is grounded in a personal tragedy, which Lockridge withholds until late in the novel, confronting only there one of the most personally troubling of the "what if"s. Late in the day, Stiles tells Shawnessy, "My father had died before I was old enough to remember him. When I was only ten years old, my mother died. In that death, Jerusalem Webster Stiles knew the secret of life—which is death—and never after added to his wisdom though he added to his words. And with that act, also, he left Raintree County and went East, where he had roots. Now, as you know, he came back to Raintree County when he was a young man, but he never came back home. He learned early, with the bitterness of the homeless child, that the earth cares nothing for our grief, and that even our mother who cared for us in life cares nothing for us in death. We care for her and keep her image alive in our brief world of memory and grief, but she doesn't care for us any longer. She has forgotten us. She doesn't remember our face. . . . This is the autobiography of Jerusalem Webster Stiles, which may be said to have ended when he was ten years old."

Lockridge knew Freud's essay, "Mourning and Melancholia" and in an unpublished note on the Perfessor's psychology speaks of "the infantile and unadjusted grief for the loss of one's mother." He knew that grief can turn pathological and that one must work through it.

Shawnessy hopes to overcome the terrible force of the Perfessor's utterance "by a myth of homecoming and a myth of resurrection. . . . Grief is the most beautiful garland given to love." But his memory shifts back to the death of his own mother in 1877, which had left him bereft, with only a half-written rejected manuscript, a guidebook to the Centennial Exposition, some old photographs and crumpled telegrams, and a "mothy personal legend" about the raintree.

For both men the death of fathers is barely registered, while the death of mothers is a personal and metaphysical calamity. Lockridge's inspiration for his novel, going back to Paris days, was deeply interwoven with his sense of his mother's mortality. The novel is partly grounded in a kind of anticipatory loss. Elsie Lockridge's confidence that the dead are "*living on*" is not shared by her son. But on another level I think Lockridge identifies with the Perfessor. He may have carried with him from earliest childhood the sense of already having lost his mother.

This "what if" is among the most difficult of all for Lockridge to ask: what is left after our mothers die, or after we become dead to them?

That he asks this question enhances the probability that the writing of his novel is itself a working through of grief—of grief for all that has been and could be lost. The Perfessor's unremittent grief is portrayed as pathological. Thus, Lockridge attempts, through the catharsis and self-mastery of writing, to overcome his own novel's pervasive atmosphere of loss, to overcome the death nausea that befell him while visiting Messick graveyard with his mother in the summer of 1941. The novel is both an expression and an organizing of his emotional life.

But there's an even more calamitous loss for Shawnessy, if not for the Perfessor: the death of Nell. Though occurring chronologically before the death of Shawnessy's mother, Nell's death in childbirth— she is pregnant by Garwood—is narrated only in the novel's final pages, as Shawnessy confronts in memory his greatest loss.

Why it is greatest will take us to the heart of the warmly expressed values of *Raintree County,* which has been something other than a long day's journey into night.

Lockridge's novel is a search for sustaining values in the face of death and desolation. Without embarrassment it asks large questions.

The largest is, What survives the ruins of time? It's a question both personal and metaphysical. The Perfessor would seem to have the edge in the great debate, scoring point after point. But Shawnessy gamely holds on in a narrative where sexual vitality and mythic vision contend as best they can with mortality and cultural decline.

~

Sex is an idol in *Raintree County*. In the Day episodes the menfolk gather around a pasture to watch a white bull named Jupiter mount a heifer. At the same time the Reverend Jarvey arrives at Lorena Passifee's to administer one of those orgasmic "godshouts" the local ladies are always lining up for, begging for multiple conversions. Jarvey is Zeus (Jupiter) in pursuit of Io and Europa, or Poseidon's bull mounting Pasiphaë. Their coupling, enhanced by dandelion wine, will be observed through the window by neighborhood children, just as the mating of bull and heifer is furtively watched by feminist Evelina Brown from her tower window.

There's a difference, though: what is blind and indiscriminate in the white bull is comic hypocrisy in the Preacher, who is finally undone by sex. Subjected to various frocks and hoopskirts, sex is life in this novel, sex permeates Raintree County from conception to the grave.

Growing up in pre–Kinsey Report Bloomington, Lockridge felt both the fecundity of his natural habitat and the puritan restraints of Hoosier culture. For all her advanced notions in other respects, his mother was a Christian Scientist, for whom, as Mary Baker Eddy says, "no more sympathy exists between the flesh and Spirit than between Belial and Christ."

He was greatly interested in sex, curious to hear from his friends about their sexual initiations, enjoying the humor of local folk—Jim Pennington's jokes, for instance—and reading widely on the subject. At the same time, he postponed his own sexual initiation probably until marriage, was faithful to his wife, and was rarely far from the family hearth. Earlier he had backed away when women seemed to be pressuring him sexually, less I think from puritanism than from the weight of meaning he placed on sex.

He was heterosexual but might now agree there was a homoerotic component in those strong male friendships. The ritual of male bonding in the bull-and-heifer scene—a nineteenth-century equivalent to the stag film—is as close as his novel comes to homo-eroticism on an otherwise panoramic screen.

I think it was pretty audacious for a young Hoosier from a studious, rather prudish household—a former member of Epworth League, secretary of YPB, and president of a consortium of Indiana Hi-Y's—to publish a novel that dwelt on the erotic life, as some reviewers complained, more than any previous American novel. He was not some objective sociologist of sex correcting our pious misreadings of ourselves. Rather, he was a nervy writer working up his materials to give a fuller sensation of life.

What is the meaning of sex in the novel?

The title of Elsie Lockridge's favorite childhood book, *Barriers Burned Away,* becomes a metaphor of the erotic life. The great sentimental wish of sex is to *burn all barriers away* in total unmediated ecstasy. But "Raintree County was itself the barrier of form imposed upon a stuff of longing, life-jet of the river." The "random curve of water" contrasts with the "rectilinear stone" of the courthouse, and would ideally be "the pathway of the hero of a legend, of one who rose from the Great Swamp and rode a horse of godlike appetite to the summit of Platonic forms."

But the imposition of barriers is the only way a humanly erotic life is possible, whether as incest taboos or rituals of courtship and marriage. These barriers can be either restrictive or defining, as the various love affairs in the novel show.

Not long after his dunking in the swamp, Johnny Shawnessy is compensated by the river, out of which a fabulous creature steps naked one day while he covertly watches. "On the left of the deep-fleshed hemispheres was a brown mole, pennysized. Then as the creature half turned a moment and stretched up its arms full length in the sunlight, he saw the brightnippled breasts, the wide, smooth belly, and three gold tufts of hair." Nell Gaither has ordinarily appeared in high-necked bodice and petticoats, speaking the "evasive language" of Raintree County. Suddenly she is Venus.

Johnny had earlier seen the Indiana landscape in the image of his mother, Ellen (near-anagram of Nell), as a maternal earth with its riddle of origins reinscribing the Oedipus myth. But now "it had taken for its image the Venus Callipygos in exchange for Mother Eve in her figleaf."

The novel implies that this exchange is a healthy one in the natural history of sex. It echoes Lockridge's comparative ease in marrying Vernice Baker and beginning his own family. The Perfessor in his grief over his mother's death has not resolved the Oedipal predicament.

Thus, Shawnessy's greater grief is not for his mother but for Nell, the river goddess and local girl who first awakened him to life as desire. This loss is tragic, while the other is natural and necessary.

For Shawnessy and Lockridge, desire enhances the sensation of life even *because* it attempts always to transcend its own roots in vacancy and loss. The novel conveyed both the vitality and the poignancy of desire to a generation of young readers who still remember elusive, doomed Nell rising naked from the riverbank when they've forgotten everything else.

Desire draws its nourishment from our connection with the biological landscape. The land is always there, with its river of life and Great Swamp. Emblem of female genitalia, the Swamp is the home of our nostalgia, as well as our ultimate tomb. Geography recapitulates anatomy in Raintree County, even down to the book jacket, where the living body of Nell is seen in the lush contours of the county map. Though dead and buried, she survives in the landscape. The abandoned Danwebster graveyard lying next to the river gives Shawnessy an overwhelming sense of *life*, overrun as it is by grasshoppers, grave myrtle, wild carrot, blackberries, and poison ivy.

Corruption of this sense of place threatens our collective vitality. Called an "ecological novel written before its time," *Raintree County* warned of our loss of connection with this biological planet. There's been plenty of evidence that Lockridge's environmental instincts were right—that in "mining and stripping and gutting and draining, and whoring and ravaging and rending the beautiful earth of America," we would lay waste our powers.

I take some consolation in the fact that he didn't survive to see the pastures off High Street give way to shopping malls, his old boy scout camp lose out to the freeway, and the streams and gardens in and around Bloomington polluted by Westinghouse's PCBs.

Lockridge finds meaning and value in our fierce attachments, even when they retard, wound, or destroy us. Resisting the Perfessor's maxim that "Narcissus was your only honest lover," Shawnessy thinks our attachments extend the self beyond itself. They also link us to desires, fixations, and taboos rooted in our biological evolution, before custom and the rectangular county lines imposed. And they have human meaning. Tragedy, severing the objects of our love, ironically reaffirms meaning and value in Raintree County.

Other relationships in the novel portray the perseverance of sex and love amid calamity and sorrow. And they portray how we must seek love beyond family romance, beyond the powerful field of parental domination. The attachments that make us human can also make us ill.

Some female characters have more trouble with their fathers than Shawnessy ever had with his mother. Lockridge wants multiple points of view, and except for Shawnessy makes them all female, as if to shift the balance of sensibility somewhat. We see some episodes through the eyes of Shawnessy's daughter, Eva, modeled on Elsie Shockley Lockridge as a young girl. We see others through the eyes of his second wife, Esther Root, modeled on Emma Rhoton Shockley, and of Evelina Brown, a feminist who is a take-off on those Minerva Society women at New Harmony. With this profusion of "E" names and women with green eyes, Lockridge suggests the ubiquity of Eve.

Eva idealizes her father and loathes herself for it. She can never be worthy of him. Lockridge narrates his mother's childhood jealousy, competitiveness, self-loathing, aggression, and nightmares. He doesn't narrate her life beyond the age of twelve—her sexual development is permanently arrested by the novel's time frame—but he confronts the living grownup Eva in his own mother, who half a century later still worships that father, with implications, as we have seen, for her own marriage and child-rearing. The novel is dedicated to his mother. But Lockridge would later feel that in portraying her youthful passions he had exploited and harmed her.

Hollywood deleted Eva, as well as Esther and Evelina, and made its movie around the character of Susanna Drake, who is haunted by her father's ghost in a different way. Lockridge once again has both used and altered family sources. In 1861, John Shockley, then twenty-two, married Susannah Duke, just approaching seventeen. A photograph of her shows no particular resemblance to Elizabeth Taylor, alas. Her father, originally from North Carolina, was a colorfully brutish Henry County dirt farmer, thrice-married, with fifteen children.

The Duke brothers hated know-it-all John Shockley, and played nasty practical jokes on him. John and Susannah lived together for only three months before they separated, she pregnant by then. In divorce proceedings brought in 1864, he complained that she refused to sleep or live with him, and she complained of same, her lawyer adding that "he was a disbeliever in a married life, that the vow taken in a marriage ceremony is of no moral force and not binding on any one . . . and that he belonged to the so called Progressive Society which holds to all the isms and cisms of modern fanatics and religion and morality." Susannah won custody and John promptly enlisted in the army. She lived briefly in Mississippi with relatives before returning to Henry County, possibly insane by this time, and died in 1877 at the age of thirty-three. Their son, James, lived until 1919, a Mississippi farmer.

Lockridge had to improve on all this. What if the lowly Dukes get upscaled to Southern aristocracy and Susanna Drake is made two years John Shawnessy's senior, a beautiful olive-skinned nymphomaniac? She has arrived from Louisiana, taken up residence in an elegant house in the county seat, Freehaven, and bestows laurels on Johnny when he wins the 1859 Fourth of July footrace against Flash Perkins. Later that day, very drunk, he chases her into the swamp near Paradise Lake, where on a grassy mound they make love, the dust of yellow flowers from a tree falling on his shoulders and her black hair.

Lockridge counterpoints the sex act with journalistic accounts of a disastrous balloon ascension, a perilous crossing of Niagara Falls on a tightrope, and a tourist promo on the "balsamic odors and blue skies" beneath the Mason-Dixon Line.

Promptly evicted from Eden, Johnny is forced to marry Susanna and journeys with her to New Orleans—as epic heroes have journeyed to Hades—where he sees slavery firsthand and intervenes in the ax murder of a young black man. He is otherwise well entertained, rather like Lord Byron in his Regency society phase. Then back to Raintree County, where he watches helplessly as Susanna sinks into psychosis and eventual suicide.

Although the causes differ, the description of Susanna's psychosis and Shawnessy's sense of guilt contain uncanny prophecies of Lockridge's fate. Probably on a level beneath his own awareness, he *did* intuit his own vulnerability. But I would otherwise call this foreshadowing a dramatic irony that highlights how one can *know* about mental disorder, perhaps anticipate it, yet be baffled when it is time to confront the snakes oneself. *The Snake Pit* isn't the only family novel that portrays mental illness.

In the days following his indiscretion under the raintree, Shawnessy feels as if a thousand eyes are watching him. He dreads the daily newspaper, expects it to publicize his crime, feels only greater dread for every day's reprieve. When he receives a letter from Susanna informing him, falsely, of her pregnancy, "the words said what he had always feared, what he had known would come to pass . . . Someone would come in and find him leaning insanely against this wall and would know that he was guilty of something." He feels helpless, caught by fate as time brings to birth dark events seeded years earlier—and he thinks of hopping a train to "California, on the Golden Shore!"

Shame before his mother's eyes brings on the catastrophe. She has received a letter from an informer. He knows then that he will marry Susanna. The bitter words they exchange are "merely the truncated mouthings of the Oedipean agony." She could never understand "the young man's pagan world of beauty and desire" and relents in her censure only when she fears he's about to throw himself under a train. He sees his fate—marrying Susanna instead of Nell—as a "Great Betrayal," as bringing harm to those he most loves. He hopes somehow to clear "his honor and good name before the County." Nell sensibly berates him for having too great a conscience in these matters, as Vernice Lockridge will try to talk good sense into her husband.

With some detective work, in a novel full of riddles, Shawnessy uncovers the origin of Susanna's psychosis. Her father, James, had taken a mulatto mistress to the virtual exclusion of his wife, and Susanna is probably the mulatto's daughter. As a racist she fears her blood is tainted. In some unpublished notes on Susanna's psychology, Lockridge makes it explicit that in her self-punishing nymphomania she is identifying with Henrietta and other black mistresses of her white father, compulsively asking that the sexual subjugation be repeated. She is a "black Helen," an emblem of the Old South, one race enslaved by the other. Slavery is "the mental illness of America" as well as its original sin.

Susanna's decline is marked by depression and paranoia. She spends hours alone in her bedroom. She imagines conspiracies everywhere—"they" are all plotting against her. She loses interest in sex, at least with Shawnessy. Talking about her problems proves less than cathartic, and Shawnessy, not handling things very well, would rather not listen. "He couldn't imagine a greater indignity than to go before Raintree County and confess that he was married to a crazy woman." It seemed to him "that he was groping helplessly outside his own world and trying to get back into it. He must not give up. He must go on bearing the burden of the whole implacably connected universe of himself." Susanna is eventually a suicide, who diverts attention at one key moment by falsely claiming that she is visiting her parents. Again, these are uncanny prophecies of the author's fate.

Shawnessy's second wife, Esther, is ashamed in turn at the probability that she is part Miami Indian. Esther like Susanna is dominated by her father. Gideon Root's fierce love for her is close to incestuous and seems greater than Shawnessy's own. In a scene the precise opposite of Joyce's "Evelina," literal-minded and humorless Esther suddenly acknowledges the hidden spring of her will, refuses to move out west with her father after all, and runs impetuously to join Mr. Shawnessy. Root's hands will always be on her, torn as she is between two worlds, and she is in effect seeking out another father figure.

But she still shows Lockridge's affirmative reading of human freedom—more affirmative at least than Joyce's in his short story. By dint of will and desire, we can sometimes free ourselves of dark entrapments, burning some of those barriers away and forming new structures for our lives grounded in other human attachments. Where Susanna and Shawnessy found themselves caught up in Aeschylean tragedy, Esther and he take up residence in a domestic Victorian novel, complete with gingerbread house, where marriage and family will survive.

Desire in Raintree County thus takes some dark turns before finding a compensatory haven. To reach Paradise Lake "one had to pass by the graveyard and the vanished town of Danwebster." Yet for all his ordeal Shawnessy isn't in paradise. Clearly there's been a chastening of the impassioned young man dreaming of lush-loined Nell on the Shawmucky River. Esther never even calls him by his first name; he is always "Mr. Shawnessy." The fate of desire is the institution of the family, brought forth in sorrow "for the crime of lustful love." There's both loss and gain in this, and Shawnessy by the novel's end has seen that boundaries and barriers, not wholly burned away, have given form and meaning to eros.

And the land is still there for Shawnessy, a full presence as always—the river, swamp, and tree, the rock at the limit of the land, and Raintree County itself, which gives us life and will reclaim us in the end. The warmth of our emotional life—the deepest element of a biological heritage rooted in the land—doesn't necessarily diminish, even as it takes forms other than erotic fever.

Lockridge was himself a family man whose feeling for his mother was strong and whose authorial freedom and identity were imposed on unwittingly by his father. Through his reading of Freud and more so through personal experience, he knew the threat of family romance. Writing is a therapy; the various sexual relationships in the novel show him working through Oedipean entrapment and still earlier torments. He had already contended with them well enough in his personal life. At a rather early age he found his living Nell Gaither—not having to settle for an Esther—and set up a family of his own.

Thus he sacrificed the youthful vagabondage of Paris days for domesticity, in a warmer marriage than his father or Grandfather Shockley had experienced. Faithful husband, provider, and father of four, he found in domesticity the structures that regulated the currents of a fearfully strong emotional life—a life he continued to express through fiction.

And like Shawnessy he had a resource beyond eros to sustain him. Mythic consciousness—grounded less in feeling than in imagination—is another human power in Lockridge's novel answering to the ruins of time.

~

As a young child, Rossie was touring the old cemetery at Frankfort, Kentucky with his father and asked, "Are all the people buried here great men?"

When father and son played their homemade game of heroes, "The Rossiteers," their list included Ulysses, Hercules, Atlas, Helen of Troy, Theseus, Jason, Mercury, Bellerophon, and many others, mythical and historical, who crop up again in *Raintree County*.

The novel is an often comic testing of criteria, as Shawnessy from boyhood on ponders who and what is great. His purported grandfather Thomas Carlyle asks the same questions in *Heroes and Hero Worship*, with his own list of heroes, including Shakespeare. Johnny Shawnessy hears of many dubious candidates for Greatest Living American, from James K. Polk to Henry Clay to Zachary Taylor. Lincoln comes off as more likely. *Raintree County* is somewhere between heroic and anti-heroic fiction, as Leonard Lutwak has noted. It doesn't dismiss heroes altogether but redefines their nature and mission in an era when the river gods have been chased away by freight trains.

Some readers may find annoying the dreams of glory entertained by an adolescent who silently aspires to be Shakespeare: Johnny is a high-flyer like Bellerophon and Icarus, who hungers for beauty and greatness. His hopes are sometimes downright messianic, as he imagines himself a prophet bringing a new religion into an America still weighed down with Old Testament and other moribund deities. Grandiose vision coexists with his unpushy good nature.

The narrator's language is often a sympathetic echoing of these dreams in the earlier portions of the novel. But irony is at work even there, and Shawnessy's early poetic effusions are meant to show that the Shakespearean gift isn't in evidence just yet. Some are candidates for "Lockridge's Leaden Treasury." And well before the novel's end, Shawnessy is humbled, no longer thinking himself a new Shakespeare, let alone Jesus. After losing a local election he feels he has "been rejected by his people and called a false prophet."

He isn't broken, though. What he salvages is a vision to challenge the Perfessor's cynicism—a vision rather lovely and very fragile.

Lockridge calls on much of what he most values in fashioning this vision for Shawnessy—words, legends, maps, antiquities, dreams, philosophy. He puts to good use the *Illustrated Historical Atlas of Henry County* that he took from Emma Shockley's house, revising it somewhat as the main prop in the Day episodes. Senator Garwood B. Jones has heard that the engraver, about to lose his job, introduced pornographic images into the *Illustrated Historical Atlas of Raintree County*. Only a single copy was said to have been printed before detection, with such images as a lady going into a dry-goods store stark naked except for a parasol, and a bull "showing prize-winning form in an intimate domestic scene." Moreover, "John J. Jubal's palatial home in Beardstown features an ithyphallic Aztec god instead of a cast-iron triton. The sign reading Burke House on Freehaven's leading hotel has been altered to something more pungent. And Jesus Christ surrounded by the twelve Apostles is getting ready to jump to Zion from the observation platform of the house on page 61."

Shawnessy obliges the Senator and manages early in the day to retrieve the copy, kept under lock and key at the Historical Museum. Off and on throughout the day they and others pore disappointedly over its pages, finding no such variants. Only in the final minutes before the Perfessor's departure does Shawnessy think of looking in the most obvious place: the main entrance to the courthouse on page five. In amazement they find a naked Adam and Eve tasting the forbidden fruit. "With what an exquisite feeling for paradox, an unknown artist had substituted his symbolic statue of Edenic rebellion for the stern yet necessary lady with the scales, whose upright form had ruled the conscience of Raintree County from the beginning!"

The old myths still have the power to subvert and give new life to our sober constructs, but the myth-making power itself needs constant rejuvenation. "Americans have rewritten the old epics and have added myths of their own. From the Greeks, we've taken the plural gods, the rape of beauty, the long war, the wandering and the return. From the Hebrew and Christian myth, we've taken the lost garden and the divine man," says Shawnessy.

Raintree County is itself a rewrite of that atlas, with renditions of the subversive scenes its own characters hoped to find. And it attempts to add some myths of its own. A few years before the vogue of archetypal criticism in America, Lockridge has his hero speak of America as "a new Eden," whose people are "the new mythmakers."

Unknown artists like Shawnessy add to our sustaining mythology by localizing and revising the old myths. Tree worship is found in many ancient cultures, as Frazer documents in *The Golden Bough,* and is prominent in the Genesis myth. Shawnessy's raintree is a mutation of an ancient archetype, combining trees of life and knowledge in the sacred grove. It reflects the local culture's impulse to seek its own origin, to explain its own name in a county where no raintrees have yet been found. The legend claims some historical grounding—perhaps Johnny Appleseed planted it—yet is anchored in human imagination and our need for myths of miraculous origin.

Shawnessy won't look too closely at his own myth, and the Perfessor reinforces this, saying that if they made an excursion and actually found the raintree, "we'd sit there and have a couple sandwiches and after an afternoon of contemplating the tree, we'd go back home with sunburnt noses and ants in our pantses, no wiser than before." The Perfessor is a comparative mythologist who could write *The Golden Bough* himself, as the narrator hints, but who sees through literal claims and thinks the age of myth is drawing to a close. "I wish I could believe in sacred places. . . . But beauty and the gods can't survive the era of Darwin and the Dynamo. All lovely things are old things."

Shawnessy's reply draws on much of Lockridge's own philosophy of language and literature, in the making since high school days. It owes much also to Ross Lockridge Senior, who could conduct a group of folks out into some featureless cow pasture and convey a brooding sense of place by evoking the legend that still haunts that ground. Language is a direct link with our origins, our own etymology. As a boy, Shawnessy felt he "had sprung into being from words in an immense blackbordered book on the parlor table." He and other poets are in search of "dawnwords" that would return us to the primitive garden of the race, "back to the parent Word." But most words are like palimpsests, layered over deceptively and in need of the poet's delving. The language of poets dissolves the distinction between words and things, ideally giving us a more intimate sense of reality than our own random experience with it and putting us in touch with our aboriginal selves.

Shawnessy believes in miracles in the sense that the raintree is "no more nor less miraculous than any other tree—and all trees are miraculous. . . . Every county in America has its secret place and every American life its Delphic cave." Being itself is miraculous—"the world is a perpetual creation" in which all selves participate. "Each Self is a Universe, and no universe is possible without God."

In a sense the Perfessor has the novel's last word because it is he who earlier dubs Shawnessy an "endlessly courageous dreamer." Lockridge's conception of the dreamer turns out to be something other than moonshiner. The dreamer is the mythmaker, and in the social sphere the mythmaker has legislative powers. In dreams begin responsibilities. Dreamer-novelist Lockridge wants his book to be read by Americans because "it will do them good—goddam them."

Shawnessy has been aware of the mythic texture of his own life, interpreting it as he goes. In beating Flash Perkins in the footrace, he lives out the myth described by Frazer that one hero must usurp another, often killing him. In making love to Susanna under the raintree and paying for it mightily, he lives out the Genesis myth. In returning from the war after having been reported dead, he lives out the myth of Lazarus. In being rejected by his own people after a period in the wilderness, he lives out the myth of Christ, almost crucified again by indignant local townsfolk led by Jarvey. It's up to the Perfessor to point out that Shawnessy has lived an American myth, Hawthorne's Great Stone Face. In his stay-at-home decency he has proved to be the hero of Raintree County.

Caught up in these myths that interpret his life, does Shawnessy have any heroic power of his own? It's clear the narrator doesn't grant this single person much direct influence beyond the classroom. Rather, he's America's representative dreamer, who has maintained his sanity while failing as an individual writer. He sees himself as part of a larger collective enterprise, the creative building of the Republic throughout the ages.

The Perfessor narrates at length his amiable "History of Mankind": e.g., "The female of the species was beginning to lose the hair around her vestigial tail because the male of the species liked it better that way and chased the ones with the bare behinds. This is called Natural Selection."

Shawnessy replies with "The Legend of Raintree County," a

fablelike account of a child's growth into mythic awareness. It lacks the Perfessorial punch, but the moral of it, as interpreted by Shawnessy and also by Lockridge in an unpublished note, is that the greatest human institutions are grounded in fictions that have been made real through collective human will. "From this premise all begins: that science and all the world are unavoidably human. Everything exists by the authority of that sturdy republican, the Self. The world in which we live lives in us. To look outward at the farthest star is to look inward into oneself. We are merely exploring our immense cupboard," says Shawnessy.

Lockridge adds that "what we call primeval nature, Eden, is already completely humanized. . . . The very conception of that which is primitive [is] a rather poetic human notion. Even the so-called War of the Species is not really a war, the combat for survival is not a real combat. Darwin makes it so." Human institutions like the Republic, History, and Science are all human projections rich in metaphor that attempt to rescue us from chaos and old night.

Strictly speaking, these institutions begin as illusions. The trick is to dream better, to purge the world of the bad dreams of slavery, genocide, and environmental rape—to dream the myth of freedom as prelude to investing it literally in our institutions. This is a radical mythic humanism or cultural idealism. One can find its roots in Vico and Schiller, and it's not unlike what the modern critic Northrop Frye would later elaborate. Shawnessy's hope is that our best imaginings can become literal, worked out in history and culture. For better or worse we think up our institutions; they are not inevitable in the nature of things. The great human illusions "were created by centuries of struggle."

In his own small schoolteacherly way, but with the prophetic vision of the poet, Shawnessy contributes to the dream of the Republic. The hero isn't precisely this single person Shawnessy; it is the collective of people who help make and sustain myth in an age of its dimming, and Shawnessy in this novel is but their representative visionary. The age—Shawnessy's and by implication our own—is in decline through a failure of imagination.

The Perfessor calls this a "beautiful and brave fable." Its vulnerability is everywhere registered by him. In an era of disillusionment, where is any evidence the dreamer is prevailing? Where's the executive will for all this? Doesn't a mechanical universe reclaim the whole experiment in the end? Lockridge was bringing his novel to a close just as the world press was peering into the Nazi ovens. After this, how entertain Olympian hopes for the human race?

Lockridge's hope for his own novel is that in evoking the old names and singing the myth of the Republic, he can move Americans to return to origins, to revere the nourishing earth and democratic vistas. In a grander way and speaking not only to Hoosiers, he hopes to fulfill the dreams of his own father. Like Whitman, he writes with the conviction, first enunciated in Longinus, that the end of art is not only to teach and delight but to transport.

But *Raintree County* is after all only a book, published for a season like other books, and how much can one have riding on a book? When Shawnessy is branded a false prophet, he picks up and goes on with his scribbling and schoolteaching. Could Lockridge be as resilient as his own hero?

~

What *is* this book? Lockridge made fun of his father's literary sensibility, which he thought hadn't advanced beyond a fondness for James Fenimore Cooper. Yet *Raintree County* shows just as much the imprint of father as of mother. She had more to do with the cast of characters, he, ironically, with matters of vision and literary form. I'll make some large claims for the novel that have no necessary connection with value judgments—claims I would think true even if the novel were deemed a large-scale fiasco.

One reviewer complained that Lockridge should never have been permitted by his editor to retell the whole of Hawthorne's "The Great Stone Face." It slipped by her that the entire novel is based on this story. Lockridge does his best to make things fairly obvious, by contrast at least with much modernist fiction. Clearly he doesn't succeed with all readers.

I'd call this an incorporative more than an allusive novel, and contrast it with *Ulysses*. As any teacher of the great novel knows, Joyce relies on his reader's familiarity with everything in western culture from *Agenbite of Inwit* to modern Irish street slang. Even before the semester's first bomb scare, it's clear in any American undergraduate class that his confidence is misplaced—happily for the teacher, who now has something to talk about. Much discussion of modernist texts must be taken up with footnoting allusions. Joyce would have alluded once or twice to Hawthorne's tale and left it to us to spot it, then grasp its significance.

But the lament out of which *Raintree County* emerges is precisely that the wealth of western myth, history, and literature is growing dim to modern memory. It must be invoked and recited. Our hope is in memory.

Recited. This is where Ross Lockridge *Senior* begins to leave his mark. When Shawnessy meets a naked woman on a slab in the post office, the narrator makes clear the incorporation of the Oedipus story: "She lay on her stomach, chin propped on hands. . . . Her eyes were a great cat's," and she asks Shawnessy, "What creature is it that in the morning of its life—." If we are trained to take pleasure in spotting allusions, we'll say, "Oh my god, this is too obvious!" But Lockridge means it to be obvious. A reader on another park bench may never have heard of the Riddle of the Sphinx.

Ross Lockridge Senior would tell his children, grandchildren, and Hoosier audiences all the old stories from scratch, as if everyone were hearing them for the first time. When his son invokes the Golden Apples of the Hesperides, he creates a context in which the story of Atlas and Hercules can be briefly told. Not counting on his reader's intimate knowledge of Frazer, he has the Perfessor tell the story of the Golden Bough and the woodland lake at Nemi. And when Reverend Jarvey is telling "The Oldest Story in the World," Lockridge has him recite substantial passages from the Book of Genesis.

This incorporative method extends to the texts of American history and well beyond. Shawnessy's great work for the July Fourth festivities is his organization of the Grand Patriotic Program, the whole flyer for which is printed in the novel. General Jackson reads the Declaration of Independence, portions of which are quoted. Many years earlier, Shawnessy first read the Gettysburg Address in a newspaper while he was visiting a Chattanooga whorehouse with Flash Perkins and the Perfessor. Lockridge prints most of the address in counterpoint to Flash Perkins's singing: "If you got a gal that's a mite tew fat, You kin melt her down with a dance like that!" Flash dances a jig with whores while the Perfessor recites obscenely revised classical texts.

If this isn't quite what Ross Senior has in mind for these master-pieces of eloquence, his son makes up for it. After all, Shawnessy takes schoolchildren on historical tours. He was "on the spot" where history was made, from the burning of Atlanta to the assassination of Lincoln to the great railroad strike of 1877. When Senator Jones calls Lincoln a "clownish country lawyer" whom Booth made great, Shawnessy intones that there are few hard facts of history but "there are some words in the right context. Perhaps the office of the histo-rian is to rebuild an accurate context around the few great words that survive."

Lockridge builds imaginary contexts around great words that have survived—from history, literature, philosophy, and religion to journalism, folklore, and folksong. Like his father, he hopes to rean-imate them with words of his own.

He gourmandizes other texts with the same gusto he brought to Madame Pernot's dinner table. There are so many sources, "running the gamut of the so-called Great Books ancient and modern," that he thinks the question of comparative influence "pretty well adds out." But he does single out *The Republic,* the Bible, the Homeric epics, the Greek tragedies, Shakespeare's plays, Hugo, Flaubert, Tolstoy, Emerson, Whitman, Wolfe, Hemingway, Dos Passos, Joyce, and Mann. He should have added Frazer and Freud. Somewhat more off-beat titles leave their imprint—*Uncle Tom's Cabin, John Brown's Body, Barriers Burned Away,* the *Elsie* series, *Alice's Adventures in Wonderland, Before the Footlights & Behind the Scenes, Ten Nights in a Barroom, Through the Dark Continent, The Life of Jesus, The Education of Henry Adams, Gone with the Wind,* and especially his father's rejected novel of the Old Northwest, *Black Snake and White Rose.*

Raintree County devours a plurality of such authors and titles, of literary and nonliterary genres, without being particularly bookish. Again, what *is* it?

Lockridge himself thought the genre problematic. Early into its composition, he reflected on its style, thinking it more an epic than a novel. But he goes on to surmise that it's "a new form, an art form mingling the characteristics of many previous genres, drama, poetry, novel, short story, legend, dream, logomyth."

Many other genres and subgenres that crisscross his book could be added: satire, parody, romance, pastoral, lyric, tragedy, elegy, comedy, farce, gothic fiction, sentimental fiction, *Bildungsroman,* historical fiction, agrarian fiction, realistic fiction, detective fiction, the dime cowboy novel, the fairy tale, the folk tale, folk dialect, song, prophecy, oratory, scientific and pseudoscientific treatise, natural history, memoir, autobiography, confession, travel literature, philosophical dialogue, exegesis, epistle, anthropological and sociological discourse, aphorism, essay, journalism, cinema, the photo album, the county atlas, pornography, blasphemy, cartography, the outline, the testimonial, the riddle, the variant. (In this biography I've tried to imitate his method somewhat.)

Some critics, spotting the hand of other writers and the imprint of one or another literary form, have called the novel "derivative." Lockridge wants it to be obvious that his novel *is* derived—from a multitude of sources. He wants the reader to recognize them. This is his method. Joyce and Wolfe will be most frequently mentioned by reviewers, more so than Whitman. He feels he's incorporated these authors among many others and gone his own way. Where in the House of Literature, he will ask, do you find anything quite like my book?

It's not only the formal variety—it's the scope of the thing and what he hopes to embody. He tells the Houghton Mifflin publicity people that, among other impossibilities, he wishes to "express the American Myth" in an American version of *The Republic,* to dramatize "the vast dualism between materialism and idealism," to make a study "of the synoptic character of human personality," to embody the "social, anthropological, and sexual characteristics of 19th-century American life," to "provide a living document of the religious and political 'rites' of the American people" and thus incorporate American culture into one novel to an unprecedented extent.

To this end he deliberately uses many American archetypes—the New Eden, the Frontier, the Republic, the Fall from Innocence, the Fear of Miscegenation, and character types such as the Innocent American Hero, the Dark Lady and the Light, the Capitalist, the Frontiersman, the Evangelical, the Feminist, the Statesman, the Perfessor. He revises these archetypes to make some ironic point or to individualize them. Nell Gaither may be offspring of the Good

Good Girl, but she's also erotic, her pale skin has a blemish, she fools around with someone other than our hero, and makes a practical compromise in her marriage.

All of this in a novel he hopes will be widely read for its story values—a page turner. Enough! or Too Much!

There's now a term for this kind of thing, not yet to my knowledge applied to *Raintree County*. In 1957, Northrop Frye coined the term "encyclopedic form." Simply put, he means works that attempt to embody the entire life cycle and culture of a people, written by one or more scribes who presume to reach beyond the merely personal to a vision of the whole. In canonical literature, Frye alludes to the Bible, the eddas, the *Mahabharata,* the classical epics, the *Divine Comedy, The Canterbury Tales, The Faerie Queene, Don Quixote, Paradise Lost, Pilgrim's Progress, Prometheus Unbound, Don Juan, Moby-Dick, The Cantos, Ulysses, Finnegans Wake,* and *A la Recherche du temps perdu.* There is often a mélange of genres in encyclopedic works—a totality of form as well as of represented reality.

In modern American fiction the encyclopedic work most discussed has been Thomas Pynchon's *Gravity's Rainbow,* with its internationalist perspectives and a cast of some three hundred. Others have included John Barth's *The Sot-Weed Factor,* William Gaddis's *The Recognitions,* and Joseph McElroy's *Women and Men.*

I'll avoid value judgments, yet make another kind of large claim that will sound inflated coming from a son of the author. It seems to me that *Raintree County* is the most ambitious attempt at encyclopedic form in American literature.

Any such attempt must necessarily fail in completeness. (Aesthetic failure in greater or lesser degree is equally assured.) Where are the gays, Chicanos, and Mormons in Lockridge's novel? Where do we find a character evil enough to hint at the horrors of Dachau? Some will say the genius of American fiction is gothic, and that this novel is insufficiently gothic. And so on. The Perfessor's constant undercutting of Shawnessy's epic ambition, and Shawnessy's failure ever to complete his epic, are the narrator's own acknowledgment that such projects must always fall short.

Still, Lockridge aspires to what his novel itself implies is an impossibility. He will write the grand work his own hero fails to write. The encyclopedic impulse has always been basic in him as in his father, who wrote a seven-volume local history for *all* of Indiana, not just a few corners of it. When MGM asks him to cut the City Section, he will refuse; his novel is more than a pastoral. He'll incorporate—in addition to the Midwest—the East, the South, and the myth of the Western Frontier. And sex is part of life, and so are dreams, and so is disillusionment and religious doubt. He feels it all belongs in his novel.

Some readers will say he used the novel as a dumping ground for all he knew. He himself criticized Benét for trying to pack too much into *John Brown's Body* and felt he was instead portraying that fraction of American life that represented the whole.

Frye makes an observation telling in its implications for Ross Lockridge, Jr. Writers of encyclopedic works usually write only one in a lifetime. I think it follows that for the writer of encyclopedic ambition, the problem of "What next?" must be in large measure stressful. It may feel, for a time at least, as if there's nothing more to say. Might be wise to postpone such a project till the gout is setting in.

Besides encyclopedic form, there's another metaphor of modern criticism that's helpful here: Mikhail Bakhtin's "carnival." In early drafts Lockridge called a central portion of his novel "The Marketplace," and much of this Russian critic's study of Rabelais is a matter of what one finds in that part of town. In folk culture—with its pageantry, fairs, banquets, farces, parodies, curses, bodily grotesqueries, obscenities, blasphemies, vital laughter—we find the vernacular languages that challenge official language. Rabelais's great book is a vernacular rout of Ciceronian Latin. Bakhtin finds the genre of novel the great arena for representing "dialogic" struggle among various languages or discourses, all linked to their own power bases, professions, and social classes. These languages jostle one against the other and assault the official language of a particular culture.

I'll make another claim for *Raintree County:* it's among the most carnivalesque of American novels. Only one critic, Darshan Maini, has so far noted this aspect of Lockridge's novel. Early on, though, Mary Jane Ward, trying to cheer her cousin up, praised the "change of style according to the mood, setting, characters etc., and it seems to me that few of the reviews I've seen have made enough of this ability to create whole vocabularies suitable to each situation."

It's the use to which this polyphony of styles and voices is put that makes the novel carnivalesque.

A lively subversive quality is found throughout and accounts for much of the fuss the novel caused in 1948. Fat belching Grampa Peters sits on "his big dumb behind" while a woman is screaming upstairs in labor: "Well, Jeeeeeeeeeesus God in Heaven, Dear Lord! git rid of it, sister!" At graduation exercises Johnny Shawnessy gets the usual dose of sentimental tributes, but Garwood Jones writes, "Tew hoom it may consurn: The owner of this book is wun of my closest pursonal ennumies. I hev no reluctuntz in recommending him fer enny kind of ordeenary household work inclooding ginneral carpentry (his fabreekations are noomerous and unsurpassed), but vurgins over fiftee wood dew well to keep him out of there drawers. Signed, Rube Shucks."

As soon as the Perfessor steps off the train, he asks for the privy ("the Boylston Chair of Oratory and Rhetoric") and talks philosophy with Shawnessy while taking a crap. Public ceremonies are subverted by firecrackers under hooped skirts, weddings are hazed with a violence well beyond rude fun, county fairs are rife with quacks and fakirs.

The Perfessor is an emanation of that culture: his title was applied "to all the glib, fraudulent creatures who appeared at carnivals and festive anniversaries to sell hair tonic, quick success, and brand-new sexual potency to the common folk. . . . It was a title of respect for an itinerant wizard who robbed the people by sheer power of language."

The dream sequences are more carnivalesque than Freudian, and more grotesque than celebratory. In one, the Philadelphia Centennial Exposition of 1876 (inspired in part by the trip Lockridge took with Malcolm Correll to the 1933 World's Fair) is transformed into a Roman holiday, where bodies are torn and trampled by chariots. Shawnessy then finds himself in "an Egyptian temple where stone idols to lascivious gods stood between brownstone columns. Priestesses naked except for belts of the brown tobacco leaf scattered gold coins at the base of an idol of pure gold, which, changing slowly, became Mr. Cassius P. Carney, the high priest of the temple, in ceremonial robes stained with tobacco juice."

In the dozens of different types of language—from Hoosier dialect to sentimental effusion to reportage to philosophical dialogue—Lockridge implies that much of the vitality of American life is its linguistic variety. It's a democracy of language—and the language of hicks is as expressive in its sphere as Shawnessy's is in his.

There's a threat, though, in Senator Garwood Jones's official utterance (when he talks to his buddies he reverts to his lively "profane" style). Shawnessy feels almost swept away by Jones's hypocritical pomposities on the podium and begins to doubt his own speech. And the older Cash Carney's and the General's speech is dry, stumbling, and empty. The linguistic vitality of Raintree County folk can turn fake, it can be drained, it can become official.

Language also gets Lockridge in trouble with his reader, especially in the earlier chapters, where Shawnessy's boyhood is narrated in childlike syntax, and where Shawnessy's adolescence is narrated in linguistic purple. Some readers have assumed this language must be laid directly on the author's doorstep, not honoring—as in Joyce's *Portrait of the Artist*—the sometimes distant ironies. Shawnessy never shakes those adolescent yearnings altogether. But there are many languages in the novel, not just Shawnessy's in his various incarnations.

Shawnessy's great poem would be a return to "dawnwords" with their hint of Edenic rebellion. So dreaming, he would be the poet of the people, and his own poem would tell of their "vast and vulgar laughters, festive days, their competitions, races, lusty games. Of strong men running to a distant string. Of their rights and their reforms, religions and revivals. Of their shrine to justice, the court house in the middle of the square. Of their plantings, buildings, minings, makings, ravagings, explorings"—indeed the carnivalesque work that Lockridge has written for him.

Lockridge liked the people of Indiana, and this affection is expressed in the largely affirmative folk portraits of the novel. Yet he sees their vitality under siege, just as America itself has an uncertain future in an era dominated by the flesh of iron.

~

In a novel both encyclopedic and carnivalesque, one might expect chaos and sprawl. More than any other word, Lockridge would hate "sprawling"—an epithet fixed to his novel by reviewers, nosing out "obscene" and "blasphemous." He rather liked sprawl in Hugo, but was convinced his own novel had intricate, discernible, meaningful form. Anybody in whatever walk of life can have such and such a vision, and espouse values others find exemplary or disgusting. But artistic form is the special province of the artist, and to have it impugned is the unkindest cut of all.

There are problems with the novel, but I don't think formlessness is one of them. It has a large-scale symmetry. More to the point here, each of its five phases finds a parallel in the life of its author, though not planned with that in mind.

Early morning of July 4, 1892, Mr. Shawnessy visits the Historical Museum and recalls his life to age nineteen—from 1839 to 1859. This is the period of beginnings, the opening of the quest of the hero, and dreams of love and literary fame. The principal woman is Nell Gaither, the visitor is Senator Garwood Jones, and the principal myths are the Garden of Eden and Actaeon's spying on Diana at the river's edge. The historical period extends from Native Americans and early settlers to the conquest of the West. This is not a conventional historical novel where history is a backdrop or frame for the hero. Lockridge's linkage is more intimate: Shawnessy's life is a repetition through analogy of the nation's history. So during the period of hopeful westward expansion, Shawnessy comes into self-awareness, learns to love the land and heroic myth, and overhears a woman giving birth.

We find a parallel in Lockridge's own life in his Fort Wayne and early Bloomington days, his own trip out West, his own "legends in a class-day album," his courtship of Vernice Baker, and his desire to become a great writer.

In the late morning, Mr. Shawnessy receives his next visitor, the infidel Perfessor, and recalls his loss of innocence in marrying Susanna, who supplants Nell as principal woman. He leaves Raintree County, journeying South into a mythic equivalent of Hades, confronts injustice and insanity, and becomes a father. His sense of identity grows through suffering. Historically, this is the period, 1859 to 1863, from John Brown's raid on Harpers Ferry to the Battle of Gettysburg and a House Divided. Shawnessy's wedding to Susanna is simultaneous with the execution of John Brown, and she gives birth when the firing begins on Fort Sumter.

In Lockridge's own life this second phase roughly parallels the years 1933 to 1940, when he left Indiana for ancient parapets abroad, suffered a life-threatening illness that entailed his own fall from innocence, married, became a father, and wrote an epic poem of sickness, nightmare, and the coming of the Second World War. But his fate was preferable to his hero's: Europe in 1933–34 proved a richly laden festal board instead of a Hades, and he married his Nell.

In the early afternoon Mr. Shawnessy orchestrates the Grand Patriotic Program, honoring his next visitor, General Jacob J. Jackson. Shawnessy remembers his years as a soldier, 1863 to 1865, from the Battle of Chickamauga through Sherman's March to the Sea to the end of the Civil War. Mythic subtexts include the Trojan War and the wanderings of Odysseus.

The biographical equivalent of this third phase is Lockridge's composition of his novel itself, his own Grand Patriotic Program, during the years 1941 to 1946, when he "hid behind a thousand skirts and let J.W.S. bleed for me all over the thousands of MS. pages of *Raintree County*."

In the late afternoon Mr. Shawnessy welcomes the final visitor, financier Cassius Carney, and remembers his sober postwar years, 1865 through 1877, including the period in the City of New York when he courted the actress Laura Golden. Mysterious, empty, and tarnished, she is the principal woman of the City Section. Shawnessy is himself tarnished during this Gilded Age of American history, with its greed, exploited labor, and uninspired post-Lincoln presidencies. He almost loses touch with his own aspirations and the great human riddles. Myths include the Sphinx and Golden Calf.

Biographical parallels to this fourth phase are both direct and prophetic. In 1947, Lockridge will go to New York City for what proves to be the most calamitous moment in his career. In response he will revise the City Section, darkening its tone. Thereafter he will feel himself an exploited laborer and have a falling-out with his publisher over how to divvy up the spoils.

The novel's fifth and final phase is the homecoming, as Mr. Shawnessy attends the evening meeting of the Waycross Literary Society, where the subject of discussion is the myth of the Golden Bough, the fate of heroes. Mr. Shawnessy is targeted as scapegoat by a tar-and-feather mob led by Reverend Jarvey. Thanks to the deft Perfessor's Malacca cane, he escapes the fate of Christ, the sacrificial god-hero. Postponed until now are the pivotal moments of Shawnessy's life. It is a homecoming of memory in this time-drenched novel as he recalls the great footrace, his loss of virginity to Susanna, the death of his son, his homecoming after being reported dead, his discovery of Nell's tombstone, and his homecoming from New York City upon the death of his mother. The memory of love and grief is restorative, as trauma has converted to personal strength through the mercies of time. In his present domesticity—with his children and Esther, a new Eve with Native American blood—he sees the perpetuity of human aspiration through tragedy and across generations. Still the courageous dreamer, he bids farewell to the Perfessor, whose leavetaking is the mirror image of his own emotional homecoming amid complex recognitions of loss and gain.

Here the parallel to Lockridge's own life is a blatant and terrible irony, for in early 1948 he too will come home to Indiana, feeling rather like someone soon to be tarred and feathered. As the Perfessor prophesied, it will be a homecoming of death.

Wishing his novel never to come to a full stop, Lockridge creates verbal linkages among all sections, often undercutting lyrical crescendos.

The train bore him steadily on, stopped briefly at Three Mile Junction, and then continued—beyond the point, he thought, where he had been accustomed to notice the cupola of the Court House.

BUT THE TIME COULD NOT BE LONG NOW,

COULD NOT BE LONG UNTIL

THE

[new section]

AWAKENING, the Perfessor snorted. He looked bewildered, clutched at his face, and then, touching his pince-nez, seemed instantly to recover his composure.

—God! he said. Garwood should bottle and sell that stuff. I haven't had such a good snooze in weeks. Well, program's over, I see.

Lockridge won't put a period to the end of his novel. He wants it never to end. So after the final dream vision that brought his wife to tears, instead of punctuation he prints the contours of the Shawmucky River—which on close inspection are his hero's and the Perfessor's initials, "JWS," in cursive script. The Shawmucky is the river of life, and Lockridge has attempted a novel in which life flows from summer to distant summer everlastingly—in a miraculous cycle of life and death that always brings more life. Shawnessy, like Nell Gaither, becomes one with the green map of Raintree County in this warmly humanized landscape.

In an era when serious fiction has been mostly concerned with anti-heroes and subversion of heroic ideology, *Raintree County* holds tenaciously, amid the desolations that pervade it, to heroic possibility. "It is this posture that places Lockridge in a tradition of hope that wins few readers in these times," writes Leonard Lutwack. In spirit it would open up a path *not* taken in subsequent American fiction, though in form it is the predecessor of such meganovels or postmodern fiction as *The Recognitions, Gravity's Rainbow, The Sot-Weed Factor, Miss MacIntosh, My Darling, The Sunlight Dialogues,* and *Women and Men.*

I feel the novel is sane. Its comedy tempers elegy, its recognitions temper the daydreaming, family romance is survived, and its hero no longer thinks himself a Shakespeare. Shawnessy's grandiose dreams have been transmuted into another type of questing, larger than personal, as he places his faith instead in the vitality of the many-voiced people, the land that nourishes them, and the myth of the Republic, tarnished but alive.

Shawnessy survives in the end, his epic unfinished and no publisher in sight. Proxy for his creator, Shawnessy has lived through the worst that Lockridge could imagine for him: warfare, the decline of the Republic, a lost election, the failure of his personal ambition to become a great writer, the death of parents, of his first love, of wife and son, and symbolically even his own death in the swamp and army hospital. He has emerged damaged but whole, no longer the son but now a "father and preserver" in the landscape of his birth, and still a believer in the miracle of being.

Throughout his suitcase full of manuscript, Lockridge has tested his hero with these "what if"s, extending his own limited personal experience of tragedy and failure. He seems to be asking "what then" would happen should fate sever the objects of his own love and ambition.

My father wanted his novel never to end. The endlessly courageous dreamer declined all terminal punctuation. But the subtext of courage is fear, and the portfolio of dreams includes nightmare. No, my father hadn't quite imagined the worst for his hero, and—in his final revision of the novel—he added that punctuation after all.

IX

Snake Pit in Paradise

Manistee, Michigan, Summer, 1946–Fall, 1947

My father was Mary Jane Ward's tag-along at the 1946 IU Writers' Conference. Not yet published, he wasn't invited to the opening luncheon on July 8. And he politely declined his father's advice about enrolling in Mary Jane's fiction workshop. But he was seen in low profile at lectures and faculty parties over the next several days, sitting crosslegged on the floor and schmoozing with his cousin. Published in March, *The Snake Pit* was second on the nation's best-seller lists and first on Chicago's, had been sold to 20th Century-Fox, and was a Dual Selection of Book-of-the-Month Club. When Mary Jane visited the Lockridge house out on High Street, Elsie Lockridge greeted her with the family's most celebrated faux pas: "Mary Jane, you certainly hit the crackpot!"

Mary Jane had sent the manuscript of her novel to the Harold Ober Agency, which represented her two previously published novels, and had received this reply: "Dear Mrs. Quayle: I am sorry to make a negative report about a book of yours, but Mr. Ober and I have been discussing [*The Snake Pit*] and the problems this book presents and have decided it would be wiser not to offer it. I think you could hardly have picked a more difficult subject to write about and neither of us feels that you have been really successful with it. Also books about insanity or mental breakdowns are not popular at best and the recent publication of Carlton Brown's *Brainstorm* has, I am afraid, killed the chances for another book for quite a while . . . Sincerely yours, Ivan von Auw, Jr."

Mary Jane was resigned to shelving the novel but her husband, Edward Quayle, sent it to Random House. When Mary Jane went to New York to sign her contract, Bennett Cerf spent "a whole afternoon trying to persuade her to change the title, because, I said, 'Women buy most of the novels—and they hate snakes!' Thank God, she told me to go to hell. Now, of course, *snake pit* is part of our language." Within months the novel was an international sensation, eventually translated into sixteen languages. The precise number of suicides at the Harold Ober Agency has never been disclosed.

She advised her cousin Ross therefore not to get a literary agent—a lawyer for tax purposes was enough—and to deal directly with his publisher. I wonder how the string of subsequent events might have been altered if only Ivan von Auw, Jr. had heard the cash register when he read Mary Jane's manuscript.

At the conference, her students were mostly middle-aged folks who had been unable to get published but barraged her wistfully with questions about defending literary property and handling tax and libel problems. Short-story writer MacKinlay Kantor reinforced such concerns, telling them that little fiction comes about through "yeasty personal fermentation" and when it does it's rarely fit to print. The writer's routine motive is profit. For Kantor, the seasoned professional, the writer's life was prudently everything that Ross Lockridge's life was not.

Born in 1905 to a jewelry dealer and a suffragette in Fairmount, Indiana—now better known for native son James Dean—Mary Jane Ward spent her youth in and around Peru, Indiana, living for a time in a house rented out by Cole Porter's family. As a young girl she filled nickel notebooks with stories that were based, like her many novels to come, on local observation and firsthand experience. She enjoyed comparisons with Jane Austen, but as one who sketched a portrait of Dreiser while he spoke at Northwestern University, she was also indebted to modern realism. *The Tree Has Roots* (1937) is an academic novel that features the staff—secretaries, janitors, waitresses—instead of faculty and administrators. *The Wax Apple* (1938) narrates the imagined life of a cashier employed at the Chicago Elevated Railroad. (Mary Jane and her husband were both Norman Thomas socialists.) In 1946, she was completing *The Professor's Umbrella,* occasioned by the notorious anti-Semitism of Northwestern's president.

Her mental collapse in 1941 began as sleeplessness and a case of nerves, leading to a verbal incoherence that abruptly severed her from her normal speaking self. Some doctors at first thought she'd been overdosed with thyroid extract, others later diagnosed her as schizophrenic. But she was probably suffering from an affective disorder. The sudden incoherence suggests instead the onset of a manic episode in a manic-depressive—someone suffering from bipolar illness.

The power of *The Snake Pit* lies in its understated, humorous, but terrifying account of incarceration from the perspective of the patient herself, who doesn't understand why she is in the state hospital and undergoes electroshock, drug, and talk therapies, each of them an assault. The setting is no more ingratiating than the Chicago meatpacking yards Upton Sinclair described four decades earlier in *The Jungle.* Ward satirizes textbook Freudianism and declines any diagnosis of her heroine.

The outcome ironically vindicates the hideous homeopathy of the snake pit: "Long ago they lowered insane persons into snake pits; they thought that an experience that might drive a sane person out of his wits might send an insane person back into sanity." Virginia Stuart Cunningham recovers her sanity as a kind of survival instinct when she confronts, as a patient, horrors greater than any she could have imagined outside the institution.

The novel was prompting a national debate about mental illness and the quality of mental health care. "People go to a psychiatrist as secretly as they go to an abortionist," Ward's narrator complained. Publicity people at Random House were nervous about the autobiographical angle, so she wrote them that if her novel "does anything to help people to see that mental illness is indeed an illness and not a malicious attempt on the part of the patient to disgrace his friends and relatives, I'll be very pleased." Her own mother thought the novel disgraced the family and had urged her not to attach her name to it.

Ward doesn't wish to identify Rockland State Hospital as the Juniper Hill of the novel, but "at the same time it would be grotesque to deny that I was ever inside of a mental hospital as a patient. I couldn't possibly have written *The Snake Pit* before my illness."

My father was finding his parents' household not much more suited for work than your average snake pit and his big triumph did little to alter family dynamics. Lillian was now in full-time residence, having given up her depressing work at the Indiana Woman's Prison in Indianapolis for depressing work with the Monroe County Welfare Department in Bloomington. Sharing the master bedroom with her insomniac mother, she seemed jealous of the attentions given us kids. Vernice told her husband that in Lillian's eyes, "unless the kids are perfect, they are B-A-D!" When my father asked if he could borrow her car for the conference, Lillian said no—that car was *her* car. He walked.

He did negotiate release of a family car for an outing to Henry County. Jeff Wylie was still working on story possibilities for *Life*. Since he and my father were both back home in Indiana, they planned an on-the-spot tour of "Raintree County" to pioneer a picture spread. On July 13, Jeff, his wife Betty, Ernest, my parents, and my grandmother drove up to the old National Road, then east to the county. My mother was excited to be entering the living landscape of the novel. She knew the house in Straughn from their honeymoon, but not the other exotica she had typed her way through. On the way, happy to be back in Indiana, Ernest entertained the others with everything he hated about Boston—the stinking school, Mountfort Street, Lee Oliver—and spirits were very high.

First they walked around the Victorian courthouse at New Castle, with its statue of blindfolded Justice, and then into the macabre historical museum, described in my father's Dream Section. "In the cases of the museum, he had seen stuffed birds and animals, varnished fish, pioneer cradles, primitive scythes, tallow lamps, candleholders, slates, spinning wheels, arrowheads, tomahawks, moccasins, stone knives, belts of wampum, cultivating sticks, firebows, stone wheels, crude steam engines, firearms, light bulbs, typewriters." These were the "ancient deposits of life" amid which the Dreamer seeks a "sacred relic," the "sainted mummy, hidden in an unsuspected case."

They skirted hog wallows to reach the old Messick graveyard, and Ross helped the women, all in dresses, over the barbed-wire fence. Jeff noticed that "Lockridge was almost ecstatic, for it was like visiting the graveyard at Danwebster in his book." He found the fallen tombstone of Benjamin Franklin Shockley, killed in the Civil War, and on the spot decided to send it to his Uncle Frank in Pittsburgh. "He lugged the stone through the tangled weeds and heaved it over the fence. To his consternation the brittle slab broke in two. 'Judgment for sacrilege!' he exclaimed."

The Blue River near Knightstown was only a trickle, with shiny pebbles where there had once been water, and Ross was disappointed. It wasn't how he'd remembered it. Betty said, "Well Ross, look it's summer, it's been dry, and it will fill up. Places change."

In Straughn, Jeff photographed him and Vernice standing like proprietors in front of the old Shockley house where they'd spent their honeymoon. Then to the rural Old Home Place, deserted and moldering, with its large glacial boulders. Betty was getting tired and said she'd stay in the car. Very sternly, Vernice replied, *"Betty! This is the Old Home Place. You have to get out!"*

Back home it became clear they had to get out of Bloomington—the Old Folks were too much for them and they for the Old Folks, my father said. For one thing Elsie was vexed whenever our wing of the family started its routine singing at the dinner table. And the summer was proving socially taxing, with numerous reunions of families and friends. On July 15, he sent out an SOS to Larry Wylie, who was spending the summer with Anne's parents on Lake Michigan near Grand Rapids. He was "completely behind the eight-ball" in his efforts to revise the book, due in only ten weeks, with publication now set for April 1, 1947. Could Larry possibly find a place up there, under three hundred dollars for the season? He misses Wylie's companionship and talk. "I've been a strangely preoccupied—perhaps almost obsessed—personality for about five years, while I built the quaint perspectives of *Raintree County*. In a way, I never really lived in Boston but all the time in the legendary landscape of my book."

He sometimes took Jeanne, Ernest, and me on walks down High Street to Covenanter graveyard and beyond. We would drop in on the Andersons, who were descended from Kentucky slaves. He struck them as sensitive to racial issues and Ruth Anderson appreciated his attempt to make them feel better about their poverty. "Well, you should see how we used to live when Vernice and I were first married—we used store boxes for furniture."

Vernice's old schooldays friend Nota Scholl came over with her husband, John McGreevey, an aspiring young writer. Nota had sent Ross her husband's sonnet on Thomas Wolfe, and Ross had replied that, alas, she was married to a poet. But during this visit Ross seemed to John distracted, going through the polite forms, his mind somewhere else. John expressed concern to Nota afterward.

My father was getting more and more nervous about the novel, assuring Houghton Mifflin that he would put his "last licks in on the book between now and October 1." Vice-president Lovell Thompson wrote to say that "anything you can do to speed up your part of the program will be gratefully received by the production and promotion ends of Houghton Mifflin Company." Editor Dale Warren wasn't exactly helping out. He had already given Ross Lockridge four books for pleasure reading, including *Sons and Lovers,* all of which my father dutifully read. He then sent others. "I don't know whether this is a summer for reading or not, nevertheless I am sending you a few of the recent Houghton Mifflin offerings, which may not come amiss." And Paul Brooks sent him *Amateurs at War,* which my father pronounced "a fine compilation which I have read with profit."

What was nagging him was the fate of the 356-page Dream Section that ended his novel, which Houghton Mifflin was urging that he drop. Earlier he had written them portentously that the issue "is one of great importance to me, the book, and possibly the future of American letters; and it is one upon which I beseech no sudden or rash decision but the most sober and careful consideration on the part of my editors." He thinks Joyce's Walpurgisnacht in *Ulysses* is "too clinical and pedantic and plain undramatic, though it pioneers the way. *Finnegans Wake,* not in any true sense a dream, is a retreat from the responsibility of communication. . . . You see, all through the book my purpose has been the opposite of Joyce's. He by his own confession attempted to make the simple obscure, having, as he expressed it, a natural antipathy to 'aquacity.' My whole intention is to make the obscure simple." His own use of dream material has in any event originated, he says, not in Joyce but in Freud.

More than a coda, the Dream Section recapitulates the structure of the earlier novel in a new key. We move, he says, from Myths of Origin to the Growth of Identity to Wars of the Republic to the City of the Gilded Age to Homecoming. "All the symbols of the book at last achieve a rich confluence . . . We now pass through the looking glass of the map of Raintree County, and we are in the world where for the first time in the book, time no longer exists: the past and present (instead of shuttling back and forth as in the Day and Flashback passages) become simultaneous and identical." Dropping the Dream Section would leave the narrative intact but undo one third of the novel's conceptual apparatus.

What is the Dream Section like? Lockridge claims new intensities here and sometimes he is right. Reverend Jarvey's slaying of his own father, only hinted at earlier, becomes vivid in the guilt-ridden dream. "The baptismal font was full of the old man's clotted blood, which had gushed in a hideous flood from his dead body. . . . Sooner or later the members of the congregation would smell the stench, or someone would go down a little too far and see the old man's stiff hand sticking out, and the jig would be up."

On one occasion Shawnessy is transformed into a black man who is about to marry the mulatto Susanna, when "several fat white men in ku-klux-klan robes, pig eyes through white eyepieces, rushed him and grabbed his arms." They lash him to the head of an iron bedstead. "SECOND TYPICAL SOUTHERNER, fat, young, friendly smile and nice teeth, high friendly voice, 'Come on, boys, le's ball this buck, and then take turns on that little bitch. Hell, I ain't had a good black fuck for a week.' "

The Battle of Gettysburg is fought again by walking corpses, John Shawnessy is crucified on a telegraph pole, the petals of the raintree in the City turn into coins, Shawnessy enters a patent office where all the world's dead bodies are stored and classified, he asks all the questions of Shakespeare one would wish answered, he encounters several eminent Victorian men who have been transformed into women, and he floats down the yellow waters of a river atop the huge old atlas of Raintree County.

The dream format invites such conceits and transmutations, but my father is more at home with its accommodation of farce. Shawnessy floats through his dream world, never until the end in control of events or getting what he wants. Improving on reality, he finds himself in bed with Nell Gaither on their wedding night. "Give me lips, lover. Thrust home," she cries. Suddenly Garwood Jones appears, drunk, fully clothed, smoking a cigar and lying squarely in the middle of the bed: "Don't mind me, john. As best man, I'm very happy to lend any little service I can to you and the missus. Mind if I take a turn at the throttle?" Before Shawnessy has finished protesting, additional uninvited guests start showing up, first the president of the Ladies' Sitting and Sewing Society, then schoolchildren, then a cousin from Spokane, then a committee from the Ladies' Aid, then a delegation from the Baptist Church, then the county school board, then Reverend Jarvey, then his father and Bobby Burns and veterans of the Grand Army of the Republic.

The homecoming sequence begins with the Perfessor pressing a button and one by one blowing Garwood Jones, Cash Carney, General Jacob Jackson, and finally Shawnessy and himself off the Fourth of July speakers' platform into outer space, where they all reassemble on a red, white, and blue rocket and chew the fat. Down below, "some remains of cities were visible, here and there a human hand, and now and again a wheel or a bottle, but, as far as eye could see, no living thing." The Perfessor says, "Frankly, I think we got off the old ball just in time." Garwood Jones says, "Move over, boys. Here, john, let me take a spin at the controls. Remember—I'm still president." Shawnessy politely asks Evelina Brown to read the minutes of the last meeting of the Waycross Literary Society. And looking over the side of the rocket, the Perfessor says, "You know, there's one good thing about this: It's possible at last to be definitive about the human race. (Hawking and spitting over side of rocket) In a word, we stank."

Elsewhere, at the Centennial Exhibition, the Perfessor as barker auctions off Lockridge himself. "Now, ladies and gents, don't go away—we've a special offer for you today: a certain terrific professor of english—and everything else from jesus to jinglish; back from the wars without any hurts, after hiding behind a thousand skirts; faces the world with a pleasant smile, absolutely devoid of guile; took first

honors and fat degree, at harvard, paris, and old pedee; juggles figures and facts and balls, imitates barnyard animals; fast and facile to
parse and pun, jack of ten languages, master of one; converses of
cabbages, kings, and crops, lallapaloosas and lollypops; good for
thirty additional years, with quips and quotes running out of his ears;
equipped with ribbons and recommendations, a beautiful wife and
nice relations, scads of children and dissertations on everything since
god was a greek, from homer's thunder to keats's squeak . . . Ladies
and gentlemen, near and far, we're knocking you down this shining
star at——(Rapping with gavel) Sold! For a good five-cent cigar!"

Beyond farce Lockridge can return in dream to the time in
Raintree County before there were human beings and county lines,
when the earth was shining, pregnant, and unpolluted. Elsie can re-
visit the world of her early memories, denying her father's mortality.
"And now she was approaching the little house behind its white
fence. She paused with her hand on the gate. . . . If now she entered, she would see them there. Her mother would be working in
the kitchen where the smell of sealing wax lingered forever. The lost
elsie and the forever lost ernest would be in the middle room reading . . . And if she went behind the house, she would see the sunlight
falling through the apple trees. She would see the outhouse filled
with clippings, and the barn, and the narrow backfield stretching to
the railroad."

In the dream, time is a plenitude of luminous moments that can
always be repossessed instead of a one-way tendency toward ruin. In
the dream, Shawnessy finally overcomes nostalgia as history yields to
prophecy and he plants a renewed myth of the Republic in the soil
of Raintree County.

What was my father to do with all this? He had written the novel
with the Dream Section always in mind, storing away images and episodes in separate files as he went. He knew his invention sometimes
flagged and had told Houghton Mifflin that he would try to compress
it. Clearly it wasn't an easy read. The narrative element was spo-
radic. Without the lucid critical roadmap he gave his publisher, it
would likely appear a jumble to many. He thought Joyce failed in the
"responsibility of communication." Was he about to fail too?

In late July, his father, Ernest, and he once again returned to
camp on the Eel River, which he had plucked "wriggling from Miami

County and transplanted to the composite landscape of Raintree County." He still hadn't done any revising to speak of, and wasn't letting on to Houghton Mifflin. He gave Ernest a hunting knife and taught him to shoot the old Winchester, using coffee cans as targets. He confessed to shooting groundhogs there as a boy. With the skill of Hawkeye, Ross Senior found yet more arrowheads. Ernest photographed his father in profile sitting pensively on the mythical Shawmucky. A decision about the novel was silently being made that weekend.

Back in Bloomington, my father wrote Paul Brooks matter-of-factly on July 29 that he would drop the Dream Section. He planned to keep as a coda only the final passages Vernice had wept over, prefaced with a little more. But this immense verbal structure would otherwise cease to exist.

Five years earlier he had abandoned *The Dream of the Flesh of Iron* with little expression of regret, as if he were freeing himself of it. He was much more attached to his Dream Section, and it was a lot to give up.

A few weeks earlier he had insisted that it was bound indissolubly to the larger novel and could be removed only with great injury to the whole. The future of American letters might depend on it! What did it mean that he could already change his mind and come to agree with his publisher? What *was* the integrity of this five-volume mass of words if it could become overnight a candidate for such surgery?

～

As usual, Larry Wylie delivered. He and Anne found a cottage for my family on Lake Michigan in the old lumber town of Manistee—a cottage that would become much more than a summer retreat. "Good old Larry! I am reminded of one of the old nineteenth century copybook maxims: 'Remember well and bear in mind / A constant friend is hard to find. / And when you find one that is true / Change not the old one for the new.' . . . The really nice thing about it all is that with our car we'll be in easy visiting distance of you kids. Let's have a *Réunion des Anciens Elèves du Groupe Delaware!*"

The car was a dark blue Hudson older than its years, either '40 or '41—my father didn't know which—and I remember him driving this our first family car proudly up the driveway at the Lockridge house. He liked cars. It was a seller's market and a local resident had taken him for nine hundred dollars. He and my grandfather tried to plaster over some cracks in this piece of scrap metal.

Early on August 10, we started up to Manistee, 430 miles north. Twenty miles out of Bloomington we were on an uphill bridge near Martinsville when the gearshift fell off in my father's hand. Happily the car at full throttle could go only forty-five miles an hour, and many fewer uphill. He let the car roll down backward out of harm's way, stopped, and quietly looked around for the screw. He was tense, but like the fictional T. D. Shawnessy he took a hopeful view of the situation. A car that had survived this long would surely get us to Manistee. In retrospect this moment—the only memory I have of the trip—has become an omen.

My mother watched the reflection of car and family in storefront windows as we wheezed and snorted by. She was afraid we looked like a bunch of Okies. At ten-thirty that night we rattled into Manistee. The surf was pounding in the cold wind and lights were on in the small cottage at 101 Lakeshore Drive. Ernest and I slept on the porch the first night. We awoke early the next morning to the sound of foghorns and looked at the mist over the lake, only one hundred yards away. Enchanted, we saw the long pier leading to the lighthouse, and across the road a large playground in the white sand. Whenever I hear a foghorn today I'm transported to that porch. We were in Paradise.

In the nineteenth century, Manistee was a prosperous town, with more than a hundred lumber companies devastating the great area forests, earlier the home of Ottawas and Chippewas. When they ran out of trees, the lumber barons packed off, leaving some elegant decaying Victorian houses on "the Hill" and a depressed depopulated community of some 7,000 inhabitants. When my family arrived there, a new resource for plunder had been found: sand dunes were being dumped onto long conveyer belts, escorted to the lake, and hauled off to Detroit for windshields. And Morton Salt was busy mining underneath it all. To the eye of an environmentalist this paradise was a ravaged industrial sump.

Yet in 1946, with the help of some reforestation, nature was holding its own. The air, lake, and sand seemed clean, and Ernest,

Jeanne, and I hiked up and down the beach and climbed over the surviving magical dunes to the north. Even the sand conveyer belts were enchanting. For Ernest the nightmare of Mountfort Street seemed really over.

Our father soon became the still center of this invigorated household continuing its great adventure. With only three small rooms, the cottage offered no refuge from family. He set up his desk in one corner of the living room and faced away from the lake as he got down to work. So absorbed was he that it could take several tries to get his attention. He was a quiet, even-tempered man at his station, once again ceaselessly typing from morning to night. He never raised his voice amid all this, but on occasion, to escape the tumult, would take work with him and quietly slip into the back seat of the Hudson.

A few days after our arrival he finished "An Album of Raintree County" and dispatched it to Dorothy Hillyer. I cannot look at it without weeping. His motive was purportedly to suggest formats for publicity. But it is more a photographic rewrite and memorial of his own novel, with photographs of Henry County and the Eel River, of Vernice and him at Rivervale and on their honeymoon, of Paris days—with antique embroidered designs in pencil and lyrical quotations from the novel.

(In mid-March, 1948, Dorothy Hillyer will return to Vernice Lockridge "under separate cover a beautiful and remarkable little album which Ross loaned to us and which has been carefully preserved in the safe. In the light of tragic event, it is almost unbearably touching for it is the mirror of love and youth and very sunny days. Of course you know it, but I want to prepare you for its arrival.")

On August 13, Paul Brooks wrote that he was pleased by Ross's decision to drop the Dream Section. Under separate cover he was sending another recent title from Houghton Mifflin's list, Thomas Heggen's *Mister Roberts*. "It's a first novel in which we have a lot of faith. I have an idea you'll enjoy it." My father thanked him— Heggen's novel was both tragic and "riotously funny, the mouth of the masque turned up on one corner and down on the other. It's an utterly absorbing book, and it completely lifted me out of *Raintree County* for a few hours."

Houghton Mifflin would send along still other titles, including new books by John Dos Passos and E. B. White. We see here how a publisher congenitally differs from an author. For a publisher, the "list" is much of the house identity, and to ask a new author to "sample" it is part of a genteel process of induction. Writing is a labor from which one can always take a break. The new author will add yet another title to an ever-expanding list.

My father like other authors wasn't interested in adding yet another title to some damned list. He was asking all those other titles to *move over!* And any other titles the company was obliged to produce that same season didn't really exist. Writing his own book— and finishing it—was a matter of ultimate concern on which the universe hung. Yet good boy that he was for the time being, he sandwiched in the house titles.

He brought up again the title of his own novel. Houghton Mifflin was still calling it *The Riddle of Raintree County.* Covering all bases, and even discounting some alternative titles he feared they *might* come up with, he put in another vote for simply *Raintree County,* expending four single-spaced pages on the issue where others might have settled for a paragraph. Dale Warren wasn't convinced: " 'Raintree County' seems too abrupt, staccato, geographical for a work of this length and 'incalculable richness.' " Warren proposed to Paul Brooks the title *That Was Raintree County.*

Neighbors in Manistee were finding Ross Lockridge a quiet, shy man who kept largely to himself. In late summer of 1946, his social life was restricted to the Wylies and some friends of theirs, Harry and Louise Armstrong, an older couple who lived on "the Hill" in an exotic concrete-block house covered with ivy and graced with antique statuary. Harry Armstrong was a commercial artist whose avocation was to paint nude portraits of his wife and, covertly, naked women in bondage.

His wife, Louise, was Manistee's most unpopular citizen. She had published a book in 1938 with Little, Brown entitled *We Too Are the People,* describing in unflattering terms the locals' response to the Emergency Food Relief program she had administered earlier in the decade.

Ernest, Jeanne, and I gaped at the nudes while our parents conversed on the patio with the Armstrongs and Wylies. Larry Wylie was happy about this renewal of their friendship. Ross Lockridge had been both his student and a sort of younger brother, but now the relationship seemed reversed, and he took pleasure in his friend's success. He saw a marked contrast between Ross Senior and Ross Junior. For the historian, like many enterprising Hoosiers, the State of Indiana was sufficient unto his ambition. Making it meant recognition of townsfolk, local newspapers, the state legislature, and the governor. But Ross Junior, like Larry Wylie himself, looked beyond the banks of the Wabash, and now his friend appeared to be making it in the larger public sphere.

They exchanged visits a few times before the Wylies returned to Haverford, and he and Ross would walk up and down the dunes alone, talking. Ross seemed relieved to escape for a few hours the cramped cottage, noisy kids, and writing table. Larry had been kept in the dark about his friend's novel and now he asked about it. Ross replied quietly: "Well, it's hard to define because it's everything. It's a novel, but it's more than a novel. It's an essay but it's more than an essay. The only thing I can compare it to is Plato's *Republic*—but it's better than that."

Slightly jolted, Larry Wylie kept silent, thinking that after all his friend might be right. Ross seemed to him somewhat like Hugo— "*C'est une force de la nature*"—and there was otherwise no evidence of derangement. The comment was made matter-of-factly without personal egotism, if also without Ross's characteristic humor or irony.

Afterward Larry expressed some fears to Anne. How would Ross handle it if critics didn't go along? He had also asked his friend a question he would come to regret—one that Ross responded to vaguely—"What are you going to do next?"

Mary Jane Ward and Ed Quayle visited two days in early October on their way to New York. My parents still kept no booze in the house, so their visitors fixed that and my father warmed to Ed's excellent martinis. His friendship with his cousin was deepening.

Upon arriving in New York, she ran into some trouble of her own with this question "What next?" Her new manuscript, *The Professor's Umbrella,* was not being warmly received at Random House. Her editors, Robert Linscott and Bennett Cerf, thought it lacked the personal investment of *The Snake Pit* and would disappoint her enormous readership. She was being forced to revise radically.

My father consoled and advised. "I suppose something like this was inevitable as you begin your career of competing with the author of *The Snake Pit.* . . . In the long run you've got to write the way you feel and are, and any effort on the part of your publisher to make you over in the image and likeness of some long-term best-seller ideal of their own could be very detrimental both to them and to you. It is entirely possible to write non-best-seller novels without being a minor novelist." He advised her to take her time with this new novel in any event—and "create a real void of anticipation."

The lukewarm reception of *The Professor's Umbrella* tempered the pleasure Mary Jane and Ed took in their celebrity tour of New York, despite the Algonquin, the Stork Club, and conversation with Bennett Cerf and Eleanor Roosevelt, not to mention Danny Kaye's wife and Ginger Rogers's mother. She spoke about her cousin to Cerf, who had already spoken with Dorothy Hillyer at Houghton Mifflin and planned to allude to the novel in his *Saturday Review* column.

When my father heard that somebody at Houghton Mifflin had described him to Cerf as "another Thomas Wolfe," he was deeply upset and fired off letters to Cerf, Mary Jane, and Houghton Mifflin. (We Lockridges, as usual, had no private telephone and long-distance calls were made collect at the park across the way.)

The comparison was "pure poison. . . . Nobody *wants* another Tom Wolfe. One was quite enough," he wrote Hillyer. "Wolfe was helpless in a job of construction; his novels just flowed along over the experience of his life, while *Raintree County* is a remarkably close-woven and elaborate job of dramatic construction and planning." He was much more influenced by Joyce and Mann among the Europeans, and equally by Dos Passos and Hemingway among contemporary Americans. "A lot of tributaries have been drowned in the Mississippi of my book."

He added, prophetically, that "critics are much influenced by labels like that, and often these tags get on early and stick."

He was relieved in one respect by Cerf's column of October 26. "At Houghton Mifflin I found the ebullient Dorothy Hillyer, back from a triumphal tour to the Coast, babbling jubilantly over a new manuscript just turned in by Ross Lockridge, Jr. It is called 'The Riddle of Raintree Country' [*double sic*], and will not be published until 1948. Lockridge, a cousin of Mary Jane Ward, of 'Snake Pit' fame, has been working on it for five years, without telling a soul what he was doing—and still has considerable polishing to do. 'It's longer than *Gone with the Wind,*' said Dorothy. 'And better than Tom Wolfe,' added Dale Warren."

Okay. But what was that about 1948?! Mary Jane could take her time, but he expected his novel to come out in May or June, 1947, at the latest to take advantage of the July Fourth *Life* spread.

And for reasons more important. On October 31, he sent up the first yellow flag concerning his health. "I have about half-killed myself to meet a tentative schedule laid down by Lovell Thompson and others," he wrote Dorothy Hillyer. "I say 'half-killed' advisedly, as I am really down and out right now and have been for a couple of weeks. Though I haven't yet babbled of green fields and pronounced last words, my fingers have been twitching at the sheets and my throat makes funny noises. I'm trying to find a medical doctor with a degree in Manistee who will hazard a guess as to how long I have to live. I don't think it will be 1948, judging by the way I feel right now, and I want to be alive when this book comes out. No kidding, I feel terrible, and I keep thinking dismally of Keats's lines: 'When I have fears that I shall cease to be Before my pen has gleaned my teeming brain,' etc. . . . I thought the Wolfe cry in Cerf's article was perfectly all right. Just now I don't mind resembling Wolfe in any way, except one. He's so terribly posthumous." The novel had better come out in mid-1947 as planned!

He had misquoted Keats, writing "shall cease" instead of "may cease."

Dale Warren cautioned him to take a rest, and Brooks calmed him down with a letter of November 14 assuring that his was the company's "big novel for '47"—albeit the manufacturing department has increased the lead time and they must have the revised manuscript by "early December, if we're to stick to our schedule." He added his regrets concerning Ross's shaky health: "Once the book is published we should all go on a rest cure together. But by then we'll only have begun to fight."

My father replied that all was well once again—the problem was merely with his eyes, one being even more perfect than the other. To his parents, who had visited for several days in late

October—hoping to make amends for the domestic tensions of July and August—he wrote more revealingly. "The doctor found nothing organically wrong, which was reassuring, and my rundown condition was put to the nervousness, aggravated—or, indeed, brought on—by eyestrain." Vernice was monitoring this "nervousness" with some concern.

On November 30, he dispatched the first two volumes to Houghton Mifflin, with the promise that the rest would come as soon as he and Vernice had done some retyping. The novel was enormously revised beyond "the wholesale murder of old Vol. V." "This last effort on the book bled me white creatively," he told Hillyer. He enclosed a detailed four-page summary of the revisions plus "Some Suggestions about Typography, Layout, Design, etc." He has made major structural revisions. He has deepened the characterizations of Nell and Susanna. He has added an entirely new episode—John's and Susanna's honeymoon journey south—thereby giving the "southern point of view" and embracing still more American geography beyond Indiana. And here and there he has sneaked in just a few short dream sequences, old and new. Thereby the novel "retains its subconscious world."

And—of larger import—he has changed the names of several characters. He had been using family names, such as Emma, Elsie, Frank, Ernest, and John Wesley, plus real Henry County place names. He very much wishes to cleanse the novel of these—and the reasons will prove deeper than a fictional convention.

Shortly thereafter he received distressing news from Paul Brooks, who thought the chances "practically nil" that a book of this size could be ready for publication in June or July of 1947, citing compelling technical reasons. As for the *Life* Fourth of July spread, "From what I know of *Life,* the chances of this going through are actually very small."

My father found this unacceptable. The sour note first sounded in the Wolfe cry now approached real discord in his letter of January 1, 1947. If April 1 was no longer possible, surely July 4 still was. "I'm violently opposed to seeing the early summer publication abandoned without at least a gallant effort. I can't agree that the LIFE possibility is small. Such chances are small or great depending on the material promoted and the way it's promoted. I have a way of promoting things I believe in so that they come true, and I have no doubt Houghton Mifflin works the same way."

Beyond the missed *Life* opportunity, there would be the problem of how he'd feed his family. "People ought not to think of me as the typical irresponsible young author who can suspend time and twist himself into pliant knots while waiting for his first novel to come out."

Brooks politely ignored all this in his reply, thanking him for the New Year's Day letter and warning that when he arrived in Boston in mid-January—to follow his novel through the early production phase—he should not expect them to have made great headway on the revised manuscript.

My father was anxious at not receiving reassurances from Brooks this time about the publication date. Though a little late in finishing the revision, he felt he'd held up his end of things. Why were they so damned *casual* about it?

Well, he had finished his novel at last, and needed only to tend to small editorial and production matters in Boston. He had learned from Captain Hubbard's film version of his New Harmony pageant not to leave production to the producers. And it's clear he wished to stay in literal touch with his novel—he couldn't bear simply to pack it off on a train. He would be there for all final editorial and production decisions.

But the period of incessant creative labor that had begun in the summer of 1941 was over at last—he thought. He could now confront "that mysterious interim after the Muse sinks back exhausted and before the printed book is on the stands." He and Vernice sent off the final two volumes and, on January 11, he sent Dorothy Hillyer a tired one-word telegram: "FINIS."

~

An imaginary exchange I wish had taken place sometime or other: "Dear Ross: I've not had a chance to read it, but some editors here believe we are sitting on a potential masterwork in *Raintree County*. Perhaps we should alter the conventional production schedule accordingly, in light of this unusual opportunity. Why not take another year or two in revision to assure that you do not sell yourself short, and let us think of bringing it out sometime in 1950, surely a date with its own symbolic weight? As for the *Life* spread, do keep in mind that 1950 has a July Fourth of its own. We have the Houghton Mifflin Literary Fellowships to encourage new talent and are prepared to offer you a stipend for two years running, not merely an advance, to free you of teaching responsibilities. We think the novel should sit and age awhile, like a fine wine. Please think it over. Sincerely, Lovell Thompson, Vice-president."

"Dear Lovell: I read your letter with great dismay and have discussed it with Vernice. We are prepared to sever all ties with Houghton Mifflin and I have written to Bennett Cerf, just one of many editors who would be less prone to break faith with the author of *Raintree County,* a book this country needs sooner than later, etc. etc. Sincerely yours, Ross Lockridge, Jr."

This exchange of letters is—in my imaginary scenario—followed up by Lovell Thompson's request via telegram that Ross Lockridge make a collect call to his office. "Really, Ross, this isn't journalism. Why not be sure the book doesn't go to press half-baked? If it's a book for the ages, who the hell cares whether it comes out in 1948 or 1950? What's the rush?"

"Well, Lovell, I begin to see your point. Maybe I should slow down a little. I've had a case of nerves from all the stress and strain. Look, burn that last letter. I'm sorry I wrote it. Yeah, let's think in terms of 1950. What's the rush? I'd be sort of sorry to finish the book so soon anyway. Vernice'll be relieved. Now about that stipend . . ."

~

On January 13, 1947, my father departed Manistee with Ernest in the decrepit Hudson. Ernest had had an earache so bad that work on the novel was halted an entire week in early December while both parents administered sulfa and worried. It was decided the climate was taking its toll, and he'd better stay the winter months with the Lockridges back in Bloomington and enroll in third grade there.

Ernest was close to tears. One day his father had asked him if he'd like to hear something of what he'd been writing. Before this,

Ernest had admired his father more for his drawings, those Hallow-
een dragons for instance, than for the book. His father apologized
first because there were some bad words in it, the sort of language
Ernest could use only at risk of having his mouth washed out with
soap. Then he stood and gave a dramatic reading of the episode
where John Shawnessy and his buddy Flash Perkins are pinned down
by Confederate soldiers, and Flash is shot clean through and slowly
dies, gurgling, twisting, and laughing. "Hell, I can lick any man here!
I can outrun any man in Raintree County! Hell, where I come
from—Where I come from, why, hell, where I come from—."

Ernest was caught up, stunned. It was better than the movies.
For the first time he came to understand what his father had been
doing all these years—there could be nothing greater than this.

And now he had to leave his father. Not long on the road, the car
began swaying as if the steering mechanism had failed, and then it
"began to float all over the road," flying along backward and just
missing a stout mailbox before coming to rest on the shoulder. The
Hudson wasn't wholly to blame. Ernest's father hadn't noticed the
ice on the road.

After a stayover in Indianapolis with Shockley and Mary Kay,
where his parents picked up Ernest, our father departed by rail for
Boston. Arriving at Mountfort Street on January 15, where he had
arranged with his subtenants to hole up in one bedroom for the duration, he discovered he'd forgotten the crucial folder, "Revision
Plans." "Strange oversight," he wrote Vernice. Setting out to control
the early production phase of his novel, he wasn't entirely in control
of himself.

The subtenants had installed that modern convenience the telephone, so he began lining up meals with friends and neighbors and
called Houghton Mifflin, where the reception was warm. Dorothy
Hillyer was already two thirds of the way through the revision. "It
looks wonderful—just wonderful," she said, adding, "There may be
a few little things." "The big news," Ross told Vernice, "is that I have
a big cocktail engagement with the editors at Houghton Mifflin at
Dale Warren's apartment."

This affair at the Ritz came off well. "We talked about my book
most of the time. The motto around H.M. really is 'Love that book!'

They refer to it just casually now among themselves as The Great American Novel. 'Which volume are you on?' " they ask one another.

During the next several weeks my father worked sixteen hours a day, sending exuberant, affectionate letters to Vernice about his reception and the smooth if arduous production process. "People are crazy about *Raintree County*. The new Susanna is universally acknowledged to be a knockout. . . . The new Nell absolutely enchanted Craig Wylie, who was the completely fresh man on the MS . . . and he says he can't even imagine the book without that terrific New Orleans section. He wonders how I got along without it in the first draft. That's how well I built those sections during those months in the front room at Manistee . . . Everybody around here treats me like the prince of the earth . . . and the general impression is that *Raintree County* is an all-time phenomenon."

He was being put up in a small office right along with the copy editor, where he made his presence felt throughout the company, by today's standards a small family-like concern in a building not much larger than a townhouse. Hillyer told him that they almost never invited an author into the house—"that ordinarily the author is a 'damn nuisance' to have around, but that my manuscript was so important and so elaborate that they wanted me to be there for decisions and to avoid trouble with correcting galley, and besides she said they thought I'd be fun to have around."

The private response of the Houghton Mifflin staff was mixed. Production people tended to like him, promotion people to tolerate him, and editorial people to find him a damn nuisance. Editor-in-chief Paul Brooks found him ebullient and often laughing but a humorless person where he himself was concerned. Editor Dorothy Hillyer, who sent him the warmest letters, would tell John Leggett years later that he was a "difficult, withdrawn, wispy sort of man," perhaps a homosexual. (She herself was outgoing and ample.) "Ross was quite capable of fussing eighteen hours a day over that manuscript. He was *in love* with it, almost sexually."

And editor Craig Wylie (amid this wealth of Wylies, no apparent relation to Larry or Jeff Wylie but a cousin of high school classmate Louise Wylie) felt that Lockridge was "an extraordinarily (even for an author) egotistical boy" who came to life only when the subject was his novel. Invited to a dinner party at the Wylies' home in Weston, my father disgraced himself before a company of literati and two very uptight neighbors by claiming that he and Shakespeare had confronted in one instance a similar dramatic problem—and he had bettered the Bard.

Craig Wylie felt he *almost* got away with it because of his youthfulness. But Wylie's wife, Angie, read the evening differently. She thought Lockridge was "very funny" and said it all "with a laugh," that he was not an "egotist" but an "enthusiast of his own novel" who "couldn't believe the success he had had"—as if to say in astonishment, "Look at this thing I've done!"

There were different ways of reading the author of *Raintree County,* who at this dinner party was clearly tipsy on something more than his book and Houghton Mifflin's own highest praise. But the cook hired for the evening made one indisputable judgment: "That young boy sure ate a lot!"

The wretched bibliography course he'd taken at Harvard, and a lifetime of fascination with the physical being of books, made him virtually a fellow employee of the production staff. He already knew about bookmaking and knew what he wanted, coming to Boston armed with maps, drawings of trains rolling by cemeteries, and *The Illustrated Historical Atlas of Henry County.* For design ideas he gave them a copy of *The Old Fauntleroy Home* with its embossed golden raintree and the street map of New Harmony, warning that "the Curse of the Shawnessys" would be on anybody who read a word of it. He knew he liked antique typeface and he knew he disliked quotation marks, preferring the Gallic dash. Vice-president Lovell Thompson wanted the cover in Harvard crimson, but Assistant Professor Ross Lockridge wanted it in green and gold, and got them. Terry Baker and others in production thought his ideas made sense.

He wished to be author of the whole book, not just the words. It was a question of identity—for, as Baker saw it, Ross Lockridge *was* his book.

Jeff and Betty Wylie invited him to their large Victorian house on the coast in Hingham a few times during this period. They were offering him a vacation, but he would come with typewriter and manuscript. Another visitor said that when Ross was typing upstairs it sounded like a train going through the house.

Alas, he had discovered the novel wasn't so finished as he thought. While admiring the book, Craig Wylie gave him a long list of queries, historical and stylistic, and suggested some deletions. And my father was undertaking larger structural revisions to boot. As he handed it over for copyediting he was rewriting it yet again. "I still lack a little of putting my last mark on *Raintree County*," he confessed to Vernice on February 1, explaining why she hadn't heard from him for a week. He'd have to stay at least a month longer than anticipated.

Meanwhile, back in Manistee I had stopped asking when Daddy was coming back and was getting used to his not being around the house. A wonderful snowfall could make up for anything. Grandma Baker had come up to fill in for him—in an unwitting rehearsal for what was to come. My mother and she were getting better acquainted at last.

My father spread my funny talk, as transcribed by my mother, all over Houghton Mifflin. "The other day Jeanne was feeling very sorry for her broken doll and said 'Poor 'ittle fing.' Larry laughed & said 'Jeannie said 'Poor 'ittle fing.' I asked 'What do *you* say, Larry?' He answered 'Poor 'ittle sing.' "

But as usual Ernest was reaping the larger share of paternal attention, privileged as the only one of us ever to get direct written communication from our father. "Dear Ernest: I thought you might want to know what's happening along Mountfort Street. The other day I was walking to our building when suddenly a small boy shot out of an alley running with all his might and two larger boys after him. On looking closely at this boy, I saw that it was none other than our old friend Henry Miller. I said, 'Hello, Henry,' and Henry immediately began to walk under my arm, while the two bigger kids slunk off, muttering things under their breath. 'How is the William McKinley School these days, Henry?' I said. 'It stinks,' Henry said. 'Who's your teacher now, Henry?' I asked. 'Bucktoothed Murphy,' Henry said. 'She stinks.' 'Is she hard on you, Henry?' I asked. 'She pulls your hair and hits your knuckles with a ruler,' Henry said . . . It wasn't many days after that, that I came out of our apartment building and saw a small boy stirring with a stick in a puddle of dirty slush right in front of the mailbox in the gutter. It was Errol, who is bigger now but no better looking. 'What are you doing, Errol?' I asked. 'Fixing it so that cars will get stuck in this mud,' Errol said. Same old Errol."

Harry Armstrong, no father surrogate, dropped over regularly to take my mother shopping and asked if she would pose nude. Of course not, but she was willing to be photographed in bare shoulders. "As it was I felt slightly undressed," she wrote her husband. "He wanted me in a sort of Madonna pose."

In 1989, I sorted through Harry Armstrong's nudes, chains, and manacles in the dusty attic of the Manistee County Historical Museum. In one painting a naked woman tied to a tree has the unmistakable head, face, and hairdo of unsuspecting Vernice Baker Lockridge, screwed onto another woman's small-breasted body.

Similarly, my father posed at this time for his book jacket in Boston, but was disappointed with the results, as usual calling the smiling ones "atrocious." For one of them he had chosen as a prop the recent Houghton Mifflin title *Nothing to Fear*. He too was secretly making use of the image of Vernice Lockridge, who had once posed nude for him. Like Armstrong he didn't cast her as a Madonna. "I woke up one morning in a feverish fury at 4:00 A.M. and sketched the most beautiful book jacket—simple but terrific—you ever saw. You're in it."

He found time to look up a couple of old friends, and both were disturbed by what seemed a change in him. "Had dinner with Steve Tryon the other night and a good chat," he wrote Vernice on February 21. "It seems likely that he will go back to Simmons as a full professor, or possibly to Boston University. His book hasn't been written, of course." Tryon had a different feeling about the evening, sensing his old friend gloated over his own triumph and condescended to Tryon's less glamorous career. This was the last time Tryon ever saw Ross Lockridge.

My father also looked up his Harvard acquaintance Dick Scowcroft, who had spent that delightful evening with him shortly after acceptance of the novel. Now instead of sharing excitement with a fellow novelist, he was "intense, joyless, justifying the novel's greatness to imaginary critics."

Then, as if confirming what he had written of the fatal arrow that can ambush the artist in the round of daily work, he ran into Dorothy Hillyer one day in early March. She told him of an enormous prize being offered by Loew's Incorporated, parent company of MGM, for film rights to an outstanding new novel. Diggory Venn, in promotion and public relations, gave him the rules and entry forms. Venn and Hillyer urged him to enter.

First held in 1944 in a highly publicized campaign to corral valuable literary properties, the contest would be increasing the award in 1947 to $150,000 for the author, $25,000 for the publisher, with several escalator clauses that could bring the total to $275,000 for the author. The sum $150,000, the equivalent of $1,050,000 in 1993 currency—with escalators, close to $2 million—was the world's largest literary prize.

My father was unimpressed. At first he thought he shouldn't enter. Having no agent and dealing directly with his publisher, he studied the contest rules and his Houghton Mifflin contract. Unlike his father, Ross Junior read the fine print. The rules guaranteed no role to the author in scripting or production, and he was an author who wished to control his novel's fate to its extremities. He noticed that the previous winning novels were "flashy, vulgarly constructed novels with an obvious eye on the movies," and no distinguished films had yet resulted. He wished to script any film adaptation himself.

And he wasn't even impressed by the spondulicks. He'd heard of novels selling for more. Surely overestimating the appeal his novel would have for movie companies, he thought he could get $300,000 in a free sale.

And there was an ambiguity, he noticed, as to how the MGM division of monies between author and publisher related to his Houghton Mifflin contract. This stipulated that the publisher would receive 15 percent of proceeds resulting from the "sale" of motion picture rights. But he wondered whether an "award" was the same thing as a "sale." Would Houghton Mifflin be entitled to 15 percent of his $150,000, or—as he thought more probable and just—would the $25,000 bonus to the publisher satisfy the contract?

Even more important, Mary Jane Ward had been permitted to spread income from her movie rights sale over a number of years, thus evading a severe tax bite and setting herself up for a virtual lifetime of writing free of financial worry. My father had a family to support and didn't wish to go back to college teaching. He knew that, like Mary Jane with her *Snake Pit,* he wouldn't necessarily pull off a string of best-sellers. Again, was an "award" comparable to a "sale" in this matter, and would he, like Mary Jane, be able to spread the income?

He wanted to settle these questions and was prepared not to enter the contest if he didn't like the answers. Shortly before he left for Manistee, he requested a meeting with the editor-in-chief. A New Englander who had been president of the *Harvard Lampoon* and class orator of the class of 1931, Paul Brooks had entered Houghton Mifflin as an apprentice editor upon graduation. He would deal with several famous authors over the years, briefly including my father's nemesis, Thomas Wolfe, who was shopping for a new house after breaking with Scribner's and showed up at Brooks's office with trunkloads of unsorted manuscript wrapped in dirty shirts. One trunk contained rolls of toilet paper.

Regarded by some in the publishing world as rather "frosty" and "patrician," Brooks was still well known for his integrity and taste and his dedication to developing a quality list. My father entered his office with a sense of occasion—and would recite a few months later to Brooks himself exactly what was said, as he remembered it.

He had his Houghton Mifflin contract in one hand and the MGM contest rules in the other. He began by telling Brooks he wanted a clarification of his contract in terms of the MGM award. Brooks interrupted to say that his contract could not be renegotiated—but my father said he wasn't asking for that, only clarification.

"I then opened the two documents and read the pertinent clauses, pointing out that the Award provided $150,000 for the author and $25,000 for the publisher as the initial, basic, and only sure guarantees. I said that I considered that these two sums should represent our 15% and our 85% of the initial payments and I wondered if I had your agreement. You said, 'Look, Ross, if we win all that money, we can easily make a division satisfactory to everyone.' I said, persisting, that nevertheless I would like to have a clarification of it as it was after all a lot of money and it was important to me, at least, to know how it might be administered. You will recall, of course, that no motion picture deal can be made on *Raintree County* without my approval. You repeated in the same words that 'a division satisfactory to everyone could be made' if we were 'lucky enough' to win that Award. You smiled paternally, I smiled, and that was that. I then decided to enter the MGM Contest."

My father exaggerated in that his decision wasn't based on this interview alone. Via Hillyer and Venn he also got reassurances from John McCaffery, the MGM representative for the contest, that the income could indeed be spread over a number of years. And Hillyer told him that any author distinguished enough to win the prize would naturally be approached by Hollywood to help out on the movie.

And there was yet another compelling reason to enter. The winner was to be proclaimed throughout the nation on July 11, 1947—his and Vernice's tenth wedding anniversary. He decided to tell her nothing of the contest. If he lost, there would be no damper on their anniversary. If he won, what a great gift to pull out of his hat!

In the few remaining days in Boston he worked around the clock to get the last revisions to Laurette Murdock, the copy editor, rewriting to the end. Whether or not at the publisher's suggestion, he toned down some passages, linguistically mopping up the overflow semen, for instance, that fell on the ground during the mating of the bull and heifer. Houghton Mifflin had by now agreed to call the novel simply *Raintree County*.

Finally, on March 14, he handed over the last pages of Volume Four. The creative effort begun in 1941 was at last at an end, this time for sure—he thought. The galleys of earlier sections were supposed to start arriving in Manistee for proofing only one week later—but this was a mere secretarial labor. Bound copies would be made available to book clubs by July 1, with publication now set for September 1, 1947.

He left Boston the evening of March 14 for the trip to Manistee, by way of Indianapolis, carrying two boxes of caps for Ernest's gun. There he picked up the Hudson left with his brother Shockley. Ernest was still too ill to return to Manistee. Near Grand Rapids he stayed over at the Stileses' house, where he left a thank-you note for the fine bourbon he had guzzled. Mr. Stiles merrily concluded he had drunk from the bourbon bottle containing watered-down crème liqueur, meant to fake out their alcoholic maid—and my father's naïveté became legend among the Stileses and Wylies. He bought a purse for Grandma Baker in Grand Rapids and went on his way.

He'd been promising Vernice that when he returned, his ardor would create a general thaw of the Michigan snows. He showed up on the porch in Manistee pale and thin. He lay quietly on the couch. But at least he had finished the darned novel!

~

Once again the Muse sank back exhausted. As a matter of compulsion, my father continued the ritual forms of work bereft of its creative substance. There remained production matters he could still tend to, for instance, and an exhausted author sent exhaustive letters to Martha Stiles and others on minutiae of the book's design, tossing about technical language like a pro. Most of his recommendations were followed.

A month's delay of the galleys reinforced an emergent pattern. Having handed his book over to the publisher, he felt an increasing sense of peril about its fate. He feared they would screw up. A corporate mentality might take over and usher his book through routinely, with insufficient attention to details that can mean all the difference. Hardly the bubbling optimist that Cloise Crane had taken him for in Paris, he feared what the gods and executives would do to his book, once his own power over it was diminished.

Thus, he attempted to control all dark contingencies through the mails, becoming an unabashed cheerleader for his own novel, sending letters in triplicate, reminding Houghton Mifflin of deadlines and opportunities, and challenging corporate decisions. Sometimes he was right, sometimes wrong.

Worries began with the delay in galleys that could indeed imperil entry into the MGM contest, with a deadline of May 29, and it could imperil early consideration by the book clubs. Fretfully waiting around, he did what normal academics often did in those days with their summer vacations: he started reading Proust. And he flew a kite. And he took walks with Ernest, who returned to Manistee at the beginning of April. And he had another set of portraits taken in Manistee, hoping for better results.

On April 19, the galleys started arriving. He and Vernice proofed all 143 of this batch in three days. He apologized to Martha Stiles for the long letter that accompanied their return. "I'm being very particular and fussy about these things now as this is my last crack at *Raintree County,*" adding that this letter was his "last will and testament" concerning it. Perhaps the phrase was occasioned by his imminent thirty-third birthday.

Uncorrected galleys for the MGM contest were ready for entry by its official opening of May 12, and my father sent six letters and one telegram to various people at Houghton Mifflin in a twenty-four-hour period, getting ahead of all contingencies and advising them how the novel might be most advantageously presented to the judges—for example, letting it slip out that *Life* was considering a spread.

*Un*like normal academics, he finished reading Proust cover to cover, writing Mary Jane Ward that it was "a magnificent opiate for the dull periods of your life" and scribbling in his copy that "Proust doesn't give experience but the analysis of experience. *Remembrance of Things Past* is really a tremendously long psychological essay with illustrations drawn from the author's life." Even so he couldn't help but think that his own novel compared disadvantageously with it in psychological penetration, especially since he had dropped the Dream Section.

A shorthand note in the back cover hints at something beginning to torment him: "The difference between my next book and Raintree County is that this book will be untrammeled and absolutely honest. It will be psychologically much more profound and daring. It will be more of our age than Raintree County and it will record the characteristics of our age . . ."

He was beginning to see deficiencies in his novel. And in addition to Proust, he had begun to worry about competing with the author of *Raintree County.* What would he do for an encore?

As was his principle, he had avoided reading anything about Proust until he'd read the author firsthand. He was then surprised to learn that Proust was homosexual and that some female characters were based on male lovers. My mother registered the first evidence of pathological fear. He began to worry that people might see a homosexual dimension in *Raintree County.* Would they think him, like Proust, a homosexual? She tried to talk him out of it.

On May 14, he received the title page of his novel. "It acknowledges in print for the first time that I am the author of a book," he wrote Dorothy Hillyer. "This left me gasping." Even this pleasure was tarnished, though, because the publisher had included a blurb: "Indeed it evades definition for it attempts no less than a complete embodiment of the American Myth. It is the novel Walt Whitman might have written of his America."

My father was upset. He acknowledged to Hillyer that the blurb was insightful—he'd given up writing a dissertation on Whitman to embark on his novel, and indeed most of what people were already calling Wolfean was really Whitmanian. But for reasons of "stinking personal vanity," he'd prefer not to be compared to anybody else.

And there was something else. Whitman could never have written this novel. The poet "was extremely protean in sexual matters, and while all sexual symbolism is indefinitely reversible, sex is played straight in *Raintree County*, both on the surface and in the subliminal meanings of the book." He feared, in effect, that the comparison might falsely imply that he was homosexual.

He wasn't a repressed homosexual—a diagnosis no longer fashionable, in any event—nor was he intolerant of homosexuals. The episode was symptomatic of roving fear, still relatively mild, fixing now on one thing, now on another. The fear concerning homosexuality soon passed, but he remained uneasy about the pervasive sexuality of his novel.

On May 19 he and Vernice, having worked around the clock, finished proofing the last of the galleys. "My job's about done," he wrote Lovell Thompson.

He then sat down to write his autobiography. For promotional purposes, Diggory Venn had asked him to supply such a sketch, as well as an account of how he wrote the novel. He put three carbons in the typewriter and quickly batted out two lengthy documents, "Some Biographical Facts about the Author of *Raintree County*" and "The Story of *Raintree County*." He wrote Hillyer on the 24th: "This stuff will gag you—it did me—I could hardly get myself to do it."

Given a format for self-promotion, he casts himself in the third person, propped up by comic hyperbole that he nevertheless hoped was true. Before his novel has even seen the light of day, he speaks of himself assuredly as the "famous son" of two distinguished Hoosiers. "A product of the public schools of America, Little Ross always led his class . . . Ross the Older produced memory training results in his youngest son which were little short of fantastic . . . To this day, he types at better than a hundred words a minute and writes everything, including poetry, at the typewriter, to which he exists in a sort of centaur relationship. . . . He raced a mysterious cyclist for thirty miles into the City of Marseilles, where in a state of collapse he discovered that his opponent was a recent champion of the Grand Tour de France." (He exaggerates: in his 1934 notebook he recorded that the race was 28 kilometers.) He glides over tragedy and setbacks—no mention of his brother Bruce, and the year of illness in 1935–36 is quickly subsumed into a brief paragraph on his "lost years" as an IU grad student. The labored humor and self-satire don't fully disguise the grandiosity. Even allowing for the promotional contexts, he's not in control of his persona here.

The account of his novel's composition is more grandiose still, as he speaks of its coming into being with a sense of occasion that one might reserve for a virgin birth or new millennium. He explains that remark to Wylie on the banks of Lake Michigan: among other items on his checklist, he has tried to "write the American *Republic,* in which the relation between the life of the Individual and the life of the State would be studied and interpreted in terms of ideas and by a process of dialectic resembling in some ways that of Plato's *Republic.*" Not imitative, his novel is "emulative," "proposing to do for the American Culture what the Platonic *Republic* did for the Greek Culture, *The Magic Mountain* for disintegrating and warring European cultures, *Ulysses* for the modern obsession with supranational and subliminal areas of human behavior and culture.

"*Raintree County* cannot and should not be called in any real sense 'a first novel' or an experimental book. Because of the time and care spent on its evolution, its techniques are assimilated and entirely successful." "This creative process was like the explosion and flight of a rocket, which in a few luminous seconds exhausts the planning and preparation of months." "The author of *Raintree County* is probably the least temperamental artist of his stature who ever lived. He could work with entire concentration with any amount of noise around him, providing that it was good-natured noise."

My parents at their wedding reception at the Lockridge house, July 11, 1937.
It was a simple Depression-days ceremony, followed by a honeymoon on the
Indiana lakes and in the old Shockley house at Straughn.

LEFT: Hugh Baker at seventy in a characteristic pose.
RIGHT: Shockley Lockridge had a great influence on his younger brother, Ross.

The Dream of the Flesh of Iron was a 400-page epic poem written in 1939-41. Ross Junior writes in the basement of his parents' house, surrounded by the eclectic sources he worked into this strange unpublished work.

LEFT: Malcolm Correll *(left)* was my father's best friend, going back to boy scout days.
RIGHT: Ross Lockridge, Sr. in a characteristic pose.

Camping on the old Lockridge farm was Ross Senior's favorite diversion. He and his son are photographed by three-year-old Ernest in the summer of 1942.

LEFT: Vernice Lockridge in 1947. She retyped the manuscript of Raintree County and was its first reader.

RIGHT: *Nothing to Fear* is the title of the book my father holds for this publicity shot of 1947.

LEFT: Cousin Mary Jane Ward visited us in Manistee in the fall of 1946, the year her autobiographical novel, *The Snake Pit*, became a national bestseller.

RIGHT: The Lockridge family reunion on September 21, 1947, could boast two nationally spotlighted writers. Ross Senior felt "shaded by these new Lockridge literary lights."

LEFT: At MGM studios on November 25, 1947, my parents appear happy and relaxed. But by this time my father was in a deep depression.

RIGHT: In our new house, my family and I, in my sailor suit, posed for *The Indianapolis News* on January 2, 1948. My father, then in the hospital, was said to be upstairs recovering from "influenza."

An autograph party at L. S. Ayres department store in Indianapolis on January 20, 1948, was the setting for the last known photograph of my father.

After the funeral on March 9, 1948, Ross Senior surveyed the old fireplace in the south yard. On this spot his son had gained some of the inspiration for *Raintree County*.

Survivors, in our first photograph after the tragedy, taken in the early spring of 1948. My father had spread fertilizer on the lawn, which resulted in some healthy weeds.

Monty Clift had sufficiently recovered from his near-fatal automobile accident to give autographs to my siblings and me, on location near Danville, Kentucky, summer of 1956.

The two Nell Gaithers, Eva Marie Saint and Vernice Lockridge, at the world premiere of the film *Raintree County* in Louisville, October 2, 1957. The most accessible member of the cast, Saint was also the only one who seemed to know her lines.

"Now briefly the river lay again across his life, opaque and green, a serpent water. . . . He would be that dreamer, and he would have perhaps again his ancient and eternal dream. . . . Of a quest for the sacred Tree of Life. Of a happy valley and a face of stone—and of the coming of a hero. . . . Of beauty risen from the river and seen through rushes at the river's edge. . . . And of all its summers when the days were long."

Many authors daydream of such stuff being said of them in print, and quickly check the fantasy. In a period of exhaustion, incipient anxiety about his novel's stature, and a sense of powerlessness now that final galleys had been dispatched, my father was coming close to a delusional state of mind, in this instance unwittingly encouraged by Diggory Venn, who had given him a routine assignment. Delusion is kept in check by humor and conscious imitation of hyperbolic conventions—but just barely.

Ben Ames Williams had a similarly high opinion of his own 1,514-page novel, the Civil War saga *House Divided*, and Paul Brooks thought he might as well take out an ad announcing that, in the opinion of their authors, both these novels on the Houghton Mifflin list were superior to *War and Peace*.

On May 26, my father, this least temperamental of artists, received a letter from Brooks informing him that publication would have to be put off to January, 1948. *House Divided* was scheduled for publication in the fall of 1947. Since Williams was an established writer, his novel would automatically go to the top of the charts. Brooks sensibly concluded the two novels shouldn't be published at the same time.

Impatient to get his novel out and feeling he had again labored unremittingly to meet a false deadline—and why hadn't they foreseen this conflict?—my father was once again dismayed. "Dear Paul: Frankly, I would be shocked to see *Raintree County* set now, without further ado, for January 1, 1948, publication." Tacitly, he believed his novel far superior to anything Williams might write and urged that it be allowed to compete with *House Divided* now for the Book-of-the-Month Club. If William's novel were entered alone at this time and selected, it would lessen the chances for his own costly novel being adopted a few months later—and Book-of-the-Month Club needed to upgrade its list, having in *Raintree County* a rare opportunity to merge literary stature with popular appeal.

Brooks politely overlooked the letter's tone, informing him that his and Williams's novels had both already been sent in galleys to Book-of-the-Month Club.

My father wrote back contritely that January 1 would be fine. "I hope you have relished the style and perfection of rhetoric in my two recent letters, since they had no relation to reality. Just warming up for my next novel. . . . I promise that the disgusting spectacle of this author's-love-affair-with-his-own-book is about to end."

The month of June required, he lamented, the "patience of Job" as he waited to hear from BOMC and MGM and *Life*, while instructing Houghton Mifflin as to how his novel might be advantageously described to BOMC judges behind the scenes. There was otherwise little to do. Midmonth he took Ernest to Indianapolis for diagnostic tests on his septum, arranged for, as usual, by the family doctor, Uncle Bob Peters. Briefly back in Bloomington, he dropped in on his friend Don Smalley, in whose house he had begun his novel in 1941, and spoke vaguely of a new novel he had in the works—one that would, for the first time, "do justice to Freud."

Houghton Mifflin wished to drop the "Jr." from his name, which would then be more "dramatic." He much regretted having to say no, explaining that his father's name was "virtually public property" in Indiana.

Mary Jane Ward and Ed Quayle were now in Hollywood, giving free advice on the filming of *The Snake Pit*. "Your Hollywood adventure turns me green," he wrote them. "I am afraid that I am American to my fingertips, and Hollywood remains to me a kind of dreamland, all the more exciting because I know it's so fantastically bogus." Mary Jane was photographed in conference with the lead, Olivia de Havilland, who, she lamented, had the unfair advantage of professional makeup. The Hollywood script departed from the novel radically, providing a pat Freudian explanation for its heroine's woes, but she and Ed were taking this well enough—after all, this was Hollywood.

Then on June 27 a momentous telegram arrived from Paul Brooks, asking my father to call Houghton Mifflin immediately. He loped over to the park telephone, called collect, and spoke with Hillyer and Brooks. Hurrah! MGM would award him the $150,000 prize!

There was a hitch—he'd have to make some additional cuts that Houghton Mifflin thought reasonable. My father, with less than a hundred dollars in the bank, replied, "This Award is not won yet. I do not propose to cut the book." He had finished it, and that was that.

Hillyer relayed this news to a surprised Carol Brandt, the New York and European head of the story department at MGM, who was administering the award from her enormous New York office in the Loew Building on Broadway. It was decorated with the set from *Berkeley Square*. Brandt asked that Hillyer bring Lockridge to New York as soon as possible. Surely he would change his mind.

My father agreed to meet with MGM representatives and was forced to tell Vernice what was up, forgoing his anniversary surprise. The next morning he boarded the train for Boston, where he met with Hillyer and others. He then left for New York and took a taxi from Penn Station to the St. Regis, where MGM had reserved a large air-conditioned suite for him.

Negotiations began over lunch at the restaurant Voisin, where he was joined by Hillyer. Carol Brandt was flanked by John McCaffery, the principal judge for the prize, who was a magazine editor and well-known radio commentator on "The Author Meets the Critic." When he read the galleys he had said immediately, "This is the book. It's a work of genius, and if we are going to give a prize, this is the book." On first meeting him at the restaurant, McCaffery sized Ross Lockridge up as "tense, mercurial, verging this way and that way, and not at all surprised that he had won the prize. . . . Ross was in a state of tremendous exhilaration and excitement . . . and he was upset by the fact that I believed his novel had to be cut . . . and he said 'No, I won't take the prize. I will reject it.' "

The main reason for the cuts was not aesthetic. Book-of-the-Month Club was unlikely to take a book this costly to produce, and without a book club sale *Raintree County* would not have the popularity MGM demanded of its prize-winner. They wanted 100,000 words out, the equivalent of an ordinary novel. The college instructor was holding his liquor well enough to say no, casting a pall over dessert, but arrangements were made for dinner that evening in Carol Brandt's apartment at the St. Regis.

During the afternoon at his office, McCaffery looked over the galleys with him, letting him know that he too was a small-town boy and genuinely admired the novel. But for the sake of getting the book club contract, MGM wanted him to drop the entire City

Section. And how about cutting all those Eva chapters? She didn't add very much.

But my father's encyclopedic design required the city as well as the country, and MGM didn't know it was asking him to dump his own mother. Amy Loveman, another contest judge and one with Book-of-the-Month Club ties, said it "cried out for cutting." She had submitted a two-page hit list, including the great footrace—one of the novel's pivotal episodes.

At the catered dinner that evening, convened at six-thirty, it was again three against one as my father stood his ground amid a cloud of cigarette smoke. Brandt was a hard bargainer. Without a minimal cut of 50,000 words, she would not award the prize. She was baffled that a poor unpublished college instructor with a wife and four kids could be this resistant to sudden wealth and fame. In those days, the sum was sufficient to put us all on easy street. He had admitted to McCaffery that he was down to a hundred dollars when the news arrived. And she was surprised that he was refusing the advice of his editor, the greatly respected Dorothy Hillyer. Houghton Mifflin had much to lose in the matter.

The evening wore on past midnight, with all parties taking breaks to lie down in adjacent bedrooms. Carol Brandt said, "We aren't getting anyplace. We're just repeating ourselves." My father replied, "Carol, you sound as if you'd consider it an improvement to cut *War and Peace.*" "Yes, I certainly would!" she replied. She proposed that someone else cut the book for him. He refused. MGM would put him up with an editor in a suburban home in Connecticut and in one week they could weed out 50,000 words. He refused. She said, bluffing, "Well, let's all have a cigarette, and forget the whole thing."

By the time the battle had dragged on to four in the morning, Dorothy Hillyer had lost all sympathy: "I never saw anyone so stubborn." McCaffery admired his nerve. They ended in deadlock. But my father said he would think it over some more and give his final decision at Carol Brandt's office at nine-thirty, later that morning. He then sent a night telegram to his wife, telling her to be at the park telephone booth first thing in the morning. The two spoke, my father telling her what was up and asking how she would feel were he to decline the prize. Unhesitatingly my mother said yes, she would support that decision. *"You should not sell your soul,"* she said.

344

McCaffery, Brandt, and Hillyer waited nervously while Lockridge kept them waiting. He was thinking it over. In declining, he'd be giving up not only the $150,000 of income spreadable over ten or more years, but also several escalator bonuses—$25,000 if the novel was selected by Book-of-the-Month Club, $25,000 if it won the Pulitzer Prize, and up to $75,000 for sales beyond 25,000 copies, for a formidable $275,000, not to mention the $25,000 to the publisher and the enormous boost in sales that would come from the national publicity over the prize and later from the movie itself. And then there was the $50,000 advance from BOMC if it was a Main Selection, more likely if the judges were confronted with a shorter book—all this beyond the ordinary royalties he'd be getting from Houghton Mifflin! This was quite a bit for a family man to sacrifice. And it weighed on him too that he'd be letting down his publisher. If he had a free hand in the revision, maybe he could even improve the novel. And they did tell him he would have minimally an advisory role in the making of the movie.

There was an unspoken motive too, I think, that underlay these and all subsequent dealings with MGM and Houghton Mifflin. My father feared that this novel alone was his masterwork, that he had said it all there, that another financial opportunity like this would not come his way, and that family and career—if indeed he did have any other books in him—would have to rest on the proceeds from this book alone.

When he appeared, forty-five minutes late, Brandt thought he looked cheerful and chipper, while Hillyer thought he looked very pale. My father asked again if the prize money could be spread over a number of years. "Absolutely!" said McCaffery. He said he would require a free hand in cutting it himself. Brandt agreed to this. My father then announced he'd cut the 50,000 words and accept the prize.

Amid the congratulations, Hillyer could see even then that Ross regarded this as a Faustian pact. He would write his brother Shockley, "That high-pressure, ulcer-making, glamor-ridden world into which I was catapulted in New York is best seen via the movie marquees. It's not worth the price of admission."

He asked if he could call his wife from the office—she would be waiting at the phone booth—and Brandt offered him a phone in relative privacy next to the Steinway. Nonetheless, she and Hillyer eavesdropped and heard him tell Vernice that he had accepted the prize and now she could buy that washing machine. They didn't understand that it was his little joke.

~

McCaffery told him that with all this money he should get some legal advice, and he recommended Martin Stone. My father promptly walked off to Stone's office at 10 Rockefeller Plaza, while McCaffery called ahead to recommend this client and also warn that Lockridge was a pain in the ass.

One year his junior, Stone was an enterprising, enthusiastic lawyer who dealt with many writers. He produced the radio show "The Author Meets the Critic," and had had Mary Jane Ward on the program. In press releases, Random House had been assuring potential readers, falsely, that the author of *The Snake Pit* considered novelwriting "merely a sideline to her major occupation of being a housewife." Stone was surprised when she indeed looked like one.

He was sitting in his office on the morning of July 3 when the young author from Indiana stormed in—unforgettably. He pulled an enormous stack of galleys out of an old briefcase and said, "Here's my book!" Within minutes, Stone knew that this unpublished writer had won the MGM prize, that the movie was to be produced on an unprecedented scale, and that his novel would certainly be a BOMC selection.

But that wasn't what mattered most. What mattered most was the Pulitzer Prize. This would be a critical recognition more important to Lockridge than Hollywood and the book clubs, and he expected it.

He *knew* all this money would be flowing in, and he needed to have the income spread out to support his family over the next several years. Would Stone help, and incidentally would he read the book in galleys as soon as possible?

Galvanized by all this, Stone was quick to say yes. As my father wrote Mary Jane, "Unless I miss my guess, he's a grand guy, eager to get me—and we made absolutely no contract or percentage arrangements. I didn't even pay a retainer. He is simply to handle all my legal problems—and they are multitudinous—in setting up the contract with MGM, renegotiating my contract with H.M., licking my income tax problem, etc., etc." He was happy not to hand 10 percent over to some literary agent.

He called the good news to Jeff Wylie—*Life*, which wasn't doing a July Fourth spread, might take note of this development. Jeff invited him to Hingham for the holiday weekend. On the way he lost his glasses, and his behavior there seemed an odd mix of good spirits, dutiful citizenship, and distractedness. He went sailing and played ping-pong, winning as usual. On the beach he found a wallet containing money and arranged through the police for its return to the owner. But he wasn't able to get the novel out of his mind.

He and Betty walked together over a deserted nine-hole golf course nearby and he told her it was like walking into the green landscape of his book jacket. When they and a larger group were going into a restaurant, she asked why he was walking oddly. "I'm developing a walk so that when I go down the street people will say, 'There goes Ross Lockridge.' " After all, in one week he'd be a celebrity and he needed some eccentricities. Betty thought he was only *half*-clowning. At the fireworks behind the Hingham high school he was edgy and asked, "Betty, why aren't you afraid? They frighten me." "Ross, they're just fireworks!" she said, noting the irony that this was someone about to become famous for a Fourth of July novel. It worried her slightly—he seemed to have a low threshold of fear.

That Sunday he called Houghton Mifflin and complained that no one answered. Betty reminded him it was Sunday. He called again later, and this time she said, "Look, Ross, everyone at Houghton Mifflin has died." When he left for Boston the next morning he forgot his shorts.

Soon to be wealthy, he decided to buy Vernice a special anniversary present and, during a stopover at Houghton Mifflin, enlisted Dorothy Hillyer, Diggory Venn, and Martha Stiles to accompany him. Vernice had spoken of wanting a nice pen and pencil set, but Diggory said that would never do. The four walked up Park Street hill to Trefery & Partridge, where tray after tray of fine ornaments was set forth. Ross kept saying, "That's not Vernice." Finally he seized on a lovely set of bracelet, ring, and brooch in jade and gold—his greatest single splurge.

Back in Manistee, he was "more pooped out than I have ever been in my life, my glasses lost, my morale shot," he wrote Mary Jane. "It was the agreement to return to the book creatively (or non-creatively) that virtually killed me at the time and took all the sweet out of the prize." He resented the task at hand and for several days did nothing. Part of his resentment lay in the recognition that McCaffery was right—the City Section could use some work. He had thought so himself. But because it was a judgment made for non-aesthetic reasons—mainly to shorten the book for the book club judges—McCaffery wasn't entitled to it. How dare tinsel town tell him what was wrong with his book!

Paul Brooks was sitting in his office after hours on Friday, July 11, when he received a call from Carol Brandt's office. MGM had decided to announce *two* winners, *Raintree County* and another novel, Marietta Wolff's *About Liddy Thomas*. Through the usual method, he got hold of my father, who had a firm oral commitment from MGM. Editor and author agreed this breach of promise was unacceptable. "In a three-way hookup with their office," Brooks would later write, "I read from their own statement of the contest rules [that only one winner would be announced], hung up, and awaited the Monday morning papers with some trepidation."

That evening, their tenth wedding anniversary, my father presented the jade jewelry, with a note. "For the real heroine of *Raintree County*, in green and gold, the colors of her book, from Ross on our 10th wedding anniversary"—to which my mother would later append the words, "our last." She cherished the jewelry.

On the evening of Monday the 14th, the story came through the wire services. *Raintree County* was announced the sole "winner," and the other novel would get only a "special prize" and an undisclosed amount for movie rights. MGM was still embarrassedly debating whether to call Wolff's novel a "co-winner" or something else. My father wrote Brooks: "Good thing I smelled a rat in that MGM announcement situation. You were a brick, Paul, in the way you handled that half-baked proposal to rob us of 90% of the publicity value of the contest. Many thanks for what must have been a formidable ultimatum to Hollywood, judging from the rapid rightabout."

(As narrated years later in *Ross and Tom* and *Two Park Street*, Brooks recalled that MGM intended to split the *money* evenly between the two, not simply announce two "winners," and that the house had in effect rescued half the prize for its author—which fact Lockridge failed to appreciate throughout their later dealings. But this was clearly not my father's understanding then of what was at stake. He had been told by McCaffery in a telegram that his $150,000 was assured; the crisis was instead a matter of nomenclature. MGM was trying at the last minute to lure another valuable literary property into its camp—and away from the likes of 20th Century-Fox—by offering to label it too a "winner" in its press release. But MGM must have been negotiating for this title *outside the financing of* the Award. As is clear in my father's letter to Brooks, the announcement of two "winners" would have robbed him of "publicity," not cash. He would otherwise have been in no mood to enjoy his wedding anniversary the night of July 11! My mother never heard at the time of any intent on MGM's part to divide the booty.)

My parents listened to the announcement of the award on the evening news. A few minutes later they had their first taste of fame when the editor of the *Manistee News-Advocate* knocked on the front door and took pictures amid much household confusion. He wrote the only accurate story to appear anywhere.

The next day the prize was treated as a big deal throughout the nation, apparently hard up for news. The three major Boston papers headlined it. "POOR TEACHER WINS $150,000," proclaimed *The Boston Post*. "Ross Lockridge, Jr. Former Professor of English at Simmons College, Given M-G-M Award for First Novel 'Raintree County,' Written in Boston—Down to $100 When Told Good News. Says, 'Now I Guess I Can Buy That Washing Machine for My Wife.'"

The United Press version appeared everywhere: Lockridge "stepped up to the receptionist at Houghton Mifflin and set a cumbersome, battered suitcase on her desk. 'Here's my novel,' he said. Lockridge fumbled a minute with the suitcase catch and then lifted the cover. Out tumbled dozens of neatly typed sheets of manuscript. The editors cheered. But it ran 600,000 words. Lockridge set to work cutting it to 300,000. . . . So scant were his funds when he left the train at the Pennsylvania station that he walked the 21 blocks to meet the M-G-M officials."

Kate Smith talked up these angles on her radio show and Mary Jane sent a telegram from Hollywood. Gregory Peck had said to her,

"It must run in the family"—which her husband thought had to count as a witticism coming from an actor without a script.

Betty Wylie was ironing the shorts Ross had left behind when Jeff came in with the banner headlines. She put the iron down and said: "Damned if I'll iron these shorts!" The local Hingham newspaper had its own little angle: the prize was virtue rewarded, coming after the poor young author had returned that lost wallet.

Ross Senior and Elsie first learned of it when the IU *Daily Student* called them. Ross Senior "went around for days repeating over and over, 'It's like a dream! Is it really true, Elsie?' "

Hundreds of letters and telegrams poured in and a steady stream of cars slowly cruised past our cottage. My mother felt we were suddenly living in a goldfish bowl. Several literary agents offered services, actors begged for roles, con artists advertised oil wells, and a ministerial group inveighed against having too much money.

My father did—and did not—see the humor in all this. Throughout his novel, he satirizes journalistic enhancements and deflations. Now he was himself the target and was proving thin-skinned. "Thus, *Raintree County* finds its way at last into the consciousness of the American People, along with Roosters, Seals, and the Hippo at the Hub Zoo," he wrote Jeff and Betty. "Such is the reward for the long, conscientious labor spurred by a desire for fame. You can have this kind of fame. Of course, we are enjoying the riches—or thinking about 'em anyway. We are planning to wear shoes now most of the time and even get an indoor toilet."

He was mildly irked with publisher and film company for planting those stories about the washing machine, the one hundred bucks in his bank account, and the 21-block walk to the St. Regis. He felt he had become the "gaunt scrivener of Mountfort Street."

But he was deeply dismayed at the report that he had agreed to slash his novel in half, and on July 16 and 17 he sent letters to all suspects—three to leading suspect McCaffery, three to other leading suspect Diggory Venn, two to Paul Brooks, two to Dorothy Hillyer, and one to Lovell Thompson, enclosing in some instances duplicates of letters being sent the others—"the usual Lockridge saturation technique," he called it. And he enclosed also a four-page "Statement on the revision of *Raintree County*."

He fears these stories are "officially inspired"—and indeed people at Houghton Mifflin and MGM *were* delighted by them. He hates the implication that his novel was first dumped on Houghton Mifflin's desk as an "unpruned jungle" that could be slashed through at the whim of editors. Reviewers, like other people, have a "herd complex," and they will quickly assume he is yet another Thomas Wolfe pretender in need of a Maxwell Perkins. His book is "lavish" but it's not "diffuse," and he hasn't been "cutting" it, rather "revising" and "improving," which has resulted in some compression. Initially 600,000 words, it is now 500,000, and when he's finished it will be 450,000—hardly wholesale slaughter.

Telling Diggory Venn that the publicity has got off on the worst possible footing, he adds, "If I were a reviewer and acquired such advance impression of a book by a lanky, pipe-smoking (I do not smoke), tweedy, slightly moronic (reckon I kin git muh wife that there washin' machine now) ex-college hack down on his luck, I would expect some kind of sloppily written, sloppily edited, oversized, half-baked horror."

Editors, MGM, and friends alike told him to calm down—the novel would speak for itself. Exhausted, he settled in once again to revise it. Never had a writer been "paid that much for the words he wouldn't say." Now then, how remove 50,000 of them?

He hadn't got very far when Sheilah Graham in her "Hollywood Chatter" column announced the cast for *Raintree County*. "Gene Kelly is not playing the lead, as reported, in Metro's prize-winning movie 'Raintree County.' Robert Walker gets the role. And here is the rest of the lineup—Lana Turner, Ava Gardner, Janet Leigh, and Keenan Wynn."

MGM people had assured him he'd have minimally an important advisory role in the production, and here was the cast already being announced, and one he didn't like!

At the same time, Mary Jane wrote him from Hollywood, "If you are feeling the way I did, you'd probably like to crawl in a hole and pull it in after you. Let me assure you that the feeling increases." And regarding her stay in Hollywood, "It was an experience all right, but the next time I put in six weeks of effort for any movie company, sans salary, I'll know it! It wouldn't have been so bad if I hadn't felt so frustrated. It may be that I accomplished a little something, but any similarity between the movie version of *The Snake Pit* and a novel of the same name will pretty much be coincidental."

Fair warning. So on July 24, without prior consultation, he mailed a single-spaced four-page letter to Louis B. Mayer. He begins with blarney about MGM's discernment in having selected his great novel, not a word of which was written with the movies in mind. "But assuming that the enclosed gossip has some basis in fact, I feel that it might be to everyone's advantage to consult the author of *Raintree County* before plunging headlong into a motion picture based upon that book."

He reminds Mayer that English films these days are regarded as superior to American. His novel gives Hollywood a chance to reverse this. It could be turned into pure corn, but "I do not anticipate that this will be done. I am convinced that MGM and that you, Mr. Mayer, as the powerful representative of this great empire of art and money, are entirely capable of seeing that my book is turned into the type of motion picture which it deserves to be."

He then makes a "personal appeal" to Mayer, asking that he be "permitted to have a share commensurable with his importance as the author of such a book." He says half-jokingly that people have told him that "when I devoted myself to the novel, I robbed the American screen of a first-rate scenarist." And he closes by chastising Mayer for permitting the cast to be announced before a script exists, indeed before he's even finished the novel.

The letter "blew Mr. Mayer's hat right off," and he immediately called Brandt and McCaffery to find out about this boy who presumed to tell him how to run his business. They tried to pacify him and got hold of Dorothy Hillyer to see what could be done about Lockridge. In turn she wrote him to say that the letter had been received as tactless and undignified.

My father replied to Brandt and McCaffery, defending his letter as written with "an honest but—shall we say—awkward sincerity. . . . As for my innocent offer to help in the picture, forget it." He was content to let MGM "do the job without the least 'advisory help' from the cinematically inexperienced young man who wrote the book. No doubt I vastly exaggerated the value of some ideas I had about the motion-picture possibilities of the book."

But to Brooks, he said he was glad he wrote the letter, "as it confirms for me early and with finality, an impression that I was reluctant to accept—that the best thing any writer of real stature and importance can do is to stay away from Hollywood."

In early August, Thompson and Brooks sent a letter and a telegram telling him to hurry along with the revision so that new galleys could be made in time for a meeting of BOMC judges on August 30. My father was whittling down the episodes inspired by his mother, but mostly he was at furious speed rewriting the City Section, not just cutting it, and he replied by telegram that 35,000 words would be out by August 11. But "HARDLY 50,000. IS THAT OK?" Hillyer wrote Brooks, "Paul—35,000 would be quite dishonest. Ross has an amazing forgettery."

Indeed the memoranda behind the scenes at Houghton Mifflin and MGM were increasingly barbed. "Authors are such interesting people—why we love our work." "I guess he is impervious to anything but a harpoon, which I shall be happy to wield again as occasion warrants." "Isn't it lovely to have someone so full of instruction!!" "I can see no reason to bother anybody with this screed from Ross."

Ross explained that he was speaking only of the early BOMC submission—of course he'd meet the MGM demand eventually, but "I'm a tired boy. You understand, I suppose, that I would do anything short of sheer artistic suicide to get out from under this book. So if I don't quite meet these time schedules, you will understand that six and a half years of effort have played me out and I'm not quite up to it physically."

He wasn't. He was losing appetite and weight, was increasingly quiet except for the pounding he gave the typewriter. To Vernice he began to worry aloud that maybe his novel hadn't been that good all along—how otherwise explain all the complaints he received and the fact that he made it better every time he returned to it?

Domestic affairs didn't conspire to help much while he was writing in one month the equivalent of a short novel, finishing off the last of the 20,000 pages of typewriter paper he had bought in 1941. I shared the living room with him for two weeks with a strep throat. Then Terry Ross appeared to have swallowed a safety pin and my father rushed him to the hospital for X-rays. Then his desk collapsed under the weight of manuscript plus at least one child, breaking the typewriter. Then four of his wife's relatives visited unexpectedly for four days during chilly weather, bringing the number of cottage inhabitants during the day to ten.

In the midst of this, Lillian Rixey of *Life* wrote him on August 5 that the great magazine had at last decided to do a spread. They must have found the old tombstones, weeds, and cow pastures of Henry County less riveting than the novel itself. They were going to publish an excerpt they would call "The Great Footrace," with payment to the author of $2,500, an entire year's salary at Simmons. "We are very happy to present it in LIFE, which as you know rarely uses fiction." Happily my father hadn't cut the footrace. He told his folks it was "a rather charming, readable *genre* scene" and warned them about the profanity.

What was he doing with the City Section? The city heroine of the finished galleys, Terry O'Rourke, was a young third-rate New York actress, closed up in façade and fearful of intimacy, whose bedroom was a hall of mirrors. Residing as an unrecognized poet in New York during the Gilded Age, Shawnessy desired her passionately, just as he desired to know the city. Though she rejected him, there was still the possibility of breaking through, of forcing her to love by dint of his own passionate seeking and her latent poignant tenderness. There was hope of finding the real Terry O'Rourke within. But he received a telegram telling him his mother was dying back in Indiana, and the relationship broke off.

In July of 1947, O'Rourke found herself on the cutting room floor, bumped by a new character.

Lockridge couldn't "return to *Raintree County* without fathering some completely new and unexpected progeny." The offspring this time was Laura Golden, who was "causing some extraordinary *bouleversements* in the life of Mr. John Wickliff Shawnessy," he told Hillyer. Golden is a celebrated actress with her own troupe who fascinates Shawnessy, but he has little desire to possess her—indeed he's frightened by this willful, enigmatic woman and would just as soon escape her boudoir. He's no longer a poet but a would-be playwright who can't finish the fifth act of his play, *Sphinx Recumbent*, written for her. And indeed Laura assumes the demeanor of the Sphinx, symbolic of the unknowable in the human personality. Her boudoir is the Forbidden Room, the folklore my father hooks up with the Riddle of the Sphinx. She lives for her career and, in the midst of the murderous Great Railroad Strike in Pittsburgh, is only concerned to have her props returned safely to New York. Hating the world of men, she sends Shawnessy packing, without any suggestion of the redemptive power of love or a core of human identity waiting to be unlocked.

I think that after his night in the smoke-filled room in New York my father returned with less of a drain-the-dregs-of-life feeling about the city. And though the real-life Carol Brandt had, I am sure, little in common with Laura Golden, she may have added some shades to this willful new character, stylized but unsentimental.

My father took far fewer words to fashion Golden than he had Terry O'Rourke—he thought the concept was clearer. He looked at the new, darker City Section and liked it better than the old. MGM couldn't claim any credit for this improvement. If he had cut the whole thing, as they wanted, he would have "left a hole in the book big enough to drive the Queen Mary through." The new elements "seemed to be waiting around for me to discover them—so that once again I have had the peculiar feeling," he told Hillyer, "that in a way I am the historian of *Raintree County*, its inspired reporter, rather than its author-creator."

On August 20, he finished his book yet again—except for proofing the new galleys. He and Vernice calculated the reduction of words and decided to declare it more than 50,000. He had fulfilled his commitment. He wired McCaffery, "LOCKRIDGE THE VANQUISHED VICTOR DROPS EXHAUSTED AT FINISH."

～

He tried to relax for his and Vernice's first vacation since the summer they married. One hundred yards away there was a lake, and he spent some time out there with his family. He invited his parents and Lillian to come up, and caught up on his personal correspondence, bringing Don Blankertz and others up to date and answering some fan mail.

It's clear from these letters that he was *ashamed* of winning the MGM turkey—great authors don't ordinarily get rich off Hollywood, and he feared friends and relatives would infer that his novel was tripe. "Don't let this prejudice you against the book—or the author," he asked of Blankertz. But he was pleased to tell Mary Jane that he too had arranged for a lifetime of financial security on the profits of a single book. "The money terms on the MGM thing are pretty beautiful. They are absolutely committed to a spread of the money in any way I want it."

He agreed to play tennis with a neighbor and dragged in afterward beet-red, hyperventilating, and clobbered. Vernice was dismayed to see the physical decline of this old competitor.

A new acquaintance throughout the fall was Jack Stiles, a young writer and the brother of designer Martha Stiles. When asked for advice on two unpublished manuscripts, my father took time out to read them and comment. In late August, he sat on an old green rocking chair at the Stiles cottage at Dunewood north of Manistee, drinking beer and rocking so vigorously that Stiles's wife "thought he'd rock a hole right through the floor!" He said there was no doubt that *Raintree County* was the greatest American novel. "Then he stopped, looked out at Lake Michigan, chortled and said, 'No, I'm a lousy writer.' "

The habit of work was hard to break and he continued sending letters to Houghton Mifflin, MGM, and his lawyer. Within three days of mailing the revision, he told Dale Warren at Houghton Mifflin that he was "squaring off" on another novel. "All I can say about it now is that it will definitely knock the spot off *Raintree County*, which knocked the bloom off me."

He had begun to worry about the family response to his novel's treatment of sex and religion, and especially his mother's response to his use of family background. He was, among other things, making her grandfather into a literal bastard and her father a divorcé, and he'd revealed some of the most intimate things about her own life— her father worship, her jealousies, sexual fears, frustrations, and nightmares. He had been giving Houghton Mifflin strictest orders not to divulge the family background to the press. At the same time he was telling them of the precious archival material he hoped they could eventually make use of in promotion.

The novel's dedication was so far dual—to his mother and his wife. His father was never in contention. But on August 26, he sent

Hillyer a new dedication. "For my Mother, Elsie Shockley Lockridge, This book of lives, loves, and antiquities." He explained that he had originally intended to dedicate it to her alone, and that "my wife's special relationship to this book really does merit something besides a dedication. . . . Besides, it is increasingly clear that I'm going to have another book of at least equal importance to dedicate to my wife before very long."

She would get her own page. "I wish to acknowledge the assistance of my wife, VERNICE BAKER LOCKRIDGE, whose devotion to this book over our joint seven-year period of unintermitted labor upon it was equal to my own. Without her, *Raintree County* would never have come into being."

Meanwhile Martin Stone was looking into that matter of the MGM money spread. My father wrote McCaffery, "I know that you and I had a perfectly clear understanding on that point, and Martin has assured me that there will be absolutely no difficulty there." In late August, Stone got back to Ross with the bad news. McCaffery had consulted with MGM lawyers, who informed him that income from an "award" could not be spread over many years.

Oops! Sorry about that. By Stone's calculation, this meant the award was worth about half of what it otherwise would have been. MGM worked hard to contain my father's indignation. It puzzled him that the representatives of the award could have been in error on a point so fundamental. They had used a "false lure"! First he had been shut out of a role in the script and production, and now he had visions of the better part of his loot being carted off by the taxman.

He would turn to his publisher for some kind of compensation. Them he could trust.

He was thus somewhat frazzled when his parents and Lillian arrived in early September. He had arranged a cottage down the street, $35 for the week. Jeanne got sick and had no appetite, and the Lockridges offered to take care of her at their cottage. The Hoosier remedy wasn't chicken soup. It was tough red meat. They gave her little pieces, which she chewed and chewed and couldn't swallow. "Eat. Swallow this meat. Eat this!" said Aunt Lillian, now so large she filled the entire kitchen.

While they were there, the September 8 issue of *Life* arrived, with "The Great Footrace" occupying eleven pages of text along with nine illustrative cartoons. "In LIFE last week John Chamberlain pointed out that the current crop of American novels is generally poor. LIFE takes pleasure in presenting on these pages an exception to that rule."

The excerpt made use of American West folklore and the ancient myth that to become a hero one must kill a hero. My father tried to frame how Mary Jane and Ed should read it. "It is deliberately styled to catch certain clichés of American life and character, in keeping with *Raintree County*'s 'mythic' aspirations." It wasn't representative of the larger book, he assured them.

Anxious about its reception on other grounds, he began to worry what people on the street would think of him. He was losing his nerve.

Happily, he passed the first test—his parents. "Dad and Mother happen to be visiting us just now and read the LIFE excerpt while here, their first acquaintance with *Raintree County*," he wrote Mary Jane and Ed. "I must say they took it very well, especially Mother. Dad, as you may know, never advanced beyond James Fenimore Cooper in his literary appreciations (but don't, for Christ's sake, quote me) and is a perfect prude where literature is concerned (literature should not resemble life), and we think he was profoundly shocked at first because some of the characters said goddam and took drinks. After he read it ten times, he got over this and said that he enjoyed it more each time and was beginning to find it funny."

It was a successful visit, with Grandpa performing to great acclaim at the Manistee Rotary Club. My father's qualms somewhat subsided. After their departure Jeanne looked around the cottage for her grandparents and Aunt Lillian. "Those darn kids. They gone, doggone it!"

Brooks sent along my father's $2,500, minus Houghton Mifflin's 15 percent commission for acting as his agent in the *Life* spread. My father was jarred, feeling he and Jeff Wylie had done most of the legwork. He thanked Brooks for "the neatly truncated check" and suggested he get another excerpt printed "and really earn that commission!"

Life sent along a reader's response. "Sirs: It is disheartening to think that a magazine as reputable as *Life* would publish as profane a story as that by Ross Lockridge, Jr. Is nothing in life sacred in these postwar days? An international criminal devised scientific methods to dispose of human bodies with as little regard for human life as if those millions were flies. A fellow countrywoman of his had men killed merely that she might have their tattooed skins for lamp shades. . . . And now we have an article in a leading publication dragging in the mud the name of the Savior of Mankind. . . . Very truly yours, George E. Carrothers (A Hoosier)."

My father tried to convince his parents that this sort of thing was unworthy of formal refutation. "If I had ducked and crawled and sidestepped on every issue that life presents and tried to please this person and that person and this camp and that camp all through my book, I would have a book that wouldn't be worth the powder it would take to blow it up."

Martin Stone was trying to renegotiate my father's contract with Houghton Mifflin and conclude the one with MGM in time for a nationally distributed newsreel of the award presentation, starring the impudent author and a placated Louis B. Mayer. "I am to be whisked to Hollywood for this charade and whisked back again—something like the magic carpet of the Arabian Nights."

On September 17, Paul Brooks quietly dismissed Stone's assumption that Ross Lockridge would receive the full $150,000 of MGM monies, and Houghton Mifflin only $25,000. "So far as I know, there has never been any question about the division of the proceeds from the award. According to contract, Houghton Mifflin owns the motion picture rights and may sell them upon approval of the author, paying the author eighty-five per cent of the proceeds. This has no connection whatever to the $25,000.00 specifically awarded by M-G-M to the publisher." In addition to their $25,000 bonus, Houghton Mifflin was therefore entitled to $22,500 of the author's prize—which bite in 1993 dollars was the equivalent of $157,500.

From these words catastrophe unfolded.

On September 20, before he'd heard from Stone, our father drove Ernest and me to the Methodist Church in Paw Paw, Indiana, next to the Eel River, for the annual Lockridge family reunion. Approaching seventy, Grandpa had written him that he was concerned about what he would be doing in his "few remaining years." His Historical Institutes were ending for the season and he'd not made further plans. He thought we should all camp on the old Lockridge farm by the Eel River.

"Surely you will feel the significance of this." It was on that spot that it all began for his son. "There is sure to be a lot of publicity, sooner or later, about your Daniel Boone days with your dad, which may do me a lot of good, as well as you. Certainly something must have gone into you during those early Nimrod, campfire, story-telling days with your historically minded DAD, that helps to account for your triumphant venture into historical romanticism—or whatever *Raintree County* is."

By now he knew his son's career had gone into an orbit well beyond his own. He hoped there might be enough reflected glory to reinvigorate his own career. In poor health, he hated the idea of retirement.

So we four pitched a tent on Brenton Webster's old farm and spent the night. In the morning I too learned to shoot the Winchester. Grandpa told me if I were defending myself against bears I'd get only one chance to hit my mark. Then we drove off to the church, where Mary Jane Ward had arrived, and a reporter and a photographer from *The Indianapolis Star* were ready to cover a hick reunion that could boast of two nationally spotlighted writers.

My father asked Mary Jane if he could speak with her, and, telling Ernest and me to go off and play, he walked with her down to the sycamore-shaded banks of the Eel where they could have some privacy. There he filled her in on the various strands of the developing plot—the good possibility of a book club selection, for instance, that would make amends for the tax burden he faced with the MGM award—and swore her to secrecy on various matters that didn't seem to require it.

She was distressed. He seemed changed. Most of this was pretty good news, yet he seemed anxious and depressed. How would he take it, she wondered, if the news turned *bad!* Her husband wrote their lawyer shortly thereafter that "the poor fellow is still so confused that he has no plans or idea what he is going to do next."

In the basement of the small country church, we ate fried chicken. My father, Grandpa, and Mary Jane were photographed digging into custard pie and laughing it up. Afterward there was a service upstairs where Grandpa recited the same poem he had read thirty-one years earlier at Paw Paw cemetery, and my father spoke wittily about how various Indiana sites would be appearing in his novel, especially the Eel River, renamed the Shawmucky. His brother Shockley and others chuckled through it, and his mother said he made the day. It was only an audience of fifty relatives, but he had felt obliged to speak from notes. Mary Jane Ward declined to speak at all.

The next day the *Star* carried the story at the top of the front page, with the pie-eating photo: "WRITING LOCKRIDGES TAKE TIME OUT FOR TYPICAL HOOSIER REUNION." Ross Junior was "at work on his second novel. But he isn't ready to talk about it yet." We were possibly moving to California. Between my father and Mary Jane, "the future of Indiana literary supremacy seems to be in willing hands." By the "writing Lockridges," the reporter meant only the "two luminaries." He didn't include Grandpa.

Upon our return to Manistee, September 22, my father found a letter from Martin Stone enclosing the letter from Paul Brooks. It was a debacle.

The next day he fired off an 8-page, 4,500-word letter to Brooks, and on the 25th, a two-page supplement. Stone "has requested me to write to you fully, explaining exactly what my position is on the whole matter of the MGM Award."

Why wasn't Stone writing these letters himself for his client? As a lawyer rather than a literary agent, he was convinced of Lockridge's eloquence in representing himself on the stand. Here was a client who knew what he wanted, who seemed a brilliant accountant, and who remembered all details and conversations with cinematic recall.

In great detail, down to precisely quoted dialogue, he "recites," as it were, the entire lamentable history of the MGM award, from Dorothy Hillyer's first mention of it and encouragement that he enter, to the conversation he'd had with Brooks in his office, to the all-night session at the St. Regis, to MGM's false assurances.

Targeting MGM, and by implication Houghton Mifflin, he writes: "I am frank to say that I do not understand people who do not keep their commitments. It is an unalterable rule with me never to have anything to do again with people whose word is simply not to be trusted. My own word, once given, is as good as a bond. I need only to be reminded of it—if I have forgotten it—and I would blush with shame if I left any stone unturned to make it good."

His only previously recorded expression of total outrage occurred in the winter of 1934, when he thought the hotel proprietor in Genoa was changing the terms of his and Lamorey's overnight stay. If his own father was a pushover in contractual matters, he wasn't going to be.

He then argues that if anyone was acting as an agent in the MGM contest, *he* was, not his publisher. He had planted the seed of the *Life* excerpt, "a possibly vital factor in the MGM Award and certainly helping in book-club possibilities." He had gone to New York and reluctantly agreed to cuts. His "own personal exertions have played the leading part, have had the main responsibility for the success achieved." The $25,000 bonus to the publisher is given in the expectation that it would be used in promoting the book, but my father reasoned that it would simply displace an equal sum that would already have been budgeted on such a large, important book. This $25,000 he regards as his gift to his publisher.

But even if Houghton Mifflin were acting as his agent, his lawyer tells him, "and I believe it is so, that a very strong legal probability exists that HM is no more entitled to my part of the MGM Award than I am to theirs, until specific agreements are made between us as to how we shall share it." It is, after all, an "award," not a "sale," and not covered in their old contract. (He'd learned this distinction the hard way with respect to taxes. And to be sure, earlier winners were photographed being presented with what was reported to be the full award to the author.) The $150,000 and $25,000 happen to represent approximately an 85/15 percent split. To make that split precise, he proposes they add the total amount and so split it (his take would then be $148,750).

He then threatens to withdraw any future books from Houghton Mifflin, saying that the most valuable property in this is not his novel but "the human property attached to it—namely myself, not simply because after all an author is his book, but because of the creative potential rolled up in me." In his letter two days later, however, he promotes his new novel. "It will be simply nothing like *Raintree County*, except that it will have an equal grandeur of design, though it may not be quite so long."

Stone was "disturbed" that Paul Brooks could be certain of the legalities now, when he was so vague about them at the meeting in early March when my father pressed him for details of how the MGM money would be split. Brooks could not even remember that meeting.

These letters went beyond what editors come to expect of difficult authors. Brooks didn't communicate in writing with Lockridge again for three weeks, dealing by telephone instead with Martin Stone. My father began twisting in the wind, losing sleep and obsessing. Hearing at last from Stone on October 10 that Houghton Mifflin wasn't giving on the issue, he wrote Brooks, "I cannot get it out of my mind that either I am being dishonest about this—and I am in a position to know that I'm not—or else Houghton Mifflin is."

But he's prepared, on advice of counsel, to make a concession. He'll let them have their 15 percent of his $150,000 if they will decline to take 15 percent of the escalator bonuses for the Book-of-the-Month Club, the Pulitzer Prize, and the extra dividends given for sales exceeding 25,000 copies. If all this materialized, Houghton Mifflin might otherwise collect 15 percent of $25,000 for BOMC, the same for the Pulitzer, and up to $11,250 for the sales—adding up to a possible $18,750, which my father noted wasn't equal to the assured $22,500 he was relinquishing to his publisher. But he was willing to take a chance on these as yet unmaterialized bonuses.

Martin Stone thought his publisher wasn't entitled to 15 percent of the BOMC and Pulitzer awards anyway—so the main concession Houghton Mifflin would be making was in its percentage of the MGM bonus for large sales. My father did these tedious calculations in pencil on the inside cover of his copy of *House Divided*.

He would tell Mary Jane that money wasn't the object. Rather, "my determination to get certain 'symbolic' concessions from my publisher caused me to write some pretty severe letters. I felt worse about them than anyone else." For all my father's tightfistedness, I believe that he did see the dispute as a matter of principle.

More than that, it questioned his *identity* as a great author. He was taking Houghton Mifflin's behavior as an assault on his identity.

Family man that he was, he had come to think of Houghton Mifflin as a sort of ideal professional family into which he had been inducted. Though only five years older, there was something "paternal," as he said, about Paul Brooks, and Dorothy Hillyer was his "fairy godmother," and he had thought himself the favored youngest son, their great young author to whose ears he could safely mouth the most outrageous praise of his own novel—because they all agreed it was that great. Now he felt like a client they could make money off of, whose own words and pleadings meant nothing. This treatment confirmed his own growing doubts about his novel's worth.

Early the morning of October 14, having slept poorly for three weeks, he called Brooks, who seemed to go along with his new proposal. He was surprised and buoyed up by this easy turnabout and sent off a letter of thanks. "I can only express inadequately how pleased I am—how heartwarming it is—in these degenerate days to find a guy who is willing to stand by his word. . . . The nice thing about all this is that the faith and pride I have all along expressed to my wife about my editors at Houghton Mifflin have been *amply* vindicated." Hillyer got a similar epistle.

But Brooks had just come back from a week's vacation when he took Ross's call, and hadn't had a chance to refresh his mind on the issues. He worried after the call that Ross may have been overly optimistic about the acceptability of his new proposal, so he checked out the bonus provisions. Later that day he called Martin Stone, who on October 15 sent Ross a telegram. "SPOKE TO BROOKS LATE YESTERDAY. HE MET WITH COLLEAGUES AT HOUGHTON MIFFLIN. EVERYONE AGREEABLE YOUR RECEIVING 100% OF POSSIBLE BOOK CLUB PRIZE AND PULITZER PRIZE. HOWEVER, THEY ARE (QUOTE) ADAMANT (END QUOTE) ABOUT REFUSING TO SURRENDER 15% MGM MONIES BASED ON SALES. SUGGEST YOU CALL ME AFTER YOU RECEIVE LETTER FROM BROOKS WHO IS WRITING YOU SEPARATELY."

My father didn't wait for Brooks's letter. Instead he wrote six pages of barely contained rage. It reads as if his mind were ready to hemorrhage.

That word "adamant" really got to him. My mother listened to him typing into the night, her stomach in knots. He just wouldn't come to bed, he thought they were cheating him, he *couldn't get it out of his mind* that they were cheating him. They had no respect for his book or for him, he was no longer their brilliant young author but a piece of meat.

He scribbled at the top: "This letter must be read by all the editors at Houghton Mifflin—aloud preferably—and a joint decision reached. Ross Lockridge, Jr." He reviewed yet again the history of the dispute, saying of the initial interview, which Brooks could not remember, that "I am not the kind of guy to ask a man like Paul Brooks to stand up and deliver the boy scout oath . . . My wife Vernice and I bitterly and seriously discussed the—to us—ugly position into which I was thrown of depending upon my sole word for an assurance that was apparently repudiated—or forgotten and therefore repudiated." He has given up his $22,500 but in not making the concession on the bonus for large sales, "Houghton Mifflin now 'adamantly' proposes to give up *exactly nothing.*"

Even so he tells them he is writing Stone to accept all their terms on a new contract. "This document if and when drawn up should have a border of black ink around it, as in it will repose, cold and recumbent, my faith in my publisher. It is only fair to add, however, that on this point Vernice and I have given each other a solemn promise, which we shall carry out immediately in such tentative but palpable form that we couldn't go back on it if we wanted to. This promise—coming from a man who is not aware that he has ever broken a promise so solemnly given to himself or another—is that Houghton Mifflin Company shall *never* have another big book by the author of *Raintree County.* Do not misread your man—do not misread your man."

This letter crossed in the mails with a temperate one from Brooks written the same day, at last explaining Houghton Mifflin's position to him directly in writing. "Apparently there have been misunderstandings and I'm quite willing to accept any blame for my part in them. They seem to hinge largely on a conversation which, I'm sorry to say, I simply cannot recall."

Brooks says, concerning their unwillingness to waive their share in further payments contingent on sales, that "I am certain that I could not defend any other point of view either to myself or to my associates here." He regards their concessions on BOMC and the Pulitzer as real—they *are* entitled to their percentage, he says—and he reminds my father of how much time and expense they've put into the manufacture of his book. Also, a literary agent would be taking 10 percent of everything, and they are taking only an additional 5 percent as the publisher's share of motion picture rights. He very much doubts Ross could have gotten a larger sum from some other movie company. They are looking into the possibility urged by Stone of spreading his Houghton Mifflin royalties (this clause would indeed be written into the new contract). And he mentions the enormous response they're getting from booksellers around the country. An advance edition of 50,000 copies should be ready by November 21.

On Sunday, October 19, my father made a collect call to Brooks at his home, accepting his terms and apologizing at length for his behavior. Brooks assured him he understood, such misunderstandings were routine. (He knew they weren't.) My father wrote the same day, "Paul, your forgiving attitude will be remembered by the author of *Raintree County*, and your faith in his book will be repaid with another book sooner, I think, than you would guess. Thanks again for helping a young guy out of a hole he dug for himself. . . . Here's to a great editor and a great house!" He enclosed a check for the collect call, which Brooks would return.

But the next morning he called again during breakfast to tell Brooks that a letter, written before their telephone conversation, would be awaiting him at the office. He asked him to destroy it unread. "Routine, I replied in effect. Eventually he hung up, assured. When I reached my office, a fat, sealed letter lay on my desk. Then followed the only rewarding moment in this tedious sequence. I took the unopened letter to the office of our sales manager, Hardwick Mosley. He knew that much of the year's sales would depend on Lockridge's book, he knew of the trouble I had been having with him, but he knew nothing of the weekend telephone conversations. 'I've had enough of this,' I said, showing Hardwick the unopened letter. 'I don't care whether we publish him or not.' Whereupon I tore the letter into shreds and dropped them into his wastebasket. His expression at that moment remains vivid after almost forty years."

That same day my father wrote Hillyer, "Never, never again. Honey, you have no idea how I bled on this thing. . . . Just a case of sheer literary shell-shock, strangely abetted by confusing circumstances and some bad advice—though that's off the record. Paul was simply magnificent . . . I confided my case to Mary Jane Ward, had to, they thought I was taking a drubbing——but I know now that I was just drubbing myself."

What Brooks and Hillyer did not know was that he had simply given up, he still believed Martin Stone and Mary Jane were right. He had written that last letter in rebuttal to Brooks's letter of the 15th. But after sending it off, and still in deep anguish and rage, he had talked it over with his wife and decided "to throw in the towel."

The night of October 20, he once again failed to sleep. The next morning his wife was alarmed at a change in her husband. This was something different from the nerves and anxiety that had been keeping him up all night, or the anger that was channeled into all those letters she never read. That morning, October 21, he had trouble swallowing food, and his skin had a strange pallor, and when he tried to speak he could hardly be heard, and he said that something was wrong with his vision, that the world didn't look right to him somehow. His wife was terrified to see all vitality drained from this man, the Hero of Raintree County, her funny, romantic, driven husband who had taken her and the children on a great adventure. Surely that spirit would be restored, surely this young hero and endlessly courageous dreamer would be there again for her at the river's edge.

X

"Flu or Something"

Hollywood and Bloomington,
Fall, Winter, 1947–1948

In late October, 1947, Ernest had a new bicycle and needed instruction. His mother told him that his father wasn't well and mustn't be disturbed. The Manistee cottage was subdued. The man who always sat at the typewriter and sang while doing dishes was replaced by someone always lying down or slowly shuffling around. He was no longer impervious to our routine skirmishes and yelps—he was fragile. Soft-spoken before, his voice was now flat.

During the months in Manistee, Ernest, Jeanne, and I had already sensed this was a preoccupied man doing his necessary work. We hadn't heard about fathers who had hours to spend horsing around with their kids. Maybe we instinctively wished for more, but what attentions we got seemed enough, and he was always there.

A neighbor, Mrs. Hubble, was our baby-sitter and leader of the local Loyal Temperance Legion, who complimented our parents for always coming home sober. Hearing her tributes to the Legion, Ernest had decided he wanted to join it. His parents said okay, so he was supposed to give a memorized speech before the adult membership. When the day came he had told his father he felt too nervous, and "he said that I didn't have to—that we could just go for a walk in the dunes, and that's what we did."

Early one morning I had walked into my parents' bedroom and was invited to sit up in bed between them. My father showed me a sketch he was making of a train passing by a cemetery. It would be found at key chapter endings throughout his novel, the train symboling time, the cemetery eternity. I spent the next two years drawing trains.

When he returned from New York in July of 1947, he brought me some painted postcards of the Empire State Building, Radio City Music Hall, and other attractions. Three years later I gave the postcards centerfold treatment in a scrapbook. I must have treasured these small attentions.

Jeanne remembers only dramatic moments of rescue and desertion. Screaming in her crib after she had been bitten above her right eye by a mosquito, she watched her pajama-clad father hurry in and squash it, and saw her own blood spread against the pale blue wall. Then there was the time that Mr. and Mrs. O'Connor, our landlords, who worried that their tenant was working too hard, organized an outing to Suttons Bay north of Manistee. When we piled into the Hudson our father closed the door on Jeanne's thumb. Though the injury was slight with no cut, he apologized warmly, ran into the house, and came back with a symbolic Band-Aid. Jeanne felt less angry at him—she knew she wasn't supposed to put her fingers in the hinges—than guilty for having held things up.

And one time she was following behind him as he walked with two companions on the beach. She waded along on a sandbar, suddenly fell into water up to her chin, and thought she was going to drown. When she emerged in guilty terror, her father was still deep in conversation and hadn't noticed the close call. A father could leave you behind, she learned.

Jeanne cannot remember much close physical contact with him, nor can I, though our mother says we had it. Our fund of distinct memories of him is rather small. Still, where Ernest loved and worshiped him, to us he was a quiet kindly presence. Jeanne and I spent much more time with our mother, who looked forward to the book's completion, when her husband would be freed up. He hoped to return to France with the entire family then.

Back in Indiana he had been well-known throughout his adult life for his rapport with kids—he was informal and joked around, learned their names, took them spelunking, and could speak their language. "Hey, Goliath!" he would say. He and his wife hadn't decided against having still more children.

But now something was wrong with our father.

On Friday, October 24, he got a telegram from Paul Brooks asking him to call collect. Henry Seidel Canby, chairman of the Book-of-the-Month Club jury, had informed Houghton Mifflin that *Raintree County* was their unanimous choice for Main Selection of January, 1948. This came with a guarantee minimally of 333,333 additional hardcover copies, a $50,000 minimal royalty, and the $25,000 MGM bonus. My father received this news with little surprise or elation.

There was a hitch. The judges wanted some cuts. The printing schedule required that the revisions be made in three days, and he should call Canby to find out what cuts they had in mind.

The BOMC judges had had their own patience tried by the tumultuous production history of this novel. They had received galleys back in May, only to be told to stop reading—it was going to be revised, and would they please return the unrevised galleys? The writer Christopher Morley had lugged the three heavy volumes up to his country house and he wrote Amy Loveman that the stamps sent for return postage had stuck together: "Tell Hogtown Mifflin from me that they can heave to in a high sea."

Still, when Morley got the new galleys, he wrote BOMC founder Harry Scherman, "In spite of my prejudice against it, for its enormous length—and I still think it doesn't need to be so long—I find it a remarkable book. I think it better under control than Tom Wolfe, for instance."

He worried, though, that the readership would be offended by all the sex. "If I were the editor I'd be inclined to remove the unpleasantly sniggering episode of the bull & heifer. . . . [The novel] is very largely an erotic fantasy, often very beautiful too, but in a way that will surely offend many readers." Fearing that the "mass-reading public is likely to be either bewildered or pained by it," he was willing to go along with the other judges but wished "to inject a serious note of caution."

(When BOMC readers did indeed object to the novel on "moral" grounds, Morley replied personally to one of them—on March 7, 1948. "See, with all its crudities, the beauty and belief of the great American scene that he tried to suggest. See its vulgar filling-station comedy and its large rump-shaped Walt Whitman contours. . . . But also see—or else fall back on niceypie—its burdened and burning sincerity, its burlesque of American emotionalism, and its anger at American hypocrisy. If these never occurred to you, you aren't a reader [there aren't many] but a consumer.")

From the park phone my father called Canby at his home the next day. The judges were enthusiastic in the main but very much hoped he would cut the smattering of dream sequences plus some of the new City Section. By this time benumbed and expecting such requests as ritual, my father said he'd see what he could do. He spoke politely without warmth or gratitude, demurring only when Canby gave a figure of the several thousand words they hoped he would cut. Canby replied, "My God, boy, you've got an eleven-hundred-page book!"

For the next three days around the clock, he once again revised his novel. By now over half of it had gone from galleys into permanent plates at the manufacturers, and he sent Brooks a telegram to stop everything. Most of the short dream sequences were already set, and he and Brooks decided these must stay unless BOMC absolutely insisted. It would otherwise cost several thousands of dollars and take weeks to reset. But the judges also disliked the scene in the new City Section where Laura Golden sexually rejects Shawnessy. Canby told him they unanimously found it "sour." So, as my father put it, "the author unanimously agreed to take it out."

He had meant it to be "sour." It was to limit the hopes expressed elsewhere for human intimacy and to suggest that Shawnessy's charms didn't prove fatal to all women. And the five City flashbacks were meant to parallel the five acts of a Shakespearean play. But he was too tired to fight, and thought maybe they were right anyway, and maybe he hadn't pulled the scene off. He had lost confidence in his book.

So he snipped the whole thing out, pared down an adjacent dream sequence, joined two Day episodes, and spliced the book back together again. The sour rendezvous in Golden's boudoir up the marble staircase is preempted by a telegram, "JOHN WICKLIFF SHAWNESSY: COME HOME. MAMMA IS DYING." His departure leaves Laura distraught, somewhat out of character as well as sorts.

On October 28, he finished his novel yet again. "This is my last gasp in Raintree County," he told Brooks, adding, "I'm pretty beat up (flu or something) and hope I won't have any more excitement or pressure for a while."

He then sent a letter to Canby, full of the blarney that, as in the letter to Mayer, was a species of contempt. Mentioning that he has "had a touch of flu, I think," he apologized for having sounded so complacent on the phone, saying that to be a BOMC choice meant more to him than any other honor, blah blah, and that, as for the board of editors, "I can't imagine a more balanced, experienced, and brilliant meeting of minds anywhere in the field of letters. An old BMC member myself, I have never complained of commercialism in BMC choices . . ." But he had complained to Houghton Mifflin editors of precisely this—one reason he thought his novel might not get the nod.

He also responded to several matters Canby had brought up. Yes, the City Section was much influenced by Mark Twain's and Charles Dudley Warner's *The Gilded Age*—his heroine too is named Laura. No, he was much aware of the danger of sentimentality, and the Perfessor was "the book's antidote for sentimentality . . . My real intention, whether réussie or not, was to make *Raintree County* a book in which sentimentality was the subject of the book—and not its unconscious mannerism."

Exhausted, he was still able to send a satiric letter off to Hillyer that gives little evidence of authorial torment. It would become apparent in coming months that he could fake people out about his state of mind—he could call on one or another of those old Lockridge personae. Here I think he was also trying out some self-therapy while still capable of it, satirizing his own messianism.

"My God, Dorothy, is all this really happening?" He thinks only one additional award could come his way. He would find himself speaking to someone over the phone who sounded like John McCaffery, only two octaves lower:

—Hello, Ross, this is God speaking.

—Hello, God. What's up?

—Why, Ross, my child, I think you'll be pleased to hear that I've just had a little meeting with Myself and have decided to select your book for Our Book-of-the-Cosmos Club.

—Gosh! That's wonderful. What century?

—Why, the Twentieth Century Choice, son. I'm going to do the review Myself.

—Swell. There's no one I'd rather have do it. I'm acquainted with some of Your own works, of course, the Bible, and all, and—

—Don't mention it, son. It's a pleasure. Of course, there are a few little deletions that I would like to see made—not to shorten the book, you understand, though My God, boy, why do you write such long books!—no, not to shorten it, but just to improve its artistic character. Now I've had some experience in these matters, been around a little, think My judgment is worth considering, and of course if you don't do it, We can always take Hemingway's forthcoming opus in place of yours.

—Well, just what do You have in mind?

—It won't be hard—I'm merely suggesting that you pull out the character named Professor Jerusalem Webster Stiles and patch up the book a little. Course there's an element of time. You only have to 1960 to do it.

—I've always sort of liked that character, fairly important to the book, sort of involved with the book's basic meanings, and—

—Remember, boy, all I have to do is issue a fiat. I just plain don't like that character. He's a discredit to your book . . . Don't let Me catch hair nor hide of that infernal rascal in your copy. . . . You're bought, boy, bought. Good-by, son, and keep your nose wiped. I think you have real promise.

Within his publisher's family, he had proved a delinquent son. His anger toward them, never satisfactorily resolved, had now turned inward and he felt guilty and ashamed, sending off several apologetic letters about having made it "tough on everybody because of my exaggerated faith in the book and, no doubt, over-valuation of the awards due it."

He told Mary Jane, "Honey, I've already had more grief and suffering out of success than I ever had in all my years of obscurity and hard work. In fact, all during that time I was happy and free from any pressures except the compulsion to write." In arguing with his publisher, he "suffered for everybody involved, and seem to have developed a talent for it. I've had—for me—a marvelous case of nerves and am not wholly settled down yet."

Fears about his own family's reaction to the novel now intensified and he told Mary Jane to tell *him* that the novel "stinks" but to "rave like hell all over the place" to his parents about how he has glorified the novel's "family elements." He was a delinquent in this family too: he didn't attend his father's seventieth birthday celebration on October 26, telling them that he'd had a contract dispute that "was both spiritually and physically exhausting to me." He sent a tribute to be read.

Grandpa was delighted to hear he would be mentioned on the book jacket—"His father, Ross Lockridge, Sr., introduced him to history"—but said he now felt like Methuselah and could only hope for five more years, hitting it on the button. My father, to help make these years good ones, began laying the ground for large annual donations to the IU Foundation for continuation of the Hoosier Historical Institutes.

But this matter of family reaction to the book—especially his mother's—was weighing on him. So he asked her up to Manistee in early November to read the book. "I hope she takes it like a brick," he wrote Mary Jane. He thought that if only she liked it, all would be well, the last fear quieted. "Ernest and I are both 'beat up' and Mother can bring us around," he wrote his father.

Upon her arrival he drove her to a Manistee hotel, out of reach of us kids. "It's your book, Mother," he told her. "You'll notice that I haven't dedicated it *to* you—it's written *for* you and I want it to have your approval before it's published." She dutifully read page proofs in three days, reporting at the end of each day that it was going very very well indeed. Elsie knew her son was under the weather, and this was no time for qualified praise.

She said the character John Shawnessy embodied perfectly the spirit of her own father—and also of her youngest son. Shawnessy's intense idealism prevailed over the Perfessor's cynicism. The portrait of Eva—of herself—she found moving and true. The "rough" portions were a natural outgrowth of characterization, and unlike her husband she had no trouble with the cusswords. (By now Grandpa had sent an indignant reply to a detractor of "The Great Footrace.") She expressed no qualms about the eroticism. Everything was fine, just fine, it was a brilliant book, a great book.

She had a way of calming him down, and his wife watched with relief and hope as Elsie would go to the icebox to bring some soothing milk back for her nervous, depressed son.

But, as Elsie would confess years later to her homecare nurse, she was very bothered by the sex and religious satire. She never fully accepted it to the day she died. I think this reservation was indirectly communicated to her son during this visit and in the months that followed.

Her ministrations at the time included something other than soothing talk and milk. She began talking Christian Science during this visit in early November, reading Mary Baker Eddy to her son in what was implicitly an antidote to the novel's errant paganism.

During her visit, my parents decided to go to California. We couldn't take another cold Michigan winter, and they needed a vacation. They didn't yet know where we were going to live, or what they were going to do with all the money. They would check out California—look at real estate, enjoy the weather—and by the by check in at MGM studios to see how movie plans were coming along. We kids could be left with relatives.

Neither had ever been to California and it seemed a glamorous prospect for my mother, who loved the movies and enjoyed hearing about the stars. Mary Jane and Ed had been writing them of their adventures out there only a few weeks earlier. My mother hadn't had a vacation since the summer of 1937. Surely it wouldn't just be chasing after the book again.

So on November 8, her husband sent off five letters to Houghton Mifflin people, telling them he was California-bound and mentioning in each that he was still convalescing from "flu." He bought a new suit, his wife two outfits, and on the 11th we climbed into the Hudson for Indiana. On the way our grandmother played number games with us kids and talked religion with her son. "No pill like the Gospel," she said. At Martinsville, we were met by relatives, and my parents returned to Indianapolis, where they checked into the English Hotel, across from the Soldiers and Sailors Monument. Elsie had made arrangements for her son to see a Christian Science practitioner.

Terry Ross was dropped off at our Uncle Leon's house in Martinsville, Jeanne and Ernest went to the old Lockridge house on

High Street, and I stayed with someone more famous throughout greater Bloomington than either my father or my grandfather—my Uncle Harold Mumby, former Bloomington High School football and wrestling coach and recent mayoral candidate. This was still part of our great adventure, we guessed. Our father said we might move out to California, where it was always sunny and we'd have orange trees in our yard. But we didn't fully understand why our parents were leaving for California without us.

~

The next day Ross Lockridge, Jr. visited Mrs. Myrtle Ayres, Bachelor of Christian Science, in the Circle Tower. He told his wife afterward, "Well, it's a good feeling to know somebody's thinking of me." Mrs. Ayres would be praying for him in the coming weeks, for a fee. His wife was willing to go along with anything that seemed to bring her husband peace of mind. But they had been raised in the Methodist Church, and she feared Christian Science was a desperate measure.

Before leaving the English Hotel he wrote to Craig Wylie, one editor at Houghton Mifflin he hadn't yet got around to thanking. The letter is ominously elegiac. He thanks Wylie for his "permanent contribution to a book which I hope may live, not for what I personally was able to give to it but for what Humanity gave to it. I've been through a period of sickness—nearly beat me down, spirits low and everything, but I seem now to have the Perfessor firmly by the collar and am dragging the scamp willy-nilly out of the Great Dismal Swamp into which you will recall JWS refused to let him descend. We are all children when we are sick, and like children our discernments are simpler and clearer.

"Just now I sit in a hotel room looking out upon the *Circle* in Indianapolis, in the middle of which rises the famous monument discussed in the opening pages of 'Fighting for Freedom,' the Civil War battle section of *Raintree County*. The stone men are there, the bronze guns, the monoliths and symbolic shards of that legendary era that I attempted to recreate in *Raintree County*. So the past lives and moral convictions survive even in pieces of humanly altered matter—like the Gettysburg bullet you gave me on that memorable evening spent at your home with your *lovely, lovely* wife. We are planning to travel slowly, Vernice and I, across the Republic."

It's as if he'll once again be traveling through his novel's landscape, but in a kind of posthumous existence where he surveys both novel and landscape as memorials to a vision and vitality that have deserted him.

They first drove up to Elgin, Illinois, where Mary Jane and Ed were living on a nearby farm. They had discovered in the few months since moving there that the farmer's life was not for them, and they were already getting ready to sell. My father's appearance alarmed them. He was thin and quiet and had a bad cough. He and Vernice had no definite plans about where and how long they would stay in California. There was a vague possibility we would all move there. My father seemed to take no pleasure in the upcoming journey. He worried about what Hollywood was doing with his novel and about being hounded by the press. Mary Jane tried to convince him that a writer in Hollywood isn't quite the lion he might be in New York. Hanging around the *Snake Pit* sets, she was sometimes taken for an actress who had failed to get a part.

After a two-day visit they left the Hudson behind the barn and boarded the noon train at Chicago for their trip across the Republic. Going in style, they had their own compartment and tried gamely to have a good time. They sang "California, Here We Come!" and other songs, and my mother began to take heart. She was herself happy to take a breather from the kids. They owed themselves a second honeymoon for all the years of hard work and child-rearing. In Wyoming her husband pointed excitedly to some running deer and seemed not quite so depressed.

Arriving in Los Angeles on November 18, they rented a Ford and set out looking for a place to stay, deciding against an upscale $24 per night recommendation from Mary Jane and Ed. They had been living on only a $1,500 additional advance given them in June. And my father wished to keep his distance from MGM for a while and simply take a vacation, though he had brought his typewriter.

Driving through North Hollywood, they alighted on the Pepper Tree Lodge at 5909 Lankershin Boulevard, where they holed up in Room 19 for the next three and one half weeks. It was a modest two-story motel with small clean rooms, feathery pepper trees, and a coffee shop where they would take most of their meals. They liked it.

When I stayed overnight at the Pepper Tree Lodge in the summer of 1989, it had sadly fallen from its already modest standard. Now a place for Saturday night assignations, it had clientele so tough-looking that I pushed the wobbly laminated furniture up against my door.

The weather was beautiful, they needed no wraps, and they drove off to see the sights, going first to the ocean and then fighting terrible traffic to Hollywood and Vine. They visited the Rose Bowl, empty, and began looking through real estate magazines, appalled at the prices. My mother wondered how they could advertise something as a "ranch" when it boasted only two city lots.

Near their motel my father soon found a Christian Science Reading Room and started dropping by. Whatever the merits of Christian Science as an independent theology, there is no aggregate of beliefs more antithetical to the values of *Raintree County*, with its celebration of the natural world, its pagan delight in the body, its irreverence, its claims for self and ambition, its mythic vision. To drop by that Reading Room was to begin renouncing all that had mattered most to him in his book, and psychologically it entailed a regression—the child in him yielding to maternal direction and care.

He made a list of resolutions. Speaking of his novel, he says, "I should exclude it from my thoughts or if I think of it at all, simply pick it up and read one of the optimistic 'sweet' parts of it." He will "continue searching thoughts into the nature of the Self and of God, and the nature of Divine Love and Power, à la Christian Science, along with readings in the Bible." "Confidently and fearlessly face every contingency of life, strengthened by reliance on God, knowing the essential error of every dream of anxiety, fear, etc., and your ability to meet and master every problem in a material world, where strength of Spirit is always adequate.

"Look at some residences in California, but consider also the possibility of returning to Bloomington around Xmas." "Believe always in the possibility of miracle, the awakening from the bad dreams into the good dream. Follow always the best, most courageous impulses of your nature." "Begin extensive planning on a new book—

planning of characters, situation, etc., whenever you feel at all like touching the necessary materials."

He continues, in the vein of metaphysical wishful thinking, "The real Self is invulnerable, cannot be touched. The time comes—the time *will* come—when that which disturbs will seem unimportant— will somehow be divested of its importance, will cause only a memory of anxiety. God created a candid universe, and the real universe of God is good. Whoever works with the intention of discovering the good, the beautiful, and the true has no reason for self-immolation."

Within days he took time out from his "rest cure" to dispatch two defensive "statements." The first, "A Statement about Some Real-Life Backgrounds in *Raintree County*," he sent to his mother and Uncle Frank Shockley. Roving fear had now fixed on the response of his uncle and of Henry County generally. To Uncle Frank he wrote, "I won't disguise the fact that I have practically worried myself sick over the question of the use of family backgrounds." The various weaknesses and misdemeanors of the hero John Shawnessy are more akin to his own weaknesses, he says, than to any in the real-life John Shockley—Frank's father. He hopes other members of the Shockley family will share Frank's liberal attitude toward the novel's "sex, profanity, and seeming irreverence."

He assures Uncle Frank that he is keeping the family and Henry County background secret until they themselves permit any disclosures. In this "Statement," which Frank and his mother could release to the press if they chose, he claims that John Wesley Shockley was used only as a pattern for fiction. All the misdemeanors of his youth, before he became an old schoolteacher, are fictional. This tacitly gets the family off the hook with regard to drunkenness, fornication, bastardy, and miscegenation.

Puzzled, Frank Shockley, who never read novels anyway, sent back a telegram: "LETTER RECEIVED AND AWAITING BOOK. DO NOT WORRY ABOUT PITTSBURGH SHOCKLEYS."

"A Statement about the Underlying Purposes of *Raintree County*," sent to his parents, Houghton Mifflin, some friends, and Indiana newspapers, is even more dismaying. It is a Christian Science misreading of his own novel—sad evidence of an author who has lost his nerve and not unlike what my father had himself written as a sophomore of Chaucer's retraction: the "importunate spectres" of his cast of characters wouldn't let him alone, and in the end "his deeply rooted morality and religious zeal ran him down and compelled him to renounce his best works." Knowing that authors shouldn't make such retractions is no help when he feels compelled to make one of his own. Letting them know he's "still recuperating from a real tough bout with the flu," he tells Brooks and Hillyer to use the statement in the event the novel gets blacklisted by religious groups. He hopes not to be banned in Boston.

In it he says his novel "reproduces the manners of a world of erring human beings. The book itself does not condone profanity." He talks of the novel as a simple combat between good and evil, spirit and matter, with spirit winning out over matter in the end, Shawnessy defeating the Perfessor. "To the impure, all things are impure. The impure characters of *Raintree County* tend to take their sex that way." But the real lesson is that "mere sex is transcended in love and resolved at last in moral and spiritual values." The town of Waycross, after all, is shaped like a cross, and "the book's final position is identical with the teaching of Jesus."

His mother liked this "statement." He had the objectivity to call it a "pious little document," but it emanated from a deep fear.

On November 25, they finally made contact with MGM and drove to the studios in Culver City. MGM people were surprised to learn the Lockridges were in town, and in North Hollywood of all places. MGM would have put them up more lavishly had they known. Carey Wilson, producer of *The Postman Always Rings Twice*, whose *Green Dolphin Street* had been released only four days earlier, welcomed the two warmly and invited them to his office for talk and a photo opportunity. Wearing the flamboyant tie that would crop up in most subsequent photographs, my father stood over Wilson, pointing to a place in some script as if to make a fine point that may have escaped the producer.

Grasping at positive responses, he wrote his folks that Wilson "is a tremendous personality, full of great feeling for the book. He talked with us for an hour about *Raintree County*, which he said had moved him as no other book ever had. He said that this book was like reliving your own life again—that the hero was Everyman . . ."

Then my dapper parents were photographed smiling at each

other next to an MGM limousine. Nothing in these pictures suggests someone in pain.

And for my mother this day was indeed thrilling. They were escorted to some sets, including *Easter Parade*, where Judy Garland and Fred Astaire were rehearsing. They got a glimpse of Peter Lawford walking by, and they were introduced to Esther Williams. While her husband was taken into meetings with MGM personnel for the afternoon, she was escorted to the commissary, where she saw Angela Lansbury and then Elizabeth Taylor descending the staircase, waving beautifully to someone across the way. It seemed that the years of unintermitted labor were yielding a different kind of life.

Meanwhile, what was going on in those meetings? Louis B. Mayer was out of town that week and would return the next. In addition to Carey, my father met with Kenneth MacKenna ("chief of script—or something like that") and Voldemar Vetluguin, head of the story department, who initiated the MGM Novel Award, soon to be declared one of the company's big short-lived fiascos. Indeed, Ross Lockridge arrived in Hollywood at Loew's darkest hour. With few recent hits and many fat-cat executives and lackluster producers, its income had been plummeting since 1946.

No reaction to Ross Lockridge among the now deceased people who met him has yet surfaced—Ted Turner's lawyers have denied me access to files and a Hollywood researcher turned up nothing. The sum total of what I know comes from Vetluguin's starlet fiancée at that time. The magnate held Ross Lockridge, Jr. in high esteem and wondered, "Where can he go from here?"

My father was sending upbeat news to his parents and only humble, appreciative words to Houghton Mifflin. He was apparently well behaved at the studios. Wilson told him that the Susanna figure had "great cinemadramatic possibilities." "They asked my opinion on how the show should be done," he wrote his parents, "and I gave them—very diffidently—a few ideas. We are invited to come back to MGM any day (the biggest studio in the world) and see any film we want to, especially run for us. We have appointments of a business nature next week—there will be some more picture-taking, and perhaps the newsreel, for which a script has already been written."

The next day was momentous—the first copy of *Raintree County* arrived special delivery, and my parents held it there in Room 19 of the Pepper Tree Lodge. It was Thanksgiving Day and they took their dinner at the Lodge. Each inscribed the book to the other on the page acknowledging my mother's contribution.

"I give with everlasting love my share of *Raintree County* to you, my husband. To Ross, whose love is my love, whose life is my life. Vernice."

"For Vernice my beloved wife, her own copy of *Raintree County*, the book whose life has been a consummation of our wedding—'two with one heart'—Given with the undying love of the author. Ross."

To Paul Brooks he wrote, "We have it! All the years of dreams, hopes, and hard work held at last between two covers in the right hand! After millions of words, you will be happy to hear that the author of *Raintree County* was simply speechless. Vernice goes around sort of cradling the book from time to time. Our fifth baby! The cover designs, end-papers, etc., are just bewilderingly, wordlessly beautiful. We can never thank you all enough for the faith, effort, tact, and guidance that brought my seven years' dream to such a beautiful consummation."

He sat down to read it through.

His father was reading it back in Bloomington. Ross Senior knew his son needed some bolstering and sent a series of telegrams. "FIRST 100 PAGES READ EVERY PAGE FULL OF THOUGHT AND INTEREST EVERY SENTENCE A GEM AM VASTLY PLEASED—DADDY." "300 PAGES RC GROWS STUPENDOUSLY JUST WONDERFUL AND THRILLED—DADDY." "RC FINISHED. THRILLED WITH GRIPPING INTEREST OVERWHELMED WITH AWE INSPIRING PHILOSOPHY. DADDY." Instead of lying down as usual on the pillowed davenport, he had read it sitting up in a straight-backed chair.

His son expressed pleasure at these telegrams and wrote his father, "I feel about the book a little the way Harriet Beecher Stowe did about *Uncle Tom's Cabin*—what is good in it the hand of God seemed to direct—and I wrote better than my own frail mortal capacities."

Though not trained in the higher criticism, his father then sweated out a letter of reflection on the novel, praising it in highest measure. "The comprehension of psychology, philosophy, economics, diplomacy, war, religion, romance, sex, etc. challenges the myriad-minded Shakespeare." He is grateful for the book jacket mention—he the "hopeful Dad, who foresaw, or believed, even in our Boy Scout campfire days on Kenapocomoco that this promising younger son would be the realization of some of his own cherished dreams and visions." He sees something of his own Historic Site Recital method in its pages.

And he insists that his son and daughter-in-law get some rest. "I feel blissfully assured that you don't have a thing on earth to worry about as to the public reception of RC. It is done and over. You are through with it; and certainly you and Vernice deserve, and must have, a long and relaxing rest. It is very clear to me why you spent seven blood-sweating years—burning your young hearts out with inspired work and soul-killing drudgery. Now it is all paying off. . . . I commend to you the assurance of the Psalmist—The Lord shall preserve you from all evil. He shall preserve thy soul. The Lord shall preserve thy going out and thy coming in from this day forth and even forever more."

It was the most emotional outpouring he had ever received from his father. He responded in kind, trying to put into words what so far baffled him about his own state of mind. "I never thought of mere commercial or contemporary success in writing *Raintree County* but tried to create a book for Humanity. Strangely enough, at the very pinnacle of RC's remarkable prepublication success, the strength that enabled me to write it seemed to desert me, and I have been at odds and ends with myself. During this time, however, I have reminded myself of the grand old truth, 'Whom the Lord loveth, he chasteneth.' "

His father was disturbed by his son's suggestion that he was being justly chastened. "Surely you have no need for feeling 'chastisement' other than the natural payoff by Mother Nature, for too intense and long continued concentration. . . . Really, you and Vernice may well rank as miracle workers; and now that your great compelling quest is fully consummated, it is inevitable that you should feel a let-down. Be assured that your God-given strength—(for it was nothing less than that) will be restored in full measure—and very soon, I hope."

By the time he received this letter, my father had finished rereading his own novel. There were some typos. The book was only words on the page now, no longer the vision that brought them into being.

He told his wife quietly that the novel wasn't so good as he had thought it was.

When she picked it up to start reading—really reading instead of typing it, and hoping to reassure her husband—he told her to put it down. He wanted it out of his sight. Shaken, she put it down.

Even now the cutting of the novel wasn't over. Book-of-the-Month Club invited him to be honored guest at their Christmas party in New York and, by the way, asked his permission to cut a line. On page 152, the Perfessor says, " 'Nature puts no premium on chastity. My God, where would the human race be if it weren't for the bastards? Wasn't Jesus God's? Pass the perfectos, John.' Completely stunned, Johnny passed the cigars." BOMC wanted to drop "Wasn't Jesus God's?"

My father obliged, despite the fact that the deletion makes it implausible that Johnny would then be "completely stunned" by the Perfessor's utterance. He wasn't up to a fight on this one and probably repented the witticism himself by this time. Houghton Mifflin followed suit and cut the offending sentence but couldn't stem the blasphemy that had already been uttered in 50,000 prepublication copies.

They went to services at a local Christian Science church, where my mother was uncomfortable with the testimonials. He himself said nothing at the service, just watched.

He was continuing to muse theologically at the typewriter during their North Hollywood stay, as a way into a new novel. This is someone who only months earlier wrote to Hillyer that the greatness of Hemingway over other American writers of the first half of the century lies in the value of *story*. Now he approaches a new novel with the conviction that it must be "worked out first on a religious and philosophical basis."

These musings may give the impression of quiet meditations, rather lovely and sometimes wise. They are actually the words of someone in despair trying to argue his way back to life. Error, mortality, and sickness are not the work of the Devil but "of a strange time-ensnared being, mesmerizing himself in a mortal dream. Through this dream come the glimpses of divinity." He tries to convince himself of the miracle of being, "that every being and every perceived form and every word and deed is in a sense the sacred testimony of the miracle. Our life is an accumulated memory of the miracle of our existence in time . . . Remember always that God vouchsafes us a world. We cannot type the typewriter or look at our poor face in a mirror or talk with another person or see a car pass except as this Universe is eternally endowed with possibility by our own mysterious and divinely authorized power of perception."

He continues the debate he had had with Crane in Paris about fate and freedom. Now the issue is whether he can free his own mind from dark forces that seem to have trapped him from within—or more simply, whether he can get out of this rut. "It is possible to regain one's excitement about Life. One is not the creature of blind impulses, a random shoot from the great swamp, sustained briefly in a mesmeric dream of love and suffering and death. The human world has exactly the beauty, loyalty, and love that we attribute to it."

How can he be so sure? Well, of course he isn't sure, or he wouldn't be talking this way. But he tries to read his own life in a way that affirms its potential freedom. "We look back over our life and see the highly personal and diversified character of it. There is a temptation to see too much pattern in it, a pattern imposed by the mortal mind, a psychological error, by which mind seems to hem itself in with inevitability." The Greeks see fate as "a simple objectification of man's supposed inability to escape himself," which an enlightened Christianity rejects.

So he can indeed escape from his own psychology, the snake pit of his own brain. "The supposition that we are the fools of our inexorable unconscious personality formations is basically incorrect. These patterns are mortal—but they do not touch our immortality. . . . How to rise above mere psychology—or mortal mind—to a divine psychiatry?"

And what is the artist-writer to do in the light of these recognitions? He dares hope first that *Raintree County* may not be scorned by the public after all. "That which was done for Love, for Life, for Eternity, for God cannot be evil in any part of it. And the whole achievement will awaken in all who read it the respect which a detached, living, magnificent creation of human beings seeking life and love and happiness and a good strong faith always awakens."

But he looks beyond *Raintree County* to an antithetical fiction. "The artist, like the mystic, achieves an air of detachment about the mortal world, recording its mortal beauty and its convulsions in a temporal sequence, which we may call narrative." In his new ordering of things, all that is less than divine is less than real, and therefore not the real subject matter of the artist. Indeed, matter itself is unreal. To gain this detachment, the artist "must lay down the burden of the ego."

But for him the ego is not so much burdensome as depleted, and there is nothing left to write. In these and subsequent musings, he almost never uses the personal pronoun. His sense of identity shattered, he lacks the power to say "I." He speaks of "one" or of himself in third person.

In this desperate effort to convince himself of the unreality of his own suffering, he has talked himself out of any plausible direction for a new novel.

I think he turned to Christian Science because of the shame and guilt he now felt about having exploited his mother in this erotic, blasphemous book. He had used her and her family for his own ends—he had written of their lusts, dark secrets, and failures. He now felt that instead of celebrating the family tree, he had betrayed his mother for his ambition and egoism, violating the unwritten rule against the airing of dirty laundry. It felt even like a sexual intrusion, the violation of a taboo against uncovering his mother's and the larger family's nakedness. It felt like an act of aggression, the dark underside of his idealization of her. He had lost the writer's ruthless sustaining egoism that all life is fair game for the ends of art. He would try to expiate this crime by means of his mother's own religion, which conveniently derealizes sin, sickness, and death. He would try to resume the role of good son, which his novel had ended.

Why should he otherwise be so upset about what his Uncle Frank thinks? Who the hell cares about what Uncle Frank thinks? Or what Henry County will now think of the Shockleys? It seems preposterous! But he felt that he had undressed in public not only himself but his own mother—and by extension all those Shockleys and other Henry County folk.

Once depression has set in, it can trigger a cluster of fears that symbolically represent it and that are only indirectly related to underlying causes. These fears seem irrational to those of us outside the depressive's world but have a compelling logic to its trapped inhabitant. Had there been no depression, what Uncle Frank or Henry County or even his mother thought of the novel would have been at most a mild anxiety. But there was a ceaseless feedback of cause and effect, now that the descent into madness had begun.

In letters home, following that initial visit to MGM Studios on November 25, he spoke of the various business meetings he was having with the film people, and he told Paul Brooks that he was "in constant touch" with them. Actually they never revisited the studios. Instead there were a few phone calls. His future connection with the film remained vague—at most it was to be a paid "advisory" role. Before a notary public on November 29, he signed the MGM contract sent him by Houghton Mifflin, which didn't require a personal appearance at MGM.

Whatever happened to that awesome newsreel of Louis B. Mayer presenting the award to Lockridge? Mayer was back in town after Thanksgiving. But my father wasn't invited to make the newsreel, and he began to feel that he was being given the brush-off. It's likely that Mayer refused to appear with the boy who had told him how to make a movie. He let it be known that Lockridge should be kept at a safe distance.

Near the end of his stay my father had no more confidence than before in what MGM was going to do to his novel. He was scheduled, though, to have another meeting with Carey Wilson on December 15.

My mother thought she could see some signs of improvement in her husband as they continued low-key activities, driving around and taking walks here and there. In a splurge, they went to the Brown Derby. They had given up all thought of finding a place to live in California, recognizing that the real estate search had been a flirtation with a future they knew all along wasn't for them. They resolved to return to Bloomington, and my mother wrote her sister Clona to look for a house.

As the town's most famous bank teller, to whom everybody told everything, Clona Nicholson didn't take long to get wind of an almost brand-new house on South Stull Avenue, with seven large furnished rooms and full basement, a cottage out in back, and a separate garage, going for $24,000. My parents immediately decided to buy it, sight unseen. A check for $122,500, my father's share of the MGM monies less his advance, was sent by Paul Brooks to Clona at the Citizens Loan and Trust Company on December 11, and it was simply a matter of writing a check on this balance when he got back home.

He attended to income tax matters, sending a long letter on December 4 to Martin Stone, asking about the 15 percent of his gross income for 1947 that he wished to give his father via the IU Foundation. He also asked about payment for his wife's labors—"I look upon her as my collaborator . . . I think she would be *entitled* to a third of the money from the book, in terms of actual work expended upon it." He closed with a P.S.: "As I have been a bit under the weather, I've worried about the estate tax proposition. How much of our actual 'take' after taxes are removed am I permitted each year to 'bestow' on members of the family—and how is this done?"

The national press finally caught up with Ross Lockridge in North Hollywood. UP Hollywood correspondent Virginia MacPherson dispatched a story that owed much to previous revelations. "It may not last, but Hollywood finally has clashed headlong with a young man who refuses to be impressed. Lana Turner? You can have her. All he wants is to find out where he can buy a new washing machine. His name is Ross P. [*sic*] Lockridge. And he's something of a celebrity himself. His novel, 'Raintree County,' won the M-G-M annual prize novel contest and was grabbed up by an Eastern publisher. Now it is slated for a Book of the Month Club spot. All of which makes him the latest social lion on the Movieland horizon. A rich lion, too. 'Raintree County's brought him $225,000 so far. Producer Carey Wilson, who's going to turn it into a movie, speaks his name in hushed tones. But young Lockridge is letting M-G-M down. He didn't blow into town on the Superchief, as some authors of best-sellers do. He rattled in with his battered blue sedan—and a second-hand one, at that. What's more, he didn't even let the powers-that-be know he was coming. They'd have taken the red carpet out of storage for Lockridge. He didn't give 'em a chance. The studio keeps a swanky mansion all dusted and ready for visiting bigshots. Lockridge could have moved his wife and four kids in, bag and baggage. He checked in at a little motel on the edge of town. First thing any celebrity does is allow himself to be escorted around

the glittery Sunset Strip nightspots—on the studio's expense account. Lockridge hasn't even seen the outside of Ciro's. He's been
too busy lining up a new washing machine for the missus."

So they would be returning to Bloomington after all. My mother
saw some hope in this—they would be on familiar turf, and her husband's strange fears would surely be calmed there. They would have
their own lovely home at last. There were a few more days before
that meeting with Wilson. Maybe now they could relax.

Then on December 12, with no apparent provocation, he exclaimed that they had to leave—to leave right away! He didn't know
how much longer he could stay in control of himself, he feared he
was losing his mind and might not make it home.

During this their second honeymoon—whose script should have
told of glamour, corny adventure, and recovery—he had only become worse, much worse. He seems to have suffered a sudden panic
attack. In shock, my mother helped him pack up.

They checked out of the Pepper Tree Lodge and headed for the
train station. Once again they took a private compartment. But it no
longer felt like high style and there was no singing on the way home.

∼

Nota Scholl and John McGreevey were on the short list of friends
to whom they had right away mailed out complimentary copies from
North Hollywood. They were now living in Phoenix, where John
was continuity chief for an NBC station. Like all my parents' friends
they had been following the brilliant career, mostly cheering. But
John, whose own career as a writer would soon take off, had seen
some disturbing signs beyond that first meeting with Ross Lockridge
the summer of 1946. Even before he'd read it, he thought this wasn't
the sort of novel that wins an MGM Award or becomes a BOMC
Main Selection. Such books are sitting ducks for serious critics, and
he felt Lockridge's ambition was more along the lines of a *Ulysses*
than a *Gone with the Wind*. Lockridge was in for big trouble with the
critics, he feared.

After he sent the novel, Ross mailed them his "pious statement."
He had awakened Vernice in the middle of the night and asked, "Nota
has read the book?" She replied, "Yes, honey. You had a note from her

and John." And he said, "I wonder what she thinks of me now?" His fears were widening to include the most unlikely of people.

This pious statement bothered John and Nota, but they still assumed their friends were stopping by to celebrate. They weren't prepared for the Ross Lockridge who stepped off the train with Vernice for an afternoon's visit. He was frail, withdrawn, depressed. At their adobe house, John and Nota tried to joke about MGM, about the brush-off he'd been given there, about how writers are always treated that way by Hollywood. Ross laughed along but it didn't ring true to them—it was forced and hollow. For Nota, who had known him as someone at whose fire others warmed their hands, the transformation was startling.

John was shocked to learn then that Ross had made his original agreements with Houghton Mifflin and MGM on his own and was still strictly without a literary agent. He seemed like someone who hadn't had a chance to develop any armor. The novel was the first thing he had sold and it was monumental. So much of himself was invested in it that he surely needed all the more protection.

My father had always had at least the armor of satire and humor, and he had resilience—but under extreme stress these had fallen away.

Nota's and John's qualms went unspoken for fear of upsetting their friend still more. It's hard enough to know what to say to a depressed person. But they, and others after them, were also bewildered at the irony of a radiant dream turning to nightmare before their eyes. Can this be happening? Should we say something? Should we interfere? Before Nota could resolve to take Vernice aside and ask what was wrong with Ross, it was time to leave.

As the train crossed the Republic back to Chicago, my father's fears worsened. It was like a perpetual stage fright as he prepared to confront an unseen audience both uncomprehending and malign. It was as if a very private person were undressing in public, as if the unhoused ego were naked before all. In *The Dream of the Flesh of Iron* he had written of the shame of the naked child among fully dressed adults. And his state of mind was reminiscent of his own character Susanna, who imagined that "they" were plotting to get her. There were physical symptoms too that felt rather like the general debilitation he suffered during his severe illness of 1935–36. Whatever this was, it felt life-threatening.

When they returned to Mary Jane's and Ed's farm near Elgin on December 15, he was in very bad shape. Not seeing his book out, he concluded they hadn't liked it, and though they praised it up and down, he knew it was a complete failure. He disappeared into an up-stairs bedroom and, making no excuses and expressing no anger, simply lay there. My mother took food to him in his room for the next couple of days and Mary Jane left food around, hoping he might pick it up. He didn't wish to join them downstairs, he didn't wish to talk about his MGM experience. As Mary Jane would write, "It was an ill man's inability to react to outside stimuli. His physical reactions were slow—a man who had always been vibrating with energy had become apathetic." He got a Manistee prescription for sleeping pills refilled, and yet he wasn't sleeping.

During this stopover, Ed Quayle seemed to take every opportu-nity to get Mary Jane out of the house, and my mother sensed that he feared this cousin's illness might trigger a relapse in Mary Jane.

Something had to be done, so they all talked it over. My father asked if he and Vernice could simply stay on the farm for an extended period of time. He felt he couldn't confront Bloomington and the larger family in this state of mind. But Mary Jane and Ed had just sold the farm and were getting ready to give over occupancy. He won-dered if there might be a rest home or sanitarium nearby where he could lie quietly—Vernice could stay with them and they could bring him over every evening for dinner. Ironically, though she was now renowned throughout the land for *The Snake Pit*, Mary Jane had just returned to the Chicago area and didn't know what to recommend—and was of course wary of snake pits. She could find out, though, and did know one area psychiatrist.

My father agreed that he needed psychiatric care but said that this should all be channeled through his Uncle Bob, who always han-dled his health problems going back to his scarlatina.

My mother called Dr. Peters, saying that Ross needed some doc-toring, maybe a psychiatrist. Uncle Bob exclaimed, "Oh, you don't want *that!*" She feared they'd made a mistake. Mary Jane confirmed that her cousin was totally exhausted and in need of psychiatric care.

Uncle Bob thought it was probably the sleeping pills and insisted they bring Ross to see him in Indianapolis. Mary Jane wasn't pushing for a stay in the Chicago area anyway, and my mother hoped we kids, whom she missed and worried about, might bring our father around. So Mary Jane and Ed drove my parents to Indianapolis, stopping in Elgin to buy some Christmas toys.

In Indianapolis, hearty Uncle Bob could see nothing wrong with Ross that a good beefsteak wouldn't fix, so he and Aunt Marie with my parents led the Quayles across town in heavy traffic to an abominable steakhouse. My mother felt things were going from bad to worse. The last thing her husband wanted was a big steak dinner. But he was agreeable enough at dinner, and the good doctor had his hunches confirmed. Afterward he started to climb into the Quayles's car as if to escape, but my mother reminded him that Uncle Bob was going to drive them on to Bloomington.

My younger brother, Terry Ross, not yet two, had spent the month with Leon and Mary Baker in Martinsville, where he stayed mostly in a room outfitted with large toys and dolls he found frightening. He was unhappy. Lying on the floor, he heard footsteps coming down the hallway, whereupon a tall man stooped down and swiftly carried him away high on his shoulders. This liberating moment, the night of December 18, 1947, is the single memory Terry Ross would retain of his father.

Indiana newspapers, often in touch with Ross Senior, lost no time requesting interviews with his son. This was a moment for Hoosier pride. "NOVELIST LOOKS AT HOLLYWOOD, DECIDES TO LIVE IN INDIANA." "Ross F. Lockridge, Jr., author of the forthcoming epic novel of America, 'Raintree County,' and his wife, Vernice, arrived in Bloomington last night from California . . . Attempting to recuperate from influenza and a general run-down condition resulting from publication of his intensive work of six years' duration and his trip to Hollywood, the 33-year-old native son this morning rested at his father's home on South High Street. He is planning to devote the entire holiday to his children and their Christmas, without making any appearances or be part of any public recognition or celebration. A glamorous and personable figure in New York and movieland because of his soar to fame with his $150,000 prize-winning book, Mr.

Lockridge knew that in coming home, local folks would treat him just like always."

Elsie and Ross Senior were relieved by Bob Peters's decision that psychiatric care and hospitalization weren't needed. Their son acquiesced in this also. He had disappointed his uncle, who had urged him to become a doctor, but he had never challenged his medical judgment, and wasn't up to challenging anything now. My mother saw the Lockridge family, including her husband, immediately close ranks around the notion that they all should take a hopeful view of the situation.

She had never seriously challenged that family in its wisdom. From her teenage days she had admired Ross Senior and Elsie for their intensities, intellect, and devotion to their youngest son. But she knew they were set in their ways. She had had mental illness in her own family, with her sister Imogene, and knew firsthand its potential severity. She had tried to elicit what was wrong with her husband and he would say things to her unlike anything he said to others—they were strange words she couldn't understand.

Elsie may have had a master's in psychology but she resisted clinical psychiatry on religious grounds and was already reading more Mary Baker Eddy to her son. Uncle Bob had told Elsie that *Vernice* was probably the one who was having the "nervous breakdown." Ross Senior thought there was nothing wrong that self-discipline and rest wouldn't cure.

Isolated, my mother felt something had to be done and decided to give Uncle Bob one more try on December 19. When Harold Mumby stopped over with me, she handed him a furtively written letter and asked him to smuggle it out. It contained the closest contemporary description of Ross Lockridge, Jr.'s state of mind:

"Dear Uncle Bob, I thought I'd better report to you. Ross didn't sleep last night. He said he dozed a little. He is no better. It amazes me how he is able to put on a front as he did last night at supper. This morning he talked with a reporter for about half an hour very intelligently. But he just isn't in this world.

"I had a walk & talk with him this morning & if you can't read this it is because my hand is shaking.

"His fears are now transferred from family worries to the fears he spoke of yesterday. He says if this terrible 'thing' happens the world will come down around our ears. The result would be of colossal proportions. He speaks of himself as being an innocent person being chosen as an example for this wicked age. He has mentioned for some time now that his life had taken on a remarkable pattern. Things or forces are going to destroy him. He feels that his whole life has been one of compulsion & that he couldn't help doing the things he has done—as writing the book so that it would harm those he loves the most.

"He doesn't talk to anyone the way he talks with me. He is quiet & preoccupied but what he does say to other people makes sense but he has to force himself.

"He really has been so much worse since we got on the train for the purpose of coming home.

"When he got to Elgin he was afraid he couldn't live through— without breaking down or cracking up—seeing the family. That's the reason we were puzzled & I felt that he needed some special treatment—whatever that might be.

"So you see, Uncle Bob, Ross whom we all love so much just isn't himself & if anything can be done please do it before it is too late.

"For God's sake don't tell *anyone* all this & *don't* let Ross know I've written you! I'm afraid he won't trust me anymore & that's the only way he seems to be comforted at all.

"I hope this letter doesn't upset you too much, but I'm afraid I'm desperate. Love, Vernice."

Uncle Bob was persuaded by this appeal and spoke by telephone with Elsie and Ross Senior. He thought they'd better give psychiatry a try. Both parents were reluctant, for different reasons, but neither was bull-headed. Like many Christian Scientists, Elsie allowed of exceptions. Her own life had been saved back in Fort Wayne days when she refused treatment for appendicitis, and her husband—for once acting beyond his authority within the household—dragged her downtown for an emergency appendectomy.

Ross Senior was reluctant to acknowledge that his son could be suffering from mental illness, yet assented to Robert Peters's reasoning that it couldn't hurt to give psychiatry a try. He was reassured when the doctor said that, because of the shame associated with mental illness, his son should check in under an assumed name. Yes, it wouldn't help this novel on which Scuffie had worked so hard if its author were known to be in the nuthouse on publication day.

With no will of his own, my father agreed to all of this. So Robert Peters arranged for his admission to Methodist Hospital in Indianapolis. The admitting doctor would be Murray De Armond, a neuropsychiatrist who had recently been chief of staff at Indianapolis General. The family gathered in the kitchen to pray for Ross Junior.

Before entering the hospital, he wrote several checks, including one for $25,000 to his wife for "services rendered in research, stenography, etc. for *Raintree County*," one for $24,000 to Carl Snoddy as payment in full for the new house, the interior of which they still hadn't seen, plus $4,500 for the unseen furnishings, $1,700 as an initial installment to the IU Foundation of monies earmarked for his father, a $98.20 payment on his life insurance, and $5,000 for Martin Stone's legal fee—about which he muttered to his wife, "I didn't think he did that much."

On Thursday morning, December 23, Elsie and Vernice drove Ross up to Methodist Hospital and dropped him off. It was agreed that, for the sake of maintaining cover, the family would not directly communicate with him during his stay—but speak through Uncle Bob. My mother winced as she watched him walk up alone to the hospital entrance, where he signed in under the name of Charles E. Duncan of Rochester, Indiana, wife Veronica.

Charles E. Duncan? I asked several of his friends about this colorless name, which my mother thought he must have chosen for that very reason. Don Blankertz surmised that I might find it somewhere in *Finnegans Wake*, Ted Grisell that it might derive from the Duncan Orchards, where he and Ross had had a footrace years earlier.

A year after I had recovered hospital records, I was going through microfilm of old Bloomington newspapers and came across a front-page story in the Bloomington *World-Telephone* for December 16, 1947, two days before my parents' return from California. "CORONER TO GIVE SUICIDE VERDICT IN DUNCAN DEATH." George Earl Duncan, a local man, was survived by his uncle, Charles Duncan. My father, a big one for the local newspapers, would have read this recent issue upon his return. The complex of associations here suggests he was already feeling impelled toward suicide, while resisting it too.

He was unwilling to give a history to anyone until Dr. De Armond arrived, preferring "to wait and make one recital of his troubles. . . . He looks sad and unhappy." Dr. De Armond knew this was Ross Lockridge, Jr. and took his patient's personal history. "In Sept 1947 the patient had a 'let down' in which he was aware of a change in his feeling. He says it seemed as if he had lost contact with the world although this does not appear to be a process of depersonalization. There has been a tendency to avoid social contacts and he fears and dreads to face the ordinary daily problems. He has lost some weight, appetite has been below par, sleep poor and disturbed by harassing dreams. Past illnesses have been insignificant. P[hysical] E[xamination] reveals a well developed, well nourished male who has no complaints except he doesn't know what has happened to him. Neurological examination—normal. Heart normal. BP 120/ 74. Psychiatric examination shows good insight—no evidence of hallucinations or delusions. He is fearful, depressed, has lost confidence and feels helpless to straighten himself out. Impression: Reactive depression."

"Reactive depression" in 1947 was a nonpsychotic diagnosis indicating most frequently a response to a current situation, especially loss, often aggravated by a sense of guilt for personal failures. It was differentiated from "psychotic depressive reaction" because of the absence of malignant symptoms such as delusions, hallucinations, and suicidal ideation. In the early 1950s it was regarded as a "neurotic," not psychotic diagnosis, but a clinical psychologist in 1947 wouldn't even go that far necessarily, regarding this type of depression as an isolated but exaggerated response to loss or disappointment in an otherwise healthy person.

De Armond didn't elicit the kind of talk my mother was hearing, which was nothing if not deluded. It's pretty clear my father was instead undergoing what is today termed a "major depressive episode with psychotic features," whose dire symptoms include an inability to feel pleasure, insomnia, psychomotor retardation, fatigue, recurrent thoughts of death, and inappropriate delusional guilt—not to mention constipation and impotence. Among the cognitive dysfunctions, as one student of depression puts it, is the belief "that great and terrible misfortunes will befall the patient, his or her family and friends, and even the world—all because of something the patient has/has not done in the past or will or will not be able to do in the future. In sum, the patient's thinking is dominated by the themes of failure, guilt, self-blame and condemnation, hopelessness, and sin . . ."

This depression was probably *not* the aftermath of any "manic" episode, such as his cousin Mary Jane Ward seemed to suffer as a manic-depressive. The term "manic" in the colloquial sense has not been frequently used by people who knew my father—ebullient, driven, pacing around, yes, but not manic. As for pathological mania, he never exhibited manic speech, with its disorganization and incoherence and continuous flow. Nor did he ever lose concentration and become "distractible," going off on all sorts of tangents. Nor was he given to "increased sociability, which includes efforts to renew old acquaintanceships and calling friends at all hours of the night," to quote the *DSM-III-R.* Nor did he engage in frenetic activity such as "buying sprees, reckless driving, foolish business investments, and sexual behavior unusual for the person." Episodes of euphoria were quickly overtaken by a sense of how much more work he had to do. In affect and behavior, he didn't seem manic—he was quiet, coherent, focused, and productive during those months following acceptance of his novel, if certainly nervous and excitable.

The letters to Houghton Mifflin, written during the "disgusting spectacle of this author's-love-affair-with-his-own-book," reflected not mania but what psychologists today call "grandiosity." Even if his novel *was* better than *The Republic,* it was grandiose to be talking this way.

De Armond's probable misdiagnosis didn't have major immediate implications for treatment in 1947, because even reactive depressives in those days were routinely given what is today regarded as treatment of last resort for psychotic depression. De Armond was interested not in depth analysis but in rapid alleviation of symptoms.

During the first five days of hospitalization, my father received insulin coma therapy, now obsolete, in cautious amounts each morning, and the sedative Seconal in the evenings. This wasn't bringing him around—he remained quiet and depressed—so De Armond moved to electroconvulsive therapy.

In 1947, electroconvulsive therapy was still of the "unmodified" variety. The patient is fully awake when electrodes are fastened to each side of the forehead. An electrical current is sent through the brain which renders the patient unconscious and induces a grand mal seizure, with tonic-clonic muscle spasms throughout the body. In today's modified procedure a total anaesthesia is used beforehand and muscle relaxants guard against fractures of spine and limbs. Through a mechanism not understood, this still controversial procedure can alleviate depressive symptoms in some patients for a period of time.

On the morning of December 28, my father was given no breakfast, which Mary Jane Ward had come in 1941 to understand was the give-away that this was shock day. As she wrote in *The Snake Pit*, "They put a wedge under her back. It was most uncomfortable. It forced her back into an unnatural position. She looked at the dull glass eye that was set into the wall and she knew that soon it would glow and that she would not see the glow. They were going to electrocute her, not operate upon her. Even now the woman was applying a sort of foul-smelling cold paste to your temples. What had you done? You wouldn't have killed anyone and what other crime is there which exacts so severe a penalty? Could they electrocute you for having voted for Norman Thomas? . . . Now the woman was putting clamps on your head, on the paste-smeared temples, and here came another one, another nurse-garbed woman, and she leaned on your feet as if in a minute you might rise up from the table and strike the ceiling. Your hands tied down, your legs held down. Three against one and the one entangled in machinery. She opened her mouth to call for a lawyer and the silly woman thrust a gag into it and said, 'Thank you, dear,' and the foreign devil with the angelic smile and the beautiful voice gave a conspiratorial nod. Soon it would be over. In a way you were glad."

My father prepared for his treatment with particular dread because he was already mildly phobic about electricity. When he was twelve, he had received a bad jolt from a lighting fixture in the second-floor bathroom. But by now he was willing to undergo anything to get well.

Electrodes having been fastened, Dr. De Armond—a kindly man and hardly a devil despite his penchant for prefrontal lobotomies—administered current to a level sufficient to induce a grand mal seizure. My father didn't totally lose consciousness—in agony he felt the current enter his brain. This wasn't supposed to happen. Dr. De

Armond had assured him he would feel no pain and lose consciousness immediately. Debilitated, he was wheeled out. A nurse observed that he "volunteers very little information or conversation." Besides the fear and the pain, he had found it humiliating.

He did communicate later that day with his old Delaware Group companion Curt Lamorey, in a shaky, cramped hand with insertions. "Dear Curt, Just a note hoping that you have received by this time a copy of *R.C.* Read it sympathetically. By the way, I write from a hospital, being knocked out by too much success or something. As it seems likely that I may be laid up for a long time, it's advisable that you write very *circumspect* letters to me (until further notice). My family (older folk) opens and reads all my mail now, since I'm a celebrity. By the way, being a celebrity is the least fun I've had for a long time. Everything's in a mess, and it seems too late to lead a reformed life in order to get out of it. Stick to the quiet paths and be a good boy is my advice. All my best, Ross."

This is the only letter from my father during his hospitalization that has come to light. That he really does think his suffering is a chastisement cuts through the low-battery humor here. His novel is now something to apologize for. The electroshock is apt punishment.

I know of only one book for sure that he took along—the King James Bible. To preserve his anonymity from nurses and interns he tore out the title page with his and his wife's names inscribed. On the inside back cover he listed Psalms 10, 32, 38, and 51—lamentations over the wages of sin and petitions for eternal mercy. "For I will declare mine iniquity; I will be sorry for my sin. But mine enemies are lively, and they are strong: and they that hate me wrongfully are multiplied." And in the text he bracketed Psalm 136: "O give thanks unto the Lord; for he is good: for his mercy endureth forever."

It took the single electroconvulsive treatment for my father to begin talking his way out of the hospital. He would tell his wife he made a conscious effort to appear improved. As if he were a student once again, he endeavored to give the right answers and speak rationally. "A little more cheerful today," noted the nurse on the 29th. On the morning of December 30, he underwent his second treatment, once again not wholly losing consciousness. But he didn't otherwise complain to De Armond or staff about the ordeal, continuing to give only good reports, telling them he had had a good night's sleep and acting cheerful.

The nurse's entry suggesting the greatest activity in the Hero of Raintree County throughout the hospitalization reads: "Looking for fountain pen. Things [sic] he lost it somewhere." He noticed memory problems right away, a side effect of the therapy.

Meanwhile, back home in Bloomington we were preparing to move into the new house on Stull Avenue. Reporters had been pressuring for stories, so my mother agreed to let an *Indianapolis News* reporter come to the house even before we were settled in. Her own hopes had risen. Though she had not heard directly from her husband, the word from his parents via Uncle Bob was that he was improving. She had acted, and her husband was now in the hands of Indianapolis medical professionals. She could be in a good mood for this reporter.

The two-lot yard was raw, with few trees and sticky red clay on the sidewalks. We children knew this house had to be a step up, because we had a dumbwaiter, an intercom, and a fake fireplace with fake wood. We cased out the large basement, suitable for our anarchies. There were just a few other houses on the block and a big sinkhole down the way. My mother admired the fine wood paneling and large comfortable rooms, though any decorator's impulse was thwarted by all the furnishings, mostly pseudo-antiques. We all liked the house, but it felt odd to be there without our father, and the posed family portrait that appeared on the front page of the evening *News* on January 2, 1948, captured something of our hesitancy and malaise.

"TYPIST-MOTHER OF 4 IS SUCCESS STORY HEROINE," it read. The lengthy upbeat article narrated the happy story from the beginning, emphasizing Mrs. Lockridge's heroic typing labors, her poise and beauty, and a "shy friendliness" that makes a "new acquaintance feel he has known Mrs. Lockridge for years. . . . 'We used to mark everything down in a notebook—even the nickels we tossed to the organ grinder in Boston,' Mrs. Lockridge laughed happily." She pointed out that she did now have that washing machine. As for the novel, "Yes, I know the story pretty cold—but Ross could repeat it word for word." She and Elsie said Ross was planning another novel but they didn't know what it would be about.

"Flu or Something"

Where was Ross Lockridge, Jr. during this interview? "Mr. Lockridge was upstairs in bed. The doctor ordered him to stay there when an influenza attack threatened to get the best of him. Mrs. Lockridge confessed that a little nervous tension also had reacted. Mr. and Mrs. Lockridge both are anxious to watch public reaction as the book is released Monday." Actually he was receiving his third electroconvulsive treatment that morning.

I admire my mother, whose conscience in matters of honesty is deeply ingrained, for bringing off this charade.

Another charade was going on behind *her* back. Dr. Peters, who dropped by to see Ross Junior frequently, told Ross Senior and Elsie, but not their emotional daughter-in-law, that their son was undergoing shock treatments. Both were outraged and decided to exert pressure to get him out of the hospital. They didn't tell Vernice what was going on. Dr. Peters himself was ambivalent: there was potential family shame in this incarceration. Some of these sentiments were passed along to Dr. De Armond, who thought he could see improvement in this patient anyway, despite the small number of treatments so far. The nurse's clinical record for January 3 reads, "Pt cheerful & responsive. Wants to go home." On the 4th, he was "anxious to go home," hoping both to duck out of a fourth treatment and to escape the hospital in time for publication day, January 5.

In his progress notes Dr. De Armond wrote that "his improvement was prompt and after three treatments it seemed to justify a trial in his social activity. He was released on January 4, 1948." He held to his earlier diagnosis of "reactive depression." The possible conditions upon dismissal were listed as "Recovered, Improved, Unimproved," and the doctor wrote "Recovered."

Uncle Bob and Aunt Marie drove him back to Bloomington, and Uncle Bob asked the family to be in touch if there was a relapse. But my father was resolved never again to set foot in a mental ward.

∼

The morning of January 5, 1948, the long-sought, now dreaded publication day, my father psyched himself up for the role of home-town celebrity writer. "Ross Lockridge Jr., the *Raintree County* author, emerged this morning from almost complete seclusion while

401

recovering from an illness to help along the initial sales of his novel in Bloomington. . . . Mr. Lockridge declared himself now recovered from a general run-down condition, and ready to handle all his business connected with the book."

He went to the IU bookstore and autographed copies. He had said all along he wanted to have his first autograph parties in his home state. Henry Remak, his old graduate student friend with whom he'd performed skits at Le Cercle Français, ran into him just as he was leaving. Remak was pleased to see him but before he had a chance to speak, his friend reintroduced himself. "Hi, I'm Ross Lockridge." Taken aback, Remak replied, "Well, Ross, you don't have to tell me that, you know. I would have recognized you." My father smiled, stopped for just a few seconds, said, "I'll be seeing you," and hurried off. That was a strange encounter, Remak told his wife thereafter—Ross seemed pressured and distracted.

That evening he and my mother dropped off a few autographed books at the houses of some friends, including the Smalleys. Don Smalley wrote his wife, "This evening at eight o'clock in came Ross Lockridge bearing a copy of *Raintree County*. He was out distributing complimentary copies and couldn't stay . . . He hadn't heard you were in Washington, asked me to give you his regards. He looks somewhat older, very confident, sure of himself, as he naturally would be, considering his success. He said he'd drop back some day soon for a long talk. After he'd left, I read the inscription: 'To Don and Ruth, in whose [little] house I began this novel in 1941.' Nice? Nice. A unique and interesting collector's item, if Raintree County proves another Gone with the Wind. A pleasant item in any case." Don had silently edited out the word "little."

My father was thus at times able to act like his old self, probably hoping that his inner state of mind would catch up with the masquerade. There was little reason to be glum. On the 6th, he received a telegram from Paul Brooks: "FIRST EDITION OF FIFTY THOUSAND SOLD OUT BEFORE PUBLICATION."

We moved into the new house and Ernest and I watched wide-eyed as our father and Uncle Harold stood in the kitchen drinking two beers left in the refrigerator. Ernest had taken his Loyal Temperance League seriously and told them they shouldn't do that. We kids took over the house, fascinated by the dumbwaiter and the broken intercom. We ran riot in the basement.

Raintree County was destined to be only the world's *second*-most-influential book published on January 5, 1948, by a Bloomington author living in that particular section of town. Alfred Kinsey lived just up the way on First Street. Wardell Pomeroy, one of two co-authors of *Sexual Behavior in the Human Male,* was an acquaintance of my father's in college and lived less than half a block away from us. Both books were getting enormous attention in the national press. "Apparently Mr. Kinsey and I," remarked my father, "have made Bloomington the sex center of the universe."

In the late Forties, more attention than today was paid novels in the press, with a greater sense of occasion on publication day. Here was a novel that checked in with great prepublication hype right at the beginning of the year. Could this indeed be that mythical beast the Great American Novel? In a dreary period in postwar America, with the Cold War setting in, a vital fiction was something the reading public seemed to crave.

The initial round of reviews—hundreds upon hundreds of them—was largely encomiastic. The *Chicago Tribune*, *Herald Tribune*, *Philadelphia Inquirer*, *Indianapolis News*, *Cleveland News*, and others issued their reviews in full-page spreads, many in color with quaint illustrations of the novel and handsome photographs of Ross Lockridge, Jr. Some reviewers said yes, this is the Great American Novel. Others in prominent places like *Time* and *The Saturday Review of Literature* said it at least announced the arrival of a major new figure in American letters, the equal of Dreiser and Sinclair Lewis, and the end of a slump in American fiction.

Right away Houghton Mifflin started sending the reviews to Bloomington, and my father wasn't cheered. So much of the praise spoke of the novel's great "vitality," yet its patterns and its moral vision were getting little commentary. Some reviewers spoke of it as "amorphous" and "sprawling." And virtually nobody noted his method of incorporating a multitude of voices, even corny ones, into an American polyphony.

Instead they spoke only of "influences"—the influence of Wolfe and Joyce and Whitman, especially Wolfe. Many thought him better than Wolfe—at doing what *Wolfe* did. In the midst of their raves, many reviewers complained of the lack of strict chronology, especially the delayed climaxes. One recommended skipping ahead and reading them out of sequence. Others disliked the omission of quotation marks.

Even the Book-of-the-Month Club blurbs found the judges carefully dissociating themselves from their own unanimous selection. "There may be more classical, more profound, novels published this year, but certainly none more remarkable than *Raintree County*. We have had no such eruption of the American imagination since Tom Wolfe's day," wrote Henry Seidel Canby. "Mr. Lockridge writes profusely and seems to go off the rails whenever he feels like it. . . . Here is a vital novel, rich in characters, close to the soil and American history, puzzling sometimes, too verbose for my taste, but what I would cut some other reader would insist upon keeping." Canby didn't mention that he'd exacted his own cuts already. (My father later thanked Canby, saying that he was "overgenerous to a young man's book in some ways.") BOMC judge Clifton Fadiman opined, "Sure, it's too long, but that fault issues from a noble passion to get everything in." And John Marquand, "Many readers will be tempted, I believe justly, to skip some of its interpolation. Nevertheless . . ."

The Book-of-the-Month Club shied away from my father's racy book-jacket design. Instead of a naked woman embedded in the landscape, we find Adam and Eve in full Victorian dress doing a minuet as Eve prepares to receive an apple from an accommodating snake.

Only Charles Lee of *The New York Times Book Review* came close to saying what my father wanted to hear. The novel's various "levels are so intimately interrelated that they develop with a kind of breathtaking simultaneity." He noticed its massive structure, contrapuntal design, and layered symbolism and called it "an achievement of art and purpose, a cosmically brooding book full of significance and beauty."

But my father didn't take real pleasure even in this. He had already been found out as fraud and imposter. From within his depression, he heard only the pans. A widely disseminated review by UP reviewer W. G. Rogers, who had to read a book a day, ended: "The author's reward for his hard work was well over $200,000. Our reward as readers for our hard work is boredom; I kept falling asleep."

And *Newsweek*, like many, was hostile to the book-jacket blurb that this novel attempts "a complete embodiment of the American Myth." "*Raintree County* is indeed a novel of 'heroic proportions.' It is also as loose at the joints as Paul Bunyan himself or a first draft by Thomas Wolfe. It spurts words like a nicked vein. It spreads everywhere, like beer slopped on a table."

The killer, though, was the southern novelist Hamilton Basso's review in *The New Yorker*. My father had said to Martin Stone back in July of 1946 that the MGM Award and BOMC would financially prop up his future writing career and get him a popular audience. But what he really wanted was a *succès d'estime*. He wanted the recognition of the respected critics and journals. He wanted the Pulitzer Prize. *The New Yorker* was a prestigious magazine where an emerging author might hope for recognition.

As it turned out, Basso's review became a major embarrassment for *The New Yorker* itself. "American fiction writing has for a long time been building up to 'Raintree County,' by Ross Lockwood, Jr. (Houghton Mifflin), a novel that has just been published. It is, it seems to me, the climax of all the swollen, pretentious human chronicles that also include a panorama of the Civil War, life in the corn-and-wheat belt, or whatnot. . . . Merely to get all this within the covers of a book is something of an accomplishment, like the feats performed by those sideshow performers who swallow nails, beer caps, open safety pins, and broken light bulbs. But Mr. Lockwood's real achievement is the way he has put his book together. . . . I don't see why the publishers of this book didn't go the limit and provide a compass. . . .

"Mr. Lockwood's book is full of Wolfe, by whom he seems to be, rather unfortunately, hypnotized, and it is also full of Joyce, Faulkner, and Lawton Evans' 'Essential Facts of American History.' Now that you know this much about the thing, which happens to be the Book-of-the-Month choice for January, you will not be surprised to learn that it won the last Metro-Goldwyn-Mayer Novel Award, for it's just the sort of plump turkey that they bake to a turn in Hollywood. . . . This is Mr. Lockwood's first novel, so there is still time for him to learn that bulk is not accomplishment, that fanciness is not literature, and that Thomas Wolfe, while an excellent man in his way, had defects that look absolutely terrible second-hand."

My father was not in the state of mind to laugh this off. As a Lockridge myself, I know how it feels to be mistaken for a "Lockwood." And here was that great vision he had in Paris in the spring of 1934—this novel into which he had written all that meant most to him and on which he had labored so many years—derided in one of the most respected periodicals of the land. Other errors in the piece betrayed that Basso had only skimmed the novel, but that was little consolation and there was no recourse in a magazine that didn't print rebuttals. My father didn't have the energy for rebuttals anyway. He feared the Bassos of the literary world might well be right.

Ross Senior went to Elgin to retrieve the old Hudson from Mary Jane and Ed, who were moving to Evanston, and while there told them of his son's terrifying experience in the hospital—with strictest orders that Mary Jane not tell her side of the family about it. He confessed he was feeling old and feared he'd have to give up lecturing. Mary Jane laughed as she reminded him that his mother, the big talker Charlotte Wray, had never given it up.

He did look weary and old to them as he set out in the Hudson. It stopped, started, and stopped several times en route, and though Grandpa kept refilling the radiator it gave up the ghost for good near Fowler, Indiana.

My father had it towed the rest of the way and, on January 7, traded it in on a new car, a four-door Kaiser, in which he took some pride. A couple of days later he and my mother in their finest attire set out in this brand-new car for an autograph party at L. S. Ayres department store in Indianapolis. They were not far out of town when the car started to list and sway. A back wheel was barely hanging on to the axle. They thumbed a ride home and called off the party.

On January 9, he made out a check for the tax on the MGM monies, which had proved to be not spreadable. Calculated by the New York law firm of Cohen, Bingham & Stone, it was for $47,321.51, or $331,250.57 in 1993 dollars.

Then on the 11th, Uncle Harold drove him, my mother, and me up to Manistee to close up the cottage and retrieve some belongings. The roads were icy and my mother was worried as we drove well into the dark. The cottage had no heat and we froze through the night. The next day my father started to dump the original *Raintree County* manuscript in the small coal burner in the kitchen. It wasn't only to warm the place up, it was to destroy the evidence.

Dismayed to see this behavior in an antiquarian who treasured old parchments and had labored so hard on this manuscript, my mother asked why he was burning it. "Well, it's really better not to have too much," he muttered. He kept a small portion, apparently at random, and wrapped an old belt around it.

He and I went over to the O'Connors' that afternoon to pay the rent and say good-bye. Mrs. O'Connor was upset by the change in him—he looked years older, he was sad and solemn. She asked about the trip to California. He said he'd had a good rest but hadn't been at all well. He sat in their rocker, looking at the floor, slowly shook his head, and said, "I don't know just what's wrong, but something's wrong."

Mrs. O'Connor thought he meant physically. But surely he would feel much better after getting settled in the new home. As he tied my scarf to go, she asked him not to forget them in their little town. He replied, "We've spent the happiest years of our lives right here in Manistee and probably the happiest we ever will know."

But Manistee had turned into a snake pit. He meant that he had been happiest when writing his book. And now the book was *gone*.

When Brooks sent him a new printing, in which for economy's sake the handsome green and gold binding had been replaced by a beige and brown one, he didn't even object. "Autumn has come to the raintree," wrote Brooks—not knowing how right he was.

On the lecture circuit, author and critic John Mason Brown spent much of the day with my father on January 15. He wasn't able to get out of him what his plans were for his next novel. The young author was puzzled by all the talk of Thomas Wolfe in the reviews. The next day Brown told an audience in Indianapolis that "for a man who has met with sudden and amazing success, Ross Lockridge, Jr. is the most modest and unassuming author I've ever met."

Instead of his usually expansive epistles my father started sending out tired plaintive notes to friends, with no details of what was ailing him. To Larry and Anne Wylie on the 16th, he wrote that he thought Charles Lee's *New York Times* review "was the one which most nearly expressed what I intended to do in the book, though what an author intends and what he actually accomplishes are of course two different things. . . . We have been really topsy-turvy here in Bloomington, where we are trying hard to establish a new home in the crush and stress of publication events. I have been severely ill and am thoroughly knocked out from too many years of the same kind of work or something, but we hope to get into the clear soon." And to Jeff Wylie he wrote, "I expect you could take me in ping pong without any trouble at all right now—or anything else."

He still didn't *know* what was wrong. The word "depression" existed, of course, but was even less understood then than now. Though De Armond had used the word in his diagnosis, it is found nowhere in my father's subsequent papers. He felt he had suffered what was called then a "nervous breakdown" from too much "stress and strain" and told his wife that if anyone had said a year earlier that he would have a nervous breakdown, he would have found it unimaginable.

Mary Jane Ward herself didn't use the word "depression." She had written to Vernice, the day before he entered the hospital, that Ross was suffering from "extreme fatigue" and "exhaustion." "Fatigue certainly can be very serious, can play all sorts of devastating tricks on the body and on the mind, but it can be licked." We don't commonly think even of "clinical" depression as playing tricks on the mind, of creating delusions—but these are among the terrible spawn of this still mysterious, calamitous illness.

A deep irony in my father's story is how much he *knew* about various fatal arrows that lie in ambush, yet how powerless he was to defend against them when in the grip of major depression. He *knew* that even Chaucer can lose his nerve and retract his best work, that Byron and Napoleon had taken terrible risks in their egoism and fame and paid for it in homecomings of death, that Hugo risked being ridiculous for his sublime overreaching, that his own hero Wanderfell risked insanity in his idealism and isolation, and that he himself had a messianic impulse that could justly be satirized. He *knew* Freud and the perils of family romance, of sibling rivalry, of not completing the work of mourning, of identifying with lost or dead persons, of regression to a pre-Oedipal state. He knew the vulnerability of the "naked, shivering, unhoused ego."

He knew from his own previous illness that one can confront

death and come out the stronger for it. He knew from his cousin Mary Jane Ward—ironically a national spokesperson for greater understanding of mental illness—that a Lockridge can endure incarceration and triumph in dignity over mental illness. He knew by heart those lines of his beloved Whitman, "O despairer, here is my neck, / By God, you shall not go down!" He knew the philosophical weaknesses of Cloise Crane's fatalism.

He knew Mary Jane Ward shouldn't compete with the author of *The Snake Pit* and should take her time getting her next novel ready. He quite agreed with her that Hollywood wasn't worth taking seriously and that, in a larger perspective, contract disputes are trivial. His hero John Wickliff Shawnessy was able to maintain his perpendicular despite a failed literary career. He knew that critics can get it wrong, and that even Keats can get panned.

Finally, he knew that you can't go home again, and thought he knew better than Wolfe that the past, as the "ghost residence of the dead events," is not all there is to time.

For all this knowing, though, he felt like a sick child, baffled by his illness. I have written of him as a driven but capable person. In a psychotic depression he no longer knew anything and no longer willed anything. His insights into Chaucer and mental illness—and all his other capable words and acts that have had elements of foreshadowing throughout—now come clear and fall away as terrible dramatic ironies.

On Tuesday, January 20, he and Vernice tried again to keep a date with L. S. Ayres for an autographing party. The press showed up for the gala event. Mr. Riker, who ran the bookstore, was sitting in his office when he was informed that Lockridge had arrived and was standing in men's furnishings. Mr. Riker said, "I'd better go and see." The reporter followed along and thought Lockridge looked like a man interested in a bargain on socks as he stood there with an uncertain expression.

Was he able to get any work done these days? "No," he mumbled. "Sickness . . . and moving . . . and one thing . . ." "Somehow he gave the impression of a small boy standing in the wings, ready to go on stage for his first Children's Day performance at Sunday School. He smiled like one expecting to fall on his face the next moment."

Of his book he said, "It's hard to read. You sort of have to work at it." He sat down to receive the long line, mostly women, and started to fire off signatures rapidly. *The Indianapolis News* carried on its front page later that day the most memorable photograph of my father's career, and also his last known photograph. With flamboyant tie but tired expression he sits at the center of a crowd of standing Hoosiers, those people whose good opinion in his illness he feared losing. With their fur and hats and scarves and perms, they stand in decorous contrast to the naked, languorous woman on the book jacket. Some of them have the joyless expression of anxious consumers. What is it that they want or think they are getting? For whom was *Raintree County* written? Did they get past the naked lady on the stone slab in the post office on page 4? Did the novel get to some of them, transporting them for a few hours beyond the dreary torpor that I have come to associate with that period of our national life?

Three figures look directly at the camera—one a young man with a smiling countrified Hoosier face, T-shirt under jacket, another a respectable older lady in the background. And then a vulnerable young girl peeking out from behind my father. Somehow I identify with her, partially obscured as she is by my father's head and a little puzzled by everything. His life had darkened now and the shade it would cast on my own life, and that of my family, would prove unending.

And yet the girl's face is also alive and expectant, almost impish, and my father's is tired but hardly angry or sinister. The signatures he gives away are tokens of a larger generosity he shares with all writers who, in their pride, attempt to give us something that might endure. And like my siblings I still sense, through it all, his generosity even as a father. His legacy to us has been more light than shade.

My family came down with the flu the next week. Only my father didn't catch it. Naomi Dalton made a house call on January 27—fee $3, which works out to 60 cents per sick person. Standing in the doorway, my ailing mother almost said something to her about how the really sick person in the house was her husband. But they weren't alone and the moment slipped by.

Three days later her husband showed up without an appointment at Naomi's office. He was anxious and left the office to walk around the block instead of waiting. Upon returning he told her he had run out of sleeping pills prescribed by his uncle. He didn't wish to talk about his insomnia—he was not, after all, her patient—but could she give him a prescription? She was uneasy—he seemed depressed and less affable than usual. So she wrote a prescription for a nonlethal amount of Veronal.

On January 30 and 31, he sent out another round of plaintive notes to old friends and responses to fan mail. To Malcolm Correll he wrote that he was "so 'sat on' by old Father Fate these days that I haven't anything good to say for myself. What with family trouble (new house, sickness—mainly me, children everywhere as usual, etc., etc.), celebrity trouble, and general exhaustion from too many years too hard at the same thing, I am far from the old Lockridge just now and am trying hard to get out of the woods. Believe me, Fame—if you can call it that—ain't what it's cracked up to be."

And to an Indiana resident who tangled hard with the novel, finding its characters compelling, its eroticism painful, and its philosophy inconclusive, he wrote: "Believe it or not, I agree with every sentiment in your letter. Any young presumption which may have gone into the book (there was far too much) is quite gone. Like you, I agree that no one can answer the questions raised in RC. . . . Just now I am a very tired author—feel much less a success, no doubt, than yourself and millions of others. As your letter so justly expresses it, success can only be measured in fullness of life."

He had resumed visiting Myrtle Ayres, C.S.B. His wife objected, she didn't think visiting a Christian Science practitioner would work. "It does *Mother* so much good," he replied. She exclaimed, "But she's not the one who is sick!"

On Tuesdays throughout February, my parents drove to Indianapolis to see Myrtle Ayres and her associate, Miss Bibbs, in the hope that this would bring him around. Medicine had had its chance, had failed, and now it was religion's turn—such was Elsie's reasoning. It had the result of shutting down communication among all parties. Anything was better than a return to the hospital, so my father himself wanted to try this religious therapy.

My mother was again isolated in her doubts. To seek medical help would be to go behind his back again, and the last time she broke this rule her husband had dearly paid for it. So for the time being she accepted the ground rule: Christian Science, not medical science, was now the protocol, and everyone would look for signs of improvement.

Her husband had decided, ominously, that she should learn to drive, so he would drive up, see the practitioners, and have her take the wheel back. She hated passing the cemeteries.

With success came that modern contrivance the telephone, and my parents were learning its disruptive power. In addition to hate mail, my mother was screening calls, which included many requests for speaking engagements. In the midst of our domestic flu epidemic, my father had received a letter from Nanette Kutner, a freelance New York journalist, requesting an interview for *Today's Woman* magazine. He declined, citing poor health. She persisted, called long-distance, got past my mother, and asked him to reconsider. "Long-distance" gave her some authority, and my father relented.

In 1932, Kutner had published *Middle Class,* a morality tale in which an ordinary American family inherits a South African diamond mine out of the blue and doesn't know how to handle sudden wealth. When the heroine tries to show off her tasteless new brownstone, she rightly falls to her death down the elevator shaft. The moral seems to be that middle-class folks shouldn't try being aristocrats. Kutner herself didn't know how to handle money. Estranged from her husband, she was a well-off only child who had reached adulthood without knowing how to boil an egg or iron a blouse—and in driving a Cadillac, shopping at Bergdorf's, residing at the King's Crown Hotel, and eating out most of the time, she was living beyond her means.

A press agent had told her that Lockridge thought he was the great American genius, so she was surprised by his wistful boyish modesty. Our living room had the "neat, barren look of a freshly decorated hotel parlor." She praised the novel—"It's like a symphony"— and my father complained about the *Newsweek* and *New Yorker* reviews. "I don't think those fellows read the book through." He told of the labors of composition. "Now that it's finished I feel . . . like having been eight years pregnant." She asked him about the new book. "He said it was 'terrible going.' He pointed to an adjoining pine-paneled room and his paper-littered desk"—actually a card table in the downstairs bedroom. He hadn't put his office in the small rear cottage because a graduate student couple was renting it when we moved to Stull Avenue.

"I asked if he had done anything in the recent war. 'Had too many responsibilities. Physical disabilities . . . ,' he mumbled. Vernice's fresh voice took up the cue. 'I can tell you *I* was glad when he was rejected. I was in the hospital having my [third] baby.' He was still mumbling, something about not having wanted to stand on the sidelines while the rest of the world . . .'"

She met the rest of the family—Elsie, wearing her Phi Beta Kappa key, my sister Jeanne, running in and out to ask if it was time to pass the cookies, Terry Ross, "dressed and diapered by his writer father," and Ross Senior, who she had heard from IU faculty was "an extreme extrovert." Kutner decided that "all the Lockridges were normal, nice, pleasant, kind; as American as the 'Elsie' books, as banana splits and apple pie, as Thanksgiving dinners, and fireworks on the Fourth. And as smothering as your Aunt Tillie's feather bed." Jeanne must have been too aggressive with those cookies.

This reading was hardly compatible with what she said of my mother. "I looked closely at Ross Lockridge, Jr.'s patient echo. Her young, soft beauty, her sweet dignity masked the quiet granite-like stubbornness I encountered when I asked a question she did not want to answer." " 'She's Nell Gaither,' Ross told me. 'She definitely influenced Nell.' But Johnny Shawnessy never married Nell; his heroine was an unattainable dream."

My father drove her back to the Graham Hotel. She noticed he drove badly, "with sudden stops and starts. On the wheel his hands were nervous and unsure. He looked thin and pinched. 'I can't sleep,' he said, 'I take sleeping pills. . . . I haven't slept since I won those prizes.' " She thought he ought to get drunk. My father, who rather liked Kutner, told *her* to grab a couple before dinner.

She would return to Bloomington a few weeks after *Today's Woman* yanked her chatty article from press at the last minute—this time for *The Saturday Review of Literature*.

～

Kutner didn't know what the normal, nice, American-as-bananasplits Lockridge kids were doing in the basement. I prevailed upon a couple of little girls from a Christian Science household to take off their clothes and run naked. Perhaps I heard of this sport from scurrilous peers at Elm Heights kindergarten. My sister was in on it too, and all of us were whooping it up one day, when our father appeared at the top of the staircase and beheld the bacchanal.

Years later when I described this episode to John Leggett, I thought I had a memory of my father laughing. I'm sure now that he didn't laugh. He quietly told the girls to get dressed and go home. The laughter was my guilty wishful revision.

He was often in the house in early 1948 but mostly lying down looking at the ceiling. After the electroconvulsive therapy, his electricity phobia greatly worsened and the new house was an ordeal. It had new rugs and lots of static, so he dreaded touching objects. He could barely turn lights on and off and would allow his room to become dark rather than brave the light switch.

He didn't blame De Armond for anything, and even sent him an inscribed copy of his novel. De Armond thanked him and hoped he was resting up from "pressure activity." He also didn't blame Houghton Mifflin, telling his wife that if it hadn't been the contract dispute, it would probably have been something else. He blamed himself.

I have wondered why he didn't compare notes with Mary Jane Ward on his hospitalization and continued illness. Their correspondence resumed briefly, only on the literary level. He sent her a letter in early February praising *The Professor's Umbrella*, published by Random House to respectable reviews. "Mary Jane, it's a wonderful book—humane, delicate, sensitive, deeply felt . . . You know how dearly and deeply indebted we are and always shall be to you both— two of the world's really wonderful people."

And she wrote at length on *Raintree County*, telling him where even the encomiums were falling short, praising the story, which "carries the reader on and on, as if borne on a great river," and its "mystical and yet entirely realistic handling of Time," and its multiplicity of styles. She stopped short of highest praise, though— nothing about Shakespeare and Homer.

I think the two now shied away from the real issue—madness. He feared getting into any discussion that might send him back to the hospital and didn't wish to let on that her course of action had failed and he was giving his mother's therapy a try. Though Mary Jane knew her cousin had been ill, even she didn't wish to acknowledge how severely. She had told him that she was on stand-by should he need help. The cry for it would never come.

He continued shopping for groceries, rounding up us kids at dinnertime, and sitting at his card table. Occasionally he wrote. But mostly we remember the darkened bedroom and him often lying on the bed, looking at the ceiling. One time he crossed the street to summon Jeanne to dinner. She was visiting her Christian Science chums and refused to come downstairs after several pleas. He lost his temper and switched her. Jeanne still feels guilty about it.

In early February, Uncle Harold started taking Ernest and me to Sunday School and Ernest began a tiny sentence-a-day diary. *February 8:* "I have just started to go to sunday school. I will be a new boy there." Memorandum: "I must do evry thing my mother tells me and my father." Many of his subsequent entries find him sick and staying home from school.

My parents were not sharing a bedroom. Still not sleeping— despite medication—my father worried about keeping her awake. He slept in the downstairs bedroom-office, while my mother slept upstairs in the master bedroom, where she could keep tabs on us kids.

And he wasn't holding up his end of book promotion. In early February he received a telegram from Paul Brooks. "BELIEVE RAINTREE'S SALES WOULD BENEFIT BY YOUR PERSONAL APPEARANCE IN THE EAST. PUBLICITY DEPARTMENT HAS SEVERAL TENTATIVE PLANS FOR APPEARANCES IN NEW YORK AND BOSTON . . ." He wrote back that "for an indefinite period, the book will have to hobble along on its own merits as I am under doctor's orders to take it easy—that is, as easy as I can with the hullaballoo going on around here. We have had a good deal of sickness in the family during the last two months, with me as the leading contender." Disappointed, Brooks replied graciously. But nobody at Houghton Mifflin through all of this had yet divined just how ill their author was.

Ross Senior had his own therapy for his ailing son—recitation. He proposed a friendly competition. His son would rememorize the entire Declaration of Independence, and he would rememorize the entire Constitution.

His son didn't feel like doing this—it was an added burden—but he endeavored to please his father, who was after all only trying to help. My father tried to please everybody. I watched one day as he paced up and down the long living room at Stull Avenue, reciting, while Grandpa knelt like an acting coach, intently watching and suggesting gestures and inflections. But my father couldn't memorize anything, not even Patrick Henry's speech, which he had recited all over Indiana as a youth. Depression had been compounded by the aftereffects of electroconvulsive therapy.

Christian Science and recitation were thus the improbable alternatives offered up by Elsie and Ross Senior, always in character.

Out of a sense of obligation to Bloomington, my father accepted a couple of local speaking engagements. He dreaded them. On February 10, he spoke at the IU Faculty Club. "LOCKRIDGE TO MAKE INITIAL SPEECH TONIGHT." It was a brief low-key narration of how the novel got written and a tired response to his critics. He disclaimed any intention of writing the Great American Novel—there are "much stronger candidates for that legendary distinction." He complained of the emphasis in reviews on Wolfe—if anything, his novel has too much pattern and there are so many predecessors that they add out. He was unhappy that some readers were finding the novel difficult, and conceded it takes some work. It could "go on being rewritten and cut and revamped *ad infinitum* and to good advantage." Russell Noyes, his master's thesis advisor and an admirer of the novel, had the feeling that Ross Lockridge didn't really have much to say.

In the question and answer period, he was asked what he was going to write next. "I wish I knew," he replied.

Earlier that day he had written a "Sketch for a book of Philosophy." It was one way of finessing the question of what new novel he had in mind: why does he have to write a *novel?* This "Sketch" is a meditation far darker than anything the Perfessor ever spouted. It's a renunciation of everything John Wickliff Shawnessy ever believed in, turning once again on the issue of fate and freedom. Unlike his desperately wishful meditation in Hollywood, with its echoes of Mary Baker Eddy, his conviction now is that we are governed by Fate in a world that is mostly a living hell.

"Is a human being really free?" he asks. We begin in unfreedom, not having asked to be born, and for the rest of our lives, down to our personality itself, we are the result of forces not of our choosing. "It seems probable that all is inexorably caused, though some of the causes are of course subterranean and obscure." (A few years earlier he had instead written that an "infinity of physical and reactive and causal possibilities becomes chance again. The past is not a closed circuit.")

If we have no free will, how do we judge one another? "Life has a biographical aspect—observed by others. It has also its inexorable autobiographical aspect, which each knows for himself, and none can know for him—just as no one feels another's pain, another's fear, another's madness, etc. No one may be blamed for the course that his life takes. He is simply responding to whatever forces internal or external dominate him, having always made him what he is." Fate reaches down to our very thoughts and beliefs—we aren't responsible even for what we think.

So what happens to the great questions of ethics, God, and immortality? There is a practical, not absolute, truth in teachings of religion since it is through inappropriate "ambition, narcissism, vanity"—his own sins—that so much evil comes into the world. Psychiatry is more correct than religion in locating these evils in the mind rather than in the Devil. He concludes that wisdom consists in "unselfing oneself as far as it is possible to do so."

Yet the metaphoric Devil is certainly in charge of this planet, he thinks, discarding once and for all Mr. Shawnessy's and his own father's visionary reading of human history and the Republic. The enduring religious truths have done nothing to improve the lot of humanity. God he now calls merely a "hypothesis" who "remains strangely absent from his creation." "The lost lives are those that are torn apart by forces of self, and our American Twentieth Century is thus the living hell of many lost lives, incurable except by the deaths that they can never know but only seek through the ticking seconds of eternity. To these lost lives," of which he clearly counts himself one, "let others be charitable. . . . Whatever is is. And though life may have many blessings, it may also be the greatest curse imaginable."

He sees the dark truth of Calvin that the elect and the damned are chosen from all eternity. There is no justice in this. Our fate is not according to our deserts. He has now discovered himself to be one of the damned.

He had had a friendly debate with his wife about the afterlife. She feared that once you're dead, you're dead, and that heaven and hell are states of mind now, in the land of the living. He always held out for immortality. But now he thinks the total destruction of consciousness in death is more likely. "No individual can affirm anything with certainty except his own life. It is certain also that he will die, but he will never know this death. It is something he intellectually anticipates, but it will never exist for *him*. Death is nothingness from the internal or subjective point of view."

My father isn't depressed because he's discovered these truths. Rather, he's "discovered" these truths because he is depressed. He is also preparing the conceptual framework for the end of all suffering. The sins of his personality are not his own, so why should he continue to suffer for them? In death he will not confront hell. It will be nothingness. He works to quiet the final fear—of death itself—and he seeks absolution for the guilt he feels at the prospect of self-murder.

Our father in the coming days exhibited some bizarre behavior. He was frequently inspecting knives in the kitchen. And one day he was opening and closing some empty cupboards—as if in bleak revision of John Shawnessy's utterance that to explore the great cosmos is to look into our own "immense cupboard." At first somewhat amused, his wife asked him what he was looking for, and he replied, in dead seriousness, "I'm looking for a way out."

He told her that he'd begun to think something was wrong with his physical brain, not just his mind. Something was wrong with his *brain*. Could it be syphilis? He told her that maybe he'd caught syphilis during his year in Europe, cutting himself while shaving over a dirty sink in a moving train. My mother wasn't dumb, you don't catch syphilis that way.

This is the only other evidence I've come across that there may have been a sexual encounter in Europe, though not with one of those Ivy League types. But depressives sometimes had precisely this irrational fear—that they had somehow or other caught syphilis. If he did in fact link it to an early sexual encounter, it seems likely he would have had himself tested without blabbing beforehand to his wife.

He went up to Indianapolis and had Uncle Bob arrange a test. It was negative. He told his wife that instead of mental illness he wished he had some "respectable" disease, like tuberculosis.

Another infernal speaking engagement was scheduled for February 17, this time Ladies Day at the Bloomington Rotary Club. My mother and his parents were there for it, sitting at the speakers' table before 180 guests at commodious Alumni Hall. His script for this was sloppily typed, with scribbles. He had given a stirring performance in this same hall back in 1932 when he played Patrick Henry. My mother watched him limp his way through the talk.

All that was good in his novel he owed to his parents, wife, and Bloomington, he said. "My own contribution to the book was its demerits no doubt . . ." Once again he told the history of the novel's composition, this time with a humility quite unlike the comic pomposity of the history he gave the publicity people at Houghton Mifflin. With the ladies in mind, he told of the tumultuous domestic circumstances but could conjure up only one small anecdote—of the scare they had when Terry Ross seemed to have swallowed a safety pin. It wasn't vintage Lockridge.

Having made dutiful orations to both town and gown, maybe he could take a breather. But it was not to be. The morning of February 19—the same day that the 37th Indiana High School State Basketball Championship Tournament began—the Associated Press carried to many of the nation's newspapers an attack on *Raintree County* by one Reverend Alfred Barrett, S.J., a Fordham professor. The Reverend had a flair for language reminiscent of some comic tirades in my father's discarded Dream Section.

In his opinion, having been "bedeviled" by *Raintree County*'s "1066 pages of bombast, rank obscenity, materialistic philosophy, and blasphemous impudicity," he concludes that "this book not only fails artistically, but patently falls within the general prohibition of the Index. It is a book inimical to faith and morals. For most readers it may well be a proximate occasion of sin. . . . The devil had a lot to do . . . with the writing of this book. . . . The Professor is the most sympathetically presented character in the novel and the author had a field day writing his racy obscene blasphemous talk. No reviewer has, so far as I know, called attention to the extremely objectionable attack against Christianity and Christ on page 1027 and thereabouts.

419

The virgin birth, the Resurrection, the virginity of Mary, the divinity of Jesus Christ Himself are derided in terms of lascivious and unquotable blasphemy. . . . I have long doubted the literary discrimination of the Book-of-the-Month Club judges. *Raintree County* is the one rotten apple that ruins their whole barrel for me. From now on I choose my own books."

The Bloomington *World-Telephone* interviewed Lockridge the same day. He "hated to see anyone acquire such a viewpoint," mentioning that the Perfessor is balanced by Shawnessy, who he insists is more Christian than pagan. In his novel the Perfessor had, with greater wit and finesse than the author could now muster, disposed of Reverend Jarvey, the whited sepulchre who led a mob bent on tarring and feathering John Shawnessy.

The attack prompted a discussion in the New York *Herald Tribune* and other newspapers about the Catholic Index. The *Trib* noted that in the 1940 edition of two thousand proscribed titles, an American novel had not yet made the list. Lockridge might soon be in the august company of Voltaire, Rousseau, Gibbon, Hugo, Balzac, and Zola.

Malcolm Correll would later be astonished that his old, often irreverent, friend had taken no delight in the fracas. The "Perfessor" in him was dead. Houghton Mifflin had on tap the "pious statement" he had drafted out in Hollywood just for this sort of thing, so it was sent to major newspapers and the Associated Press. BOMC let it be known that one objectionable sentence had been cut from their edition.

In shorthand, probably about this time, he wrote, "One might as well speak out, and bravely, about one's book and other things—one cannot possibly commit any graver errors than one has already imagined."

The attack triggered an avalanche of hate mail, which my mother intercepted and tossed as best she could. Her husband was in no shape for this. Houghton Mifflin and BOMC were coming in for their own hate mail. "Gentlemen: The book you have published & are responsible for before God—'Raintree County' is obscene—blasphemous & a sacrilege—And you will each one be held accountable before God for the moral harm done by such a disgusting book." Readers' columns had already been full of this sort of thing. "To the Editor of *The Indianapolis News:* Have just read *Raintree County* and am now going to bury it in my garden. It should make good fertilizer. It's too putrid to leave unburied."

Shortly thereafter my mother awakened earlier than usual one morning and went downstairs. In the living room, her husband was standing next to the large Funk & Wagnalls dictionary with his back to her. Something was odd. He was dressed in his best suit. She offered him breakfast and afterward he quietly returned to his bedroom. Of course he had been acting strangely, so she put it out of her mind.

It wasn't until weeks after his death that she was looking through the dictionary and discovered what he probably had on his mind to do that morning and what she had unwittingly intercepted. She found tucked away a note in a shaky hand which read, "Dearest, Have gone for early morning walk to clear head. Love, Ross." On the back he had written, "The purpose of *Raintree County* is to present life in its many-sided variety with idealism triumphant. An irreverent character in a book does not mean an irreverent book. In any event it is an old and good rule that every reader is entitled to his own opinion of a book."

They were still visiting the Christian Science practitioners. He was assuring his wife there was some hope in this and she feared undercutting what hope he had. If Elsie and Christian Science did have this positive effect on him, she suggested that maybe he should move out to the Lockridges' for a spell. But not long after their session in Indianapolis on February 24, he admitted to her—as he had once before out in Hollywood—that he was not one bit better.

This was no revelation. Her husband in unguarded moments had been saying the most lamentable things to her. "I feel no human emotion. I only know that I love you and the children." And when he was lying down one day, he said, "These beautiful children, and there's nothing I can do for them." And "How did I ever think I could get away with writing such a book?"

He was not prepared, though, to stop these visits to the practitioners. He himself could think of no options between Christian Science and a greatly dreaded return to the hospital. Wary of bringing an unstable Mary Jane Ward back into this dismal picture, my mother could think only of Naomi Dalton as someone to turn to, but she kept this possibility to herself. Ross didn't want medical help. Then too, Naomi was an old high school friend, a local general practitioner and obstetrician. What could she tell them that the august psychiatrists in Indianapolis couldn't? But she silently decided to seek out Naomi's counsel. She didn't know that Ross had already asked Naomi for a prescription, as yet unfilled because he had stopped taking sleeping medication—probably in deference to the practitioners.

She continued to love the new house—it was like a mansion—but he seemed to have no feeling for it at all. She leaned on the kitchen sink one day looking out the window and told him how much she loved the house. And he said he was so glad—with an intonation that implied he had taken care of the family and we would have a good place to live after he was gone.

Despite all this, he was able to get up when visitors called and put on an act. His parents were ever optimistic, seeing signs of improvement every day.

On February 27, Paul Brooks sent him a telegram: "NUMBER ONE FICTION BEST SELLER HERALD TRIBUNE LIST MARCH SEVENTH GOOD GOING." These were for regular Houghton Mifflin sales alone, not counting the enormous BOMC distribution. My father took no pleasure in this.

The Baker side of the family had its own therapy. Practical-minded Aunt Clona suggested he get out and do some late winter yardwork. It was a good time to spread fertilizer. So my father got a spreader and set to work. Kinsey associate Wardell Pomeroy happened by. Many years later he would write that he had known Lockridge before he went East "to teach and write his novel, in seven years of tremendous and shattering toil. I remember seeing him after he came home, rich and famous, raking autumn leaves apathetically in his front yard, a strangely bent and broken man just before his tragic death."

Other friends had similar sightings. John Robert Moore, eighteenth-century scholar and his old chess partner, hadn't finished reading *Raintree County*. Like many members of the IU faculty, he didn't much like it. Buying the groceries was one of the few tasks my father could still perform. "He was pushing a cart at the A & P grocery store, and his shoulders drooped as I had never seen them do before. His face was gray and haggard, and his eyes were dull and almost sunken. I begged him to take a vacation immediately, and I offered him a key to our cottage on the shore of Lake Erie, which would have been delightful at that late season. I wished I could have told him that he was one of the greatest writers who ever lived—he wanted to hear that, and he would have believed it from me." Like many of my father's friends, Moore would soon put the half-read novel down, not having the heart to read on.

On March 1, he stopped at Jim Pennington's gas station and had the tank filled on his Kaiser. Pennington complained to Don Smalley that Ross Lockridge wasn't much fun anymore. He used to like a good dirty joke with the rest of them.

On Tuesday, March 2, my parents headed off as usual to the Christian Science practitioners. My mother had tried to arrange for Elsie to go with him instead, so that she would have an opportunity to go see Naomi Dalton and speak at some length about her husband. But he insisted that she come along as usual. She put off her visit to Naomi for the time being. It could wait a few more days.

Myrtle Ayres found much improvement in her patient. It was their best meeting, she felt. He laughed heartily, she would recall shortly thereafter, and "expressed more assurance that [the Christian Science way] was just what he needed, and that he would be able to work it out." He feared he would be forced once again to undergo "that horrible experience," electroconvulsive therapy, "and I assured him that he didn't need to go through with it—and that if he would call us or come to us, day or night, we would take him in and help to protect him. He chuckled and said, 'Well, if I don't get this, it won't be your fault, will it?' . . . I am sure he was better that day than he had been at any time, and was free to say so."

After my father's session she and Miss Bibbs called my mother in from the waiting room. They had never spoken with her alone. While her husband waited outside, she was given a rosy report on her husband's progress. *"No!"* she exclaimed. *"He's not one bit better!"* Miss Bibbs told her not to express that opinion to her husband—he needed encouragement.

Upon walking out onto the crowded sidewalk, her husband said, "Look at all these happy people." Why could he not feel their happiness? They all looked pretty grumpy to my mother.

Throughout the first week of March, Ernest was sick again, missing school, and feeling rather mournful. "I shall not forget the good times I had at Manistee," he wrote in his diary.

He could hear his father sometimes playing Stephen Foster songs on the gramophone. And his father liked the old hymns. Hearing "Rock of Ages" on the radio one day, he spoke to our mother of its consoling age-old truth.

Frequently he walked out to the old High Street house. His mother continued reading the Bible to him, and his father coached him in recitation. He would lie down sometimes on his old bunk bed in the small sleeping porch. Thinking back on his fears as publication day had approached, he said to his mother, "Sometimes it seems to me as if I wrote my book in a vacuum—that nobody else would ever read it but us." And he told her, "I wish I could go back to childhood." To his father he said ominously in early March, "It looks as if God sustained me until I had finished my work." Even so they continued to think he was coming out of it.

Josephine Piercy, a member of the English department, called to invite him and my mother to a small dinner party on the following Monday, March 8. A cellist might play for the group. My father accepted. She didn't know him well but admired the novel greatly, and tried to make a small joke by way of compliment. "I've looked hard through your book to find something bad, and I am disappointed." He didn't seem to get it. He sounded very hoarse and she thought maybe he had a cold.

About this time he wrote a letter to his Boston friend Aharon Arsenian that was more detailed about his state of mind than he was otherwise letting on. According to recollections of it four decades later, he complained about how nervous he was, always pacing back and forth, how he felt the pressure of getting another novel under way, and how he was claustrophobic back in his hometown, where everything seemed drab and joyless.

He wrote also of feeling very guilty about his wife, who had labored so many years for him on the book. What was he able to offer her now?

The Arsenians were alarmed and debated inviting him to come East. It wasn't a simple matter of environment, of course. My father became ill next to a beautiful lake and only worsened out in fabulous Hollywood. He took the depression with him back to Bloomington.

Having exhausted the visionary nineteenth-century Indiana landscape in his novel, he now found the real twentieth-century landscape colorless and flat like his life. His novel had become a false prophecy. The homecoming was a mistake—not because of Bloomington's particular atmosphere but because it felt to him as if he had come full circle. In his depression, homecoming felt like a closing down of his life within the orbit of his parents. It was the symmetry of fate that he was returning home to die.

On the morning of Thursday, March 4, he was walking out to his parents' house once again, passing Don and Ruth Smalley's house. Smalley, a Trollope scholar who had just finished editing Browning's "Essay on Chatterton," had very much hoped to like *Raintree County*. Along with many other literary people in academe, he didn't. Part of it was the Great American Novel hype, which he thought created a false expectation. But he was also disturbed by the novel's seeming revelation of a personality that wasn't quite the one he had come to know as Ross Lockridge—a sane and discerning person possessed of brilliant whimsy. At the time, he thought the novel fevered, hectic, and fraught with unanswerable questions of self-definition. Still, he very much liked Ross Lockridge and upon spotting his friend haled him in.

That evening he wrote to his wife, Ruth, of the encounter. "He is looking in ill health and years older. I told him I'd read *Raintree County* and he asked how I had liked it. I adroitly started praising my two favorite spots: the scene near the beginning where the woman is giving birth to a child abovestairs and the men are commenting downstairs in front of the store and Johnny is listening in. The other: Johnny getting lost and wandering outside his world. Ross said they were two of his own favorites. I said I didn't know what it showed that I picked two places so early in the novel. He said, 'Reader fatigue' and grinned. He said he didn't write the book chronologically, however, or as the pages progress, and so I wasn't praising his early work at the expense of his later. He is cagy on saying much and went no further into that one. I told him he was somewhat like Browning's Lazarus—having seen heaven and now having to get adjusted to earth once more (the grind of producing another work). Then I said the analogy was not altogether fair or accurate. He said it fit pretty well."

Smalley was trying to be kind, finding something to praise without any wholesale dishonesty. My father could tell his praise was measured and gave his friend an easy way around potential embarrassment by alluding to "reader fatigue." Smalley had the impression, in any event, that Lockridge was just being polite and was wholly apathetic about anything one might say of the novel. He was "stooped and thin and hollow-eyed."

Their friendship had been based on mutual drollery, so Smalley kidded him about the naked woman on the book jacket, not knowing this was Lockridge's own handiwork. His tired friend, unable to join in the mirth, didn't let on. Smalley made just a few more critical observations, unrecorded and now forgotten.

The Lazarus analogy was apt. My father confronted the grind of producing another book back in the real world, and he felt as if he were already dead, a kind of zombie in a posthumous existence. He told his friend—as Smalley would remember in another letter to his wife, a few days later—that he had "wanted so much to believe that *this* book, not any future book of his, would be remembered and even read a hundred years from now." He soon excused himself, saying he was late in getting to his parents'.

∼

What kind of new work was my father now attempting? He had accumulated some papers, with headings like "Plans for additional creation" and "Beyond RC." He had a working title, *A Valley in the Years*, a partial outline, a couple of episodes, and a cast of characters that included a Christian Science practitioner. Mostly written on the back of old *Raintree County* carbons and unfinished letters, some of these papers have odd typographic patterns, tiered like "pattern" poetry, as if he were doodling with the typewriter.

It was the worst possible direction for a new novel: a thinly disguised autobiography, from Fort Wayne days to the present. If there was one psychic space he needed to be free of for the time being, it was his own.

He felt right away that he was competing with the author of *Raintree County*. The question was, After writing an encyclopedic novel, what more did he have to say? Simply to admit of the question confirmed his fear that the earlier novel was a failure. The new novel "will vie in magnitude with RC and surpass it in naturalness and lifelikeness, without loss of poetic quality. This book will actually have more detachment perforce and will embody in it the beauty and the chastened classic quality lacking to the other." It will be "a graver work, a sober evocation." It will be "more plausible" and have "a much richer cast of characters." It will be "a work in which I can take more pride."

My father had told Don Smalley that his next novel would "do justice to Freud," and as he geared up to write an autobiographical novel he had the Freudian grammar in mind. During his last illness, there's no evidence he ever thought psychoanalysis a likely therapy—his suffering felt more like a total disabling of brain and body than a neurosis reachable through talk. It felt more like "flu or something." I think too that the prospect of opening up to an analyst may have been unnerving to someone who already felt his privacy invaded. And Protestants are less at ease in this kind of confessional than are Catholics and Jews. He would do the analysis himself. For a blocked writer, after all, the best therapy would be writing.

Since he decided to die rather than write this novel, I'll sketch a reading for him based on issues of identity and aspiration, building on his own hunches in these late writings, mostly avoiding the Freudian vocabulary but making use of some professional opinion I've sought out. It's unsettling as well as presumptuous to put the shade of one's father on the analyst's couch—for one thing, I lack proper certification. But it seems in keeping with his own interest in psychology, and in keeping with the goal I set myself—of bringing whatever light I could into a deep mystery.

Some light comes from seeing how my father's life, which had always seemed to me unique and impenetrable, exhibits some patterns of development that are familiar to anyone who has taken Psych 101. Most theorists today link the quality of our self-esteem to the first three to four years of life, when the mother's influence is dominant. Born into maternal dependency but also into a kind of womblike symbiosis where boundaries between self and other haven't yet formed, we briefly feel a sense of omnipotence—if we are lucky enough to have mirroring intuitive mothers. My father described this state in "Emergence"—the fantasy that begins *The Dream of the Flesh of Iron*.

But such bliss must soon yield to separation anxiety at the dawning recognition of boundaries. Since the mother must also be the source of withholding, we may contend with our own disappointment or rage by means of a compensatory idealization of her. I've come to think that Elsie Lockridge may have seemed to her children to withhold too much, even love itself, and that this may ironically have launched my father's idealization of her. For all her strenuous efforts, she was perhaps not a "good enough mother" in the conventional sense.

But I'd add that without her unconventional and visionary encouragement of her youngest child's imagination, he might, with his great constitutional energies, have devolved into a politician, or worse.

All mothers, whether warm or cold, influence our aspirations. By fusing early on an idealized image of our mother with our idealized self-image, we seek both her love and our self-love in becoming what we feel is her highest wish for us. Thus our aspirations may point simultaneously in opposing directions—regressively toward the mother as we attempt to regain that sense of omnipotence, and creatively toward self-affirmation, exploration of the world into which we've been thrown, and productive work.

Some of us hold on to these aspirations fiercely—hoping to confirm our powers in a world that feels no remorse in trouncing us. We may fail to modify these hopes in terms of a more realistic self-assessment.

Fail? This is the issue. The commonplace view of maturity is that we learn to accept our limitations, tone down our aspirations, and agree that our lisp disqualifies us for TV anchorperson. Our self-worth becomes less vulnerable thereby.

Great personal striving that declines such compromises often implies inordinate self-love, and artists rely on this enabling pride in great measure. It is one source of their vitality and creative well-being. But striving also implies a deficit, a perfection never reached, and such people may in the end suffer not from too much self-love but from too little. They may find they cannot rest from their labors, behold what they have made, and see that it is good.

So should Ross Lockridge, Jr. have been talked out of trying to write the greatest book ever? Should he have been made to see that he need not pursue this implacable, unrealistic, visionary goal?

For all the price that he paid and that his family paid with him, I would not have had him make this accommodation.

By the time he was four or five he was identifying with various older males in the family. Not just his father, but his two brothers as well. And also his dead grandfather, the poet John Shockley, whom his mother worshiped. Worship of parent generations has been a trait of the Lockridge and Shockley families. Ross Senior's own worship of the noble dead took infectious hold in his youngest son.

Among these four male figures the most telling identification was with the dead brother, Bruce, whose career was a blank. In emulation of his living brother, Shockley, who had a flair for writing, Rossie would fill in for this special lost life, making real as a great writer what in his Grandfather Shockley had been only potential, and also doing "greater deeds than his father ever did before."

When at age five he witnessed what others in Fort Wayne found strange—that his parents didn't visibly mourn the loss of their eldest son—he confronted the spectre of his own dispensability. But rather than impute to them either a lack of love or pathological denial, he came to see their sturdy composure as a symbol of great idealism and hope, of a very American refusal, as Whitman said, to "go down." His life as a writer would be in part a continuation by other means of this resistance to time and death—his own refusal, his own idealism, his spirited denial of the ultimacy of death. And yet like Whitman, whose greatest poem is an elegy, this idealism was vulnerable, was anchored in loss, and he was haunted by the shade of his brother whose death had not elicited tears.

Beyond family dynamics, I've said that there was another motive, an intrinsic one and more powerful, in his becoming a writer—a motive so simple that it can be overlooked or falsely explained away. From his earliest years in the culture of this family, he *loved the art of story-telling.* His novel would far exceed the psychological dynamics that entered into its making. In him as in other artists, the self-reflections of Narcissus give way to the yearnings of Icarus. Freud himself acknowledged that "the nature of artistic attainment is psychoanalytically inaccessible to us."

So certain features of my father's emotional life were shaped early on—the fear of abandonment and investment in homecomings, the nostalgia and sense of loss, the belief in special destiny, the idealism, the wish to please and not overtly challenge authority, yet the exuberance and will to excel beyond all measure, and the secrecy of his great ambition. This ambition was tucked away from his everyday persona, which struck some as rather modest, just as the hero of his novel would be both the domestic Mr. Shawnessy and the prodigal dreamer mr. shawnessy. And an alter ego to both of these was the satanic Perfessor, who had lost his mother at an early age and lived forever in her shade.

Though his aspiration at age seven to become a writer may have been fashioned partly in response to maternal withholding, it was something he could in turn withhold from his mother, nurturing it secretly. It was ironically his self-defining resistance to her. If both parents tended to see him fulfilling aspects of their own frustrated wills, he would fulfill them on his own terms.

Though refusing to acknowledge fully Ross Senior's influence, he took measure of this character, who was never a potent rival in his mother's eyes. The child's own birth in 1914 assured that Ross Senior would henceforth sleep alone. My father loosened the Oedipal tie sufficiently to marry well—a woman unlike his mother—and have a normal sex life. In his novel he describes how Mother Eve must give way to Venus Callipygos, and how fathers must give way to lovers and husbands. *Raintree County* isn't an unconscious manifestation of such trials, it explores them, acknowledging that they are never fully resolved.

The fictitious John Shawnessy works through the pain of maternal separation—both in infancy and after his mother's death—and accepts limits in his erotic and creative life. He overcomes any pathology in his self-love, haunted as he is by his ideal self, mr. shawnessy, who wishes to write the epic of his people but never gets around to it. In the end it's a collective self—not the self-intoxicated John Shawnessy—who keeps alive the great mythic enterprise of the American Republic.

My father, though, completed his own epic. His twenty-pound manuscript seemed at first to answer to his greatest hopes for himself, as the grandiose letters written to his editor upon completion of the novel show. But his estimate of the novel was as vulnerable as his self-worth, given the ruthlessness of these ideals. Grandiosity is a flip side of depression.

To be vulnerable isn't yet to be ill, and I think it was only in the stress and exhaustion of finishing the book again and again, combined with the relentless sequence of events that followed its acceptance, that his vision failed him and he became ill. He said that he had been heart-whole in writing the book, that he had never been happier, and his widow and I believe him.

The story of his life after first completing the novel in the spring of 1946 was one of incremental stress, coming wavelike with the series of false finishes, and culminating in the contract dispute. Stress was both physical and emotional. He felt like a prisoner at the typewriter trying to write his way out from under his own enormous book, and he bled himself white.

More important, stress was conceptual or cognitive. The false finishes made him doubt the integrity of this beloved novel—the more he revised, the more imperfect it seemed. And the publicity surrounding the MGM Award treated him more like James Whitcomb Riley than Thomas Mann. Public perception grossly contradicted wishful self-perception, and he became fearful.

But it was the contract dispute with Houghton Mifflin that made stress in this cognitive sense finally intolerable. Besides adding to his physical and emotional exhaustion, the dispute was an assault on his very identity. No longer the favored son in the house, he confronted a family that seemed willing to cheat him. They must have no real regard for him. They wouldn't have done this to Hemingway. Now he had even less status than an amanuensis, and the resentment he had never expressed toward his own father exploded one-hundred fold toward his publisher. All feelings of omnipotence and grandiosity were frustrated and his self-worth was gravely wounded.

So wounded that he lost his very identity as writer and sank into unutterable depression. He could hardly speak the personal pronoun. He had become a shade. When he threw in the towel, the aggression that this soft-spoken person was directing toward his publisher turned inward. He was guilty and ashamed.

In the aftermath, the object of my father's love—this book of his own making and so much an expression of his own identity—seemed cheapened and unworthy. A spiritual testament had been fought over for money. And from late October, 1947, on, he felt a kind of cosmic stage fright as publication day approached. Set in plates and no longer under his control, the novel would expose him as an imposter.

In this state of mind, he came to feel that his novel had been grounded less in love than in aggression. To some degree it had been aggression against his father, for his simple patriotism, conventional morals, and insistence that *he* was the writer in the family—but this hardly mattered now. More so, it had been aggression against his mother—against her religion, her sexuality, her father worship, her very being—for which he felt intense shame and guilt. Whatever her praise of the novel, he felt he had deeply harmed her in this implicit rebellion against her.

The therapeutic value of writing this novel was not the equal of the devastations that followed, when a private person came to feel he was exposing his and his mother's unseemly inner lives to the nation. As a friend has suggested to me, it was not success that destroyed him but his inability to use success as a declaration of independence, his inability to move beyond private rebellion, enacted in his closeted compositional labors over the years, to sudden public witness of that rebellion.

His life had already taken on the stamp of tragic fable when external circumstance cooperated so heartily with his own dangerous drivenness, as if the gods *were* out to get him. Just when everything seemed to open up, his novel warmly accepted for publication and no more sackcloth and ashes, his life ironically began to be thornhedged in. It just so happened that Mary Jane Ward's agent had dumped her and she advised her cousin not to bother with agents; it so happened that he was persuaded to enter the MGM contest; it so happened that Paul Brooks thought it unnecessary to specify in advance how the booty was to be split; it so happened that Martin Stone felt his client could best argue his own case.

And the dispute with his publisher just so happened to coincide with completion of the novel. To finish a work of art is to lose it, and when an artist has loved the work over so many years it may feel like grief to give it up. This novel had focused his energies—erotic, aggressive, artistic. Where earlier he urgently wanted it sent out into the world, he now felt the pain of separation. The novel itself had abandoned him. John Shawnessy, the Perfessor, Susanna, and even Nell and Eva had become mere shades for their author at the very moment they were coming into life for a nation of readers. And at this moment of creative loss, his publisher seemed to abandon him as well.

So he now read his own life as a shameful tale of "ambition, narcissism, vanity," as he put it in these late writings. A sense of loss was compounded with a total collapse of self-worth. It was a dark moralistic Freud whom he now brought to bear on his shattered life. It had all been an exercise in narcissism, chastised in the end. "And so he became one who watched life but did not realize that he was always really watching himself. . . . None ever looked so long with such a silent, dangerous intentness at his own image." At the same time he felt that he hadn't chosen his own personality and was being unfairly punished, even "sacrificed."

This man who had served as consultant to Dr. Ames, read widely in psychoanalytic literature, and created the psychotic Susanna was otherwise baffled by his own illness. And in 1948 the psychiatric profession itself had small grasp of this type of depression, with little to offer in therapy.

He hoped that a return to his mother might lessen the shame, purge the guilt, and restore his powers—hence his desperate, regressive try at Christian Science, rather like the Dreamer in *The Dream of the Flesh of Iron* returning to the maternal lake in the end. He would try to resume the role of good son, as if the novel had never been written. But the metaphor was wrong. The lake was really a snake pit.

And he was once again in that campfire circle with his orator father—the character who had dogged him all his life, who had thought of him as an amanuensis, who down to his very name had been reluctant to grant him a separate identity, and whose career he had been groomed to carry on. He had tactically freed himself of this father, whose stature had diminished in his eyes as he matured intellectually. But back in Bloomington for a homecoming of death, he felt imposed on once again.

His depression was as deep as his aspirations had been absolute, and maybe there's a cruel sense of proportion here. But I've wondered why after several months it showed no signs of lifting.

It may be that he was being hit by yet another force out of his control—his genes. This wouldn't explain the meaning or even the proximate cause of his depression, but it might help explain its severity and persistence.

During the past two decades many researchers have argued, of course, that depression is a specific biological illness, if often triggered by externally induced stress. The most used therapy is antidepressant drugs, nonexistent in 1947. In my father's case "stress" would consist of the unremitting weight of circumstance that followed upon the initial completion of his novel and that bore down upon his vulnerable self-worth. Mary Jane Ward and Ross Lockridge, Jr. were double second cousins (Lockridge brothers had married Wray sisters)—and a genetic bias could have been introduced from the Lockridge and/or Wray side. My father didn't have manic episodes, and didn't have the great fluctuations of mood characteristic of manic-depressives. He was well known for both ebullience and a stable temperament. But there's no ruling out a genetic or biological bias toward major depression, and there was enough stress in his life to trigger it. In theory you can get stuck with both vulnerable self-worth, acquired largely through circumstances of your upbringing, and a susceptibility to depression as a gift of your genes.

Depressives project a dark world, seeing sinister patterns and events in their ordinary lives as a way of symbolically explaining the catastrophic mood to themselves. The course of my father's life now seemed death-ridden to him from the beginning, the novel that he was fated to write harmful to those he loved—especially his mother. Its warm, fig-leafed eroticism and witty irreverence were now the blatant obscenities and blasphemies that Father Barrett said they were. His thinking had become as delusional as the priest's.

He wasn't depressed because he couldn't get a second novel going. Rather, he couldn't get a second novel going because he was depressed. This second novel was therefore plotted as a reparation of self-worth in a suicidal person. He would write to prove to himself that he was still a writer.

He should have started with haiku. Instead, in a twenty-page outline, he projected a vast autobiographical novel more inclusive than his failed first novel. His story would be told by the "Cosmic Historian," who "enters everywhere" and speaks "as if the Universe became a voice." The Historian would explore depths "below the depths merely psychological of the Joyces and Prousts." From his perspective, "how little and vain is a temporary combat over money, contract, etc.——the things that people in the world contend over. For the years will come, they will come . . ." With his own "ironic, gentle, omnivorous, omnipotent personality," the Cosmic Historian would "dig back into the archaeology of a life," he would be the "antiquarian of a personality," and this life would be my father's own, projected as an Everyman of the twentieth century.

Born at the beginning of the First World War, my father came into public life after the end of the Second. And just as the life of John Wickliff Shawnessy mirrored the convulsions of the nineteenth century, so Ross Lockridge, Jr. sees his own life now as mirroring the twentieth.

Its literal story beneath the allegory would be the very one that I have been telling in this biography.

It would begin with the death of his brother Bruce, out of which he now sees all the rest unfolding. In the last days of his life, my father was drawn inexorably back to that early death which prefigured his own. It would begin on the tranquil Avenue of Elms, Creighton Avenue in Fort Wayne, whose backdrop was the Great War. It is in this city that his brother Bruce drowns, that his house catches fire, that there is a great strike at the mill, that he falls in love with Alicia Carpenter, that he decides to become a writer, and that through "the brutality of fate" his personality is set by the age of ten.

The story would move along to Bloomington, where the young adolescent in a "corridor of young wishes" experiences close friendship, intense love, and the "drunken dreams of fame." Here the love of a young woman is fixed on him and, despite some passage of time when they are not together, this love is a constant in his life. The Cosmic Historian will portray the culture of Bloomington during the Twenties and Thirties, out of which the hero emerges. During these years the strongest presence in the hero's life has shifted from mother to father.

In Europe, wandering over "ancient parapets," the hero absorbs the waning vitality of the Old World in "brutal young affirmation," and back home, in the illness that lays him flat in 1935–36, he mirrors the sickness of the modern age, the dream of the flesh of iron, that is overtaking Europe and will spread to the world at large—in fascism, consumerism, and industrial assault on the "changing beautiful earth."

After the cataclysm of the World War the hero approaches public life with the spirit of affirmation intact, only to take a "plunge into notoriety." His challenge to the culture of Bloomington—a microcosm of American life—endangers him and seems to be exacting a sacrifice.

Such was the outline of his new novel. The more hopeless and powerless he felt, the more messianic he became in his imagery and rhetoric. The problem with this narrative was that it all pointed to his own sacrificial death. He was caught up in the same web of Fate that had killed his brother.

In actual composition, drafting only two episodes—the loss of Alicia Carpenter and the death of his brother—he didn't get his hero out of Fort Wayne. "His life began in a street of majestic elms. There were some earlier memories, it is true. He remembered how he walked on a high porch, and names that were to grow old in his life and gradually close him in with familiarity and at last with sadness [and finally with terror] moved about him clothed in their material substance."

The bracketed words he penciled out, as if to pencil out the terror itself—the shadowy forms of the old Lockridge family.

The "murmurous summery womb" of this avenue of elms had now become entombment in his own self. "None ever looked so long with such a silent, dangerous intentness at his own image." Thus the dangerous narcissism took hold that—in early 1948—he ruefully felt had governed his life from the beginning.

He could not see the generosity, only the egoism, of his own *Raintree County*.

This self-entombment was his fate—fate now defined as "man's inability to escape himself," and it was sinisterly at work, "weaving its patterns around the little brownshingled house."

As a boy he was strongly aware of his brother Bruce, handsome, laughing, blue-eyed like his mother. Then he confronted the tragic death. "The thing had already happened. It had happened in a time aloof from the time of the small boy who played in the yard, it had happened in a separate and eternal time that was in a sense the only time that ever was, it had happened, and the griefhoarse words could not take it back."

He could see in the years thereafter that his mother and father didn't weep over the grave. They felt there was a purpose in this death, that Bruce was somehow "living on" with them now. My father saw his own life in the story of this early death and its aftermath. Around his own life was webbed "the death of the boy in the womb of waters. . . . For if the world is to be saved, it shall be through sacrifice, through the giving of oneself. It shall be saved through death, through agony." In his mother's response to Bruce's death he sees a metaphor of resurrection, of eternal life. And he could see that his mother would not weep for him either.

Bruce had died for him. He speaks of the "blood-sacrifice, the death that waits, fate springing rampant from the accumulated years. . . . The story is of this death and its deep unconscious, symbolic, and philosophical meanings. For this one dead, another dedicated to eternal life."

In his suffering, my father's sense of identification with Bruce deepened—the vital brother whose death now seemed to have been destined so that he, Ross, might live more abundantly. He hadn't mourned him at the time—he was only five, and that death in late June, 1919, had interfered with the Fourth of July celebration. He had to beg Shockley to take him downtown to the fireworks. But he learned to mourn, as I too from the age of five learned to mourn my father.

In the logic of despair, he began to see his own death as a gesture that might renew the lives of those for whom his own life had become burdensome, people he loved and yet had harmed by his novel—his mother whose life he had exploited, his wife who had patiently worked with him all those years, and those beautiful children for whom he could do nothing. There was one thing still that he could do, one thing that would expunge all that was sullen and sinful in him and atone for the shame he had brought on his family.

And he felt resentment at the fate that had brought him to this end, and at family members, especially his parents, who now reminded him only of his dead enormous failure, and who stood along with all the other shades that hemmed him in—in terror. All those he loved had borne him to this early crucifixion at the age of thirty-three.

He thought of his brother, at peace and loved by all for his sacrifice, Bruce, the most affirmative person he had ever known. A family man, he longed to join him now. "Always after he had visited Lindenwood Cemetery and had followed the winding drives to the place where his brother was buried, the boy loved cemeteries. Nothing else seemed to him so quiet, lovely, peaceful, and so full of the meaning of human life as these places of death. An indefinable longing filled his heart when he stood in these places where the ground was full of stones with letters on them. Lindenwood Cemetery—beautiful Lindenwood."

XI

"Hail and Farewell
at the Crossing"

Bloomington, March 6, 1948–Spring, 1948

A great day for Bloomington despite the drizzle and cold, March 6, 1948, was Regionals day of the Indiana High School Basketball tournament. Coach John Brogneaux's Purple Panthers of BHS, having won their sectional games, had been drilling on the Martinsville hardwood earlier in the week. They would be facing Terre Haute Wiley there in the afternoon and hoped to advance to the finals in the evening.

In the morning my father worked on a tax return for my mother and had her make out a check for $544.22 to Internal Revenue. He went out to mail the return and buy the weekend groceries, and after lunch told his wife he'd take Ernest, sick as usual, and go listen to the Regionals out at his parents'. Lillian was a big sports fan, and she and her brother sometimes listened to the radio together. His mood had in no way improved in recent days, but he was able to carry on slowly the daily business of life—shopping, doing dishes, paying bills, cutting our hair, buying a bed for Terry Ross, a toy baby carriage for Jeanne, and a squirt gun for Ernest. It's a rare Hoosier who is not a fanatic about high school basketball, and my mother was cheered to hear of this plan.

Ross Senior that afternoon passed the old IU Library and chanced to look up at the carved inscription over the entrance. "A good book is the precious life-blood of a master spirit." He had a strange premonition. "That's the way it is with Scuffie," he thought.

Arriving home, he found him there, listening to the game. Things were going well for the Panthers. Watched over by troopers, a frenzied crowd of four thousand was on its feet much of the time as the Purple Five defeated Terre Haute, 44–42. They would face Solsberry in the finals that night.

Ross Senior and Elsie, inveterate optimists, had continued to see improvement in their son, which my mother—of a more realistic midwest family—didn't see at all. She was the only one with whom he could put down his guard and cease performing. Elsie discerned this afternoon, though, that not even basketball was lifting his spirits. "What's bothering you, Ross, can't you tell your mother?" she asked. She got him to laugh a little. He then, as I have learned, spoke words to her that are forever lost—words that hinted at his darkest inclination, words she didn't fully hear, words that would come to haunt her.

Ross Senior looked forward to seeing him again the following afternoon, when they would continue their important recitation work. His son was coming to the point where maybe he'd be able to accept some more speaking engagements. His old fraternity, Phi Gamma Delta, intended to firm up some plans with him on Sunday.

Late in the afternoon he told Ernest that it was time to go. Ernest protested but his father said he was tired and had things to do. Ernest did his best to obey him these days—this father who had become so solemn. His mother had told him, "Daddy's sick and we have to help him get well." Once she explained it in a strange way. "Daddy is a genius, honey, and things just hurt him easily."

They passed the old stone and metal sundial that had been at the Shockley house in Straughn. GROW OLD WITH ME, THE BEST IS YET TO BE. I RECORD ONLY THE SUNSHINE. The father's shoulders were stooped and he smiled and patted his son gently as they got into the Kaiser. Ernest felt closer to his father now than he had even that day on the huge sand dune in Manistee when he explained the facts of life.

When they got home, the Bloomington *World-Telephone* for March 6 had arrived. I think the tired author put it aside for the time being.

At five-thirty we settled into our evening meal—swiss steak, vegetables, milk, and dessert. Our quiet father ate well, with seemingly good appetite. Finished by six o'clock, he and our mother did the dishes, he played with us briefly and returned to his card table. Ernest had some fun pretending to shoot Mom and me with a small lead replica of the Empire State Building.

Our father wrote a letter to Jonathan Bingham, an associate of his lawyer, Martin Stone.

"Dear Bing, The final return for Vernice has been sent in to the Collector of Internal Revenue. For the purpose of estimated income tax you may confine your problem to myself, as Vernice is not currently performing any secretarial labors for me and may not again— enough to justify a salary, as her hands are full otherwise and when I resume writing seriously I may employ a secretary and relieve her of this burden. The validity of the large payments made her in the past is still maintainable, simply because she did the work. Considering her important share in the work and the fact that her compensation is made only once in terms of the large revenue from the book, I believe the government will accept our interpretation. Many thanks for your fine handling of these matters. As for my estimated income tax return, make it out on the sole basis of $20,000.00 certain to be paid from Houghton Mifflin. At the moment I do not anticipate other revenue and adjustments can be made later as necessary. Cordially, Ross."

When I resume writing seriously . . .

He then made out a check for $67.07 as payment of his life insurance premium and one for $1.90 for furnace filters. He carried over the balance of $4,332.61 to the next checkbook stub, for check number 36, never written.

He had before complained to Vernice of how fast their monies were going. He had begun on December 13, 1947, with a balance of $122,500, and he was now down to less than five grand. Of course they had a house to show for it, and Vernice now had more money in the bank than he, and more was on the way, but still it seemed a dispiriting depletion of the riches he had hoped would sustain a lifetime of writing. And now, whatever he had tonelessly said to Bing, he felt he had no more books in him anyway. He was depleted.

Having dealt with these matters, I think he then opened the evening *World-Telephone*. His novel hadn't been much mentioned in the local papers for a couple of weeks. But this edition contained a prominent editorial by editor and owner Blaine Bradfute, intended as a defense of *Raintree County*.

Few in Bloomington took *The New Yorker* and few had seen or heard of Hamilton Basso's pan in early January. Bradfute, though, decided Basso should be refuted, and to that end quoted a lengthy portion of the pan.

The novel is "the climax of all the swollen, pretentious human chronicles that also include a panorama of the Civil War, life in the corn-and-wheat belt, or whatnot. I don't know what started the trend. It may be the temper of the age, or it may simply be that publishers do better with thick books than with thin ones. At any rate, the crest has been reached." Bradfute quoted more Basso, ending with the critic's observation that "it contains, along with the smorgasbord already noted, a play-by-play account of a couple of Indiana Fourth of Julys, vast stretches of philosophical thought, three love affairs that involve haystacks, a considerable amount of swimming in the nude, a girl who has a mole, a girl who has a scar, and a girl who seems to be completely unblemished."

Bradfute's refutation was limited to pointing out that Basso hadn't read closely—the girl who seems unblemished actually has a torn earlobe. Indeed Lockridge knows lots about nineteenth-century earlobe piercing.

This would not have been the refutation my father hoped for. Meanwhile, there in the sight of all the hometown folk was the dread review once again, his book ridiculed in a famed eastern magazine by a prominent critic and fellow novelist.

Mom had thought she would just put us kids to bed, but then she remembered that Uncle Harold was going to take Ernest and me to Sunday School the next morning. I was bathed by her and then it was Ernest's turn to bathe alone. While he was in the bathroom, she found her husband sitting in Ernest's and my easy chair. I think I was in and out of the room as they conversed, doing my little boy things.

Her husband seemed worse, more depressed than ever. "Well, what shall we do, what am I going to do?" he asked. He wasn't any better, he said. He feared he was never going to get any better.

She tried to be encouraging and told him that they should just "carry on," one of his expressions, and he would get better. She reminded him of what he was still able to do—the shopping and chores and family business, for instance.

Her father always told her that the blues get you nowhere, but while saying all this, she knew she was herself discouraged—and feared she wasn't being upbeat enough.

I didn't register any of this. But I did hear him casually say, "I'm going out to mail some letters." He said he'd stop by his parents' house afterward and listen to the evening game.

My mother was standing at the front door as he walked out. "It was raining and I told him to come back and I had him put on his overshoes and he kind of smiled at me. And then he went on out the door, and right at the door I said, 'Why don't you come sleep with me tonight.' And he smiled again and he said, 'Well, maybe I will.' " And he left.

My mother was a little apprehensive. But this was a man who his entire life always did what he said he was going to do. *You could depend on what he was going to do.* She turned to her ironing. She hoped he would enjoy the evening game. She vowed she would discuss her husband with Naomi Dalton the following week to see if there were other medical options.

When Ernest and I bedded down, Ernest put the Empire State Building statue on the night stand between us so that he could clunk some old robbers if they broke into the house and tried to steal anything. And that night he dreamt he and his father were on a boat, drifting languidly down a river together. His father was telling him things and confiding in him, making him feel grown up.

Up in Martinsville, the Solsberry Hornets chilled the Regional title hopes of BHS early in the game, but with Bobby Dobson and Jim Dearring shoveling in the coal, the Panther Express jumped ahead, and took a commanding lead. The die was cast by half time, with BHS leading 22–14, and in the end they had swatted the Hornets, 60–35. It was a great night for the BHS Panthers, who would now advance to the state semifinals.

My mother continued with chores and sometime later turned on the radio to listen for the end of the game, which came around ten o'clock. She waited awhile, knowing her husband might chat with his folks for a few minutes afterward. They were night owls. Getting close to 11 p.m., when he still wasn't home, she called the Lockridges. Lillian answered, and my mother asked whether her husband had started home yet.

Lillian said he hadn't even been there that evening.

Alarmed, my mother told her to stay on the phone. She went to the back door and from the kitchen turned on the light over the side door to the garage. She hurried outside in the drizzle and approached the glass-paned side door. Halfway there, she heard a car engine running.

Upon opening the unlocked side door, she turned on the interior light, and in horror through the dense suffocating fumes saw her husband sitting upright in the back seat.

A vacuum cleaner hose was attached to the exhaust pipe and was funneled into the small left rear window. Her husband had stuffed a rag in and around this ventilator window.

She rushed in to turn off the ignition, threw open the large garage door, and pulled her husband out of the back seat. You get strength at certain times, she always said, and she pulled him by his shoulders through the garage door onto the loose crushed rock. "Ross! Ross!" But he didn't respond, he didn't seem to be living.

She screamed for help and some lights appeared in neighbor windows. But nobody came out. She ran back into the house, where an apprehensive Lillian was still on the phone. Ross was probably dead, hurry over, she cried. She then called the Bloomington Fire Department, which logged the call at 11:13.

"Can you do anything for carbon monoxide poisoning?" she asked frantically of fireman Noble Henderson, adding that her husband had tried to kill himself. Firemen Ray Collier and Paul Lentz were dispatched to the scene. Lentz was Vernice Baker's old neighbor on Lincoln Street, who always said of her to his wife, "There goes my girl!"

She ran back to her husband in the cold. He still wasn't breathing. In a family car, the Lockridges—Ross Senior, Elsie, and Lillian—beat the fire truck and the police, and they knelt over Scuffie, lying face up on the cold wet gravel. They decided to get him into the kitchen. The firemen and police arrived just as they were attempting to carry him from the driveway.

By this time Lillian had already removed the vacuum cleaner hose and the rag and had thrown them in the large trash can behind the garage.

Paul Lentz looked with surprise at my mother when they had carried the body into the kitchen. He asked, "Is that you, Bake?"

He and Collier set to work with an inhalator. My father's limbs had already begun to stiffen and it was difficult to maneuver the body into position. The lips were cherry red.

They worked the inhalator with my mother kneeling alongside. "Don't let him go, Paul!" she cried. Lentz and Collier were certain Ross Lockridge was already dead, but they kept at it. Dr. Robert Lyons, Monroe County coroner, arrived shortly after 11:30, pronounced him dead, probably as of 9:30, and asked the firemen to step away from the body.

But my mother refused to let them stop. "Please, please, keep on working!" Lentz and Collier soon exhausted themselves, so the police radioed back and two more firemen arrived and labored for a time. The efforts to revive him lasted one hour and ten minutes. Finally, Collier and Lentz led my mother into the living room and told her that her husband had died. She collapsed in shock as they tried to console her.

Meanwhile, the neighborhood was lit up with fire trucks and police cars. The word had got out, and reporters were everywhere. Neighbors were gathering around and passing the news, "He killed himself!" We children slept soundly through it all.

Lillian had had considerable work with the police at the Woman's Prison in Indianapolis and, speaking to reporters in her grief, tried to carry off her desperate little cover-up. Ross Senior backed her up. As she would later tell the FBI, she did it to protect the children and the feelings of Vernice. The police asked my mother if she had had a fight with her husband. "Oh no!" she said.

The official story—in various mangled versions—was that Ross Lockridge, Jr. had been found in the *front* seat, the garage lights on, with the driver's door ajar and his left leg protruding. Thus, he might simply have lost consciousness or bumped his head while exiting. The speculation began that he was listening to the Regionals on the car radio and forgot to turn off the ignition. The problem with this theory was that my father economized on extras in his Kaiser. There was no radio.

With reporters apparently talking to reporters and know-nothing neighbors, a few sensational elements were added: the doors had been locked and heroic efforts by neighbors and Ross Lockridge Senior were enlisted to break into the garage—though glass panes to the side door oddly hadn't been broken. I think my father didn't lock the doors to garage or car because he knew his wife would then have to break the window panes. He went about the task efficiently in the dark. He had once remarked to Malcolm that carbon monoxide seemed like a quick and painless way to die.

A car engine in that garage cannot be heard from the house. This was no cry for help. But I don't think he made up his mind to do it until late the evening of March 6. There was no rise in spirits during his last days, something commonly observed in people who have already decided on suicide.

When his friend Vincent Hippensteel died back in 1934, he had speculated that it was a suicide disguised as an accident to spare his mother's feelings. His own body language in death was now unambiguous—he meant the suicide to be known to his mother and everyone else for what it was.

As all coroners know, family cover-ups are routine when suicides occur within the home. In most states, including Indiana, such cover-ups aren't prosecuted—a rare gesture of legal compassion. That evening, after the body had been removed and the Kaiser towed, Dr. Lyons sat with the family in the living room and told them it all pointed to suicide. He would conduct an autopsy, though, to check for a heart attack or stroke. The family kept mum about the hose and back-seat position of the body, hoping he would somehow render an accidental-death verdict.

Autopsy "reveals slender white male." The "odor of exhaled air when chest was compressed was unusual and suffocating." "Skull—meninges normal, slight increased spinal fluid, cerebral tissue unusually friable; cerebellum seemed more normal in consistency. On section of cerebral hemispheres, no evidence of brain tumor found." Everything else was normal, except that the blood was "cherry red and did not coagulate." "Verdict, suicide by asphyxiation by carbon monoxide gas."

So had my father's genius been enmeshed in that friable cerebral tissue? The coroner, not a trained pathologist by today's standards, seems to have suspected organic brain disease. "Friable" is sometimes used in describing carcinomatous tissue. But he then ruled that out.

In the modest zip-around billfold on his person that night were two photos of his wife, including the one taken just before their marriage, one of us kids with our tricycles and scooter, and one of himself smiling. And there was Naomi Dalton's unfilled prescription for Veronal.

My mother searched around the house for a note. She didn't really expect one—"he knew I would understand." He felt he would never get well, he had lost all hope, he would expect her now to carry on. But next to his typewriter there were some papers in a manila folder, the writings on his new autobiographical novel, with the episode of the death of Bruce. And on the very top there was a typed statement.

On the back of it, he had crossed out another half-hearted defense of his novel. "The question of technique is an involved one. Most readers, plunging headlong into RC, get promptly lost and emerge, as many reviewers did, with the belief that it is a completely amorphous book. Well, I don't deny that it is difficult to read and that it may be technically very faulty—but I do demur a little at the suggest [sic] that it is amorphous or patternless. If it is confusion, it is planned confusion."

Always frugal with paper, he had typed his final statement, his "Ultimate Philosophy," in rough draft on the other side.

"Let no one blame another one. A man is an accumulation of many men, of all mankind quartered in a now, inescapable, unasked for, absolute, ultimate. Good and bad are human discoveries. The universe is neither good nor bad. It does not care about the individual human being. It is he who learns care and who is taught good and bad from infancy. There is nothing that we are that is not taught us by our bodies, by events, by other men. God is man's desire that good have an absolute guarantee. Once man became aware of death, learned anticipation, acquired knowledge, God became necessary as the guarantor of good, as the promise that made human life possible and tolerable. And thus there are good people, though whether they are good for reasons other than the compulsions of their experience or not, remains unanswerable. As for the evil, as for those who lose their grasp on the stuff of life, who become unable to cope with their world, are they to blame or are they not also the victims of long circumstance?

"As for the miracle of being—it is of course a miracle, but it is not necessarily a good miracle. Some lives are fortunate, and some which seem fortunate become involved in agony, and who shall say whether this is through their own fault or not? Just as poets are born so, the brave are born so, and the cowardly are born so. That is, they are born to their fate. No one blames the child of less than ten for the errors of his personality, but link by link he is bound to the grown man."

"Not necessarily a good miracle." With this sad paradox, the Hero of Raintree County asked for forgiveness, locked as we all are in a universe governed by a Fate that is indifferent to human need and desert. He was ten years old when he left Fort Wayne, the errors of his personality already confirmed, he tells us, and his life essentially over. Likewise, his "Perfessor" had been ten upon the death of his mother: "In that death, Jerusalem Webster Stiles knew the secret of life—which is death—and never after added to his wisdom though he added to his words."

Compelled by forces within and without, the Hero of Raintree County had fallen into cowardice, agony, and evil—evil without culpability. He absolves of blame all those who have impinged upon him, making him what he is.

The note may or may not have been written that day. It was perhaps a contingency draft, written not long after his "Sketch for a book of Philosophy," just as he had probably made contingency plans with that vacuum cleaner hose. It was an old one, probably the same he had used years earlier out on High Street for asphyxiating moles.

My mother had asked him to sleep with her that night. She didn't bed down alone. Her mother-in-law joined her in the upstairs bedroom. It was the indifference of Fate that sleep visited neither one.

~

"Today is a mournful day. My father has died and left us," wrote nine-year-old Ernest in his diary on March 7. And the next day, "I have cut my diary on account of my father's death." His final "memorandum": "I shal never forget the good times I had with my father. I think he was the best man alive. He will b put in history. He taught me about all the things I have learned but he is still with us. I loved him very much so u see that it is a sad day."

Our father's friends were mostly astonished at the news, which came simultaneously with the *Herald Tribune*'s announcement that *Raintree County* was now the number one national best-seller. Many heard of his death Sunday on Walter Winchell and other radio news programs. In Morocco, Curt Lamorey got word from fellow Delaware Group member Ed Mitchell. Curt thought it *inconceivable!*— this laughing, affirmative, capable person the least likely in the world to kill himself. In Phoenix, John McGreevey was outside on a stepladder when a novelist friend drove up and asked him if he'd heard the news. "No, I've been cutting oleanders." "Well, you'd better come down from that ladder." Marion Monico sent a telegram: "DEAR VERNICE THROUGH TEARS MY HEART GOES OUT TO YOU." In Chicago, Malcolm Correll got word from his mother—"Well I hate to say it but he took his own life." What seemed incomprehensible to Malcolm and others was that this ardent sports fan would kill himself before finding out if BHS had won the Regionals.

Jack Stiles, would-be novelist, remembered they had discussed Virginia Woolf up in Manistee only months earlier, and Ross Lockridge had said he found suicide inconceivable for himself.

Mary Jane Ward and Ed were dropped in on unexpectedly by friends who thought the Quayles could use a drink. "We came as soon as we could, as soon as we heard the terrible news, we're so sorry about it, oh, dear, didn't you hear it on the radio?" "Hear what?" "That your cousin committed suicide!" "What cousin?" And Mary Jane added nervously, "Well, if you mean you actually heard that about *Ross,* I know it's wrong. That station's always making mistakes." She stared at the drink in her hand while Ed called Vernice.

Many felt inappropriate guilt—Josephine Piercy because she worried that her dinner invitation might have felt like an additional pressure, Larry Wylie because he thought that if he had only been there he might have helped his friend, and Jeff Wylie because he had told Ross that the very imperfections of his novel gave promise of even greater work in the future. Now there was to be no future work.

And Don Smalley regretted having made that Lazarus analogy.

"What I wanted to say to him, but couldn't because it would sound so patronizing," he wrote his wife on March 8, "was that he showed such great promise for the future, that he was inevitably in a period of depression, like Sheridan, who was said to be afraid of the man who wrote *The Rivals* and *The School for Scandal*. And now no words can help, and I am so very very sorry I said anything derogatory of his book, though what I said could probably not have made an iota of difference one way or the other. Sorry, sorry, sorry, sorry—sorry for the hurt lad, the gallant, optimistic boy who poured out his soul in public and got it walked on by people. . . . The prize was to the swiftest, but the prize cup was filled with hemlock. . . . I guess all I have said is that Ross is dead and I am very very sorry that it is so."

And some felt resentment, because Lockridge in killing himself had killed something of them too.

The question has always been "Why did he do it?" With my father as with other suicides, I think the more appropriate initial question is "How did it happen?" For someone in a state of abject despair, the compulsion to die can be overwhelming. I don't believe any ordinary criteria of blame apply. But in the end it was still an act. He was not killed by others, he killed himself.

"MOURN DEATH OF YOUNG AUTHOR." "Death came into our community Saturday night and tapped a young man of genius, Ross Lockridge, Jr., on the shoulder—and this earthly end of a brilliant individual was made doubly sad as death was self-summoned," editorialized *The World-Telephone*. My father's age at death made the Jesus analogy a commonplace. "As young Jesus of Nazareth died to make good the words of his teachings, young Ross Lockridge died in a modern 1948 manner to make present-day readers believe in his purpose in writing *Raintree County*."

Reverend McFall of the First Methodist Church came to our house to plan the funeral. My mother remembered how her husband had responded so deeply to "Rock of Ages" over the radio, and she wanted that. McFall started to say the words, and she broke down, knowing she'd never make it through the ceremony if they sang it.

Flags were at half mast throughout Bloomington on March 9, and in the vestibule at the First Methodist Church my father lay in an open cherry casket before the two-thirty ceremony began. Malcolm Correll walked in and paused, reluctant to look at the corpse for fear

450

that would forever usurp the living image of his beloved friend. A mutual acquaintance saw him standing at the far end and pulled him vigorously over to the coffin, saying, "Sure looks different, doesn't he?" Malcolm saw how his friend had aged in the few months since they had seen one another, and for the first time he noticed Ross's hair was thinning.

Vernice Baker Lockridge stood with an overflow crowd in the church where seventeen years earlier she had first met Ross Lockridge. She and Ross Senior and Elsie maintained a proud composure during the service that followed. Reverend McFall quoted from a letter the son had written his father early in his depression: "During this time . . . I have reminded myself of the grand old truth, 'Whom the Lord loveth, he chasteneth.' And I have vast comfort and strength from a direct reliance on the Scriptures and the great symbolical truths everywhere expressed in the Old and New Testaments. When our own strength deserts us, there is a greater strength." Lockridge was the young idealist John Wickliff Shawnessy.

My mother would always be grateful for the words of Bloomington's wisest person, William Lowe Bryan, IU's president emeritus, who way back in 1913 had encouraged Ross Senior to embark on a career in public speaking. These words came closer than any ever have to the heart of the tragedy that had taken place before her astonished eyes.

He wasn't reconciled, he said, to the loss of this brilliant young jewel of the University. "The book, I think, consumed him. Like Walt Whitman, he wrote with a vast emotion, a great laughter. He renounced technical art forms. It burst forth from him, this book, like Emerson's 'Volcano's Tongue of Flame.' This thing, so filled with a great emotion, was written with an impassioned mind through a long time. It was written with a passion that burns up a man. I think that was it. It resulted in a deadening of the emotions—I would I could say that better. There's an exhaustion of whatever it is that is the mother of emotion, so that the ordinary impulses of youth, of joy and satisfaction, are dead for a time."

The very mother of emotion was exhausted—Ross had said such words himself, she remembered.

Afterward the funeral procession made its way up to Rose Hill Cemetery, where two thousand people witnessed the graveside ceremony. Ross Lockridge, Jr. was to be buried next to Hugh Baker. It was sunny, with a powder blue sky, and there were the first signs of spring as the grass was beginning to green on the slopes. "In the high March afternoon," wrote a reporter, "the body of the poet was given to the earth. There was silence for the final prayer. Below the cemetery hill came the muffled sound of the town, where the court house flag flew at half mast and black crepe was draped about the poet's book in the bookstore window on the square."

There was some acrimony. Ross Senior and Elsie both blamed Robert Peters—the hospital stay had worsened their son, they thought. Uncle Bob and Aunt Marie, for their part, blamed Elsie and her Christian Science, and felt snubbed at the funeral. And there was denial on the part of many that it had even been a suicide. Uncle Bob called the inquest a travesty. Mary Jane Ward too was never told of my father's unambiguous thoroughness in self-murder, and for the rest of her life maintained it was an accident—her cousin was always careless about turning off the car engine. Bennett Cerf almost ran a column on the possibility that it was an accident.

To Shockley Lockridge, whose stories had inspired his brother's writing career at the age of seven, this second loss of a brother deepened his emotional reserve and quiet. He, like Ross, had undergone a terrible illness—alcoholism. But unlike Ross he had survived and flourished. His brother's death baffled him. It was like "the riddle of the Sphinx," he thought. He hadn't guessed how deep the depression was. Probably his brother had thought "he might become a burden to the family. In the arcane confusion of a sick mind flashed a noble impulse: to subdue this final indignity to himself and his loved ones by taking arms against a sea of troubles and by opposing end them." Of his father, Shockley wrote that "in Ross Jr.'s achievement he had a realization of all his own aspirations. Now he has only memories."

My father was right. His mother never wept for him. To her he was always with her, living on. But to the day she died, she felt remorse for not fully hearing what her son Ross seemed to intimate that Saturday afternoon, just as she had reproached herself for failing to tell Bruce to take a rope to the river. When, years later, she confessed her great error to her homecare nurse, she asked the nurse never to tell another soul what her son had said that day. To my torment, the nurse has kept the promise before the eye of God, never telling her own husband, let alone me.

And my father was right about his wife, who had strengths many hadn't fathomed—he knew she'd raise the kids and take comfort in them. Like his grandmother Emma Shockley, she would find spiritual sustenance in her widowhood. And proceeds from the novel supported the family for two decades.

What he imagined would come of his children I do not know. Perhaps he thought his wife would find a more suitable father for them.

Back at the Lockridge home on High Street that afternoon, the family talked about the tragedy. During the service that he wasn't allowed to attend, Ernest had been cutting rings around young trees with his jackknife. Ross Senior told Uncle Frank Shockley that after having been "driven by an impelling force to write," his son confronted "a complete blank—felt he might live to be 70 and never do anything further with his life."

The tired historian led some reporters down into the old south field, where the stone-ringed fireplace was filled with ashes. He stood at the edge in his crumpled baggy suit and looked down. "We started having bonfires here about 24 years ago," he said. It was on this spot that he and his son rehearsed their speeches, where Scuffie was Patrick Henry. It was on this spot that so much of what went into the novel came into being. He recalled too the bonfires on the Eel River, and the Winchester rifle he'd given Scuffie at age twelve. "We scarred up plenty of trees playing Daniel Boone in those days." He turned away from the stone circle. "I think his work was done. His reward came quickly. His wife and children will be well provided for. I think his work will endure."

It was on this spot that my grandfather tried to evoke the spirit of his dead son, the strong voice subdued now, for there was no life in those ashes, no echo from the cold stones.

～

Houghton Mifflin sent two midwest representatives to the funeral, whom my mother did not receive warmly. These two were the first people she'd ever met from the company—the others were simply names from a legendary cast in which her husband had seemed to play for a time the leading role. They had seen photographs of her and he often spoke to them of her. This was Nell.

On March 12, she wrote in longhand, "Dear Mr. Brooks, I want to thank you and Ross's other Houghton Mifflin friends for your kind expressions of sympathy. . . . The long years of intense work, the terrific pressures of the past year, and finally the intolerable delay in publication were more than Ross could stand . . . Perhaps I should not write such a letter, but somehow I feel impelled to do so. I feel that if I speak now perhaps another such tragedy might be avoided. Of course, I realize that it may be a long time before there is another man with Ross's spirit and ability, but if such another one should appear, everything should be done to preserve him.

"I feel no bitterness in my heart, nor any regret, because, as Ross kept saying, everyone did what he considered right and what he felt had to be done. No one could anticipate—least of all Ross—what would happen.

"Ross died as a result of overwork, but he suffered much from what he called the Sickness of this Age—materialism—which he had so hoped to counteract in some small measure by giving *Raintree County* to the world.

"I feel no bitterness nor regret—only a profound sense of loss and loneliness which is made tolerable only by the memory of Ross's own very real faith in God and the eternity of a man's soul.

"Strangely enough, I found Ross's typewriter broken this morning. It lasted just long enough for me to compose the report of his death. It almost seems that it was meant to last just long enough for Ross's work to be done."

If such another one should appear, everything should be done to preserve him . . . The quiet chastisement in this letter was far exceeded elsewhere. Years later Paul Brooks wrote of how some critics thought *Raintree County* would have been a better novel if Lockridge had been forced to do some cutting. "On the other hand *The Writer* magazine, following his suicide, published an open letter: 'Dear Mr. Brooks: You have killed your author'—by making him cut his manuscript. Sometimes you can't win."

"As for what people say here," Don Smalley wrote his wife on

March 13, "They have begun to blame the Lockridge family, mother and father, and say that they are queer people, too."

My mother was contending with mail. One was a hate letter to her husband that arrived shortly after his death, and she wrote to reassure the woman that he hadn't seen it and she need not fret that she had caused his death. Another was a letter to her from the Christian Science practitioner Myrtle Ayres, who thought her husband's death could not have been suicide. "I do not accept the verdict given about your little boy. There was never any indication that he was having that sort of argument at all. . . . I hope you will feel that Science can mean something to you, because he was free to express to me that it was the thing he wanted and I feel sure he would have wanted his children to have the Christian Science Sunday school. So, maybe you can see your way to go on with your study alone and help the children to have what he felt he wanted to give them." My mother says her reply was unprintable.

But she was also deluged with sympathy letters and couldn't bring herself to answer more than a fraction. Her mainstay in a bleak period was her witty, practical sister, Clona Nicholson. Late in her life, Clona suggested I write the story of Ross and Vernice. It would be a love story, she said. When she was on her deathbed in 1988, I promised her I would.

One day Ross Junior said to his wife, "You have a talent for love." She laughed at first. "Do you mean physical love?" she asked. "No, I don't mean that," he said.

"We had good years," she would tell me. "I was happy. I felt a part of what he was doing."

Raintree County marched on without its author, leading most bestseller lists through April and May of 1948 before falling away. Its bizarre postpublication history continued with its nationally publicized seizure and empoundment, beginning on March 20, by the Philadelphia vice squad, led by one Craig Ellis. Five booksellers were arrested. The vice squad was following the lead of Fordham's Reverend Barrett. Lockridge's suicide seemed to many a manifestation of God's taste in literature, vindicating those who denounced the novel as obscene and blasphemous.

Delegations of priests and ministers lined up in Federal District Court in eastern Pennsylvania to denounce the novel as "lewd, obscene, licentious, filthy and indecent." Houghton Mifflin fought the seizure handily, arguing that priestly celibates lack the credentials to judge in matters of sex.

Only two weeks before Houghton Mifflin prevailed in court, on October 31, 1950, vice-squad chief Craig Ellis put a bullet through his brain, leaving a suicide note. "I have failed as a leader. My wife did not know of my laxity. I suppose my pain has made me mad. I pray God will help any I may have caused regret."

Nanette Kutner returned to Bloomington following Ross Lockridge's death to interview my mother and grandparents for *Saturday Review*. "Escape from Main Street" appeared in June of 1948. In it she blamed the restrictive Indiana environment for the suicide. He should have gotten out of town. "No matter where he went, he should never have lugged Bloomington along." She thought of Thomas Wolfe's cry, "Don't let them get you!" "They 'got' Ross Lockridge, Jr., because he was a sweet person, lacking ruthlessness, the prerogative of genius."

The Pulitzer Prize for fiction in 1948, for which my father would have traded in a dozen MGM Awards, went to James Gould Cozzens's *Guard of Honor*.

If the fertilizer he spread on the lawn that winter grew more weeds than grass, there were happier reminders of the great heart that had dreamt on the banks of the Eel River. We planted a small fragile raintree close to the garage and would always maintain a proprietary attitude toward raintrees wherever they spring forth, with their golden blossoms and comforting shade. I watch the raintrees in New York's Washington Square Park survive season after season, raining their blossoms down on many junkies and some students.

In June of 1948, New Harmony once again put on the pageant that my father had tossed off in the spring of 1937 to raise some cash for his upcoming marriage. The festivities began with a street dance in the shower of the Golden Raintree, seven hundred of which blossomed then in the small town. Five thousand people made the pilgrimage, and the pageant was dedicated that year to its own author. A tribute was read. "This pageant was one of the first revelations of his literary skill and artistry. He gave national prominence to our beautiful tree by naming his distinguished novel after it. Our performance is a memorial honoring his genius . . ." The performance ended in the Dance of the Tree of Golden Rain, with hamadryads in green, yellow, red, and brown depicting the seasonal cycle of the famous tree. My sister was a Flower Bearer and danced with a tall dark Rappite man. Ernest stood on a branch of a raintree dedicated to his father, with his mother looking on. They were both smiling.

Amidst its legacy of death, Ross Lockridge, Jr.'s novel remains the record of human festivity, of the strongest impression of life. I imagine my father's spirit approaching his own tombstone, as his hero John Wickliff Shawnessy did in *Raintree County.* "He took hold of the top of his tombstone and tugged on it. It was firm as if it had taken root. He gritted his teeth and pushed and pulled. The stone wanted to stay there. With a great effort he tore it loose from the earth and pushed it over. It fell flat, curiously solid and inert, the words staring up. In a fury of effort, he picked it up and carried it to the brow of the hill and rolled it down."

We all wish he could have toppled that tombstone at the last minute, that he could have held on until spring and summer, when the raintrees would have been once again in bloom. Other books would have come. And probably other children as well. He couldn't have known it then, but the depression would have lifted. His argument about fate was unanswerable—after the fact.

"Authors survive in their books," said one editorial following his death. In current critical thinking, this is extremely naïve. You can't find an author in a book anymore. But I continue to look for my father there, and think that those old metaphors about authors pouring themselves into books or writing their hearts out sometimes hit home. He saw himself as the pleasant photographer "who did not seem at all disturbed by the confusion in which he worked," and who "prepared to trace with a radiant pencil a legend of light and shadow, some faces on the great Road of the Republic." In the end he was disturbed indeed, having lost his grasp on the stuff of life.

But he grasped it hard while he wrote, and like any writer he lives again by virtue of the human sympathies aroused in readers whenever the old book is dusted off. "So he would plant again and yet again the legend of Raintree County, the story of a man's days on the breast of the land. So he would plant great farms where the angular reapers walk all day, whole prairies of grass and wheat rising in waves on the headlands. So he would plant the blond corn in the valleys of Raintree County. Yes, he would plant once more the little towns, Waycrosses and Danwebsters, and the National Roads to far horizons, passing to blue days and westward adventures, and progress, the cry of a whistle, arcs of the highflung bridges, and rails and the thundering trains. Hail and farewell at the crossing!"

Notes
and
Acknowledgments

Chapter I.
Epilogue: Bloomington, Indiana, 1948–1993

This chapter is largely based on my memory and on that of my mother, Vernice Lockridge Noyes, and my siblings Jeanne, Ross III, and Ernest. Without their own devotion to it from the beginning, *Shade of the Raintree* could never have been written. They were close readers of each draft as well as characters in its pages. The book was written with their tears and love and hope.

Pablo Neruda mentions Ross Lockridge in the poem "I Wish the Wood-cutter Would Wake Up" ("Que despierte el leñador"), translated by Robert Bly, in *Neruda and Vallejo: Selected Poems* (Beacon Press, 1971).

Excerpts from the 1974 letter of James A. Michener to John Leggett are reprinted by permission of James A. Michener. John Leggett graciously encouraged me to make use of his papers accumulated during the writing of *Ross and Tom*, all of which are in the University of Iowa Special Collections. He was given access to whatever materials in the family files he wished to see, including the writings of my father's illness, but my mother declined to discuss her husband's final day. Wallace Stegner's letter to the editor concerning *Ross and Tom* appeared in *The New York Times Book Review*, September 29, 1974. Whatever my disagreements with John Leggett's portrait, I wish to acknowledge his contribution warmly.

Edward Dmytryk's comments are found in *It's a Hell of a Life but Not a Bad Living* (Times Books, 1978). He was interviewed by Elwy Yost of TV Ontario, an admirer of *Raintree County*, who recommended that Dmytryk sometime read the novel his film had been based on. Some material concerning Montgomery Clift comes from Robert LaGuardia's *Monty* (Arbor House, 1977) and Patricia Bosworth's *Montgomery Clift* (Harcourt Brace Jovanovich, 1978). Generous with her time and expertise, Stacey Behlmer of the Margaret Herrick Library, Academy Foundation, provided me with a large amount of archival material dealing with the MGM production. I am also much indebted to

Stephen V. Russell, who has the world's largest private collection of *Raintree County* film memorabilia, and to James Tamulis, another formidable collector.

Ross Lockridge Senior's letter to Herbert Heimlich after the death of his son is quoted by permission of the Indiana Historical Society. I am grateful to Helen Augspurger for making available her correspondence with Ross Lockridge, Sr. after 1948, which is now in the Indiana State Library. The unsigned newspaper article on whether the Lockridge children would follow in their father's footsteps appeared in the New Castle *Courier-Times,* September 3, 1957. Other materials, including Elsie Lockridge's Tommy and Zippy stories, remain in the family archive.

For those interested in the impact of suicide on survivors, a good place to begin is *Suicide and Its Aftermath: Understanding and Counseling the Survivors,* edited by Edward Dunne, John McIntosh, and Karen Dunne-Maxim (W. W. Norton, 1987).

Biographers and critics alluded to or cited include John Leggett, *Ross and Tom: Two American Tragedies* (Simon & Schuster, 1974); James Baldwin, "The American Myth," *New Leader* (10 April 1948); Joseph Blotner, "*Raintree County* Revisited," *Western Humanities Review,* 10 (1955–56); Fred Erisman, "*Raintree County* and the Power of Place," *Markham Review,* 8 (1979); Donald Greiner, "Ross Lockridge and the Tragedy of *Raintree County,*" *Critique,* 20 (1978); Howard Mumford Jones, "Indiana Reflection of U.S. 1844–92," *Saturday Review of Literature,* 31 (12 June 1948); Joel M. Jones, "The Presence of the Past in the Heartland: *Raintree County* Revisited," *MidAmerica,* 1976; Nanette Kutner, "Ross Lockridge: Escape from Main Street," *Saturday Review of Literature,* 31 (12 June 1948); Charles Lee, "Encompassing the American Spirit," *New York Times Book Review,* 4 January 1948; Darshan Singh Maini, "An Ode to America: A Reconsideration of *Raintree County,*" in *Essays in American Studies,* ed. Isaac Sequeira (U.S. Educational Foundation in India, 1992); William York Tindall, "Many-leveled Fiction: Virginia Woolf to Ross Lockridge," *College English,* 10 (November 1948).

Chapter II.
"Avenue of Elms": Fort Wayne Days, 1914–1924

Quotations from Ross Lockridge, Jr. on his Fort Wayne experience are taken from post–*Raintree County* writings of early 1948. As yet I've not been able to trace an "Alicia Carpenter"—if she reads this I hope she'll get in touch—but find mentioned in *The Miner Reporter* an "Evelyn Carpenter." My father slightly changed some other names in these late writings. Other sources include "Some Biographical Facts About the Author of *Raintree County*" (1947) and notebook entries of 1935–36. *The Demon with the Fiery Tongue* is obviously a farrago of traditional fairy tales. My grandfather used to tell me similar ones and Shockley's lost fairy tales probably influenced it. The "fiery tongue" may come directly from "The Fall of the House of Usher," while the name "Cherry" comes from *Pinocchio*, given him by his uncle Ernest Shockley for Christmas, 1922. His early engagement with cinema and music is narrated in a college essay of 1935, "A Discussion of Ten Musical Compositions and Their Composers." I had assumed Shockley Lockridge tossed his own stories written as a college freshman, but was pleased to find them in the family's Fort Wayne archive. All of the above are now in the family archive in Bloomington.

For assistance with Ross Lockridge Senior's papers I am grateful to Bruce Harrah-Conforts and Melissa Carey of the Indiana University Archives, Noraleen Young of the Indiana State Library, Lisa Lussier of the Indiana Historical Society, and Rosemary Alsop of the New Harmony Workingmen's Institute. Some papers remain in the family archive. His biography *Theodore Thieme: A Man and His Times* (1942), commissioned by his boss at the Wayne Knitting Mills long after he left the company, fills out the Fort Wayne setting and narrates the strike. For vivid recollections of Ross Lockridge Senior, I am indebted to Mildred Neff, Herman B Wells, John Purman Banta, Harry Davidson, Richard M. Davis, Doris H. Devine, Nina Reifsnyder, Alice Fleener Smith, Glen Ludlow, David Repp, and many others. His father Brenton Webster Lockridge's eight surviving farm ledgers are in the family archive, as are Robert Bruce Lockridge's letters of 1902–3.

Elsie Shockley Lockridge's Oklahoma short story and "The Sayings and Doings of Our Two Sons, Bruce and Shockley" are in the family archive, as are the love letters of John Wesley Shockley and Emma Rhoton (1875–77), and other Shockley materials mentioned. Elsie Lockridge discusses her son's early decision to become a writer in her 1949 talk, "Henry County Real Life Background of *Raintree County*."

My father borrowed quite literally from his mother's life for the Eva portions of *Raintree County,* from which I've quoted in describing her girlhood. *The Narcissus,* Peru High School yearbook, 1900–5, is in the Peru Public Library; I am grateful to Charles Wagner, Director, for photocopies. *The Cauldron,* Fort Wayne High School yearbook, is in the Allen County Public Library of Fort Wayne; the 1919 edition contains Robert Bruce Lockridge's only known surviving essay, "At the Y.M.C.A. Conference." The Allen County–Fort Wayne Historical Society has *The Miner Reporter,* two photographs of Ross Junior in the Peltier historical pageant, Elva Gaskill's "A History of the Miner School" (1952), and Minutes of the Historical Society's early meetings with Ross Lockridge Senior in attendance.

Ella Geake narrated the episode concerning her to my father in a congratulatory letter of January 27, 1948. Mary Jane Ward's portrait of the Lockridge household and Shockley Lockridge's account of the Montessori apparatus are contained in letters of 1968 and 1969 to John Leggett, in the University of

Iowa Special Collections. The deaths of the two Robert Bruce Lockridges are narrated in detail in contemporary local newspapers and elsewhere.

For genealogical information, I would like to thank Lloyd D. Laughridge, Oscar Lochridge, and other staff members of *The Lock-On,* the enterprising newsletter of the Lockridge family (with variant spellings). Catherine Lippert has also been very helpful.

The judgment that closes out this chapter—that there was probably something disconnected in Elsie Lockridge's early nurturing of her youngest son—was confirmed independently by Dr. Kenneth Lewes, clinical psychologist, by Herbert Hendin, M.D., Executive Director of the American Suicide Foundation, and by Roslyn K. Pulitzer, A.C.S.W., psychotherapist. Details of their analysis are given in Chapter X.

Taped interviews with John Crane, George Crane (who wrote of the death of the younger Bruce Lockridge in one of his nationally syndicated columns decades later), Mildred Crane Palmer, Lillian Bradway Henley, the late Marie Lockridge Peters, Robert Masters, Kay Lockridge, Anne Lockridge Sales, my siblings, and my mother helped fill out the contexts of this chapter.

Chapter III.
"Legends in a Class-Day Album":
Early Bloomington Days, 1924–1933

Naomi Dalton, Louise Moore Strain, Dorothy Smith McCrea, and F. H. Latimer have described student life at Finley School in letters and interviews.

In a series of letters to me and a taped interview conducted over many days, the late Malcolm Correll, Emeritus Professor of Physics at the University of Colorado, Boulder, provided a good portion of the information and episodes involving my father in boy scouts, high school, and his early college years. This chapter and later ones owe much to his warm and precise recall of his friend.

Edwin Fulwider, Louise Wylie Campbell, the late Ben Siebenthal, Carl Martz, Becky Brown Martz, the late Lillian Setser Burnett, the late Jean Fox, Nota Scholl McGreevey, Donald Binkley, Morris Binkley, Alice Lloyd Binkley, Virginia Barnard Deupree, the late Joseph Deupree, Georgia Adams Coppock, Elloise Kunz Hiatt, Majora Kunz Gondring, Norma Kunz Waller, Mary Murphy Taylor, Mary Blankenship Baker, Peggy Woodburn Crowder, Verlin ("Bud") Miller, Ruth Bradt Wilson, Joseph D. Coppock, John B. Thomas, Jr., and Vernice Lockridge Noyes filled out these years. My friend Walton Francis provided access to the papers of his deceased mother, Peggy Bittner Francis.

I talked my reluctant mother into handing over her line-a-day diary for 1930–33, as well as her personal correspondence with my father, to be excerpted later. The diary has room for only one or two sentences per day; a few longer entries are found at the back. Her Memory Book (full of playbills, the

Girls' Council Code, banquet menus, and so on), Hugh Baker's diary, Ross Lockridge's unpublished high school stories, his high school journal, copies of *The Reflector,* "The Tributaries," and the immortal classroom note passed back and forth between Malcolm Correll and Georgia Adams are in the family archive.

My father's descriptions of Bloomington are found in the fragmentary discarded novel *American Lives,* scattered throughout the *Raintree County* manuscript at the Lilly Library of Indiana University. I am grateful to Saundra Taylor, Curator of Manuscripts, and to William R. Cagle, Lilly Librarian, who has been developing the Ross Lockridge, Jr. Collection at the Library. My father's description of his wrestling career is contained in a letter to the Bloomington *Evening World* (July 5, 1940). The dialogue concerning shorthand between Ross Junior and Senior is taken from his "Biographical Facts" of 1947, in the Houghton Library, Harvard University. Pam Service located BHS and other materials for me at the Monroe County Historical Society Museum.

My father had only the second-highest grade point average in his high school class; fellow Four Musketeerer Don Binkley nosed him out. Marsha Fritch of Monroe County Community School Corporation recovered my father's academic records.

My portrayal of the African-American experience in Bloomington was influenced by longtime resident and family acquaintance Ruth Anderson Carter and by Frances Gilliam's *A Time to Speak: A Brief History of the Afro-Americans of Bloomington, Indiana, 1865–1965.*

For my father's early college experiences, I am indebted to Laurence Wylie, Emeritus C. Douglas Dillon Professor of the Civilization of France, Harvard University, for an extended taped interview.

Edith Brown Siebenthal and Mary Eloise Humphreys Dillin very kindly gave me access to my father's letters to them. He was so oblique in his courtship that Edith Brown was never aware he thought they were dating, as distinguished from being "just friends."

The early IU years are filled out by Maurice Felger, Aline Robinson, Ted Grisell, and Ralph Gettelfinger. For information concerning the 1932 Historic Site Recital tour, I am indebted to Mildred Neff. Accounts of the trip to the Chicago World's Fair of 1933 are found in Malcolm Correll's letters to me, as well as my father's letters to Mary Eloise Humphreys, Edith Brown, and his brother Shockley.

Chapter IV.
"A Richly Laden Festal Board": France and Italy, 1933–1934

Ross Lockridge's family, Vernice Baker, and Laurence Wylie carefully stored his letters from Paris; thirty-four, of which thirty-three survive, were sent to his family. I've stepped aside somewhat in this crucial chapter to let some of his representative voices emerge. Unfortunately, most of his letters sent to the forty-odd other recipients have been lost. This was not necessarily a generation of "savers."

He himself was a saver and kept most letters sent to him abroad; inferences can be made about his own. These include letters from Laurence Wylie, the late Malcolm Correll, Edith Brown, Mary Eloise Humphreys, Robert Masters, the late Antoinette Billant, and others. His mother, Elsie, wrote forty-nine letters, his father Ross Senior, thirty, his sister Lillian, four letters, and various other family members a lesser number.

Lockridge used two small green notebooks, Cahier I and II, on his excursions; three larger notebooks in which he logged recipients of letters and "to do" lists; and "Follies of France," his poetical compositions for the year. He kept his voluminous French *dissertations* and thesis, and also made a photo album with detailed inscriptions. All these materials are in the family archive. The account of the vision in the flat on rue d'Ulm comes from "The Story of *Raintree County*" (1947), in the Houghton Library, Harvard University. Blandine Blukacz-Louisfert, *Le Conservateur aux Archives Nationales en mission auprès du Rectorat de l'Académie de Paris,* supplied archival information on *Le Cours de civilisation française de la Sorbonne.*

The wonderful Delaware Group itself contributed much. John Leggett first contacted members in the late 1960s, and I have made good use of letters he received, and of notes he made on interviews with people no longer living. These are in the University of Iowa Special Collections. The Alumni Records Office of Dartmouth College, Associate Alumnae of Douglass College, Bryn Mawr College Archives, Alumnae House of Vassar College, Alumnae Association of Mount Holyoke College, alumni or alumnae associations for Sweet Briar, University of Pennsylvania, Wellesley, Wells, and especially Jean Brown, acting University Archivist, the University of Delaware Archives, all assisted me in contacting Delaware Group members.

I am chiefly indebted to Curtis Lamorey, who permitted me to tape a lengthy interview; there's little he doesn't remember about that year. Amanda Macy Gelpke, Edward Mitchell, Huntington Harrison, Huldah Smith Payson, Mary Marks, Grace Carter, Beverly Hill Furniss, and others contributed also. By the way, the couple who displaced my father from his suite aboard the *Scythia* got married and are now enjoying their grandchildren. Jack Parsons and Charlotte Watkeys married but divorced.

John Leggett's chapter on the year abroad is one of the stronger in *Ross and Tom,* though he requested only excerpts of Ross Lockridge's voluminous letters from Paris. He preferred to rely on Delaware Group perceptions and tried to get in touch with all Delaware Group members, who responded with vivid recollections. Yet I would like to single out this chapter as representative of the larger portrait and discuss its assumptions. When he initially wrote to

Delaware people, he asked, "I wonder if you have any recollections of him—what he was like during that year, who among you saw the most of him, and any incident that might illustrate the reaction of this bright, though innocent, young Hoosier to that bath of European culture and sophistication."

Some members, notably Lamorey, objected to the assumption of an innocent abroad, as well as to a certain underestimation in "bright." Some others responded according to cue. Though a Hoosier among Easterners, he wasn't any more "innocent" than the others and was regarded by many as sophisticated in his own way. For one thing, he already knew perhaps more about European culture than anyone in the group; it was the first trip abroad for most of them, and he was fairly steeped in European book-learning. But this continued to be the underlying assumption of Leggett's chapter—the naïve Midwesterner among more sophisticated Easterners.

With regard to the portrait of Ross as naïf, Donald Smalley noted that one of Ross Lockridge's personae was "to play at being simple," and people could be taken in. To be sure, he also had qualities of hope, enthusiasm, and intensity of purpose that could come off as innocent to more world-weary observers. And he always took pride in being a Hoosier.

Leggett added some psychological shading to the chapter in noting that Ross Lockridge was "goaded by a specter of failure." Lamorey objects to having this insight attributed to him and doesn't believe it. I'd agree with Leggett—as most people with great ambition must negotiate a fear of failure—but would resist any implication that fear of failure or desire to do his parents' bidding was the mainspring of his drive.

On the small point of Ross Lockridge's introduction to alcohol—which Leggett says was a big occasion in an English pub—we've seen that this had already happened back in Chicago. Leggett's account is an instance of novelization. Curt Lamorey says Ross took to alcohol casually on the *Scythia*. But he was fascinated by young *women* drinking.

Leggett emphasizes Lockridge's eager return to Indiana as soon as the term was up, while "the majority of the Delawares had an eye on the political clouds and guessed this might be a last chance to see the France they had been studying about all winter." Actually only a handful of the Delaware people stayed over—six or seven; the prearranged ocean liner was awaiting them and most didn't have extra funds. And most were women whose parents paid a special "chaperonage" fee to ensure their daughters' virtue throughout the year; their after-hour activities were carefully monitored. These parents weren't about to let their daughters stay over unchaperoned, prey to European lusts. (I've served twice as Director of NYU in London and know something about this, even in these days.) I've narrated the circumstances that compelled Ross Lockridge's return; it wasn't homesickness for Indiana. He had managed by then to pack in more travel on the Continent than most of his classmates. And it will also be clear in the sequel that he didn't "turn

his back" on the experience. Leggett doesn't narrate the substantial counterevidence.

He also writes that "Elsie hoped that Ross would choose someone with a
more intellectual background [than Vernice Baker], perhaps one of those girls
who were always hurrying along faculty row clutching a violin case, someone
more like herself." But Elsie's letters to her son—which Leggett didn't ask to
read—demonstrate quite the opposite.

While in Italy, Ross "was not much moved by the sight of old buildings
and old masters," writes Leggett. But the rhapsodic letters on the Italian trip
as well as Lamorey's own witness show otherwise.

As for the weighty matter of my father's virginity, for once Leggett goes
too far in the opposite direction, crediting him with loss of virginity in the
spring of 1934, for which there is lamentably little evidence. Malcolm
Correll, Curtis Lamorey, and Laurence Wylie—his three closest friends—all
discounted this story, in part, I think, because it undercut their sense of their
friendships. My father was unnervingly explicit in telling these three about his
sex life—and all three say there's no way they wouldn't have known. Especially, of course, Lamorey, who was on the scene. His cousin Robert Masters
never heard of it either, and nobody else in the Delaware Group corroborates
such an initiation.

The story came from Richard Scowcroft, an admirable acquaintance of my
father years later, who heard it from him when the two of them were well into
a bottle of bourbon one night in 1947 (see Chapter VII). Leggett's first instinct
about this purported lapse in virtue was probably closer to the mark—that Ross
was just talking, with a bit of wishful thinking. Since Scowcroft didn't proffer
any details, Leggett's account of a woman's resolute seduction of the Hoosier
virgin was invention in any event. The particular woman he silently guessed
must have been the seducer that spring—from a "prestigious Eastern women's
college"—couldn't even remember, in the late 1960s, that Ross Lockridge had
not joined the rest of the group on their spring excursion to Italy.

Leggett's inferences, based on the limited evidence he made use of, were
plausible, but they were frequently novelistic. He prefaced his biography with
the comment, "I am a novelist and I believe that forceful biography employs
all the techniques of the novel; those of setting, narrative, characterization and
subjectivity. I believe in the biographer's right, within a limit, to portray his
subject's reaction to experience, and the limit is truth, insofar as that can be
determined from evidence." Some will say I'm simply writing a different
novel. But I'll be depositing for the record an annotated copy of *Ross and Tom*
in the Lockridge Collection at the Lilly Library, Indiana University, indicating
factual errors (I count about eighty in the "Ross" part) and clear instances of
"novelization"—not "interpretation" but instances of narrative bridges and interior monologue where no direct substantiation exists or where there is
counterevidence (I count about sixty of various lengths).

The passage on Victor Hugo that I have translated reads: *"Considérons, par exemple,* Les Misérables, *qui contient presque toutes les qualités d'Hugo, le meilleur et le pire—cette immense oeuvre, remplie de descriptions interminables, de digressions, d'épisodes superflus, nous offrant réalisme, romantisme, sentimentalité, artificialité, lyrisme, satire—bref, tout en tout—arrive à force de cette ampleur même à donner une sensation de noblesse épique et de génie divers. . . . Plus un génie aspire au sublime, plus il risque de tomber lourdement dans le ridicule."*

Chapter V.
"Dream of the Flesh of Iron": Bloomington, 1934–1940

A copy of *The Dream of the Flesh of Iron* is in the Lilly Library, Indiana University. The rough draft of some 2,500 pages is in the family archive. This draft is of greater interest than the incomplete poem he submitted to Houghton Mifflin, because it reveals a full history of composition—sources, methods, patterns of revision, several pages of running self-criticism, and some poems he omitted, including "The Marvelous Garden." (Apparently he thought a pastoral poem out of place in this urban epic.) In her unpublished doctoral dissertation, "The American Epic Tradition and *Raintree County*" (Syracuse University, 1973), Delia Clarke Temes makes some good contrasts between *The Dream of the Flesh of Iron* and the novel.

Though he includes quite a bit of free verse and some stanzaic forms of his own, he tries to salvage what he can from traditional forms. The workhorse of the poem is the Spenserian stanza! The Dreamer finds himself in a vault:

> I stood among the boxes, leprous and black,
> Unseamed, split, sagging, ripped, broken, and scarred
> With gaping fissure, ragged hole, and crack.
> All that was lustred to a burnish hard
> Was blotched with the Sickness, tettered, blistered, and marred,
> Consumed, encrusted, soiled, a rot, a stench,
> Flinders and scobs, roin, rubbish, mouldy shard,
> Heaped up confusedly in gutter and trench,
> Burst in a fall, crushed by a stone, split from a wrench.

My father sometimes kept count and could pour forth a baker's d
these things in a single sitting and not be breathing hard.

All other unpublished materials of my father—his academi~rnice
Hitler satire, shorter poems, the plays, *Byron and Napoleon* debooks,
Russell Noyes, rough drafts of the *Pageant of New Harmony*, mily archive.
Lockridge, notebooks, bluebooks for his philosophy co
photo albums, and his eulogy of Emma Shockley—are

John Robert Moore's observations are found in letters to John Leggett, in the University of Iowa Special Collections.

I am much indebted to Mary Louise Gilman, Words and Puzzle Editor of the *Journal of Court Reporting,* who was able to decode a good percentage of my father's shorthand in various manuscripts and book margins. With a photocopier that enlarged and darkened the faint pencil entries, I was able to provide her with a text that was still unintelligible to several other Gregg shorthand experts. His shorthand had become idiosyncratic since high school days. I thank Morris Miller for putting me in touch with her.

Letters of Ernest Vivian Shockley to his mother, Emma, are in the possession of Ernest Vivian Shockley, Jr., who has been very helpful in giving me information on his wing of the family. Ross Lockridge Senior's seven-volume local history of Indiana is unpublished and in the New Harmony Workingmen's Institute, along with many of his unpublished writings on New Harmony. The rough draft of *The Old Fauntleroy Home* is in the Indiana State Library, as are the letters to Ross Senior from Miss Fauntleroy. His unpublished novel, *Black Snake and White Rose,* is in the family archive.

The epistolary record of these years is spotty; my father kept letters from Malcolm Correll, Curtis Lamorey, Marion Monico, and Cloise Crane, but his letters to them, with the rare exceptions cited, were lost. The censored letter of 1934 to Lamorey fell out of a French novel in 1990. Marion Monico, a professor of French and Italian at Connecticut College, died in 1976; her family kept her professional correspondence and destroyed the personal. One of the two articles she published, in addition to a monograph on French drama, was on Racine and suicide (*PMLA,* June 1955). Crane died with no survivors except his mother in 1970.

I am particularly indebted to Marguerite Young for a taped interview. Her lyrical history of New Harmony, *Angel in the Forest,* appeared in 1945, and *Miss MacIntosh, My Darling* (1965)—conceived on a gigantic scale like *Raintree County*—makes use of the New Harmony setting in its later chapters. Others ⟨inter⟩viewed for this chapter include: Jane Owen, Herman B Wells, Elizabeth ⟨⟩le, Josephine Elliott, Mae Beth Shockley Mock, the late Donald Smalley, ⟨th⟩e Lloyd Binkley, Morris Binkley, Ruth Armstrong Correll, the late ⟨Joh⟩n Correll, the late Donald Blankertz, Dorothy Dugdale, Naomi ⟨⟩ Henry Remak, Laurence Wylie, Ted Grisell, Donald Carmony, ⟨⟩ Ro⟨⟩geon, Robert Menke, Dorothy Collins, Nota Scholl McGreevey, Don⟨⟩nette Billant, Edwina Patton, Dorothy Rey, Agnes Elpers, Aline ⟨⟩ Mi⟨⟩thy Smith McCrea, Jane Butcher, Janet Dunn, Doris Seward, ⟨⟩ Harmony. J⟨⟩cilia Wahl, Henry Wahl, and Vernice Lockridge Noyes. ⟨⟩ letter requesti⟨⟩ and Dorothy Moore Spore sent me recollections of New ⟨⟩ Jr., the late Cha⟨⟩roeder, editor of the *Indiana Alumni Magazine,* printed my ⟨⟩iscences and has helped in other ways. John B. Thomas, ⟨⟩slog, the late Lawrence Froberg, Wendell Phillippi,

Dorothy Thompson Letsinger, Susan Spriggs, Rachel Jones Haggard, Jean McGriff Fox, Alice Miller, Emily Wheelock Reed, Frances McNutt Nelson, Lois Jaggers, Ruth Allison Coates, Helen Thomson, Ralph Hughes Brown, and Hugh Highsmith wrote me about their recollections of Ross Lockridge Junior and Senior at Indiana University. John Robert Moore, Leo Dowling, Frank Davidson, Helen Judson, A. C. Judson, and Stith Thompson—all now deceased—wrote to John Leggett in 1969. The great athlete Charles Hornbostel was slowed by Parkinson's disease and died before I could interview him.

Chapter VI.
Starting Over: Cambridge, Bloomington, Boston, and Cape Ann, 1940–1943

The fragmentary manuscript of *Raintree County* in the Lilly Library, Indiana University, contains, on some versos, approximately two hundred pages of the discarded novel originally entitled *American Lives*. This includes "Notes on Joyce, etc." A few other pages are in the family archive. Other unpublished writings mentioned here are also in the family archive: the voluminous type-written notes on my father's reading, the Harvard essays, and the dismissive commentary he made on his own epic poem.

A three-page document, "Incidents to Weave into *American Lives*," gives a detailed itinerary of the trip to Henry County that he took with Elsie Lockridge in August, 1941. This is fleshed out with his circumstantial narra-tive account of the trip that I pieced together from pages of *American Lives*. He also annotated pictures from this excursion and others for the family albums, which I have made use of throughout this chapter. His annotated copies of *The Web and the Rock, You Can't Go Home Again, Leaves of Grass, Ulysses, Finnegans Wake, War and Peace, The Magic Mountain,* and other works read during this pe-riod are in the family archive.

Both Ross Lockridge and Vernice Lockridge wrote letters to the Lockridge family during these years, and letters to each other during their sep-aration in spring, 1942. Letters from Ross Senior and Elsie Lockridge survive except for the year 1940–41. Extant letters from my father to the late Donald Blankertz are now in the Lilly Library. With one exception, all letters written to Blankertz after November, 1942, are lost. Louise Wylie Campbell graciously sent me copies of letters that she wrote to her mother in 1940–41, with con-temporary descriptions of the Lockridge household in Cambridge. I am grate-ful also to Mrs. Harwood Picard. A letter from Thaddeus Ames and Ames's résumé as of 1941 are in the family archive. He never did write the book.

The internal memorandum rejecting *The Dream of the Flesh of Iron* is among the Houghton Mifflin materials donated to the Houghton Library at Harvard, which also has a letter from Ross Lockridge to Hyder Rollins. Another letter to Rollins is in the Harvard University Archives. Jerome Hamilton Buckley gave me the Kittredge anecdote and described Harvard in the early 1940s. Walter Jackson Bate wrote me about hearing my grandfather speak and meeting my father.

I'm not sure how much he saw of Perry Miller or F. O. Matthiessen; the reading list for his study of Whitman largely followed recommendations in a 1941 letter to him from IU professor Frank Davidson, whose course in American literature he had audited as a graduate student, taking extensive notes in shorthand. He typed up summaries of critical and biographical studies of Whitman but his own commentary is mostly confined to glowing marginalia in his copy of *Leaves of Grass.*

The views expressed by the late Anne Stiles Wylie and by Rachel Tryon are found in accounts and transcriptions of interviews in John Leggett's papers at the University of Iowa Special Collections. I emphasize these views because they had considerable impact on Leggett's portrait and help explain it, given the relatively small sample group he consulted. Some acquaintances at the time thought Rachel Tryon jealous of her husband's friendship with Ross Lockridge. But her views and those of Anne Wylie contain at least a measure of truth, as I have indicated.

Ross Lockridge's experience at Simmons College is documented in the Simmons College Archives, which Megan Sniffin-Marinoff, Archivist, and Peter Carini made available to me. The archives supplied me with *Simmons News* and *Fenways* articles on and by my father and other pertinent material, including a scrapbook on him. Naomi Scott Pfeiffer graciously gave me a lengthy interview. June Whitfield Hill took scrupulous notes on his 1942–43 course in American literature and sent me a copy of the whole set, while Nancy Shaw Esty gave me her annotated two-volume *American Poetry and Prose,* ed. Foerster and Lovett, which he assigned in another course. Some students—Nell Dickinson, Nancy Shaw Esty, and Evelyn Bennett Shore—gave me copies of their written coursework with his comments and corrections (of which more later). I am indebted to Kathryn Olga Daniels, daughter of the late Beatrice Alper Daniels, for copies of her mother's essays with comments by Ross Lockridge and an essay her mother drafted on him shortly after his death. Dorothy O'Keefe sent me a reminiscence written in 1958. Shirley Friedman Roffman sent clippings.

Many students gave vivid portraits: Evelyn Bennett Shore, Betty Borgeson Lotz, Doris Carter Ufford, Barbara Kridel Greenberg, Janice Liverpool Hale, Constance Ramsdell Blair, Barbara Finberg Korn, Constance Leighton, Wini Rubin Mason, Bernice Diamond Levinson, Lucienne G. Feldman, Janice White Sander, Anne Bailey Keller, Sybil Yamins Goldberg, Barbara Chesley Roberts, and Priscilla DePetris. Judith Matlack, a colleague of my father's at Simmons, wrote John Leggett concerning him. I am also indebted to Mary Murdoch and

Doris Linnell for interviews, and to Bruce Le Roy, Director Emeritus of the Washington State Historical Society, for information on Warren Tryon.

Taped interviews with Vernice Lockridge Noyes, Ernest Lockridge, the late Donald Blankertz, the late Donald Smalley, Edith Helman, Josephine Arsenian, John Arsenian, Jean Arsenian, the late Warren Tryon, and Laurence Wylie helped fill out these years.

Chapter VII.
Writing *Raintree County:* Boston, Cape Ann, and South Byfield, Fall, 1943–Spring, 1946

In 1947, my father wrote his own account of the composition of his novel, "The Story of *Raintree County,*" for use by Houghton Mifflin's promotion department. The calamitous correspondence between him and the publishing house from mid-1946 through early 1948 amounts to almost a thousand pages, by far the larger portion from Ross Lockridge, and the equal of a couple of short novels in itself. It is now in the Houghton Library, Harvard University. Houghton Mifflin has granted me permission to quote from their part of the correspondence. I would like to thank Vicki Denby of the manuscript department for her assistance. Selections from original readers' reports, ordinarily kept under lock and key, were released by Paul Brooks in 1947.

Among the many synoptic American histories Ross Lockridge read and annotated were S. E. Morison's and Henry Steele Commager's *The Growth of the American Republic,* Bernard De Voto's *The Year of Decision, 1846,* and Margaret Leech's *Reveille in Washington, 1860–1865.*

The Shockley family materials and the correspondence between Ross and Vernice Lockridge and Bloomington folk are in the family archive. I am indebted to the late Edward Quayle, husband of Mary Jane Ward, for retrieving my father's letters to her; she kept almost none of her other personal correspondence. Her professional correspondence and other papers are in the Special Collections of Mugar Memorial Library, Boston University, to which I am indebted for materials in coming chapters. The portrait of Ross Lockridge by Betty Underwood was given my brother Ernest by her son, Douglas. Correspondence with Francis ("Jeff") E. Wylie is in the Lilly Library, Indiana University.

John Leggett's papers in the University of Iowa contain correspondence and accounts of interviews with Jeff Wylie and Richard Scowcroft. Both wished to revise certain aspects of their encounters with Ross Lockridge as narrated in *Ross and Tom.* In addition to my interviews with them, I have profited from interviews with Paul Brooks, Edith Helman, Kingdon Grant, Donald Blankertz, and Warren Tryon, as well as family members.

Chapter VIII.
Author in the Epic

All quotations are taken from *Raintree County* as published by Houghton Mifflin in 1948. In the next chapter I'll be discussing some deleted passages, including the dream sequence that originally ended the novel. Lockridge's commentary on his own novel is found in a variety of texts: principally the original manuscript in the Lilly Library, "*Raintree County:* A Critical Estimate," "The Story of *Raintree County,*" and correspondence with Houghton Mifflin.

I owe much to previous critics of *Raintree County,* such as Darshan Maini, Donald Greiner, Delia Clarke Temes, Fred Erisman, and Joel Jones, whose work is already cited; also Park Dixon Goist's "Habits of the Heart in *Raintree County*" (*MidAmerica,* 1986) and Gerald Nemanic's "Ross Lockridge, *Raintree County,* and the Epic of Irony" (*MidAmerica,* 1975). Greiner is the first critic to discuss the irony that Shawnessy fails to complete his epic yet survives in the end, while Lockridge completes his epic but does not survive. I think Leonard Lutwack's "*Raintree County* and the Epicising Poet in American Fiction" is the best structural analysis to date of the novel (*Ball State University Forum,* 1972). My discussion of the novel's structure builds on and somewhat modifies his reading, in which he was assisted by Elizabeth Yoder. Northrop Frye discusses "encyclopedic form" in *Anatomy of Criticism* (Princeton, 1957). Mikhail Bakhtin's *Rabelais and His World* was suppressed for many years in the Soviet Union and elsewhere; it first appeared in English in 1968.

For information on Susannah Duke, the real-life Susanna Drake (better known as Elizabeth Taylor), I am indebted to Professor Thomas D. Hamm, Archivist of the Lilly Library of Earlham College. He is himself distantly related to the Dukes, has the photograph of Susannah mentioned herein, and provided information that came orally from Lola Ledbetter, a granddaughter of Ester Jane Duke Scott, Susannah's sister. He provided genealogical information and recently turned up the divorce proceedings of John Shockley and Susannah Duke in the Henry County (i.e., Raintree County) courthouse in New Castle (i.e., Freehaven), Indiana. Much of this information was presumably given by word of mouth, or in writings now lost, from Elsie Shockley Lockridge to Ross Lockridge, Jr.

For other information on the Henry County background of the novel, I am indebted to Evelyn Clift and Mildred Davis, curators of the Henry County Historical Society, and to Donald E. Hamilton, Tom Woodward, and William Gulde. Susan Neville of Butler University put together an informative pamphlet, *Raintree County, 1983,* based on a class project. Herbert L. Heller explores the background material in *Historic Henry County* (vol. III, 1982).

The anecdote concerning young Ross in the Frankfort, Kentucky, cemetery was narrated by his father to Lois Taylor Becker.

The *Illustrated Historical Atlas of Henry County,* in the possession of my family, has no variants suggesting Edenic rebellion that I've been able to spot—so far.

Chapter IX.
Snake Pit in Paradise: Manistee, Michigan,
Summer, 1946–Fall, 1947

The manuscript of the discarded Dream Section of *Raintree County* is in the Lilly Library of Indiana University. Only a handful of people have ever read it. I'm unsure about its literary merit but feel Houghton Mifflin was right that it would have sunk the novel as popular fiction.

The late Edward Quayle wrote me at considerable length concerning his wife, Mary Jane Ward. I am indebted also to James Sweet. The film version of *The Snake Pit,* produced by Darryl Zanuck, directed by Anatole Litvak, and starring Olivia de Havilland, Mark Stevens, Leo Genn, and Celeste Holm, appeared in late 1948. It was the cover story of *Time,* December 20, 1948. Ward's accounts of the Paw Paw reunion and episodes in the next chapter are contained in an unpublished personal memoir, *Snake Pits Revisited.* Written late in life, the memoir is not always accurate.

Jeff Wylie described the 1946 visit to Henry County in a profile on Ross Lockridge, Jr. published in *Book-of-the-Month Club News* (December, 1947) and various newspapers. It was the best single piece of writing on the author to appear in his lifetime.

I am indebted to the Manistee County Historical Museum for access to its attic and for information on the town.

Just as my father read and admired *Mister Roberts,* so Tom Heggen read and for the most part admired *Raintree County,* which Paul Brooks had sent to him. John Leggett narrates that Lockridge's suicide was a "crushing loss" to Heggen, though they had never met. With all the publicity heaped on Lockridge, he felt a kinship and had thought of writing him. Heggen drowned in his bathtub in 1949 after an overdose of barbiturates. I gather there is no evidence that Heggen's act was imitative of Lockridge's.

Despite repeated petitions, the door was closed in my face by the Turner Broadcasting System, which owns the MGM Story and Legal files housed in Atlanta. Andrew J. Velcoff, Deputy General Counsel, cited inadequate staff and unspecified "legal reasons" as grounds for withholding all files relating to my father and *Raintree County.*

Brandt & Brandt Literary Agency declined to answer my inquiry. In a letter to John Leggett, the late Carol Brandt objected to certain inaccuracies in *Ross and Tom,* which I have taken into account here.

In telling of the homecoming from Boston in March, 1947, John Leggett remarks on how Ross came "unquestioningly by way of Indianapolis," whereas there were more direct routes back to Manistee—more evidence that Indiana was the hub of the universe for him. I must ruin a good story: my father was actually picking up his car, left in Indianapolis after dropping off Ernest.

In laying grounds for the argument concerning my father's patricidal guilt, Leggett says that when the *Life* excerpt appeared on September 8, 1947, Ross was alarmed at not hearing from his parents: "Confirming Ross's worst suspicions there was no response at all from Bloomington and each day the silence grew more howling. . . . He guessed that his father had read the excerpt and reacted with a glacial silence that had enveloped the household, that while the offense he had taken was outwardly a moral one—How could the boy have breached these well-established fences of decorum?—he had been hurt in a far deeper way. First, five years of mutiny and then he had been licked grandly in the pages of *Life* magazine. There was no way to be patronizing about that, no way to pass that off. It was a stab at his father's vitals" (p. 151). But as we have seen, Ross Senior was actually *visiting* Manistee when the excerpt appeared and tried hard to get over his scruples about those cusswords. There's no evidence that Ross Junior ever worried very much about his father's reaction to the book. His mother's reaction was another story. Leggett's version is "novelization."

I am indebted to Leggett for notes taken on interviews with people no longer living, including Dorothy Hillyer Santillana and Carol Brandt. He taped an interview with John McCaffery, also deceased, who took large credit for the cutting of *Raintree County*, almost as if he were its Maxwell Perkins. His actual participation was limited to that single day in New York. My account of the night at the St. Regis is based on these materials plus my father's own detailed accounts in two letters to Paul Brooks, one letter to Mary Jane Ward, one letter to Donald Blankertz, and one letter to his brother, Shockley.

Ralph Sipper, president of Joseph the Provider Books, graciously made photocopies available to me of my father's correspondence with John McCaffery. McCaffery seems to have destroyed all letters written after August 26, 1947, which would have shown my father's indignation on learning that McCaffery had misinformed him about spreading the MGM income for tax purposes.

Paul Brooks's account of his dealings with Ross Lockridge is found in *Two Park Place: A Publishing Memoir* (Houghton Mifflin, 1986), pp. 75–83, from which I have quoted. Martin Stone said his legal files were destroyed in a garage fire and my father's apparently voluminous letters to him went up in smoke.

During interviews with me more than four decades after the contract dispute, Martin Stone was still confident he and my father had a strong case against Houghton Mifflin but he couldn't remember the particulars; and Paul Brooks was still confident Stone and Lockridge had no case at all. Brooks didn't wish to discuss the dispute beyond what he had written in *Two Park Place*. I don't know which side would have prevailed in civil court but have sometimes wondered what the interest would be on $22,500, compounded since 1947.

A copy of Ross Lockridge's egregious letter of July 24, 1947, to Louis B. Mayer is in the Houghton Mifflin correspondence at the Houghton Library, Harvard University. He had sent a duplicate to his dismayed publisher.

I am indebted to Mary James, Joyce Miller, and Mildred Kopis of the Miami County Museum, Peru, Indiana, for making available to me the three volumes of original *Raintree County* galleys. This is the only extant set I know of and contains the original City Section, starring Terry O'Rourke.

Interviews with Paul Brooks, Martin Stone, Betty Wylie, Jeff Wylie, Nota Scholl McGreevey, John McGreevey, Laurence Wylie, Ruth Anderson Carter, Martha Stiles Lawrence, Morton ("Terry") Baker, the late Edward Quayle, the late Angie Wylie, the late Warren Tryon, and family members have been important in this chapter.

A Ross Lockridge letter of August 21, 1947, to Donald Blankertz was discovered by Marcia Scanlon during our search of the barn mentioned in Chapter I. It is the only extant letter to Blankertz after one written on November 29, 1942. But the correspondence was active during all the intervening years, and remained so up to my father's death. In addition to matters literary, the lost letters would have articulated his response to world events—the dropping of the atomic bombs and the opening of the Nazi concentration camps, for instance. He became a reluctant correspondent while he was writing his novel, but always replied. He would get a letter from Blankertz and mutter to his wife, "I thought I just wrote him." In the 1947 letter he tells Blankertz of his good fortune and closes, "I therefore recommend that you go on with your writing, camerado." Blankertz told me that in a subsequent letter my father said the greatest blunder he ever made was to accept the MGM Award.

Chapter X.
"Flu or Something": Hollywood and Bloomington, Fall, Winter, 1947–1948

Book-of-the-Month Club materials on *Raintree County* and my father's letter to Henry Seidel Canby are in Butler Library, Columbia University. Christopher Morley's letters and commentary are quoted courtesy of the Estate of Christopher Morley. The original version of the "rejection scene" in the City Section, with the original heroine, can be found in the printer's copy of the novel at the Lilly Library, Indiana University, and in the three-volume galleys in the Miami County Museum, Peru, Indiana. But I have been unable to recover the revised version of this rejection scene with the new heroine, Laura Golden— cut at the insistence of BOMC—and rely here on what my mother and father said concerning it.

The account of what Ross Lockridge, Jr. said to his mother when she came to Manistee to read the manuscript is taken from a newspaper interview with her, by Harriet Ferguson of *The Indianapolis Times,* two days after the novelist's death.

I am grateful to the late Angie Wylie and to her daughter Jennifer Wylie for making available a copy of my father's letter to Craig Wylie.

Mary Jane Ward's account of her experience with Ross Lockridge, Jr. and Vernice Lockridge—from their first visit to Elgin through the funeral—is found in her unpublished memoir, *Snake Pits Revisited.*

All late writings of Ross Lockridge, Jr. alluded to in this chapter remain unpublished and were contained in the file labeled by my mother, "Writings when Ross was ill," in the family archive.

Because I have been denied access to MGM files, I have been unable to determine just how much contact Ross Lockridge, Jr. made with MGM, telephone or letters or otherwise, during his visit to Hollywood in November and December, 1947. Except for my mother, all people who might have known are apparently dead. I appreciate the efforts of Dick May on my behalf. Once again, my thanks to Stacey Behlmer of the Margaret Herrick Library, Academy Foundation, as well as to Joan Cohen of Legwork, Ned Comstock of the University of Southern California Library, Joel Rane of the Louis B. Mayer Library of the American Film Institute, and Felice Earley of New York City.

Vernice Lockridge's letter to Robert Peters describing her husband's state of mind, smuggled out of the Lockridge house in December, 1947, was thought to have been long lost. It was found among Shockley Lockridge's papers in 1989.

I am grateful to Ted Grisell, M.D., longtime friend of my father, for his very considerable assistance in locating the Methodist Hospital's health records concerning his stay there, and also for the interpretation of them. The late Dr. Murray De Armond may also have kept his own physician's records. Efforts to locate these failed and they were probably destroyed with his other files. Given the nature and brevity of my father's psychiatric treatment, these would not have been pages of depth analysis. Murray De Armond is said to have been "chagrined" upon hearing of Ross Lockridge's suicide—he really hadn't thought him that ill.

The literature on depression is vast and controversial. A handy recent title, *Depressive Disorders: Facts, Theories, and Treatment Methods* (1990), edited by Benjamin Wolman and George Stricker, is rich in bibliographical material, and begins with descriptions of no fewer than six current "theories": biological, psychoanalytic, existential, cognitive/behavioral, psychosocial, and genetic. From this volume I have quoted Jerold R. Gold's "Levels of Depression," on cognitive dysfunctions of depression. The American Psychiatric Association's first "Diagnostic and Statistical Manual" of "Mental Disorders" was published in 1952. The *DSM-III-R* was published in 1987. In most of the literature on the subject, there is little effort to describe depression from within the patient's agonized consciousness itself, as distinguished from symptomatology. William Styron's *Darkness Visible* (1990) is a remarkable exception, with certain close parallels to my father's experience, and also some marked differences. Kay Redfield Jamison's *Touched with Fire: Manic-Depressive Illness and the Artistic Temperament* (1993) argues the pervasiveness of the syndrome in artists, composers, and writers. The relationship of manic-depressive to narcissistic disorders (discussed below) remains a gray area, however.

The effectiveness of electroconvulsive therapy is still debated. For opposing views and extensive bibliographies, one can consult proponent Max Fink's *Convulsive Therapy: Theory and Practice* (1979, 1985) and Peter Breggin's *Electroshock: Its Brain-Disabling Effects* (1979). The senior Lockridges' outrage upon hearing of the shock therapy and their efforts to spring their son loose from the hospital are described in Mary Jane Ward's unpublished memoir.

In "An Author Wrecked by Success: Ross Lockridge, Jr." (*University of Hartford Studies in Literature,* 1978), Leonard Manheim notes the prevalence of nakedness and primal scenes in *Raintree County* and, following Erik Erikson, sees its author regressing from Oedipal guilt to the more primordial level of shame. "The Ross Lockridge pattern is rather one of *shame and doubt* arising from a maladjustment in the period of anal development which would normally in a well-developed personality lead to *autonomy*. This muscular-anal pattern merges imperceptibly into the third, locomotor-genital, pattern of the first oedipal period. . . . Shame and doubt, it will be remembered, are the negative aspects of the second (muscular-anal) epigenetic level, as guilt is the negative aspect of the third (locomotor-genital) level"(!). To be sure, my father felt considerable shame as well as guilt. But unlike Manheim, I think sex in his novel is more vital than pathological.

The diagnostic term that most conforms to the illness I am describing in my father is "narcissistic disorder." It is descriptive of him only up to a point.

I have already acknowledged (Chapter II) the assistance of Dr. Kenneth Lewes, Herbert Hendin, M.D., and Roslyn K. Pulitzer, A.C.S.W., in connection with the inference that there was probably something disconnected in Elsie Lockridge's nurturing of her youngest child. This is consistent with the additional inference that my father ultimately manifested symptoms of a narcissistic disorder. According to current theory, such a disorder can usually be traced to the quality of maternal care during the pre-Oedipal years. (In emphasizing the mother and the "*pre*-Oedipal" years, I differ from John Leggett, who finds the source of my father's vulnerability more in the "Oedipal triangle," where his relationship to Ross Senior is crucial.) Lewes and Hendin independently gave me generous professional commentary on a late draft of the manuscript, which has influenced the latter part of this chapter. They thought it wise not to stick my father with a diagnostic label—it could limit discussion and is only a classificatory shorthand—and I agree.

Freud's essay "On Narcissism" appeared in 1914, the year of my father's birth. Freud thought narcissists untreatable because they wouldn't yield to the transference—their "libidinal cathexes" were too self-directed to be redirected to the analyst. Freud didn't say much more about narcissism, nor did anybody else until the 1950s.

A popular error about narcissists is that they are too much in love with themselves, but as theorists and clinicians note, it's fairer to say that they don't love themselves enough. What they love is an "ego ideal" that eludes them, that always finds them missing the mark. Narcissistic striving is grounded in *vulnerable* self-esteem, where grandiosity cohabits with shame and depression. I believe that of the nonbiological clinical diagnoses available to us today, "major depression related to narcissistic disorder" has the greatest explanatory force with respect to my father's illness late in life.

I would not otherwise call him a narcissist because his personality was larger, his affections more social, and he was so damned Christian, always helping out. In his case the term would pertain more to structures of consciousness and object relations than to the quality of his personality.

Otto Kernberg's textbook narcissists may have made superficial social adjustments but are intrinsically cold and manipulative in their pursuit of admiration—from others whom they contradictorily devalue. They are often promiscuous in social and sexual dealings and don't keep old friends, are envious, are deficient in sympathy and incapable of love. With a great sense of entitlement, they are flighty in their work. Their achievements, which may glitter at first, are actually shallow and empty. Worse, they refuse to mourn when their analyst takes a vacation.

To most people who knew him, my father had a warmth of feeling for other people and a curiosity about the natural world, which he revered. His ego ideals didn't limit his sympathies. And he worked unceasingly for everything he got. As some theorists following Heinz Kohut have argued, Kernberg doesn't sufficiently allow for how our ego ideals can connect creatively with the world—in my father's case, through the visionary commitments of art. In his impassioned novel he expressed a wealth of feeling for the people of America—for mothers, fathers, lovers, children, soldiers, neurotics, hicks, and poets. Writing the novel was for him a way of working beyond narcissistic to social reality.

My reading in narcissistic theory has included such titles as Otto Kernberg, *Borderline Conditions and Pathological Narcissism* (1975, 1985, 1992), Heinz Kohut, *The Analysis of the Self* (1971), and Andrew Morrison, ed., *Essential Papers on Narcissism* (1986), which includes essays by Freud, Annie Reich, Alice Miller, Arnold Rothstein, and others. Christopher Lasch's well-known books, *The Culture of Narcissism* (1978) and *The Minimal Self* (1984), connect narcissism with dubious trends in American culture; interestingly, my father himself lamented many of the same trends—consumption, commodification, and "the fading of a durable, common, public world."

Revision of narcissistic theory with respect to issues of sex and gender has focused on how its patterns differ in males and females, but has not yet greatly challenged the central role of the mother's nurturing in its etiology. But challenges on other grounds to assumptions that mothers alone must be indicted for the results of parenting may be found in such recent titles as Diane Eyer's *Mother-Infant Bonding: A Scientific Fiction* (1992) and Jane Swigart's *The Myth of the Bad Mother* (1991).

In addition to hundreds of reviews of *Raintree County* sent to the author or his family by Houghton Mifflin, I have made use of a large archive gathered by Ray Lewis White for his article *"Raintree County* and the Critics of '48," in *MidAmerica* (1984), and made available to me by David D. Anderson, Director of the Society for the Study of Midwestern Literature. Professor Anderson has begun holding colloquia on the novel, and excellent essays by him, Dean Rehberger, Douglas Noverr, and others are forthcoming.

The New Yorker sent a letter to Houghton Mifflin about Hamilton Basso's review, in which Lockridge was called "Lockwood" throughout, but this letter is not in the archive at Harvard's Houghton Library.

My father's words and behavior at his Manistee landlord's house during our return there in January, 1948, are described minutely by the landlady, Mrs. O'Connor, in a sympathy letter to my mother in March, 1948.

The reporter for the *Indianapolis News* story of the Lockridges in their new house was Louis Hiner, Jr.; the reporter for my father's L. S. Ayres book-signing party was Fremont Power.

The description of what was said in my father's last meeting with the Christian Science practitioners is found in a letter to my mother from Myrtle Ayres, C.S.B., of March 17, 1948.

Wardell Pomeroy's description of Ross Lockridge, Jr. is found in *Dr. Kinsey and the Institute for Sex Research* (1982). Josephine Hendin made the observation to me concerning my father's inability to use success as a "declaration of independence."

I am grateful to the late Donald Smalley and to his former wife, Ruth Visher Frechtman, for copies of the remarkable series of letters Donald wrote Ruth from January 5, 1948, through April 9, 1948. Smalley's agonized response to my father's death, narrated in the weeks that followed it, is witness to the impact the suicide had on my father's friends and contemporaries.

For sending me letters my father wrote in his final weeks, I would like to extend warm thanks to Mary C. Cline, Jane Butcher, Kathryn Olga Daniels, Mrs. Robert E. Coates, Glenn Cantrell, Virginia Barnard Deupree, Jeff Wylie, Laurence Wylie, Curtis Lamorey, Wini Rubin Mason, Ruth Correll, and the late Malcolm Correll. I would especially like to thank Jean Arsenian and John

Arsenian for their graciousness in allowing a search of their premises for the lost letter my father wrote to Aharon Arsenian in early March of 1948.

Shockley Lockridge not only went against the family grain with respect to politics; he also rejected its habit of holding on to all family papers and photographs. Upon the death of his mother in 1961, he discarded many of these, even tearing in two a photograph of his parents on their honeymoon. His father's papers had already been donated by then. Though he carefully preserved some of the key documents quoted throughout—for which I will always be grateful—he once again discarded a large percentage of the family papers and photographs in his possession shortly before his death in 1986. Very few of his mother's or his sister's papers survive, and it is impossible to say what else was lost. His daughter Anne Lockridge Sales believes there was little of real consequence and that he would have preserved everything directly related to my father.

Interviews with Nota Scholl and John McGreevey, the late Edward Quayle, Henry Remak, the late Donald Smalley, Wardell Pomeroy, Lillian Mumby Chitwood, Naomi Dalton, Margret Beardslee, Ernest Campaigne, the late Malcolm Correll, Laurence Wylie, Josephine Piercy, Josephine Arsenian, John Arsenian, and Jean Arsenian were important in this chapter.

Chapter XI.
"Hail and Farewell at the Crossing":
Bloomington, March 6, 1948—Spring, 1948

Various accounts of my father's last evening are found in the *World-Telephone, Bloomington Daily Herald, Indianapolis Star, Indianapolis News,* and a few other regional newspapers, as well as the news syndicates. The only reliable account is my mother's, given me in a taped interview late in 1988, subsequently confirmed by the FBI file on my father. Lillian Lockridge's role in the removal of evidence is made clear in her interview with FBI agents, who were trying to determine if her brother might indeed have been murdered, as the death threat to his male heirs claimed. She fessed up. The agents noted that "the above facts concerning the finding of the hose, the rag and the position of the body in the rear seat of the car were concealed from the coroner at the time of his investigation, and this information is not known outside the family except as revealed herein."

I am grateful to the family of the late Robert McCrea—the lawyer who handled my father's estate and who married Dorothy Smith, a friend of my parents from an early age—for giving me access to his safe, where my father's final letter, written to Jonathan Bingham, was found.

I didn't hear about or come across the Bradfute editorial that quoted a large portion of Basso's *New Yorker* pan until a couple of years ago, when looking through microfilm at the Monroe County Public Library. We had kept newspapers containing obituaries but not newspapers from the day of the suicide. To my knowledge nobody had ever noted this startling "coincidence." My mother was herself unaware of this editorial, which probably served as a trigger. Any number of other trivial jabs might have served eventually, given his unremitting depression. Hearing from Shelley that Keats's death had been caused by a pan in the *Quarterly Review,* Byron wrote: " 'T is strange the mind, that very fiery particle, / Should let itself be snuffed out by an article."

There was one report, years later, that he had been seen the night of March 6 listening to the Regionals down at the old Book Nook, where Hoagy Carmichael composed "Stardust," and that he left at half time, when BHS had an 8-point lead. Somehow I would like to believe this, but have found no corroboration. (If anyone saw him at any time on March 6, 1948, I'd like to hear from him or her.) We know he carried out one half of what he told his wife he intended to do that night—he mailed those letters.

Richard Lewis of *The Indianapolis Times* wrote a moving account of the funeral from which I have quoted.

I am indebted to Dennis Troy, Monroe County Coroner, who made available to me the autopsy report and other papers on my father and discussed various legal and physical aspects of the case.

I remember reading somewhere the "open letter" accusing Paul Brooks of killing his author but, as my book goes to press, I haven't been able to locate it in *The Writer* magazine. In any event the author(s) of this letter could have known very little of the novel's publishing history. Brooks speaks of this episode in *Two Park Street,* p. 80.

I would add a postscript here on the lives of a few people who have figured prominently in this book. Malcolm Correll was one of seven plaintiffs in the landmark Supreme Court case of 1952 that declared the Oklahoma loyalty oath unconstitutional. He became Chair of three physics departments and was President of the American Association of Physics Teachers. He died in 1992. His wife, Ruth Armstrong Correll, was elected Mayor of Boulder in 1977 and was responsible for the "green belt" that has protected the city against urban sprawl. Also living in Boulder is Robert Masters, a retired Air Force colonel and college administrator. Two years after my father's death, Laurence Wylie returned to France, where he lived with Anne and their two sons in the small Provençal village of Roussillon. His delightfully informal and widely read sociological study, *Village in the Vaucluse* (1957), was influential in making even the French aware of French village life. His brother Jeff Wylie still resides in Hingham with his wife, Betty. Now retired from Time-Life and MIT, he has been researching the family of Abraham Lincoln. Donald Blankertz authored books on marketing and was for many years Dean of the Wharton School before his death in 1990. Warren ("Steve") Tryon, Professor of History at Boston University, continued to live in Rockport, Massachusetts, and authored and edited books on American history before his death in 1989. Curtis Lamorey once again resides in his hometown of Barre, Vermont, following a long career in international business. Among the titles during Paul Brooks's subsequent years at Houghton Mifflin were Winston Churchill's six-volume *The Second World War* and Rachel Carson's *Silent Spring*. In retirement he is active in environmental causes, and most of his own books concern nature and conservation.

After 1948, Lillian Lockridge got out of social work and found professional and personal satisfaction as a popular elementary school teacher. She even managed to lose some weight.

In 1967, I spoke with Mary Jane Ward concerning my father's death. She still wished to believe it an accident, and I myself did not know at that time the precise physical circumstances. After 1948, she published four more novels, *A Little Night Music* (1951), *It's Different for a Woman* (1952), *Counterclockwise* (1969), and *The Other Caroline* (1970). The last two deal once again with mental illness. She was hospitalized for extended periods three more times—in 1957, 1969, and 1976—before her death in 1981.

The literature on suicide, like depression, is vast. Among recent titles, in addition to the classic texts in John Donne, Emile Durkheim, Edwin Shneidman, Sigmund Freud, and Karl Menninger, I've found the following helpful: Herbert Hendin's *Suicide in America* (1982), A. Alvarez's *The Savage God* (1970), Howard Kushner's *Self-Destruction in the Promised Land* (1989), Ronald Maris's and Bernard Lazerwitz's *Pathways to Suicide* (1981), and *Suicide: Understanding and Responding* (1989), edited by Douglas Jacobs and Herbert Brown. In a study of imitative suicide, based on the number of suicides during the month following nationally publicized suicides, D. P. Phillips reports that after the death of Marilyn Monroe there was an increase of 197.5 suicides over the expected crop, while after the death of Ross Lockridge, Jr. there was a *decrease* of 11.5. (See the Jacobs and Brown volume, p. 95.)

Interviews with Iris Lentz, the late Malcolm Correll, Curtis Lamorey, Barbara Kerr, Martin Northway, Margot Dowling, and family members were important in the writing of this chapter.

I would like to thank occupants of my parents' old domiciles for letting me rummage around: Susan Thornberg, Alice Moore, Laura Gilman, Heidi Carlson, Mark Knapp, Francie Hill, Philip Hill, Joan Zirker, Malvin Zirker, Bruce O'Connor, Martha O'Connor, Ann Fisk, Barry Marshall, and Dee, Tina, and Steph.

Several people helped in the transcription of interview tapes and often offered me their impressions: Jane Stoloff, Roy ("Chip") Benjamin, Sheila McLaughlin, Derk Kinnane, Ellen Mackenzie, and Marcia Scanlon.

This book could not have been written without the encouragement of some loyal friends, relatives, and professional acquaintances, beyond those mentioned already. Susan Fox read the manuscript carefully chapter by chapter during its composition with the ear and eye of a poet-novelist and the warmth

Notes and Acknowledgments

of a close friend. Its strengths owe much to her. My cousins Kay Lockridge and Anne Lockridge Sales generously donated financial assistance early on, as well as many insights into our family. Kay Sales located valuable family materials in our Aunt Marie Peters's family Bible. Rebecca Lockridge sent me some of my father's books, including *The Sherwood Anderson Reader* (1947), which contains important personal shorthand. Elizabeth Steele, Emeritus Professor of English at the University of Toledo, began a biography of my father in the early 1960s, abandoned a few years later; she graciously sent me her complete file. George Thompson, Humanities Librarian at the Bobst Library, New York University, gave me assistance on everything from tracking down wills to calculating the worth of 1947 dollars. I owe much to Aileen Ward, whose wonderful biography of John Keats often came to mind while I relived my father's life. Josephine Hendin, Americanist and novelist, read the manuscript and engaged with it strongly on many levels; among other things she helped me discern certain patterns in my father's relationship with his parents. Martin Mueller and Laurel Richardson, who have had the dubious good fortune to marry into the Lockridge family, gave the manuscript searching critiques, with perspectives both professional and intimate. The novelist Joseph McElroy read and reread the manuscript, offering everything from stylistic improvements to conceptual challenges. He encouraged me to get more of myself into the book. For her insights into family structure and the psychology of composition, I am grateful to the novelist and essayist Erika Duncan, who gave the manuscript a sensitive reading. Without the keen editorial eye and wide-ranging knowledge of Beena Kamlani, this book would have been a poorer thing. Thanks also to Marjorie Horvitz for her proofreading labors. I would like to thank my agent, Robert Lescher, for his early encouragement and professional expertise, and my editor, Al Silverman, for his enthusiasm and wise counsel.

For assistance with the photographic archive, I would like to acknowledge Mark Simons, Paul Riley, Sharon Nelson, and Beverly Sympson of Indiana University Media and Teaching Resources, as well as John Goodheart of the IU Department of Photography and family friend Marvin Carmack. Other work was provided by Galowitz Photographics of New York City and Terry Clark of Indianapolis.

Additional thanks go to Margie Appleman, Philip Appleman, James Binkley, Petey Brown, Carolyn Carlson, Mary Cates, Alfred David, Linda David, Sheila Emerson, Bernard Fried, Marilyn Gaull, Nina Gershon, Lois Gilman, Day Gleeson, Janet Gregg, Walter Gregg, the late Tom Haas, Sandra Haller, Tulle Hazelrigg, Susan Jones, Takis Kayalis, William Keach, Melinda Koyanis, Lynka Kroll, Lilach Lachman, Donald Lamm, Starling Lawrence, Arthur Levine, Hank Levy, Judith Linhares, LindaAnn Loschiavo, Lisa Madden, James Madison, Marcia Marvin, Ann Murray, Stephen Orenstein, Debrah Pearson, Cynthia Ross, William Rusin, Michael Scanlon, Stephen Spretnjak, Roger Straus, Enid Stubin, Patricia Swain, Stephanie Tevonian, Dennis

Thomas, Valerie Wise, Arthur Wrobel, Joan Wylie, Betty Yearley, my colleagues at New York University, members of the Biography Seminar, and especially my old classmates at Bloomington High School and University High School.

One morning late in 1988, having finished a scholarly project I'd worked on for many years, I spoke with Marcia Scanlon, a painter and sculptor, about what I might write next. With some apprehension I had jotted down "biography of my father" on a short list of other topics more bookish in character. Right away and with great warmth she chose the biography, and I set to work later that day. For this early encouragement and much more, the book is dedicated to her.

Index

Abbreviations:
RLJ: Ross Lockridge Junior
RC: Raintree County

Adams, Georgia, 75, 81–82, 86,
  89–90, 106
Adams, Henry, 282; *The Education of
  Henry Adams,* 299
Adler, Alfred, 206
Akins, Hubert, 116, 139
Alpert, Hollis, 17
Ames, Thaddeus Hoyt, 206–7, 237,
  433
Anderson, Ruth, 315
Anderson, Sherwood, 201
Aquinas, Thomas, 229
Aristotle, *Poetics,* 165, 229
Armstrong, Harry, 322, 333
Armstrong, Louise, *We Too Are the
  People,* 322
Arnold, Matthew, 237
Arsenian, Aharon, 38, 222, 253,
  424
Arsenian, Jean, 222, 261
Arsenian, John, 222, 261
Arsenian, Josephine, 38, 222
Astaire, Fred, 381
Austen, Jane, 311
Auw, Ivan von, Jr., 311
Ayres, Myrtle, 376, 411, 423,
  455

Baker, Alexander Leon, 80, 103,
  249, 375, 392
Baker, Aubrey, 80, 83, 103
Baker, Hugh, 78–80, 81, 83, 174,
  180, 216, 253–4, 452
Baker, Imogene, 80, 81, 82–83, 393
Baker, Lillie Thrasher, 30, 78,
  79–80, 81, 82, 106, 180, 216,
  262, 332, 337
Baker, Morton ("Terry"), 331
Bakhtin, Mikhail, 302
Baldwin, James, 11, 13
Balzac, Honoré de, 211, 420
Barth, John, *The Sot-Weed Factor,* 301,
  308
Barrett, Alfred, 419–20, 434, 455
Basso, Hamilton, 405–6, 442, 482–3
Bate, Walter Jackson, 194
Baudelaire, Charles, 211
Beach, Sylvia, 133–4, 140
Beatley, Bancroft, 216, 263
Benét, Stephen Vincent, 155, 212,
  259; *John Brown's Body,* 153,
  299, 302
Benny, Jack, 196
Bergen, Edgar, 196
Bergson, Henri, 152

Index

Berryman, John, 194
Bierce, Ambrose, 201
Billant, Antoinette, 164
Bingham, Jonathan, 441
Binkley, Donald, 84–85, 465
Bittner, Peggy, 85–86, 91, 142
Blankertz, Donald, 38, 173, 174,
    181, 200, 207, 208–9, 210,
    211–2, 216, 218, 219, 223,
    226–7, 232, 238, 250,
    258–9, 280, 355–6, 395, 477,
    483
Bloomington, Indiana, 7–8, 14, 29,
    36, 44, 55, 68–107, 424–5,
    435–6, 456
Blotner, Joseph, 12–3
Book-of-the-Month Club, 4, 31, 310,
    341, 342, 343, 344, 345, 353,
    363, 370–3, 384, 404, 420
Borderland, 61
Boston Post, 38, 349
Bosworth, Patricia, 19
boy scouts, 41–42, 49, 71–72, 383
Bradfute, Blaine, 442
Bradt, Ruth, 86, 105
Brandt, Carol, 343–6, 348, 352, 355
Brookhouser, Frank, 11
Brooks, Paul, 261, 265, 270, 315,
    319, 321, 322, 325, 326, 327,
    330, 335–6, 341, 342, 348,
    350, 353, 359, 361–7, 370–2,
    382, 387, 388, 402, 407, 415,
    422, 432, 454, 476, 483–4;
    Two Park Street, 348–9
Brown, Carlton, *Brainstorm,* 310–1
Brown, Edith, 97, 142
Brown, John, 10
Brown, John Mason, 407
Browning, Robert, 134; *Childe
    Roland,* 160
Bryan, William Lowe, 46, 451
Buckley, Jerome Hamilton, 194
Bunyan, Paul, *Pilgrim's Progress,* 301
Byron, George Gordon (Lord), 173,
    174–6, 289, 408, 483; *Childe*

Harold's Pilgrimage, 176, 185,
    280; *Don Juan,* 201–2, 280, 301

Caldwell, Erskine, *God's Little Acre,* 29
Calvin, John, 417
Canby, Henry Seidel, 370–2, 404
Capote, Truman, *Other Voices, Other
    Rooms,* 11
Carlyle, Thomas, 275; *Heroes and
    Hero Worship,* 292
Carmichael, Hoagy, 76, 268
Carpenter, Alicia, 63–64, 90, 183,
    435, 436, 462
Carroll, Lewis, *Alice's Adventures in
    Wonderland,* 299
Carter, Henry, 102, 158, 165, 166
Cather, Willa, 201
Cerf, Bennett, 311, 323, 324–5,
    328, 452
Chamberlain, John, 358
Chapman, John (Johnny Appleseed),
    25, 47, 100, 294
Chaucer, Geoffrey, *The Canterbury
    Tales,* 102, 301, 380, 408
Christian Science, 5, 27, 28–29, 49,
    52, 218, 241, 284, 375, 376,
    378, 379–80, 384, 386, 412,
    414, 415, 416, 421, 426, 452,
    455
Christianity, 10, 11, 50, 84, 92, 121,
    124, 159, 230, 292, 293, 295,
    380, 385, 419–20, 450
Citizen Kane, 236, 269
Civil War, 62, 233, 240, 241,
    277–8, 306, 376
Clark, George Rogers, 247
Clemens, Samuel (Mark Twain), 201,
    220, *The Gilded Age,* 372
Clift, Montgomery, 15–19, 50
Coleridge, Samuel Taylor, 275, 279;
    The Rime of the Ancient Mariner,
    78, 207
Collegiana, 88, 89, 91
Collier, Ray, 444, 445
Confidential Magazine, 14–15

488

Index

Cooper, James Fenimore, 297, 319

Corneille, Pierre, 131, 135

Correll, Ruth Armstrong, 151, 171, 223, 483

Correll, Malcolm, 101–5, 109, 116, 118, 124, 137, 143, 155, 156, 171, 172, 208, 209–10, 223, 263, 280, 303, 411, 420, 446, 449, 450–1, 464, 483

  high school days with RLJ, 72–74, 78, 84, 86, 88, 89–90, 95

  warns RLJ of rival, 129

Cozzens, James Gould, Guard of Honor, 456

Crane, Cloise ("Jack"), 109, 112, 115, 127, 130, 137, 160–1, 208, 280, 337, 385

Crane, George, 42, 57

Crane, Hart, 211

Crane, John, 41, 57

Crane, Mildred, 63

Crane, Stephen, 174, 201, 241; The Red Badge of Courage, 209

Croce, Benedetto, 152

Crowther, Bosley, 17

cummings, e. e., 165

Daladier, Edouard, 124, 125

Dalton, Naomi, 68, 75, 214, 410–1, 421–2, 443, 447

Dante, Aligheri, The Divine Comedy, 166, 301

Darwin, Charles, 281, 294, 295, 296

Dean, James, 85, 311

De Armond, Murray, 395–401, 408, 414

Debs, Eugene, 58

Delaware Foreign Study Group, 104, 108–9, 125, 127, 128, 197, 319, 466–68

depression, 290, 312, 386–7, 390–4, 396–401, 408–9, 416, 418, 424–5, 431–4, 452, 457, 478–9

Dickens, Charles, David Copperfield, 160; Great Expectations, 97; Pickwick Papers, 164

Dini, Gennaro, 112, 119, 130–1

Dinklage, Katherine, 62, 63

Dmytryk, Edward, 16, 18, 461

Donahue, Winston, 34–35

Dos Passos, John, 201, 209, 212, 299, 322, 324; U.S.A., 219–20

Drdla, Franz, 89

Dreiser, Theodore, 4, 22, 26, 201, 211, 220, 311, 403; The Titan, 159

Dumas, Alexandre, The Count of Monte Cristo, 60

Eddy, Mary Baker, 241, 284, 375, 393, 416; Science and Health with Key to the Scriptures, 49

Edison, Thomas Alva, 91

Eel River, 25, 43, 60–61, 178, 215–6, 318–9, 361, 453

Eliot, T. S., 153, 211–2; Sweeney Agonistes, 212

Ellis, Craig, 455–6

Elpers, Agnes, 155, 173

Emerson, Ralph Waldo, 10, 211, 220, 299, 451

Epworth League, 83, 86, 89, 285

Fadiman, Clifton, 404

fate and freedom, 39–40, 137, 160–61, 385, 416–8, 436, 447–8

Faulkner, William, 201, 405; Absalom, Absalom!, 13

Fauntleroy, Mary Emily, 162–3, 168, 177

fear, 208–9, 226, 290, 338, 347, 373–4, 393–4, 432

FBI, 34–35, 482

Felger, Maurice, 101–2

Feltus, Catherine, 87, 105

feminism, 13, 52, 163, 287

Finley, Martha, the Elsie series, 299

Fitzgerald, F. Scott, 201

Flaubert, Gustav, 135, 211, 299
Foley, Celia, 62–63, 234
Fort Wayne, 41–42, 47, 49, 56–64,
    181–2, 187, 189–90, 228, 230,
    435–8, 448
Foster, Stephen, 30, 424
Frazer, James George, *The Golden
    Bough,* 294, 298, 299, 307
Freud, Sigmund, 21, 39, 144, 185,
    187, 206, 231, 236, 266,
    285–6, 289–90, 291, 299, 342,
    408, 427–30; *Interpretation of
    Dreams,* 180–1, 315; "Mourning
    and Melancholia," 282; "On
    Narcissism," 480
Frost, Robert, 194
Frye, Northrop, 296, 301, 302
Fulton, Robert, 79
Fulwider, Ed, 72

Gaddis, William, *The Recognitions,*
    301, 308
Gardner, John, *The Sunlight Dialogues,*
    308
Gardner, Ava, 351
Garland, Hamlin, 210
Garland, Judy, 381
Gettelfinger, Ralph, 102, 103
Gibbon, Edward, 420
Gilman, Mary Louise, 37, 470
Goncourt, Edmond and Jules de,
    211
Grable, Betty, 240
Graham, Sheilah, 351
Gray, Thomas, "Elegy in a Country
    Churchyard," 69
Green, John, 17, 19
Green Pastures, 99
Greenslet, Ferris, 257, 259
Greiner, Donald, 13, 36, 474
Griffith, D. W., 169; *Intolerance,* 187,
    236, 269
Grisell, Ted, 37, 158, 478
Guest, Edgar, 165

Hale, Will Taliaferro, 164–5, 181
Hardy, Thomas, 38; *Jude the Obscure,*
    137
Harrison, Benjamin, 179
Harrison, William Henry, 47, 179
Harvard University, 10, 180, 193–4,
    200–3, 210, 216–7
Havilland, Olivia de, 342
Hawthorne, Nathaniel, 10, 19, 201,
    259; "The Great Stone Face,"
    220, 234, 271, 295, 297
Heggen, Thomas, 475; *Mister Roberts,*
    20, 21, 321
Held, Serge Simon, *La Mort du fer,*
    159, 185
Helman, Edith, 260–1
Hemingway, Ernest, 201, 202, 208,
    209, 211, 220, 227, 299, 324,
    384, 431
Henley, Lillian Bradway, 62
Henry County, Indiana, 9–10, 31,
    50–51, 203–5, 210–11, 232,
    239, 243, 269, 313–4, 354
Herald Tribune, 4, 420, 422, 449
Hervey, Allen, *Anthony Adverse,* 159
Hillyer, Dorothy, 256–60, 261, 264,
    265, 321, 324–7, 329, 330,
    334, 336, 339, 343–6, 347,
    350, 353, 361, 364, 372
Hippensteel, Vincent, 85, 89,
    149–50, 446
Hitler, Adolf, 128, 175, 182, 184,
    201, 203
Hodnett, Edward, 256
Hollywood, 15–16, 40, 342, 351,
    375, 377–89, 390, 392
homecoming, 270, 271–2, 307, 425
Homer, 10, 237, 239, 281, 318,
    414; *Iliad,* 57, 135, 299;
    Odyssey, 57, 135, 242, 299, 306
homosexuality, 99, 115, 266, 284–5,
    338–9
Hornbostel, Charles, 102–3, 104,
    106, 118, 124, 129–30, 137,
    138, 149, 154, 183, 184, 471

Index

Horne, James, 45
Houghton Mifflin, 13, 22, 29,
    132–3, 199, 200, 238, 256–61,
    315, 321–2, 324–7, 329–37,
    359, 381, 384, 420, 453–4,
    456–7, 473
  contract dispute with RLJ, 361–7,
    431
Hubbard, Captain, 169, 171, 327
Hudson, W. H., 259
Hugo, Victor, 134, 185, 299, 305,
    323, 408, 420; Les Misérables,
    60, 135, 165, 469
Humphreys, Mary Eloise, 95–96, 97,
    106, 149, 158, 244
Huxley, Aldous, Point Counter Point,
    159

idealism, 10, 152–3, 155, 300,
    428–9
An Illustrated Historical Atlas of Henry
    County, Indiana, 170–1, 293,
    331
Indiana University, 10, 44, 46,
    51–52, 59, 70, 72, 155, 310

Jackson, Ruth, 109, 118
Jackson, W. A., 194, 203
James, Henry, 259
Jeffers, Robinson, 211, 212
Jones, Howard Mumford, 11
Jones, James, From Here to Eternity, 29
Joyce, James, 140, 199, 201, 227,
    231, 281, 299, 300, 318, 324,
    403, 405, 435; "Evelina," 290;
    Finnegans Wake, 229, 301,
    315–6, 395; Portrait of the Artist,
    304; Ulysses, 11, 22, 38, 133,
    220, 228, 229, 235, 264,
    297–8, 301, 315, 340, 389
  RLJ's critique of, 228–30
Jung, Carl, 206

Kantor, MacKinlay, 311
Katzenjammer Kids, 81

Kaufman, Millard, 15, 17, 18, 24
Keats, John, 106, 121, 134, 156,
    175, 183, 185, 218, 275, 318,
    325, 409, 483
Kinsey, Alfred, 29, 284; Sexual
    Behavior in the Human Male,
    14–15, 403
Kipling, Rudyard, 71, 165
Kittredge, George Lyman, 194
Kunz, Elloise, 87, 105
Kunz, Majora, 87
Kutner, Nanette, 38, 412–3, 456;
    Middle Class, 412

LaGuardia, Robert, 18–19
Lamorey, Curtis, 108–9, 115, 118,
    119, 130, 136, 141, 150–1,
    172, 187, 197, 203, 208, 280,
    362, 399, 449, 466, 484
  in Italy with RLJ, 119–23
  Paris manifestations, 125–7
language, 13, 166–7, 294, 299,
    302–4
Lansbury, Angela, 381
Lawford, Peter, 381
Lawrence, D. H., Lady Chatterley's
    Lover, 110; Sons and Lovers, 315
Lee, Charles, 11, 404, 407
Leggett, John, Ross and Tom, 20–24,
    225, 330, 348, 414, 461,
    466–8, 475–6, 479
Lentz, Paul, 82, 444, 445
Lewis, Sinclair, 201, 259, 403; Main
    Street, 159
Life magazine, 4, 21, 185, 268–9,
    313, 326–7, 338, 342, 347,
    354, 357–9
Lincoln, Abraham, 43, 76, 100, 279,
    292, 298, 299
Lindsay, Vachel, 212; "The Congo,"
    224
Linscott, Robert, 323
Littlefield, Dorothy, 109, 110, 118,
    125
Little Turtle, 25, 47, 100

Index

Lockridge, Anne Shockley, 117, 118, 247

Lockridge, Brenton Webster, 43, 49, 145, 195, 360

Lockridge, Charlotte Wray, 43–44, 58, 145, 148, 169, 215, 406

Lockridge, Earl Butler, 104, 119–20, 129, 145–8, 178

Lockridge, Elsie Shockley, 3, 5–6, 26, 33, 43, 44, 45, 47, 56, 60, 62, 64, 67, 69, 70, 75, 77, 87, 100, 107, 108, 139, 140, 169, 170, 173, 180, 196, 210–1, 215, 219, 223, 231–2, 240–1, 242, 246, 247, 254, 262–3, 266–7, 268, 284, 314, 344, 350, 356–7, 395, 400, 413, 428, 432, 437, 448, 451, 452; "For Things Worth While," 54–55; "Henry County Real Life Background to *Raintree County*," 27–28; "The sayings and doings of our two baby sons, Robert Bruce and Vivian Shockley," 52–53

belief in immortality, 172, 217–8, 230–1, 452

after death of RLJ, 27–28, 452–3

response to RLJ's depression, 374–5, 393, 394, 401, 411

as Eva in *RC*, 27–28, 287

final conversation with RLJ, 440, 452–3

and RLJ's illness of 1935, 156–8

influence on RLJ, 65–66, 252–3, 427–9

in *The Inheritors*, 145–8

letters to RLJ in France, 116–7

life to 1914, 49–55

pedagogy, 53–54, 91–92, 224

response to *RC*, 262, 357–9, 374–5, 476

RLJ's awareness of her mortality, 132–3, 282–3

as story-teller, 27

visits to Henry County with RLJ, 203–5, 313–4

Lockridge, Ernest Hugh, 3–4, 25, 26, 29, 31, 32–34, 174, 181, 193, 195, 196, 206, 215, 218, 222, 234, 244, 245, 249, 250, 254, 262, 266, 275, 313, 315, 318–9, 320–1, 322, 336, 337, 342, 368, 375–6, 402, 439, 440, 441, 442–3, 453, 457, 461

diary, 415, 424, 448–9

RLJ's letters to, 213, 332–3

RLJ's raising of, 223–6, 251–2

RLJ reading *RC* to, 328–9

Lockridge, Georgie, 43

Lockridge, Jeanne Marie, 6, 7, 8, 29, 30, 32–34, 240, 241, 245, 249, 250, 254, 262, 315, 321, 322, 332, 357, 358, 375–6, 413, 414, 415, 439, 457, 461

early memories of RLJ, 369

Lockridge, Kathryn Delana (Kay), 26, 219, 247

Lockridge, Larry Shockley, 3, 8, 29, 31–32, 218, 223–4, 234, 237–8, 241–2, 245, 249, 250, 251, 262, 315, 320, 322, 332, 353, 360, 368–9, 375, 402, 442, 443

Lockridge, Lillian Louise, 6, 28, 35, 42, 54, 58, 60, 62, 65, 70, 75, 108, 139, 169, 173, 180, 197, 201, 213, 240, 241, 247, 249, 254, 263, 313, 355, 357–8, 439, 443, 444–45, 484

Lockridge, Mary Kay Geake, 219, 240, 247, 329

Lockridge, Maud, 43

Lockridge, Robert Bruce (d. 1903), 44–45, 102, 215

Lockridge, Robert Bruce (d. 1919), 45, 48–49, 52–53, 54, 56, 59, 65, 72, 239, 254, 277, 340, 429, 447

character and upbringing, 57–58

drowning of, 41–42
subject of RLJ's unwritten novel,
  230–1, 435–8
Lockridge, Ross Franklin, Jr., *passim;*
  "To Adolf Hitler, by An
  American Admirer," 179; "An
  Album of Raintree County," 7,
  321; *American Lives,* 37, 40, 201,
  210, 226–7, 230, 231–4, 238,
  280; "Some Biographical Facts
  about the Author of *Raintree
  County,*" 339–40; *Byron and
  Napoleon,* 173; *The Demon with the
  Fiery Tongue,* 64, 185, 462–3; *The
  Dream of the Flesh of Iron,* 40, 180,
  183–90, 194, 198–200, 232,
  236, 319, 390, 427, 433, 469;
  "Follies of France," 134; *The
  Harrisons,* 178–9; *The Inheritors,*
  146–8; 1931 Journal, 90–92;
  juvenilia, 93–94;
  "Kenapocomoco," 178;
  "Lockridge's Leaden Treasury,"
  165, 292; *Metchnikoff,* 154; *A
  Pageant of New Harmony,* 167–70,
  243, 267, 327, 456–7;
  "Rhapsody in Words," 166–7;
  "Sketch for a book of
  Philosophy," 416–8, 448; "The
  Story of *Raintree County,*" 339–40;
  "Ultimate Philosophy," 6, 447–8;
  A Valley in the Years, 426–7,
  434–8; *Wanderfell: A Tragedy in
  Four Acts,* 154–5, 169, 190, 408
accomplishments and character,
  10–11
as American writer, 39–40
analysis of, 427–34
anxiety at mother's response to
  RC, 356
bicycle tour of France, 128–9
at Chicago World's Fair, 104–5
and cinema, 18, 61, 71, 186, 236
as college instructor, 163–4,
  216–7

contract dispute with Houghton
  Mifflin, 29, 334–6, 359, 361–7
courtship of Vernice Baker, 77–78,
  85–90, 99–100, 105–7, 127–8,
  129–30, 137–9, 144–5
and culture of Bloomington,
  68–92
on death of brother Bruce, 42,
  230–1, 436–8
death of, 443–8
decision to be a writer, 67
dreams recorded in shorthand,
  180–83
editorials on, 4, 450, 457
elementary school education,
  62–63, 68–69
failures and set-backs, 63–64, 73,
  75, 91, 95–96, 103, 127, 134,
  150–1, 156–9, 161, 169–20,
  176, 178, 179–80, 200,
  431–33
as father, 223–26, 368–9, 410
hospitalization, 395–401
on French literature, 135, 211–2
freshman and sophomore years,
  96–104
on heroic myth and history,
  60–61, 292–7, 358
in Hollywood, 377–89
in Italy, 119–23
illness of 1935–36, 155–61, 278,
  390–1
meeting MGM reps in New York,
  343–6
Paris *manifestations* of, 1934,
  124–7, 150
and politics, 150, 174–5, 187,
  193, 202–3, 276, 297. 300
reading, 60, 133, 135, 159, 210–1
religious sensibility of, 229–31
revising *RC,* 315–6, 318–9, 332,
  325–6, 336, 343–6, 350–1,
  354–5, 371, 373–4, 384
on time, loss, mourning, 34,
  132–3, 217–8, 227–8, 236,

Index

Lockridge, Ross Franklin, Jr. *(cont.)*
279, 282–4, 430, 432–3,
436–8
  track and cross-country, 102–3,
  118, 128
Lockridge, Ross Franklin, Sr., 5,
21–22, 51–52, 55, 60, 70–71,
108, 129, 169, 180, 182–3,
194, 195, 196, 203, 215, 219,
240, 249–50, 254, 263, 267,
291, 318–9, 320, 340, 342,
350, 406, 413, 439, 444, 445,
446, 451, 452, 453; *A. Lincoln,*
76; *Black Snake and White Rose,*
178, 299; *George Rogers Clark,* 76;
The Labyrinth of New Harmony,
177; *La Salle,* 76; *The Old
Fauntleroy Home,* 22, 161–3, 331;
The Story of Indiana, 26; *Theodore
Thieme: A Man and His Times,* 463
  contrasted with RLJ, 77, 323
  after death of RLJ, 25–27
  as employment manager, 46–47
  enlisting RLJ in history projects,
  161–3, 178–9, 246–7
  Historic Site Recitals, 47–48,
  100–1
  influence on *RC,* 294, 297–302
  influence on RLJ, 66, 76–77, 188,
  265, 429–30, 433
  letters to RLJ in France, 115–6,
  139–40
  life to 1919, 42–49
  in *The Inheritors,* 145–9
  response to *RC,* 357–60, 374,
  382–3, 476
  response to RLJ's depression and
  death, 394–5, 401, 415–6, 453
Lockridge, Ross Franklin, III, 6, 16,
29, 32–34, 227, 229, 254,
353–4, 375, 392, 413, 419,
439, 461
Lockridge, Vernice Baker, 3, 5, 6–7,
15–17, 73, 91, 94, 95, 96,
101, 108, 109, 134, 136, 142,

143, 149, 150–1, 154, 160,
169, 172, 173, 174, 178, 180,
181, 182, 183, 185, 190, 213,
218, 221–2, 227, 234, 241–2,
261, 267, 270, 277, 289, 313,
319, 321, 327, 336, 347, 348,
353, 357, 365, 375, 395, 408,
430, 437, 440, 441, 451, 461
  in Cambridge with RLJ, 193–8,
  200, 202, 203
  death of father, 254
  after death of RLJ, 28–31, 453
  early years, 80–83, 85–88
  early relationship with RLJ,
  77–78, 85–90, 99–100, 105–7
  final conversation with RLJ, 442–3
  and RLJ's illness of 1935–36,
  156–9
  inscribing *RC,* 382–3
  interviewed during RLJ's
  hospitalization, 400–1
  RLJ's letters from Boston to,
  329–30, 332, 333
  letter to Paul Brooks, 454
  as Nell Gaither in *RC,* 16, 244–5,
  277, 286, 291
  nude portrait on *RC* book jacket,
  333
  response to RLJ's depression, 326,
  367–8, 393–4, 411–2
  as typist for RLJ, 194–5, 244–5,
  255, 441
  wedding and honeymoon, 170–1
  during RLJ's year in Europe,
  117–8, 124, 127–8, 129–30,
  137–9
Lockridge, Vivian Shockley, 42,
52–53, 54, 57, 58, 62, 65, 70,
240, 247, 254, 268, 329, 336,
345, 429, 437, 482
  alcoholism and recovery, 76, 219,
  452
  short stories, 59
Logan, Olive, *Before the Footlights &
Behind the Scenes,* 299

Index

Longfellow, Henry Wadsworth,
  Hiawatha, 60, 221
Longinus, 297
Louisville, 17, 44–45, 79, 80
Loveman, Amy, 344, 370
Lutwack, Leonard, 292, 308, 474
Lynd, Robert and Helen Merrell
  Lynd, *Middletown,* 70
Lyons, Robert, 5, 445, 446

McCaffery, John, 336, 343–6, 348,
  349, 350, 352, 357, 372, 476
McElroy, Joseph, *Women and Men,*
  301, 308
McFall, Merrill, 450, 451
McGreevey, John, 315, 389–90, 449
MacKenna, Kenneth, 381
MacLeish, Archibald, 211
MacPherson, Virginia, 388–9
Macy, Amanda, 109, 110, 118, 137
Mailer, Norman, *The Naked and the
  Dead,* 11
Maini, Darshan, 13, 302
Mallarmé, Etienne, 211
mania, 312
Manistee, Michigan, 319–21, 406–7
Mann, Thomas, 27, 201, 227, 299,
  324, 431; *Death in Venice,* 238;
  The Magic Mountain, 280–1, 340
Marquand, John, 404
Marquis, Don, *Archy and Mehitabel,*
  159
Martin, Charlotte, 196, 197
Martz, Carl, 72
Marvin, Lee, 19
Marxism, 153, 281
Masters, Robert, 60–61, 67, 118,
  219, 483
materialism, 153, 185, 300
Maupassant, Guy de, 59, 211
Mayer, Louis B., 19, 352–3, 359,
  372, 381, 387
Melville, Herman, 4, 201; *Moby-
  Dick,* 13, 93, 121, 301
Menger, Edna, 88

Methodist Church, 43, 49, 74, 77,
  78, 79, 86, 96–97, 170, 376,
  450–1
Metro Goldwyn Mayer, 4, 15–19,
  380–81, 387
  Novel Award, 334–6, 342–6,
  348–50, 353, 357, 359, 361–7,
  405, 477
Millay, Edna St. Vincent, 220
Miller, Perry, 210
Milton, John, 439; *Paradise Lost,* 44,
  301
Mitchell, Edward, 111, 118, 449
Mitchell, Margaret, *Gone With the
  Wind,* 15, 159, 299, 325, 389,
  402
Michener, James A., 22–23
modernism, 133–4, 153, 154, 166,
  297–8
Molière, 115, 131; *Le Bourgeois
  Gentilhomme,* 164
Monico, Marion, 118, 142–3, 154,
  172, 187, 201, 449, 470
Montessori, Maria, 49, 54, 66
Moore, John Robert, 97, 158, 164,
  176, 422
Moore, Louise, 69, 71
Morley, Christopher, 370–1
Mumby, Beulah Baker, 79, 80, 82,
  103, 268
Mumby, Harold, 376, 393, 402, 406,
  415, 442
Mumford, Lewis, 241
Murdock, Laurette, 336
myth, 229–30, 234, 281, 292–7, 358

Napoleon Buonaparte, 91, 173,
  174–6, 408
narcissism, 261, 273, 287, 417,
  427–34, 464, 479–81
Neff, Mildred, 100, 101
Neruda, Pablo, 4, 461
New Harmony, Indiana, 10, 25, 100,
  161–3, 167–9, 177–8, 187,
  219, 243, 247, 262, 287, 331

Index

New York City, 143, 186, 189

The New Yorker, 405–6, 442, 481, 482–3

The New York Times, 5, 20

Nicholson, Clona Baker, 79, 80, 82, 103, 106, 107, 149, 170, 180, 217, 387–8, 422, 455

Niebuhr, Reinhold, 38

Norris, Frank, 201, 210

Noyes, Helen, 249, 250

Noyes, Russell, 30, 173–4, 176–7, 180, 203, 416

O'Connor, Hazel, 369, 407

Oliver, Lee, 251, 313

Olney, Austin, 257

Owen, Robert, 163, 168

Parsons, Jack, 118–9, 160, 183, 184

Peck, Gregory, 349–50

Pennington, James, 203, 284, 423

Perkins, Maxwell, 351

Pernot, Felix, 112, 125

Pernot, Jeanne, 112

Pernot, Madame, 111, 112, 130–3, 141

Peters, Marie Lockridge, 43, 145–8, 401, 419, 452

Peters, Robert, 156, 247, 342, 391–2, 393–4, 395, 400, 401, 452

Phantom of the Opera, 71, 186

Phi Gamma Delta, 44, 59, 76, 98–99, 440

Piercy, Josephine, 424, 449

Plato, 194; *The Republic,* 22, 202, 285, 299, 323, 340

Poe, Edgar Allan, 4, 59, 153, 211; "The Raven," 78

Pomeroy, Wardell, 403, 422

Porter, Cole, 44, 311

Pound, Ezra, 153, 211; *The Cantos,* 301

Power, Tyrone, 77, 217

Presley, Elvis, 35

Proust, Marcel, 22, 257, 435; *À la Recherche du temps perdu,* 301, 337, 338

Pulitzer Prize, 345, 346, 363, 456

Pynchon, Thomas, *Gravity's Rainbow,* 301, 308

Quayle, Edward, 311, 323, 342, 350, 360, 375, 377, 406, 449

Rabelais, François, 302

Racine, Jean, 115, 131

racism, 63, 88–89, 288–90, 315, 316

Raintree County, 4, 8, 157–8, 215–6, 223, 225, 271–309, 449, and *passim*

   acceptance by Houghton Mifflin, 256–61

   as American archive, 39

   authorial self-portrait in, 246, 273, 275–6, 278

   the carnivalesque in, 302–4

   characterization of Shawnessy, 275–9

   characterization of the Perfessor, 280–4

   city section, 354–5, 371

   composition of, 235–40, 242–6, 250, 253, 255–6

   conception of, 132–3

   critical reaction to, 11, 403–5

   dream section (discarded), 236, 253, 254, 264, 313–4, 315–9, 321, 338, 475

   as ecological novel, 9, 286

   empoundment by Philadelphia vice squad, 455–6

   encyclopedic form in, 297–302, 426

   as Great American Novel, 12, 13, 121, 133, 403, 416, 425

   and myth, 292–7

   raintree motif, 242–3

   and sex, 14–15, 284–91, 300

   structure of, 305–7

Index

Raintree County (the film): 15–19, 272, 287, 302

Rank, Otto, 206

Rapp, George, 163, 167

Rawlings, Marjorie, 201

religion, 152, 281–2, 284, 292, 295, 417–8

Remak, Henry, 164, 402

Renan, Ernest, *The Life of Jesus,* 299

Rhoton, Franklin, 50, 204, 232

Riley, James Whitcomb, 25, 210, 224, 431

Rimbaud, Arthur, 154, 185, 211

Rivervale Methodist Church Camp, 78, 94–96, 105–6, 143, 160

Rixey, Lillian, 354

Robinson, Sid, 102, 103

Roe, Edward Payson, *Barriers Burned Away,* 210–1, 285, 299

Rogers, W. G., 404

Rollins, Hyder, 194, 200, 201, 202

Roosevelt, Eleanor, 324

Roosevelt, Franklin Delano, 174, 193, 247–8; *Nothing to Fear,* 7, 333

Roseman, Sydney, 110, 142

Rousseau, Jean-Jacques, 178, 420

Royce, Josiah, 152

Russell, Bertrand, 193

Saint, Eva Marie, 16, 17

Sandburg, Carl, 212

Santayana, George, *The Last Puritan,* 159

Saroyan, William, 38, 201, 227; *The Human Comedy,* 224

Sartre, Jean-Paul, *Nausea,* 36

Sassoon, Siegfried, 209

Saturday Review of Literature, 324, 413, 456

Scanlon, Marcia, 38, 477

Scherman, Harry, 370

Schiller, Friedrich von, 296

Scholl, Nota, 82, 86, 87, 106, 143, 315, 389–90

Schricker, Henry, 177–8

Schwartz, Delmore, 194

Scott, Naomi, 239

Scowcroft, Richard, 194, 257, 260, 265–6, 333

Setser, George, 68–69

sex, 14–15, 84, 86, 139, 181, 182, 266, 284–91, 300, 370, 430

Shakespeare, William, 10, 11, 106, 121, 134, 150, 158, 200, 202, 229, 272, 275, 278–9, 292, 299, 308, 331, 371, 414

Sharp, Fred, 74, 280

Shelley, Mary, *Frankenstein,* 185

Shelley, Percy Bysshe, 121, 173; *Alastor,* 185, *Prometheus Unbound,* 301

Sheridan, Richard, *The Rivals,* 450; *The School for Scandal,* 450

Sherwood, Dan, 106, 164

Shockley, Benjamin Franklin, 273, 314

Shockley, Emma Rhoton, 50, 58, 62, 92, 132, 133, 144–5, 159, 166, 170, 172, 204, 231, 233, 239, 274, 293, 453
   as Esther Root in *RC,* 290–1

Shockley, Ernest Vivian, 51, 60, 62, 159–60, 173, 201, 204, 210–1, 226, 231, 233, 236

Shockley, Frank William, 51, 144, 170, 204, 240, 314, 379, 386

Shockley, James, 288

Shockley, John Anger, 209, 219

Shockley, John Wesley, 49–50, 62, 92, 132, 142, 144–5, 148, 160, 170, 172, 204, 205, 226, 231, 239, 240, 273–5, 291, 356, 379, 429
   marriage to Susannah Duke, 288
   as prototype of hero of *RC,* 133, 233–4, 275
   as writer, 273–5

Shockley, Mae Beth, 144

Shockley, Susannah Duke, 50, 205, 287–8, 474
   as Susanna Drake in *RC,* 287–90

Shockley, William B., 204, 205, 239–40, 275, 356

Siebenthal, Ben, 69, 71

Simmons College, 10, 180, 201, 206, 210, 216–7, 219–20, 245, 248, 263, 354

Sinclair, Upton, 201; *The Jungle,* 312

Skeleton, George, 63–64, 85

Smalley, Donald, 180, 203, 276, 342, 402, 423, 425–6, 427, 449–50, 454–5, 467, 481

Smalley, Ruth, 203, 276, 402, 425, 450, 454

Smilin' Through, 61

Smith, Dorothy, 69

Smith, Huldah, 118, 136

Smith, Kate, 349

Sorbonne, 114, 135, 140–1

Spenser, Edmund, 102, 189, 275; *The Fairie Queene,* 185, 301

Stanley, Henry, *Through the Dark Continent,* 299

Stavisky, Serge, 125

Stegner, Wallace, 21, 194

Stein, Gertrude, 201, 220

Stevenson, Robert Louis, 71, 97

Stiles, Jack, 356, 449

Stiles, Martha, 337, 338, 347, 356

Stone, Martin, 346–7, 357, 359, 361, 363–7, 388, 395, 405, 406, 432, 441, 476

Stowe, Harriet Beecher, 10, 239; *Uncle Tom's Cabin,* 299

Straughn, Indiana, 53, 61–62, 144–5, 159, 206, 271, 318, 440

Sturgeon, Robert, 164

suicide, 5, 8, 33, 154, 225, 290, 421, 446, 450, 462, 484

Swinburne, Algernon, 165

Swindell, Larry, 13

Synge, J. M., *Riders to the Sea,* 140

Sypher, Wylie, 263

Tarkington, Booth, 26

Taylor, Elizabeth, 16–19, 381

Tecumseh, 47, 100, 164

Theocritus, *Idylls,* 253

Thieme, Theodore, 217

Thomas, Norman, 47, 312, 398

Thompson, Lovell, 315, 325, 327–8, 331, 339, 350, 353

Thompson, Stith, 153

Thorne, Alice, 87, 89

Thorpe, James, 45

Thrasher, Theodore, 79–80

Tindall, William York, 11

Todd, Mike, 17

Tolstoy, Leo, 165, 201, 209, 234, 299; *War and Peace,* 208, 341, 344

Tryon, Rachel, 222–3, 225

Tryon, Warren ("Steve"), 207–8, 214, 216, 221, 222, 238, 240, 248, 249, 250, 251, 256, 257–8, 280, 333, 483–4

Turner, Lana, 270, 388

Turner, Ted, 25, 381

Underwood, Betty, 256–7

Updike, John, 40

Valéry, Paul, 135

Vegler, Ferdinand, 41–42

Venn, Diggory, 334, 336, 339, 341, 347, 350, 351

Verdun, 115, 187

Verlaine, Paul, 211

Vetluguin, Voldemar, 381

Vico, Giambattista, 229, 296

Virgil, 10, 122, 135, 205; *Aeneid,* 76

Voltaire, 420

Wagner, Richard, *Tristan und Isolde,* 160

Walker, Robert, 351

Wallace, Lew, 26

Ward, Mary Jane, 56–57, 58, 215, 267, 302–3, 335–6, 338, 346, 348, 351–2, 356, 373–4, 375, 377, 406, 409, 421, 432, 434,

Index

449, 452, 473, 484; *The Professor's Umbrella,* 312, 323, 324, 414; *The Snake Pit,* 19, 258, 260, 263, 289, 310–3, 323, 324, 325, 342, 360–1, 398; *The Tree Has Roots,* 268, 311; *The Wax Apple,* 311–2
career to 1946, 311–3
initial rejection of *The Snake Pit,* 310–1
RLJ's response to *The Snake Pit,* 260
and RLJ's depression, 414–5
RLJ on their early relationship, 267–8
Warren, Dale, 259, 264, 315, 322, 325, 329, 356
Watkeys, Charlotte, 110, 118–9, 120
Wayne, Anthony, 47, 100
Wells, H. G., Julian Huxley, G. P. Wells, *The Science of Life,* 186
Wharton, Edith, 220
Wells, William, 47, 100
White, E. B., 322
Whitman, Walt, 4, 10, 12, 155, 199, 201, 202, 211–2, 220, 232, 234, 239, 259, 265, 297, 300, 339, 370, 403, 429, 451; *Leaves of Grass,* 210, 218, 299, 409
Whittier, John Greenleaf, *Snow-Bound,* 69
Who Wouldn't Be Crazy? 87–88
Wild, John, 202
Willard, T.A. *The City of the Sacred Well,* 72
Williams, Ben Ames, *House Divided,* 341, 363
Williams, Esther, 381
Williams, Jay, 14–15, 24
Willkie, Wendell, 193
Wilson, Carey, 380, 389, 399
Winchell, Walter, 196, 449
Wolfe, Thomas, 4, 12, 201, 208, 212, 220, 232, 265, 299, 300, 315, 324, 335, 339, 351,
403–4, 405, 407, 416, 456; *Look Homeward, Angel,* 13; *The Web and the Rock,* 228; *You Can't Go Home Again,* 228
RLJ's critique of, 227–8
Wolff, Marietta, *About Liddy Thomas,* 348
Wood, Grant, 259
Woolf, Virginia, 449
Wordsworth, William, 207
World's Fair of 1933, 104–5, 303
World War I, 56, 183, 233, 264
World War II, 183, 202, 208–10, 218–9, 221, 224, 250, 251, 269, 477
Wylie, Angie, 331
Wylie, Anne Stiles, 197–8, 223, 225, 238, 314, 319, 322, 323, 407
Wylie, Betty, 313–4, 331, 347, 350
Wylie, Craig, 330–1, 332, 376–7
Wylie, Jeff (Francis E.), 96, 268–9, 313–4, 331, 347, 350, 358, 408, 449, 483
Wylie, Katherine, 96–97
Wylie, Laurence, 96–97, 108, 109, 113, 128, 143, 180, 187, 197–8, 208, 214–5, 238, 263, 268, 280, 314, 322–3, 340, 407, 449, 465; *Village in the Vaucluse,* 483
encourages RLJ to go to Paris, 104
tells RLJ of teaching position at Simmons, 201
arranges cottage in Manistee, 319
Wylie, Louise, 99, 150, 196–7, 199–200, 330
Wynn, Keenan, 351

Yeats, William Butler, 153
Young, Marguerite, 26, 177; *Miss MacIntosh, My Darling,* 309, 470
YPB, 86–87, 97, 105, 285

Zinsser, William, 17
Zola, Emile, 211, 420

499